EATING ASIAN AMERICA

Eating Asian America

A Food Studies Reader

EDITED BY
Robert Ji-Song Ku,
Martin F. Manalansan IV,
and Anita Mannur

NEW YORK UNIVERSITY PRESS
New York and London

NEW YORK UNIVERSITY PRESS
New York and London
www.nyupress.org

References to Internet websites (URLs) were accurate at the time of writing.
Neither the author nor New York University Press is responsible for URLs
that may have expired or changed since the manuscript was prepared.

FOR LIBRARY OF CONGRESS CATALOGING-IN-PUBLICATION DATA
PLEASE CONTACT THE LIBRARY OF CONGRESS

ISBN: 978-1-4798-1023-9 (cl)
ISBN: 978-1-4798-6925-1 (pb)

New York University Press books are printed on acid-free paper,
and their binding materials are chosen for strength and durability.
We strive to use environmentally responsible suppliers and materials
to the greatest extent possible in publishing our books.

Manufactured in the United States of America

10 9 8 7 6 5 4 3 2 1

Also available as an ebook

CONTENTS

List of Figures and Maps   vii

Acknowledgments   ix

An Alimentary Introduction   1
    Robert Ji-Song Ku, Martin F. Manalansan IV, and Anita Mannur

PART I: LABORS OF TASTE

1. Cambodian Donut Shops and the Negotiation of Identity in Los Angeles   13
    Erin M. Curtis

2. Tasting America: The Politics and Pleasures of School Lunch in Hawai'i   30
    Christine R. Yano (with Wanda Adams)

3. A Life Cooking for Others: The Work and Migration Experiences   53
    of a Chinese Restaurant Worker in New York City, 1920–1946
    Heather R. Lee

4. Learning from Los Kogi Angeles: A Taco Truck and Its City   78
    Oliver Wang

5. The Significance of Hawai'i Regional Cuisine in Postcolonial Hawai'i   98
    Samuel Hideo Yamashita

PART II: EMPIRES OF FOOD

6. Incarceration, Cafeteria Style: The Politics of the Mess Hall   125
    in the Japanese American Incarceration
    Heidi Kathleen Kim

7. As American as Jackrabbit Adobo: Cooking, Eating, and   147
    Becoming Filipina/o American before World War II
    Dawn Bohulano Mabalon

8. *Lechon* with Heinz, Lea & Perrins with *Adobo*: The American   177
    Relationship with Filipino Food, 1898–1946
    René Alexander Orquiza Jr.

9. "Oriental Cookery": Devouring Asian and Pacific Cuisine   186
    during the Cold War
    Mark Padoongpatt

10. *Gannenshoyu* or First-Year Soy Sauce? Kikkoman Soy Sauce and the   208
Corporate Forgetting of the Early Japanese American Consumer
Robert Ji-Song Ku

PART III: FUSION, DIFFUSION, CONFUSION?

11. Twenty-First-Century Food Trucks: Mobility, Social Media,   231
and Urban Hipness
Lok Siu

12. *Samsa* on Sheepshead Bay: Tracing Uzbek Foodprints   245
in Southern Brooklyn
Zohra Saed

13. Apple Pie and *Makizushi*: Japanese American Women   255
Sustaining Family and Community
Valerie J. Matsumoto

14. Giving Credit Where It Is Due: Asian American Farmers   274
and Retailers as Food System Pioneers
Nina F. Ichikawa

15. Beyond Authenticity: Rerouting the Filipino Culinary Diaspora   288
Martin F. Manalansan IV

PART IV: READABLE FEASTS

16. Acting Asian American, Eating Asian American: The Politics   303
of Race and Food in Don Lee's *Wrack and Ruin*
Jennifer Ho

17. Devouring Hawai'i: Food, Consumption, and Contemporary Art   323
Margo Machida

18. "Love Is Not a Bowl of Quinces": Food, Desire, and the Queer   354
Asian Body in Monique Truong's *The Book of Salt*
Denise Cruz

19. The Globe at the Table: How *Madhur Jaffrey's World Vegetarian*   371
Reconfigures the World
Delores B. Phillips

20. Perfection on a Plate: Readings in the South Asian   393
Transnational Queer Kitchen
Anita Mannur

Bibliography   409

Contributors   425

Index   431

LIST OF FIGURES AND MAPS

Figure 5.1.   The founding chefs of HRC.   106

Figure 5.2.   The cover of Janice Wald Henderson's *The New*   110
               Cuisine of Hawaii.

Figure 5.3.   Alan Wong's loco moco.   114

Figure 6.1.   Santa Anita Assembly Center cafeteria.   128

Figure 7.1.   Filipinas learn how to make baking powder biscuits.   154

Figure 7.2.   Eudosia Juanitas and her children in their   158
               vegetable garden.

Figure 7.3.   Filipino asparagus cutters celebrate the end of   161
               the asparagus season.

Figure 7.4.   Bibiana Castillano's restaurant.   164

Figure 7.5.   Pablo "Ambo" Mabalon's restaurant.   165

Figure 10.1.   Kikkoman's Golden Anniversary advertisement   210
               published in the *New York Times.*

Figure 14.1.   Nectarines at Kozuki Farms, Parlier, California.   277

Figure 14.2.   Golden Bowl Supermarket, Fresno, California.   279

Figure 14.3.   Boxes and storage shed at Kozuki Farms,   283
               Parlier, California.

Figure 14.4.   California Department of Labor safety poster   285
               written in Hmong.

Figure 17.1.   Puni Kukahiko, *Lovely Hula Hands*, 2005.   325

Figure 17.2.   Lynne Yamamoto, *Provisions, Post-War*   326
               (Pacific Asia and U.S.), 2010.

Figure 17.3.   Michael Arcega, *SPAM/MAPS: World*, 2001.   328

Figure 17.4.   Keith Tallett, *Tattoo Williams (Watufaka)*, 2010.   330

Figure 17.5.   Keith Tallett, *Mobile Taro Lo'i* (Camo design), 2010.   335

Figure 17.6.   Trisha Lagaso Goldberg, *Eshu Veve for Olaa*   338
                Sugar Company, 2011.

Figure 17.7.   Alan Konishi, *Yellow Peril (Remember*   340
                Pearl Harbor?), 2006.

Figure 17.8.   Mat Kubo, *Big Five* (full view and detail with   342
                pineapple open), 2004.

Figure 17.9.   Gaye Chan and Nandita Sharma, *Eating in Public,* 348
                Free Garden at Kailua, Hawai'i, 2003–2012.

Figure 20.1.   A "perfect" dish comes together. Frame enlargement 398
                from *Nina's Heavenly Delights* (2006).

Figure 20.2.   The "perfect dish," which tastes like "shite," is 399
                thrown into the trash. Frame enlargement from
                Nina's Heavenly Delights (2006).

Figure 20.3.   "Love in a Wet Climate." Frame enlargement   401
                from *Nina's Heavenly Delights* (2006).

Map 3.1.   The Chin family in North America, 1935–1946.   56

Map 3.2.   The Chin family in China and North America,   68
                1935–1946.

Map 4.1.   Los Kogi Angeles, 2010–2011.   83

Map 4.2.   The Void, 2010–2011.   85

Map 4.3.   Kogi's most common locations, 2010–2011.   87

ACKNOWLEDGMENTS

The familiar food-related adage cautions, "Too many cooks spoil the broth," which may be true, but not for this book. A great number of "cooks" have had their hands in the completion of this collection. First and foremost, we thank the seventeen contributors for their enthusiasm, diligence, creativity, erudition, and friendship.

We thank Eric Zinner, editor in chief of New York University Press, who believed in our project and pushed us to finish it. We also thank production editor Alexia Traganas and assistant editors Ciara McLaughlin and Alicia Nadkarni for their support and guidance throughout the completion of this book. We are grateful for the constructive feedback from the two anonymous readers of our manuscript. Their thoughtful comments and suggestions have improved this book immeasurably.

We would be remiss if we did not acknowledge the Association for Asian American Studies, as our participation in the 2010 meeting in Austin, Texas, and the 2011 meeting in New Orleans, Louisiana, provided the original impetus for the teamwork that culminated in the publication of this book. We thank the AAAS officers, conference organizers, and members for their intellectual support and personal friendships.

Finally, we three editors would like to make the following personal acknowledgments.

Anita: I wish to thank my colleagues at Miami: Yu-Fang Cho, Nalin Jayasena, Mad Detloff, Luming Mao, and Gaile Pohlhaus for their generous intellectual feedback. My thanks to Jason Palmeri and Lisa Weems for an ever evolving context for critical eating in southwest Ohio, and for their continued support and encouragement, I thank Michael Needham, Julie Minich, Bill Johnson Gonzalez, Allan Isaac, and Cathy Schlund-Vials.

Martin: I want to express my gratitude to Lisa Nakamura and Kent Ono, who were especially supportive during my research. Special thanks to Bill Johnson Gonzalez, Allan Isaac, Jose Capino, Rick Bonus, and members of the Filipino American studies "mafia" for their social and scholarly camaraderie, especially during delectable meals, spicy chats, and warm boisterous laughter.

I dedicate my work to my parents and family for providing unconditional love amid feasts of adobo and *sinigang*.

Robert: To all those who I've cooked for this past few years, thank you for enjoying my food. Thank you especially to our apocryphal Momofuku *bo ssam* gang (Kevin Hatch, Matt Johnson, Julia Walker, and Deanne Westerman). My gratitude goes, too, to my Asian and Asian American studies cohorts at Binghamton University: Immanuel Kim, Sonja Kim, Cynthia Marasigan, Rumiko Sode, Roberta Strippoli, and Lisa Yun. My love goes to Nancy, Eliot, and Oliver.

An Alimentary Introduction

ROBERT JI-SONG KU, MARTIN F. MANALANSAN IV,
AND ANITA MANNUR

Understanding and apprehending Asian American food experiences begin and end with the body. The category *Asian American* is a historical U.S. federal census designation that rests in part on the long history of what might be described as the Foucauldian control and discipline[1] around the movement of Asian bodies to America, in part on their toil in various agricultural fields and plantations, fruit orchards, fisheries, and salmon canneries in Hawai'i, California, the Pacific Northwest, and the South. That these same bodies sweated and slaved over hot stoves and small kitchens to produce many of America's ubiquitous ethnic take-out food establishments—Chinese, Thai, Indian, Middle Eastern, Japanese, and so forth—is neither coincidental nor incidental.

Many people in the United States, including the students in our Asian American studies and food studies classes, often wonder whether Asians became a prominent part of the American food landscape because of their ancestral homelands' *intrinsically* delicious foods. Or perhaps Asians are exceptionally devoted not only to eating good food but also to the entrepreneurial aspect of food, that is, to the business of producing and distributing food. Or perhaps Asians are "naturally" great cooks, just as they are popularly perceived as "innately" good at math. Simply put, is the love of food an indelible—and inescapable—part of the Asian DNA?

This book is a reminder that social, political, economic, and historical forces, as well as power inequalities, including discriminatory immigration and land laws, have circumscribed Asians materially and symbolically in the alimentary realm, forcing them into indentured agricultural work and lifetimes spent in restaurants and other food service and processing industries. While race is often popularly understood as a function of skin color and other physical attributes, critical race scholars like Michael Omi and Howard Winant,[2] have demonstrated that racial meanings and the processes of racialization permeate all facets of social discourse. We suggest that this is especially true for most matters related to food. The tendency to equate racial features with gastronomic expressions is so persistent that a person's race is commonsensically equated with what he or she ingests. The short—if not apocryphal—version of the nineteenth-century French gastronome Jean Anthelme Brillat-Savarin's much celebrated and quoted classic dictum, "you are what you eat," has often been interpreted as meaning that an individual is, first and foremost, marked and signified by his or her food habits.

To define a person or a group of people principally by the food they eat is, however, to uncritically and narrowly essentialize them through the corporeal terms of gustation and digestion. Also, those marked in such a way come to embody the foods and the corresponding values and meanings attached to them. Consider the racialized motives in perpetuating the image of African Americans eating fried chicken or watermelon, as Psyche Williams-Forson points out in *Building Chickens out of Chicken Legs: Black Woman, Food, and Power* and Kyla Wazana Tompkins illustrates in *Racial Indigestion: Eating Bodies in the 19th Century*.[3] Consider also the irksome question Asian Americans often confront: "Do you eat dogs?" When asked of those of Korean, Filipino, Vietnamese, Chinese, or Cambodian ancestry, this question is rarely posed in good faith; rather, the motive behind such a question is not to know but to accuse.[4] On the one hand, the controversy over the practice of eating dogs—especially in places like the United States where the distinction between what is pet and what is food is understood as affectively stable—is about the taxonomy of different types of humans. On the other hand, this controversy is about determining who is a "real" American and who is not, what sort of cultural practice is "mainstream" and what is exotic, and what sort of food is disgusting and what is palatable.

The problem of equating personhood with food was part of the final episode of the popular HBO series *Sex and the City*, which aired for six seasons between 1998 and 2004. Charlotte—one of the four main female characters in search of white, heterosexual, bourgeois, urban bliss—has been despondent because of her struggles with infertility. One evening for dinner at home, she lays out several unelegant boxes of take-out Chinese food on an otherwise elegant dining-room table. She calls her husband to dinner and immediately apologizes for ordering Chinese instead of cooking the meal herself. Her husband, however, is unexpectedly cheerful as he produces an envelope and announces that he has "something from China, too." He takes out a picture of a baby—the Chinese baby that the couple has been waiting to adopt. Overcome with tearful joy, Charlotte cries out, "That's *our* baby!"

This scene from a popular television show illustrates the slippage between personhood and food. A racialized discourse that renders "Chinese" and "China" as provenance and a stand-in for not only a hasty meal but also an adopted baby serves as a reminder of the insidious ways in which race has become embedded in our everyday orchestration of bodies, meanings, and food. Not merely a descriptive category for people and nation, China—or things "Chinese"—is also regarded as a commodity to be bought, possessed, and ingested. The prerogative of multicultural cosmopolitanism is such that we can now "order" Chinese food from a Chinese take-out and have it delivered to our home; we can also "order" a Chinese baby from a Chinese adoption agency halfway around the world and have her delivered to our home as well.

Senses, emotions, and affects constitute the corporeal frame through which the vexed relationship between Asian Americans and food is mediated. In the United States, the racialization of Asian Americans is often expressed in terms of bodily sensibilities and sentiments. The "trope" of the smelly and unwashed immigrant permeates discourses about citizenship and immigrant assimilation. It is telling that when Southeast Asian refugees were relocated to the United States during the late 1970s and early 1980s, the primers given to them to help them adjust to American life included tips on hygiene. Among the many lessons was reducing the odor of their food, especially when frying fish and using exotic ingredients that might offend their American neighbor's delicate sense of smell.

Food Studies and Asian Americans

The study of food, foodways, cuisine, and gastronomy has emerged as an important site of inquiry in fields ranging from literature to anthropology, from sociology to history, and from film studies to gender studies. Journals such as *Food and Foodways* and *Gastronomica* have helped disseminate and promote both discipline-centered and multidisciplinary scholarship on this subject. At the same time, Asian American studies has become an important presence in the academy, with intellectual projects that offer new ways of understanding the social, cultural, political, and economic realities of what it means to be an American and a citizen of the world. This anthology is a collection of new scholarship in Asian American studies that examines the importance of centering the study of culinary practices and theorizing the racialized underpinnings of Asian Americanness. The twenty scholars represented here have inaugurated a new facet of food studies: the refusal to yield to a superficial multiculturalism that naively celebrates difference and reconciliation simply or primarily through the pleasures of food and eating.

Asians in the United States have long been associated—often reluctantly or against their will, as well as voluntarily or with pleasure—with images of and practices regarding food. Starting in the days of the Gold Rush, Chinese

Americans opened restaurants that catered to both Chinese and non-Chinese clientele. Asian Americans have been important workers in American food and agricultural industries: Japanese Americans and Filipino Americans, for example, played pivotal roles in the West Coast's produce and cannery industry before World War II. Chinese, Thai, Indian, and Japanese restaurants can be found in both small towns and big cities across the country. Words like "chop suey," "sushi," "curry," and "kimchi" have become part of the American popular imagination to the extent that contentious notions of ethnic authenticity and authority are marked by culinary and alimentary practices, images, and ideas. Dishes like General Tso's chicken, California roll, SPAM *musubi*, tandoori chicken, and Korean tacos have come to signify the confused and ambivalent relationships between mainstream American consumptive desires and Asian American assimilative dreams.

Although the linkage of Asian Americans and food has been a dominant motif in both American materiality and imaginary, the academy has been slow to respond. In addition, despite the abundance of Asian-themed cookbooks, the scholarly treatment of Asian—let alone Asian American—foods and food practices is relatively rare, at least compared with studies of European food. Moreover, the studies that do exist usually focus on a specific Asian nation or ethnic group rather than the broader categories of regional Asia, pan-Asia, or Asian diaspora. Examples are Lizzie Collingham's *Curry: A Tale of Cooks and Conquerors*; E. N. Anderson's *The Food of China*; Katarzyna Cwiertka's *Modern Japanese Cuisine*; Emiko-Oknuki-Tierney's *Rice as Self: Japanese Identities through Time*; Theodore Bestor's *Tsukiji: The Fish Market at the Center of the World*; Judith Farquhar's *Appetites: Food and Sex in Post-Socialist China*; and Mark Swislocki's *Culinary Nostalgia: Regional Food Culture and the Urban Experience in Shanghai*. (The majority of these, furthermore, concern East Asian—principally Chinese or Japanese—gastronomy.) Most of the examples of diasporic or transnational food scholarship are edited volumes, such as David Y. H. Wu and Tan Chee-beng's *Changing Foodways in Asia*; David Y. H. Wu and Sidney C. H. Cheung's *The Globalization of Chinese Food*; Katarzyna Cwiertka and Boudewijn Walraven's *Asian Food: The Global and the Local*; James Watson's *Golden Arches East: McDonald's in East Asia*; Sami Zubaida and Richard Tapper's *Culinary Cultures of the Middle East*; and Krishnendu Ray and Tulasi Srinivas's *Curried Cultures: Globalization, Food, and South Asia*.

Among the few scholarly treatments of Asian American food and food practices, the more notable include Krishnendu Ray's *The Migrant's Table: Meals and Memories in Bengali-American Households*; Andrew Coe's *Chop*

Suey: A Cultural History of Chinese Food in the United States; Jennifer Ho's *Consumption and Identity in Asian American Coming-of-Age Novels*; Wenying Xu's *Eating Identities: Reading Food in Asian American Literature*; and Anita Mannur's *Culinary Fictions: Food in South Diasporic Culture*. (While Jennifer 8. Lee's *Fortune Cookie Chronicles: Adventures in the World of Chinese Food* is a valuable contribution to the study of Asian American food, its merits are more journalistic than scholarly.)

To date, this volume is the first book-length collection of scholarly essays to consider how Asian American immigrant histories are inscribed in the production and dissemination of ideas about Asian American foodways. *Eating Asian America* describes the cross-articulation of ethnic, racial, class, and gender concerns with the transnational and global circulation of peoples, technologies, and ideas through food, cooking, and eating. We acknowledge the critical work by Sidney Mintz on sugar, Gary Okihiro on pineapple, and Andrew Dalby on spices,[5] noting the immense power food production, distribution, and consumption wields.

Food is intimately connected to the histories, cultures, and communities of Asian Americans. While it is true that Chinese food is the ultimate "ethnic" American fast food, the juxtaposition of ethnic "otherness" with mainstream America's "normalcy" in the figuration of Asian American gastronomy is a telling example of how difficult it is to overcome the marginalized image of Asian Americans as perpetual foreigners. One notable gap in the literature on food systems is the relationship of food to labor, especially as it relates to Asian Americans. While social and labor historians have long documented the movement of migrant labor from Asia to work in the agricultural fields in the United States as the beginning of Asian American immigration history, food studies scholars have often overlooked this crucial topic. Instead, Asian American labor is related to food *service* more than to food production, dissemination, and consumption in America. The banality attributed to such persons as "the cook," "the dishwasher," "the busboy," and the "delivery boy" hides the racializing tendencies of such tropes and images. We argue that discussions about Asian American foodways and cuisine are undergirded by questions of power, race, gender, class, ethnicity, and sexuality.

These questions in turn cut across the many approaches to theorizing food in a transnational and diasporic framework. The methods of inquiry into food have traditionally diverged along disciplinary lines. Scholarship in the humanities and social sciences concentrates on the relationship of food, gender, and sexuality. Literary and film studies often analyze particular scenes, with little attention to the larger political or social factors shaping the food's preparation, consumption, or production. In contrast, works from the social sciences, particularly anthropology, center on the ritualized significance of food and what food can tell us about the power relations and organization of particular societies, though without explaining how food entered the cultural or social imagination through film or literature. This book brings together food scholars in different fields in conversations about similar questions that arise in different types of texts; it celebrates the inter- and multidisciplinary nature of food studies while at the same time examining its limits and possibilities.

We believe our anthology is the first to bridge the fields of food studies, cultural studies, area studies (Asian studies in particular), gender and sexuality studies, and Asian American studies (as part of the larger project of American ethnic studies, which includes African American studies, Latina/o studies, and Native American studies). We consider and critique the ways in which the immigrant trope pervades and persists in the American imagination and representation of Asian Americans. The twenty chapters of this volume interrogate in various ways the image of Asian Americans as being from "elsewhere" and how, through culinary contexts, they have been assimilated into the national fabric of normality and whiteness. Accordingly, this anthology asserts that Asian American foodways are located not in the intersection of culinary traditions alone but in the conjunctures of racial, gendered, sexualized, and classed hierarchies.

The Organization of This Book

Our journey through the culinary landscape of Asian America begins with stories of the labor and efforts of Asian Americans individuals and entrepreneurs who have found sustenance in the food-service sector. Part I begins with Heather Lee's story of Chin Shuck Wing, a wage laborer in New York City's service industry, who eventually became a lifelong restaurant worker during the 1930s. Christine Yano (with Wanda Adams) brings to life the voices of Asian Pacific American "cafeteria ladies" from the Ewa-Waipahu school district in Hawai'i. Through interviews with this now retired group of women, Yano and Adams argue that the "school lunch"—a topic that has come under great scrutiny in large part because of First Lady Michelle Obama's interest in school lunch programs—was the basis of a locally defined form of "culinary citizenship" predicated on an ideology of America rooted in a Pacific-Asian historical matrix.

In their chapters, Erin Curtis and Oliver Wang analyze the historical and structural foundations of Cambodian-owned donut shops and Korean-owned

Kogi taco trucks in Los Angeles. Samuel Yamashita maps the emergence of Hawai'i's regional cuisine in an Asian American framework, establishing a context to understand the contribution of Hawai'i-based chefs. Collectively, the five chapters of part I set the stage for the story of food in Asian America: about labor and about the pioneering efforts of men and women, refugees, and immigrants.

A picture of Asian American food pioneers would not be complete without an examination of the longer history of food in the context of U.S.-Asian relations, both domestically and abroad. Specifically, when we think about the historical circumstances in which Asian American foods were consumed and produced, we must consider the effects of wars and imperialism on the racialized and often racist contexts of Asian American bodies. In part II, Heidi Kim argues that during World War II, this context was most acutely experienced by Japanese Americans in internment camps. Her discussion of the camps' mess halls illustrates how the site of communal dining functioned as ideological battlegrounds on which notions of Americanness were negotiated.

In their chapters, Dawn Mabalon and René Alexander Orquiza Jr. examine the ways in which American colonialism transformed the Filipino diet. Mabalon addresses questions about the kinds of food that sustained migrants who settled in the United States before World War I, particularly the diets of Filipina/o immigrants on the West Coast and in Alaska during the first decades of the twentieth century. Orquiza, in contrast, explores the attempt by American reformers to transform the culinary knowledge and practices in the Philippines during the forty-eight years of U.S. imperialism. Robert Ji-Song Ku and Mark Padoongpatt offer a different Asian American critique. For Ku, the ubiquitous Kikkoman soy sauce and its history in the United States tell a fascinating story about when and where Asian Americans entered the mainstream. Mark Padoongpatt's analysis of "Oriental cookery" during the United States' Cold War intervention in Asia and the Pacific similarly argues that interest in Asia came before the arrival of large numbers of Asians and against the backdrop of hostility toward Asian bodies. Through and against the disciplinary mechanisms of anti-Asian sentiments in the United States and Asia, the five chapters in part II discuss where and when food became an index to think about Asian Americans entering the U.S. imagination.

If meanings of America are never stable, then meanings of Asian America are even more precarious. Attending to the varied culinary formations in "Asian America," the chapters in part III put the category of Asian America itself into crisis. How do foods become marked as "Filipino," "Korean," or "Thai"? What makes "foodies" into experts on what foods are "authentic" and what "fusion" is? Valerie Matsumoto examines how the multifaceted culinary work of nisei women beginning in World War II affirmed ties of ethnic culture and community while demonstrating resilience in the kitchen. Nina F. Ichikawa asks why "American" landmarks like California cuisine, the health food movement, and New York green groceries are *not* seen as Asian American milestones. Is it due to accidental oversight, intentional exclusion, or self-exemption? Might there be a confused logic that prevents certain kinds of contributions to "Americanness" from being defined as "Asian American"?

If indeed some cuisines are deemed to be discernibly "Asian," what is it about Filipino food in Queens, New York City (as Martin Manalansan ponders) or Uzbek foods in neighboring Brooklyn (as Zohra Saed muses on) that make us think more expansively about who and what constitutes authenticity *within* Asian American foodways? More specifically, to what extent does the notion of authenticity become both a refusal to engage difference on its own terms and a form of nostalgia? Taking us back once again to the scene of food trucks, this time in Austin, Texas, Lok Siu asks what Asian Latino fusion and the food-truck phenomenon of the twenty-first century can reveal about immigration, mobility, and the intersecting histories of Latinos and Asian Americans.

Finally, part IV shifts from the ethnographic and historical to the literary and the artistic. The explosion in recent years of novels, cookbooks, and cultural representations of Asian American foodways has produced much critical material. The chapters here look at the possibility of using food to read the multifaceted dimensions of Asian American subjectivity and personhood while also imagining more expansive definitions of Asian America.

Beginning with the organic farmer, Jennifer Ho examines how Don Lee's novel *Wrack and Ruin* brings together the ecocritical, gastronomic, and artistic imagination. Margo Machida's chapter on the visual gastronomies of food establishes how concerns about food politics, access to natural resources, and issues of sustainability have been fashioned into subjects for contemporary Hawaiian visual artists of Asian and Pacific American descent. Denise Cruz juxtaposes a reading of Monique Truong's *Book of Salt* with the reality television show *Top Chef* to consider the multiple meanings of the Vietnamese and Vietnamese American chef.

With South Asian ingredients at the center of her culinary map, fabled Indian chef Madhur Jaffrey reimagines the global power and reach of South Asian cooking in Delores Phillips's chapter. Then, in the last chapter, Anita Mannur juxtaposes two South Asian diasporic texts, *Nina's Heavenly Delights* and *Bodies in Motion,* to examine how a narrative of queerness might realign the ways in which food and cooking are constructed as an implicitly hetero-normative formation.

The twenty chapters of this anthology cover new ground in Asian American food studies. By focusing on the many struggles across various spaces and temporalities, they bring to the fore the potent forces of class, racial, ethnic, and gender inequalities that pervade and persist in production of Asian American culinary and alimentary practices, ideas, and images.

Notes

1. Of the many works by Michel Foucault, see especially *Madness and Civilization: A History of Insanity in the Age of Reason* (New York: Vintage Books, 1988), *The Order of Things: An Archaeology of the Human Sciences* (New York: Vintage Books, 1994), *Archaeology of Knowledge* (New York: Vintage Books, 1982), *Discipline and Punish: The Birth of the Prison* (New York: Vintage Books, 1995), and the three-volume *The History of Sexuality* (New York: Vintage Books, 1988–1990).

2. See Michael Omi and Howard A. Winant, *Racial Formations in the United States: From the 1960s to the 1990s* (New York: Routledge, 1994).

3. Psyche Williams-Forson, *Building Houses out of Chicken Legs: Black Women, Food, and Power* (Chapel Hill: University of North Carolina Press, 2006); Kyla Wazana Tompkins, *Racial Indigestion: Eating Bodies in the 19th Century* (New York: New York University Press, 2012).

4. See Frank Wu, "The Best 'Chink' Food: Dog Eating and the Dilemma of Diversity," in *Gastronomica Reader*, ed. Darra Goldstein (Berkeley: University of California Press, 2010), 218–31.

5. Sidney Mintz, *Sweetness and Power: The Place of Sugar in Modern History* (New York: Penguin, 1986); Gary Y. Okihiro, *Pineapple Culture: A History of the Tropical and Temperate Zones* (Berkeley: University of California Press, 2009); Andrew Dalby, *Dangerous Tastes: The Story of Spices* (Berkeley: University of California Press, 2000).

PART I

Labors of Taste

1

Cambodian Donut Shops and the Negotiation of Identity in Los Angeles

ERIN M. CURTIS

When the communist Khmer Rouge regime came to power in Cambodia in 1975, Ted Ngoy, a major in the Cambodian army working at the Cambodian embassy in Bangkok, fled with his wife and three children "aboard one of the first refugee airplanes to leave Asia for the [United States] West Coast."[1] "All the way over we just talked about having enough pigs and chickens to take to the market," Ngoy later told the *Los Angeles Times*. "That was my dream."[2] The family joined the more than fifty thousand Vietnamese and Cambodian refugees. They relocated to, were processed in, and moved out of Camp Pendleton in Oceanside, California, before the end of 1975.[3] Ngoy found employment as a janitor, sweeping floors at a Lutheran church in Tustin, California. To make ends meet, he also took two other jobs.

It was during his night job as a gas station attendant that Ngoy first encountered the pastry that would alter his fate. According to the *Los Angeles Times*, a fellow worker left Ted in charge one evening while he "ducked over to a nearby donut shop to bring back some sugary snacks. 'I didn't know what it was, but I liked it,' he recalled of the treat. 'I took some home and my kids liked it, too.'"[4] The next day, Ngoy went to the donut shop with $2,000 in cash he had raised from selling his possessions in Thailand and offered to buy the store. "'They turned me down,'" he later reported.[5] Undaunted, he attempted another purchase, this time at a branch of the popular West Coast chain Winchell's Donut House. Employees at the store promptly enrolled him in a management-training program. After a year spent managing a Winchell's in Orange County, Ngoy was able to save enough money to purchase Christy's Donuts in La Habra, California. By the mid-1980s, he owned more than fifty Christy's locations, a donut empire stretching from San Fernando to San Bernardino and from Monrovia to Newport Beach—in other words, across the entire five-county Los Angeles area.

Ted Ngoy and his family suddenly found themselves at the forefront of a vibrant local food culture. They now were the owners and operators of a successful donut chain in a city with hundreds of donut shops[6] and a populace "mad for" the fried confections.[7] More important, Ngoy is credited with both inspiring and creating a major ethnic business niche in Los Angeles.[8] In addition to operating his own chain, Ngoy sold donut shops to more recent arrivals from Cambodia. Following his example, these new owners developed systems of extending credit to fellow refugees who continued to come to California throughout the 1970s and 1980s, allowing them to open their own stores. Through this process, the Cambodian community quickly gave Los Angeles the distinction of having more donut shops than any other city in the world.[9] Their transformation of Southern California's food culture did not go unnoticed. As Seth Mydans reported in the *New York Times* in 1997,

> Cambodian refugees have, with little fanfare, virtually taken over the doughnut business in California, making it their primary route into the local economy.... Cambodian immigrants have opened one small shop after another, cutting deeply into the business of large chains like Winchell's Donut Houses, which once dominated the California market. Today, industry analysts say Cambodians own about 80 percent of the doughnut shops in the state.[10]

Writing in the *San Francisco Chronicle* in 2004, Kim Severson increased that estimate to 90 percent.[11]

This chapter tells the story of how and why the donut, a popular staple of so-called traditional American cuisine since the nineteenth century, became linked to Cambodian refugees in twentieth-century Los Angeles. Using interviews with donut shop owners, donut shop workers, and members of the Cambodian community, in addition to archival evidence, I examine the historical and structural foundations of this business niche. After explaining why Cambodians found this business model particularly advantageous, I describe the strategies they used to make it successful within a relatively short period of time. Finally, I explore the role of donut shops in the negotiation of identity for Cambodian refugees in the United States.

In addition, I raise questions about the relationship between Asian immigration, the urban built environment, and food cultures. Using Cambodian donut shops as the sites where local, national, and transnational histories intersect, I explore the development of relationships among a new group of Angelenos, Los Angeles, and Asia, highlighting the role of donut production and consumption. I show that donut shops (and perhaps even donuts themselves) serve as sites of cultural negotiation. Cambodians reimagined the traditional ethnic business niche in a form that reflects the physical and cultural landscapes of Los Angeles. In doing so, they demonstrated the ability of immigrant entrepreneurs to successfully negotiate, adapt, and modify business practices and consumption patterns. Accordingly, I suggest that immigrant entrepreneurs can also reshape our understanding of the role of food and food enterprises in the construction and contestation of ethnic, cultural, and urban identities.

The Advantageous Donut: Popularity

The ownership and operation of donut shops offer two major advantages over other occupations: their preexisting popularity and their economic viability. Before Ted Ngoy ever tasted his first donut, a widespread, highly visible, and readily available donut business infrastructure and donut culture already had succeeded in Los Angeles. The city's heavy reliance on automobiles and the eventual development of an extensive freeway grid, which, according to British design historian Rayner Banham, offered a "comprehensible unity" and "a language of movement, not monument,"[12] to otherwise "polymorphous landscapes,"[13] gave rise during the early and mid-twentieth century to a new retail architecture that included supermarkets, strip malls, and drive-ins.[14] The earliest fast-food establishments, including donut shops, thrived in this commercial environment. In 1936, a mere five years after the first retail donut and coffee chain opened on the East Coast, a trade publication, *Doughnut Magazine*, ranked California sixth in the nation for donut consumption, declaring, "Of all the states in the territory which extends from the Rockies to the Pacific, California has the highest annual total consumption of donuts—10,039,569 dozens," adding with some fervor that "the lusty, growing doughnut business has abundant room in which to grow and expand."[15]

This observation proved prescient: the men and women who flocked to Los Angeles both before and after World War II to take jobs in the growing aerospace[16] and tire industries[17] helped make donuts a favorite local treat and donut shops a standard feature of the retail landscape. By 1950, industry analysts considered the California donut market as separate from that of the rest of the United States, even going so far as to identify a regional taste profile: "They really live it up on the West Coast, where the preference is for 'crunch' doughnuts. These tasty tidbits are rolled in nuts, cocoanut, or cake crumbs. True to California tradition, they're spectacular—real big."[18] In 1979, as increasing numbers of Cambodian refugees entered Los Angeles, an industrywide survey ranked San Diego and Los Angeles as having the first and second highest densities of donut shops in the nation.[19] Shortly thereafter, the success of Cambodians in opening new donut shops caused Los Angeles to surpass San Diego. Simultaneous growth in what Edward Soja refers to as "high technology industries" combined with an "even greater expansion in low-paying service and manufacturing jobs"[20] during this period meant a steady supply of customers for Cambodian donut shops and a constant demand for donuts. In 1995, Seth Mydans noted that "defying California's health-food trend . . . the number of doughnut shops in the state grew by 55 percent from 1985 to 1993, even as consumption fell by nearly 10 percent." He added, "In Los Angeles, for example, there is one doughnut shop for every 7,500 people compared with 1 per 30,000 more common elsewhere in the country."[21] Cambodians found a successful business model and then made it work harder and better.

The Advantageous Donut: Economic Viability

Donut shops had another advantage: a relatively low and attainable cost of ownership and operation. Although an associate of Ted Ngoy's named Scott Thov reported that opening a small store in the 1990s required an initial investment of about $80,000,[22] recent arrivals used various means to accumulate the necessary capital relatively quickly. According to Hak Lonh, a Cambodian film director with two aunts and numerous cousins in the donut business, many refugees worked low-wage jobs (e.g., Ngoy's stint as a janitor) until they could combine their savings with loans obtained through informal credit arrangements.[23]

In many cases, friends and family provided additional funds, often in the form of direct loans. Helen Chin, a retired donut shop worker who spent fifteen years in the business, used money she earned as a seamstress to help her husband's niece and nephew open the store in which she later worked.[24] Family and friends also contributed less tangible forms of support. For example, shop owner Nally Yun told a *Sacramento Bee* reporter that she and her husband Roger lived with their parents "so we could save some money and fly on our own wings."[25] Apprenticeship arrangements, in which a more experienced baker or store owner would train a newcomer to the business, also were common. Susan Chhu, who runs Sunrise Donuts in Rosemead, California, reported that friends who owned donut shops trained her husband to bake and helped them set up their business shortly after their arrival in the United States.[26] Allen Dul of Mr. Steve's Donuts in Rosemead embarked on a sort of reverse apprenticeship: hiring a friend with experience in the donut business in order to learn how to operate the shop he had recently purchased.[27]

The Yuns raised a portion of the necessary money to buy their shop, Howard's Donuts, through a *tong tine*, another common source of capital. The *Bee* describes a *tong tine* as an "informal lending club that allows immigrants to pool their money."[28] In the *Houston Press*, Claudia Kolker elaborates:

> This is how it works: typically, anywhere from six to thirty friends will contribute a pre-determined sum at weekly or monthly meetings. Then, through lotteries or a group decision, each member gets a chance to collect the whole pot. After drawing the money, he or she keeps paying the installments until each group member has had an opportunity to take home the accumulated money. Only when a cycle finishes may a new member sign on or participants drop out. More often, though, the same participants begin again. In some groups, they take their place in line by lottery; in others, they may compete with secret bids of ten or fifteen dollars that go back to the pot.[29]

The *tong tine* has many different names[30] and is common among Asian, African, and South American immigrants. Los Angeles community business developer Namoch Sokhom described Cambodians' specific adaptations of the practice using a theoretical example:

> Let's say Mr. Sok needs $10,000 for a down payment to buy a donut shop. He has been known in the community to be upright and trustworthy. In January 2012, he calls a meeting of ten close friends who know how to "play" and can put $1,000 each per month. Thus, for January 2, 2012, Mr. Sok is the *mei tong tine* (the mother or the head of *tong tine* . . .) and he gets the full $10,000. In February 2, 2012, if the *kon tong tine* #1 (the child of . . .) needs the money and she bids the highest against the other 9 *kons tong tine*, let's say 5% . . . then she wins. She will get a total of . . . $9,500. In effect, she pays the interest up front. She is considered "dead," i.e. she will not be able to bid anymore for the rest of the pool period. On March 2, 2012, *kon tong tine* #2 also need the money and bid at 4% and the highest, so then he will get $9,800 . . . #2 is now "dead" also. And so forth. On October 2, 2012, *kon tong tine* #10 will not need to bid and after a long wait and 10 months pay ($1,000, $950, $980 . . .) now #10 get a sum of $10,000.[31]
>
> If Mr. Sok needs more than $10,000 he could organize at the *tong tine* with a head of $5,000. If 10 members, he would then get $50,000. In the U.S., $1,000 is most common and easier to find a member to join, and 15 members or less. If he needs more than $15,000 he can organize two pools.[32]

The titles of the participants in a *tong tine*—"mother," "head," "child," and so forth—as well as the groups' relatively small sizes indicate that these business arrangements could bring Cambodian refugees together in a kind of kinship. Thus, in terms of trust, obligation, and social bonding, this type of lending may not differ widely from the forms of family monetary support described earlier.

Of the many strategies employed by Cambodian refugees for raising capital to buy donut shops, the *tong tines* were perhaps the fastest, most economical, and most effective. The Cambodian variation of the arrangement allowed refugees to swiftly receive and pay back money. The loans were both tax free and interest free, supporting Kolker's assertion that informal lending clubs exist "to save money, not to make it."[33] Perhaps most important, they made cash "quickly available to those who couldn't otherwise get credit."[34] As Sokhom notes, *tong tines* were common for "Cambodian who cannot get a bank loan or did not know how."[35] In Lonh's words, being able to "kind of avoid the bank"[36] through personal savings, the help of friends and family, or the support of a *tong tine,* allowed Cambodians swifter access to independent business ownership with lower initial expenditures and fewer long-term costs.

Furthermore, the equipment, supplies, and labor required to run a donut shop are inexpensive. The necessary machinery for automated donut production, continuously streamlined since its invention in 1920,[37] is cheap and eliminates the need for costly labor or extensive training. The required staples—flour, sugar, and oil—also are plentiful and even cheaper. Prepared donut, glaze, and filling mixes—introduced in the late 1920s for use with automated donut-making equipment and frequently reformulated throughout the twentieth century—ensure a uniform product, allowing workers with no prior knowledge of pastries to master the baking of donuts in a short amount of time and also lowering labor costs.[38] Like the restaurant owners that Miri Song describes in *Helping Out: Children's Labor in Ethnic Businesses,* donut shop proprietors relied on the labor of their children, other relatives, or friends in order to further reduce expenses.[39] Indeed, a family of just three to five people could manage a shop independently.[40] If additional labor was necessary, extended family and friends usually provided it. Chhu and her husband ran their shop with "just family"[41] for many years, relying on the aid of their three children until each of them left home. With the business firmly established and family unavailable, they began to "hire part time,"[42] employing Latino or fellow Chinese Cambodian workers. Dul's daughters often take care of Mr. Steve's Donuts on Sundays, allowing their father an occasional day off.[43] Lonh describes his cousins helping out in his aunts' shop, and Chin's daughter Christina Nhek remembers folding boxes alongside her mother as a child.[44] Refugee assistance programs rarely fund child care, and being able to include children in the work of a donut shop allows parents to earn an income when they may not be able to do so otherwise.[45]

The Successful Donut: Hard Work

Having recognized the economic advantages of owning a donut shop, Cambodian refugees set about buying franchises, opening independent stores, and expanding the donut business in California so prodigiously that by the mid-1990s, industry insiders expressed fears of supersaturation:

> "In my computer, I have 2,400 Cambodian doughnut shops in California," said Ning Yen, 39, who started with a small shop and now owns an $8 million business distributing doughnut-making equipment. "I think it's already too many now," said Mr. Yen, a disciple of Mr. Ngoy, "and people are fighting each other for business. They just kept opening doughnut shops, and there is not enough demand for them all."[46]

Established California donut chains such as Winchell's also expressed displeasure with their increased competition:

> Nancy Parker, president of Winchell's, said her company was now down to 120 outlets in California. Before the Cambodian influx, Winchell's had more than 1,000 outlets in the western United States, mostly in California. "Where we had one Winchell's shop, they now have three or four Cambodian shops," Ms. Parker said. "They were very happy with a much lesser volume."[47]

In 2002, Winchell's even began renovating stores and increasing its advertising budget in order to compete more effectively with Cambodian donut shops.[48] Shop owners relied on three businesses strategies for their success. The first, and perhaps most important, was the willingness of donut shop owners and laborers to work hard. The second was an emphasis on frugality and practicality, and the third was the shops' integration into local neighborhoods.

Whether they viewed it positively or negatively, Cambodian donut shop owners and workers, almost without exception, cited hard work as key to the success of their businesses. Chhu reported that for about fifteen years, she and her husband regularly worked twelve-hour days, six or seven days a week, at

Sunrise Donuts. They worked even harder in their previous shop, which was their first.[49] Unfazed by the long hours, Chhu noted that her customers dispelled any potential monotony: "We see different people every day."[50] She also openly speculated that she could handle hard work because of her experience during the rule of the Khmer Rouge.

In contrast, Dul was dissatisfied with the hard work he encountered after leaving the jewelry business to buy a donut shop. He and his wife, Belinda Chhem, each have put in seventeen hours a day, "eight days a week," in their new venture, he joked. "Too many hours a day, right? Four months, so far I lose thirteen pounds,"[51] he added. Both concluded that in terms of workload, owning a donut shop compared unfavorably with the other jobs they previously held, including Dul's stint as a jeweler and Chhem's work in health care. Chhem even moonlighted in a donut shop for some time and found the twelve-hour shifts easy compared with the never-ending concerns of ownership.[52]

The Successful Donut: Practicality

Applying the kind of frugality found in a *tong tine* to the daily business of running a donut shop also helped Cambodians succeed. Lonh asserted that shop owners constantly find ways to economize in their daily routines. For example, he told of his aunts' uncanny talent for stretching dough to its limit, saying, "For one little batch, they can get a week's worth of doughnuts."[53] In the documentary *Cambodian Doughnut Dreams*, shop owner Leng Hing's advertising budget allows for only a single rubber stamp, which she uses to manually apply her store's name and address to every box of donuts. She expresses hope that this strategy will net new and repeat customers.[54] Similar tactics, such as relying on popular California donut varieties in order to ensure consistent revenue, helped bolster the success of other donut shop proprietors.

Another form of frugality manifested as a kind of resistance to change: Cambodian donut shop owners rarely changed their menus or remodeled their shops. Although this tactic had initial advantages, after more than thirty years in the business the ongoing refusal of donut shop owners to innovate may have hurt more than it has helped. As Sokhom complained:

> They run the business in the sense that they don't upgrade, they don't really . . .
> the younger Cambodian may say, "OK, I'm going to rebuild, repaint, remodel,"
> but some doughnut shop I say the last fifteen years I've been in, it's the same.
> Never get a drop of paint. Maybe a neon sign, but that's about it.[55]

In addition to occasionally putting up a neon sign, some donut shop owners were willing to diversify their coffee menus in order to compete with Starbucks and other specialty coffee purveyors.[56] Though he appreciated this nod toward change, Sokhom noted that this might not always be the most practical choice:

> They may add some coffee, some coffee machine, espresso. Those are expenses, some six, seven thousand dollar. You know, how many cup do you have to sell to recoup, right? You are selling not like Starbucks, but you buy a Starbucks machine, so not so smart. I mean, a regular . . . because people go there expecting a dollar a cup, not three dollars, so now you buy a machine that Starbucks sell for three, four dollar and you buy the same machine but you cannot sell three dollars, so how long does it take to recoup? And the people going there maybe not really conscious about . . . people that go to donut shop is the people who have about two dollar for breakfast . . . and not so picky.[57]

Here Sokhom is touching on the most important reason that donut entrepreneurs favored practicality over innovation: it not only saves money; it helps build and maintain a large base of regular customers. According to shop owners, rather than through novelty, they retain these regulars by offering good customer service and consistently fresh, high-quality donuts.[58]

The Successful Donut: Location

Cambodian donut shops retain customers because they become well integrated into the neighborhoods that they serve. With their small size, location on most major thoroughfares, and frequent placement in shopping centers, it is not difficult for a donut shop to become part of a local resident's routine. Most customers of Cambodian donut shops patronize stores near their homes and places of employment. "They live around here," as Dul put it.[59] Since shop owners and workers spend long hours in their businesses and often live nearby as well, they know their regulars well and can predict their habits and expectations. Chin reported that she knew what kind of donut each of her regulars preferred and would do her best to have it ready for them.[60] Over time, Chhu observed a correlation between her customers' ethnicities and the time at which they would arrive at the shop: "You know, most Hispanic people, they come early and then Asian people, like after eight."[61] Among Dul's regular customers were elderly men who "sleep and wake up early,"[62] often arriving at Mr. Steve's Donuts at 3:30 A.M. Even though it meant extending his already grueling hours, Dul often let them in. In general, the relationships between

Cambodian donut shops and their neighborhoods appear to be friendly and largely free of the tensions frequently observed between Korean grocery stores and their customer bases in Los Angeles.[63]

Cambodian donut shops also succeeded because of their provision of local spaces within an extremely large and racially diverse global city. Chhu now has a working knowledge of six different languages in order to communicate with customers from varying ethnic backgrounds.[64] In addition, customers can be found playing games and whiling away long hours in the stores' limited seating. Donut shops also—sometimes grudgingly—provide a place for jobless and homeless people to spend time without spending a lot of money, a valuable service in a city with a large homeless population frequently restricted from occupying public space.[65] As Sokhom pointed out, "[Donut shops] serve a big community that is really low income."[66]

Donuts and Identity: Cambodian Culture

Cambodian donut shops give their owners and workers a unique means through which to negotiate their identities as both Cambodians and refugees living in the United States. They do so by providing spaces in which entrepreneurs and their employees can partake of Cambodian culture, promote Cambodian values (particularly the concept of survival), and navigate American culture. Spread throughout Los Angeles, each store serves as a small oasis of Cambodian culture, a virtual franchise of such enclaves as Little Phnom Penh in Long Beach (which grew from seven families in 1975 to eight thousand residents by 1981 and is still the largest Cambodian community in the United States)[67] and Valerio Gardens in Van Nuys.[68] Recent immigrants can work alongside family, friends, or, at the very least, others with the shared language, ethnicity, and experiences of escaping Cambodia and enduring what Aihwa Ong refers to as "the exigencies of coping and getting through life"[69] in the United States. Many shops contain small Buddhist shrines[70] (Duc's shop prominently placed a Buddha next to the cash register, for example), while others display posters of Khmer slogans or art above cases of crullers and maple bars. Lonh described his aunts' donut shops as both gathering places for his extended family and places where he can find someone to translate the lyrics of classic Khmer rock songs.[71]

Donuts and Identity: Survival

Donut shops evoke a value particularly dear to early Cambodian refugees: survival. As Sucheng Chan points out in *Survivors: Cambodian Refugees in the*

United States, first-generation Cambodian immigrants self-identify as survivors, and they value their survival and that of their families above almost everything else.[72] The actual means of survival matters less than the survival itself. In fact, donut entrepreneurs often have disdain for their product. In *Cambodian Doughnut Dreams*, store owner Bunna Men expresses contempt for the entire business, saying, "I don't like anything about donuts, but I have to do, for a living."[73] Men appears to be using the word "living" in two ways: while he indicates that he has to make donuts in order to earn money, he also is referring to living in the most literal sense. Donut shops offer a means of owning tangible property and reaping the benefits of one's own labor, two things that had been taken away by the Khmer Rouge. They also give families that have undergone horrific experiences of separation and loss an opportunity to bond more closely. Chhu noted that one of the best things about running a donut shop was that it helped keep her family close together.[74] Again, donut shops have allowed families to survive independently with minimal outside help and almost no institutional interference. Minimal interaction with a new and unknown government is another marker of survival for a population recently brutalized by its authorities. Lonh summed it up best: "Donut shops are the keystones of survival for the Cambodian community."[75]

Donuts and Identity: American Culture

Besides preserving and promoting aspects of Cambodian life and Cambodian values, donut shops also offer a chance for refugees to negotiate aspects of life in the United States. They can become familiar with an American business model (and, to a limited extent, American foodways) while employing a Cambodian work ethic that emphasizes hard labor and long hours. Workers can practice English, albeit with a somewhat limited vocabulary. (As the *New York Times* reported, "The first English words that Ly Yiv learned . . . were the names of donuts: twist, glazed and jelly, chocolate, buttermilk and old-fashioned.")[76] They can network, share stories, and offer advice to one another. Donut shop owners and workers can interact with other Los Angeles residents from a variety of class and ethnic backgrounds and thereby situate themselves within the city's complicated social landscape. Chin told stories about residents of a wealthy neighborhood adjacent to her shop who became not only regular customers but also benefactors who gave generous tips to help her family.[77] At the same time, she endured her customers' open racism and contempt for her refugee status.[78] As a whole, the practices of Cambodian refugees in donut businesses are reminiscent of Ong's description of Cambodian refugees negotiating American citizenship in institutional settings: "In official and public domains—refugee camps, the welfare state, the court system, community hospitals, local churches, and civic organizations—refugees become the subjects of norms, rules, and systems, but they also modify practices and agendas while nimbly deflecting control and interjecting critique."[79] The Cambodian donut shops of Los Angeles serve as similar sites of contact with American customs, but storeowners and workers also use these spaces to assert a Cambodian identity, suggesting that Ong's argument extends to commercial as well as institutional spheres.

Conclusion

In little more than thirty years, Cambodian donut shops have become important sites of cultural negotiation in Los Angeles. Recognizing their economic potential and viability, Cambodian entrepreneurs have parlayed a popular treat into a thriving commercial concern through the successful application of core business strategies and adaptation to their particular locale. In doing so, they have created spaces that simultaneously embody their memories of the past and aspirations for the future and allow for the negotiation of overlapping identities. It is important to note, however, that with very few exceptions, the first generation of Cambodians to come to the United States does not see itself as having a privileged relationship to a uniquely Cambodian American identity through donuts. Instead, they continue to identify themselves primarily as survivors and to see donuts as a means to two ends: a living for themselves and a wider range of opportunities for their children.

The global financial crisis of the early twenty-first century has threatened the ability of Cambodian donut shop entrepreneurs to rely on their businesses for survival, particularly as the first generation of refugees ages and looks toward retirement. In addition, the cost of supplies and rent has risen dramatically,[80] decreasing the amount of profit that a donut shop can yield at any given time. "Right now, economy not so good," Chhu stated.[81] Sokhom explained, "So instead of ten days, now you have to do eighteen day or twenty day to pay just the rent."[82] Furthermore, because of the stagnant real estate market, donut shop owners who once expected to retire by selling their properties can no longer rely on this plan. According to Sokhom:

> Now suddenly they lose almost everything. Because if I want to buy a donut shop from you, I'll look at the cash flow. So suddenly the rent was $1,500 and now it's $3,000. So your donut shop is almost half as much. Your donut shop can,

say, sell for $200,000, now $70,000, nobody want to buy it. And so, if I've been building up my expectation and my hope that my donut shop is going to give me enough money to enjoy vacation, whatever I have dream about, $100,000 in my hand . . . it's not possible now.[83]

Rather than retiring, many owners have had to continue working even though their "bones are creaking."[84] To make matters worse, they now face a greater likelihood of health problems but rarely have health insurance. Sokhom noted:

I mean, for me, it's very sad, very . . . the sad part is, you thought they are well set, they are ready to retire. These are the people who work so hard, rarely take vacations, mostly open shop ten to sixteen hours a day, don't have health insurance most of the time—none, actually, none.[85]

Even Ted Ngoy has fallen on hard times. In 2005, the *Los Angeles Times* reported that the man who stated that he "created the doughnut world" was "broke, homeless, and dependent on the goodwill of his few remaining friends"[86] due to a series of personal, political, and financial missteps.

Yet despite these recent difficulties, Cambodian donut shops have not entirely lost their luster. Allen Dul purchased a shop during the financial crisis in part because the donut is a fairly "recession-proof"[87] commodity. Entrepreneurs still take pride in their businesses, and the Cambodian community in Los Angeles still regards them with respect: "I think the most satisfying is you are well recognize when you go to a wedding, you go to the temple . . . people recognize you, because it's a step up. Whether or not your shop make it or not make it, but in the meantime you enjoy it.[88] Though their future is extremely uncertain, Cambodian donut shop owners persist in the face of hardship much as they always have, and their stores still provide a place in which to navigate these new challenges. "Now people know that business is hard," said Sokhom, "but it was that old feeling, still keep them going."[89]

Notes

1. David Haldane, "A Real Horatio Alger Story: Refugee Built Empire on Doughnuts," *Los Angeles Times*, December 18, 1988; available at http://articles.latimes.com/1988-12-19/business/fi-434_1_doughnut-shop.
2. Ibid.
3. *Los Angeles Times*, "Last of Refugees Leave Camp Pendleton," November 1, 1975.
4. Haldane, "A Real Horatio Alger Story."
5. Ibid.

6. An industry survey reported that in 1979, the city of Los Angeles had 720 donut shops. Including the surrounding counties that make up the greater Los Angeles metropolitan area would increase this number substantially. See Ralph Chapek, Inc., *1979 Donut Industry Survey* (Santa Barbara, CA: Ralph Chapek, Inc., 1979).

7. Mary MacVean, "Krazy Kravings," *Salon*, March 10, 2000; available at http://archive.salon.com/travel/food/feature/2000/03/10/kreme/index.html.

8. See Haldane, "A Real Horatio Alger Story"; David Haldane, "Voices from the First Generation: The Ngoy Family," *Los Angeles Times*, November 5, 1989; available at http://articles.latimes.com/1989-11-05/magazine/tm-1171_1_united-cambodian-community; Seth Mydans, "Long Beach Journal; From Cambodia to Doughnut Shops," *New York Times*, May 26, 1995; available at http://www.nytimes.com/1995/05/26/us/long-beach-journal-from-cambodia-to-doughnut-shops.html; and Paul Mullins, *Glazed America: A History of the Doughnut* (Gainesville: University Press of Florida, 2008), 89–90.

9. MacVean, "Krazy Kravings." According to MacVean, 1,650 of the United States' 9,743 doughnut shops were located in Los Angeles as of November 1997. These numbers vary from source to source, however.

10. Mydans, "Long Beach Journal."

11. Kim Severenson, "The Hole Truth: Can America Build a Better Doughnut? Does It Need To?" *San Francisco Chronicle*, March 17, 2004; available at http://articles.sfgate.com/2004-03-17/food/17418894_1_doughnuts-krispy-kreme-fried-dough.

12. See Mike Davis, *City of Quartz: Excavating the Future in Los Angeles* (New York: Vintage Books, 1992), 73.

13. Ibid.

14. See Richard Longstreth, *The Drive-In, the Supermarket, and the Transformation of Commercial Space in Los Angeles, 1914–1941* (Cambridge, MA: MIT Press, 2000); Richard Longstreth, *City Center to Regional Mall: Architecture, the Automobile, and Retailing in Los Angeles, 1920–1950* (Cambridge, MA: MIT Press, 1997); and Richard Longstreth, *The American Department Store Transformed, 1920–1960* (New Haven, CT: Yale University Press, 2010).

15. Doughnut Machine Corporation, "Doughnut Possibilities in the West," *Doughnut Magazine*, March/April 1936, 6–7.

16. According to Joseph E. Libby, "In the decades following the Second World War, Southern California became the most powerful geo-political region in the United States. Much of its political and economic strength was due to its preeminence in the fields of aerospace and defense related technology. By the early 1960s, more than forty percent of the billions of Federal dollars spent on research and development went to California's aerospace industry." Joseph E. Libby, "To Build Wings for the Angels: Los Angeles and Its Aircraft Industry, 1890–1936," *Business and Economic History* 22 (1992): 22.

17. "God and Man seem to have conspired to make Los Angeles the future hub of the tire world," the *Los Angeles Times* declared in 1919 when the Goodyear Tire and Rubber Company announced the opening of a twenty-million-dollar tire factory in Los Angeles. See *Los Angeles Times*, "Twenty-Million-Dollar Tire Factory Coming to Los Angeles Soon: Goodyear Builds Plant," June 29, 1919. Ten years later, according to the *Times*, the factory was producing almost two million tires a year. See *Los Angeles Times*, "Fourteen Million Tires Made: Local Plant Celebrates Tomorrow," June 23, 1929. In 1947, the factory was still growing and announced further expansion to its

facilities. See Lynn J. Rogers, "Automotive Highlights and Facts," *Los Angeles Times*, January 19, 1947.

18. Monsanto Company, "The Ubiquitous Doughnut," *Monsanto Magazine*, February/March 1958, 31.

19. Ralph Chapek, Inc., *1979 Donut Industry Survey*.

20. Edward W. Soja, *Postmodern Geographies: The Reassertion of Space in Critical Social Theory* (London: Verso, 1989), 192. Soja includes "engineers, scientists, mathematicians, and technical specialists" among the members of the high-technology industries. Soja also notes,

    Between 1970 and 1980, when the entire USA had a net addition of less than a million manufacturing jobs and New York lost nearly 330,000, the Los Angeles region added 225,800. In the same decade, the total population grew by 1,300,000 but the number of non-agricultural wage and salary workers increased by 1,315,000, making the region by far the world's largest job machine, a position it has continued to hold in the 1980s.

21. Mydans, "Long Beach Journal."

22. Ibid.

23. Hak Lonh, interview by Erin M. Curtis, Los Angeles, March 2011.

24. Helen Chin, interview by Erin M. Curtis, Long Beach, CA, December 2011.

25. Stephen Maganini, "Surviving the Killing Fields: Cambodians Find Success in California," *Sacramento Bee*, May 5, 1995.

26. Susan Chhu, interview by Erin M. Curtis, Rosemead, CA, December 2011.

27. Allen Dul, interview by Erin M. Curtis, Rosemead, CA, December 2011.

28. Maganini, "Surviving the Killing Fields."

29. Claudia Kolker, "Dipping in the Money Pool," *Houston Press*, March 30, 1995.

30. The Vietnamese term for such an arrangement is *hui*, and the Ethiopian term is *ekub*. See Kolker for a broad treatment of the subject.

31. Namoch Sokhom, e-mail to Erin M. Curtis, January 2, 2012.

32. Ibid.

33. Kolker, "Dipping in the Money Pool."

34. Ibid.

35. Sokhom, e-mail.

36. Lonh, interview.

37. For more on the invention of automated doughnut-making equipment, see Mullins, *Glazed America*; and Sally Levitt Steinberg, *The Donut Book: The Whole Story in Words, Pictures & Outrageous Tales* (North Adams, MA: Storey Publishing, 2004).

38. For more on the history of prepared doughnut mixes, see Mullins, *Glazed America*; and Steve Penfold, *The Donut: A Canadian History* (Toronto: University of Toronto Press, 2008).

39. See Miri Song, *Helping Out: Children's Labor in Ethnic Businesses* (Philadelphia: Temple University Press, 1999).

40. Mydans, "Long Beach Journal."

41. Chhu, interview.

42. Ibid.

43. Dul, interview.

44. Christina Nhek, interview by Erin M. Curtis, Long Beach, CA, December 2011.

45. A 1985 refugee policy report cited a correspondence between large family size and lower workforce participation, observing,

This relationship between household size and employment can be explained in two ways. First, it is more difficult for families with large households, especially when most of the household members are children, to support themselves on the type of employment that is generally available to refugees—minimum wage jobs. Second, in large households with young children, it is more difficult for all adults to seek employment since at least one will usually have child-rearing responsibilities. As discussed below, child care programs are not generally funded through the refugee program.

See Susan S. Forbes, *Adaptation and Integration of Recent Refugees to the United States* (Washington, DC: Refugee Policy Group, 1985), 11.

46. Mydans, "Long Beach Journal."
47. Ibid.
48. Mark Ballon, "A Hole in Their Dreams," *Los Angeles Times*, April 4, 2002.
49. Chhu, interview.
50. Ibid.
51. Dul, interview.
52. Belinda Chhem, interview by Erin M. Curtis, Rosemead, CA, December 2011.
53. Lonh, interview.
54. Chuck Davis, *Cambodian Doughnut Dreams*, documentary film, Throughline Productions, 1989.
55. Namoch Sokhom, interview by Erin M. Curtis, Los Angeles, November 2011.
56. For more on the competition between Cambodian donut shops and major chains such as Starbucks after the turn of the twentieth century, see Ballon, "A Hole in Their Dreams."
57. Sokhom, interview.
58. According to Dul, the best advice he received about running his own donut shop was to focus on top-notch customer service and fresh products. As a result, his shop has a large number of regular customers.
59. Dul, interview.
60. Chin, interview.
61. Chhu, interview. Chhu added that African Americans tended to arrive early and that the local Chinese population frequented her shop in the afternoon.
62. Dul, interview.
63. For more on the relationship between Korean groceries and the neighborhoods of Los Angeles, see Nancy Abelmann and John Lie, *Blue Dreams: Korean Americans and the Los Angeles Riots* (Cambridge, MA: Harvard University Press, 1997). These tensions were observed most strikingly in the destruction of Korean shops during the 1992 Los Angeles uprising. Abelmann and Lie warn against speculating generally about their source, however:

Nowhere is the distance between ideal and reality greater than in the dominant media framing of the "black-Korean conflict." The popular account of the interethnic conflict reifies essentialized views of the two ethnic groups and fails to make sense of the concrete structures of opportunity they face. Facile ethnic and cultural generalizations are drawn, and class divisions within each group are passed over in silence. Although we do not deny that tensions exist between African Americans and Korean Americans, we criticize the dominant "black-Korean conflict" frame by considering its place in the American ideological crucible (x).

64. Chhu, interview.

65. See Davis, *City of Quartz.*

66. Sokhom, interview.

67. Rebecca Trounson, "8,000 Refugees Make Long Beach Cambodian Capital of U.S.," *Los Angeles Times*, December 27, 1981.

68. John Nielsen, "Cultural Wall Confines Cambodians," *Los Angeles Times*, April 14, 1985.

69. Aihwa Ong, *Buddha Is Hiding: Refugees, Citizenship, the New America* (Berkeley: University of California Press, 2003), xvii.

70. Lonh, interview.

71. Ibid.

72. See Sucheng Chan, *Survivors: Cambodian Refugees in the United States.* (Urbana: University of Illinois Press, 2004).

73. Davis, *Cambodian Doughnut Dreams.* Not all storeowners and workers share Men's opinion. Chhu recalled her first taste of a donut positively: "I said 'It's good. It tastes good and we can eat every day.'" She still eats donuts for breakfast daily.

74. Chhu, interview.

75. Lonh, interview.

76. Mydans, "Long Beach Journal."

77. Chin, interview.

78. Chin, interview.

79. Ong, *Buddha Is Hiding*, xvii.

80. Sokhom, interview. According to Sokhom, the cost of rent for a donut shop has risen from $600 to $1,500 in 2007 to currently about $3,000, an increase of two to five times the original amount in an extremely short period of time.

81. Chuu, interview.

82. Sokhom, interview.

83. Ibid.

84. Ibid.

85. Ibid.

86. Sam Quinones, "From Sweet Success to Bitter Tears," *Los Angeles Times*, January 19, 2005.

87. Sokhom, interview.

88. Ibid.

89. Ibid.

2

Tasting America

The Politics and Pleasures of School Lunch in Hawai'i

CHRISTINE R. YANO (WITH WANDA ADAMS)

[Food is] a marvelously plastic kind of collective representation. . . . In its varied guises, contexts, and functions, [food] can signal rank and rivalry, solidarity and community, identity or exclusion, and intimacy or distance.

Arjun Appadurai, "Gastro-Politics in Hindu South Asia," 1981

February 2009, Kabuki Restaurant and Delicatessen, Waimalu Shopping Center, Aiea, Hawai'i, 11:00 a.m. I am here with Wanda Adams, former food editor for the *Honolulu Advertiser*,[1] and fourteen retired "cafeteria ladies" (school cafeteria managers) from the Ewa-Waipahu school district.[2] Wanda and I have been invited to one of their regular lunchtime gatherings. Mrs. Oshiro, the woman in charge, greets us and ushers us through the dark, nearly empty restaurant to a section in the back, which is noisy with the chatter of familiarity. Wanda and I are the last to arrive. In local Japanese American fashion, if an event is to start at 11:00 a.m., most people are there by 10:45 a.m. We are quickly seated at the end of a long table of women, all looking to be in their sixties or seventies, primarily of Japanese (including Okinawan) ethnicity.[3] They greet us warmly and present each of us with a lei. Mrs. Oshiro interrupts the buzz and asks us to introduce ourselves and explain our project on school lunch. Everyone listens attentively, some nodding, others looking a bit puzzled or vaguely disinterested. After Wanda and I speak, waitresses begin serving lunch—miso soup, rice, chicken teriyaki, *tonkatsu* (breaded, fried pork cutlet), *namasu* (vinegared sliced cucumber, carrot, daikon), potato salad, and *tsukemono* (pickles). The chatter resumes, mixed with the soft murmurs of eating. This is not a boisterous bunch, but a group comfortable in their own long-standing friendship and shared experiences on the cafeteria line. They pay attention to the food. After the restaurant meal, one of the women serves a dessert that she made—"Frog Eyes" (pasta, canned pineapple, Cool Whip, instant pistachio pudding, canned mandarin oranges).

I talk intermittently to the woman seated across me, who retired in the last few years, but am content mainly to watch and listen. Wanda, though, works the room. She is a bit of a celebrity: people know her through her newspaper column on food. She asks for recipes and the women gladly oblige, not necessarily on the spot, but with promises to send them to her. They are pleased by her attention, which acknowledges their expertise.

The cafeteria ladies, along with Wanda, exchange the common talk of those who have been professionals in the food business for their entire lives. These are not high-flying chefs, but earthbound cooks and managers who have run school cafeterias. They have fed a good number of Hawai'i's children, five days a week, approximately forty weeks a year, for decades. They have come to know the children well, just as the children know them, often by name. They—and the food they served—form part of the ties that make the school a homey place. Many of their cafeterias still bake their own bread, even after the advent of pizza, nachos, and chocolate milk. These women have become identified in part by the foods that they learned to cook in large quantities, often faced with the challenges of received ingredients, calling on resourcefulness, culinary know-how, and a certain deft creativity. They know how to think on their feet, in the kitchen, stirring a twenty-quart pot of local stew. Sharing recipes with one another in portions of one hundred, three hundred, five hundred servings, their careers have been built on the power of food not only to sustain and nurture bodies but also to comfort, teach, and draw close those creating and sharing the contents of the cafeteria tray. In a land like Hawai'i, with a high cost of living and an immigrant population base, working mothers are the norm, and those eating lunch at school form the great majority of students. These women have thus played a large hand in molding the food experiences of generations in Hawai'i. What they have cooked and served have become part of the taste of childhood.

As anthropologist Arjun Appadurai notes in the epigraph beginning this chapter, food is a powerful, semiotic device that draws people together and also keeps some apart, etching in lines of inclusion and exclusion. This chapter draws on the lessons of food to do just that. I focus on these women ("cafeteria ladies"), the food they served, and inevitably the children they fed as a historical node centered on what I call *culinary assimilation*, learning the ways and tastes of national citizenship through food. Serving school lunch in a place like Hawai'i meant serving the taste of a particular version of America, especially for a postwar generation in the early days of statehood. This was not macaroni-and-cheese America, nor was it hot dog-or-hamburger-in-a-bun America; rather, this was an America of its own making in a local context of the many Asian cultures and indigenous Pacific base that formed Hawai'i's ethno-racial mix. This version of school lunch meant a hot meal that more often than not included rice: America with its own local Asian-based twist. Although this may not have been blanket assimilation on the order of language (e.g., "speak American" campaigns), its sensory and emotive force provided a kind of sub-jective assimilation convincing eaters that they were partaking of a dominant force and, quite critically, that it tasted good. School lunch represented a mid-day lesson in deliciously shared citizenship. It mattered less that the food itself may not have been exactly what was served in Kansas. It mattered more that the food represented something different from (even better than) home that tapped into larger aspirations of belonging. Indeed, this was not yet an era of ethnic-cultural resilience but an era of eager, hungry Americanization in Hawai'i and elsewhere.

In this chapter I analyze ways in which school lunch became the basis of locally wrought, culinary citizenship—representing its own version of America founded on principles of a Pacific-Asian–based multicultural history. I base my findings on formal and informal interviews with those who have been involved in school lunch in Hawai'i, on newspaper columns, and on my personal experi-ence while attending public schools in Honolulu in the 1960s.[4] I consulted the online Child Nutrition Archives oral history project of the National Food Ser-vice Management Institute, including six interviews conducted by Dr. Josephine Martin in 2007 with food service managers from Hawai'i.[5]

The chatter that lingers in my ears from the Kabuki Restaurant lunch sparks the idea of such cafeteria talk of times past in Hawai'i as a site of multiply wrought, locally based, widely shared interaction centered on eating. School lunch—primarily that found in public schools in the late 1940s to 1970s—forms part of the common experience known as "local" culture. At least for a generation of those who grew up in Hawai'i in a time when most cafeterias made their own dishes, that genre of cuisine known as "school lunch" carries fond memories of a hot meal in the middle of the day, nostalgically repre-sented by these Japanese American cafeteria ladies. Ask those who grew up during that period and they can easily recall the smell of the food emanat-ing from the cafeteria and the eagerness with which they approached school lunch. For some (especially from lower-income areas in the state), it was the only hot meal of the day. The smell, taste, and memory of those lunches are wrapped up in the images of the Japanese American cafeteria ladies. Although many of the women gathered at Kabuki Restaurant may be too young to have been the actual cooks in the late 1940s to early 1970s, they still carry the cul-tural weight and pride of their predecessors.

I focus my study on public elementary schools because they are the site of the consumers' greatest shared experience—that is, more students ate the school lunch served in cafeterias in elementary school than in higher grades, during which there may have been more options (e.g., eating lunch off-campus), more rebellious attitudes toward institutions, and more menu variety. Elementary schools may also be the site of heightened parental and public concern, with expectations of control over nutrition, diet, and, possibly, culinary socialization. Food as a source of Americanization may hold particularly true in the years leading up to and immediately following statehood in 1959.

Cafeterias in Hawai'i, as elsewhere, operated under particular mandates: (1) utilize federally distributed food surpluses from the U.S. Department of Agriculture; (2) adhere to the federal government's nutritional requirements; and (3) produce food that children will eat. This chapter describes the ways in which these conditions were addressed by school cafeteria managers (primarily Japanese American), becoming part of the culinary assimilation for both those planning and making the food as well as for the generations of children consuming it. The food served in cafeterias differed from that of the many homes that make up multicultural Hawai'i. I look at ways in which historical conditions and prestige systems—sociocultural, political, economic—give particular meanings to the food.

Talk Story about School Lunches, Past and Present

School cafeterias have long been the site of much talk, whether it is about the latest friendships or last night's TV show or the quality of the food. School cafeterias have also been the subject of much talk, particularly in the last few decades in the United States when alarm bells of childhood obesity have pointed a finger directly at the food served in that most public of institutions, schools. In her book *School Lunch Politics*, social historian Susan Levine cites the stigma of feeding America's children as part of the National School Lunch Program, a social welfare policy instituted in 1946 under the auspices of the U.S. Department of Agriculture.[6] The general picture that Levine paints is that of dreary cafeterias, institutionalized (soon-to-be-corporatized) food, and docile children.

The case of Hawai'i, by contrast, is startlingly different from—yet related to—Levine's description. Cafeterias in public schools in Hawai'i in the late 1940s to 1970s were known not for the blandness, but for the savoriness, of their food: older adults wax nostalgic over school lunches; specific schools were known for their lunches; and cafeteria managers—typically Japanese

American women like those gathered at Kabuki Restaurant—gained reputations for the recipes they developed, which sometimes marked the start of a family legacy of expert food preparation and future careers in the restaurant business. Wanda Adams's weekly column in the *Honolulu Advertiser* regularly featured readers' requests for recipes for dishes served in school cafeterias.[7] Some of these differences may be the product of social and institutional conditions in Hawai'i, including a high proportion of working mothers, a relatively low proportion of children bringing lunch from home, public schools with full kitchens, and heavily subsidized school lunch programs (a long-standing twenty-five cent price tag for a meal).

The rosy era of the nostalgized school lunch in Hawai'i is long gone. Although the smell of homemade bread still wafts from some cafeteria kitchens, more likely children are served food similar to that found across the United States—and, more important, face many of the same issues of tight budgets (including closing some kitchens and consolidating meal service to regional distribution centers), well-founded nutritional concerns, and children's fast-food tastes. Highly public campaigns in the 2000s, such as Berkeley restaurateur and locavore activist Alice Waters's Edible Schoolyard Project, which brings school-grown produce into the cafeterias; followed by First Lady Michelle Obama's White House garden to promote healthy eating, especially for children; have brought to stage center the concerns about school lunches.

In fact, talk that ties children's meals to politics has occupied common ground through time and space. As sociologist Gary Fine was quick to point out: "The connection between identity and consumption gives food a central role in the creation of community."[8] And what better institution to control the creation of community through food than the education system through which all citizens must pass? Thus school cafeterias, the governments that oversee them, and the cafeteria ladies who make many day-to-day decisions play key roles in community making. This community founded on food finds its greatest strength where there is the highest level of participation, as was the case in Hawai'i's elementary public schools in the postwar/statehood era.

Researchers, politicians, and cafeteria ladies alike recognize the power inherent in controlling what children eat. The idea of culinary assimilation does not surprise but is tied to citizenship in terms of hunger, consumer choices, and prestige systems. School lunch provides lessons for both children and cooks. Anthropologist Anne Allison analyzes what she sees as Japanese statist ideology tying mothers to children in regard to the *bento* (boxed lunch) that they prepare.[9] Through a properly made *bento*, mothers learn how to perform as good mothers before the eyes of the state-linked educational system; children also learn the expectations of maternal involvement in school affairs. Conversely, a hastily prepared, ill-planned *bento* suggests inattentive parenting, which creates shaky foundations for a strong citizenry in both body and mind. Mothers heed the ideological lessons: this is about not only nutrition but also mandatory attentiveness, commitment, and labor. Indeed, it is about citizenship.

Japanese, American, and other educational systems are right to focus on the school lunch as critical to individuals, families, communities, states, and nations. Growing bodies need the most nutritious food that institutions can offer. Impressionable minds need to learn about nutrition (and politics) by way of the school lunch in order to learn lifelong practices of healthy eating and being. Furthermore, children may lead families into consumption patterns through some of the lessons from their school lunches, whether they are what constitutes a complete meal to preferences for certain dishes to developing a taste for the cafeteria's cooking. Indeed, anthropologist Eriberto P. Lozada Jr. finds that children may be the decision makers in determining the restaurants or the particular kind of food that a family eats.[10] Although this may be true, especially in the present era of global food industries and heavy advertising aimed toward children, even school lunch—if admired, as was the case in postwar Hawai'i—may be the subject of such favor. One woman in her seventies recalls her children attending a public elementary school in Honolulu and insisting that she make spaghetti at home just the way the cafeteria ladies made it.

Alice Waters writes about her Edible Schoolyard Project using the headline "Want to Teach Democracy? Improve School Lunches."[11] The same may be said with even greater fervor about the years following World War II. At a time when patriotism ran high for the general population, as well as tenuously for Japanese Americans—that is, when citizenship had to be earned, maintained, and displayed—wartime remnants of unease cannot be overlooked. Japanese Americans in Hawai'i during wartime may not have faced large-scale internment because of their numbers, but they understood well their position as potential enemy aliens. Just as they lived under campaigns to "Speak American," so, too, school lunches may be said to promote notions of "Eat American" or at least to taste it in one's cafeteria tray.[12] Needless to say, Japanese Americans were not the only ones to catch the fever of broad-scale assimilation in postwar Hawai'i.[13] With the campaign for statehood heating up (including a race with Alaska to become the forty-ninth state), the parallel culinary side of that fever may be seen in the workings of the cafeteria tray. Schools worked hard as the site for teaching the populace how to speak standard English and other lessons of American citizenship and also how to eat American and taste the victory of the flag. School lunch in Hawai'i could thus be seen as a civic achievement.

The Food They Served: Hawai'i-Based American Food

The civic achievement of school lunch may not have been a conscious administrative decision to serve American food (or its interpretation). Rather, cooking and serving American food in large quantities was part of the training of cafeteria workers and heads, as well as an expectation of the public. Moreover, even as I interpret school lunch during this time period as a form of "tasting America," I recognize the polyglot, sometimes haphazard, nature of what was actually served. Thus, this is not strictly a top-down, governmentally designed plate but one shaped by available ingredients (including an assortment of U.S. Department of Agriculture surpluses), federal nutritional requirements, cafeteria ladies' interpretation of local menus and tastes, and the children's ephemeral palate. In his discussion of national culture and food in Belize, Richard Wilks provides a useful table entitled "Polarities of Food Culture."[14] He contrasts two interactive, interdependent polarities of Lived Practice and Public Performance as cooking versus cuisine, meals at home versus public banquet, working class versus elite class, and local versus cosmopolitan. The case of school lunch in postwar Hawai'i may be positioned between these two, existing as everyday food (cooking, not cuisine), eaten publicly in institutionalized settings (school cafeteria), and serving primarily non-elite working-class foods but with aspirational connotations (assimilation to a local version of American national culture). Wilks makes the point that national cuisine typically emerges through a dynamic interaction between polarities like these. So, too, a Hawai'i version of American national cuisine emerged through such an interaction.

An examination of school lunch menus from that period reveals the predominance of Western food and the relative scarcity of Asian-based dishes.[15] Even though there may not have been Asian dishes, there typically was rice—that is, white, short grain, Japanese-style steamed rice[16]—served with a variety of foods. As was common during that period, there was less emphasis on fresh foods and more emphasis on industrial food, from canned fruit cocktail to pudding mixes. And there always was white whole milk, even if a significant portion of the population may not have been able to digest this properly because of lactose intolerance.[17] Just as the cafeteria trays had convenient compartments for each of the dishes, so, too, the menus reflected such divisions so that each meal comprised a protein, a starch, a vegetable, a fruit, and milk.

What is relatively absent from the school lunch menus in Hawai'i is what might be considered a staple of lunches elsewhere in the United States: sandwiches. I argue that at this time, lunch planners—whether dietitians, cafeteria ladies, or managers—held a particular notion of the food that constituted a meal and would satisfy eaters. The emphasis in Hawai'i rests on rice (short grain, steamed, Japanese style) and its constitutive role in the idea and place of a "hot meal." According to food historian Rachel Laudan, in the state of Hawai'i, the amount of rice consumed every year averages sixty pounds per person (including children), in contrast to the average of nine pounds a year for persons in the continental United States. Clearly, rice makes the meal. The taxonomic contrasts between a sandwich (cold, dry, light, old) and a hot meal (warm, moist, filling, fresh) suggest the relative lack of appeal of the former and the great, even emotional, appeal of the latter. I base this not so much on surveys and hard data but on informal conversations over the years with parents and children in Hawai'i. According to them, one of the best things about the school lunch was that it was a hot, filling, and thus satisfying meal.

People remember the cafeteria experience and food well. On August 4, 1996, the *Honolulu Advertiser*, then the largest newspaper in the state, ran a long feature based on responses of readers to the question of "You Know You're Local If. . . ." At least half the entries concerned food, many of which can be traced in some form to school lunch, from the dishes they ate to the cafeteria ladies who served them. Most notably, readers expressed their preference for eating rice (short grain, Japanese style) with everything, including Western starches—rice with spaghetti, rice with macaroni or potato salads, rice with tuna casserole. Although this kind of rice-based meal can be found throughout Hawai'i, the school lunch experience and the rice that goes with it became emblazoned as identifiers of being local. Accordingly, what was served at schools subtly helped develop the style and taste known today as "local food."

Throughout her tenure as the *Honolulu Advertiser*'s food editor, Wanda Adams's "Food for Thought" column was besieged with pleas for school lunch recipes. Some requests were easy to satisfy: Spanish rice (by far the recipe most often sought), shortbread cookies, beef niblets (a corn-and-beef brown stew), peanut butter crisscross cookies, sweet-sour spare ribs or sweet-sour pork (see the appendix to this chapter). Others—baked lemon chicken from Ka'ahumanu Elementary, date bars with crumbly topping from Kamiloiki School, malted-top brownies from Likelike School, crispy morning toast from Ka'iulani Elementary, peanut butter bread (coffee cake) from Kapalama Elementary—were never located. Researching the files of the School Food Services office in Kaimuki in the early 2000s, Adams quickly learned that these recipes were likely to remain lost unless they happened to be handed down within the cafeteria managers' families.

Before schools began to share their central kitchens in the 1970s, there was only a sketchy central repository for recipes. Adams was told by Food Services personnel that cafeterias were operated independently, recipes were created by cafeteria workers from whatever ingredients were available, and many were never recorded or the records were destroyed or lost. Furthermore, many of the recipes would be impossible to replicate exactly even if they existed, as the cafeterias used surplus foods provided by the U.S. government and some of these were quite odd. The cheese, butter, and nut butters one might expect, but maybe not the dehydrated wheat flakes or rolled wheat, powdered milk and eggs, and canned stewed beef chunks. And even common foods might be altered in texture and flavor: chicken, fruit, potatoes, and sweet potatoes arrived flavored and canned. "Horrible stuff!" recalled one former cafeteria manager.

Those public and private school food service programs that received the ingredients were nonetheless required to use them, so cafeteria recipe designers had to be very creative. "People didn't know what we put in there: bulgur wheat in crusts, almond butter in the spaghetti sauce, peanut butter in meatloaf," said Teri Jean Kam-Ogawa, a former cafeteria lady and now a child nutrition specialist with the School Food Services program. One well-known cafeteria lady, the late Chieko Okamoto, whose recipes are in the Food Services files, even made a cake with split peas. Kam-Ogawa said that one reason that popular crisps and cobblers were served so often was that the cafeterias were rarely given, and rarely could afford, fresh fruit. Cobblers, crisps, betties, and crunches were readily made in bulk and used up sweetened canned fruit, oatmeal, flour, and butter from the surplus stores, as well as leftover bread and rolls. Similarly, files of the American School Food Service Association's *School Lunch Journal* show ingredients like sauerkraut hidden in chocolate cake, powdered milk as the basis of butterscotch blanc mange (a cornstarch pudding), cottage cheese in yeast rolls, and dehydrated sweet potato flakes in cookies.

Tasting this version of America thus relied heavily on the cafeteria ladies' ingenuity and general cooking expertise, masking surplus ingredients, trying different recipes, and shouldering the responsibility of creating a hot meal every day for hundreds of children with as little monotony as possible. This was explicitly not home cooking. But it was comfort food that made school into a homey place through the lunch break in the middle of the day.

Cafeteria Ladies as the Domesticating Presence

A significant part of remembering school lunch in the 1996 *Honolulu Advertiser* article and through talking with people rests on what I call the domesticating presence of the cafeteria ladies. One "local" writes: "You know you're local if . . . you remember the names of the 'cafeteria ladies' at your school."[18] In Wanda Adams's food column, requests for recipes were "local," as demonstrated by reader Arlene Almaida Santiago, who reeled off the names of the cafeteria ladies at her school, Kalihiwaena Elementary: "Mrs. Sato, Mrs. Brown, Mrs. Santos, Mrs. Shishido." Clearly, cafeteria ladies made an impression on the children who stood in line for their food, an impression that was gendered and, to an extent, racialized.

Although the school lunch program, like much of the rest of prestatehood and early statehood culture, was dominated by *haoles* (whites), almost all its workers (cooks and, later, cafeteria managers) were of Asian ancestry (Japanese, Okinawan, Korean, Chinese, Filipino) and almost all were women (thus the term "cafeteria ladies"). Some people of Portuguese and Hawaiian ancestry also worked in school kitchens, whose racial mix became the image of the cafeterias. Notably, the racial mix of the kitchens was not reflected in the food, but it did offer an important civics lesson: even if one were of Japanese ancestry, one could (and should) cook and eat not necessarily the food of one's ancestors but the food of citizenship—that is, American.

Kilihune Matsui, whose Chinese American mother studied to be a cafeteria manager, recalled that on some days, cafeteria managers were allowed to take home leftovers. Her family was thrilled to get something other than "the same old Chinese food." "My mother learned how to 'do *haole*' and would make her own cream puff pastry shells and bake her own angel food cakes," Matsui said. The family learned to eat dishes that Matsui's girlfriends would not touch, such as creamed tuna or salmon loaf. Matsui's mother, like others who attended the cafeteria manager–training programs of the time, was taught by *haole* home economists, many from the continental United States. Thus the cafeteria ladies brought their training in Western/American dishes to their places of work as well as their homes. In parallel with an earlier generation of Japanese (American) maids to *haole* families who learned American housekeeping and cooking and brought these home to their own families, these cafeteria ladies themselves became agents of assimilation.

Matsui's mother's story underscores the importance of home economics as an educational path that led the cafeteria ladies to their eventual careers. The course of study known as home economics was the product of an 1899 conference in Lake Placid, New York, where women activists developed a curriculum whose goal was twofold: to achieve respect for and create careers in what was then defamed as "women's work"—cooking, cleaning, and household management—and to help disadvantaged families fight malnutrition and the ills associated with "uncleanliness." The movement took on momentum, became a common course of study from grade school to college, and was a socially acceptable career choice for women, like that of teaching and nursing.

In the first half of the twentieth century, homey versions of the five "mother sauces" of classic French cooking dominated home economics cooking curricula: béchamel ("white sauce"), espagnole ("brown Spanish sauce"), hollandaise ("mayonnaise"), velouté ("light stock sauce"), and vinaigrette ("French dressing"). These sauces became the basis for much of the cooking by career home economists. Another influence of home economics that changed immigrant and first-generation palates was a focus on heavy proteins—beef, pork, chicken—in larger portions than is usual in Asia and on dairy foods, particularly milk. This was because rickets and other nutrition-related diseases were common in some areas, so the concern was getting enough nutritious food to eat. In Hawai'i, these recipes and Western-style approaches were taught to budding cafeteria managers who may never have experienced anything like them in their Chinese, Japanese, Korean, Hawaiian, Filipino, or even Portuguese homes.

Portrait of a Cafeteria Lady (Interview with Wanda Adams)

Some cafeteria ladies became famous within their small circles, and some of their recipes have appeared in community cookbooks over the years. One of these was Mrs. Eleanor Kim Tyau, a Korean American who was born in 1915 in Kona on the island of Hawai'i, moved to O'ahu as a child, and married a Chinese man at age nineteen. Tyau first came to Wanda Adams's attention through a request from Shirley Okino, whose husband craved the salad dressing known to Saint Louis School boys of a certain generation simply as "Mrs. Tyau's Sauce." When the food page put out a call for the recipe, versions came in from all over. It was a straightforward salad dressing of the sort popular in the early twentieth century under the title "French Dressing," tomato and oil based. But there was something about the way she made it that had the boys drizzling it on everything, from rice to cooked vegetables, bread to broiled meats. Here is her story, based on an interview conducted by Wanda Adams when Tyau was in her nineties.

Eleanor Kim Tyau first worked as a maid and cook ("not by choice; it was what I could do"). A Mrs. Edwards from the Department of Education was impressed with her work and urged her to go the University of Hawai'i to get a degree in food services management. "She said you can train anybody to be a cafeteria manager, but you need a degree to be a food services manager," Mrs. Tyau recalled. However, Mrs. Tyau became pregnant and so could not become a full-time student. Instead, when she was twenty-one, she attended a two-year cafeteria manager program taught at the central Honolulu high school (McKinley High School) taught by a Mrs. Foxall.

Upon graduation, Mrs. Tyau's first assignment was at Kalihi-waena School, where she remained until World War II. As everyone was expected to turn their hand to war work, she was assigned to the cafeteria on the campus of Saint Louis School (a Catholic Marianist school for young men), which had been turned into a civilian defense canteen, a feeding station for war workers (students took their classes and meals at McKinley High School during this period).

This would be the beginning of a fruitful thirty-seven-year career at Saint Louis School; when the war ended, the school asked her to stay on as a concessionaire. An independent businesswoman, she was contracted not only to provide meals for students but also three meals a day for the boarders and the priests and brothers who taught there, and lunch for nonboarding students. A sports lover, Mrs. Tyau also found time to cook for the various sports teams and to provide meals for class reunions. She remained touchingly grateful that coaches and athletes were kind to her developmentally disabled son; in return, she fed them well and helped raise funds for the teams.

At one point, she supervised a staff of twenty to accomplish this.

For the much-loved Saint Louis Carnival fund-raiser, she made gallons of kimchi (hot and sour fermented cabbage) and *taigu* (dried salt cod marinated in sesame oil, paprika, Korean red pepper powder, and honey and dressed with sesame seeds). "I used to buy the codfish in hundred-pound crates and soak it and pick out all the bones myself," she recalled, shaking her head at the work she was capable of then. She made hundreds and hundreds of jars of each dish annually for the sale, carrying on from the late 1940s until her retirement in the 1970s. "But I just never seemed to make enough of it."

Despite her fame for kimchi and *taigu*, Mrs. Tyau said she doesn't recall cooking much that "I could truly say was Korean or Japanese; it was more Western stuff—stew, curry, meatloaf, baked chicken, spaghetti." However, she did acknowledge that Asian ingredients played a role in many of these Western recipes and that both teriyaki chicken and teriyaki beef were standards.

Her specialties included sweet-sour spareribs, beef stew, lamb curry (she bought whole carcasses and cut all the meat), baked spaghetti (with bacon in the sauce and cheese on top) and an invention of her own called "Spanish beans," which was cubed luncheon meat and fresh green beans, stewed in tomato purée with onions, garlic, and soy sauce, and thickened with a poi (mashed and fermented taro root)-based batter. ("I didn't like flour or cornstarch"; see appendix.) Desserts ran to chocolate sundae pie (Spanish cream with bitter chocolate curls), peach and apricot pie, marble cakes (yellow cake with chunks of chocolate and chocolate frosting). "It was all very simple food, but the boys liked it," she confessed.

The Legacy of School Lunch: Plate Lunch, Local Identity, Nostalgia

The plasticity of school lunch as an icon in postwar Hawai'i suggests both shared local identity based on the common experience of a public school education, as well as subdivisions of a place-based identity dependent on the particular school (and its lunch) of one's childhood. Neighborhoods can be identified by their physical and socioeconomic location and also their shared school meals. These identities and memories interact synesthetically through the smells of the apple brown betty baking, the sounds of the cafeteria trays, the smell and taste of milk that came out of an individual-serving carton, the texture of the Spanish rice on one's tongue, the smoothness of the concrete floor underfoot, the cool touch of the stainless steel counters, and the distinctive odor of sour milk that pervaded certain areas of the cafeteria.

School lunch is a common experience of locals of a certain age, as well as the way they ate it, which reflects local practice. One does not eat all of one thing at a time (nor, in general, is one supposed to skip anything, such as peas or cooked carrots). Instead, one samples the meat, starch, and vegetable together, each bite reconstituting the well-balanced cafeteria tray contents, saving dessert for last. One could interpret this style of eating as reflecting a local ethos of a "melting pot" or, more to the point, a "plate lunch." Although this interpretation may sound overdetermined and trite, it follows what anthropologist Dafna Hirsch finds in her analysis of hummus in Israel: "[In] the Israeli manner of eating hummus (referred to in Hebrew as 'wiping,' distinct from Palestinian 'dipping'), the entire bodily hexis involved in its consumption . . . manifest the main qualities that Israelis like to associate with 'Israeliness': informality . . . but also sociability."[19] In other words, the very manner of eating school lunch in Hawai'i, as in eating hummus in Israel, may be interpreted as linked to identity.

Until child labor laws intervened in the 1970s, students in both public and some private schools were required to render one or two days' service a year to the school lunch program, generally serving food or milk, punching or collecting lunch tickets, and performing other simple tasks. Even this becomes part of the remembered experience of school lunch—whether of one's own labor (and legitimately missing class) or recognizing one's friend on the other side of the counter serving. Lori H., who attended Lunalilo Elementary School on Oʻahu, recalled this practice without resentment—fondly, in fact. In a 2009 e-mail to the *Honolulu Advertiser*, she remembered that these students got free lunches and generally an extra dessert and thought that wearing black hair nets was hilarious. They enjoyed the chance to sneak their friends extra large servings of the "really good stuff" (such as, she said, mashed potatoes, considered "exotic" because then the dish was rarely served in island homes). Rochelle Uchibori said the long hours of "cafeteria duty" "gave me a better appreciation of and insight into the hard work it took to bring us those meals."

"Nani," who went to Manoa Valley Elementary in the 1950s, remarked during a phone call to food editor Wanda Adams, "They fed us so well. It was so much better than anything the schools are making now." Another man, a McKinley High School graduate of Okinawan heritage, whose mother was a cook, jokes that he knew only three "Okinawan" dishes when he was a child: meatloaf, spaghetti, and mac and cheese. Years later, he asked his mother why she cooked that way, and she said that those dishes were the ones she learned to cook, first in service as a maid in a *haole* household and then in the school system working in the cafeteria. She emphatically added, "Plus, I wanted my children to be Americans."

The legacy of school lunch of postwar Hawaiʻi may be seen most clearly in the evolution of the plate lunch: a sectioned plate of rice, meat dish, and macaroni salad. The plate lunch has become an icon of local culture, notably in a touring exhibit (1997/1998), "From Bento to Mixed Plate," curated by the Japanese American National Museum. Further iterations of the iconicity of the plate lunch can be found in food scholar Rachel Laudan's *The Food of Paradise: Exploring Hawaii's Culinary Heritage*,[20] Wanda Adams's *The Island Plate*,[21] and journalist Arnold Hiura's *Kau Kau: Cuisine and Culture in the Hawaiian Islands*.[22] Hiura's documentation of the genesis of the plate lunch in postwar Hawaiʻi includes historic sharing of plantation *bento* (lunch) among workers, pushcart peddlers serving hot lunches to dock workers, lunch stands and wagons selling plate lunches, drive-ins, and restaurants. He does not mention the role that school lunches had in creating the expectation of a hot meal in the middle of the day, shared with one's peers while seated at a long table. Some people still call it the highlight of their day.

Concluding Thoughts on Culinary Citizenship:
Becoming Americans in the Cafeteria

In an article entitled "The Gourmetization of Hummus in Israel," anthropologist Dafna Hirsch discusses the meanings given to and political claims made of hummus: "The meaning of hummus for Arab-Jewish relations is not given, but is a matter of the way in which it is used by social actors."[23] Here, too, debates may flare over the nutritional value of plate lunches past and present or the degree to which they were local (Pacific Asian based) versus American food or how they navigated the space between public and private. As in Hirsch's discussion of hummus, so, too, our discussion of plate lunch in Hawai'i is based most significantly on the way in which the school lunch—or the idea of it—is used by social actors, including the state, educators, cafeteria ladies, and the children past (now adults). School lunch for baby boomers and older in Hawai'i represents their shared experience, the stuff of nostalgia for a time when people talked about assimilation as if it were a proud and necessary achievement.

For this older generation, school lunch was not laden with concerns about nutrition. Rather, the plastic tray and small carton of milk carried with them some of the best-remembered, everyday, not-home, comfort food of one's childhood. This is the food that people would never expect their mothers to make. Rather, it was the food that they went to school to eat and, years later to talk about. Here lie the practices of talking with one's mouth full. School lunch became its own genre of food: similar to but not replicating that found in many family-style restaurants in Hawai'i.

But how did school lunch provide such a fulsome mouth in postwar Hawai'i? I return to some of the features of Appadurai's epigram with which I began this chapter: rank and rivalry, solidarity and community, identity or exclusion, and intimacy or distance. School lunch during the statehood era provided a means of inclusion, generating identities that changed through time—as members of a particular neighborhood school, as members of an island-based state, as fledgling Americans, as a generation of aging baby-boomers. These identities were not without rivalries, sometimes pitting school against school on the basis of their lunches, sometimes correlating with the socioeconomic class of the neighborhood. But the rivalries themselves became points of pride and affiliation.

The mouths filled with talk of school lunch in Hawai'i are replete with emotion, intimacy, and overwhelming affection. They speak person to person; they speak, too, in the public forum of nostalgic newspaper articles and food columns. The objects of such affection are the Spanish rice or the shortbread and often the women who made them, the cafeteria ladies like those with which I began this chapter. Those mouths are still talking, as are the women themselves. When they talk about the good old days, the subject inevitably turns to food. Good old days may never have been quite as good as people remember them, but this is where the nostalgized school lunch and the opportunity to taste this version of America now called "local" find their way to center stage. As an everyday, every-person shared experience, the Hawai'i school lunch of the postwar era embeds mundane, assimilationist rhetoric in the intimacies of the heart and stomach.

This is where culinary citizenship comes alive—or at least did for a generation that grew up with dreams of becoming American. Even before one could march with stars and stripes in hand, one could at least participate in acts of assimilation daily. The achievement of the postwar school lunch in Hawai'i was that it created citizens through taste rather than through didacticism. Cafeteria ladies knew all too well that in order for children to eat their peas, they had to savor them and return every day wanting more. School lunch lessons taught clearly that politics may be best swallowed when mixed with a hearty dose of pleasure.

Appendix: Frequently Requested Recipes

The following are some of the recipes documented from school or cafeteria worker files or recreated from "skooldayz" memories by food writer and editor Wanda Adams.

SPANISH RICE

   2 cups uncooked long-grain white rice

   3½ cups half water and tomato water (drained from canned tomatoes, see below)

   ½ green bell pepper, minced

   ½ medium-large onion, peeled and minced

   ½ cup stringed and chopped celery

   2 pounds ground beef (less than 20% fat), lightly browned, fat drained

   1 (28-oz.) can plus 1 (15-oz.) can peeled, chopped tomatoes, with juices (use some juices to cook rice, remainder in casserole)

   1 (6-oz.) can tomato paste

   2 teaspoons salt

   2 tablespoons sugar

   1½ tablespoons Worcestershire sauce

   2 teaspoons mild chili powder

   In a large saucepan or Dutch oven, bring water/tomato water to a boil, pour in rice, bring to boil again, cover, and turn down to low, steaming until liquid is absorbed. In a very large bowl, stir together rice, bell pepper, onion, celery, browned ground beef, tomatoes with juices, tomato paste, salt, sugar, Worcestershire sauce, and chili powder. Spread in a 9" × 13" baking dish and bake at 325° for 40 minutes or until cooked through.

Makes 16 servings.

Source: files of the Hawai'i State School Food Services program

SWEET-SOUR SPARE RIBS (OR PORK CHUNKS)

4 to 5 lbs. pork spare ribs (with "soft" bones) or chunks of pork butt
Seasoned flour (optional, see below)
2 cloves garlic, crushed
2 to 3 inches peeled fresh ginger, grated or minced
½ cup soy sauce
½ cup brown sugar
½ cup white vinegar
1 (20-oz.) can pineapple chunks in juice
Cornstarch (optional, see below)
Sesame seeds for garnish (optional)

Approach 1: Cook on stovetop with thickened gravy: Lightly dredge the spare ribs or pork chunks in flour seasoned with salt and pepper. In a large Dutch oven, fry pork pieces in vegetable oil; drain fat. Add garlic, ginger, soy sauce, brown sugar, vinegar, and pineapple juice; cook over medium heat, simmering 30 to 40 minutes or longer until pork is tender; add pineapple chunks toward the end of the cooking time. Thicken juices with cornstarch, as desired (whisk in cornstarch, bring juices to a boil, turn down heat ,and serve).

Approach 2: Cook in oven with thin gravy: Marinate pork with ginger and garlic in soy sauce, brown sugar, white vinegar, and pineapple juice for at least one hour, turning occasionally. Preheat oven to 325°. Place pork mixture in a large, heavy Dutch oven and bake in oven for 30 minutes; stir and turn meat; and cook another 30 minutes until pork is very tender. Add pineapple chunks toward the end of the cooking time.

In either case, serve hot with steamed rice; garnish with sesame seeds, if desired.

Makes 8 to 10 servings.

Optional: Add 1 star anise during cooking or ½ teaspoon Chinese five-spice powder. Early recipes also routinely used Aji-no-moto (MSG).

Source: files of the Hawai'i State School Food Services program
and various community cookbooks

MRS. TYAU'S SPANISH BEANS

Drizzle of oil or spurt of vegetable spray

1 lb. ground beef or finely chopped luncheon meat or ham or raw bacon

1 small onion, chopped

2 cloves garlic, minced

2 tablespoons soy sauce

2 teaspoons sugar

2 (15-oz.) cans green beans (or equivalent defrosted frozen beans or steamed
fresh beans, cut into 1½-inch lengths)

2 (8-oz.) cans tomato sauce

¾ to 1 cup thin poi

Cooked rice

In a large, deep sauté pan or wok, heat vegetable oil or vegetable oil spray over medium-high heat; add meat, lower heat to medium, and brown meat. Drain away excess fat (reserving a little for caramelizing the vegetables). Fry onion and garlic over medium to medium-low heat until onions are limp and translucent. Add soy sauce, sugar, green beans, tomato sauce, and meats, and cook until heated through. Thicken juices with poi.

Makes 4 to 6 servings.

Source: The late cafeteria manager Mrs. Eleanor Tyau, Saint
Louis School

BEEF NIBLETS

2 tablespoons canola or other vegetable oil

2 pounds cooked pot roast, roughly chopped

3 cloves garlic, minced

1 round onion, sliced

1 to 2 cans low-sodium chicken or beef broth

2 drained cans or 1 bag frozen corn

Cornstarch for thickening gravy

Salt and pepper to taste

Brown beef in oil; add garlic and onion. Pour in broth, and simmer until beef is tender. Add corn. Whisk together 1 to 2 tablespoons juices with 1 tablespoon cornstarch (more if the dish is very juicy). Season to taste with salt and pepper.

Makes 6 to 8 servings, with mashed potatoes or rice.

Source: Phyllis Dolim Savio, former student, Saint Anthony
School, Wailuku, Maui

KAIMUKI HIGH SCHOOL HAWAIIAN CURRY

6 tablespoons margarine or butter

1 medium onion, finely chopped

2 teaspoons peeled and finely chopped fresh ginger

6 tablespoons flour

1½ teaspoons salt

1 tablespoon curry powder

2 cups room-temperature milk

1 cup room-temperature coconut milk

3 cups cooked shrimp, chicken, veal, lamb, or fish

Condiments: sliced bananas, chutney, chopped preserved ginger, chopped nuts, sieved hard-boiled eggs, crumbled bacon, grated and toasted fresh coconut

Melt margarine or butter and sauté onion and ginger. Add flour, curry powder, and salt; blend thoroughly. Gradually add milk, stirring constantly. Cook until thickened and smooth. Add shrimp, meat, or fish, and cook just until heated through. Serve with hot rice and condiments.

> Source: *Seventeen* magazine prize-winning recipe from Kaimuki High School cooks. School lunches usually didn't serve condiments, but very light, unspicy, white sauce–based curries were common.

BAKED SPAGHETTI

¾ package of dried spaghetti

1 lb. hamburger

½ medium onion, chopped

3 cloves garlic, chopped

1 can button mushrooms, with liquid

1 package spaghetti sauce mix

1 (6-oz.) can tomato paste

1 (15-oz.) can tomato sauce

1 tablespoon butter, softened

Spices to taste: basil, oregano, garlic powder, or salt

Shredded cheddar cheese

Preheat oven to 300°. Cook and drain spaghetti; toss with a little olive oil to prevent sticking. Some schools cut the cooked spaghetti into short lengths; others left it whole. Brown hamburger and drain fat. Add onions and garlic, and simmer until onion is limp and translucent. Add mushrooms with liquid. Make spaghetti sauce according to package directions, and add paste and sauce. In a large bowl, combine spaghetti, hamburger/onion/garlic mixture, and spaghetti sauce. Spoon into a buttered 9" × 13" baking dish. Top generously with cheddar cheese. Bake at 300° for 30 minutes (do not cover).

Makes 8 to 10 servings.

Source: Files of the Hawai'i State School Food Services program and Bev Pace

Notes: Mrs. Eleanor Tyau memorably fried chopped, uncooked bacon with hamburger for this dish. Many cafeterias made their own *pomodoro* (tomato sauce) from scratch and used spices and garlic very lightly because of children's timid tastes.

APPLE BROWN BETTY

4 cups coarsely chopped day-old bread (or dry chopped bread in 325° oven)

½ cup butter, melted; plus 1 tablespoon softened butter for dish

4 tart cooking apples, peeled, cored, and thinly sliced

⅓ cup brown sugar

1 tablespoon fresh lemon juice

1 tablespoon grated or finely chopped fresh ginger

1 teaspoon ground cinnamon

3 tablespoons apple juice

Whipped cream or hard sauce*

Preheat oven to 375°. Lightly butter a 2-qt. casserole or baking dish. In a large bowl, drizzle melted butter over chopped bread. In another bowl, combine apples, brown sugar, lemon juice, ginger, and cinnamon.

Assemble brown betty: Spread one-third of buttered bread crumbs in casserole dish; top with one-half of apple mixture. Sprinkle with 1 tablespoon apple juice. Repeat bread and apple layers. Top with remaining bread.

Cover with foil and bake for 30 minutes; uncover and bake another 30 minutes. Serve warm with whipped cream or hard sauce.

* Recipes for classic hard sauce, a thick mixture of soft butter and sugar, can be found online or in older cookbooks.

Source: Files of the Hawai'i State School Food Services program

Notes

1. Wanda Adams is a former food columnist of the *Honolulu Advertiser*. Besides her experiences as a journalist, she brings the perspective of her own background as someone who grew up on Maui in the 1950s and 1960s in a Caucasian family, first attending

Catholic school and then public intermediate and high schools. The *Honolulu Advertiser* was one of two dailies in Honolulu until it was sold in June 2010.

2. The Ewa-Waipahu district of Honolulu county (island of Oʻahu) encompasses a broad area characterized generally by lower socioeconomic strata than central Honolulu, with a racial-ethnic admixture that reflects the presence of the U.S. military (white, some black), former agricultural workers (Filipinos, Japanese), and younger families seeking cheaper housing (white, other Asian).

3. My attribution of ethnicity to these women is in part by their names (although these are married names), in part by the way they look (although it might be difficult to distinguish other women of Asian ancestry), and in part by the reputation of those who worked as cafeteria ladies (primarily those of Japanese ancestry—including Okinawan—but also some of Chinese or Korean ancestry). Of the fourteen present at the lunch, only one woman was not Asian. All the others' names were Japanese: Doi, Fujita, Kakazu, Kiyabu (Okinawan), Kondo, Maeda, Nakasone (Okinawan), Oshiro (Okinawan), Saito, Sugai, Tanabe (2), Wakatsuki.

4. My intention in beginning this project was to write a full history of school lunch in Hawaiʻi, beginning with the establishment of the public school system, and to that end, I turned first to archival data for documentation. Unfortunately, to my knowledge, that documentation does not exist, especially since records have been regularly expunged by the School Food Services office in Honolulu. Although the documented history—and my goal of a book—has thus been lost, I have attempted a partial retrieval through interviews with older cafeteria managers and patrons.

5. These interviews are available online at http://www.nfsmi.org. The women interviewed were (alphabetically): Janice Low (ethnicity unknown, but likely Chinese American), cafeteria manager and other food-service positions in school lunch programs on all six islands of Hawaiʻi since 1977; Donna Matsufuru (Japanese American sansei), school food service supervisor for the state of Hawaiʻi and various positions in food service from 1972 onward; Doris Yaeko Mau (Japanese American nisei married to a Chinese American), retired cafeteria manager (thirty-eight years since the 1960s) and past president of the Oʻahu School Food Service Association; Nancy Miura (Okinawan American nisei originally from Maui, Honolulu Vocational School degree in school food service management), retired cafeteria manager, past president of the Oʻahu School Food Service Association, and various school food service positions since 1954; Peggy Nakamoto (Japanese American, Honolulu Community College degree in cafeteria management), retired cafeteria manager and past president of Oʻahu School Food Service Association, and various school food service positions since 1968); and Sue Uyehara (white, originally from Louisiana, married to Okinawan American; M.A. in public health and nutrition from the University of Hawaiʻi), state director of the Child Nutrition Program since 2006. I found this information in interviews and photographs.

6. Susan Levine, *School Lunch Politics: The Surprising History of America's Favorite Welfare Program* (Princeton, NJ: Princeton University Press, 2008).

7. See the appendix for Adams's sampling of recipes.

8. Gary Allen Fine, *Kitchens: The Culture of Restaurant Work* (Berkeley: University of California Press, 1996), 1.

9. Anne Allison, "Japanese Mothers and *Obentos*: The Lunch Box as Ideological State Apparatus," in *Food and Culture: A Reader*, ed. Carole Counihan and Penny Van Esterik (New York: Routledge, 1997), 296–314.

10. Eriberto P. Lozada Jr., "Globalized Childhood? Kentucky Fried Chicken in Beijing," in *The Cultural Politics of Food and Eating: A Reader,* ed. James L. Watson and Melissa L. Caldwell, (Oxford: Blackwell, 2005), 163.

11. Alice Waters, "Want to Teach Democracy? Improve School Lunches," *Huffington Post,* September 3, 2009, available at http://www.huffingtonpost.com/alice-waters/want-to-teach-democracy-i_b_276420.html (accessed January 25, 2012).

12. Roland Kotani, *The Japanese in Hawaii: A Century of Struggle* (Honolulu: Hawai'i Hochi, 1985), 98; Eileen Tamura, *Americanization, Acculturation, and Ethnic Identity: The Nisei Generation in Hawaii* (Urbana: University of Illinois Press, 1994).

13. Nor was this the first time that public authorities had recognized the significance of molding citizens through food. An earlier campaign during the 1920s and 1930s emphasized the Americanization of Hawai'i's multiethnic population through food, with home economists and public schools leading the way. See Rachel Laudan, *The Food of Paradise: Exploring Hawaii's Culinary Heritage* (Honolulu: University of Hawai'i Press, 1996), 101.

14. Richard Wilks, "Food and Nationalism: The Origins of 'Belizean Food,'" in *Food Nations: Selling Taste in Consumer Societies*, ed. Warren Belasco and Philip Scranton (New York: Routledge, 2002), 70, table 1.

15. The following are some school lunches from around 1960 culled by Wanda Adams from Hawaii State School Food Services menus:

    MENU 1
    Spanish rice with ground beef
    Wax beans
    Crisp relishes
    Tangerines or orange slices
    Drop biscuits with butter or margarine
    Milk
    Vanilla pudding

    MENU 2
    Lasagna
    Tossed salad with chopped egg and dressing
    Chilled fruit cup
    Buttered French bread
    Milk
    Butterscotch brownie

    MENU 3
    Baked spaghetti with meat and cheese
    Brussels sprouts
    Carrot sticks
    Sliced peaches
    Poppy seed rolls with butter or margarine
    Milk
    Peanut butter–raisin cookies

MENU 4
    Oven-baked crispy chicken
    Cole slaw
    Garlic French bread
    Cherry streusel dessert
    Milk

16. Japanese short grain rice is standard in Hawai'i, eaten not only with Japanese food but also with everything from chicken to spaghetti. Long grain rice, by comparison, is eaten primarily with Chinese food.

17. The rate of lactose intolerance among those of Asian ancestry is notoriously high, sometimes estimated at 90 percent or more.

18. Sent in by Mildred Kobayashi of Wahiawa, whose aunt was a "cafeteria lady." "You Know You're Local If . . . ," *Honolulu Advertiser*, 1996, D:1, 3.

19. Dafna Hirsch, "'Hummus Is Best When It Is Fresh and Made by Arabs': The Gourmetization of Hummus in Israel and the Return of the Repressed Arab," *American Ethnologist* 38, no. 4 (2011): 619.

20. Laudan, *The Food of Paradise*.

21. Wanda A. Adams, *The Island Plate: 150 Years of Recipes and Food Lore from the* Honolulu Advertiser (Waipahu, HI: Island Heritage Publishing, 2006).

22. Arnold Hiura, *Kau Kau: Cuisine and Culture in the Hawaiian Islands* (Honolulu: Watermark Publishing, 2009).

23. Hirsch, "'Hummus Is Best,'" 827.

3

A Life Cooking for Others

The Work and Migration Experiences of a Chinese
Restaurant Worker in New York City, 1920–1946

HEATHER R. LEE

[Chop suey][1] is no longer merely a casual commodity. It has become a staple. It is vigorously vieing [*sic*] with sandwiches and salad as the noontime nourishment of the young women typists and telephonists of John, Dey and Fulton Streets. It rivals coffee-and-two-kinds-of-cake as the recess repast of the sales forces of West Thirty-fourth Street department stores. At the lunch hour there is an eager exodus toward Chinatown. . . . To them the district is not an intriguing bit of transplanted Orient. It is simply a good place to eat.

Bertram Reinitz, "Chop Suey's New Role,"
New York Times, December 27, 1925

The kitchen in which I had to work was a very long one. There were six huge ranges in it each having two very deep and large fire boxes. . . . Since the ranges had to be gotten ready and kept at the highest degree possible of heat for the cooking of dinners for more than a thousand guests, I had to remain in front of the six sizzling hot ranges from four o'clock in the [morning] until seven-thirty in the evening. This was as you may well suppose most exhausting. My legs got so blistered from the intensity of the heat that I soon had to put on woolen underwear despite the fact that it was the Summer season. While it was uncomfortable nevertheless it did keep the heat from striking my bare legs and so they no longer got so painfully blistered. . . . As you can see this made a most strenuous ten-hour working day for me in that all too hot kitchen. At the close of each day I was too exhausted to desire to eat or even sleep.

Chin Lee, "Along the Way," unpublished memoir, ca. 1949

On December 27, 1925, *New York Times* columnist Bertram Reinitz published a special piece entitled "Chop Suey's New Role."[2] As the designated cultural and social commentator for this widely circulating newspaper, Reinitz used the approaching New Year to reflect on "the changes of character and custom that this sizable city has lately undergone." "At the lunch hour," he marveled, "there is an eager exodus toward Chinatown." With the throngs of clerks, secretaries, and sales ladies descending on Chinatown, it seemed as if everyone had gotten the office memo on where to eat lunch. This curious trend of people streaming into Chinese restaurants caused him to ponder the place of Chinese food in the New Yorker's diet. In his words, "[c]hop suey has been promoted to a prominent place on the midday menu of the metropolis." By the 1920s, Chinese food was no longer the exotic cuisine of Chinese immigrants, as it was once regarded. Both the masses of people eating Chinese food and Reinitz's commentary signaled that Chinese food was novel only because it had become so familiar. This depiction of Chinese food's popularity among New Yorkers, who were among the earliest patrons of Chinese restaurants in the country, can be seen as an official declaration: New Yorkers could no longer live without Chinese food.

While Reinitz and the average New Yorker at a Chinese restaurant paid no attention to the people serving him or her, the army of cooks and waiters feeding the "eager exodus" demands explanation, because so many of them worked illegally in the United States. In the 1920s, each of the three hundred Chinese restaurants in New York City maintained a Chinese staff of five waiters and four and a half cooks to deliver piping hot plates of chicken chop suey, beef chow mein, and Chinese roasted pork. In all, 307 Chinese restaurant owners and 3,275 cooks and waiters worked in the state of New York. These are astounding figures, given that Chinese workers were officially barred from entering the country.[3] Between the enactment of anti-Chinese legislation in 1882 and its repeal in 1943, only international businessmen, students, teachers, and diplomats could legally pass through America's gates. Despite these restrictions, the Chinese managed to recruit workers from China to staff the hundreds of restaurants operating in the city. Once the workers reached the United States, the work for them was physically demanding. Cooks worked ten or more hours over stoves that were kept at the "highest degree possible" so that food orders could be made in an instant. After working under these conditions for seven days a week, the cook quoted at the beginning of this chapter felt "too exhausted to desire to eat or even sleep." Focusing on the experiences of one Chinese restaurant worker over his lifetime, this chapter shows that Chinese restaurants were not just palaces of consumption, as Reinitz presumed, but were also sites of a complex network of chain migration, labor, and familial obligation. I follow Chin Shuck Wing through his years as a wage laborer in New York City's service industry.[4] Between his arrival in the United States in 1935 and his death in 1987, Shuck Wing worked at a variety of restaurants, cooked for the U.S. Air Force, and briefly operated Jim Lee's Laundry on Manhattan's Upper West Side. During these fifty years, Shuck Wing never returned to China to see the wife and children he left behind, although he maintained a financial and emotional relationship with them through remittances and letters. From his experiences, we learn that Chinese restaurant workers led dual lives—toiling in the United States while dreaming of China.[5]

Shuck Wing provides a case study for understanding how the Chinese endured horrible work experiences like those described by the line cook. Like so many Chinese immigrants, Shuck Wing came to the United States because he put his family before himself. He worked in small, family-run businesses that turned a profit only because the owners paid themselves and their relatives very little. When Shuck Wing discovered the hard life ahead of him, he turned to his relatives for emotional support. Through regular letters to one another, the Chin family persuaded Shuck Wing and the other Chin men in the United States to persevere for the sake of their families. By compelling Chinese immigrants like Shuck Wing to accept untenable work conditions, the transpacific Chinese family networks were able to secure cheap laborers who put Chinese food on customers' tables.

Leaving Home: How Did Chinese Restaurant Workers Get Here?

For men like Shuck Wing, coming to the United States was as natural as getting married, fathering children, or dying. For generations, the Chin family had been sending young, able-bodied men from Dragon Village, a small village on the southern coast of Guangdong Province in China, to Southeast Asia, Canada, and the United States. In North America alone, Shuck Wing had forty-seven relatives and friends in fourteen cities—most of whom ran family businesses in San Antonio, Texas, and Tucson, Arizona (see map 3.1). In fact, Shuck Wing followed in his own father's footsteps. When Shuck Wing left Guangdong in 1935, he had reached the right stage in his life to take his father's place in the United States. He was twenty-four years old and had gained some business experience as clerk in the village grocery store.[6] He was married and had young children to clothe, feed, and educate. Shuck Wing knew from his elder relatives that he could support his young family better as a laborer

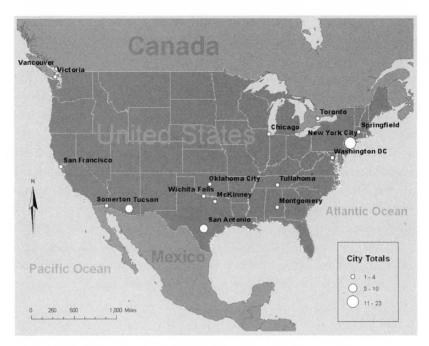

Map 3.1. The Chin family in North America, 1935–1946. Source: Bachelor's Apartment, 111 Mott Street Collection, Museum of Chinese in America, New York, NY. Map by the author.

in America than as a clerk in China.[7] Moreover, his father, the family head and breadwinner, had passed away abroad, and his remains were en route to Dragon Village.[8] Since Shuck Wing's older brothers, cousins, and uncles were already in the United States, it was time for Shuck Wing, the family's next youngest male, to take this well-worn path overseas.

The Chin family sent its men abroad to find stable work because working the land in China no longer provided a secure livelihood. Shuck Wing came from an area in southern China that had been shaken by an agricultural crisis. Although the land was neither abundant nor fertile enough to feed its population, the population of Taishan County had quadrupled between 1838 and 1920, placing a heavy burden on the unproductive farmland. Indeed, the county needed 60 percent more land to meet Taishan's basic needs, which meant that its farmers produced only half the grains needed for local consumption. The dire situation forced these farming people to seek work off the land. In 1890, 100,000 Taishanese were full-time farmers; 300,000 were part-time farmers and also worked in commerce or industry; and 200,000 engaged in commerce and industry exclusively.[9] "A farmer lives a strenuous life and makes little money," stated a man from northern Guangdong, who repeated a common local aphorism: "A business man usually makes more money, especially if he has luck and is helped out by relatives or friends."[10]

Like their neighbors, the Chins decided that farming alone would not suffice. Although the family held on to its farmland, they left the actual farming to landless tenants who shared their harvest with the Chins.[11] Freed from the land, the Chin family went into trade, purchased more land, and funded young men to travel abroad for work.[12] Of all the ways the Chins diversified their economic ventures, sending young men overseas had the largest impact on the family income. During Shuck Wing's first year abroad, he sent home $134.50, or about two months' salary for a cook, which in 2012 would be worth $2,161.[13] The Chins' neighbors also benefited from their men working overseas. In 1935, the year that Shuck Wing left for the United States, more than one-fourth of the entire Taishanese population worked abroad and, on average, contributed 81.4 percent of their families' annual incomes.[14]

U.S. immigration laws (Chinese Exclusion Laws) prevented Chinese immigrants like Shuck Wing from entering the United States legally, however, reducing Chinese immigration for sixty years, during which only merchants, teachers, tourists, students, U.S. citizens of Chinese heritage, and some of their wives and children, could travel between the United States and China. Shuck Wing got past immigration officials in San Francisco by posing as the son of a U.S. citizen because his uncle, Chin Ton in Tucson lied on his behalf. As an American citizen, Chin Ton had the right to sponsor his children to join him in the United States. In January 1935, Shuck Wing initiated this illegal process by sending a letter of request to his uncle and six identical head shots of himself for Chin Ton to use when filing immigration papers. That Shuck Wing knew to include the photographs signaled that he understood the immigration process and was prepared to face the challenges and dangers of coming to America illegally.[15]

Sending for Shuck Wing was an expensive and time-consuming process that Chin Ton, a successful and generous businessman, undertook in fulfillment of his familial obligations. By the time Shuck Wing's letter arrived in Tucson in February 1935, Chin Ton had already brought three sons to the United States and taken three return trips to China. Upon receiving Shuck Wing's letter, he informed the Chins in San Francisco that Shuck Wing was coming as his son. He then hired Oliver P. Stidger and Lewis A. Root to file immigration papers for Shuck Wing at the Angel Island Immigration Station in San Francisco Bay. Meanwhile in Arizona, Chin Ton drew up several sets of affidavits for him and his sons that claimed Shuck Wing, "now living in China [and desiring] to come to the United States . . . is the natural son of . . . Chin Ton."[16] On September 9, 1935, Samuel Wright, an immigration agent at the Texas Immigration Bureau in El Paso, interviewed Chin Ton to verify his citizenship status. Next, Edward L. Haff, the district director of immigration in San Francisco, and the American consul general in Hong Kong received transcripts of this interview and Chin Ton's affidavits for their evaluations of Shuck Wing's application.[17] In a letter dated October 2, 1935, Chin Ton told Shuck Wing to start saying his good-byes. "[Since] you are so anxious to join us I am sending you the affidavit together with Hongkong [sic] bank draft amounting to $250 through the On Lung Co. You can start your journey any time you desire."[18] Ten months, multiple transpacific letter exchanges, and several hundred American dollars later, Shuck Wing had secured the proper documents and overcome the first obstacle en route to the United States.

With his immigration papers in order and a small allowance in hand, Shuck Wing started the long and arduous journey to America. In November 1935, he bade farewell to his wife, children, mother, and extended family at the gates of Dragon Village and left on foot with a suitcase and folded mattress.[19] After walking one and one-quarter miles to the Ng Hip railway station, he boarded a train to Bok Gai and, from there, traveled by steamship to Hong Kong. He went to the American consulate in Hong Kong for a health inspection and vaccinations, as well as to present Chin Ton's affidavit. Cleared to board a U.S.-bound steamship, Shuck Wing wrote Chin Ton one last time before the SS *President Coolidge* set sail on November 30, 1935.[20] Nineteen days later, Shuck Wing landed at Angel Island Immigration Station, the main processing center for Chinese immigrants.[21] The immigration bureau detained Shuck Wing on Angel Island for thirty-three days while deciding whether he was Chin Ton's son. As Shuck Wing waited in the Chinese barracks, Samuel Wright interrogated Chin Ton and his sons for two days in Tucson about the Chin family and Dragon Village, hoping to detect evidence of fraud. On January 20, 1936, the Board of Special Inquiry ruled in Shuck Wing's favor: "The testimony is in general agreement. . . . I believe that the evidence of record should be accepted as reasonably establishing the relationship claimed between the applicant and Chin Ton."[22] After six weeks of travel and another four and half weeks of detention, Shuck Wing had earned the right to join the Chin men in America.

Dishing Out Chop Suey: What Was It Like to Work in a Chinese Restaurant?

Because Shuck Wing spoke no English and was now an ocean away from Dragon Village, the Chin family in North America helped him settle into his new life. The day the U.S. Immigration Bureau released Shuck Wing from its custody, he rode the *Jeff D. Milton* ferry from the detention center on Angel Island across San Francisco Bay.[23] His friends and family awaited him at the Chin family clubhouse in Chinatown at 150 Waverly Place. A four-story building, the family headquarters housed Tsui Gee Chong and Co., an all-purpose trading company, on the ground floor and new arrivals and passersby on the fourth floor. On the middle two levels, the Chin men socialized, exchanging news about people in China and information about business opportunities in the United States. Through these fellow wanderers, Shuck Wing heard about jobs in New York City and booked a ticket east through Tsui Gee Chong and Co. As he planned his next move, he received a disheartening letter from an uncle back in China. The Chins had lost their bid to buy a fertile plot of land in Dragon Village, and the family was not earning enough to make ends meet, so his uncle had decided to leave for Southeast Asia. Motivated by news of this hardship, Shuck Wing continued eastward to pursue job leads in New York.[24]

In New York, the first Chinese restaurants date to the 1870s and catered almost exclusively to the city's early Chinese immigrants. Located in the triangular intersection of Mott, Pell, and Doyers Streets known as "Chinatown," a half dozen Chinese eateries served the everyday food of rural, southern China to Chinese laborers and "lower classes of white people."[25] For special occasions, Chinese merchants threw large banquets for their clansmen at one of New York's "high-class" Chinese restaurants. Ordered several days in advance, these extensive meals included as many as forty courses. Guests savored these indulgent repasts in lavishly appointed dining rooms, on whose walls hung scrolls of Chinese poetry and maxims. "Chinese lanterns are suspended in reckless profusion from every available point," commented Louis J. Beck, a journalist who wrote a book on New York's Chinatown. "The most gorgeously decorated and illuminated buildings in Chinatown are those occupied by these restaurants."[26] Located in the heart of Chinatown on Mott and Pell Streets, these eight high-end restaurants were busiest on Sundays when "the Chinese laundrymen of New York and neighboring cities come in [to Chinatown] for a general good time."[27] In the United States, Chinese laborers earned decent wages and could afford to eat foods that had been too expensive for them in China. On their days off, Chinese laundrymen indulged in food and the company of their peers at the same restaurants as Chinatown's business elite.[28] While some Americans also patronized these restaurants, these early restaurants did "not cater to any other trade than [the] Chinese," because other customers added little to the restaurants' bottom lines. Wong Chin Foo, a writer and contemporary of Louis Beck, deduced that Chinese restaurant keepers paid no heed to white customers because "[the] Chinaman frequently orders two-dollar and three-dollar dishes, while the American seldom pays more than fifty or seventy-five cents for his Chinese dinner."[29] Moreover, Chinese patronage of Chinatown restaurants indirectly supported a diverse array of food businesses throughout New York State. Farmers in the Bronx, Queens, and Long Island supplied fresh produce, and Chinatown grocers imported preserved foods to feed a growing population of Chinese immigrants who craved a taste of home.[30]

Within twenty years of New York's first Chinese restaurants, some Chinese entrepreneurs had established a specialized set of restaurants to serve New Yorkers who were curious about the city's "Chinese colony."[31] During the late nineteenth century, newspapers like the *New York Times*, the *New York Tribune*, and the *New York Sun* regularly published articles on New York's Chinese, a fascinating topic to readers because the Chinese were still considered recent and exotic arrivals to the city.[32] Bertram Reinitz's predecessors who wrote for major New York newspapers taught their readers to dine at Chinese restaurants. In their articles about New York's intriguing newcomers, they promoted Chinese food as exciting and delicious and helped readers through their first experiences with a cuisine they probably found intimidatingly different from their usual fare. Journalists published the addresses of tourist-friendly restaurants, described and evaluated the dishes, and gave instructions on using chopsticks. Enough New Yorkers accepted these invitations to try Chinese food that tours through Chinatown grew into a specialty business. Former policemen and English-speaking locals organized tours of "slummers" or "rubberneckers"—as tourists were called—to see the Chinese temple, hear a snippet of Chinese opera, gawk at opium addicts, shop at a knickknack store, and, finally, to dine at a Chinese restaurant.[33] Of all the items on a Chinese restaurant menu, "slummers" relished chop suey. Cantonese for "different pieces," chop suey is made of bite-size pieces of meat and vegetables in a brown gravy and is served over rice or noodles. This simple dish originated in southern China, where most Chinese immigrants, including Shuck Wing, came from. A series of prominent articles on a Chinese diplomat who preferred chop suey to Anglo-American foods during his goodwill tour of the United States ignited a "chop suey craze" in New York. By the 1920s, as Reinitz observed, chop suey had become an American staple. "Chop suey joints," small restaurants specializing in the dish, opened all over New York. In 1925, George Chappell, a contributor to *Vanity Fair,* noted that these restaurants were "naturally somewhat Americanized" because "their patronage [was] largely American and not Chinese."[34]

In 1936, Shuck Wing easily found work at an Americanized Chinese restaurant because the vast majority of New York's Chinese restaurants were small, family operations in need of labor. During the 1920s and 1930s, three relatives started a restaurant by pooling together a few thousand dollars.[35] The partners divided the roles of manager, accountant, and head chef, so that each person assumed the duties for which he was best qualified. The manager was the most charismatic and spoke the best English of the partners. As the public face of the restaurant, he greeted customers, interacted with vendors, and mediated interpersonal conflicts among staff members. The accountant had sufficient math, reading, and writing abilities to manage the business records, which included paying employees and suppliers and keeping the company balance sheet. The head chef needed to be physically robust, since running the kitchen was the most physically taxing and dangerous duty.[36]

Clearly, a staff of three could not possibly feed the "eager exodus toward Chinatown" that Reinitz described, so the partners counted on their countrymen to fill the labor gaps. In New York City, the average Chinese restaurant crew was 42 percent kitchen and 42 percent wait staff, with the partners making up the remaining 16 percent of the workforce. During the Great Depression, 248 restaurants were in operation, employing more than 2,400 Chinese restaurant wage workers, which constituted a significant portion of New York City's Chinese population.[37] Even during the Depression, newcomers like Shuck Wing could land a job in a Chinese restaurant because of the robust demand for Chinese food.

In this line of work, getting the job was the easy part; *doing* the job was the hard part. For two years, Shuck Wing was employed "to prepare and cook chop shuey [*sic*] and other chinese [*sic*] dishes."[38] Line cooks worked "a most strenuous ten-hour" day over "sizzling hot ranges." Many Chinese restaurants around Times Square stayed open late to catch post-theater diners and had two shifts of workers. Owing to scheduling or management errors, line cooks in these restaurants sometimes worked back-to-back shifts. Moreover, some cooks worked for "dictators" who believed verbal insults and bullying were "the only way to get things done correctly." The "dominating type" of manager "even tells [their cooks] how a dish should be prepared." When the abuse became unbearable, the "chef changed his working clothes and left."[39] Managers treated their kitchen staff disrespectfully because many of them believed that cooking was an unskilled occupation. In the words of one Chinese, "A person who knows how to prepare a dish of chow mein or chop suey or any other Americanized version of a Chinese delicacy is not considered a chef by the Chinese."[40]

Like the kitchen staff, waiters "felt exploited" by their bosses, who made unreasonable demands of them.[41] One waiter oversaw four to five tables, each of which seated two to six people. During the mealtime rush, waiters received orders from customers, headwaiters, and cooks in "rapid succession." A waiter had to scribble on his waiter's pad or memorize a string of orders: "Olive and celery—shrimp cocktail—soup—tea—chow mein—steak—coffee—pie—ice cream—water."[42] He had to get the orders to the kitchen and the food to the right table in the correct sequence of courses. This task was made harder by the fact that Americanized Chinese restaurants served both Cantonese and American dishes. Therefore, waiters had to learn the American foods their restaurants served and also how their customers liked them. While meals in China were also organized into courses, American meals followed a different logic, which waiters were obliged to understand when serving their customers.[43] The dizzying mess of demands and commands made one inexperienced waiter so confused that he was literally "run[ning] around in circles." On top of all this, new waiters received no training. Anyone who asked for help often got the cold shoulder from his colleagues. One waiter, who was looking for coffee cups, was told he "should have been there an hour earlier to find out where the different things were kept." This was especially true if a waiter needed something from the kitchen, whose staff was working under constant pressure and in extreme heat to get the food cooked and plated as fast as possible.[44]

A Collective Bargain: Did Chinese Restaurant Workers Demand Better Work Conditions?

For all their sweat and toil, Chinese restaurant workers were among the lowest-paid workers in the food service industry, which included a broad spectrum of full-service restaurants and partial-service establishments. New York's Chinese restaurant workers made 30 percent less than the average food service employee. According to the 1930 U.S. Census, the average eating establishment spent twenty-four dollars on staff wages for every hundred dollars earned in sales. In contrast, the Rice Bowl Restaurant, a popular Americanized Chinese restaurant in New York's Chinatown, spent seventeen dollars on wages for every hundred dollars earned in sales.[45] Chinese restaurants were full-service businesses, meaning that customers were waited on at their tables from the beginning to the end of their meals. Yet the staff in Chinese restaurants earned wages comparable to those of workers in lunchrooms and cafeterias, which streamlined the service to provide cheap meals. If Chinese restaurant workers as a whole made 30 percent below the national average, Chinese cooks and waiters fared even worse owing to the hierarchy of pay in their restaurants. Each partner took home a hundred dollars a month, which was padded by a 10 percent dividend on their investment. A talented and hardworking cook might earn as much as a partner, although most line cooks earned between sixty and seventy dollars a month. Headwaiters earned sixty dollars, and waiters, about fifty dollars a month, tips included. Most Chinese restaurants were too small to hire busboys or dishwashers, so the entire staff pitched in to clean up the restaurant at the end of the workday.[46] Newcomers like Shuck Wing fell into the lower end of the Chinese restaurant pay scale.

Whereas many wage workers turned to unions to address their workplace grievances in the 1930s, Chinese workers could not benefit from membership in American labor unions because of their racially exclusive policies. In 1891, the American Federation of Labor formed the Hotel Employee and Restaurant Employee Union (HERE) to improve the hours, wages, and benefits of workers in the hospitality industry. Struggling through its first ten years, HERE became "a permanent fixture in the industry" and numbered 65,000 members by World War I.[47] Its membership, however, excluded "Chinese and Negro workers" who worked alongside whites or in racially segregated hotels and restaurants.[48] The Chinese and blacks were excluded from HERE because its parent organization, the American Federation of Labor (AFL), was formed to protect white male workers. In fact, the AFL organizers saw immigrant, black, and Chinese workers as competitors they wanted to eliminate from the field. Samuel Gompers, the AFL's founder and longest sitting president, lobbied the U.S. Congress to pass legislation that ended free immigration to America. In 1902, Gompers wrote a caustic pamphlet entitled *Meat vs. Rice: American Manhood against Asiatic Coolieism*, which portrayed Chinese immigrants as parasites eating away at white working-class masculinity. When the Chinese Exclusion Laws were due to expire in 1892 and 1902, union organizers used this rhetoric to persuade American policymakers that the "Chinese Must Go!" in the name of defending the white male breadwinner.[49]

HERE tackled poor labor conditions in Chinese restaurants by pressuring their owners to hire unionized white workers. Throughout the 1920 and 1930s, HERE mounted a series of successful strikes in New York that raised the minimum wage to twenty dollars a week, excluded tips from wages, and limited the workday to nine hours for waiters. HERE negotiated these changes with the New York Restaurant Keepers Association and the National Restaurant Association, neither of which represented Chinese restaurant owners. In 1935, the union won a major ruling from the Industrial Commissioner of New York State to raise the state's minimum wage for food service employees.[50] Emboldened by this victory, HERE tried to force Chinese restaurants to comply with state regulations. The AFL picketed the Merry-Go-Round Restaurant, a large Chinese restaurant in Greater New York, and several other Chinese restaurants in Brooklyn, demanding that the management hire HERE members. Merry-Go-Round's owners, Harold Stern and his Chinese partner, conceded to the AFL's demands by hiring unionized waiters at five dollars a day and giving cooks a raise of five dollars a month. Since few of the union workers were Chinese, it is very likely that racial conflict between the management and employees was responsible for this experiment failing. In 1937, the New Fulton Royal Restaurant opened at Merry-Go-Round's old address with a nonunionized, Chinese staff.[51]

Racial exclusion alone does not explain the failure of the labor movement to redress exploitation in Chinese restaurants. Even when the AFL tried to organize Chinese food servers, it failed because the primary conflicts transpired between Chinese restaurants rather than within them. In 1939, after the Merry-Go-Round experiment, AFL leaders approved Local 211, a racially segregated branch for Chinese workers. The mission of Local 211 was to unionize Chinese small business employees, promote solidarity between Chinese and Americans, fight racism against the Chinese, and "eliminate mutual distrust between workers and employers."[52] The last plank of this agenda shows how little the AFL leadership understood the Chinese restaurant industry. While union organizers correctly recognized ill feelings between employees and their employers, they mistakenly interpreted them as the result of class conflict. The vast majority of Chinese restaurants were small family partnerships staffed by friends and relatives. In other words, everyone was invested in the restaurant's success for the good of the family. Even the Chinese Left, which was sympathetic to the AFL's efforts, recognized that union organizers falsely characterized employee-employer relationships. Responding to the AFL's unionization drives, Chu Tong, the English-language secretary for the Chinese Hand Laundry Alliance, and Zhao Jiansheng, a writer for the progressive newspaper *China Salvation Times*, pushed for trade guilds instead of unions as the more appropriate solution to the problem of exploitation that stemmed from competition among Chinese businesses. Unions represented employees before employers, whereas trade guilds mediated between businesses and treated everyone working in one business as generally sharing the same interests.[53]

Long before the AFL and HERE took an interest in Chinese restaurant workers, the Chinese established their own organizations to regulate the food industry. Founded in 1932, the Chinese Restaurant Association negotiated with government agencies on behalf of the Chinese over regulatory changes, whose confusing and discriminatory nature threatened to undermine the Chinese restaurant industry.[54] Serving a similar purpose, the Chinese Hand Laundry Alliance formed in 1933 to battle a municipal ordinance in New York that would have financially crippled Chinese laundries with a twenty-five-dollar licensing fee and one-thousand-dollar security bond.[55] Both organizations believed they represented their employees and employers equally in their efforts to defend Chinese small businesses. After the formation of Local 211 by the AFL, the Chinese Restaurant Association changed its name to the Chinese Restaurant Workers and Merchants' Association to reflect its commitment to workers who had been members since its formation. Another Chinatown organization, the Chinese Consolidated Benevolent Association (CCBA), resolved conflicts among restaurants, the major point of contention among them being territorial claims to city blocks.[56] This two-tiered organizational structure protected the Chinese restaurant industry from threats that emanated from both inside and outside the Chinese community.

Tensions existed between restaurant employees and owners even if they were not based on class antagonism. Chinese restaurants were collective enterprises. Many restaurant owners helped relatives come to the United States with immigration papers and loans. Shuck Wing's journey from Taishan to New York is just one example of how much immigrants and their relatives invested in the expensive and time-consuming process of immigration. As established immigrants, restaurant owners granted jobs in their restaurants to their brethren, who in turn provided cheap and reliable labor. This chain of favors bound restaurant employees to employers. Moreover, Confucian notions of obedience reinforced these new immigrants' sense of debt. In rural agricultural societies like Taishan, the family hierarchy organized people into positions of power and deference, in which the older males held authority over young males, women, and children. In Chinese-run businesses in America, this social order shaped workplace relationships to resemble family relationships in China: elder male relatives were employers and in positions of authority, while young relatives were employees and subservient to their elder relatives.[57] Restaurant workers who suffered through years of low pay, long hours, and hard work out of deference to their employers also grew to resent their superiors. Shuck

Wing and his relatives had plenty to gripe about, though they were too polite and too political to vent their frustrations openly. Instead, the Chin men made veiled complaints in their letters to one another about having "no free time," earning too little, and being in poor health.[58] The close world of dependence among the Chins, however, necessitated that the employees of Chin family businesses keep their mouths shut in front of their superiors. The bonds of family complicated relations between employer and employee, thereby making conflicts in Chinese restaurants qualitatively different from those in a work-place of strangers.

The tensions simmering just below the surface of a Chinese-run restaurant erupted when employees wanted to form their own restaurants. In some ways, conflict was inevitable because the aspirations of employees and the wishes of employers were at odds with each other. While restaurant owners desired cheap labor for their restaurants, the workers saw their jobs as a means to an end. Newcomers like Shuck Wing migrated to the United States because they dreamed of showering their loved ones in China with luxury, and many hoped to achieve wealth by operating a restaurant. But there was not enough room in the restaurant industry for every aspiring cook and waiter to have his own restaurant. Established Chinese entrepreneurs realized this and created organizations that protected the industry from becoming oversaturated. One of the major functions of the CCBA was to minimize competition among restaurants. As the "general authority and great power" in Chinatown, the CCBA regulated the restaurant industry by forcing all major business trans-actions to go through it, or "the deal [would not be] recognized by the Asso-ciation as legal."[59] The CCBA arbitrated disputes and stipulated the distance between restaurants, with the intent of protecting the industry for the greater Chinese community. To some Chinese, the CCBA was the strong arm of the Chinese elite, and it certainly behaved that way by sending hired men to bully the Chinese who refused its dictates. Its executive board mediated the turf wars from a broader vantage point, however, than did those personally involved in interbusiness disputes.[60] Often times, these goals clashed with the ambitions of the Chinese thinking of a future for themselves and their fami-lies in China.

Ironically, it was Shuck Wing's family, rather than the CCBA, that blocked his path to self-employment. Throughout his time in the United States, Shuck Wing considered opening his own business on several occasions, but the end of World War II presented an especially big window of opportunity. He regarded the war's end as his ticket out of the U.S. Air Force, into which he had been drafted. He and one of his brothers were looking for a restaurant "on a big main street" in downtown San Antonio, Texas. On December 10, 1945, Guang Yan wrote that he had found a "chop suey restaurant" that its owner was willing to sell for $6,000. He invited Shuck Wing to "come take a look" and decide if they were "getting a good deal" for the business.[61] Shuck Wing, however, never bought this restaurant and never moved to Texas. Instead, he returned to New York after the war and worked in various service industry jobs until he grew too old, dying at a boarding house at 111 Mott Street in 1987. There is no document to explain what stopped Shuck Wing from opening a restaurant, although we do know that important figures in his life opposed this venture. Upon learning about Shuck Wing's intentions, his mother asked him to be cautious: "I advise you to fully investigate your opportunities . . . so that you avoid being tricked by other people." His brother Guang Lin also opposed Shuck Wing's plans, ordering that his professional ambitions "should wait," reminding him that his greatest contribution to the family came from respecting commands from his elders. Or in the words of his mother, "work hard and come home soon"—ask for nothing more and do nothing less.[62]

Life beyond the Kitchen Doors: Why Did the Chinese Endure Such Hard Work?

The family dispute over Shuck Wing's intended restaurant was a classic conflict of the individual versus the collective. The twist in this story is that Shuck Wing sought to serve the Chin clan by opening a restaurant, a move that key relatives regarded as selfish and damaging to family harmony. Indeed, the Chins reacted strongly to Shuck Wing's plans because allocations of any family member's capital and labor affected the entire family and, therefore, needed to be carefully measured. During this era, the Chinese in China and the United States survived through collective action. This concept of "interdependence" motivated people like Shuck Wing to migrate to and make a living in the United States. Da Chen, a sociologist working in both the United States and China during the interwar period, described this commitment: "The peasant in South China is not an individualist. He feels himself bound to his sires and to his progeny by a blood relationship that involves both duties and benefits."[63] That is, the Chinese viewed the world and their place in it through the needs of the entire family. Reality, however, did not always conform to this ideal. As a result, the Chins sought ways to keep the family intact through challenges that shook the delicate ties spanning vast geographies.

Shuck Wing's family faced the difficult challenge of being scattered throughout North America and southern China (see map 3.2). To maintain a sense of

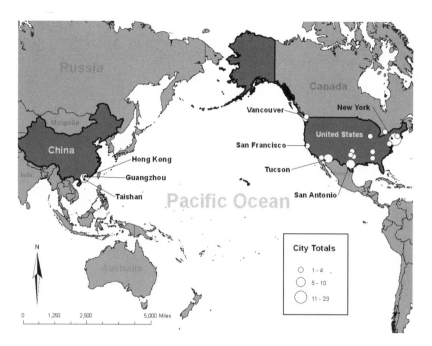

Map 3.2. The Chin family in China and North America, 1935–1946. Source: Bachelor's Apartment, 111 Mott Street Collection, Museum of Chinese in America, New York, NY. Map by the author.

family unity, the Chin men regularly wrote to one another about both mundane and extraordinary events in their lives. While Shuck Wing served in the U.S. Air Force, he wrote or received one letter a week, which amounted to 186 letters over 161 weeks.[64] The Chins benefited from the U.S. government's investments in mail delivery during World War II to ensure that its military personnel stayed in touch with their loved ones. After 1937, because the Japanese occupation had made communication with Taishan very difficult, the Chins relied on the U.S. postal service to relay news from China in their letters to one another. Shuck Wing's male friends and relatives in New York and Washington, DC, sporadically got bundles of mail from relatives in China. In total, they forwarded twenty-four letters that were meant for Shuck Wing to Tarrant Airfield in Fort Worth, Texas, where he was stationed. Shuck Wing's mother managed the household in his absence and needed his consent about decisions regarding schooling and marriage for his children. Unable to read or write, she counted on her educated nephew to send her wishes to Shuck Wing through the transpacific letter network. The role of men in this communication network should be striking to us today, because these men assumed the duties of women in Western cultures. In short, the Chin men held the transpacific family together through their correspondence.[65]

Shuck Wing embraced letter writing as his form of expression. He had attended the village school for two years as a young boy in Taishan but lacked the skills to write confidently as an adult.[66] As a result, even though Shuck Wing owned only a dozen books, two-thirds of them were on writing, including several dictionaries—both Chinese to Chinese and Chinese to English—and a letter-writing manual. Careful with his wording and calligraphy, he drafted letters before committing to a final version for the people listed in his little green address book.[67] His family would have understood the generosity of such gestures because they knew how precious his personal time was while he served in the military. In one letter, Shuck Wing openly lamented that "it [was] a hard life working as a cook in the barracks," rising at 4:30 A.M. to bake fresh bread and retiring after midnight when the cleaning was done.[68] In addition to "being worked harder than beasts of burden," the Chinese in the military faced "racial discrimination" and other forms of "unfair treatment" from white peers and superiors.[69] Correspondence with his family and friends, then, gave Shuck Wing temporary respite from the work, harassment, and loneliness he endured while in the military. Because the letters were his only line of contact to life beyond the barracks, he eagerly engaged in the regular exchange of letters with the other Chins in North America.

These exchanges served the greater social purpose of carrying on Chinese cultural traditions. At Christmas and Chinese New Year, Shuck Wing received cards and gifts of money from friends and relatives across North America. While Shuck Wing was stationed at Tarrant Airfield, he received nineteen holiday cards from friends and family, which, in total, contained $95, which in 2012 would be worth $1,270.[70] The money-stuffed cards were adaptations of Chinese red envelopes, gifts of money given during holidays and important life-cycle moments. In China, money trickled down the social hierarchy, from married to unmarried and from older to younger individuals.[71] The Chins in North America embraced this practice, with elder or more established relatives and friends sending Shuck Wing holiday cards while he was in the military. It is unclear to whom and how much Shuck Wing himself gave, since his money cards do not survive, though the unused holiday cards that he left behind suggest that he, too, observed this custom.[72]

The Chins also used letters to control the actions and behaviors of family members who threatened to break from the cycle of "duties and benefits." Away from the village and the close watch of relatives and friends, those living in North America had more freedom to live for themselves than they had ever experienced before. Loneliness and hard work pushed some men to find pleasure in gambling and extramarital affairs.[73] Shuck Wing was not immune to such temptation. In 1939, Shuck Wing met Vera Bartlow while working at Jim Lee Laundry, and the two began a relationship that continued through some of his time in the air force. Bartlow was a white sales clerk and lived just around the corner from the laundry. While Shuck Wing was stationed at Tarrant Air Field, they exchanged letters every few weeks and met during his furloughs. Shuck Wing occasionally supported her financially.[74] When news of his relationship with her spread through the family grapevine, his relatives intervened to remind Shuck Wing of his obligations to the Chin family. Guang Lin, his older brother in Washington, DC, pressured him to end the relationship:

> I can tell [what's going on] without you saying anything—concealing is very difficult because the rocks can be seen when the water is clear. In my opinion, why not confess. It's better than hiding the truth. . . . I have some words of advice for you—in this society, you should know the way to deal with people and things. Being unethical, immoral, and unappreciative . . . you must then correct what you have done in the past, cleanse your heart, and determine to be a man; to study should be the order of your life as well as the establishment of a sense of obligation. Be cautious of becoming a prideful, arrogant, and selfish man.[75]

To Guang Lin, Shuck Wing needed to renew his commitment to the family. Extramarital relationships with local women were not uncommon and sometimes tolerated as a consequence of families sending men to work abroad.[76] They were unacceptable, however, if they interfered with men's abilities to financially support their families in China. At the time of Guang Lin's reproach, Shuck Wing was unable to send money home and unwilling to maintain communication with his mother, behaviors that threatened to dissolve the social pact that bound him to China. If he abandoned his family in China, another male relative would have had to assume Shuck Wing's responsibilities. Therefore, his relatives had a stake in convincing him to maintain his duties as a son, husband, and father.

As a means of maintaining family cohesion, letter writing was an imperfect tool for keeping people in the fold because it also occasionally alienated them from the family network. During his first ten years (1937–1946), Shuck Wing remained true to his purpose for coming to the United States. He received twenty-two requests for money from relatives in China and sent back money on sixteen occasions. In 1939 alone, not long before communication to Dragon Village was cut off, Shuck Wing sent home $250, which in 2012 would be worth $4,129.[77] He also participated in the cultural life of the village by doing favors for relatives, who in turn helped his mother with family affairs. Shuck Wing improved his family's social standing among the seventeen families in Dragon Village by sending gifts of cash and goods from the United States to elders in China.[78] Local power brokers returned the favors with small loans when his family was in need. But in 1946, Shuck Wing abruptly cut off contact with people in China. He stopped writing and sending money, and eventually his family quietly disappeared from his life. In the last surviving letter, dated June 24, 1946, his daughter wrote to thank him for the money she had received and to describe how she had spent it. She reminded him that Mrs. Chin, her grandmother and Shuck Wing's mother, had a birthday soon and wished for her father's return.[79] As far as we can tell from the records, Shuck Wing neither replied nor returned to China. He lived out the remainder of his life separated from his family and working wage jobs in New York City. After ten years, Shuck Wing had broken away from the transpacific social network that had embraced him so tightly.

Conclusion

The transpacific family network that sustained the Chins through years of separation was a delicate web. Letter writing imperfectly extended a culture of obligation into the everyday lives of wage earners who worked for their relatives in small family businesses across the United States. As a Chin family wage worker, Shuck Wing felt his relatives' disapproval when he made plans that might have severed his overseas ties. Chins from across the globe sent letters that guided Shuck Wing away from opening his own restaurant and persuaded him to end his relationship with Vera Bartlow, the white sales clerk. His relatives meddled in Shuck Wing's life because he played a critical role in the Chin family's collective struggle for success. The family had invested much time and money in bringing Shuck Wing to the United States, which his relatives believed obligated him to accept a life of sacrifice for the family. His service to the Chin family as a dutiful laborer was essential to making the Chin family businesses in North America profitable. Accordingly, he was asked to surrender himself to the collective and to become one of thousands of Chinese workers who cooked and served Chinese food to American consumers. In death as in life, Shuck Wing was just another worker.[80]

As a man who cooked for others, Shuck Wing provides a case study for understanding Chinese restaurant operations during the era of Chinese Exclusion. My examination of Chinese restaurant life puts a face and name to the anonymous and forgotten masses whose labor built the Chinese restaurant industry into what it is today. Given that the Chinese restaurant industry continues to grow and that the Chinese can easily find work in it, Chinese of all backgrounds—from educated professionals to semiliterate manual laborers—share the experience of cooking over sizzling stoves or waiting on disgruntled customers. Yet the information about this prevailing experience is limited to autobiographical or literary portraits of restaurant life and statistical reports on Chinese occupations. As a close study of one Chinese restaurant worker in New York, I hope to have sharpened our historical understanding of this common Chinese American experience by humanizing the work of feeding the "eager exodus toward Chinatown." By studying the barely articulated and unquantifiable aspects of the experience for Chinese restaurant workers, we learn that these anonymous bachelors who dished out chop suey day in and day out have histories and aspirations that crisscross the Asia Pacific and the continental United States.

Notes

My thanks to the K-Team Writing Group for nurturing this work through many drafts and for picking through it with a fine comb in its final stages. I am deeply indebted to my dissertation committee for guiding me through the hurdles I faced while researching and writing. I wish honor to my family, especially my mother, whose love and support made this research possible. Mom, your patience and dedication to the ones you love are bottomless, and I am infinitely grateful to be on the receiving end.

1. *Chop suey* is the Chinese term for "different pieces" and is the name for stir-fried hash served over rice or noodles.

2. Bertram Reinitz, "Our Town and Its Folk: Chop Suey's New Role," *New York Times*, December 27, 1925.

3. I calculated these restaurant statistics from business information in the Chinese Exclusion Case files for New York City. I examined 115 of 225 files on Chinese immigrants who listed restaurant work as their primary occupation. From these 115 files, I gathered information on assets, gross receipts, purchases, and expenses. The restaurants included in these calculations operated in the 1920s and 1930s. These statistics calculated from these records are cited as Chinese Exclusion restaurant business data, 1920–1939. See Shepard Schwartz, "Mate-Selection among New York City's Chinese Males, 1931–38," *American Journal of Sociology* 56, no. 6 (1951): 563.

4. For the remainder of this chapter, I refer to Chin Shuck Wing as Shuck Wing to distinguish him from his brothers who share the last name Chin. I chose this romanization of the Chinese characters 甄灼榮 because he used this transliteration in his legal documents. I refer to one of his uncles by his legal English name and to his mother as Mrs. Chin. In all other romanizations of Chinese names, I use pinyin phonetics and place the family name first.

5. Madeline Y. Hsu, *Dreaming of Gold, Dreaming of Home: Transnationalism and Migration Between the United States and South China, 1882–1943* (Stanford, CA: Stanford University Press, 2000), 16–18.

6. Chin Shuck Wing file, San Francisco, January 20, 1936, 35841/7-4, Chinese Arrival File, San Francisco, Records of the U.S. Immigration and Naturalization Service, RG 85, National Archives and Records Administration, Pacific Region, San Bruno, CA. Hereafter I refer to this archive as CAF, SF.

7. Da Chen, *Emigrant Communities in South China: A Study of Overseas Migration and Its Influence on Standards of Living and Social Change,* ed. Bruno Lasker (New York: Institute of Pacific Relations, 1940), 86–89.

8. Letter from Mrs. Chin, China, to Chin Shuck Wing, USA, January 2, 1937, accession no, 2009.006.265, Bachelor's Apartment / 111 Mott St. Collection, Museum of Chinese in America, New York. Hereafter I refer to the Bachelor's Apartment / 111 Mott St. Collection as BA.

9. Hsu, *Dreaming of Gold*, 21–23, 42.

10. Chen, *Emigrant Communities in South China*, 72.

11. Letter from Zhen Yong Han, Guangzhou, China, to Chin Shuck Wing, New York, May 3, 1937, Accession Number 2009.006.008, BA.

12. Letter from Zhen Yong Huai, China, to Chin Shuck Wing, USA, April 15 1936, accession no. 2009.006.078, BA; Letter from Mrs. Chin, China, to Chin Shuck Wing, USA, January 2, 1937, accession no. 2009.006.266, BA.

13. To make this calculation, I converted the total remittances Mrs. Chin received in 1937 to Hong Kong dollars and then to U.S. dollars. In 1937, HK$1 was worth 2.116 Chinese *yuan*, and in 1939, US$1 was worth HK$5. In 1937, Mrs. Chin received 1,000 Chinese *yuan* and HK$200 from Shuck Wing. I used an inflation calculator provided by the Bureau of Labor Statistics to arrive at a 2012 U.S. dollar value for Shuck Wing's total remittances in 1937. Letters from Mrs. Chin, China, to Chin Shuck Wing, USA, April 28, 1937, accession nos. 2009.006.289, BA, 2009.006.265, BA, and 2009.006.266, BA; remittance from Chin Shuck Wing, New York, to Wu Shi Lian, Hong Kong, September 25, 1939, accession no. 2009.006.201, BA; available at http://www.bls.gov/data/inflation_calculator.htm (accessed November 1, 2012).

14. Hsu, *Dreaming of Gold*, 31, 43; Chen, *Emigrant Communities in South China*, 83.

15. Chin Shuck Wing file, CAF, SF; Erika Lee, *At America's Gates: Chinese Immigration during the Exclusion Era, 1882–1943* (Chapel Hill: University of North Carolina Press, 2003), 111–16, 131–18; Lucy E. Salyer, *Laws Harsh as Tigers: Chinese Immigrants and the Shaping of Modern Immigration Law* (Chapel Hill: University of North Carolina Press, 1995), 57–68.

16. Application for Certificate of Identity for Chin Shuck Wing, January 23, 1936; Letter from Edward L. Haff, district director, San Francisco, to Stidger and Root, San Francisco, December 20, 1935; affidavit of Chin Yee Kim, January 7, 1936; form 2508, December 20, 1935, Chin Shuck Wing file, CAF, SF.

17. Letter from R. A. Scott, inspector in charge, Tucson, AZ, to Edward L. Haff, district director, San Francisco, September 9, 1935; letter from Edward L. Haff, district director, San Francisco, to American consul general, Hong Kong, October 3, 1935, Chin Shuck Wing file, CAF, SF.

18. Chin Shuck Wing file, CAF, SF.

19. Ibid.

20. Chin Shuck Wing's health inspection card, Hong Kong, November 27, 1935, accession no. 2009.006.147, BA; Elizabeth Sinn, "Hong Kong as an In-Between Place in the Chinese Diaspora, 1849–1939," in *Connecting Seas and Connected Ocean Rims: Indian, Atlantic, and Pacific Oceans and China Seas Migrations from the 1830s to the 1930s*, ed.

Donna R. Gabaccia and Dirk Hoerder (Leiden: Brill, 2011), 225–47; application for Certificate of Identity for Chin Shuck Wing, CAF, SF.

21. Erika Lee and Judy Yung, *Angel Island: Immigrant Gateway to America* (New York: Oxford University Press, 2011), 9–15.

22. Summary report by R. W. Hanlen, chairman of the Board of Special Inquiry, San Francisco, January 20, 1936, Chin Shuck Wing file, CAF, SF.

23. Lee and Yung, *Angel Island*, 338, n. 7.

24. Application for Certificate of Identity for Chin Shuck Wing, CAF, SF; letter from Zhen Yong Huai, accession no. 2009.006.078, BA.

25. Louis J. Beck, *New York's Chinatown: An Historical Presentation of Its People and Places* (New York: Bohemia Publishing, 1898), 6–8, 48–49.

26. Ibid., 47, 49–54.

27. Wong Chin Foo, "The Chinese in New York," *The Cosmopolitan*, June 1888, 304.

28. Michael Diehl, et al., "Acculturation and the Composition of the Diet of Tucson's Overseas Chinese Gardeners at the Turn of the Century," *Historical Archeology* 32, no. 4 (1998): 19–33; Renqui Yu, *To Save China, to Save Ourselves: The Chinese Hand Laundry Alliance of New York* (Philadelphia: Temple University Press, 1992), 27.

29. Wong, "The Chinese in New York," 305.

30. "Chinese Farmers in Greater New York," *New York Times*, August 4, 1901; Warner Montagnie Van Norden, *Who's Who of the Chinese in New York* (New York, 1918), 33.

31. "The Chinese within Our Gates," *New York Times*, July 20, 1890.

32. Arthur Bonner, *Alas! What Brought Thee Hither? The Chinese in New York, 1800–1950* (Madison, NJ: Fairleigh Dickinson University Press, 1997), 33–40.

33. Heather R. Lee, "The Chinese in New York: A Look at Popular Representations of the Chinese by American Writers from 1808–1940" (master's thesis, Emory University, 2004), 74–113; Bonner, *Alas!*, 97–107; Andrew Haley, *Turning the Tables: Restaurants and the Rise of the American Middle Class, 1880–1920* (Chapel Hill: North Carolina University Press, 2011), 95–105.

34. Renqui Yu, "Chop Suey: From Chinese Food to Chinese American Food," *Chinese America: History and Perspectives* 1 (1987): 87–99; Andrew Coe, *Chop Suey: A Cultural History of Chinese Food in the United States* (New York: Oxford University Press, 2009), 160–72; George S. Chappell, *The Restaurants of New York* (New York: Greenberg, 1925), 160.

35. Chinese Exclusion Restaurant Business Data, 1920–1939; Bernard Wong, *Patronage, Brokerage, Entrepreneurship and the Chinese Community of New York* (New York: AMS Press, 1988), 116–18, 121–27.

36. Fong Yee King file, New York, September 30, 1921, file 6/436; Samuel Meisler file, New York, October 13, 1921, file 6/436; Mui Tin Yuen file, New York, October 26, 1921, file 6/579, Chinese Exclusion Acts case files, New York, Records of the U.S. Immigration and Naturalization Service, RG 85, National Archives and Records Administration, Northeast Region, New York, NY; Wayne Wong, *American Paper Son: A Chinese Immigrant in the Midwest*, ed. Benson Tong (Urbana: University of Illinois Press, 2006), 36–37.

37. Chinese Exclusion Restaurant Business Data, 1920–1939; Louis H. Chu, "The Chinese Restaurants in New York City" (master's thesis, New York University, 1939), 24; U.S.

Bureau of the Census, *Sixteen Census of the United States*, vol. 2, *Population* (Washington, DC: U.S. Government Printing Office, 1943), 157.

38. Chin Shuck Wing's Certification of Separation from the U.S. Army, September 29, 1945, accession no. 2009.006.149, BA.

39. Chu, "The Chinese Restaurants in New York City," 41.

40. Ibid.; Julia Hsuan Chen, "The Chinese Community in New York: A Study in Their Cultural Adjustment, 1920–1940" (master's thesis, American University, 1941), 55.

41. Chu, "The Chinese Restaurants in New York City," 45.

42. Ibid.; Chinese Exclusion Restaurant Business Data, 1920–1939.

43. Chu, "The Chinese Restaurants in New York City," 45–48; John Jung, *Sweet and Sour: Life in Chinese Family Restaurants* (Los Angeles: Yin and Yang Press, 2010), 62–64, 80–81, 212.

44. Chu, "The Chinese Restaurants in New York City," 45, 49.

45. U.S. Bureau of the Census, *Fifteenth Census of the United States, 1930*, Special Report, Retail Distribution (Trade Series), *Food Retailing* (Washington, DC: U.S. Government Printing Office, 1934), 23–25; Rice Bowl Restaurant account books, 1945–1948, accession no. 2006.003.648, Marcella Dear Chin Collection, Museum of Chinese in America, New York.

46. Chinese Exclusion Restaurant Business Data, 1920–1939; Chu, "The Chinese Restaurants in New York City," 48, 49–50; Beck, *New York's Chinatown*, 54.

47. Dorothy Sue Cobble, *Dishing It Out: Waitresses and Their Unions in the Twentieth Century* (Urbana: University of Illinois Press, 1991), 61–62.

48. Chu, "The Chinese Restaurants in New York City," 43.

49. Alexander Saxton, *Indispensable Enemy: Labor and the Anti-Chinese Movement in California* (Berkeley: University of California Press, 1971), 271–78; Fred Greenbaum, "The Social Ideas of Samuel Gompers," *Labor History* 7, no. 1 (1966): 42–44.

50. "Sign Waiters' Agreement," *New York Times*, May 29, 1920; "2,000 Waiters Win All Wage Demands," *New York Times*, May 31, 1922; "Tips Not Wages, NRA Board Rules," *New York Times*, November 15, 1933; "To Set Hotel, Restaurant Wage," *New York Times*, November 25, 1935.

51. Chu, "The Chinese Restaurants in New York City," 36–37; Peter Kwong, *Chinatown, N.Y.: Labor and Politics, 1930–1950* (1979; repr., New York: New Press, 2001), 88–90.

52. Kwong, *Chinatown*, 89.

53. Ibid.; Him Mark Lai, *Chinese American Transnational Politics* (Urbana: University of Illinois Press, 2010), 84-88; Yu, *To Save China*, 158–59.

54. Chu, "The Chinese Restaurants in New York City," 31; Thomas Chow, "Chinese Restaurateurs Association of Greater New York," March 22, 1937, Federal Writer's Project, WPA, New York City Unit, Racial Groups 1 Series, Microfilm Reel 66; Wong, *Patronage, Brokerage, Entrepreneurship*, 102–3.

55. Yu, *To Save China*, 32–43.

56. Wong, *Patronage, Brokerage, Entrepreneurship*, 137–42.

57. Yuen-Fong Woon, *Social Organization in South China, 1911–1949: The Case of the Kuan Lineage of K'ai-p'ing County* (Ann Arbor: Center for Chinese Studies, University of Michigan, 1984), 1–10.

58. Letter from Zhen Guang Jian, New York, to Chin Shuck Wing, Fort Worth, TX, 1943, accession no. 2009.006.120, BA; letter from Zhen Yi Yu, San Francisco, to Chin Shuck

Wing, Fort Worth, TX, June 23, 1943, accession no. 2009.006.045, BA; letter from Zhen Guang Lin, Washington, DC, to Chin Shuck Wing, Fort Worth, TX, April 19, 1943, accession no. 2009.006.005, BA.

59. Beck, *New York's Chinatown*, 19; bylaws of the CCBA, cited in Wong, *Patronage, Brokerage, Entrepreneurship*, 89.

60. Wong, *Patronage, Brokerage, Entrepreneurship*, 84–90.

61. Letter from Zhen Guang Yan, San Antonio, TX, to Chin Shuck Wing, Fort Worth, TX, December 10, 1945, accession no. 2009.006.114, BA.

62. Letter from Mrs. Chin, accession no. 2009.006.265, BA; letter from Zhen Guang Lin, Washington, DC, to Chin Shuck Wing, Fort Worth, TX, September 3, 1945, accession no. 2009.006.109, BA; letter from Mrs. Chin, China, to Chin Shuck Wing, New York, December 11, 1939, accession no. 2009.006.264, BA.

63. Chen, *Emigrant Communities in South China*, 123; Hazel Rose Markus and Shinobu Kitayama, "Culture and the Self: Implications for Cognition, Emotion, and Motivation," *Psychological Review* 98, no. 2 (1991): 224–53.

64. While Shuck Wing was in the air force, he received ninety-three letters from friends and relatives in North America. To get this figure, I counted only those letters and empty envelopes in the Bachelor Apartment / 111 Mott St. Collection that originated in North America, were addressed to Shuck Wing, and were posted or dated while Shuck Wing was in the service. I did not count the letters from his girlfriends, his relatives in China, and his unsent correspondences. Shuck Wing's letters to friends and family have been lost. Assuming that he responded to each letter, I estimate that Shuck Wing exchanged a total of 186 letters over a 161-week period.

65. For an example of letter forwarding, see the letter from Zhen Guang Yao, China, to Chin Shuck Wing, Fort Worth, TX, June 8, 1943, accession no. 2009.003.047, BA; Micaela Di Leonardo, "The Female World of Cards and Holidays: Women, Families, and the Work of Kinship," *Signs* 12, no. 3 (1987): 440–53.

66. Chin Shuck Wing file, CAF, SF.

67. Writing Guidebooks, accession nos. 2004.006.076, 2004.006.138, BA; dictionaries, accession nos. 2004.006.080, 2004.006.081, 2004.006.082, 2004.006.084, 2004.006.136, and 2004.006.137, BA; address book, ca. 1942–1945, accession no. 2006.003.083, BA; unsent letters from Chin Shuck Wing, accession nos. 2009.006.088, 2009.006.104, 2009.006.302, and 2009.006.303, BA; unused letterheads, accession nos. 2009.006.280–2009.006.283, BA.

68. Letter from Zhen Guang Lin, accession no. 2009.006.005, BA; available at http://nisei.hawaii.edu/object/io_1160630003265.html (accessed July 27, 2011).

69. Letter from Li Yuan, Camp Forrest, TN, to Chin Shuck Wing, Forth Worth, TX, October 25, 1943, accession no. 2009.006.069, BA.

70. I estimate that each holiday card contained five dollars because of references to holiday gift money of five dollars in various correspondences. Holiday cards from Zhen Guang Lin, Washington, DC, to Chin Shuck Wing, Fort Worth, TX, December19, 1943, accession no. 2009.006.066, BA; December 25 1944, accession no. 2009.006.138, BA.

71. Kin Wai Michael Siu, "Red Packet: A Traditional Object in the Modern World," *Journal of Popular Culture* 35, no. 3 (2002): 103–25.

72. Unused Christmas and New Year cards, ca. 1942–1945, accession nos. 2009.006.257, BA and 2009.006.308, BA.

73. Paul Siu, *The Chinese Laundryman: A Study of Social Isolation* (New York: New York University Press, 1987), 227–49.

74. Letters from Vera Bartlow, New York, to Chin Shuck Wing, Fort Worth, TX, August 31, 1942, accession no. 2009.006.013, BA; November 16, 1942, accession no. 2009.006.030, BA; January 4, 1943, accession no. 2009.006.048, BA; February 19, 1943, accession no. 2009.006.044, BA; letter from Chin Shuck Wing, Fort Worth, TX, to Vera Bartlow, ca. 1942–1945, accession no. 2009.006.213, BA.

75. Letter from Guang Lin, accession no. 2009.006.120, BA.

76. Hsu, *Dreaming of Gold*, 112–22; Adam McKeown, "Transnational Chinese Families and Chinese Exclusion, 1875–1943," *Journal of American Ethnic History* 18, no. 2 (1999): 73–110; Schwartz, "Mate-Selection among New York City's Chinese Males," 564–66.

77. Letters from Mrs. Chin, China, to Chin Shuck Wing, USA, November 19, 1939, accession nos. 2009.006.262, BA and 2009.006.264, BA; Bank of China remittance receipt, September 25, 1939, accession no. 2009.006.201, BA.

78. Letters from Mrs. Chin, China, to Chin Shuck Wing, USA, February 8, 1937, accession nos. 2009.006.015, BA and 2009.006.289, BA; letters from Ma Guang Shuo, China, to Chin Shuck Wing, USA, April 28, 1937, accession no. 2009.006.269, BA; May 29, 1942, accession no. 2009.006.050, BA.

79. Letter from Zhen Zhu, China, to Chin Shuck Wing, New York, June 24, 1946, accession no. 2009.006.312, BA.

80. Shuck Wing passed away in 1987 with no living friends or relatives to care for his things, so the tenants who replaced him at 111 Mott Street moved his possessions out of the way and forgot about them. A decade later, people working for the Museum of Chinese in America—located a few blocks away from Shuck Wing's old apartment—salvaged his belongings from the dumpster. The museum staff called them the "Bachelor's Apartment Collection," since his identity was unknown at the time. These personal belongings are the accumulated effects of a man who worked in Chinese restaurants and laundries from his arrival to the United States in 1935 until his death more than four decades later.

4

Learning from Los Kogi Angeles: A Taco Truck and Its City

OLIVER WANG

Local Los Angeles lore credits Raul Martinez with creating the first *lonchera*—also known as a taco truck—when he converted an ice-cream van and began selling tacos in front of an east LA bar.[1] Martinez's innovation proved so lucrative he eventually parlayed his mobile money into a popular brick-and-mortar chain named King Taco. The company still operates taco trucks on the streets of LA—you can even hire one to cater a private party—and while they rarely come up in conversations about the city's best *loncheras*, the fact that one can even have such a debate is a credit to Martinez's ingenuity.

Meals on Wheels

Estimates of exactly how many food trucks exist in Los Angeles are hard to pin down. In 2006, journalist Jesse Katz estimated there were around four thousand *loncheras* operating in Los Angeles County, enough for "one taco truck for every square mile of land."[2] A different source cites Erin Glenn, CEO of the advocacy group Asociación de loncheras, who put that number closer to seven thousand in 2010.[3] Either way, as the photo essayist Mac Kane explains, these thousands of *loncheras* can be divided between two types: "the *transient* taco truck moves quickly among lower-density locations to serve a diverse mix of needs, the *semi-permanent* truck takes on the location memory of a fixed restaurant."[4] The average Angeleno roaming the city is likely to see the former at construction sites, serving daytime laborers and can often find the latter close to bars and nightclubs (among other places), waiting to capitalize on late-night revelers.

In these ways, *loncheras* are an indelible part of the Southland's business, culture, and community, what Kane describes as "the unconscious connectors of the city . . . responding to the daily changes and needs of its citizens, piggybacking on the larger infrastructure of communication, power and transportation networks."[5] In other words, by traversing the city and occupying space (however briefly), the trucks help bring hidden social patterns into greater relief.

For example, by design, many *loncheras* seek out customers otherwise underserved by existing foodways, bringing into the open the voids and gaps in food distribution.[6] In other cases, the proximity of *loncheras* to brick-and-mortar restaurants has led to protracted battles between the trucks and fixed businesses, politicians, and the police, highlighting the contested relationships between public space and private enterprise, culinary practices and municipal laws.[7] Certainly, in a city as food obsessed as Los Angeles, *loncheras* are one of the most prominent examples of an "authentic" street cuisine, empowering socially and culturally mobile "foodies" with a sense of one-upmanship that comes with claiming to know where the best taco trucks in the city are.[8] As foodways scholar Allison Caldwell describes them, food trucks have become "traveling containers of cultural capital."[9]

Loncheras are so omnipresent that Kane argues they have attained a certain kind of invisibility through overfamiliarity: "The average resident will pass several taco trucks over the course of a day, but their ubiquity hides them in the everyday life of the city."[10] That may have been true once, but not since 2009, when a wave of so-called luxe *loncheras* emerged in the city, led by the Asian American venture Kogi BBQ-to-Go.[11]

"LA in a Single Bite"

Kogi began operating in November 2008, the brain child of Filipino American Mark Manguera, Korean American Caroline Shin-Manguera, and Korean American chef Roy Choi. Launched with a Korean-inspired short rib taco, Kogi initially struggled until the social media specialist Mike Prasad came aboard and suggested that they use the Twitter platform to reach out to potential customers, especially to update the truck's locations.[12]

As the most prominent of the new, haute-meets-street cuisine trucks (*nueva trucks*), Kogi behaved much like a hybrid *lonchera*. Although its constant movement resembled that of transient trucks, its desire to cultivate a brand memory was more akin to that of a semipermanent truck. Social media technology made this dual strategy possible. Kogi customers could either visit the company's website (http://kogibbq.com) or subscribe to its Twitter feed (http://twitter.com/kogibbq) to determine where and when the truck would appear. Especially in its early days, when Kogi had one lone truck rolling across the city, tracking it down became "like a treasure hunt," according to Kogi's public relations chief, Alice Shin.[13]

In hindsight, Kogi's strategy was a perfect trifecta of media catnip, combining cutting-edge cuisine, technology, and culture angles. As I suggested, "The Kogi storyline wrote itself: inexpensive, ethnic fusion street food with a hip, technorati twist."[14]

It also did not hurt that its short rib taco was, in the words of one customer quoted by the *New York Times*, "this Korean Mexican fusion thing of crazy deliciousness."[15] The taco begins with a griddle-warmed corn tortilla, on which are heaped finely chopped pieces of soy-sesame marinated beef short rib that would not be out of place in dozens of Korean BBQ restaurants in town. Add to that a sesame-chili *salsa roja* and a lettuce-and-cabbage slaw with chili-soy vinaigrette, all of which is garnished with a cilantro onion relish (see http://kogibbq.com/category/menu). The result is a brilliant, unexpected contrast in flavors, a sweet/salty/spicy/sour combination that fits in your hand.

This was the other story that wrote itself: how Kogi's mélange of flavors reflected Los Angeles's larger social/cultural mixtures. As Roy Choi told *Newsweek*, "These cultures—Mexican and Korean—really form the foundation of this city. Kogi is my representation of LA in a single bite."[16] Those sentiments were echoed by others, most notably the Pulitzer Prize–winning *Los Angeles Times* food critic, Jonathan Gold, who described the short rib taco as "unmistakably from Los Angeles, food that makes you feel plugged into the rhythms of the city just by eating it."[17]

The impact of these trucks goes beyond just representation. According to New York City Food Truck Association president David Weber, "Food trucks activate public space."[18] One example that comes to mind is from my second trip to Kogi in the spring of 2009, an impromptu, late-night stop in downtown Los Angeles, outside the Golden Gopher Bar. The line was easily thirty to forty people, and as I waited, I eavesdropped on and interacted with fellow customers. The two men in front of me were two twenty-something African American men, both working in marketing. Ahead of them was a pair of forty-something white gay men, and behind me, I noticed a pair of twenty-something Asian American women, each holding a small lap dog in her arms. I later wrote about that experience, noting:

> I couldn't remember ever spending even 15 minutes on an L.A. sidewalk talking and mingling with complete strangers, let alone downtown at 10 p.m. I could appreciate [*Los Angeles Times*'s] Jessica Gelt's idealism when she described Kogi . . . as "a sort of roving party, bringing people to neighborhoods they might not normally go to, and allowing for interactions with strangers they might not otherwise talk to."[19] It's tempting to see Kogi as powering a tech-driven,

heteropolitan form of sidewalk contact, forging, in urban planner Jane Jacobs's words, "a feeling for the public identity of people, a web of public respect and trust."[20]

Lest this wave of urban utopianism—fueled by short rib satiety—go too far, however, I should note that in Jane Jacobs's time, there was not the same kind of virtual panopticon of electronic surveillance watching over the sidewalk (however incompetently).[21] Likewise, as Kristin Day points out, even in the supposedly "safe" streets of Irvine, California (a popular Kogi destination), the intermingling of racialized and gendered bodies can produce an aura of fear that challenges the ideal of a neutral public space.[22]

Especially interesting to consider is how *nueva* trucks like Kogi fit into a larger history of Los Angeles's city-planning schemes that seek to create an idealized "urban experience," but in highly privatized terms and on literally private grounds. An example is CityWalk by Universal Studios, a pioneering outdoor mall design with a faux urban decor that serves as a Vegas-like simulacrum of a Manhattan-style "city street," but one that is completely private and highly surveilled.[23] Part of food trucks' draw lies precisely in their signifier of "urban-ness," not to mention culinary urbanity. Especially in Los Angeles, with its long-standing rivalries with more classically conventional cities like San Francisco and New York, there is a deep attraction to the *nueva* trucks' ability to "activate public space." As I discuss later, *which* public spaces the trucks choose to "activate" have meaningful implications for existing inequities in space, especially along class and race lines. Do the *nueva* trucks transform those borders or merely reify them?

These concerns intersect with a long history in Los Angeles of what has been described as "multicultural triumphalism."[24] Celebratory descriptions of Kogi-as-LA recall Lisa Lowe's warnings that while "multiculturalism claims to register the increasing diversity of populations, it precisely obscures the ways in which that aesthetic representation is not an analogue for the material positions, means, or resources of those populations."[25] What we have seen with the championing of *nueva* trucks and their fusion fare is that the Korean taco can become a potent symbol of a city's embrace of diversity: "the only-in-L.A. combination of two of the city's most beloved ethnic cuisines," as Jessica Gelt wrote.[26] Yet, harmony between flavors can belie the often discordant reality of urban social relations.

In this regard, I agree with the general notion that Kogi can represent "L.A. in a single bite," only it is a far more complex and fragmented Los Angeles than is often acknowledged. Jonathan Gold contends that "Kogi represents mobility in a city that worships mobility; it is a vehicle for traversing lines of race, class and ethnicity," and I would add that it defines the borders in addition to crossing them.[27]

Just as *loncheras* reveal the hidden social structures and forces that flow through the city, I suggest that the *nueva* trucks, led by Kogi, also offer a way to confront the heterogeneity of Los Angeles, where diversity and inequality alike leave their mark on the city's cartography.

Mapping Los Kogi Angeles

For all the attention paid to the social media angles of the *nueva* trucks, surprisingly few publications, either popular or academic, focus on what would seem like an obvious advantage of mobile food trucks: their mobility. As one social media–centric essay on Kogi observes, "A sense of [consumer] community goes beyond geographical parameters."[28] This is not necessarily wrong—certainly, the notion of a community, whether local, national, or transnational, is not solely bound to geography—but in the case of food trucks, whether or not they tweet, a relationship to space is integral to their entire raison d'être. Without their transient model, these trucks would simply be stationary food stands. Once they are on the move, "geographical parameters" are absolutely central.

That said, Twitter does offer a valuable source of data for investigating the travels of a *nueva* truck like Kogi. Twitter's public database allows anyone to look through as many as 3,200 past tweets, and for Kogi, that equals approximately a year's worth of tweets and, by extension, a year's worth of locations. At various times since 2009, I have used Twitter to trace Kogi's unique stops, compiling a complete list of its locations in 2010 and 2011 (but only a partial database for 2009).[29] I then used Google Maps to find these locations, creating a coverage map that displays all the places in Southern California at which Kogi has made at least one stop. I next turned to the *New York Times*'s "Mapping America" site, which allows users to overlay Google-generated maps with census block data on race, income, education, and the like.[30] In that way, I could compare patterns in Kogi's stops with demographic information about those same locations.[31]

Between 2010 and 2011, Kogi made nearly five thousand stops at more than three hundred unique locations, spread across a geographic space ranging from Santa Clarita in the north, Diamond Bar in the east, Laguna Niguel in the south, and Canoga Park in the west: more than four thousand square miles in all (see map 4.1).[32]

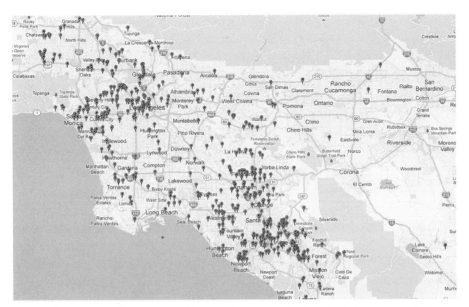

Map 4.1. Los Kogi Angeles, 2010–2011. Each marker represents a location but does not indicate the frequency of stops made at that location. Map by Terrametrics, 2012.

The following analysis should be treated as preliminary, especially because I am focusing on a small handful of observations compared with the potential depth of the data represented in these locations. In addition, I have excluded the 2012 data, so this should be treated as only a snapshot of Kogi during these two years (hence my use of the past tense when describing where Kogi "went" instead of where it "goes").

In 2010 and 2011, what I am calling "Los Kogi Angeles" was split between two large regions. Almost all of "Kogi South" was in Orange County, where it was assigned two trucks, Rosita and Naranja. "Kogi North" was served by two trucks, Roja and Verde, which covered Los Angeles, mostly north of the 10 Freeway and west of downtown, with other stops scattered throughout the sprawling county.[33] Within these regions, I identified three broad categories of Kogi's destinations (or lack thereof):

1. Magnets: locations—whether individual or grouped into clusters—where Kogi went the most often. The most popular magnets were essentially weekly stops in Venice, Granada Hills, West LA, Eagle Rock, and Orange. The most popular magnet was The Brig, a bar in Venice, where Kogi trucks stopped at least 270 times in 2010/2011.

2. One-stops: locations where Kogi stopped once, although I expanded the term to apply also to locations of two or fewer stops. Sixty percent of Kogi's locations were one-stops, not including those stops clustered around magnets. The more important one-stops were those appearing within voids.

3. Voids: large areas (a radius of more than five miles) where Kogi had a minimal presence.[34] The most obvious example is what I term "The Void"—the twenty-mile-wide band separating Kogi North and Kogi South. Smaller voids included the beachside stretch from El Segundo to San Pedro, the neighborhoods in Santa Ana / Fountain Valley located between the 405 and 5 Freeways, and the adjoining west San Gabriel Valley cities of Pasadena, South Pasadena, Alhambra, and Monterey Park.

The first time I made a map of Kogi's locations, in the summer of 2009, The Void was one of the most obvious features, not only for its size, but also because it so closely encompassed long-standing zones of class and racial segregation in the area, including the South Bay, Harbor, South LA, Southeast LA, and East LA. Map 4.2 looks more closely at The Void (shaded gray).[35]

The neighborhoods within this space are overwhelmingly African American and Latino, which took the brunt of the region's deindustrialization in the 1970s and 1980s and suffer from some of the highest concentrations of poverty and homicide rates in Los Angeles County.[36] In short, The Void covers those neighborhoods that have long been marginalized racially, economically, politically, and educationally. In that sense, the minimal presence of a *nueva* truck like Kogi is not surprising, as many other companies, institutions, and nonresidents have steered clear of The Void for decades.[37]

To its credit, Kogi did make stops throughout the region, including locations in Inglewood, Ladera Heights, Baldwin Hills, Huntington Park, Whittier, and Bellflower; by no means am I suggesting that Kogi practiced a *deliberate* policy of abandonment, let alone discrimination.[38] In fact, one of the most vocal critics of what one might term "geographically conservative" *nueva* trucks has been none other than Roy Choi.

In a May 2011 article for the *Los Angeles Times*, Gelt quotes and paraphrases from Choi's comments about how other trucks have failed to serve the city:

He says trucks need to stop congregating in the same lots and go out into L.A.'s vast outer reaches to feed neighborhoods "stacked with relatives," such as Santa Fe Springs, Downey, La Puente, Hacienda Heights, Granada Hills, Northridge, El Segundo, Torrance, Reseda and Arleta. If you "don't serve and honor the culture and soul of L.A.'s neighborhoods, what differentiates you from that Marie Callender's across the street that you are so blatantly fighting against?" asks Choi.

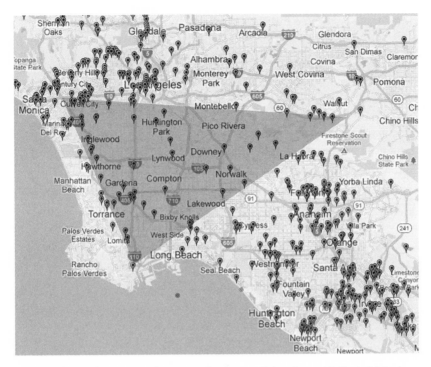

Map 4.2. The Void, 2010–2011, frequency of stops at each location not indicated. Map by Terrametrics, 2012.

On the one hand, Choi and Kogi certainly have covered a tremendous amount of ground in Southern California, seeking locations far from where many other *nueva* trucks cluster (midcity, Hollywood, West LA, and so on). Still, The Void looms in the backdrop of his comments, especially in mentioning Downey. It is true that Kogi has serviced Downey, but in 2010/2011, it was a "one-stop" location: February 19, 2010. I found no other evidence that Kogi stopped there for the rest of the year or the year after.[39] Likewise, another one-stop in The Void was Figueroa and Fifty-Ninth Street, just west of Huntington Park. As it turns out, that stop was accidental; on March 26, 2010, Kogi sent out a tweet: "Verde will continue serving @Figueroa and 59 Ave! Truck broke down here! Might as well serve u guys!! Come on by!!" In cross-checking the addresses that appear in the middle of The Void, I found that the overwhelming majority were one-stops. Map 4.3 shows Kogi's most frequent repeat-stop locations, and The Void is so clearly represented that it needs no shading.

Notably, the most popular stop in the heart of The Void was at 9325 California Avenue in South Gate, an address that turned out to be a venue regularly holding a rave party (see http://twitter.com/rvdie). That this was an exception to The Void highlighted an obvious fact of food-truck locations: trucks travel to where they think they can find customers, thus the trucks' geographic patterns suggest something about the kinds of consumers they are seeking (and where they find them) and perhaps, by extension, what kinds of consumers they may want to avoid.

One way to address these questions would have been to interview the Kogi staff themselves directly, but despite a good-faith effort to arrange such a conversation, their management politely declined my request, citing a general moratorium on interviews.[40] Instead, I relied on an inductively built profile of Kogi's customer bases by analyzing its locations, especially magnets. Map 4.3 shows the magnets at which Kogi stopped at least fifty or more times in 2010–2011, on average, stopping at each location at least once every two weeks.

The typical Kogi consumer was likely to be young (in his or her twenties or thirties), and/or upwardly mobile, and/or white or Asian. There were, of course, exceptions to this, but overall, Kogi's locations and business model seemed to cater to these people.

Youth

I began with the magnets near college campuses: the Westwood cluster (UCLA), Eagle Rock (Occidental), Northridge (Cal State, Northridge), Diamond Bar (Cal Poly Pomona), Orange (Chapman), and the Irvine cluster (UC Irvine). Then I added clusters of magnets near bars and nightclubs: Hollywood, Koreatown, Sawtelle (West LA), Abbot Kinney (Venice), downtown LA, Silver Lake, and so on.

Young people are more likely to be adopters of the necessary technology (smart phones and social media accounts) used to find Kogi and other *nueva* trucks. Also, given that popular culture trends are often driven by youth culture, it is not be surprising that such a culturally trendy movement as the *nueva* trucks would be especially appealing to younger consumers. Also, as Jonathan Gold e-mailed me, Kogi's typical consumer is someone who would see "nothing unusual about going out for tacos at 11 P.M. . . . and saw half-hour waits less as a burden than as an opportunity to socialize."

Upward Mobility

Kogi may take its inspiration from the *loncheras*, but whereas the latter cater mostly to workers with $1 tacos and $4 burritos, Kogi's markup is anywhere from

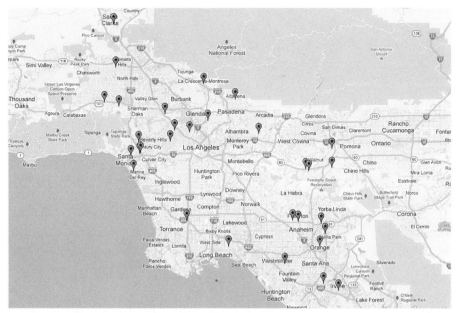

Map 4.3. Kogi's most common locations, more than fifty stops in 2010–2011. Map by Terrametrics, 2012.

50 percent ($6 burritos) to 229 percent ($2.29 tacos) higher.[41] Per item, the difference may seem negligible, but scaled up for a meal, especially for a family, it is the difference between feeding three people for $12 (*lonchera*) and for $24 (Kogi).

The major difference is that the transient *loncheras* cater mostly to blue-collar workers looking for a quick meal between work shifts; they sell convenience by going to where the workers are.[42] Inversely, *nueva* trucks set themselves up as *destinations*. As Alice Shin noted, determining where and when a *nueva* truck is going to be is akin to a "treasure hunt," and it is not just food that awaits the successful quester, it is also the bragging rights to say, "I went to Kogi." Such self-selected consumers, one might rationalize, would be willing to pay twice as much for their food, given that they have already shown they are willing to drive across town and wait forty-five minutes to buy a taco from a truck. I should note, too, that even to begin the hunt, it helps to own a Twitter-enabled smart phone and pay $400 a year for its data plan.

The *nueva* truck's transience also presumes that its patrons have access to a private vehicle.[43] Transient *loncheras* regularly travel into residential and industrial neighborhoods in search of workers to feed, but again, that is a convenience-based model. In contrast, Kogi's magnets lay mostly in commercial zones, next to, for example, Northridge shopping centers, Santa Monica office parks, and Orange saloons. These, too, are destinations, ones that typically offer amenities such as wider streets and available parking that are boons to both trucks and car-borne consumers.

It thus is not surprising that Kogi's locations maximize the possibility of drawing local consumers with either disposable incomes (office workers, shoppers, late-night revelers) or, at least, the willingness to spend limited economic capital to accrue cultural capital (college students or other young people). Likewise, where its coverage is weaker are those areas with lower household incomes, that is, where people have less to spend, particularly on food truck meals substantially marked up from *lonchera* fare.

Race

Looking at a Los Kogi Angeles map of primarily 2010 locations, overlaid with 2010 U.S. Census data on racial distribution, it becomes apparent that Kogi's top magnets were where the largest racial groups were typically white or Asian (though other magnets were located in "nonmajority" tracts). In fact, the best predictor for where Kogi's coverage thinned out is those neighborhoods with low percentages of *both* white and Asian households. That is the case in places like central Santa Ana, central and western San Fernando, central Anaheim, and, as noted earlier, most of The Void. Although Kogi stops appeared on the fringes of those voids, they were only where the demography had shifted to include more white- and Asian-populated tracts (e.g., Gardena and Torrance, which sit at the southwestern edge of The Void).

This was a challenging area to explore since I am not in a position to guess *intentionality*, least of all regarding a topic as sensitive as the racial preferences of consumer bases. For example, in my casual conversations with others about this issue, some suggested that perhaps it is an "issue of palate"; that is, the culinary tastes of Latino and/or African Americans living in these neighborhoods are less likely to embrace a Korean taco or a kimchi quesadilla. But I do not think this theory holds up to any reasonable scrutiny given that food preferences cannot possibly be essentialized so rigidly, especially when the food cultures in all these communities encompass wide ranges of flavors and ingredients. As Gold pointed out, in parts of east LA, where Kogi rarely goes, "The area was once home to a fairly substantial Nisei population, and . . . teriyaki was as familiar to the local palate as hot dogs."[44] Moreover, the argument reifies the assumption that residents in The Void self-segregate and never, for example, cross north of the 10 Freeway or east of the 5 Freeway to get a meal. It also plays into a middle-class self-image of cosmopolitanism, compared with the less refined tastes of "others" (which, in this case, has both racial and class overtones).

The correlation of race, class, and space concerns how the tracts with more white and Asian households coincide with higher median household incomes. As just noted, if Kogi's typical consumer is middle class, then it makes sense to travel to where the middle class works, lives, or plays. This correlation of race, class, and neighborhood is itself a partial product of the "cumulative advantages and disadvantages" stemming from racial privilege and policies, especially in a historically segregated housing sector.[45]

In summation, Kogi's location preferences help illuminate the social topographies of race and class in Los Angeles. Furthermore, just as faux urban malls like CityWalk and The Grove offer privatized, sanitized experiences of "city life," the decisions of *nueva* trucks like Kogi to locate in middle-class / professional spaces while bypassing hundreds of square miles of central-city neighborhoods may indicate the city's discomfort with its own urban spaces.

Asian American Foodies

The other factor not yet mentioned is the role of Asian Americans, on both sides of the truck window. Given the pan-Asian roots of Kogi's founders and the Asian influences on the cuisine itself, it is not unreasonable to assume that Kogi would seek out Asian American consumers by establishing magnets in and around neighborhoods with high numbers of Asian households. In fact, the data mostly confirm this, as I found Kogi magnets around Asian-heavy college campuses such as UCLA and UC Irvine, as well as in Asian-identified cities and neighborhoods such as Gardena, Carson, Little Tokyo, Koreatown, Westminster, and Rowland Heights.[46]

In this way, I suggest that Kogi also helped highlight the growing role and presence of Asian Americans in Los Angeles's social and cultural milieus. It is notable that Roy Choi's rise coincided with that of other prominent Asian American chefs and restaurants in the area, including Sang Yoon (Father's Office), Diep Tran (Good Girl Dinette), and Ray Byrne (Slaw Dogs).[47] It is not even that all these chefs' menus are Asian inspired—Father's Office and Slaw Dogs certainly are not—but that Asian American culinary talents are claiming space in an industry that historically has been almost completely dominated by white chefs.

This phenomenon also caught the attention of Gold, who situated it as

> part of the new movement in Los Angeles cooking, the one where Asian-American chefs claim the chicken-pot pie, the taco and the Cobb salad as their own, relating the dishes back to similar ones in Thailand, Korea and Taiwan, but

celebrating the differences in culinary culture rather than trying to bury them in a flurry of catsup and processed cheese.[48]

I agree that there has been a "new" movement afoot insofar as these personalities arose in the media spotlight in the same general time frame, but of course, this also may be part of a far older movement of Asian American cultural hybridity—chop suey, anyone?

As Samantha Barbas writes, "The story of chop suey and Chinese American dishes in the first half of the twentieth century illustrates the way that restaurants have been able to initiate, however slight, crosscultural interaction and culinary diversification," and she then points out that "food and eating establishments have often been more successful in promoting exchange between diverse cultural groups and traditions than other social institutions."[49] But Barbas also warns that "Americans' exposure to Chinese American food . . . seems to have done little to change dominant attitudes toward Asian immigrants" and that "chop suey became more popular . . . the further it moved from Chinese American people."[50] Whether our current moment represents a different balance in power remains to be seen—can one co-opt the Korean taco?[51]—but it is tempting to see the rise of Kogi, among other operations, as one in which Asian Americans are not so much "introducing" Asian traditions into the American menu as reshaping American culinary traditions by means of a polyglot method of adaptation and innovation.

Asian American consumers also have a significant but understudied role in emergent forms of what, for lack of a better term, I call "food documenting" (since it goes beyond writing). This certainly includes blogs and websites, but Asian Americans also seem to have a notable presence on restaurant review sites, such as Yelp.com. In particular, some of my friends insist that using smart phone cameras to share photos of meals is somehow a uniquely "Asian thing."[52] This may be an overgeneralization, but it is interesting to think about how some long-standing assumptions of Asian Americans—our technological prowess, for example—ends up aligning with an emergent popular discourse on food that has flourished through such digital media as blogs, review sites, and camera phone–sharing services.

Its Asian American fans have played a vocal and visible role in fueling Kogi's "buzz," and notably in the immediate post-Kogi boom of *nueva* trucks, several of the more prominent ones have been founded by young Asian Americans, including the Nom Nom Truck (Vietnamese), the Don Chow Truck (Chinese), and the Flying Pig (pan-Asian). I have no conclusions to offer, only the observation that Asian American consumers and chefs alike seem to be coalescing into a critical mass that might be able to alter the Southland's culinary land-scape. As Alice Shin posted on Kogi's website, "We don't call it fusion. But what we do call it is Angeleno. The thing is, THIS is what Los Angeles tastes like. To us 2nd and 1.5 generation Asians living in LA County anyway" (http://kogibbq.com/2010/03/ess-not-fusion/, italics in original).

Last Run of the Night

In Los Angeles, the new conventional wisdom is that the *nueva* truck craze has plateaued, either because it has become oversaturated and/or the recession has forced it to scale back.[53] Even Kogi had to downsize: from 2009 through 2011, it slowed from roughly seventy-five stops per week by five trucks to roughly fifty stops per week by four trucks.[54] Despite this slowdown, the *nueva* truck phenomenon has not shown signs of abating elsewhere. Outside Los Angeles, many other cities are experiencing their own rapid expansion, creating many of the same problems of licensing, excessive competition, and brick-and-mor-tar tensions seen in Southern California in recent years.[55]

There are many unanswered questions about what this movement means. In regard to the relationship between *nuevas* and *loncheras*, some people, includ-ing Choi, have suggested that the *nuevas* helped redeem people's previously poor opinion of *loncheras*, often derided as "roach coaches."[56] But it seems more likely that *nuevas* carved out a different niche for themselves, one that comes with culinary school pedigrees, reputations first burnished in estab-lished brick-and-mortar eateries, and the blessings of prominent food writers and publications. These all have helped make *nueva* trucks more acceptable, even desirable, to certain middle-class consumers, but meanwhile, *loncheras* continue to be as invisible as before.[57]

Another concern, especially if *nueva* truck operations are downsizing, is whether the progress of shrinking voids will also slow if these operations grow more conservative and fall back to more familiar locations. As I have stressed, many voids are located in historically underserved neighborhoods, and if the *nueva* truck movement wants to live up to the rhetoric of "representing the city," it must find ways of expanding into these areas. A truly transformative activation of public space would find a way not just to bring people from West-mont to Westwood but go in the other direction as well.

Future research could go in a variety of directions. My project was to look at a single truck and to examine and map its location data. But there are more than three hundred *nueva* trucks in Los Angeles alone and thousands of *loncheras*, some of which have also started using Twitter. I therefore hope to use this research as the basis for a collaborative project that looks more closely and critically at how food trucks relate to their cities, and vice versa. As should be evident, my analyses are highly inductive and speculative, closer to a series of critical thoughts or primordial hypotheses than firm conclusions. I find it especially revealing that whenever I have discussed my project with like-minded scholars and journalists, they suggest new directions I had never considered. It shows that mobile eateries are a rich topic on which to ruminate but one that we have only begun to sample.[58]

Notes

I would like to acknowledge the research assistance of Miriam Fraire, Danielle Abdelja-ber, and Brenda Martinez, as well as additional suggestions for this project from Oiyan Poon, Jeff Chang, Sean Slusser, Jenny Banh, Jonathan Gold, David Leonard, and Mac Kane. Thanks also to Karen Tongson, the first to mention Kogi to me in late 2008, and Linda España-Maram and Larry Hashima, my coteachers at Cal State University, Long Beach, who assigned our first field trip to Kogi.

1. Jesus Sanchez, "King Taco Got Start in Old Ice Cream Van," *Los Angeles Times*, November 16, 1987, available at http://articles.latimes.com/1987-11-16/business/fi-14263_1_ice-cream-truck. *Lonchera* is translated literally as "lunch box" but in colloquial parlance, it refers to a catering truck in Los Angeles, of which the taco truck is one of the most prominent configurations.

2. Jesse Katz, "Wheels of Fortune: Nearly 4,000 Taco Trucks Roam the Streets of L.A. Tacos Jeesy's Is Hoping There's Room for One More." *Los Angeles Magazine*, October 1, 2006, available at http://www.lamag.com/features/Story.aspx?ID=1531012. Katz's estimation combines 2,422 officially health-permitted food trucks with 1,465 formerly permitted trucks that could still be in operation.

3. Heather Shouse, *Food Trucks: Dispatches and Recipes from the Best Kitchens on Wheels* (Berkeley, CA: Ten Speed Press), 6. Shouse claims there are "3820 licensed trucks on record" and quotes another estimate, putting that number closer to seven thousand. For both Katz and Shouse, what is clear is that *non*permitted/off-record trucks are the hardest to keep track of, thus obfuscating the true number of trucks in operation on any given day in Los Angeles.

4. Mac Kane, "Taco Trucks," *Polar Inertia*, 2006, available at http://www.polarinertia.com/jan06/taco01.htm (italics added).

5. Ibid.

6. Food access is an ongoing issue in poorer Los Angeles neighborhoods, many of which rely on a loose combination of fast-food franchises, liquor stores, greengrocers, and mobile eateries to fill in the gaps left by the absence of larger, full-resource supermarkets. While *loncheras* play a part as a stopgap measure, from a community health perspective they are not ideal, given the poor nutritional content of what they often serve. See Andrea Azuma, *Food Access in Central and South Los Angeles: Mapping Injustice, Agenda for Action* (Los Angeles: Urban and Environmental Policy Institute, May 2007).

7. Ernesto Hernandez-Lopez, "LA's Taco Truck War: How Law Cooks Food Culture Contests," Chapman University Law Research Paper, 2010, available at http://works.bepress.com/ernesto_hernandez/10. Chapman University law professor Ernesto

Hernandez-Lopez conducted an in-depth exploration of the "taco truck wars" of 2008 and 2009, during which many *loncheras* came under regulatory fire from LA city officials. See also Gustavo Arellano, "Bribery, Threats, Broken-Down Vehicles, Lawsuits, Pioneers, Good Food: Tales from OC's Taco Trucks," *OC Weekly*, July 23, 2009, available at http://www.ocweekly.com/content/printVersion/479478/. *Orange County Weekly* food writer Arellano also described similar issues in Orange County.

8. The correct answer: Tacos Leo on Venice and La Brea, but only on weekends when it brings out the al pastor spit.

9. Alison Caldwell, "Will Tweet for Food: Microblogging Mobile Food Trucks—Online, Offline, and In Line," in *Taking Food Public: Redefining Foodways in a Changing World*, ed. Psyche Forson and Carole Counihan (New York: Routledge, 2011), 316. Caldwell writes about the new generation of food trucks in New York City, but there is no reason to think the same idea applies to LA *loncheras*, especially with sites like The Great Taco Hunt (http://greattacohunt.com) devoted to meticulously evaluating and documenting these traditional trucks. L.A. Taco (http://lataco.com) has a running series, *My Favorite Taco*, in which it asks local culinary and cultural luminaries to name their preferred taco trucks and stands.

10. Kane, "Taco Trucks."

11. The term "luxe *lonchera*" was coined by Arellano. See Gustavo Arellano, "Where Are the Loncheras at the Luxe-Lonchera Fests?" *OC Weekly,* September 1, 2010, available at http://blogs.ocweekly.com/stickaforkinit/2010/09/where_are_the_loncheras_at_the.php. I use the term "*nueva* truck," but they both refer to the same phenomenon.

12. Alison Abodeely, "The Kogi Effect: Food Trucks and Social Media," *allieab02*, March 19, 2011, available at http://allieab02.wordpress.com/2011/03/19/kogi-effect/.

13. Caroline McCarthy, "When Twitter Met Food Trucks," CNET, May 18, 2009, available at http://news.cnet.com/8301-13577_3-10242185-36.html.

14. Oliver Wang, "to live and dine in kogi l.a.," *Contexts* 8, no. 4 (fall 2009): 69.

15. Jennifer Steinhauer, "For a New Generation, Kimchi Goes with Tacos," *New York Times*, February 25, 2009, available at http://www.nytimes.com/2009/02/25/dining/25taco.html.

16. Andrew Romano, "Now 4 Restaurant 2.0.," *Newsweek*, February 28, 2009, available at http://www.thedailybeast.com/newsweek/2009/02/27/now-4-restaurant-2-0.html.

17. Jonathan Gold, "The Korean Taco Justice League: Kogi Rolls into L.A." *LA Weekly*, January 28, 2009, available at http://www.laweekly.com/2009-01-29/eat-drink/the-korean-taco-justice-league-kogi-rolls-into-l-a/. *Newsweek* reporter Andrew Romano was not content with just viewing Kogi through a LA filter when he wrote, "Kogi's rapid rise reflects the same cultural moment that produced Barack Obama; youthful, urban, multiethnic, wired and communal" ("Now 4 Restaurant 2.0.").

18. Kim Severson, "Should Cities Drive Food Trucks off the Streets?" *New York Times*, July 16, 2011, available at http://www.nytimes.com/2011/07/17/sunday-review/17foodtrucks.html.

19. Jessica Gelt, "Kogi Korean BBQ, a Taco Truck Brought to You by Twitter," *Los Angeles Times*, February 11, 2009, available at http://www.latimes.com/features/la-fo-kogi11-2009feb11,0,4771256.story.

20. Jane Jacobs, *The Death and Life of Great American Cities* (New York: Vintage Books, 1992), 56; Wang, "to live and dine in kogi l.a.," 69–70.

21. Andrew Blankstein and Richard Winton, "LAPD Botched Use of Downtown Crime Cameras," *Los Angeles Times*, December 24, 2011, available at http://articles.latimes.com/2011/dec/24/local/la-me-police-camera-20111224.

22. Kristen Day, "Being Feared: Masculinity and Race in Public Space," *Environment and Planning* 38, no. 3 (2006): 569–86.

23. As the CityWalk's own planners put it, the mall was designed to evoke the funky, polyglot experience of visiting Venice Beach or Melrose Avenue without "somebody on every corner with a 'Work For Food' sign." See Kevin McNamara, "CityWalk: Los[t] Angeles in the Shape of a Mall," in *The Urban Condition: Space, Community, and Self in the Contemporary Metropolis*, ed. Ghent Urban Studies Team (Rotterdam: 010 Publishers, 1999), 188.

24. Claire Kim, "Imagining Race and Nation in Multiculturalist America," *Ethnic and Racial Studies* 27, no. 6 (2004): 989, available at http://dx.doi.org/10.1080/0141987042000268567.

25. Lisa Lowe, *Immigrant Acts: On Asian American Cultural Politics* (Durham, NC: Duke University Press, 1996).

26. Gelt, "Kogi Korean BBQ."

27. Jonathan Gold, "How America Became a Food Truck Nation," *Smithsonian Magazine*, March 2012, available at http://www.smithsonianmag.com/travel/How-America-Became-a-Food-Truck-Nation.html.

28. Abodeely, "The Kogi Effect."

29. I initially began data-mining Kogi's Twitter feed in the summer of 2009, but I did not revisit this project until early 2011, by which time the second half of 2009 already lay beyond Twitter's 3,200 limit on past tweets. The Library of Congress is supposedly in the process of developing a searchable archive of all public tweets ever made. Once this goes online, I may be able to recover the complete set of Kogi's 2009 locations.

30. There are important caveats in analyzing geodemographic data in this way. First, the census data I used were based on where people live but not where they work or "play," and in a commuter-heavy city like Los Angeles, the demography of specific neighborhoods can literally shift complexion from day to evening. Since food trucks, especially *nueva* trucks, target mostly workers and people engaged in social activities, the residential census data may not accurately reflect a truck's actual clientele. Likewise, as geographic spaces, census tracks rarely conform to the same shapes and borders as areas understood as neighborhoods. In other words, our sense of a neighborhood is as much constructed through lived, cultural practice as any formal cartographic process can designate. Looking at geodemographic data is useful for developing an impression of an area, but an accurate assessment of any neighborhood at any given point in time requires metrics that census data simply do not collect.

31. A self-reflexive observation about the research process: this project came together in discrete and largely separate phases—a short journal review in 2009, a conference paper in 2011, and now a book chapter—and while I think that reflects an organic evolution, it also meant that my methodological approach came together in fits and starts. With the benefit of hindsight, I have come to see the areas where I could have improved my data management. For example, because collecting and mapping more than two years of addresses was labor intensive, I tried to expedite the process by stripping off both date and truck information. The biggest problem with that is that I lost the ability to create a useful, longitudinal database of Kogi's locations. Obviously, in any research project, there are untapped methods that seem obvious with hindsight, and as noted, this project is in an early stage. Nonetheless, I find it worth disclosing my own process of discovery

(and self-admonishment) in this process as a way of unpacking the challenges of doing research in "small batches" over time.

32. Kogi has gone farther west; in 2010, it experimented with a handful of stops in both Thousand Oaks and, even farther away, Santa Barbara, but I am treating these two locations as literal outliers.

33. A fifth truck, Azul, roamed in both regions but was taken off-line, without notice, in May 2011. I cannot find any record in Kogi's Twitter feed of how or why Azul disappeared—my presumption is that the company was forced to scale back its operations—but what was notable is that in the course of analyzing location data, Azul appeared to be the truck most responsible for Kogi's one-stops. To me, this suggested that it was used as an "exploratory" truck, sent off to new locations either to test its viability or perhaps to extend Kogi's reach during the most ambitious part of its geographic expansion.

34. Voids exist *within* the normal range of Kogi trucks. Ventura and San Bernardino Counties, therefore, would not be considered voids, since they lie outside Kogi's historical service area.

35. Numbered locations coincide with the locations mentioned in this chapter.

36. Even though these are adjoining regions, they are considerably different, at both the macro level (e.g., east LA has lower crime rates than south LA does) and the micro level (there are affluent neighborhoods interspersed, despite disproportionately low median household income levels overall).

37. Photo essayist Mac Kane examined my maps of The Void and sent an e-mail reply discussing his research on cell phone "dead zones":

    I seem to recall there being large cell dead spots in the space you have located in grey [The Void]. I am not sure if it's related to the economic forces which are the main motivators for private infrastructures (cell phones and taco trucks are fluid and respond directly to the demand on the ground) or other factor related to density of population?

    As I have noted, there is a definite correlation with household income, but there is no correlation with population density. Kane's cell phone coverage research echoes the idea that The Void is separated from entire spectra of businesses, with *nueva* trucks simply being one of many. This is not true of *loncheras*, however, especially in east LA, which has some of the highest density of semipermanent *loncheras* in the city. In other words, food trucks thrive in parts of this area, just not *nueva* trucks.

38. The same cannot be said for other private industries and government bodies.

39. Based on a cursory scan of the 2012 data, by that fall, Kogi did begin returning to Downey, with at least half a dozen stops.

40. In my correspondence with Alice Shin, she offered to let me book time with Roy Choi (the only Kogi staffer authorized to address my questions) "at a standardized rate . . . [of] $350 an hour." For ethical and budgetary reasons, I declined that option.

41. If my recollection is accurate, these prices are slightly higher than when they first started. Burritos rose from f$5 to $6, and tacos, from $2 to $2.29.

42. Kane estimates that some transient *loncheras* make up to twenty stops *a day*, moving from work site to work site.

43. Almost all Kogi stops are within one to two miles of a freeway access point. By avoiding city traffic as much as possible, Kogi gives its trucks more time to move between shifts and makes it easier for customers to reach them.

44. Gold, "How America Became a Food Truck Nation." In the interests of full disclosure, Gold interviewed me for his article, specifically to talk about the research that appears in this chapter. But in his article, he writes as though I were stating my own speculations regarding the "limited palette theory," when in reality I was relaying to him the speculations that others had given to me in casual conversation as to why The Void existed.

45. Melvin Oliver and Thomas Shapiro, *Black Wealth, White Wealth: A New Perspective on Racial Inequality* (New York: Routledge, 2006), 53.

46. The main exception is enigmatic; another Kogi void appears in the west San Gabriel Valley, from Pasadena south to Montebello. These are neighborhoods with higher household incomes *and* very high numbers of Asian households. In discussing this with Gold, we both agreed that it would be "common sense" for an Asian-themed food truck to pursue locations in Alhambra, San Gabriel, and Monterey Park; yet Kogi had only one stop in that area in 2010 and 2011 that I could find. The other mysterious void lies along LA beachside cities from El Segundo down through San Pedro. Many of these cities are affluent and similar in demographic profile to the Orange County beach cities where Kogi has a strong presence. Permission issues may have kept Kogi out of places like Manhattan Beach and Redondo Beach, but this is not clear.

47. Nationally, Roy Choi's East Coast counterpart would be another Korean American chef—David Chang (Momofuku, Ṣṣäm Bar). See Larissa MacFarquhar, "Chef on the Edge," *New Yorker*, March 24, 2008, available at http://www.newyorker.com/reporting/2008/03/24/080324fa_fact_macfarquhar.

48. Jonathan Gold, "Three Dog Night: Frank Talk about a New L.A. Food Movement," *LA Weekly*, June 10, 2010, available at http://www.laweekly.com/2010-06-10/eat-drink/three-dog-night/.

49. Samantha Barbas, "'I'll Take Chop Suey': Restaurants as Agents of Culinary and Cultural Change," *Journal of Popular Culture* 36, no. 4 (spring 2003): 681.

50. Ibid., 682.

51. Interestingly, one of the many Kogi "clone" trucks—Calbi Fusion Tacos—was purchased by the Baja Fresh chain, though, I should note, Baja Fresh's CEO, David Kim, is Korean American himself. See Lisa Jennings, "Baja Fresh Owner to Franchise Calbi Taco Truck," *Nation's Restaurant News,* October 2, 2009, available at http://nrn.com/article/baja-fresh-owner-franchise-calbi-taco-truck.

52. I happen to be one such person who does this, but it had never occurred to me that this was specific to Asian Americans.

53. Jessica Gelt, "A Wrong Turn for L.A.'s Food Truck Scene?," *Los Angeles Times*, May 6, 2011, available at http://articles.latimes.com/2011/may/06/food/la-fo-food-trucks-20110506. Gelt argues the oversaturation angle, while Clements posits the recession as a major factor. See Miles Clements, "The Find: Taco María Truck Survives the Downturn," *Los Angeles Times*, January 19, 2012, available at http://www.latimes.com/features/food/la-fo-find-20120119,0,3934262.story.

54. By the time of this writing, in the fall of 2012, Kogi's website still had four trucks listed, but only three with active daily locations. The fourth truck (Rosita) is used sparingly during the week and seems to be in service mostly on weekends (it may also be used for unlisted private catering events).

55. For examples of food trucks in other cities, see John Tanasychuk, "What's Next for South Florida's Food Trucks?," *South Florida Sun Sentinel*, January 19, 2012, available

at http://www.sun-sentinel.com/features/fl-sh-food-trucks-012012-20120119,0,365491.
story; Tim Carman, "D.C. to Propose Zones for Food Trucks," *Washington Post*,
January 20, 2012, available at http://www.washingtonpost.com/local/dc-to-propose-
zones-for-food-trucks/2012/01/19/gIQAHYZWCQ_story.html?tid=pm_local_pop;
and Danielle Dreilinger, "Somerville Scene: We Need More Food Trucks," *Boston.com*, June 10, 2011, available at http://articles.boston.com/2011-06-10/
yourtown/29643636_1_food-trucks-mobile-food-vendors-new-food.

56. See Jace Lacob, "Street Food Guru Roy Choi on Sunny Spot, Food Trucks, Kogi
and More," *Daily Beast*, December 13, 2011, available at http://www.thedailybeast.
com/articles/2011/12/09/street-food-guru-roy-choi-on-sunny-spot-food-trucks-
kogi-more.html; and Jace Lacob, "The Hunt Resumes: Interview with Bandini,
Taco Hunter," *L.A. Taco*, August 11, 2009, available at http://www.lataco.com/taco/
the-hunt-resumes-interview-with-bandini-taco-hunter.

57. For example, the esteemed Zagat restaurant guide recently ranked "LA's 10 Best Food
Trucks," and all of them are *nuevas* (http://www.zagat.com/buzz/las-10-best-food-
trucks). Likewise, food truck aggregator sites like Foodtruckmaps.com and Foodtrucks-
map.com have more than two hundred and three hundred trucks in their respective
directories; all are *nuevas*.

58. For example, I find it astounding that even though the *loncheras* figure heavily in
ethnographic and literary sketches of Latino communities, I was barely able to locate
published scholarly articles dedicated to them, let alone an entire monograph.

5

The Significance of Hawai'i Regional Cuisine in Postcolonial Hawai'i

SAMUEL HIDEO YAMASHITA

At first glance, Hawai'i regional cuisine (HRC), like other American regional cuisines, seems nothing less than a paean to the state's diverse ethnic communities and foods and to the islands' natural bounty, air, land, and sea.[1] Given the history of the Hawaiian Islands as, first, an independent kingdom (1795–1893) and then a U.S. colony (1898–1959), however, Hawai'i regional cuisine has a much greater significance.

Traditionally, fine dining in Hawai'i was assumed to be continental cuisine, which was usually found at restaurants in Waikiki. These establishments had long hired French, German, or Swiss chefs with impeccable credentials, who had been trained and apprenticed in Europe and brought continental culinary techniques, values, and traditions to the islands. Their richly sauced dishes echoed classic French cuisine and were consumed with French or, later, California wines. In theory, a fine meal at La Mer, the fabled French restaurant at the Halekulani Hotel in Waikiki, was no different from a fine meal at La Côte Basque in New York City or Guy Savoy in Paris.[2]

In contrast, because local food—what most of Hawai'i's population ate—was definitely not continental, it was denigrated, overlooked, or, at best, tolerated. Indeed, local food and continental cuisine were not to be mentioned in the same breath except perhaps ironically, as when one spoke of a "local French restaurant." Local food was denigrated simply because it was what "locals" ate.[3] During the colonial period, a "local" was someone born, raised, or educated in Hawai'i who was not Caucasian and was a member of either the indigenous Hawaiian population or one of the many groups that had immigrated to the islands to work on the plantations or ranches.[4] Typically, Hawaiians, Chinese, Japanese, Puerto Ricans, Spanish, Portuguese, and Filipinos were regarded as locals. Indeed, during this time, Hawai'i had a "rigid caste system" of racial hierarchies and distinctions, to which the colonial authorities and business elite strictly adhered.[5]

Every aspect of life in the colony was racialized: the inhabitants' political, economic, and social life, as well as their education, sports, and culture. Well-born members of the Caucasian elite attended O'ahu College (known after 1935 as the Punahou School) or a mainland (continental U.S.) boarding school and then were sent away to an Ivy League university. After marrying someone from the local elite or the mainland, they returned to take their place in one of the five major companies, known as the "Big Five," spending their free time playing tennis or golf and dining at one of several established Honolulu country clubs and reveling in the benefits of their superiority.[6] Those Caucasians who were not so well born attended one of the English Standard Schools, and then the University of Hawai'i.[7] They then entered one of several local companies, where their race entitled them to rise to a managerial or supervisory position.

Those who were Hawaiian, Chinese, Japanese, Filipino, Portuguese, Puerto Rican, or some combination of these were locals and thus inferior. Within a century after 1778, when the first Europeans arrived in the islands, the indigenous population had dropped from somewhere between 400,000 and 1,000,000 to 40,000, owing to both the diseases brought by the visitors and the impact of the profound changes in land tenure, government, religion, and culture carried out at their urging.[8] In 1893, prominent American businessmen engineered the overthrow of the native monarchy and pushed hard for the U.S. annexation of the islands, which finally took place in 1898 despite the opposition of the indigenous population.[9] A decade after the islands were annexed, the remnants of the Hawaiian population were in both physical and cultural decline, and Asians were regarded by the Caucasian elite as mere "instruments of production," akin to the "cattle of the ranges."[10] The exceptions were Hawaiians from the *ali'i*, or chiefly, class—many of whom had succeeded in preserving their landholdings and married Caucasians—and locals who had succeeded in business.[11] Most locals went to public elementary schools through the eighth grade and then started working at age fifteen, joining the large pool of plantation, factory, or dock workers. Some were lucky enough to be sent to one of the several private schools in Honolulu: the 'Iolani School, Mid-Pacific Institute, the Kamehameha Schools, or the College of Saint Louis (now the Saint Louis Schools). Kamehameha was open only to Hawaiians, and although the others were open to all groups, 'Iolani attracted many Chinese, Mid-Pacific many Japanese, and Saint Louis a combination of Hawaiian, Portuguese, and Chinese.[12] Many private school graduates attended the University of Hawai'i, and after graduating, they became teachers or entered family businesses or local companies, with a good chance of rising to a managerial position. A few attended professional schools on the mainland. Some Hawaiians and Portuguese even rose to supervisory positions on plantations.[13]

Race mattered politically, too. In 1917 Hawaiʻi's population of 228,771 was broken down ethnically as follows: Caucasian, 16,042; Chinese, 21,954; Filipino, 16,898; Hawaiian/part Hawaiian, 39,104; Japanese, 97,000; Portuguese, 23,753; Puerto Rican, 5,187; Spanish, 3,577; and other, 5,254.[14] Even though Caucasians made up only 7 percent of the colony's population, they nonetheless dominated the other 93 percent and were supported in doing so by 13,249 American soldiers and sailors.[15] Not surprisingly, as the number of servicemen increased, so too did the interracial tension. Officers responded by sending their children to private schools in Honolulu, and enlisted men got into fights with locals, often over women.[16] But even when large numbers of Hawaiians and immigrant children gained the right to vote, and thus to wield political power, many nineteenth-century notions of Caucasian superiority persisted, well into the 1950s.[17]

Caucasians and locals met as equals only on the colony's playing fields, as members of a high school team or in one of the racialized sports leagues. For example, the Hawaiʻi Major League consisted of single-ethnicity baseball teams: the Wanderers were the Caucasian team; the Chinese, or the Chinese Tigers, were the Chinese team; the Rising Suns (Asahi) were the Japanese team; the Braves were the Portuguese team; and the Filipinos formed a team later. To protect the racialized nature of the league, each team was allowed to have only two players of a different ethnicity.[18]

These racial and class hierarchies informing colonial Hawaiʻi also shaped the "food supply, culinary treatments and habits of consumption."[19] In the 1800s, Caucasians continued to eat the food they always had, but now with locally sourced meat, fish, shellfish, fowl, vegetables, fruit, and dairy products.[20] Their beef, mutton, pork, and poultry came from one of the many local ranches, and local meat was more highly regarded than meat packed in ice and shipped from the mainland. Their fish and shellfish were locally caught. One observer noted that "Hawaiian mullet, boiled, baked or fried, approaches in flavor the blue fish of the Atlantic coast." Also available were locally grown tomatoes, corn, beans, cauliflower, cucumbers, carrots, turnips, potatoes, and artichokes. Caucasians even ate taro, regarding it as "far ahead of the potato in nutrient," and enjoyed local fruit such as breadfruit, guava, and poha berries.[21] That Caucasians discovered these staples of the Hawaiian diet is hardly surprising, because as David Stannard observed,

The foods and health habits of the Hawaiians were far more salubrious than those of their European contemporaries and were even superior to those of modern Americans in their diets' nutritional value and relative lack of saturated fat, cholesterol, sugar and sodium—and, of course, in the absence from their lives of alcohol and tobacco.[22]

In time, even well-to-do local businessmen began to adapt the Caucasians' diet, although they continued to eat rice and to have their meals "cooked and served in semi-American style."

Most immigrants still preferred to eat those foods to which they were accustomed.[23] Accordingly, Portuguese made bread as they did in the old country, and Chinese, Japanese, and Filipinos made rice the center of their meal, supplementing it with local fish, pork, chicken, duck, and homegrown vegetables when they were available. Those who lived near towns or cities such as Honolulu, Lihu'e, Wailuku, or Hilo could buy locally made bean curd, bean paste, soy sauce, sausages, fish sauce (*bagoong*), and even noodles. Hawaiians and part-Hawaiians stuck to their traditional diet as well, eating poi, catching local fish, and gathering seaweed (*limu*) at nearby beaches.[24]

Hawai'i's First Restaurants

The first restaurant in the islands, Warren House, opened in 1819 at the corner of Hotel and Bethel Streets in Honolulu. The second restaurant was Butler's Coffee House, nearby in Warren Square, which began serving meals in 1836.[25] Most of the restaurants that opened between 1850 and 1900 were owned by Chinese. Some combined a bakery and a coffee shop, as did Po Hee Hong's in Hanapepe, Kauai; several were grocery or dry goods stores that had canteens, as was the case with Hew's Store and Restaurant in Paia, Maui; and a few were saloons that also served food.[26] Since most of their customers were not Chinese, these restaurants served Hawaiian and Western as well as Chinese fare. In the late 1800s, Honolulu had two notable Chinese restaurants: Wo Fat opened in Honolulu in 1882 and Sun Yun Woo in 1892. Both served Cantonese food.[27]

Beginning in the 1920s, more restaurants in Honolulu catered to both the local population and servicemen stationed on O'ahu. The first of these, the American Café, opened in 1923.[28] Sakazo Fujika, an immigrant from Hiroshima, started the Diamond Ice Cream Parlor at the eastern end of Kalakaua Avenue, which served chili con carne, hamburger steak, beef stew, and pies. Later, Fujika renamed his restaurant the Unique Lunch Room and added to his menu Hawaiian dishes like *lau lau, lomi lomi* salmon, and *pipikaula*.[29] In 1927 George C. Knapp and Elwood L. Christiansen opened the first drive-in restaurant in Hawai'i, at the corner of Kalakaua and Ala Wai Boulevards.[30] In 1929 Pang Yat Chong opened a Chinese restaurant in Waikiki called Lau Yee Chai, which, with its beautiful and well-decorated interior, attracted both locals and tourists.[31] In the 1930s, many more restaurants could be found in Honolulu and its environs, and like the American Café, many were owned and operated by the children of immigrants from the Okinawan community of Oroku.[32] In 1939 Spencer and Clifton Weaver opened the Swanky Franky hot dog stands, and from this modest beginning, they created a veritable restaurant empire that, by 1987, numbered twenty-three restaurants on O'ahu and Maui.[33] After World War II, when people dined out they usually went to a Spencecliff or one of the many Okinawan-run restaurants that opened in the 1940s and 1950s. By the 1960s the top fine-dining choices were in Waikiki: Canlis, a Spencecliff restaurant; Michel's, a French restaurant; and P. Y. Chong's Lau Yee Chai.[34]

Besides the distinctions between fine dining and local restaurants, the other peculiarity of the colony's culinary and gastronomic life was that much of the food was imported. The best of the fine-dining establishments, however, served locally sourced foods. For example, a menu from the Alexander Young Hotel, dated February 28, 1928, included "Baked Island Pond Mullet, Normandy Pommes Hollandaise," "Fresh Island String Beans," and "Hawaiian Banana Fritters." Two decades later, Richard Kimball, the owner of the Halekulani Hotel, took great pride in serving locally caught fish and locally grown vegetables and fruit. But even his kitchens served mahimahi from local waters that had been frozen after being cleaned and fileted.[35] In fact, much of what was served, even in the top restaurants, was imported, and this was especially true of both meat and vegetables.[36]

The diets of the local population also consisted of local and imported foods. They could not afford to do otherwise. Most local families ate fish that they caught or were given; chicken, pigs, rabbits, and ducks that they had raised; vegetables that they grew or bought; and fruit that they picked. Even their poi, bean curd, bean paste, soy sauce, dried shrimp, fish sauce, sausages, and noodles were made locally. But the plantation stores always stocked rice and canned goods, and although they were relatively expensive, most families kept a small supply of canned corned beef, luncheon meat, vienna sausage, tuna, and vegetables.[37] Of course, canned foods were also "American," and their consumption in the islands would have been applauded by reformers on the mainland who worked to wean immigrants away from their traditional diets.[38]

This short history makes clear that the relationship of fine dining and local food before Hawai'i became a state cannot be understood apart from the racialized nature of life in the colony. It explains why Caucasians and locals ate what they ate, the distinction between "fine dining" and "local food," and Hawai'i's dependence on imported food products and canned goods.

The August 1991 Meeting

On August 27, 1991, the regime of fine dining in Hawai'i began to change. Fourteen chefs based in Hawai'i gathered at the Maui Prince Hotel in the resort town of Wailea on the island of Maui.[39] They were meeting for the "First Hawaiian Culinary Symposium,"[40] the idea of three chefs—Roger Dikon, Peter Merriman, and Alan Wong—who earlier had flown to Kaua'i to cook together and celebrate Jean-Marie Josselin's birthday at his new restaurant, A Pacific Café. While they were there, they talked about finding a way to meet more often. Merriman remembered that he and other chefs often visited one another's restaurants and that he would

> fly to Roy's place [Roy Yamaguchi, the founder of Roy's Restaurants] and cook for a night and fly home. What it really entailed was that you'd fly in there mid-day and you'd cook your ass off; you had to cook dinner for 150 people that night, go out and have a few beers, and then fly back to your restaurant in the morning.[41]

"I realized," Merriman continued, "that we were at a disadvantage because we were islands . . . 'cause in cities guys can meet at one particular bar. Chefs often do that."[42] Although he then was relatively young, he had watched chefs interact in this way when he worked in restaurants on the East Coast and Europe.

Dikon, Merriman, and Wong all had lived and worked elsewhere. Merriman was a graduate of the University of Pennsylvania, had gone to a culinary school on the East Coast, and had worked in that area and in Germany before being hired as a saucier at Maui's Mauna Lani Bay Hotel in 1983.[43] Dikon had moved to Hawai'i in 1978 from Florida, and Wong had returned to the islands in 1986 after five years of training on the East Coast, including three years at New York City's iconic French restaurant Lutèce.[44]

Dikon offered his hotel, the Maui Prince, as a meeting place, and Merriman suggested calling the gathering a *symposium*, a word whose meaning he later confessed he was not sure of at the time. He knew that the word meant "a place where there was a lot of eating and drinking," and he thought, "That's for us."[45] Thirteen other chefs attended the meeting.

Roy Yamaguchi was the group's most distinguished chef. After graduating from the Culinary Institute of America in 1978, he worked in Los Angeles for eight years, first at L'Ermitage, famous for its classic French cuisine, and then at Michael's, known for its newer California version of French cuisine.[46] In 1987 Yamaguchi opened his own restaurant, 385 North, in Hollywood, and later that year, the California Restaurant Writers Association named him California Chef of the Year. The food magazine *Bon Appétit* featured Yamaguchi in its June 1988 issue, and four months later he moved to Hawai'i to open Roy's in a suburb of Honolulu.[47] Clearly, Yamaguchi was, as a fellow chef put it, the "rock star" of the group.[48]

Most of the fourteen chefs could not have anticipated what was about to happen, and none could have known what impact their August 1991 meeting would have on the fine-dining scene and much else in Hawai'i. Indeed, most of them were only in their early thirties and trying to make their way in a notoriously demanding business. By this time, seven were chefs at major hotel restaurants, and five had their own restaurants. Nearly all were products of local, mainland, or European culinary schools, and most had apprenticed and trained at leading restaurants in the United States and Europe.[49] The exception was Mark Ellman, who was self-taught and had worked as a personal chef for celebrities before Longhi's, an Italian restaurant on Maui, hired him in 1985.[50]

At the August 1991 meeting, the chefs considered the unhappy state of fine dining in the islands. Of special concern was restaurants' continuing reliance on imported fish, meat, and vegetables.[51] Roger Dikon recalled that when he worked at the Kapalua Bay Hotel on Maui (from 1978 to 1986), only a quarter of the vegetables and fruit served at the hotel's restaurants were grown locally.[52] Jean-Marie Josselin, who came to Hawai'i in 1984 from Paris via New Orleans to cook at the Hotel Hana-Maui, remembered, "I was in shock. It was so isolated. I was given frozen and canned food to cook with; it was like being in a professional kitchen twenty-five years ago."[53] Amy Ferguson, a native of Dallas who was hired as the food and beverage director at the Kona Village Resort in 1985, agreed, "Old World chefs were running the kitchen and preparing continental cuisine. Sometimes they even cooked with frozen produce."[54] She wondered why "they were serving Scandinavian buffets instead of [the] foods of Hawai'i."[55]

Several members of the group talked about what they did to remedy the problem. Roger Dikon began to frequent local swap meets and would return with "as much local produce as he could carry."[56] He also started growing his own vegetables in an 800-square-foot garden.[57] In 1980, Gary Strehl, a chef at the Maui Prince, arranged with other Maui chefs to have a farmers' cooperative grow "specialty items" for them.[58] Peter Merriman remembered seeing gardeners trimming the coconut trees on the grounds of the Mauna Lani Hotel and wondered what was being done with the coconuts. When he found out that they were thrown away, he asked the gardeners if he could have the ones they cut down, and when they agreed, he had them delivered to farmers in Kealakekua, who husked them. The coconut meat was then brought to Merriman in a laundry truck that made a daily trip to Kona.[59] In 1986 Philippe Padovani, the new chef at La Mer, the premier French restaurant in Hawai'i, quickly discovered fresh vegetables and fish at the markets in Honolulu's Chinatown.[60]

These stories, and others like them, raise the obvious questions: Why weren't these chefs already using locally grown tomatoes? Why weren't they serving lamb or beef raised on local ranches? Why weren't they availing themselves of the islands' locally caught fish? The Maui chefs' success in making their own arrangements with farmers and the local produce and fish markets already suggested possible solutions. At the end of their first meeting, the chefs agreed to investigate buying from local farmers, ranchers, and fishermen and to meet again soon.

Clearly, most of the chefs at the first meeting knew that these problems could be solved. From their training and work in Europe, Josselin, Padovani, and George Mavrothalassitis knew that chefs could establish mutually beneficial working relationships with farmers. Amy Ferguson had helped found what came to be known as Southwestern Cuisine in Texas in the 1980s and had seen how such a relationship with local farmers and producers could benefit them.[61] There also was the example of Alice Waters, the chef/proprietor of Chez Panisse in Berkeley, California, who had developed a similar working relationship with California farmers.

The chefs met again six weeks later, this time on the Big Island (Hawai'i). According to Peter Merriman, "We literally loaded these chefs on a bus and took them from farm to farm. Because they didn't know farms existed. I'm not gonna name names, but some of the chefs were Big Island chefs, and I'm taking them on their island saying, 'Look, here's a farm.'"[62] Looking back, Merriman acknowledged that the key issue was finding farmers willing to grow what the chefs needed and wanted. In the old days, he recalled, chefs would work through their hotel delivery departments and simply look for the lowest price, and of course, most of what they got was imported.[63] For this to change, they had to start thinking "far outside the box."

Figure 5.1. The founding chefs of HRC. Front row: Mark Ellman, Alan Wong; Middle row: Roy Yamaguchi, Amy Ferguson Ota, Jean-Marie Josselin, George Mavrothalassitis, Beverly Gannon, Peter Merriman; Back row: Sam Choy, Philippe Padovani, Roger Dikon, Gary Strehl. Photograph courtesy of Steven Minkowski estate.

This idea of chefs establishing relationships with local farmers proved hard to realize. Merriman's experience on the Big Island was typical. After he and his wife opened Merriman's in December 1988, their first problem was finding farmers willing to grow produce for them. In addition, many of those who offered their services had never farmed before. The Merrimans were saved by Tane Datta, who had been at the 1991 meeting with his wife, Maureen. Datta was a recent graduate of Guilford College, with degrees in geology, environmental studies, and alternative energy, and he had been farming on the Big Island since 1979.[64] He and Merriman looked over his seed catalogs, and Merriman marked the things he wanted. Datta then worked with the farmers who wanted to grow for Merriman's restaurant, assigning crops to each of them and suggesting where and at what elevation they could grow them. Their plots were tiny—some only 6 × 40 feet—and they used French intensive-gardening techniques.[65]

On O'ahu, Roy Yamaguchi developed a relationship with Dean Okimoto, a local farmer in Waimanalo. Okimoto had graduated from the University of Redlands in 1983 with a degree in political science and was working on his father's farm, growing lettuce hydroponically. This was a very small operation, involving only three people, and Okimoto says they were on the verge of giving up when he met Yamaguchi. But Yamaguchi advised him, "Don't quit. We'll buy herbs from you, and I want you to start growing other things." Okimoto thus became Yamaguchi's go-to-farmer, growing whatever he needed. Yamaguchi then began taking Okimoto along on his demonstrations at Liberty House, a big department store in Honolulu. He would say, "Come with me . . . and you can explain the different greens, " Okimoto remembers. "Every time we did this, I'd get five or six calls from restaurants. That's how our business started growing."[66]

Because the new arrangements had not yet been tested, the farmers had to be willing to take risks. This was the HRC chefs' second problem. Merriman recalled that he found a farmer willing to grow vine-ripened tomatoes for his restaurant, a rarity in those days. Or more precisely, he found a farmer who grew something other than tomatoes but who was willing to try growing them. Her name was Erin Lee, and she showed up one day at his restaurant with herbs.

> So Erin comes in, and she's got herbs. I'm talking to her . . . she's a very intelligent woman, and I think, "This lady's got it going on." So I tell her, we've got enough herbs. What we really would need are vine-ripened tomatoes." At the time everybody knew you couldn't grow vine-ripened tomatoes because of the fruit flies. That was a known fact. . . . So anyway, 120 days later, here comes Erin back in my kitchen with vine-ripened tomatoes. What she figured out was that if she moved to a high-enough elevation, the fruit flies wouldn't come up there. But it was always raining up there. So she put plastic over her tomatoes and irrigated. So she went to the wet side of Waimea and put in irrigation. . . . The point is that very few people go to the wet side and irrigate. She had the brains to do that. So she was selling us tomatoes for us for a number of years.[67]

The other farmers on the Big Island finally adopted Lee's model. Many of them had grown flowers until South American growers took over their markets with the help of FedEx.[68] This is an example of how globalizing economic forces in North and South America and a transnational firm—in this case, FedEx—affected a local economy on an island in the middle of the Pacific.

The HRC chefs' third problem, according to Merriman, was that forging relationships with local producers took a lot of time. An example is how he began working with Herbert M. "Monty" Richards, a well-known local rancher who raised lambs on the Big Island.

> He tried to sell us some lamb and it was frozen, and I said we really want to get fresh lamb. He said the only way you could do that would be if you bought the

whole animal. I said, OK we'll do it. That's how we got that tradition, which is now one of our signatures, of a different lamb dish every day. Now it's becoming famous: snout-to-tail is the concept. I laugh about this. Yeah, snout-to-tail is the latest thing. People are using the whole animal, whole animal contact.

Merriman worked with Edwards for twenty years and continually gave him feedback on the lambs—whether they were too small, their meat was too dry, they had enough fat, and so forth.[69]

The HRC chefs' agreement to buy local was revolutionary. It called into question how they had viewed their own culinary productions, and it was a new way of looking at food and their relationship with the land and the sea and with those who worked the land and who fished the local waters. This agreement also meant not relying solely on the big wholesalers that supplied restaurants and hotels—the Suisan Company and Armstrong Produce. Instead, the HRC chefs were imagining a foodscape that did not really exist before 1991.

Hawai'i Regional Cuisine: The First Fifteen Years (1991–2006)

The same core group of twelve chefs met several times in 1991/1992 and from time to time through the 1990s.[70] They continued to search for farmers, fishermen, and ranchers who could grow or produce what they needed. They also arranged deliveries of sufficient quantities of each product. Then they began to use in their restaurants these locally grown vegetables, locally caught fish and gathered shellfish, and locally raised beef and lamb. They even began to highlight the "local" provenance of what they were using, fully two decades before the word *locavore* became popular.[71]

The HRC chefs had larger ambitions, however. They were aware of other regional cuisine movements on the mainland. In fact, at their first meeting, they turned to Amy Ferguson, who, as part of the founding of the Southwestern Cuisine movement, had worked with its leaders: Dean Fearing, Robert Le Grande, and Stephen Pyles. Because the HRC group knew that they needed someone to help them organize and present themselves to a larger audience, they asked her how the Southwestern Cuisine chefs organized and presented their new cuisine.[72] But it was Beverly Gannon who suggested Shep Gordon, an impresario extraordinaire who was a veteran of the Los Angeles music scene and was best known as the long-time manager of the shock rock icon Alice Cooper. Gordon also was into film and had his own production company, Alive Films, whose productions included *The Duelists* and *The Kiss of the Spider Woman*. Two other things made Gordon especially attractive: first, he ran an agency that represented chefs, including the renowned French chef Roger Vergé, as well as Alice Waters and Emeril Lagasse, and, second, he lived in Kihei on the island of Maui.[73] Some of those at the meeting when Gordon was introduced remember his prediction, that only some of the HRC chefs would become celebrities and that the others would need to support them.[74]

With the help of Gordon and many others, the Hawai'i regional cuisine chefs quickly gained national attention. National food magazines began to feature them. *Bon Appétit* published more articles on Roy Yamaguchi (in 1991), as well as Alan Wong (1992) and Mark Ellman (1995). Roy Yamaguchi was inducted into the Fine Dining Hall of Fame in 1992. Janice Wald Henderson, the West Coast food writer who wrote the first article on Yamaguchi, was contracted to produce an HRC cookbook. *The New Cuisine of Hawaii: Recipes from the Twelve Celebrated Chefs of Hawaii Regional Cuisine* was published in 1994 and featured each of the twelve founding HRC chefs along with a sampling of their recipes. Several of the HRC chefs' own cookbooks followed: Roy Yamaguchi's *Roy's Feasts from Hawaii* (1995), Sam Choy's *Choy of Cooking* (1996), Alan Wong's *Alan Wong's New Wave Luau* (1999), and Jean-Marie Josselin's *A Taste of Hawaii: New Cooking from the Crossroads of the Pacific* (2000). These five cookbooks gave a national audience a chance to look closely at the new regional cuisine from what Henderson called the "last frontier in American cooking."[75] At that point, even the local media commentators began to pay attention to the HRC chefs. One of them wrote to Hawaiian Airlines offering to design their first-class meals, and all twelve chefs contributed ideas.[76] It was the beginning of HRC's close relationship with the local airlines, which survives to this day. In November 1992 Roy Yamaguchi agreed to do a local television show on HRC, and *Hawaii Cooks with Roy* first aired in October 1993.

The late 1990s and the first decade of the twenty-first century brought more recognition to the HRC chefs. In 1999 *Travel + Leisure* named Amy Ferguson's new restaurant, Oodles of Noodles, one of the fifty best restaurants in the United States, and in 2002 *Gourmet* named George Mavrothalassitis's new restaurant, Chef Mavro, one of "America's Best Restaurants." In 2004 Sam Choy's Kaloko restaurant was named a James Beard "American Classic," and in 2006 *Gourmet* named Alan Wong's one of the country's top fifty restaurants. More cookbooks were published. In 2003 Roy Yamaguchi published a second cookbook, *Hawaii Cooks with Roy Yamaguchi*, and that same year Sam Choy and the Makaha sons published *A Hawaiian Luau*, which won a local book award. Finally, in 2005 Roy Yamaguchi published his third cookbook, *Roy's Fish and Seafood*.

Figure 5.2. The cover of Janice Wald Henderson's *The New Cuisine of Hawaii*. Reproduced with permission of Mark Ellman.

The chefs' national exposure began to have another effect: they started appearing on national television. Amy Ferguson was featured in Julia Child's *Cooking with Master Chefs* in November 1993,[77] and two HRC chefs were invited to cook at the James Beard House in New York City: Roger Dikon was invited to be a guest chef there in 1995, and Gary Strehl participated in a James Beard program, "The Best Hotel Chefs in America," in 1996. HRC chefs also were paired with leading mainland chefs. In 1997, Alan Wong cooked with his former mentor, André Soltner, the chef/owner of Lutèce in New York City, for a benefit at Kapiʻolani Community College, and the next year Wong was paired with Thomas Keller, whose French Laundry was regarded at the time as the country's best restaurant, on "Grand Chefs on Tour." In September 2000, Wong and Ming Tsai were featured at the Kea Lani Food and Wine Festival. The HRC chefs also started winning the most prestigious national culinary awards: three of them won the James Beard award for the "Best Chef in the Pacific Northwest": Roy Yamaguchi (1993), Alan Wong (1996), and George

Mavrothalassitis (2003). Four others were nominated for the same award but did not win: Sam Choy (1997), Jean-Marie Josselin (1997 and 2000), Beverly Gannon (2004), and Peter Merriman (2004). Merriman's won a *Wine Spectator* Award of Excellence in 2006.

As all this was happening, most of the chefs moved at least once and many, two or three times, opening new restaurants and, often, more than one. Jean-Marie Josselin opened three restaurants: two on Kaua'i (1990 and 1994), and a third in Honolulu (1997). Sam Choy had four restaurants: three in Kona (1990) and a fourth in Waikiki (1996). George Mavrothalassitis opened Chef Mavro in Honolulu 1998. Alan Wong opened Alan Wong's in Honolulu (1995); the Pineapple Room, in the Ala Moana branch of the Liberty House department store chain, which is now a branch of Macy's (1999); and a third restaurant in Japan (2000). But none of them came close to Roy Yamaguchi, who, by January 2003, had opened thirty-seven restaurants, five in Hawai'i, one in Asia, one in the Pacific, and thirty on the mainland.

Within a decade of the August 1991 meeting, HRC was well on its way to being recognized as an exciting new regional cuisine and an important culinary movement in the islands. The HRC chefs had benefited from Shep Gordon's good advice and the attention they were getting from food writers and industry organizations such as the Hawai'i Restaurant Association. Their success has continued in the twenty-first century.

Hawai'i Regional Cuisine

A year after the HRC chefs announced the appearance of their new regional cuisine, they created a nonprofit entity, "Hawai'i Regional Cuisine, Inc."[78] Well aware of Alice Waters and California cuisine, they were hoping to establish the kinds of relationships Waters had with California farmers.[79]

Each HRC chef described differently what he or she was doing. Sam Choy insisted that he was continuing to do what he had been doing long before 1991 and that his cooking style "developed from a love for the land and an understanding of the Hawaiian culture and the other ethnic groups who live" in Hawai'i.[80] Mark Ellman explained that his version of HRC required that he "utilize as many products grown and raised here as possible and to present them in the simplest, purest manner," and he added, "I'd like to get back to what early Hawaiians were eating, and utilize these foods in mine."[81] Beverly Gannon declared that she was "committed to raising the level of quality of local produce. That's what ties HRC together. It's not about boundaries and definitions; it's a melting-pot cuisine like the people who came here."[82] Jean-Marie Josselin agreed. "I like to think I was one of the first chefs who helped improve the quality of Hawai'i's products. That's what Hawai'i regional cuisine means to me."[83] George Mavrothalassitis's "definition of Hawai'i regional cuisine is to cook the food of Hawai'i from the foods in the Hawaiian markets in a contemporary fashion."[84] Amy Ferguson's view of Hawai'i regional cuisine was simply "preserving food's integrity."[85] Alan Wong saw HRC as a medium for showcasing the dishes and flavors that he grew up with, dishes that reflected his Chinese, Filipino, Hawaiian, and Japanese roots.[86]

Given these widely divergent views of HRC cuisine, what exactly is an HRC dish? Clearly, there is no single culinary style, since each HRC chef has his or her own version. Moreover, the chefs adapt whatever they cook to their own experience, training, and regional and national origin. But all of them hope that what will be most conspicuous about their culinary creations is that they are made with the best, locally sourced ingredients, whether greens, fish, shellfish, meat, fowl, fruits, macadamia nuts, or coffee. This insistence on using locally sourced ingredients also is typical of most regional cuisines in the United States.

HRC dishes reveal unmistakable Asian influences. This is apparent, first, in the HRC chefs' cooking techniques: some use Chinese cooking techniques, such as stir-frying, steaming, or deep frying, or the Japanese practice of serving the freshest fish raw and thinly sliced. Most of the HRC chefs also try to create dishes with new flavors, using such Asian ingredients as soy sauce, hoisin sauce, fish sauce (*nam pla*), bean paste, sesame oil, Sichuan chili oil, Thai curry paste, rice-wine vinegar, five-spice powder, lemongrass, water chestnuts, dried seaweed (*nori*), black sesame seeds, kaffir lime leaves, perilla (*shiso*), and *yuzu*.[87]

From the outset, well-known Asian dishes began to appear on the menus at HRC restaurants. At first, the chefs experimented with teriyaki sauces. Several even served their own versions of sashimi, *siu mai*, tempura, and sushi.[88] Today many of these dishes are commonly found at high-end restaurants both in Hawai'i and on the West Coast. For example, at Wolfgang Puck's Spago, in Los Angeles, the first-course choices include Crispy Maine Sweet Shrimp Tempura and Marinated Japanese Hamachi and Tuna Sashimi. At Providence, a Michelin-starred restaurant on Sunset Boulevard, also in Los Angeles, kampachi sashimi is almost always on the menu. Indeed, the naturalization of Asian dishes in U.S. regional cuisines may have begun in Los Angeles, but it reached a new level with Hawai'i Regional Cuisine.

As the HRC chefs formed relationships with farmers, ranchers, fishermen, aquaculturists, and coffee growers, they added these producers' names to their menus so that diners would know they were eating Erin Lee's tomatoes, Nalo greens, Sumida Farm's watercress, and Maui Cattle Company beef tenderloin and were drinking Edward Sakamoto's vintage Kona coffees. In time, these names carried a cachet of their own, enhancing the dining experience of savvy diners at HRC restaurants. Here, too, the HRC chefs may have learned from Alice Waters and other regional cuisine chefs.

Several HRC chefs even added to their menus their own renditions of local dishes that originated with the indigenous Hawaiians or the different ethnic groups that had immigrated to the islands. Accordingly, Sam Choy made a contemporary version of the Hawaiian dish *laulau*, which is made by wrapping pieces of pork and fish in taro and ti leaves and then steaming it. Roy Yamaguchi serves miso-glazed fish dishes, a staple in the Japanese repertoire; Alan Wong offers his own version of *lumpia*, a Filipino take on the egg roll; and George Mavrothalassitis makes his own, highly refined, version of the Portuguese *malasada*.[89] What these chefs are offering is a new and positive version of some of the most humble local dishes. Although some, like *laulau*, are indigenous, others—such as *chazuke*, chicken *hekka*, *pinkabet*, and pork hash —were brought by immigrants; and still other dishes, like the *loco moco*, were created later, in Hawai'i.[90] Although many had the same name as the dishes introduced to the islands by immigrants from China, Japan, Korea, and the Philippines, the HRC versions of these local dishes were conspicuously more refined than the original versions. After all, they were made with the freshest and best ingredients and were prepared using sophisticated French techniques.

An example is the loco moco, a hamburger patty served on a bed of rice, smothered in brown gravy, and topped with a fried egg. *Loco* is Spanish or Portuguese for "crazy," and *moco* was chosen because it rhymed with *loco*. The dish may have been invented by Mr. and Mrs. Richard Inouye, owners of the Lincoln Grill in Hilo, for teenagers eager to have "something different from American sandwiches and less time-consuming than Asian food."[91] The loco moco is now a staple at fast-food restaurants throughout the state and at Hawaiian-themed restaurants on the mainland.

Alan Wong's loco moco has the same name and basic structure but substitutes famously expensive *wagyu* beef for the hamburger; uses *kabayaki* sauce, the thick, soy-based sauce used in a Japanese broiled-eel dish, instead of the brown gravy; and adds a fried quail egg. The *wagyu* beef, *kabayaki* sauce, and quail egg reveal Wong's Japanese inflection of the loco moco. In fact, his rendition of the loco moco might be described as a French-trained chef's refined Japanese riff on a humble local classic. As with this dish and so much else that HRC chefs serve, a typical dish has several linguistic layers: the name of the dish, the names of the producers of the ingredients making up the dish, and

Figure 5.3. Alan Wong's loco moco. Author's photograph.

the traces of the dish's particular cultural or national registers, which together create a culinary phenomenon of enormous complexity.

So who eats the new culinary creations of the HRC chefs? Just as there is no single style that all HRC chefs share, there is no ideal consumer of HRC dishes. The chefs who opened restaurants in Waikiki or other resort towns clearly were targeting tourists. Peter Merriman has several restaurants in resort towns, and not surprisingly, he uses cooking techniques (grilling) and garnishes (salsas) that would be familiar to any customer who was a fan of California cuisine or had eaten at Wolfgang Puck's Spago or Bobby Flay's Mesa Grill. Yet Merriman, true to his HRC ideals, faithfully uses locally sourced vegetables, fish, and, when possible, meat.

In contrast, HRC chefs whose restaurants are not in Waikiki or resort towns targeted locals. One thinks of Roy Yamaguchi's first restaurant, located in a suburb eight miles from Waikiki, or Peter Merriman's eponymous Waimea restaurant, which is ten to thirty miles from the resort hotels on the Kona coast. Both opened in December 1988 within a day of each other.

Roy's quickly developed a following, but Merriman's, perhaps because it is so far away from the resort hotels, had a harder time initially, although it now attracts both locals and tourists.

Jean-Marie Josselin opened his first restaurant, A Pacific Café, in a strip mall in sleepy Kapaa on the east coast of Kauai, but it is only six miles from the largest city on the island, Lihue, and within a mile of nearby hotels and condominiums. Bev Gannon's first restaurant, Hailimaile General Store, is the exception. It is located in Makawao on the island of Maui, twenty-five to thirty miles from the resort hotels in Wailea, Lahaina, Ka'anapali, and Kapalua. Although one might imagine that her choice was carefully calculated, Gannon explains that the Makawao site was something of a fluke—the building went on the market when she was looking for a space for her growing catering business, and she took it.[92] In 1995 she opened another restaurant, Joe's, in the resort town of Wailea, which attracts visitors who own or rent condominiums there.

The locations of the several HRC restaurants that opened in the 1990s suggest careful planning. The best example is Alan Wong's, which opened in April 1995 on the third floor of a nondescript office building on South King Street in the working-class McCully district. This location may reflect the marketing savvy of Frances Higa, who put up the capital for the new restaurant and, conveniently, owned the building. Higa, the founder of the very successful Zippy's restaurant chain, knew a lot about marketing and must have recognized that the King Street location put Alan Wong's within easy driving distance of well-to-do suburbs (Makiki and Manoa), as well as downtown Honolulu, and a short taxi ride from Waikiki. He was right. Other HRC chefs followed suit: Sam Choy opened Sam Choy's Diamond Head in working-class Kapahulu, less than a mile from Waikiki (1995); Jean-Marie Josselin opened A Pacific Café in the new Ward Center in a Honolulu industrial district going upscale (1996); and George Mavrothalassitis opened Chef Mavro half a block from Alan Wong's (1998). These new restaurants were within five miles of Waikiki and downtown Honolulu and quickly developed a following among both locals and tourists.

The HRC restaurants attracted a clientele willing to spend more than $100 to $200 for a dinner for two. Like the toniest restaurants in Los Angeles, San Francisco, Chicago, and New York City, their patrons were mostly local professionals, well-heeled tourists, or locals out for a special-occasion dinner. It is hardly surprising that these new restaurants did very well:

Bev Gannon's two restaurants grossed $1,000,000 in 1990, $2,500,000 in 1995, and $5,000,000 in 1999; Sam Choy's restaurants grossed $6,000,000 in 1996 and $10,000,000 in 1998; and Roy Yamaguchi's empire of restaurants grossed $100,000,000 in 2006.[93]

Conclusions

Hawai'i regional cuisine is important, I believe, for four reasons. First, HRC introduced and popularized the new calculus promoted by the new regional cuisines that began to appear in the United States in the 1970s, beginning with California cuisine and followed by other regional cuisines. The chief premise of the new regional cuisines is that food is better if it uses local ingredients.

This new culinary calculus also emphasized the importance of clean air, soil, rivers, and oceans and accordingly encouraged state and county officials to monitor local agriculture, fishing, and ranching even more carefully, as well as raising the general public awareness of the environment. This development was especially important in Hawai'i, whose sugar and pineapple industries were declining and whose growers were having to compete with developers for thousands of acres of vacated sugarcane and pineapple fields. Today, the impact of this new calculus is apparent in the goal of many restaurants in Hawai'i to serve food that is 90 percent locally sourced.[94]

Most important is that HRC affirms the local that once had been racialized and thus had been subordinated and denigrated. This "cultural denigration" of the "local" is the standard posture of colonizing regimes toward the cultures of those they dominated or enslaved.[95] I have suggested that HRC's affirmation of the local assumed many forms: first, it affirmed the *local produce* that the HRC chefs now use—whether vegetables, fruit, seaweed, fish, shellfish, meat, eggs, honey, macadamia nuts, or coffee. It also affirmed the *local producers* who grew, caught, gathered, and raised that produce. Most telling in this regard is that the producers' names now are on the menus of many HRC restaurants. For instance, the restaurant Chef Mavro acknowledges its long relationship with the Sumida family, which has supplied it with watercress since the 1980s. But HRC also brought *local dishes* to the tables of Hawai'i's fine-dining restaurants, even the once despised foods of the urban ghettos and the plantation camps. Moreover, the retention of the untranslated names of dishes signals to diners that what they are being served is truly distinctive and like nothing else they have seen in fine-dining establishments on the mainland or elsewhere in the world.[96]

HRC affirmed the local in an even more dramatic way: some of the HRC chefs were locals born and raised in the post–World War II American imperium. Sam Choy and Alan Wong were born and raised in Hawai'i. Roy Yamaguchi's father was in the U.S. military and was stationed in postwar Japan, which meant that Yamaguchi grew up on an American military installation. Local chefs who were not Caucasian could never have reached such prominence during the colonial period or even in the early decades after Hawai'i became the fiftieth state. But Wong and Yamaguchi had impressive credentials. They were trained on the mainland—Wong at the Greenbrier Resort in White Sulphur Springs, West Virginia, and Yamaguchi at the Culinary Institute of America in Hyde Park, New York. Both also had long and demanding apprenticeships at great French restaurants in the United States, Wong at Lutèce in New York City and Yamaguchi at L'Ermitage in Los Angeles. And both won James Beard awards.

Equally important to this discussion, the other nine HRC chefs who came from the mainland or Europe also affirmed the local. They, too, enthusiastically bought local produce, encouraged and featured local producers, and invented new versions of local dishes. They even began to hire locals to work in their restaurants, not just as waiters, busboys, dishwashers, and janitors, but also as sous-chefs, sauciers, and pastry chefs. Many of these locals are now emerging as new, great chefs and are being nominated for James Beard awards. In sum, the affirmation of the local, although it assumed many different forms, was the defining trait of the new culinary vision represented by Hawai'i regional cuisine.

HRC was nothing less than a critique of the older, Eurocentric, and racist tradition of fine dining that had existed in the islands from the late nineteenth century through the 1980s. It was also a critique of those who sustained and protected that fine-dining tradition: hotel owners, restaurant managers, chefs, consumers, and food writers. As a critique of colonial Hawai'i and its ugly vestiges, HRC was a subversion of the culinary language that originated in the metropolitan centers of the Euro-American colonial empires and that presented itself as not only superior but also universal. Read in this way, then, HRC represents an important reworking of the power relations that sustained the dominance of Euro-American culinary traditions and signaled the appearance of a new "syncretic and hybridized" and evolving regional cuisine.

Yet despite its successes, HRC has not been able to contribute in any sustained and meaningful way to the solution of the largest and most vexing postcolonial problem: the enduring legacy of the colonization of the Hawaiian islands and its genocidal impact on the indigenous population.[97] As is well known, nineteenth-century European and American visitors brought diseases that wiped out most of the Hawaiian population, reducing it from four hundred thousand to a million in 1778 to forty thousand a century later.[98] The visitors converted almost all the survivors to Christianity and denigrated Hawaiian values and beliefs. Finally, they also appropriated, with the cooperation of the Hawaiian chiefly class, most of the land in the islands, overthrew the Hawaiian monarchy, engineered the annexation of the islands, and undermined the Hawaiian way of life. The memory and traces of the Western impact on the islands pose a lasting challenge to every thoughtful person in the state.

Notes

1. I would like to thank those who generously shared their knowledge of the HRC movement with me: Wanda Adams, Sam Choy, Mark Ellman, Amy Ferguson, Hiroshi Fukui, Beverly Gannon, John Heckathorn, Kurt and Pam Hirabara, Joan Namkoong, Erin Lee, George Mavrothalassitis, Peter Merriman, Dean Okimoto, Edward Sakamoto, Russell Siu, Alan Wong, and Roy Yamaguchi. I am especially grateful to Michiko Kodama-Nishimoto, who caught many mistakes in an early draft of this paper, and Francine Wai,

who brought the Willows to my attention; and Dana and Arash Khazeni, who gave me an old menu from Alexander Young Hotel.

2. A number of chefs at fine-dining establishments were not trained in Europe. Michel Martin, the founder/owner of Michel's in Waikiki, was the most famous of those who had no training in classical French cuisine. Although he was raised in France, he learned his craft after he migrated to Hawai'i as a teenager and opened his restaurant in 1942. Another exception was the chefs at the Willows, arguably the most famous fine-dining establishment in the islands from the 1940s until 1980. It opened in July 1944 on land once owned by Hawaiian royalty and initially served only until 7 p.m. because of wartime blackout regulations. Once the war ended, it became a full-fledged restaurant, and its regulars included Arthur Godfrey of *Hawaii Calls*, and a number of Hollywood celebrities such as Dorothy Lamour and Johnny Weismuller. Yet none of its chefs had formal culinary training: they simply liked to cook. See Wanda A. Adams, "Michel Martin, 100, Shared Fine French Cuisine with the Isles," *Honolulu Advertiser*, January 19, 2008; and Wanda A. Adams, "Guide to Good Eating," *Honolulu Star-Bulletin*, April 9, 1961.

3. Food historian Rachel Laudan has written the definitive study of "local food." See her *The Food of Paradise: Exploring Hawaii's Culinary Heritage* (Honolulu: University of Hawai'i Press, 1996), 5–9, 16–103. See also Arnold Hiura, *Kau Kau: Cuisine and Culture in the Hawaiian Islands* (Honolulu: Watermark Publishing, 2009), 54–77.

4. See Lawrence H. Fuchs, *Hawaii Pono: A Social History* (New York: Harcourt, Brace & World, 1961), 38, 43–46, 59–67; and Stephen Sumida, *And the View from the Shore: Literary Traditions of Hawai'i* (Seattle: University of Washington Press, 1991), xiv–xv. Haunani Kay Trask disagrees with the use of the word "local" to describe the islands' nonindigenous population. See her "Settlers of Color and 'Immigrant' Hegemony: 'Locals' in Hawai'i," *Amerasia Journal* 26, no. 2 (summer 2000): 2; and Candace Fujikane and Jonathan Y. Okamura, eds., *Asian Settler Colonialism: From Local Governance to the Habits of Everyday Life in Hawai'i* (Honolulu: University of Hawai'i Press, 2008), 25–29.

5. Judith Kirkendall, "Hawaiian Ethnogastronomy: The Development of a Pidgin-Creole Cuisine" (PhD diss., University of Hawai'i at Manoa, 1985), 331.

6. Fuchs, *Hawaii Pono*, 43–47. The Big Five firms, which were established in the nineteenth century and dominated the colony's economic life, were C. Brewer & Co., Castle & Cooke, American Factors, Alexander & Baldwin, and Theo H. Davies. For an account of their history, see Fuchs, *Hawaii Pono*, 22, 53–55.

7. English Standard Schools were created in the 1920s and 1930s for Caucasian students whose parents wanted their children to have classmates who spoke standard English and not pidgin English, the local dialect. Entrance to these schools was based on examination, and most of those pupils were Caucasian. The English Standard Schools were part of a system of de facto segregation and were abolished in 1947. See Fuchs, *Hawaii Pono*, 274–79.

8. David H. Stannard, *Before the Horror: The Population of Hawai'i on the Eve of Western Contact* (Honolulu: Social Science Research Institute, University of Hawai'i, 1989), 7, 45, 50–75; Sally Engle Merry, *Colonizing Hawai'i: The Cultural Power of Law* (Princeton, NJ: Princeton University Press, 2000), 93–95; Jonathan Kay Kamakawiwo'ole Osorio, *Dismembering Lāhui: A History of the Hawaiian Nation to 1887* (Honolulu:

University of Hawai'i Press, 2002), 1–144; Noenoe Silva, *Aloha Betrayed: Native Hawaiian Resistance to American Colonialism* (Durham, NC: Duke University Press, 2004), 39–44.

9. The overthrow of the monarchy and annexation are described well in Osorio, *Dismembering Lāhui*, 145–249; and Silva, *Aloha Betrayed*, 123–203.

10. Fuchs, *Hawaii Pono*, 68; Consul General Moroi, "Americanizing the Japanese in Hawaii," *Mid-Pacific Magazine*, October 16, 1918; Royal Mead, "Sugar Interests in Hawaii," *San Francisco Chronicle*, July 18, 1910, quoted in Fuchs, *Hawaii Pono*, 49.

11. Fuchs reports that "as many as thirty of the early white residents married Hawaiian women of chiefly rank." Fuchs, *Hawaii Pono*, 38. See also Osorio, *Dismembering Lāhui*, 27, 70, 82, 87, 140, 153, 242.

12. The Kamehameha School for Boys opened in 1887, and its school for girls opened in 1894; 'Iolani School was founded in 1863 and is affiliated with the Anglican Church of Hawai'i; Mid-Pacific Institute was created in 1908 with the merger of the Kawaiaha'o School for Girls and the Mills Institute for Boys; the College of St. Louis was founded in 1846 by the Congregation of the Sacred Hearts of Jesus and Mary and was located first in Windward O'ahu and, after 1881, in Honolulu.

13. Fuchs, *Hawaii Pono*, 3, 57–59.

14. *The Friend*, January 1917, 3. By 1940, the number of Caucasians had risen to 25 percent of the colony's population. See Fuchs, *Hawaii Pono*, 52.

15. The military presence grew to 17,169 in 1927, 24,952 in 1937 and, after the Pearl Harbor attack, jumped to 135,907 in 1942, peaking at 406,811 in 1944. See Robert C. Schmitt, *Historical Statistics of Hawaii* (Honolulu: University of Hawai'i Press, 1962), 10.

16. W. A. Pickering to CG, Hawaiian Department, Sub: Annual Inspection, Schofield Barracks, Territory of Hawaii, Fiscal Year 1935, June 30, 1935; Adjutant General's Office Document Number 333.1, National Archives Record Group Inventory Entry Number 11, Record Group 159; and Joseph Y. K. Akana Interview, *Waikīkī, 1900–1985*, 1:11; Walter Maciejowski to Brian M. Linn, January 6, 1993, quoted in Brian McAllister Linn, *Guardians of Empire: The U.S. Army and the Pacific, 1902–1940* (Chapel Hill: University of North Carolina Press, 1997), 123, 126.

17. Fuchs, *Hawaii Pono*, 49–52.

18. Arthur Suehiro, *Honolulu Stadium: Where Hawaii Played* (Honolulu: Watermark Publishing, 1995), 25–117; Michael Okihiro, *AJA Baseball in Hawaii: Ethnic Pride and Tradition* (Honolulu: Hawai'i Hochi, 1999), 7–43.

19. Kirkendall, "Hawaiian Ethnogastronomy," 326, 352–55.

20. Ibid., 124–26.

21. Elinor Langton, "A Hawaiian Bill of Fare," *Paradise of the Pacific* 16 (April 1903): 11.

22. Stannard adds, "It is now almost certain that Hawaiians in 1778 had life expectancies greater than their European contemporaries." See Stannard, *Before the Horror*, 60–61.

23. For a detailed account of the immigrants' food and recipes, see Laudan, *The Food of Paradise*, 106–59; and Hiura, *Kau Kau*, 26–53.

24. "What Chinese Eat," *Paradise of the Pacific* 15 (April 1902): 9–10; Franklin Ng, "Food and Culture: Chinese Restaurants in Hawai'i," *Chinese America: History and Perspectives—The Journal of the Chinese Historical Society of America* (San Francisco: Chinese Historical Society of America with UCLA Asian American Studies Center, 2010), 113; and Hiura, *Kau Kau*, 4–25.

25. Robert C. Schmitt, *Firsts and Almost Firsts in Hawaii*, ed. Ronn Ronck (Honolulu: University of Hawai'i Press, 1995), 115.
26. Ng, "Food and Culture," 114.
27. Ng, "Food and Culture," 115; and John Heckathorn, "Dining—The Oldest Restaurant in Hawaii and the Newest," *Honolulu*, November 1987, 348–52.
28. Center for Oral History, *The Oroku, Okinawan Connection: Local-Style Restaurants in Hawai'i* (Honolulu: Social Science Research Institute, 2004), app. A.
29. Michiko Kodama-Nishimoto, Warren Nishimoto, and Cynthia Oshiro, *Talking Hawai'i's Story: Oral Histories of an Island People* (Honolulu: University of Hawai'i Press, 2009), 164–67.
30. Schmitt/Ronck, *First and Almost Firsts in Hawaii*, 115.
31. Clarence E. Glick, *Sojourners and Settlers: Chinese Migrants in Hawaii* (Honolulu: Hawai'i Chinese History Center, 1977), 80–81.
32. Center for Oral History, *The Oroku, Okinawan Connection*, app. A.
33. "The New Spencecliff," *Sunday Star-Bulletin / Advertiser*, June 7, 1987.
34. Alan Matsuoka, "Lau Yee Chai: Not an Ordinary Chop Suey House," *Honolulu Star-Bulletin*, March 12, 1991.
35. "Clark's Tour No. 8 Menu," Alexander Young Hotel, February 10, 1928; and Center for Oral History, *Waikīkī, 1900–1985. Oral Histories* (Honolulu: Center for Oral History, 1985), 1726–27.
36. Center for Oral History, *Waikīkī*, 1731.
37. Kirkendall, "Hawaiian Ethnogastronomy, 137; Ng, "Food and Culture," 13; and Kodama-Nishimoto et al., *Talking Hawai'i's Story*, 11, 46–48, 52–55, 72, 74–75, 83, 120, 156–57, 211–13, 225, 249, 271–72, 296–98.
38. Donna R. Gabaccia, *We Are What We Eat: Ethnic Food and the Making of Americans* (Cambridge, MA: Harvard University Press, 1998), 122–48.
39. Although fourteen chefs attended the August 27, 1991 meeting, two—René Boujet and John Farnsworth—did not attend subsequent meetings. The twelve who did are generally regarded as the Hawai'i regional cuisine core group. They are (in alphabetical order) Sam Choy, Roger Dikon, Mark Ellman, Amy Ferguson, Beverly Gannon, Jean-Marie Josselin, George Mavrothalassitis, Peter Merriman, Philippe Padovani, Gary Strehl, Roy Yamaguchi, and Alan Wong. See Alan Wong, interview by Samuel H. Yamashita, March 15, 2009.
40. John Heckathorn, "Delicious Decade," *Honolulu*, August 2001, 8.
41. Peter Merriman, interview by Samuel H. Yamashita, July 18, 2010.
42. Ibid.
43. Janet Wald Henderson, *The New Cuisine of Hawaii: Recipes from the Twelve Celebrated Chefs of Hawaii Regional Cuisine* (New York: Villard Books, 1994), 64; Merriman, interview.
44. Henderson, *The New Cuisine of Hawaii*, 12; Wong, interview.
45. Merriman, interview.
46. David Kamp, *The United States of Arugula: How We Became a Gourmet Nation* (New York: Broadway Books, 2006), 239–41, 254–61.
47. Roy Yamaguchi, interview by Samuel H. Yamashita, July 7, 2009.
48. Merriman, interview.
49. Mark Ellman, interview by Samuel H. Yamashita, October 17, 2009; Beverly Gannon, interview by Samuel H. Yamashita, October 17, 2009; George Mavrothalassitis, interview by Samuel H. Yamashita, March 17, 2009.

50. Ellman, interview.

51. Ellman, Gannon, Mavrothalassitis, Wong, and Yamaguchi, interviews.

52. Henderson, *The New Cuisine of Hawaii*, 12.

53. Ibid., 44.

54. Ibid., 74; Amy Ferguson, interview by Samuel H. Yamashita, June 29, 2011.

55. Henderson, *The New Cuisine of Hawaii*, 74.

56. Ibid., 72.

57. Ibid., 12.

58. Ibid., 96.

59. Merriman, interview.

60. Henderson, *The New Cuisine of Hawaii*, 84.

61. Ferguson, interview.

62. Merriman, interview.

63. Ibid.

64. Tane Datta, interview by Samuel H. Yamashita, June 29, 2011.

65. Merriman and Datta, interviews.

66. Dean Okimoto, interview by Samuel H. Yamashita, August 9, 2009.

67. Merriman, interview; Erin Lee, interview by Samuel H. Yamashita, June 28, 2011.

68. Merriman, interview.

69. Merriman, interview.

70. Datta, interview.

71. *ERS Report Summary*, Washington, DC, May 2010, 1–2.

72. Ferguson and Datta, interviews.

73. Grace A. Lazzarus, "Alumni Profiles: Shep Gordon," *UB Today* (fall 2007), available at www.buffalo.edu/UBT/UBT-archives/ . . . /alumni_profiles/gordon.html.

74. Ferguson and Datta, interviews.

75. Henderson, *The New Cuisine of Hawaii*, xvi.

76. Gannon, interview.

77. Ferguson first met Julia Child when she was twenty-one and already a promising chef. Ferguson, interview.

78. PalmBeachPost.com, October 13, 2009.

79. Henderson, *The New Cuisine of Hawaii*, 96.

80. Henderson, *The New Cuisine of Hawaii*, 4. Choy also credits his parents for teaching him a lot about Hawaiian food. Sam Choy, interview by Samuel H. Yamashita, April 5, 2010.

81. Henderson, *The New Cuisine of Hawaii*, 20.

82. Ibid., 32.

83. Ibid., 44.

84. Ibid., 74.

85. Ibid.

86. Ibid, 106; Wong, interview.

87. Henderson, *The New Cuisine of Hawaii*, 4–9, 12–18, 22–29, 32–41, 44–51, 54–63, 66–71, 74–83, 86–93, 96–103, 106–13, 118–26.

88. Ibid., 22, 70, 102, 108, 118.

89. See Sam Choy, *Sam Choy's Island Flavors* (New York: Hyperion, 1999), 161; Roy Yamaguchi, *Hawaii Cooks: Flavors from Roy's Pacific Rim Kitchen* (Berkeley, CA: Ten Speed

Press, 2003), 98–99, *Roy's Fish and Seafood* (Berkeley, CA: Ten Speed Press, 2005), 10, 13, *Roy's Feasts from Hawaii* (Berkeley, CA: Ten Speed Press, 2007), 109; and Alan Wong, *Alan Wong's New Wave Luau: Recipes from Honolulu's Award-Winning Chef* (Berkeley, CA: Ten Speed Press, 1999), 18, 36.

90. Alan Wong, *The Blue Tomato: The Inspiration behind the Cuisine of Alan Wong* (Honolulu: Watermark Publishing, 2010), 26–27.

91. James Kelly, "Loco Moco: A Folk Dish in the Making," *Social Process* 30 (1983): 62–63. For another version of the origins of the loco moco, see Center on Oral History, *Tsunami Remembered: Oral Histories of Survivors and Observers in Hawai'i* (Honolulu: Center on Oral History, 2000), 1:118–20.

92. Tom Yoneyama, "Getting Their Just Desserts," *Hawaii Business* 5 (1989): 34, 36; Gannon, interview.

93. Alex Salkever, "Cookbook to Perfection," *Hawaii Business* (June 1998); Alex Salkever, "A Woman's Place," *Hawaii Business* (July 2000).

94. Wanda Adams, "Merriman Planning Restaurant for Kauai," *Honolulu Advertiser*, December 7, 2007.

95. For a discussion of the linguistic and literary dimensions of this "cultural denigration," see Bill Ashcroft, Gareth Griffiths, and Helen Tiffin, *The Empire Writes Back: Theory and Practice in Post-colonial Literatures*, 2nd ed. (London: Routledge, 2001), 7–10.

96. Ashcroft et al., *The Empire Writes Back*, 63.

97. J. Kēhaulani Kauanui discusses the many proposed solutions to this problem in *Hawaiian Blood: Colonialism and the Politics of Sovereignty and Indigeneity* (Durham, NC: Duke University Press, 2008), 171–96; and Haunani Kay Trask describes the plan for decolonization offered by Ka Lahui Hawai'i and its legal foundations in "Settlers of Color and 'Immigrant' Hegemony," 13–21.

98. Stannard, *Before the Horror*, 45, 50.

PART II

Empires of Food

6

Incarceration, Cafeteria Style

The Politics of the Mess Hall in the Japanese American Incarceration

HEIDI KATHLEEN KIM

George Takei, best known for playing Mr. Sulu on *Star Trek,* is one of the most famous of the World War II Japanese American incarcerees. His autobiography *To the Stars*, little known except among Trekkers, begins in the camps when he was four and might well be his first memory. Then, when the camps were being closed, Takei's father left his family temporarily to see whether Los Angeles was still too hostile an environment for Japanese Americans. With the family separated, Takei's child memory suddenly fails completely.

> Mama says she decorated a tumbleweed with fruits and candies. She says we opened presents on Christmas morning, and she made hot chocolate for us. I remember none of that. I don't even remember the fact that we had a Christmas without Daddy. Somehow, Christmas 1945 has completely vanished from my memory.

It seems quite reasonable for a young child not to remember one quiet Christmas, but Takei makes this a lost piece of family history. His literary amnesia skillfully uses the image of a pitiful but loving Christmas as something stolen from him by his unjust incarceration, encompassing not only his father's absence but also these forgotten luxuries.[1]

Takei's concern about his family's separation, centering on a moment of consumption at "home," employs one of the chief rhetorical devices used in narrating the Japanese American incarceration. The incarceration was one of the greatest violations of civil rights in American history, based on nothing more than fear and suspicion. Japanese Americans within a hundred miles of the West Coast—regardless of age, citizenship, or even prior military service— were forcibly removed by military orders starting in 1942. *How* the 120,000 incarcerees ate, as well as *what* they ate, proved to be a particular concern throughout World War II for both those incarcerated and the War Relocation Authority (WRA) administrators in charge of the eleven incarceration camps specifically for Japanese Americans.[2]

The mess hall became the demonized cause of Japanese American family breakdown, starting with the sociological studies of the incarcerees and their own complaints in camp papers. Anthropologist Jane Dusselier's study of the foodways in the camps reveals the extent to which food became a battleground for Japanese American political agency and survival, most famously in the riots at Manzanar. However, she briefly notes, the mess halls were a more contested and resented site because of their threat to the family.[3] As I argue, an examination of the lasting discussion of the mess halls shows that they were battlegrounds of Americanization and public relations. There was an extraordinarily cohesive discourse about the dangers of nonfamilial eating, a sentimental narrative that started immediately and was given renewed force in the activism and governmental redress movement of the 1970s and 1980s. With their bad food and worse facilities, mess halls served as potent reminders that family life and tradition had been torn apart. As the Congressional Committee on the Wartime Relocation and Internment of Civilians (CWRIC) concluded in the 1980s, "The community feeding weakened family ties. At first families tried to stay together; some even obtained food from the mess hall and brought it back to their quarters in order to eat together. In time, however, children began to eat with their friends."[4]

Recollections and descriptions of the mess halls are, thanks to oral histories, now legion. Some of the cohesion of mess hall discussions is unquestionably due to the uniformly poor conditions and food from camp to camp. What has been less studied and credited because of the tacit acceptance of the mess hall as a universal evil, however, is how the dialogue regarding the mess hall in turn enabled and threatened the use of family life, especially nuclear family life, to project a public image of assimilation and Americanization. Against the image of yellow peril—in wartime, that of Japanese military hordes—the image of the family was wielded by sympathizers, administrators, and incarcerees in a number of contradictory directions to direct both outward opinion and Japanese American behavior. The mess hall served rhetorically as a euphemistic origin story for the disintegration of the family, shifting the focus away from the government's actions. At the same time, its chaos and the juvenile delinquency it supposedly bred fed racist fears.

The Incarcerated Family: Conditions and Administration

The mess hall was instantly caught between competing public images. Though the nuclear family and family table proved to be the images of choice to display

Americanness, communal living and eating was the image that proved that these dubiously regarded Americans were not being "pampered" at a high cost to the taxpayer, a rumor that plagued the WRA, particularly in 1943. In publications ranging from pamphlet to film, the WRA notes that meals generally cost much less than the allowed forty-five cents per head and were served economically "cafeteria-style," meaning that just as in schools, factories, and other large institutions, individuals lined up to obtain food from servers and carried their trays to long communal tables.[5] The "cafeteria-style" meals, portrayed to outsiders as a financial compromise that still allowed families to eat together, were seen as the heart of the camp problem for incarcerees and the WRA administrators and sociologists, as well as sympathizers.

The WRA strove for a uniform mess hall organization within the incarceration camps. Most mess halls were built to serve three hundred people and featured standard tables and benches as well as plain institutional tableware. Each hall had a dedicated cooking and dishwashing staff of incarcerees, most of whom were paid the standard $16 (skilled) or $12 (unskilled) rate per month. Incarcerees lined up at mealtimes, even in inclement weather, and, according to most accounts, ate quickly and departed as soon as possible. The crowds— particularly before the incarcerees developed habits and schedules—were the chief obstacle to family dining, as the mess halls at various times were serving far more people than they had been designed to do. In her famous memoir *Nisei Daughter*, published in 1953, Monica Sone describes her first meal at the camp in typically quasi-comic style:

> Our family had to split up, for the hall was too crowded for us to sit together. I wandered up and down the aisles, back and forth along the crowded tables and benches, looking for a few inches to squeeze into. . . . My dinner companion, hooked just inside my right elbow, was a bald headed, gruff-looking Issei man who seemed to resent nestling at mealtime. Under my left elbow was a tiny, mud-spattered girl.[6]

Mess halls in the assembly camps were generally larger, more chaotic, and dirtier.

Within the camps, Japanese Americans tried to maintain a semblance of normal social structure through community organizations such as baseball teams, newspapers, and churches. But the physical structure of the camp necessarily meant that parents had less control over their children, who in some cases were sent out into the local community for school and returned home to a communal camp with multiple outside influences rather than a protective

Figure 6.1. Santa Anita Assembly Center cafeteria. An original government photograph by Clem Albers showing a full mess hall in an assembly camp. WRA mess halls had similar designs. Original caption: "Lunch time, cafeteria style, at the Santa Anita Assembly Center where many thousands of evacuees of Japanese ancestry are temporarily housed pending transfer to War Relocation Authority Centers where they will spend the duration." Dated April 6, 1942. It is important to note that these government photos were often posed, sanitized, or censored. Many were never widely circulated. From the collection of the University of California at Berkeley, Bancroft Library, accessed through Calisphere website at http://content.cdlib.org/ark:/13030/ft958008z9/?order=1.

family home. As a source of community, food became a rare privilege, problematized by rationing; initially, there were no provisions made for discretionary food for large parties, and these had to be specially approved. The WRA stressed the political cohesion of the "blocks," units of barracks that had a common mess hall and bathroom facilities, but few of the incarcerees recollect any block identity.[7]

The deterioration of family structure caused by communal eating was partly due to the poor management of the camps and the needs of different family members. The walk back and forth, sometimes considerable for small children or the elderly, forced families to eat separately if someone stayed behind, or discouraged their walking back and forth with meals and empty plates. The disorganized assembly camps had even worse problems of long lines, overcrowding, and food mismanagement, and occasionally children ran around the camps to several different mess halls.[8] Eventually, sociologists found, "Groups based upon age and sex differences replaced the family as the traditional meal-time group, and became a set pattern in several centers."[9] They also became the organizational modes of social life.[10]

The emphasis on proper nuclear family living, even inside the camps, occasionally led to somewhat overstated ideals. In the *Pacific Citizen*, the official newspaper of the Japanese American Citizens League, columnist "Ann Nisei" offered suggestions for setting up a barrack apartment with sofa/bunks and dressers for a family of two parents and two children in a "quite large" room, 16' × 24'. The design allowed for the typical activities of "living, eating, sleeping, dressing, work and study" as well as "easy clean-up for Mother." This attitude of making the best of the incarceration imposes American home design standards onto an imagined average family of four, either a "young Nisei couple and their youngsters, or . . . an Issei couple and their teen-age children." Extended families or the all-male barracks of several camps are ignored in favor of the nuclear structure.[11] The "typical" activities include "eating," a suggestion that this, too, can be easily carried on in camp and imply an imaginary family table in this perfectly designed apartment, which notably does not include one, for most of the small space is occupied by beds and storage.

Throughout the war, there were constant pleas and talk of starting family-style dining—still in the mess halls but with guaranteed space together—some of which came to pass to an extent in certain camps. The finance and logistics of this were difficult, however, particularly with food rationing in effect. Fred J. Haller, the steward of the Heart Mountain camp, wrote in a report to Dillon Myer, head of the WRA,

> From my experience cafeteria style service is the most economical for large operations. The defense plants, the army and other large operators all use cafeteria style service. Also with the present rationing of meat and other items family style service would be most impractical as it would be impossible to insure a fair distribution. There is a certain amount of waste in both operations but it has been proven that this waste is considerably less in cafeteria style service.[12]

What even Haller, a tolerant and compassionate steward, glossed over was the spurious nature of a comparison of all-adult worker (some single-sex or day-only) facilities with facilities that for every meal had to serve people of all ages and health conditions.[13] The incarcerees' social and emotional needs thus ranked a distant second to economics. Stockton, one of the initial temporary camps dubbed "assembly centers," allowed limited experiments with "family-style service," but only for "children 6 years younger and their mothers." This concession was made more to address the difficulty of a mother carrying multiple trays, and in any case, these were the only family units that were likely to manage to eat together in the mess halls.[14]

Attempts to control the initial traffic at mess halls, which ranged from assigned shifts to ticketing to ushers, only exacerbated the problem. Kenneth Tashiro, then a teenager, vividly remembered his first meal in Gila River: "I walked down the aisle between the rows of tables and a pretty young woman directed me toward a table at which there was one space left. I hesitated, then I heard my dad say, 'Can we sit together as a family?'" The woman assented, and they were redirected to another table.[15] It seems astonishing that it was not the common practice even to attempt to send families to sit together, but such seems to have been the case. Another similarly disgruntled incarceree wrote to the Gila newspaper, "May I ask that somebody have something done about the traffic directing system now used in the various dining halls. It seems to me that this method only tends to separate families who desire to have their meals together."[16]

The WRA administrators, while relying on the nuclear family as a unit of management, admitted its sacred status at their own discretion. Family camps and family transfers took months or, in some cases, years. One woman from Hawai'i was denied the right to have her unincarcerated eleven-year-old son transferred to her care in the camp because her parental rights were abrogated by the internment. Historian Stephen Mak has shown that invocation of the unity of "family" became a tool used in the construction of incarceree/internee rights for Japanese Americans, and even more for the Latin Americans of Japanese descent who were interned in the United States.[17] Conversely, incarcerees cited anger over separated families in the camps as a primary reason that many refused to take the loyalty oaths. WRA staff members had to distinguish among "the No of protest against discrimination, the No of protest against a father interned apart from his family . . . the No of felt loyalty to Japan," to name only a few.[18] Once a number of incarcerees had been successfully "resettled" away from the coast, the WRA even restricted visits to family members still in the camps, worried about excessive administration and traveling. But when the camps were closing and some older incarcerees were afraid to leave, having lost their homes and livelihoods, the WRA forced them out, citing as one reason: "These people would have been maintained in an institutional environment which, practically all welfare students agree, is much less desirable than a system of maintenance in private homes or normal family surroundings."[19] Suddenly, it had become essential to maintain a proper familial way of life rather than an institutional one.

Yellow Peril versus All-American Families

It is difficult to summarize all the ways that the incarceration fragmented the Japanese American nuclear family structure. Some families were sent to different camps and had a lengthy wait before reuniting, as when the husband/father of the family was imprisoned first or an ill or pregnant family member was kept in a hospital temporarily while the rest of the family was incarcerated. Many nisei volunteered or were drafted for military service when the ban on Japanese Americans was lifted; 30,000 Japanese Americans from Hawai'i and the camps eventually served, and the all-Japanese American 442nd Regimental Combat Team, which served in Europe, still remains the most highly decorated unit of its size in U.S. history. Volunteer work and contract farmwork, also depicted as patriotic by the WRA and the press, occasionally employed families or couples but tended to take men away from their families. The "resettlement" project sent many young college or work-aged nisei to the Midwest and East, away from family and friends. Finally, the disagreement among family members about what to do about repatriation and the infamous loyalty oaths led to deep fissures.[20]

At the same time that camp administrators worried about the destruction of family structure by the mess halls, they also encouraged enlistment, farmwork, and resettlement, which often separated families as well. In a curious reversal of the conception of the nuclear family as keeping danger contained, these family-splitting endeavors were portrayed as useful and patriotic. Military service took older nisei away from wives and children and younger nisei away from dependent elderly parents. Farmwork was needed in order to make the camps self-sustaining, since early (spurious) criticism of the Japanese Americans being fed and kept idle at taxpayers' expense made the WRA doubly determined to promote the agricultural division. Calls for workers and volunteers appealed to a sense of duty. "America's call for food to feed her people and her Allies becomes louder and louder. . . . By [working], you will not only be helping the people in this community, but your fellow evacuees in other centers where vegetables are not being produced," proclaimed the newspaper at the Gila River camp, where the farms' abundance sometimes outran the manpower, though not the administrators' ambitions.[21] Outside farmwork was also seen as patriotic, but the separation of family was not prominently featured in calls for it. The Hirabayashi family illustrates this dispersal, son by son: Gordon, plaintiff in the landmark Supreme Court case *Hirabayashi v. United States* testing the legality of the military orders that applied only to Japanese Americans, was in jail; Ed went to work on a farm, then in a restaurant, then to a college in North Carolina; the parents were escorted to Seattle for Gordon's trial; and in their absence, Jim left for Idaho to do farmwork. Obviously, the Hirabayashi family had a somewhat exceptional source of separation in Gordon's imprisonment and trial. But the other children were widely scattered by the government's purposeful encouragement of farmwork and resettlement, something that would have been hard to imagine before the war.

Other internal demands, such as the mess hall itself, demanded the separation of families. As May Sasaki recalled,

> My mother took on the waitressing at the mess hall because they wanted a lot of help there, and they asked the camp internees to take those roles. She eventually became a head waitress, which meant she spent more hours away from home. . . . But we never could eat with family because my dad became a block manager, which then took him away to other responsibilities. So both my parents were no longer always around as they had been, and now my brothers and I were kind of left to our own devices.

Sasaki cites her family's long-standing ethic of service and patriotism, which impelled her parents to perform these thankless, ill-paid jobs even at the cost of leaving their children alone for long hours.

This fracturing was dangerous because it denied Japanese Americans one of the main available ways of demonstrating proper assimilation: the idyllic nuclear family structure. In Caroline Chung Simpson's reading of gendered narratives in and after World War II, she uses as an example Carl Mydans's feature article and photos in *Life* magazine, "the first feature article on Japanese American internment to appear in a major publication," at the late date of March 20, 1944. Simpson traces Mydans's confused rhetoric of male troublemakers and aliens versus a "muted liberal critique" of the infringement of civil rights. The former wins in Mydans's slightly menacing lead photograph of a line of unnamed Japanese American men at Tule Lake, reminiscent of the yellow peril. The second part of his article switches away from these potentially treacherous figures to the other camps, which he portrays as unabashedly wholesome. One photo shows an "idyllic scene of a middle-class American family," the nine-person Manji family cheerfully reading and playing in their cramped quarters. As a corrective to the Tule Lake rebels, Mydans "implies that . . . the wholehearted pursuit of middle-class domestic ideals impossible to achieve in the camps" will help them escape the rigid past maintained by the patriarchal structure of Japanese society.[22] As Simpson notes, the family image was—as evidenced in later memoirs—a key method of stabilization for Japanese American identity during and after the war.

Countering past images of yellow peril and perversely large families taking over farms, the nuclear family was portrayed as a thoroughly American, wholesome image. The official WRA definition of a family unit was "father, mother, and unmarried children living with the family." Widows and widowers with children, for example, were considered separate even if they were living with other relatives.[23] Mydans's Manji family portrait, which, the caption notes, is missing two sons who are in the military, presents the Japanese American family at its most Americanized and palatable, looking like any middle-class family (albeit in a smaller space). Such photos also reassured the public that the government was being compassionate, allowing American citizens to live acceptable American lifestyles. Japanese Americans thus had to demonstrate both their own Americanness and the government's upholding of that Americanness, a precarious position indeed for people forcibly segregated and incarcerated.

Wartime films and other visual media showed frightening images of masses of Japanese that bled into depictions of Japanese Americans; Frank Capra's film *Prelude to War* showed a Japanese army marching through Washington, DC, and Theodore Geisel, better known as Dr. Seuss, drew a cartoon showing a fifth column of Japanese stretching all the way up the West Coast states. The fear of not being able to distinguish loyal from disloyal, given as an excuse for the incarceration, further created the image of identity-less, indistinguishable Japanese masses. Written publications evoked these images as well, both during and after the war. General John L. DeWitt's final report, "Japanese Evacuation from the West Coast," described a "tightly-knit racial group," held together by "ties of race, the intense feeling of filial piety and the strong bonds of common tradition, culture and customs." Perhaps DeWitt's most telling descriptor is "homogeneous," a word employed to condemn the entire population. Mydans's *Life* article exemplifies this attitude, with the Tule Lake "rebels" given no names but left as an anonymous column.[24]

The mess hall thus was also a troubling site within the camps, where the incarcerees blended into an unidentifiable mass. Under its pernicious influence, the incarcerees ran the risk of familial fragmentation, which in turn risked the creation of delinquency and violence. The high volume of negative coverage of the 1943 Tule Lake riots described "an unruly mob of Japanese" nearly committing arson and murder, even though, as the WRA acknowledged, it had lost control of its press relations at this time and could not persuasively counteract these stories. "The events which took place were not anywhere near as violent or dangerous as they were commonly represented in the press," Myer of the WRA insisted, but it was too late to remove the impression that had been left. Afterward, the WRA was doubly aware that such behavior had to be carefully controlled.[25] With the cooperation of Japanese Americans in positions of influence (such as the Japanese American Citizens League [JACL] or the camp newspaper staff), the WRA saw the maintenance of a strong family structure as an effective antidote to the threat of large, discontented groups.

Fears expressed about young male resettlers reveal that the WRA believed that releasing a horde of Japanese Americans back into society without the containing family unit could be a destabilizing force. Historian Ellen Wu's in-depth study of the "resettlement" project shows that these young men, often zoot-suiters associated with violence in camps and resettled communities, greatly angered and troubled administrators.[26] The rise of juvenile delinquency was a particular fear in the camps. Reflecting fears of yellow hordes and mirroring depictions of the mostly male "pressure boys" at Tule Lake, male violence was a source of not only inconvenience and unrest but also unfavorable publicity. Thus, its transformation into favorable press by sympathizers writing about inevitable familial disintegration was crucial. As one father observed in an article in the *New York Herald Tribune* that stressed the rise of juvenile delinquency at the Rohwer camp, "I no longer provide the bread for their table and the roof over their heads. So, they say, 'why should I respect what you say and obey your word?'"[27] His feeling of inadequacy stems from his abrogation of financial responsibility, with food and the family table at the metaphorical center. Having lost control of his livelihood and physical home, his two sons, aged seventeen and nineteen, had passed completely beyond his control. Sociologists pointed out that the mother's authority had also been undercut. "Mass feeding in the mess halls eliminated the role of wife and mother in the preparation of food for the family and lessened the controls of the parents exercised at the time of the family meal."[28] Focus was thus shifted away from a violent mass identified with Japan and onto the wayward children of helpless parents.

Modern oral histories of incarcerees reflect these accounts of behavioral change, especially in male teenagers, but tend to downplay the "delinquency" and tragedy, concentrating more on survivorship. Jim Hirabayashi spoke of his meals as a pivotal experience. "I no longer ate with my parents; I ate with my peers. And so I spent most of my time outside of the family circle. And did a lot of things that I didn't normally do and wouldn't have done had the family stayed together." This resembles the start to many accounts of delinquency, but Hirabayashi does not specify what these "things" are, and his account implies that they were not grave. Bo Sakaguchi, also a teenager at the time, was even more vague about any problems.

> Families were all separated now because you went to the mess hall with your friends, your school friends. So, but because we were already teenagers, it wasn't so bad. I felt sorry for the younger kids who had, who also did the same thing, so they weren't having their meals with their parents. But for us, we were adult—well, we were young, seventeen, sixteen, seventeen, it didn't matter that much.

His nonchalance is decidedly different from the dramatization of familial separation, and the interviewer follows it up, asking, "Did this separation of families relative to meals and things, was that upsetting to the parents in families?" Sakaguchi did hesitate at that, saying, "I, I don't know. I don't know," but maintained that it was harder for those with small children who, despite their ages, were still eating apart. He then repeated a more standard depiction of the familial problems, saying, "I'm sure it didn't help the family unit per se over the long term, though I don't believe they caused problems while we were in camp themselves, maybe postwar."[29]

Incarceree May Sasaki actually got into an extended discussion with her oral history interviewer about the extent of her brother's bad behavior:

> My oldest brother loved this freedom, and he felt that now he could do what he wanted with his cohorts, and they became kind of like a gang in camp. They were not bad boys, but they certainly liked to do things that were not always things that their parents wanted them to do.

The interviewer asked for clarification, saying, "By 'gang,' nowadays we understand 'gang' to mean something where maybe young men are causing mischief and maybe criminal acts." Even though he was describing a modern understanding, this was likewise the picture in the 1940s of the unruly young men in camps, particularly Tule Lake. Sasaki hastened to dismiss the idea of criminality:

> Oh no, this wasn't anything of that. I guess you'd just call them boys sticking together, then, maybe. But in their minds they were this gang. And there were often many little gangs that sprung up, and they would have their own meetings and their own kinds of things, rituals that they would go through. . . . And yes,

he wasn't as obedient. I remember him talking back to my dad which he never did before.

These "little gangs" that Sasaki characterizes as bad boys doing silly things together were, in the wake of the Tule Lake riots, portrayed as violent, disaffected youth. Sasaki then proceeds to take this story about her brother's teenage rebellion into a perceptive analysis of the issei-nisei generational conflict as a central problem of incarceration itself, whereas complaints of juvenile delinquency at the time shifted blame to the mess halls and other evil influences of communal life.[30]

Keep the Children Safe: Resettlement as a Means to Avoid the Mess Hall

The immediate result of separating families at mealtime was supposedly child misbehavior, ranging from poor table manners to the more feared juvenile delinquency. In one of the earliest published memoirs of the incarceration (1946), Miné Okubo wrote, "Table manners were forgotten. Guzzle, guzzle, guzzle; hurry, hurry, hurry. Family life was lacking. Everyone ate wherever he or she pleased. Mothers had lost all control over their children."[31] Camp papers started reporting this phenomenon early, advising parents to restrain their children and set the example themselves. As early as September 1942, the *Gila News-Courier* reported,

> Remonstrations of abominable table manners used in the dining halls of youngsters and adults during meal hours have been heard here and there each day. Misplaced elbows, seats used as foot-rests, loud talk with a full mouth, covered heads. . . . Is this one of the demoralizing indications of the camp life? It seems so. It seems that we evacuees are doing less than we can to combat the evil influences of our community existence.[32]

Since the newspapers did not tend toward the radical—hardly surprising, given the necessity of at least some cooperation with the camp administration—this article did not probe the reason behind this "community existence" or even call for a better system of dining. It was not until May 1944, at which point the incarcerees must have felt that they had put up with this system quite long enough, that "organization of a Family table system in mess halls to encourage family ties and discourage juvenile delinquency was recommended by the Butte Community Council," one of the internal camp self-governments.[33]

Japanese American newspapers continued the theme of personal responsibility that decades later plagued memoirists. "Ann Nisei" advised parents to discipline their children through proper educational stimulation and structure. "Never miss a meal with your children, even though you know they can take care of themselves. Keep the family unit together for all meals." While this particular advice was framed as a way to model good table manners for children, the tone of the entire column suggests acute anxiety about child development as a whole away from the normal influences of the family home, such as "pets, picture magazines, toys, playmates, and all the objects in the home." Another exhorted incarcerees to create a colorful play and work area for children in the camp in order to eliminate the influence of the "concentration camp" and the "bareness and bleakness of the barrack."[34] As usual, though, the columns passed over the reasons for these absent influences, instead focusing on coping mechanisms. Likewise, deeper anxieties about the cumulative effect of these individual lapses went unspoken. As modern anthropologists observe, traditional family mealtimes serve as places to acculturate children, teaching not simply etiquette but morals, gender roles, and narrative/linguistic skills as well.[35] Yet the effect on the community as a whole was not discussed openly.

An article in the *Pacific Citizen* offered an even more vivid depiction of family life gone wrong, describing one mother's experience with her small daughter and ending by using this disturbing image to suggest an entirely different course of action.

> Dining in community mess halls taught her to squirm out of her seat and reach in front of anyone for whatever she wanted. The dessert on the table disappeared early so she got in the habit of helping herself quickly to generous portions before the others. She got in the habit of gulping her food wolfishly—we all had to almost bolt our food. . . . I couldn't teach Haruko to beg anyone's pardon or to use knife and fork correctly—everyone seemed to be violating good table manners. Once when I scolded my child and she cried, every baby in the mess hall seemed to pick it up and cried. The looks I got from the other fretting mothers stopped me from ever doing it again.[36]

Like the articles discussed earlier, this one stresses the bad atmosphere of the mess hall and its deleterious effects on children, especially with regard to table manners but also the greater evils of greed and disobedience. This woman's difficult experiences are aimed at an audience of fellow fretting mothers who would commiserate with her. The details, probably unnecessary for fellow incarcerees, add up to total agreement. Unlike the mothers in previous articles, this mother does not beg everyone else to set a good example for her daughter and other children, nor does she place blame. Instead, the article subtly offers the solution to all these problems in a revealing last sentence: "I wish I had come out a year ago."

"Coming out" of the camps refers to resettlement, a policy of dispersing Japanese Americans away from the still-proscribed military area. The WRA was strongly encouraging it, but it was not progressing at the speed the administrators had hoped. The article about Haruko appears in the JACL news section under a column entitled "Colorado Calling!" about the fertile land of Utah Lake. (Since Utah Lake is in Utah, not Colorado, the title is a little misleading.) Written by Joe Masaoka, the Denver JACL chapter leader and brother of Mike Masaoka, the national JACL president, this article's opening lines about Brigham Young and the comparison of Utah Lake with the Sea of Galilee create a call for a new exodus. Masaoka does not refer directly to resettlement, but he skillfully deploys a rhetoric of abundance and idyllic family life to extol the virtues of life on the shores of the new Sea of Galilee. He describes Utah Lake's "fruitful orchards and cultivated acres," with "children romp[ing] under shady trees," appealing to farmers and parents. Privacy and masculine dignity can also be regained, as "men build their houses nearby and life is stimulating." In contrast with the story of Haruko's misbehavior, Masaoka's utopian vision implies that refusing to resettle means damaging children's socialization, perhaps permanently, whereas a move to Utah is a move to familial paradise.[37]

Sympathizers also used the imagery of the mess hall to drum up support for resettlement. An article in the magazine *Christian Century*, which frequently featured sympathetic articles about the incarceration, noted in a familiar tone, "The usual practice is for 200 to 300 persons to eat together in a large mess hall. Thus the significance of the family is broken down." Later, the author concluded, "Parental influence is diminishing with the steady breakdown of the family." But following the standard line, this article, entitled "Empty the Relocation Centers!" exhorted readers to support the WRA in order to create more opportunities for "resettlement" in "desegregated" areas.[38] Many Christian groups supported resettlement, and the appeal to a wide Christian audience rested on sentimental family values rather than dry theories about proper minority assimilation.[39] But the idea of releasing Japanese Americans to their homes or protesting the mass incarceration still was not even entertained.

The Family Table: Three Decades of Sentimental Appeal

The popularity of Jeanne Wakatsuki Houston's 1973 memoir, *Farewell to Manzanar*, written with her husband James D. Houston, regenerated the story of the Japanese American family for the political activism of the 1980s. Although Houston's memoir poignantly tells a tale of familial decay, she also explicitly reflects at some length on the question of agency, blaming teenage willfulness as well as the incarceration for the Wakatsukis' unraveling.

> You might say it would have happened sooner or later anyway, this sliding apart of such a large family, in postwar California. People get married; their interests shift. But there is no escaping the fact that our internment accelerated the process, made it happen so suddenly it was almost tangible.

Using language found in later accounts, Houston starts with the destruction of domesticity: "It began in the mess hall. Before Manzanar, mealtime had always been the center of our family scene. . . . Now, in the mess halls, after a few weeks had passed, we stopped eating as a family." Her mother, valiantly trying to fulfill her appropriate domestic role, "tried to hold us together for a while, but it was hopeless." At home, Papa had been the one who headed the table. The children, however, enjoyed their new freedom.

> My older brothers and sisters . . . began eating with their friends, or eating somewhere blocks away, in the hope of finding better food. . . . Kiyo and I were too young to run around, but often we would eat in gangs with other kids, while the grownups sat at another table. I confess I enjoyed this part of it at the time. We all did.

By "confessing," Houston takes some responsibility for familial breakdown; we didn't resist enough, she implies.[40]

In her account, Houston notes, although she does not make much of it, that the camp administrators did worry about the effect on the family.

> A couple of years after the camps opened, sociologists studying the life noticed what had happened to the families. They made some recommendations, and edicts went out that families *must* start eating together again. Most people resented this; they griped and grumbled. They were in the habit of eating with their friends. And until the mess hall system itself could be changed, not much could really be done. It was too late. (33)

Houston's memoir, itself a mélange of the explanatory, condemnatory, and conciliatory, is at its most confused here, retreating to impersonal analysis to avoid talking any more about her family's breakdown. Rarely is Houston's tone scholarly; she almost never invokes sociologists or any other outside "experts" or sources on the incarceration. She also avoids the question of authority regarding this mess hall horde and does not mention who was sending out or loosely enforcing the edicts on families eating together.

Houston's narrative does have another, more important beginning than the mess hall. Even though the abrupt arrest of her father, a fisherman on Terminal Island, breaks up the family before they even enter the camp, she does not even mention this. Instead, several days later, when her father is charged with delivering oil to Japanese submarines, she says, "This was the beginning of a terrible, frantic time for all my family." (8) Nonetheless, she confines this "terrible, frantic time" to a finite and proportionally small section of the narrative, implying that other times, including the arrest itself, were less terrible and less frantic. When she says that her mother's weeping was terrible or that her family's disintegration "began in the mess hall," it is a false, sentimental starting place with which her mainstream audience can identify. Beginning at the beginning would require a cross-racial identification with the loss of a father dragged off by police for being a dangerous enemy alien spy. Houston bleakly concludes this section with "My own family, after three years of mess hall living"—notably, not "camp living" or even "internment living" but specifically blaming the mess hall—"collapsed as an integrated unit" (33). Even though this time also included three years of her brother's enlistment against her father's wishes, her near conversion to Catholicism, and various hardships for her family members, the mess hall retains its rhetorical primacy. The fact that the bulk of Houston's camp narrative does address her father's tragic alcoholism, illness, and loss of patriarchy makes her rhetorical stress on the mess hall all the more curious a choice. Houston was either consciously or unconsciously drawing on decades of discourse about the breakdown of the family attributed to the mess halls, but *Farewell to Manzanar*'s success ensured its continuance.

Houston's memoir is the best example of a post-incarceration adaptation of the sentimental novel's depiction of family. As numerous scholars have argued, the classic American sentimental novel may have assumed that a conventional family structure existed, but it frequently depicted its heroines in unconventional scenarios and communities that break apart the family and sometimes demand the type of cross-racial identification that Houston's narrative required of white American readers. Glenn Hendler writes, "Sentimental plots repeatedly transgress both the internal and the external limits of the family structure which domestic ideology held up as its overt ideal." The incarceration memoir, however, generally depicts such transgressions in service of its larger mission and twentieth-century audience, to introduce Japanese Americans into mainstream American acceptance. Houston and other protagonists emerge from their unconventional camp situations with new bonds of sympathy connecting them to an outward society rather than to a restored nuclear family. The normative family, however, is still assumed as a function of sentimentality, even as it may be transgressed by the narrative.[41]

It matters little that—as Stephanie Coontz has most popularly argued—the idyllic nuclear family image most powerfully identified with the next decade did not actually exist as the American norm in the 1940s.[42] Image was everything to the incarcerees who, judging from their own memoirs, might have been the only American population accustomed to dining family style. Far more likely, of course, is that sympathetic writers, both incarcerees and others, understood the power of family as a rhetorical device. The 1950s black-and-white television family, an image that undoubtedly also influenced Houston's depiction of her family table, can actually be seen partly growing out of the depictions of incarceration. Girls in home economics clubs across the country were carefully instructed in creating proper nuclear family homes, with the camps' "new type of community" held up as a sad counterexample. A 1943 magazine article asked them to consider the plight of fellow young American citizens who also liked jitterbugging and cokes. "Family life as known in the ordinary American home is largely absent. . . . As meals are served cafeteria style in mess halls, there is no dinner table around which the family can thresh out everyday problems." Once again, the lack of a dinner table, and not the lack of civil liberties, is the sentimental tragedy. But homemakers have done wonders in these sad circumstances, and "evacuee girls find that home economics, more than almost any other subject, helps them improve life in the center and gives them a firm foundation for the future." This future is one in which the "ordinary American home" can flourish for girls of all ethnicities, who will have the privilege of setting their own dinner tables.[43]

The fulfillment of this idealized image also appeared in mainstream film. In the 1960 black-and-white film *Hell to Eternity* starring Jeffrey Hunter and Sessue Hayakawa (and featuring George Takei in a supporting role), poor young orphan Guy Gabaldon is adopted by his Japanese American gym teacher's family, an idyllic nuclear family of father, mother, and two sons, an image that was too sentimental for the *New York Times* reviewer.[44] Mama and Papa Une welcome Guy kindly, and the only moment when he shows any uneasiness arises when his friend and new adoptive brother, George, jokes that they eat seaweed and octopus for breakfast; Guy is then relieved to find cornflakes and other familiar foods on a nicely set table worthy of any sitcom of the 1950s. The film takes the path of least resistance, not suggesting that Japanese food or customs can be genuinely American, but instead showing that Japanese Americans were fully "Americanized" in this area, sitting down together at the table until the incarceration breaks them up forever.[45]

Conclusion

While embracing the traditional depiction of the mess hall, more recent accounts of Japanese Americans' incarceration also reveal new details of how families circumvented the rules and preserved themselves in unsanctioned ways. The mess hall story, effective as it was, mostly ended with the family's destruction, creating a story of victimhood rather than survival. Tashiro, who had almost been separated from his family during his first meal in Gila River, writes an astonishingly frank account of his teenage years in the camp, full of pranks, name calling, sexual awakening, and friendship. Such frankness would have been unheard-of in the sentimental memoirs of the early years or in the era of redress. His recollections seem to be accurate, though, because his mother one day announced to him that he was becoming a "yogore"—an unsavory character, sometimes translated as a gangster—in the camp, and so his family was sending him to live with relatives in Minneapolis. Among other, more serious offenses, his mother tells him that the mess hall crew reported that he had loosened the caps on the salt and pepper shakers, causing people to dump the entire contents all over their food.

Tashiro's pleas and promise to behave in the mess halls did nothing to change his mother's mind. Determined to save him from the lack of structured life in camp, his mother, acting as agreed by correspondence with his father serving in France with the 442nd, speedily packs him off. Significantly, their last act as a family was to buy a chicken from a Native American. They pluck it together—Tashiro still remembers the stench of the feathers—cook it on their little barrack stove, and make teriyaki chicken for his lunch on the journey. In this narrative, it is the Tashiros' ability to buy food independently, cook it as a family, and pack it for a child that enabled him to escape the mess halls that were turning him into a delinquent. With his bento (lunch) box, Tashiro, escorted by his grandfather, heads out for his new life in the Midwest, leaving his mother and baby sister behind. Instead of a story of decay, it is the Tashiros' enduring strength as a family unit that allows them to overcome all the obstacles of the incarceration, albeit at the price of the temporary separation that closes the memoir.[46]

The disintegration of the family structure in the mess halls three times a day, symbolizing the lack of both a family home and the freedom to choose and prepare food they liked, was certainly a source of great discomfort and emotional trauma for the incarcerated Japanese Americans, making their imprisonment even more difficult. Houston's account, as well as other memoirs and testimonies, made the mess hall a subject of sympathy and interest, paving the way for the redress movement that further cast it as accepted fact. Ironically, the discourse on which the movement drew was, during the incarceration itself, much more politically double-edged. The mess hall imagery generated great sympathy from a mainstream audience and rallied the incarcerees to preserve what home life they could through a variety of methods, but for all audiences, it drew attention away from the causes and the legality of the incarceration, as well as the WRA's plans to scatter the Japanese American community as widely as possible across the rest of the country. Substantiating historians' claims that the nuclear family was not as sacred to Americans as the midcentury myth would have it, public outcries over cafeteria-style dining and familial separation came even from sympathizers only at strategic moments. The mess hall was not simply pitied, but feared. Pushing past the politics of this sentimental image exposes the depths of prejudice that caused the incarceration in the first place.

Notes

1. George Takei, *To the Stars: The Autobiography of George Takei*, Star Trek's *Mr. Sulu* (New York: Pocket Books, 1994), 62–63.
2. Following modern practice, I use the terms "incarceration" and "incarceree" rather than "internment" and "internee," which imply alien status. I also use the term "camp" or "incarceration camp" instead of the euphemistic WRA term, "Relocation Center." I refer to the "Assembly Centers" initially administered by the Wartime Civilian Control Agency as "assembly camps" to distinguish them from the WRA camps. There were other camps holding a smaller number of Japanese Americans, administered by other government entities, but I am not specifically discussing these, nor were they often spoken of publicly during the war.
3. Jane Dusselier, "Does Food Make Place? Food Protests in Japanese American Concentration Camps," *Food & Foodways* 10 (2002): 153–55.
4. *Commission on Wartime Relocation and Internment of Civilians, Personal Justice Denied.* Washington, DC: The Civil Liberties Public Educaion Fund (Seattle: University of Washington Press, 1997).
5. "Relocation of Japanese-Americans," ed. War Relocation Authority (Washington, DC: U.S. Government Printing Office, 1943), 5. "A Challenge to Democracy" [short film], War Relocation Authority with the Office of War Information and Office of Strategic Services, 1944.
6. Monica Sone, *Nisei Daughter* (Seattle: University of Washington Press, 1979), 176.
7. J. A. Krug and D. S. Myer, "WRA: A Story of Human Conservation," ed. U.S. Department of the Interior (Washington, DC: U.S. Government Printing Office, 1946), 90; and John H. Provinse and Solon T. Kimball, "Building New Communities during War Time," *American Sociological Review* 11, no. 4 (1946): 405.

8. For example, Miné Okubo, *Citizen 13660* (Seattle: University of Washington Press, 1946). 89.

9. Provinse and Kimball, "Building New Communities during War Time," 404.

10. Leonard Bloom, "Familial Adjustments of Japanese-Americans to Relocation: First Phase," *American Sociological Review* 8, no. 5 (1943): 559.

11. "Ann Nisei Says: Design for Center Living: Ideas for a Barrack Apartment," *Pacific Citizen*, October 1, 1942, 2.

12. Fred Haller, "Statement of Fred Haller, Project Steward," April 29, 1943, in Records of the War Relocation Authority, Headquarters Subject-Classified General Files, 61.620, Box 363 (Washington, DC: National Archives, 1943), 5.

13. Nor did Haller note that cafeteria-style service in other hastily constructed facilities was equally unsatisfactory. American war workers complained vigorously of the high cost and poor quality of unappetizing food at their factory canteens. See Lizzie Collingham, *The Taste of War: World War Two and the Battle for Food* (London: Allen Lane, 2011), 422–23.

14. "Family-Style Meals for Stockton Center," *Pacific Citizen*, July 9, 1942, 6.

15. Kenneth A. Tashiro, *"Wase Time!": A Teen's Memoir of Gila River Internment Camp Days* (Bloomington, IL: AuthorHouse, 2005), 28.

16. "Tom Tom: Letter to the Editor," *Gila News-Courier*, September 23, 1942, 2.

17. Stephen Mak, "'America's Other Internment': World War II and the Making of Modern Human Rights" (PhD diss., Northwestern University, 2009).

18. Quoted in Alice Yang Murray, *Historical Memories of the Japanese American Internment and the Struggle for Redress* (Stanford, CA: Stanford University Press, 2008). 79.

19. Visit restrictions are mentioned in Krug and Myer, "WRA: A Story of Human Conservation," 144; Bloom, "Transitional Adjustments of Japanese-American Families to Relocation," *American Sociological Review* 12, no.2 (1947): 201–209, cites the actual WRA regulation in 1944.

20. Perhaps most famously depicted in John Okada's novel *No-No Boy*, in which the son says "no-no" to the two famous test questions about swearing allegiance and willingness to serve in the armed forces, which sends him to jail and eventually breaks his family apart. See John Okada, *No-No Boy* (1957; repr., Seattle: University of Washington Press, 1979).

21. "Work to Eat-Eat to Work," *Gila News-Courier*, October 10, 1942, 2.

22. Carolyn Chung Simpson, *An Absent Presence: Japanese Americans in Postwar American Culture, 1945–1960* (Durham, NC: Duke University Press, 2001), 32–33, 23; Carl Mydans, "Tule Lake Segregation Center," *Life*, March 20, 1944.

23. "Rulings Clarify Basic Family Unit." *Gila News-Courier*, December 15, 1942, 3.

24. Frank Capra, "Prelude to War," in *Why We Fight*, ed. Frank Capra (U.S. War Department, Twentieth Century Fox, 1942); Theodore Seuss Geisel, "Waiting for the Signal from Home . . . ," black and white comic, *PM*, February 13, 1942; Lieutenant General J. L. DeWitt, "Japanese Evacuation from the West Coast, 1942: Final Report," ed. Headquarters Western Defense Command and Fourth Army (Washington, DC: U.S. Government Printing Office,1943), 9, 15.

25. Krug and Myer, "WRA: A Story of Human Conservation," 116–18.

26. Ellen Wu, "Race and Asian American Citizenship from World War II to the Movement" (PhD diss., University of Chicago, 2006).

27. "Japanese Voice Resentment at Arkansas Camp," *New York Herald Tribune*, July 18, 1943, n.p., from the American Civil Liberties Union Records, "The Roger Baldwin Years, 1917–1950," Seeley G. Mudd Manuscript Library, Princeton University.

28. Provinse and Kimball, "Building New Communities during War Time," 404. Such discussions of the loss of parental control were repeated for decades. One of the major accounts of the 1980s redress and reparations campaign, *Achieving the Impossible Dream*, reads, "The influence of mess hall conditions led to the deterioration of the family structure. Mothers and small children usually ate together, while the fathers ate at separate tables with the other men. Older children joined peers of their own age group for meals." The mess hall is thus placed as the primary cause for family fragmentation, but interestingly, the paragraph goes on to say, "Many husbands lost prestige, while many wives and some children gained more independence. The men were no longer seen as the financial heads of the household." These considerable economic shifts are, somewhat perplexingly, relegated to an afterthought. See Mitchell T. Maki, Harry H.L. Kitano, and S. Megan Berthold, *Achieving the Impossible Dream: How Japanese Americans Obtained Redress* (Urbana: University of Illinois Press, 1999), 44.

29. James Hirabayashi, "James Hirabayashi Interview," in *Densho Visual History Collection*, available at www.densho.org, 2008; Bo T. Sakaguchi, "Bo T. Sakaguchi Interview," in *Manzanar National Historic Site Collection*, available at www.densho.org, 2002.

30. May K. Sasaki, "May K. Sasaki Interview," in *Densho Visual History Collection*, available at www.densho.org 1997.

31. Okubo, *Citizen 13660*, 89.

32. J. N., "Table Etiquette," *Gila News-Courier*, September 23, 1942, 2.

33. "Family Table System Urged," *Gila News-Courier*, May 16, 1944, 1.

34. "Ann Nisei's Column: Child Discipline Difficult to Maintain in Relocation Camps," *Pacific Citizen*, November 6, 1943, 6; "The Children in the Centers: Should Not Be Subjected to 'Concentration' Atmosphere," *Pacific Citizen*, July 9, 1942, 6.

35. Elinor Ochs and Merav Shohet, "The Cultural Structuring of Mealtime Socialization," *New Directions for Child and Adolescent Development* 111 (spring 2006): 35–49.

36. "Center Life Spoils Children," *Pacific Citizen*, November 13, 1943, 6.

37. Joe Masaoka, "Colorado Calling!: Two Kinds of People in World," *Pacific Citizen*, November 13, 1943, 6.

38. Kirby Page, "Empty the Relocation Centers!," *Christian Century*, June 16, 1943, n.p., from the American Civil Liberties Union Records, "The Roger Baldwin Years, 1917–1950," Seeley G. Mudd Manuscript Library, Princeton University.

39. See Stephanie Bangarth, *Voices Raised in Protest: Defending North American Citizens of Japanese Ancestry, 1942–49* (Vancouver: University of British Columbia Press, 2008), chap. 3.

40. Jeanne Wakatsuki Houston and James D. Houston, *Farewell to Manzanar: A True Story of Japanese American Experience during and after the World War II Internment* (1973; repr., New York: Houghton Mifflin Harcourt, 2002), 31–34. Page numbers of quotations from this book are in parentheses.

41. Glenn Hendler, "The Limits of Sympathy: Louisa May Alcott and the Sentimental Novel," *American Literary History* 3, no. 4 (winter 1991): 686. As Hendler notes, one of the dangers of a novel that wields sympathy as a device to force the reader to identify with the heroine is that the sympathy can be misplaced. The example he gives is of the loss of self in scenes of excessive mourning, but this may also be one way to consider the displacement of sympathy on the reader's part onto the mess hall.

42. See Stephanie Coontz, *The Way We Never Were: American Families and the Nostalgia Trap* (New York: Basic Books, 1992).

43. John C. Baker, "The Relocation Center Home," *National Magazine of Home Economics Student Clubs*, September 1943, 10, 18, in Records of the War Relocation Authority, Washington Office Records: Documentary Files: Magazine Clippings (Washington, DC: National Archives).

44. Howard Thompson, "'Hell to Eternity' Is Story of Marine Hero," *New York Times*, October 13, 1960.

45. Phil Karlson, *Hell to Eternity*, DVD, Warner Home Video, 2007 (Allied Artists Pictures, 1960).

46. Tashiro, *"Wase Time!"* 143. The Tashiros were not alone in buying and cooking food as a family. Incarcerees in Gila River were allowed to go fish in the canal, and Manzanar incarcerees dared to sneak out of the camp in order to go fishing in the Sierras (as seen in the documentary by Cory Shiozaki, *The Manzanar Fishing Club* (From Barbed Wire to Barbed Hooks, 2011)). There also were stores in the camps, run by incarcerees.

7

As American as Jackrabbit Adobo

Cooking, Eating, and Becoming Filipina/o American before World War II

DAWN BOHULANO MABALON

My father Ernesto Tirona Mabalon arrived in Stockton, California, in 1963 to be reunited with his father, Pablo "Ambo" Mabalon, who had left their home-town of Numancia, Aklan, for the United States in 1929. My *lolo* (grandfather) Ambo ran a popular Filipino American diner, the Lafayette Lunch Counter, in the heart of Stockton's Little Manila. Almost immediately after he arrived, my *tatay* (father) was "itching to have dried fish" and craved his favorite variety, called *tuyo*. When my lolo stepped out one afternoon, my father threw some *tuyo* on the restaurant's hot grill. The reek of the fried, fermented fish wafted down Lafayette Street. Lolo rushed back to find angry patrons and warned Tatay never to fry *tuyo* again. After he ate, Tatay lambasted the customers. "I said, *Mabaho pala kayo*!" (You're the ones who stink!), he remembered.

> I said: When you left the country you were eating dried fish, were you not? This is what made you what you are! Dried fish! Because you are here [in America], you hate the smell of dried fish? You did not come to this country if you were eating steak in the Philippines!

For him, *tuyo* was a powerful symbol of his culture, his class, and his identity as a *provinciano,* or person from the provinces. To him, the old-timers were arrogant traitors who thought themselves too good for rice and fish.

After this *tuyo* debacle, he swore that "wherever I am, I will always eat dried fish, the old dependable."[1] My *tatay*'s story continues to intrigue me as a historian of Filipina/o American culture and community. If these immigrants come to despise the fish of their youth, then what kinds of foods sustained the 150,000 Filipinas/os who settled in the United States before World War II? How did American colonialism transform Philippine diets? Which recipes survived the journey, and which ones were transformed? Moreover, how did

147

the experience of farm and cannery work influence what they cooked and ate? What roles did gender and class play in production and consumption?

This chapter explores these questions by discussing what Filipina/o immigrants on the West Coast and in Alaska produced and consumed, and argues that what they cooked and ate made possible not only their survival but also the formation of a collective ethnic identity as Filipina/o Americans in the first decades of the twentieth century. The lack of specific Philippine ingredients and the poverty that forced cooks to improvise, embrace, and creatively adapt local resources, the extreme sex ratio imbalance in which very few women immigrated before World War II, the migratory nature of Filipina/o life, and the intermarriage and the close social ties of Ilocanas/os, Tagalogs, and Visayans gave birth to a unique Filipina/o American cuisine with cultural ties to the Philippines but with roots in the *campos,* canneries, and plantations of Hawai'i, Alaska, and the West.

Previous scholarship on Filipina/o Americans focused heavily on labor experiences, immigration exclusion, and race relations, with less emphasis on family formation, gender, class, community formation, and cultural production. In exploring the ways in which Visayan, Ilocana/o, and Tagalog emigrants became Filipina/o Americans through their food, I take to heart the call of the late historian Steffi San Buenaventura, who insisted that Filipina/o American history "should be as much a narrative of the cultural world they brought with them as it is an account of their life in the new country."[2] Studying Filipina/o American foodways allows us to explore the cultures and community that these immigrants created. "Foodways include food as material items and symbols of identity, and the history of a group's ways with food goes far beyond an exploration of cooking and consumption," writes historian Hasia Diner. "It amounts to a journey to the heart of its collective world."[3] Filipinas/os turned to their family networks and kin and to fellow immigrants to survive, constructing a social world and ethnic identity grounded in their provincial ethnic and class identities and shaped by new cultural traditions borne of the world they now inhabited. The unique Filipina/o American cuisine they created was a powerful symbol of their collective struggle to survive despite overwhelming odds.

What Filipinas/os produced in the fields and canneries and cooked and ate in the decades before World War II was shaped by the brutality of industrialized agriculture, the grinding poverty of the Depression years, pitiful agricultural wages and conditions, anti-Filipina/o racist violence, exclusion and deportation, labor repression, and an extreme sex-ratio imbalance.[4] That Filipinas/os insisted on staying in United States demonstrated that the ethnic community that they had built together in the 1920s and early 1930s gave them the resources that allowed them to survive and even flourish. Just as the Mexican Americans of whom George Sanchez writes created new identities and possibilities for themselves in the 1930s and 1940s, so did Filipina/o immigrants develop and assume "a new ethnic identity, a cultural orientation which accepted the possibilities of a future in their new land" by the 1930s.[5] The Filipina/o American community survived and insisted, even demanded, that they be part of the nation. As they built this community and created new cultural traditions, Filipina/o immigrants, like the European immigrants that Diner studied, were able to enjoy more food than ever before.[6] In this light, food became more than sustenance. According to food scholar Doreen Fernandez, for Filipinas/os since the American occupation, food has been "a vital field of study—even only as a vestige of war, as index of struggle."[7]

Eating in the Philippines at the Turn of the Century

After a brutally violent, protracted imperialist war against Filipina/o nationalists that began in 1898, the United States maintained the Philippines as a formal colony until 1946. The Philippine diet that American imperialists encountered at the turn of the century was a Southeast Asian one, with influences from China, Spain, and Mexico. More than eighty dialect and language groups and seven thousand islands meant that countless regional and local methods, resources, recipes, and styles of food proliferated.[8] For example, the rocky soil of the Ilocos region produced a cuisine based on vegetables, including *pinakbet* (vegetables with pork and *bagoong,* a fermented, salted fish paste). According to Doreen Fernandez, four flavors dominate in Philippine cooking: salty, sour, sweet, and bitter. Rice is central, she writes, and probably the most important food in the entire archipelago.

Before Spanish colonial rule began in 1565, people of the archipelago depended on staples such as seafood, goat, pork, chicken, *carabao* (water buffalo) meat and milk, rice, and fruits and vegetables such as coconuts, bananas, and mangoes.[9] Beginning in the eleventh century, Chinese traders brought noodles, bean curd, bean sprouts, soy sauce, and such dishes as *lumpia,* a roll of julienned vegetables and meats in a flour-based wrapper. Filipinas/os indigenized these Chinese dishes into such dishes as *pansit* (sautéed noodles).[10] Spanish friars and officials brought olive oil, wine, ham, tomatoes, and sausages. N. S. Fernandez notes that Spanish food became fiesta cuisine.[11] Spain ruled its Southeast Asian colony by way of Mexico, for the center of Spanish colonial rule was the galleons trade linking Mexico and the Philippines. Filipinas/os who jumped ship from the galleons in Acapulco as early as the 1500s and 1600s and made their way to Louisiana began shrimping in the bayous.[12] From Mexico came dozens of new terms, foods, dishes, and techniques: cacao, guava, avocados, *camote* (sweet potatoes), *singkamas* (jicama), and *tamales*. From Mexico came the term *adobo*, for an indigenous pickled dish in which vegetables and/or protein are stewed in vinegar, salt, garlic and spices, a method that flavors, tenderizes, and preserves, historian Felice Prudente Sta. Maria pointed out.[13] Fernandez explains that in the Philippines, adobo came to mean anything—pork, chicken, seafood, vegetables cooked in the adobo style.[14]

By the time Americans arrived, elite Filipinas/os were enjoying imported cheeses, Spanish sausages, and paté. The sugar barons in the province of Pampanga, considered the culinary capital of the Philippines, Filipinized Spanish recipes such as *arroz a la Valenciana* (sweet rice and meats cooked in coconut milk and olives), *menudo* (diced liver, pork, and vegetables), *afritadang manok*, and chicken braised in a rich tomato broth. These dishes became fiesta food and Sunday fare for elites. Fiesta desserts included *leche flan,* or crème caramel, and a variety of desserts, including *biko* and *suman*, that were made of newly harvested sweet rice, sugar, and coconut milk, called *kakanin*.[15]

Hungering for America

But these foods of the elite were not everyday fare for the vast majority of the emigrants from the provinces of Luzon and the Visayas who arrived in the United States before World War II. Seafood, rice, and/or *saba* bananas, corn, or *camote* and vegetables formed the basis of their diets. The poorest of the poor might eat only rice, *bagoong*, and/or salt. The hunger and poverty the writer Carlos Bulosan experienced and witnessed in his province of Pangasinan in the 1910s and 1920s haunted his memories. In the first part of his 1946 novel, *America Is in the Heart*, Carlos accompanies his mother to the market, where she traded her *bagoong* for rice, beans, and the rare chicken and eggs in neighboring villages.[16] A starving woman approaches them and asks to dip her cracked, dry hands in their jar of *bagoong*. What happened next shocked and humbled Carlos:

> The woman . . . ran into her house and came back with a small earthen bowl half-filled with water. Quickly she put her hands into my mother's can of salted fish, and taking them out as quickly, she washed them in her bowl of clean water. There was agony in her face. When the water had reached the deepest recesses of the cracks in her hands, the woman looked at me with forgiving eyes. Suddenly

she lifted the bowl to her mouth and drank hungrily of the water where she had washed her hands that had been smeared with salted fish. When it was empty she scraped the sediment in the bottom of the bowl with her forefinger; then she rushed into her hut to look for rice.[17]

Whether fictionalized or drawn directly from Bulosan's own experiences, the story illustrates the horrors of provincial poverty and hunger that early immigrants yearned to escape.

Bulosan was one of the thousands of lower-middle-class pre–World War II emigrants from families with small landholdings who relied on subsistence-level farming of rice and vegetables, bartering, fishing, hunting, and gathering. They lived in the densely populated provinces of Ilocos Norte, Ilocos Sur, Pangasinan, Tarlac, and La Union and on the islands of Panay and Cebu, which had almost five hundred residents per square mile but whose landholdings averaged only about an acre.[18] American colonial rule led to massive dislocations in the provinces as the local economies shifted from subsistence farming to export-oriented agriculture. Because the soil of the Ilocos region in Luzon lacks the fertile richness of the rice and coconut-growing lands directly to its south, those who managed to eat three times a day and owned a little bit of land considered themselves fortunate. One immigrant recalled that his family survived by trading with fishermen the bananas, rice, corn, and sweet potatoes that their tenant farmers shared with them. "So there's no exchange of money," he said. "It was only a matter of exchanging fish for a staple food so that everyone could live. This was the way we lived in that small village . . . a beautiful thing, yeah."[19]

For Filipinas/os in the province, a diet of fish, rice, and vegetables was not monotonous and tiresome; only hunger was unbearable. True hardship meant having no food at all. "We were lucky in that we managed to eat three times a day," recalled my *lolo* Ambo of his turn-of-the-century childhood in Numancia, Capiz province (later renamed Aklan province). There were no special family meals or celebrations.[20] "We always have lots of fish," said Camila Labor Carido of her childhood in Hinundayan, Leyte. "But we never complain, 'How come fish all the time?'"[21] For breakfast, they ate hot rolls such as *pan de sal* from the town baker. For lunch, Camila was sent to the market (*palengke*) for fresh *ginamus* (salted and fermented fish or shrimp paste) to be eaten with rice and vegetables. "Fish all the time, and maybe in a blue moon, chicken," she said. Every night, she pounded rice clean for the next day.[22]

At Christmastime and fiestas, the wealthier landowners and the middle class shared their bounty with their tenant farmers and less fortunate neighbors. This was when the poor could eat fiesta food and holiday desserts, such as sweet rice steamed in banana leaves, rice cakes, and drink hot chocolate. "Christmas was the most beautiful thing in my life back home because of all the goodies like *suman* and rice cake," remembered one Stockton old-timer: "It didn't matter how poor you were, they always prepared something for that occasion because it was special for us. . . . When we finished our meal, someone would give us coffee—real coffee, and then some chocolate, pure chocolate from the cocoa tree."[23]

Crop failures, typhoons, and droughts were disastrous for the provincial poor surviving on subsistence farming. A 1904 drought killed the crops of the family of Alberta Alcoy Asis of Carcar, Cebu, whose father farmed a few acres of sugarcane, corn, and vegetables like *sitaw* (long beans), *langka* (jackfruit), *ube* (purple yam), and *munggo* (mung beans). Her father's death in 1908 was catastrophic. "I'm very poor," she remembered. "My dad left the five acres of land to us. But we cannot plant something because we are small yet. We are seven brothers and sisters." In Cebu City, Alberta's mother encountered a recruiter for the Hawaiian Sugar Planters Association. Within weeks, the family left to work in the sugar plantations in Hawai'i, where work was plentiful but grueling.[24] Families like the Alcoys and thousands of other Ilocanas/os and Visayans responded to the burdens of population pressure, colonialism, land loss, and poverty with massive emigration.[25]

Civilization via Chiffon Cake: American Colonial Education and Food

At the center of the American colonial regime was a national public school system, with its goal of shaping loyal servants of the empire under the premise of preparation for eventual self-rule. As scholar Alex Orquiza notes in chapter 8 of this book, free public school for girls in the Philippines sought to civilize them through a curriculum of domestic science courses, which required girls to adopt white, middle-class gender roles and learn American cooking and baking, knitting, sewing, and household hygiene and sanitation. Domestic science was central to the colonial project and its civilizing mission. "That to have good government we must first have good people; that in order to have good people we must first have good homes," wrote Alice Magoon, a teacher charged with drawing up the domestic science curriculum in Zambales in 1902.[26] Domestic science (later called home economics) was a nineteenth- and twentieth-century movement of white middle-class women who sought to professionalize the domestic sphere by applying the scientific and managerial techniques of modern industrialization to domestic labors.[27]

In every town, domestic science buildings were erected.[28] Camila Labor Carido remembers bitterly how domestic science and pressure to conform to gender roles, instead of reading and arithmetic, dominated her education. "We are not educated," she remembered angrily.

> We go to school [only] to learn how to write [our] name. You are prepared [only] to take care of your husband and your children. We are just taught how to be a good wife, darn and sew, cook for your husband. That's our life in the Philippines, to serve your husband even if he kills you for not doing it.[29]

If Filipina/o bodies were deemed racially inferior to American ones, so too were their native foods. Students were taught the nutritional superiority of refined sugars, red meats like beef, animal fats, hydrogenated fats like shortenings, and highly processed foods. As a result, American food was increasingly seen as "hygienic, practical, and 'modern,' fit for the new generation," explains Doreen Fernandez.[30] Moreover, the students were instructed to eat three square meals (and avoid *merienda,* or afternoon snacks), use forks and spoons, and end the traditional practice of eating with their hands.[31] In agriculture classes, teachers pressed students to abandon crops thought inferior to American varieties.[32] As Orquiza contends in chapter 8, a combination of domestic science curricula and the marketing of American corporations like Nestlé, Lea & Perrins, and Heinz encouraged a generation of Filipinos to crave canned products such as corned beef and SPAM, white bread, pies, chiffon cakes, cookies and biscuits, salads made of American canned fruit, and mayonnaise-slathered macaroni salads. But few Filipinas/os could afford canned Dole fruit, Nestlé condensed milk, and a freezer for "Frozen Pampanga Fruit Salad"; or gas ovens, imported nuts, dates, and cracker meal for a cookie called "Food for the Gods," both of which were popularized by *Culinary Arts in the Tropics* (published in 1922 by the wives of American colonial officials).[33] Nonetheless, the domestic science curricula and American advertising made an indelible impression on young Filipinas/os by portraying life in America as a paradise in which macaroni chicken salads, steaks, biscuits, pies, cakes, and frozen fruit salad were abundant. Such a country must have seemed irresistibly delicious.

Going to the Land of Baking Powder Biscuits

To paraphrase my father, in the 1910s and 1920s, Filipina/o emigrants who were eating steak in the Philippines did not come to America, but those whose diets

Figure 7.1. Filipinas learn how to make baking powder biscuits in a domestic science class in the Visayas, Philippines, in the early twentieth century. Photograph by Frank Mancao. Courtesy of the Filipino American National Historical Society.

relied on *tuyo* and rice made their way to the United States by the thousands. The influence of American public schooling and the poverty and deteriorating economy of the provinces, coupled with the attractive prospect of gaining a college education in the United States, drew more than 150,000 Filipinas/os to Hawai'i, Alaska, and the United States by 1946. As American nationals, they could enter freely, unchecked by Asian exclusion laws. Moreover, because of traditional gender roles, most emigrants left their wives and children behind. The result was a sex-ratio imbalance of fourteen men to one woman in California before World War II. Planters in Hawai'i and farmers on the West Coast were in desperate need for cheap labor. Filipina/o populations swelled wherever there was agricultural work: the sugar plantations in Hawai'i, the salmon canneries in Alaska, and the fertile farmlands of California and Washington state. Filipinos in the navy were drawn to bases in Vallejo, San Diego, and Brooklyn. Seattle, Los Angeles and San Francisco attracted busboys and domestics, and hundreds of Filipinas/os attended colleges and universities.

Luckily for these immigrants, rice was abundant. Earlier Asian immigrants had pioneered rice farming in California and truck farming Asian vegetables. Large-scale rice production exploded in the California Delta in the 1910s with Japanese short-grain varieties, known now as Calrose.[34] Other familiar foods and staples such as soy sauce (*toyo* or *suyo*), noodles, and vegetables like bitter melon, eggplant, okra, tomatoes, sweet potatoes, and coconuts were grown or imported by Asian immigrant tenant farmers. The sweet short-grain rice called *malagkit*, prized for *kakanin* (rice desserts) was already being grown and used for *mochi* by Japanese Americans. Bay leaves, ginger, peppercorns, vinegar, and garlic were readily available. But not until after World War II could Filipina/o-owned grocery stores import products like *bagoong*, banana leaves, and *patis* (fish sauce). In those intervening years, Filipina/o cooks creatively adapted local ingredients and made substitutions when necessary. Because of the sex-ratio imbalance, Filipinos were forced to learn how to cook for themselves, which challenged traditional gender roles, and most *campo* cooks were men. Filipina immigrants' lives were grueling: they worked as laborers and *campo* cooks, in addition to raising children, keeping house, and maintaining ethnic culture.

When the Depression pushed farm labor wages down to ten cents per hour and service-sector work disappeared, Filipinas/os crowded into tiny rooms in residential hotels and shared grocery and cooking expenses. As aliens, they were ineligible for New Deal relief. Often the one or two Filipinas/os in a group of friends or relatives who had a job would support the rest.[35] To exclusionists, reports of dozens of Filipinos crowding into hotel rooms and eating unfamiliar foods in squalid conditions were further evidence that they were morally and culturally unassimilable and racially unfit for citizenship. In a front-page declaration in the Watsonville, California, newspaper *Evening Pajaronian*, Judge D. W. Rohrback claimed that Filipinos had a "low standard mode of housing and feeding." "Fifteen Filipinos will live in a room or two, sleeping on the floor and contenting themselves with squatting on the floors and eating fish and rice," a horrified Rohrback wrote.[36] Editors of *The Torch*, a Filipina/o American newspaper based in Northern California, dismissed Rohrback's insults. "To discuss the Filipino diet is stupid," the editors responded. "Each nation has a particular diet."[37]

Perhaps the uncles who loudly protested my father's stinky dried-fish lunch were attempting to distance themselves from the stereotype of dirty, emasculated, barbaric, rice-and fish-eating savages popularized by Rohrback (and by Samuel Gompers in his inflammatory 1906 tirade against Chinese workers, "Meat vs. Rice"). Some Filipinos took to extremes the relationship between consumption and Filipina/o fitness for independence. Hilario Moncado, founder of the powerful Filipino Federation of America (FFA), insisted that his members eschew red meat, labor unions, dance halls, drinking, and gambling in favor of a mostly raw, vegetarian diet. The most spiritually dedicated members subsisted on peanut juice they called *mug-mug* and a compressed bar of honey, oats, and raisins.[38] Filipino labor union leaders, whose strikes were often broken by federation scabs, derisively claimed that the diet made FFA members too weak for farmwork. But the second-generation children of FFA members, like Jean Hipolito Labuga, sometimes bent the rules. In the 1930s, Labuga used to trade her peanut butter and jelly sandwiches to her classmates for bologna sandwiches and hot dogs.[39]

Jackrabbit Adobo: Working, Cooking, and Eating in the Campo and the Cannery

By the mid-twentieth century, Filipinas/os, along with Mexicans and other Asians, had transformed California into an agricultural empire and one of the world's largest economies. By 1930, Filipinas/os comprised more than 80 percent of the total number of asparagus workers in the San Joaquin Delta region and almost 14 percent of the total farm labor force in California.[40] Filipinas/os traveled as far north as Alaska for salmon cannery work in the early summer, and as far south as the Imperial Valley to pick grapes in the early fall. Filipinas/os also followed the crops to across California to Washington State, Idaho, and Montana. These laborers picked asparagus, grapes, lettuce, sugar beets, prunes, tomatoes, peaches, apples, berries, melon, potatoes, celery, brussels sprouts, artichokes, onions, hops, and more. Because Filipinas/os occupied the lowest rung of the farm labor racial hierarchy, they received the lowest wages and substandard working and living conditions.

The America about which their domestic science teachers had bragged in the Philippines was far from the reality of the *campo,* the Filipino nickname for the farm labor camp. Filipina/o workers in the Delta and the San Joaquin Valley lacked electricity, running water, and flush toilets. They lived in segregated ramshackle wood bunkhouses, old barns occupied by animals, or abandoned boxcars. In addition to working on farms, the women also had jobs as bookkeepers, contractors, and *campo* cooks.[41] Filipina immigrants expecting gleaming, modern American kitchens were shocked to find that they had to cook over open fires and gather their own firewood and water. "I cooked for about fifty men," recalled Camila Carido.

> We used to complain because they had a bathroom in the [farmer's] house and electricity, but we had a butane stove. I used to have to carry the wood. You have to burn it because you have to cook rice, but I didn't complain. I had to help my husband. I made thirty five cents an hour.[42]

Farmers and contractors charged up to seventy-five cents per day for room and board and served the cheapest possible food—fish and rice—at a time when most workers made a dollar a day. "You have no choice," said George Montero. "You get what they cook . . . I had no car. I had no money."[43] Workers fell into debt because they were charged for room and board during the off-season. Once Filipinas/os rose in the ranks to become contractors, many took advantage of the *encloso* system, in which workers deducted expenses for things like groceries and work tools from their total earnings. The cook, who was sometimes the wife of a laborer or contractor, would also receive a cut. George Montero's workers used the *encloso* system and took turns cooking. All the expenses were divided. "We just get what we want to eat," he said. "If the men want to have roast pig, we get roast pig. Or if they want chicken, we'd just go and buy chicken."[44]

To many Filipina/o immigrants, life in America, even in the *campos* and canneries during the Depression, still occasionally afforded a richer and more varied diet than what they had subsisted on in the province. *Campo* cooking was basic: fish, either fried or in soups, stews, or stir-fries (*gisa*) of meat and vegetables. Leftover rice was fried for breakfast, with eggs and coffee. Chickens' feet, fish heads, and pigs' necks, bellies, tails, and feet were cooked as *sinigang*, adobo, as flavoring in *monggo/balatong* (mung bean stew), or *nilaga* (boiled), since these cuts were flavorful and cheap or free from the butchers and grocers who supplied the camps. A dish in Angeles Monrayo Raymundo's *campo* cooking repertoire in the 1920s and 1930s was pigs' feet cooked *adobado* style (braised with vinegar, soy sauce, and pickling spices).[45] In their parents' farm labor camp in Winton, California, Henry Dacuyan and his sister Helen remember a kitchen that consisted of two giant iron *kawa* (woks) set on brick foundations with gas jets under them and a wood stove. Helen Dacuyan Villaruz remembers cutting vegetables and washing stacks of dishes in the *campo* kitchen.[46]

To supplement these meals, Filipinas/os might enjoy the fruits of their labor: surplus peaches, grapes, asparagus, tomatoes, celery, potatoes, and other fruits and vegetables. "I used to help our boss bake bread," Segunda Reyes remembered. "And then, for the rest of our food, my husband gets potatoes, celery. He would go over there and pick up potatoes by the sack and that's what we eat all day."[47] Filipinas/os raised chickens and planted gardens. In the 1930s and 1940s on the Juanitas family farm in the Delta, the family grew long beans, *patola* (Filipino squash), bitter melon, bell peppers (the young leaves were also eaten), a green called *alugbati*, onions, garlic, water cress, okra, *gowgi* (another Filipino green vegetable), beets, squash, Chinese lettuce and cabbage, and *tanglad* (lemongrass), Violet Juanitas Dutra remembers. Her father Cirilo even made wine from local grapes.[48]

Figure 7.2. Eudosia Juanitas and her children in their vegetable garden in the San Joaquin Delta area, July 1941. Juanitas, who arrived in Stockton in 1936, grew Philippine vegetables such as bitter melon (*ampalaya*) and *malunggay* to feed her family and to sell. Courtesy of Aileen Boyer.

Filipinas/os took advantage of their surroundings to feed themselves. In the 1920s and 1930s, the waterways of the San Joaquin Delta teemed with wildlife and wild vegetables. The forests and mountains surrounding Seattle, Dorothy Cordova remembers, were rich in game such as deer, as well as greens, birds, and exotic mushrooms. Filipinas/os fished in Delta rivers for salmon, catfish, and sea bass, gathered river snails (Filipinas/os called these *sisi*) and frogs, hunted pigeons and rabbits, and foraged for greens and mushrooms. "It was great because we really weren't hungry when we lived out there [in the Delta]," remembered Anita Bautista, who was raised in the Delta in French Camp, California. "There were jackrabbits. There were cottontails. There were pheasants. There were ducks that flew in. We had the river there. The bass would be huge." Bautista's Ilocano father did most of the cooking for their large family in the *campo*. "I remember my father making the jackrabbit adobo," she remembered. "And him shooting those illegal swans out in the asparagus field. Vegetables [were] out there growing wild. The pigweed, mustard greens." The family also had a garden, chickens, and goats.[49]

In his memoirs, Alejandro Raymundo recalled that his family subsisted on rice, soy sauce, and mushrooms during the hardest years of the Depression: "1931 was depression time, and boy was it tough," he wrote. "Those who have money would buy me a sack of rice and a bottle of *soyo* and that would last me over a month." Raymundo collected tree mushrooms from willow trees. "Rice and fried mushroom," he wrote. "That's all we eat 3 times a day. Sometimes I wonder how we survived."[50] Foraging could be dangerous, however. In 1934, sixteen Filipinos died from eating poisonous toadstools they had found near their lettuce camp in San Luis Obispo County.[51] If Rizaline Raymundo's father Alejandro Raymundo was terrified that his family might starve, his children did not sense it. Many Filipinas/os growing up during the Depression felt fortunate to have any kind of food and shelter. "Hard times I wasn't aware of, we always had food on the table and a roof over our heads," Rizaline Raymundo said. "Most of the time the food was rice and mushroom, rice and fish—whatever was on the table we ate it." Raymundo said she learned how to eat fish head, shells from the river, tripe, fried intestines, chickens' feet, and frogs' legs. "You name it, we ate it," she laughed. "Filipinos have a knack for making any kind of food edible and delicious." When their supply of rice fell, Raymundo's mother turned to the *campo* cook's supply of *tutong,* the crispy bottom of the rice pot, which he stored in burlap.[52]

The wild salmon swimming through Delta streams and rivers were prized catches, although fishing for them was illegal. In her diaries, Angeles Raymundo recorded the happy fall day in 1928 when her husband Alejandro and his buddies caught huge salmon by hand as the fish struggled from the ocean up a shallow stream to lay their eggs. "He made sinigang out of the head and we fried some of the stomach," she wrote. The rest of the fish was cleaned, salted, and preserved to be shared with neighbors.[53] Jean Hipolito Labuga of Livingston, California, remembers that her father and his friends would leave at night to fish illegally. "They did this so they could feed their families," she remembered. Labuga's parents would salt and dry the fish to make it last through the winter, and Labuga's mother also dried and pickled eggplant.[54] Lillian and Violet Juanitas helped their uncles and cousins clean, salt, and dry fish. "The fish were dried on the roof and when they were stiff and completely dried, they were stacked and bagged and used to help stretch food supplies," Lillian recalled. The fish were stinky, she remembered.[55]

Massive celebrations marked the end of asparagus season in June in the Delta, and the end of lettuce in the Salinas area in early December.[56] The centerpiece of the party would be a *lechon,* or whole roasted pig (or several, depending on the size of the work crew), cooked in a pit dug in the fields. "When we finished the crop, we would celebrate the end of the season, [because] that's when everybody gets paid," remembered Moreno Balantac, who was born and raised in Stockton. Every part of the pig was used. Balantac remembered that they used the blood and organs to make *diniguan,* or pork blood stew, and fried the belly for *bagnet,* an Ilocano specialty. Balantac also learned different methods that Visayans and Tagalogs used to make *biko,* a brown-sugar rice cake. "What I learned to do was squeeze the coconut, fry the juice, and mix the residue with the rice and then bake it," he said.[57]

Seal *Adobo*, Bear *Nilaga*, and Salmon Head *Sinigang*: Cooking in Alaska

From the 1910s to the 1970s, Filipinas/os constituted the main labor force in Alaska's salmon canneries. Bunkhouse cooks prepared cheap and monotonous meals of rice alongside salmon, bottom fish, and dried seafood, according to historian Donald Guimary. Contractors closed the kitchens at 8 P.M., hoarded supplies, and forced workers to buy expensive snacks like chocolate and biscuits from the company stores.[58] Sinforoso L. Ordona remembers that in 1935 in Alaska, his work crew nearly starved. "We had those biscuits with no butter, no jelly, no coffee, no sugar, no milk, just jet black coffee and we work twelve, fourteen hours," he said. "We only have one biscuit, no eggs for breakfast." For lunch, the cook made a pot of *munggo* beans with only a handful of pigs' tails to be shared among several dozen men. "We have to fish for the pig tail, no kidding," he recalled.[59]

Filipina/o workers in Alaska scavenged and foraged for additional food. The salmon heads and tails that the cannery discarded were turned into *sinigang* (sour soup). Local crabs were caught and eaten, Ordona remembered. Workers planted vegetable gardens and scavenged for the local wild peas that Filipinas/os called *bukayong.* Some would also raise pigs, he remembered. Filipinos also resorted to illegally hunting deer, which they had to hide from their cannery supervisors. "We even kill a bear, a bear to eat, a black bear," Ordona recalled. "It's like beef." Ordona remembers that men were so hungry that they were eating berries and raw mussels, clams, and sea snails they plucked from the shore. Only a telegram reporting the death of a friend by tainted seafood stopped them.[60] Workers in the salmon canneries improvised their own *bagoong* and *patis* (fish sauce) by salting and fermenting salmon scraps in barrels. "I would salt the salmon, layer by layer, into a 25 gallon barrel made of wood," Sleepy Caballero of Stockton remembered.

> Some of the old timers would get a full size salmon and let it dry out in the shower room, or some would hang them in the enclosed porch. . . . After I filled my barrel, I would immediately go down to the post office and mail it home to my mother in Stockton.[61]

Figure 7.3. Filipino asparagus cutters celebrate the end of the asparagus season with a two-hundred-pound *lechon*, a whole roast pig, at a farm labor camp on Ryer Island in the San Joaquin Delta, June 17, 1938. Courtesy of Antonio Somera.

When Filipino cannery workers unionized in 1937, their food demands reflected their newfound power, their long years in America, and their desire for a more varied diet.[62] In the late 1930s, union representative Prudencio Mori of Local 37 told the supervisor at the Sunnypoint Cannery that their meals did not make for happy workers. "We are served eggs and rice every morning," Mori remembered. "Rice and boiled salmon at noon, rice and boiled salmon or fried salmon at night. That was the menu throughout the whole season and many people are not fed properly. They are quite unhappy." Mori demanded bacon and eggs, and jam with bread for breakfast. "Because there are some of us who have been here in the United States for so long, do not eat rice for our breakfast, we would like some bread, bacon, and eggs," he said. Mori also won his demand for turkey or chicken every Sunday.[63]

Filipino men who married Native Alaskan women adapted Philippine techniques to local ingredients. My father would "hunt moose, porcupine, ptarmigan, geese and ducks for our food," said Lisa Dolchok, daughter of a Cebuano father and a mother of Aleut and Yup'ik heritage. "He cooked with *bagoong*. He taught us to cook *adobo:* beaver meat, moose, goose, duck, or whatever meat there was at home. We ate seal meat, seal oil, and dried fish, and rice."[64] Dorothy Larson, the daughter of Jacinto Tagabao Pelagio, a native of Vigan,

Ilocos Sur, and an Iñupiat Eskimo, Lucille Gabriel, remembers well her father's cooking in Alaska. "My father did most of the cooking," she recalled. "And he used local meats for his adobo: moose meat, porcupine meat, beaver meat. . . . He dried seal meat and called it *tapa,* or jerky. And of course, we had rice."[65]

Adobo "At Least Once a Week": Eating and Surviving in the City

Beginning in the 1920s, Filipina/o cooks opened restaurants, grocery stores, and even soda fountains in Chinatowns and Filipina/o American neighborhoods. "In the United States the Filipinos never get quite satisfactorily fed unless they eat *adobo* at least once a week," declared writer Manuel Buaken in his 1948 memoir *I Have Lived with the American People.* Buaken's favorite was the Universal Café, opened in 1938 on Second Street in Los Angeles's Little Manila. There, Buaken feasted on *gulay* Ilocano (Ilocano vegetables), *ampalayang manok* (chicken with bitter melon), *escabecheng isda* (fish cooked with peppers and tomatoes), and *bagoong* with onions. "Here is a place where the pressure of racial differences is relaxed. . . . Here is a place where one hears and speaks one's own dialect without hostile or curious glances. . . . Here is a place to feed your body and relax your mind and feel at home."[66]

The Universal Café was only one of several dozen Los Angeles Filipina/o American eateries. According to scholar Carina Monica Montoya, there were many Filipina/o- owned restaurants in and around Los Angeles's Little Manila, including the Ace Café, Busy Bee, Luzon, La Divisoria, LVM Café, La Union, Lucky Spot, Moonlight, Three Stars, and My-T-Good Café.[67] More than a dozen Filipina/o restaurants also could be found in Stockton's Little Manila neighborhood from the 1910s to the 1940s, including a soda fountain, Filipinas Café, International Café, Luzon Café, Lafayette Lunch Counter, La Union Café, and Mayon Restaurant. As early as 1927, Filipinos in Brooklyn, New York, could satisfy their cravings for *adobong baboy* (pork adobo), *sinigang isda,* and *sinigang visaya* (fish in sour broth) at E. G. Lopez's Manila Karihan Restaurant at 47 Sands Street.[68] San Francisco's earliest Philippine restaurants were Las Filipinas Restaurant in Chinatown at 623 Pacific and the Manila Restaurant at 606 Jackson, both opening in 1930, and the Luzon Café, the New Luneta Restaurant, and the Baguio Café, all located in Manilatown near and/or on Kearny Street.[69] In San Diego, Filipinas/os patronized the Manila Café, downtown on Market Street in the 1930s, and then after World War II, the Bataan Café on Island Street.[70] By the 1940s, Filipinas/os in Alaska ran more than a dozen Filipino restaurants.[71]

Most of these restaurants melded regional styles and cooked very basic Philippine classics in order to appeal to the widest possible audience, while others specialized in Visayan or Ilocana/o cooking. In the 1930s, the LVM Café in Little Manila on First Street in Los Angeles served Ilocano specialties like *gulay Ilocano* (Ilocano vegetables), along with *sinigang hipon* (shrimp in sour broth), each for sixty-five cents.[72] Also in the 1930s, Bibiana Castillano's Philippine Café in Seattle's Chinatown catered to Seattle's heavily Ilocana/o community, often featuring an Ilocano favorite, *calding* (goat meat). Her daughter Dorothy Cordova recalled the time her uncles brought a goat to her house in Seattle on their way to the restaurant. "The goat just break in that door and run all over," her uncle Sinforoso Ordona remembered. "We chased him." They eventually caught and ate it.[73]

Filipina/o restaurants, grocery stores, and other ethnic businesses in Little Manilas also served as informal banks, community post offices, social halls, employment centers, and gathering points for Filipinas/os. One example was my *lolo*'s Ambo Mabalon's restaurant, the Lafayette Lunch Counter, which became one of the most enduring businesses in Stockton's Little Manila. In 1931, my *lolo* Ambo bought the restaurant, located at 50 East Lafayette Street, from Margarita Balucas, an Ilocana entrepreneur who had opened it in 1929. Mabalon offered credit and a permanent address to which customers could send their mail while they followed the crops. Lolo Ambo served food familiar to most Filipinas/os, like chicken and pork adobo, *diniguan, pancit, sinigang*, beef *nilaga* (boiled beef soup), and *sarciado* (meat braised in tomato sauce). He saved cooking fats to make his own soap, which he sold, and made his own dried beef, or *tapa*. By using local ingredients and/or ingredients like salmon and asparagus that were harvested and brought in by Filipina/o workers, he helped create a distinctive Filipina/o American cuisine in Stockton. Filipino jazz bands on their way to gigs at the Little Manila dance halls or at community events would stop first to eat at the Lafayette Lunch Counter.[74] "The first spot [we hung around at] was Ambo's Lafayette Lunch," Policarpo Porras remembered. "So that Lafayette Lunch is the oldest Filipino restaurant in Stockton!"[75] My grandfather sold the restaurant to a Filipina/o couple in 1979, and they ran it until 1983. It then was a Mexican restaurant until the city tore down the building for a McDonald's in 1999.

Many immigrants became dishwashers, busboys, and pantrymen in the hotels and restaurants of major cities, with a handful working their way up to becoming head chefs. For example, Cavite native Paul Paular worked his way up from a dishwasher to the head chef at a fine Los Angeles restaurant, eventually becoming the head chef at the luxurious Hotel Stockton in the 1940s. In his retirement, he even had his own cooking show on Sacramento local television in the 1970s.[76] Ilocano immigrant Pete Valoria became the head chef of

Figure 7.4. Bibiana Castillano (center) ran the popular Philippine Café in the Chinatown district in Seattle, Washington. She specialized in Ilocano food. This day's specialty, advertised in the window, was *calding*, or goat. Photograph courtesy of Dorothy Cordova.

Pioneer Tamale in the 1940s, a popular restaurant in Stockton, a position he held for three decades.[77] Miguel "Mike" Castillano became the head chef at Seattle's finest restaurants and retired as the executive chef of the legendary Seattle seafood chain Ivar's in the 1970s.[78]

Let's Go Chop Suey!

Filipina/o American restaurant food was satisfying, but on special occasions, many Filipinas/os would "go chop suey." For many Filipinas/os, going out for Chinese food was an important symbol of their Americanization. In the Philippines, "they used to kid us, saying, 'When you go to America you will not see any more rice there,'" recalled one immigrant who arrived in San Francisco in 1926. But "the first thing my father did when he met us was to take us to a chop suey house where there was lots of rice."[79] Anita Bautista's favorite chop suey place was Gan Chy, in Stockton's Chinatown. "We would go to celebrate special occasions such as paydays, birthdays, Christenings, end of the asparagus season, [and it was] a place to take our relatives from Hawai'i," she recalled.[80]

Filipinas/os developed a taste for Chinese food in the Chinese gambling houses. "In the afternoon, there is a table full of all kinds of food—you just

Figure 7.5. Pablo "Ambo" Mabalon, the author's grandfather (left), with a friend in front of his Lafayette Lunch Counter, circa 1940s. He ran the restaurant as the owner-cook from 1931 to 1979. Author's own collection.

help yourself," remembered Alfonso Yasonia of Lumban, Laguna, of the gambling houses in 1920s Seattle.[81] In the Delta's Chinese gambling houses, owners served tea and coffee, doughnuts, rice gruel, chow mein, soup, rice, and chop suey.[82] As scholar Heather Lee writes in chapter 3 of this book, by the turn of the century, Chinese American restaurants exploded in popularity. Most of them, as historian Renqiu Yu notes, stoked the national craze for "chop suey," the stir-fried "Chinese" dish of diced meats and vegetables. By tweaking their menus and popularizing "Oriental" decor and curtained booths, these restaurants gave the impression of being sophisticated and exotic.[83]

Chop suey restaurants were popular for several reasons. Because of the long presence of Chinese in the Philippines, many immigrants already were familiar with Chinese food, and Chinatowns often were the only places Filipinas/os could live. The food was served family style (in large bowls or platters for sharing) and with rice, so the food could be stretched. But most important, as scholar Dorothy Cordova points out, Filipinas/os were never refused service, insulted, or segregated in the back rooms, as they were at white-owned restaurants.[84] In Stockton, Filipinas/os patronized Gan Chy Restaurant at 215 S. El Dorado Street, New China Café, and, for banquets, the glamorous On Lock Sam restaurant on 125 East Washington Street. Many of the most popular chop suey houses, such as Seattle's Tai Tung (which opened in 1935) and San Francisco's Yat Gan Low advertised in Filipino American ethnic newspapers across the West Coast.

In 1934, the editors of the Salinas-based *Philippines Mail* chided Filipinas/os for abandoning their *karihans* (informal restaurants) for chop suey. "Rizal Day celebrations, birthday, wedding and farewell festivities are not complete without taking a trip to some chop suey establishment," the editors complained.[85] Sure, "we go to [Lafayette Lunch Counter] and Mr. Candelario's restaurant [the Luzon Café]," said Concepcion Lagura of Stockton. But "when they say, 'Let's go and eat!' We go to the chop suey place."[86] This attitude enraged the Luzon Café's owner-cook Claro Candelario, whose café in Little Manila was featured in *America Is in the Heart*. "One thing about the Filipino, if he has no job, he comes to beg you to feed him," he recalled. "But when he has some money, he does not go to you. You see him eating at the Chinese restaurants!" Candelario would seek out his debtors inside crowded chop suey joints. "I go to the guy and ask, "Hey, when will you pay! And he says, 'You're embarrassing me!'" he recalled. "I says, "You owe me already about $15, and here you are eating!"[87]

"Up to My Elbows Washing Rice": Filipina/o American Home Cooking

In addition to the restaurants, *campos*, and canneries, the roots of early Filipina/o American cuisine can be found in Filipinas/os' creative and resourceful adaptations. The Filipina/o American gender roles expressed in the sexual division of labor meant that food work—the labor of preparing meals—was placed largely on women's shoulders, usually mothers or oldest daughters. As Valerie Matsumoto explains in her research on Japanese American women in chapter 13, these responsibilities gave Filipinas more power to shape Filipina/o American ethnic culture. Filipina/o families often shared their meals with large extended families of male cousins, neighbors, distant relatives, and even strangers, which increased women's burdens and responsibilities. In these settings, Tagalogs, Visayans, and Ilocanas/os socialized with and married each other, blended regional favorites, and shared recipes. Accordingly, these meals shaped the ways in which Filipinas/os thought about food, ethnic culture, and their families.

The improvisation of the early Filipina/o American kitchen was a result of demographics. The lack of both elders and many ingredients gave women the burden—and also the freedom—to adapt American ingredients to Filipino recipes and to use substitutions, creativity, and improvisation. "My mother was so young when she came, she had to learn from the other women how to cook," said Eleanor Galvez Olamit, whose mother arrived in California as a young girl in the 1910s. Asuncion Nicolas left Jaro, Iloilo, to join her mother and stepfather in San Francisco in 1929. "I hate cooking," she said. "When I came to the United States, I [had] never cooked in the islands, and my mother did all the cooking." When Nicolas married at age nineteen, her thirty-two-year-old husband, a barber, gave her a cooking pot. For dinner each evening, she would copy a pretty table setting she found in *Life* magazine and boil meat and vegetables in the pot. "To me it was delicious," she laughed. Each night, Nicolas said her husband would take one look inside the pot, and say, "Dress up! Let's go chop suey!"[88]

Camila Labor Carido, who arrived as a teenager from the Visayas, learned from her friends.

> I learned from other cultures, especially cooking here [in America]. . . . The woman who cooks the *guinataan* [coconut milk soup, either savory or sweet], she is from Luzon, where Manila is. . . . And the women who come from the southern part, Mindanao, they have different cooking, too, because they have Moros [Muslims] there. They use different utensils. The women also taught the other[s] the American customs.[89]

Some Filipinas, like Cebuana former schoolteacher Segunda Reyes, grew up with servants, so *campo* life was a rude shock.

> Over here, I have to get up early in the morning, especially when cooking for the boys in asparagus—1 o'clock in the morning or 2 o'clock. . . . I have to get up and make [a] fire. We get our wood outside and we get our water outside. And I was crying. Oh, it was sad.[90]

To feed families and guests, resourceful Filipina/o cooks used animal parts that butchers, fishmongers, and grocers discarded, and they stretched food creatively. Dorothy Cordova remembers that the slaughterhouses in Seattle gave away for free pigs' heads, tripe, bellies, tails, and feet. "Pig tail makes the best *adobo*," she remembered. Her mother cooked lots of vegetables, using meat as a flavoring. She recalled that in Seattle, Filipinas/os would catch fish called "shiners," eaten raw with lots of ginger, vinegar, salt, pepper, spices, and chilis.[91] Canned goods required no refrigeration and could be stretched; a can of corned beef (*carne norte*) sautéed with onions, garlic, potatoes, and cabbage eaten with rice could feed many people.[92] The cans of salmon that workers brought as gifts were treats. Dorothy Cordova and her siblings would eat the salmon with hot rice, a fried egg, and chopped tomatoes.[93]

Evangeline Canonizado Buell's grandmother's poker group in Oakland, California, was a mix of women of Tagalog, Visayan, and Ilocana ancestry who shared recipes and brought their specialties to the weekly game. Buell recalled that the *biko and bibingka* they brought "came steaming hot out of the oven, the aroma rich and tantalizing. I could hardly wait to eat." As they played, they drank Rainier ale and talked in their different dialects about cooking "American." "When it came time to eat, I could hear all the different dialects' terms for cooked rice: *kanon* [Cebuano and Waray], *nasi, inapoy* [Ilocano], *and bugas* [Waray, Cebuano, and Aklanon for uncooked rice]."[94] Buell's grandmother taught her how to cook Filipino foods, particularly how to grate coconuts by squatting over a special iron grater attached to a box called a *kuskus*. Her grandmother devised her own recipe for *lumpia* wrappers, and she substituted canned tomato sauce for the *annatto* seeds traditionally used for coloring.

In many Filipina/o American families, Filipino food was a mix of different regional favorites or cooking styles. For Deanna Daclan Balantac, a second-generation Pinay from Stockton, Filipino food consisted of her mother Paula's Capangpangan specialties and her father Rosauro's Cebuano favorites. In Cebu, corn and sweet potatoes were the preferred starches. Rice fields and sugar plantations dot Pampanga Province in central Luzon, but compromise meant that they did not have rice at every meal. Her mother Paula Dizon Daclan was proud of her Capangpangan specialties, like cured pork called *tocino, lumpia*, and *puto* (rice cakes). "The other thing was, my dad, in the Visayas they cooked with a lot of coconut," she remembered. "So we would have lots of coconut kinds of stuff for our celebration. So it was a combination of our Kapampangan and Visayan Cebuano type cooking."[95]

Regional dishes and cooking styles were also shared widely with different groups because of *campo* cooking and the large gatherings at Filipina/o homes for dinners and celebrations. Seattle-based nurse Maria Abastilla Beltran and her brother and husband regularly hosted up to ten additional people for dinner every night. "We would cook for seven people and then [at the table] we are sixteen! . . . That's why we always cook more, because you don't know who was coming."[96] When she was first married in 1932, Camila Carido and her husband Leon rented a tiny apartment for $11 a month in Little Manila in Stockton, where they fed to up to five extra guests per night. "They would say, 'Can we sleep with you and we can help pay the grocery?' How could they afford to go to the hotel at 25 cents a night?" She remembered that one hundred pounds of rice cost $1.95 and three pounds of sea bass cost twenty-five cents. She cooked simple meals of rice, fish, and, occasionally, a fried pork chop on a kerosene stove in a kitchen without a refrigerator, with only a barrel for storage.[97]

Evangeline Canonizado Buell explained that Filipinos would bring her grandmother crates of fresh vegetables and fruits, like asparagus and tomatoes from Stockton, to repay her hospitality.[98] Deanna Daclan Balantac said that it was a family tradition to cook extra and to set the table for ten or twelve, even though her family consisted of seven.

> That's why I never thought we were poor, because we always had all these foods to feed all these people. . . . I was always up to my elbows washing rice, because you never knew who would come through the door. . . . I just knew that whenever we cooked, we had two pots of rice.[99]

Second-generation Pinay Angelina Bantillo Magdael remembered her parents whispering in the kitchen.

> My mother would say, "You don't realize our meal tonight is so limited, lucky we have enough for the children." . . . And my father would say, "Do you know that these men had not eaten for several days?" and he would say, "I'm sure our food could stretch." And somehow it did.

Dinner was sometimes only boiled rice with some milk and a little sugar.

> My sisters and brother liked it, but I could hardly swallow it and my mother would always say, "Be thankful, at least we have something to eat, when we don't have a grain of rice in the rice can, then that's when we are in trouble." And to this day, I just don't like rice pudding. It gives me sad memories.

Many Filipinas in communities throughout Hawai'i and the West Coast capitalized on Filipinas'/os' craving for home cooking, developing lucrative side businesses in which they sold *lumpia,* rice cakes, *binangkal* (a Visayan sesame doughnut), Ilocano favorites like *cascaron* (sweet rice doughnuts), banana fritters, and other desserts, or even surplus vegetables from their gardens, on the streets of Filipina/o American neighborhoods, at dances, in pool halls, and at cockfights. These businesses popularized Ilocano, Tagalog, and Visayan regional cooking amongst Filipinas/os with roots in other regions. Lucia Cordova, whose roots were in Iloilo, brought her successful fried *lumpia*–making business from Stockton to Seattle in the 1940s. When Fred Cordova brought a basket of his mother's *lumpia* to a Filipino Club gathering at Seattle University, they were a great hit, as his mostly Ilocana/o classmates had never seen *lumpia* before. When Dorothy Laigo, an Ilocana, married Fred Cordova, one of her first tasks was to learn how to make the paper-thin *balat,* the *lumpia* wrapper, on a cast-iron griddle. "I burned all my fingers," she laughed.[100]

To make ends meet, Virgilia Bantillo sold Tagalog snacks like *lumpiang sariwa* (fresh *lumpia*) and *maruya* (banana fritters) in Stockton. "My father went out with baskets to the pool hall and even to the restrooms, and he really sold it!" Angel Magdael remembers.[101] It was an all-day affair for Bantillo to make the delicate *lumpia* wrappers, using flour, water, and eggs. She sold the wrappers at ten cents apiece to other Filipinas. Her younger daughter, Leatrice Bantillo Perez, sometimes walked several miles across town to deliver them. "She'd make a hundred, so she made $10, I think, for that," Leatrice Bantillo Perez explained. "That helped the expenses, a little extra."[102] But even with side businesses, money was a constant worry for the Bantillos and other families in the 1930s. "Very unlucky day for us," Virgilia wrote in her diary on March 19, 1939. "Broke like anything. I feel blue. I shed tears."[103]

By the 1930s and 1940s, the food at Filipina/o American family celebrations had evolved into a typical Filipina/o American buffet: Philippine foods from various regions, Filipina/o American adaptations, and American foods. At Evangeline Canonizado Buell's home, a birthday party in the 1930s featured potato salad, fried chicken, sheet cake, a whole baked salmon, roast duck, meat and seafood dishes, *biko,* fried *lumpia*, adobo, and *pansit* (noodles).[104] Virgilia Bantillo's family celebrations usually included *biko, lumpia, lechon,* and *maruya*, as well as roast chicken, Virginia ham, and a sheet cake. She served roast turkey and pumpkin pie for Thanksgiving dinner, and she cooked breakfasts of grapefruit, oranges, cereal, eggs, ham and sausage, and buns with butter.[105]

World War II

World War II profoundly transformed Filipina/o American life and, as a result, the Filipina/o American table. Wartime rations meant more sacrifice and deprivation for a community still recovering from the Depression. The incarceration of Japanese Americans on the West Coast allowed Filipinos take over their empty stores and farms, and Filipino-owned restaurants and grocery stores flourished. After initially being turned away, Filipinos were allowed to join the U.S. Army, and special Filipino regiments were activated in Salinas, California, and were sent to Ford Ord in San Francisco. At the fiesta they threw when their training was over, soldiers introduced their white command-ing officers to *lechon*. After the war, the community was transformed. Citi-zenship enabled Filipinas/os to buy land, so hundreds throughout the West Coast began farming. The Filipinas who streamed into the United States in large numbers after the war further transformed Filipina/o American cuisine. Indeed, the food these new immigrants tasted on arriving may have seemed foreign. Seal *adobo*? Salmon *sinigang*?

What these newcomers could not have known was that this new Filipina/o American cuisine had taken shape as a result of several factors. Through the public schools, the American colonial regime transformed how Filipinas/os thought about food. The sex-ratio imbalance forced Filipino men to learn how to cook, a task usually left to women in the Philippines. Moreover, the lack of Philippine ingredients; conditions in the fields and canneries where Filipi-nas/os were forced to cook and eat; the abundance of unfamiliar yet delicious local foods foraged from the land and water; the coming together of Ilocanas/os, Tagalogs, and Visayans around dinner tables; and their migratory life all determined what early Filipina/o immigrants and their children cooked, ate, and considered "Filipino." The American born-children of these families ate this cuisine and knew it not as Visayan, Tagalog, or Ilocano but as Filipino. This "bridge generation"—those Filipinas/os born in the United States before World War II—connected the consumption of these foods to their identities as Filipina/o Americans and attached memory, cultural pride, and family to their consumption.

* * *

I return to my father's *tuyo*. By the 1960s, perhaps stinky *tuyo* was no longer a favorite for these Filipina/o Americans, when they could choose from an array of foods, including beef, chicken, pork, goat, a variety of vegetables, processed and canned goods, and restaurant fare. Perhaps this is why they turned against the dried fish, my father's "old dependable," that had sustained them in their provincial youth and during the deprivation of the Depression. But they never abandoned their rice. In June 1946, a rice shortage brought on by wartime rationing pushed hundreds of Filipino workers to demand rice in their daily diets or otherwise walk off the Delta asparagus fields. In fact, hundreds of the five thousand Filipinos working the asparagus that spring left their jobs, devastating the farmers.[106] My father was only partly wrong when he lambasted Filipino Americans for forgetting their roots in fish and rice!

Notes

For their assistance and inspiration with this essay, I thank Profs. Fred and Dorothy Cordova of the Filipino American National Historical Society / National Pinoy Archives, Kay Dumlao-Doherty, Garrett Doherty and Gil and Esper Dumlao for hosting me in Seattle, Christina Moretta of the San Francisco History Center, Mitchell Yangson of the San Francisco Public Library's Filipino American Center, Amy Besa, Aileen Boyer, Antonio Somera, Alex Orquiza, Emily Porcincula Lawsin, Allyson Tintiangco-Cubales, Anita Bautista, Violet Juanitas Dutra, Rizaline Raymundo and Patricia Ann Raymundo, Leatrice Perez, and Valerie Matsumoto, who taught me as a young student at UCLA to pay attention to food. I owe a great debt to the great cooks of my food-obsessed family: my *asawa* Jesus Perez Gonzales; my late *tatay*, Ernesto T. Mabalon; my mother, Christine Bohulano Bloch, my late grandma, Concepcion Moreno Bohulano, who was, like me, a public school teacher who sells *biko* and *bibingka* on the side; my sister Darleen Mabalon Kelley; my aunties and uncle; and my cousins, nieces, and nephews. What a joy to have all of you around the table!

1. Ernesto Tirona Mabalon, interview with Dawn Bohulano Mabalon, May 25, 1996, Stockton, California.

2. Steffi San Buenaventura, "Filipino Folk Spirituality and Immigration: From Mutual Aid to Religion," in *New Spiritual Homes: Religion and Asian Americans,* ed. David K. Yoo (Honolulu: University of Hawai'i Press and UCLA Asian American Studies Center, 1999), 53.

3. Hasia Diner, *Hungering for America: Italian, Irish & Jewish Foodways in the Age of Migration* (Cambridge, MA: Harvard University Press, 2001), 10.

4. The Tydings-McDuffie Act in 1934 reclassified Filipinas/os from "nationals" to aliens and limited immigration to fifty per year. Until 1946, Filipinas/os were barred from becoming naturalized citizens.

5. George Sanchez, *Becoming Mexican American* (New York: Oxford University Press, 1995), 11–12.

6. Diner, *Hungering for America*, 19.

7. Doreen Fernandez, "Food and War," in *Vestiges of War: The Philippine-American War and the Aftermath of an Imperial Dream*, ed. Angel Velasco Shaw and Luis H. Francia (New York: New York University Press, 2002), 237.

8. Monina A. Mercado, "The Geography of the Filipino Stomach," in *The Culinary Culture of the Philippines,* ed. Gilda Cordero-Fernando (Manila: Bancom Audiovision Corporation, 1976), 10.

9. Doreen Fernandez, "One Dish Wonder," April 24, 2002 (handout from Amy Besa in her cooking course in San Francisco, May 2011); Doreen Fernandez, *Palayok: Philippine Food through Time, on Site, in the Pot* (Manila: Bookmark, 2000) 6; Doreen Fernandez, *Tikim: Essays on Philippine Food and Culture* (Manila: Anvil Publishing, 1994), 62, 223; Doreen Fernandez, *Kinilaw: A Philippine Cuisine of Freshness* (Manila: Bookmark, 1991). Also see Gilda Cordero-Fernando, ed., *The Culinary Culture of the Philippines* (Manila: Bancom Audiovision Corporation, 1976); and Felice Prudente Sta. Maria, *The Governor-General's Kitchen: Philippine Culinary Vignettes and Period Recipes, 1521–1935* (Manila: Anvil Publishing, 2006).

10. Fernandez, *Tikim*, 224.

11. Ibid.

12. See Marina Espina, *Filipinos in Louisiana* (New Orleans: A. F. Laborde), 1988; and Wayne Curtis, Dave McAninch, and James Peterson, "Shrimp," *Saveur*, March 2007.

13. Sta. Maria, *The Governor-General's Kitchen,* 43.
14. Fernandez, *Tikim,* 196.
15. Enriqueta David-Perez, *Recipes of the Philippines* (Manila: Capitol Publishing House, 1956).
16. Carlos Bulosan, *America Is in the Heart: A Personal History* (Seattle: University of Washington Press, 1973), 33–34.
17. Ibid., 35.
18. Honorante Mariano, "The Filipino Immigrants" (master's thesis, University of Southern California, 1933), 14.
19. *VOICES: A Filipino American Oral History* (Stockton, CA: Filipino Oral History, 1984), n.p.
20. Pablo Mabalon, interview with Angelina Bantillo Magdael, Filipino Oral History, Stockton, CA, 1981.
21. Camila Carido, interview with Dawn Bohulano Mabalon, June 2002, Stockton, CA.
22. Carido, interview.
23. *VOICES: A Filipino American Oral History.*
24. Alberta Alcoy Asis, interview, Demonstration Project for Asian Americans (DPAA), Filipino American National Historical Society (FANHS), Seattle, WA.
25. Henry T. Lewis, *Ilocano Rice Farmers: A Comparative Study of Two Philippine Barrios* (Honolulu: University of Hawai'i Press, 1971), 24–25.
26. "Domestic Science," *The Philippine Teacher* 3, no. 5 (October 1905): 19; Records of the Bureau of Insular Affairs, Record Group 350, National Archives and Records Administration, College Park, MD.
27. Laura Shapiro's survey of the domestic science movement is the classic work on this movement. See her *Perfection Salad* (Berkeley: University of California Press, 2008).
28. *Housekeeping and Household Arts: A Manual for Work with Girls in the Elementary Schools of the Philippines* (Manila: Bureau of Education, 1911), UC Berkeley Library. Photographs and reports from domestic science classes appear regularly in the annual reports of the Bureau of Education. See the annual reports of the Bureau of Education, esp. those for 1917 and 1931, National Archives and Records Administration, Bureau of Insular Affairs, Record Group 350.
29. Camila Carido, interview with Dawn Bohulano Mabalon, February 19, 1996, Stockton, CA.
30. Fernandez, "Food and War," 241. See also Fernandez, *Palayok*; and her essays in *Tikim.*
31. From "'Forks Are Progress': Domesticity, Women, and American Education in the Philippines," paper presented by Elisa Miller, Rhode Island College, at the 123rd annual American Historical Association meeting, New York City, January 3, 2009; also see the posters of the Board of Education, General Classified Files, 1898–1945, General Records, 1914–1945, Box 746, File 1092, Record Group 350, National Archives, College Park, MD.
32. Dean Worcester, *The Philippines: Past and Present* (New York: Macmillan, 1914), 404.
33. *Culinary Arts in the Tropics,* ed. Carlos Quirino (ca. 1922; repr., Manila: Regal Publishing, 1978).
34. Sucheng Chan, *This Bittersweet Soil: The Chinese in California Agriculture, 1860–1910.* (Berkeley: University of California Press. 1989), 269.
35. Fred Floresca, DPAA interview, FANHS Seattle.

36. "Resolution Flaying Filipinos Drawn by Judge D. W. Rohrback," *Evening Pajaronian,* (Watsonville, Santa Cruz County, CA), January 10, 1930, 1.

37. Emory S. Bogardus, "Anti-Filipino Race Riots," reprinted in *Letters in Exile,* ed. Jesse Quinsaat (Los Angeles: University of California Asian American Studies Center, 1976), 52.

38. Steffi San Buenaventura, "Filipino Folk Spirituality and Religion," *Amerasia Journal* 22, no.1 (1996): 21.

39. "Hipolito Family," in *Talk Story.*

40. Mariano, "The Filipino Immigrants," 30; "Migratory Labor in California," State Relief Administration of California, California Labor Federation Papers, Folder 10, Box 15, Labor Archives and Research Center, San Francisco State University.

41. Field notes, Box 2.

42. Camila Carido, interview with Dawn Bohulano Mabalon, February 19, 1996, Stockton, California.

43. *VOICES: A Filipino American Oral History*, unpaginated.

44. George Montero, in *VOICES: A Filipino American Oral History*, n.p.

45. Angeles Monrayo Raymundo, "Filipino Americans: Forever Our Legacy," *Filipino Journal* 5, no. 5 (1998–1999), recipes, Santa Clara Valley Chapter of the Filipino American National Historical Society, 93.

46. Helen Dacuyan Villaruz, "A Story of a Filipino Family in Winton," and Henry Dacuyan, "Growing Up in a Filipino Farm Labor Camp," both in *Talk Story: An Anthology of Stories by Filipino Americans of the Central Valley of California,* Filipino American National Historical Society, Central Valley Chapter (Merced, CA: Carpenter Printing, 2008), 15.

47. Segunda Reyes, interview with Mary Inosanto, DPAA, Stockton, CA., 1981.

48. Violet Juanitas Dutra, e-mail to Dawn Bohulano-Mabalon, November 8, 2011.

49. Anita Bautista, interview with Dawn Bohulano-Mabalon, July 2001, Stockton, CA.

50. Angeles Monrayo, *Tomorrow's Memories: A Diary, 1924–1938* (Honolulu: University of Hawai'i Press, 2003), 224.

51. "Sixteen Filipinos Succumb to Poisoning," *Philippines Mail,* March 12, 1934, 1.

52. Rizaline Raymundo, interview with Dawn Bohulano Mabalon, August 2001, San Jose, CA.

53. Monrayo, *Tomorrow's Memories*, 202.

54. Jean Hipolito Labuga and Babe Hipolito Bosier, "Hipolito Family," in *Talk Story.*

55. Lillian Juanitas, e-mail to Dawn Bohulano-Mabalon, November 8, 2011.

56. Interview with Angelina Bantillo Magdael for DPAA, July 1, 1981, Stockton, CA.

57. Moreno Balantac, interview with Dawn Bohulano Mabalon, July 2001, Stockton, CA.

58. Donald L. Guimary, *Marumina Trabaho* (Lincoln, NE: iUniverse, 2006), 126; Thelma Buchholdt, *Filipinos in Alaska* (Anchorage: Aboriginal Press, 1996), 51.

59. Sinforoso Ordona, interview with Dorothy Cordova, DPAA, FANHS National Office, Seattle, September 5, 1981.

60. Ordona, interview.

61. Sleepy Caballero, "Ketchikan, Alaska Memories," Stockton FANHS Newsletter 16, no. 3 (July 2010): 5.

62. Donald L. Guimary, *Marumina Trabaho* (Lincoln, NE: iUniverse, 2006), 130.

63. Prudencio Mori, interview with Dorothy Cordova, DPAA, FANHS National Office, Seattle.

64. Buchholdt, *Filipinos in Alaska*, 81.

65. Ibid., 98.

66. Manuel Buaken, *I Have Lived with the American People* (Caldwell, OH: Caxton Printers, 1948), 232–34.

67. Carina Monica Montoya, *Los Angeles's Historic Filipinotown* (Charleston, SC: Arcadia Publishing, 2009), 28.

68. *Philippine Record,* 1927, in "Stockton" File in the National Pinoy Archives, Filipino American National Historical Society National Office, Seattle; *WPA Guide to New York City* (1939), quoted in http://www.purpleyamnyc.com/a-filipino-restaurant-in-brooklyn-in-1938/ and http://www.purpleyamnyc.com/new-research-pioneer-filipino-restaurant-in-brooklyn/ (accessed January 3, 2012). My thanks to Amy Besa for finding this restaurant in the course of her New York Philippine food research.

69. San Francisco Polk City Directory, 1930; *Filipinos in San Francisco,* ed. Filipino American National Historical Society, Pin@Y Educational Partnerships, and the Manilatown Heritage Foundation (Charleston, SC: Arcadia Publishing, 2011), 17.

70. Judy Patacsil, Rudy Guevarra Jr., Felix Tuyay, and the Filipino American National Historical Society San Diego Chapter, *Filipinos in San Diego* (Charleston, SC: Arcadia Publishing, 2010), 20.

71. Buchholdt, *Filipinos in Alaska*, 66.

72. Mae Respicio Koerner, *Filipinos in Los Angeles* (Charleston, SC: Arcadia Publishing, 2007), 23.

73. Dorothy Cordova, interview with Dawn Bohulano Mabalon, November 11, 2011; Sinforoso Ordona, interview with Dorothy Cordova, DPAA, FANHS Seattle, September 5, 1981.

74. Nelson Nagai, interview with Dawn Bohulano Mabalon, November 1999, Stockton, CA.

75. Policarpo Porras, interview with David Magdael, 1981, Stockton, CA., Filipino Oral History Project.

76. Jerry Paular, interview with Dawn Bohulano Mabalon, August 6, 2001, Sacramento, CA.

77. Pete Valoria, interview with Dawn Bohulano Mabalon, July 10, 2001, Stockton, CA,

78. Dorothy Cordova, interview; "Mike Castillano: He Fed Both Ivar and Seattle's Filipino Community," *Seattle Times,* April 10, 1992, available at http://community.seattletimes.nwsource.com/archive/?date=19920410&slug=1485661 (accessed October 15, 2012).

79. *VOICES: A Filipino American Oral History,* n.p.

80. Anita Bautista, interview with Dawn Bohulano Mabalon, August 15, 2003, Stockton, CA.

81. As quoted in Robert Vallangca, *Pinoy: The First Wave* (San Francisco: Strawberry Hill Press, 1977), 77–78.

82. Sylvia Sun Minnick, *Samfow: The San Joaquin Chinese Legacy* (Fresno, CA: Panorama Books, West Publishing, 1988), 226.

83. For the origins of chop suey and Chinese American restaurants, see Renqiu Yu, "Chop Suey: From Chinese to Chinese American Food," in *Chinese America: History and Perspectives 1987*, ed. Chinese Historical Society of America (San Francisco: Chinese Historical Society of America, 1987), 87–100; Jennifer 8. Lee, *Fortune Cookie Chronicles: Adventures in the World of Chinese Food* (New York: Twelve, 2008), 60–61; and Andrew Coe, *Chop Suey: A Cultural History of Chinese Food in the United States* (New York: Oxford University Press, 2009).

84. Dorothy Cordova, interview with Dawn Bohulano Mabalon, November 12, 2011, Seattle.

85. "Bamboo Breezes," *Philippines Mail,* December 3, 1934.

86. Concepcion Lagura, interview with Dawn Bohulano Mabalon, July 8, 2001, Stockton, CA.

87. Claro Candelario, interview with Dawn Bohulano Mabalon, February 15, 1993, Stockton, CA.

88. Asuncion Guevarra Nicolas, interview with Dawn Bohulano Mabalon, February 1996, Stockton, CA.

89. Eleanor Galvez Olamit and Camila Carido, interview with Dawn Bohulano Mabalon, February 19, 1996.

90. Reyes, interview.

91. Cordova, interview, November 12, 2011, Seattle.

92. Rizaline Raymundo, "Recipes," Dawn Bohulano Mabalon's collection.

93. Cordova, interview, November 12, 2011, Seattle.

94. Evangeline Canonizado Buell, "Seven Card Stud with Seven Manangs Wild," in *Seven Card Stud with Seven Manangs Wild: An Anthology of Filipino American Writing,* ed. Helen Toribio (San Francisco: T'Boli Publishing, 2002), 185.

95. Deanna Balantac, interview with Dawn Bohulano Mabalon, July 2001, Stockton, CA.

96. Maria Abastilla Beltran, interview with Caroline Koslosky, DPAA, FANHS, National Office, 1981.

97. Camila Carido, interview with Dawn Bohulano Mabalon, January 1996, Stockton, CA.

98. Buell, "Seven Card Stud," 200.

99. Deanna Balantac, interview.

100. Interview with Fred and Dorothy Cordova by Dawn Bohulano Mabalon, November 15, 2011, Seattle.

101. Angelina Bantillo Magdael, interview with Dawn Bohulano Mabalon, August 17, 2001, Stockton, CA.

102. Interview with Angelina Bantillo Magdael and Leatrice Bantillo Perez, December 2000, Stockton, CA.

103. Diaries of Virgilia Marello Bantillo, 1926–1946, Bantillo Family Papers, Stockton, CA.

104. Evangeline Canonizado Buell, *Twenty Five Chickens and a Pig for a Bride* (San Francisco: T'Boli Publishing, 2006).

105. Diaries of Virgilia Marella Bantillo, 1926–1938, Bantillo Family Papers, Stockton, CA.

106. *Stockton Record,* June 9, 1946.

8

Lechon with Heinz, Lea & Perrins with *Adobo*

The American Relationship with Filipino Food, 1898–1946

RENÉ ALEXANDER ORQUIZA JR.

If you had sat down to dinner at the Manila Hotel in 1936, only a few dishes on the menu would have been Filipino. Most of the items—the olives in the India relish, chicken gumbo soup, braised sweetbreads, squab casserole, beans, carrots, potatoes, and petits fours—were so classically French that you easily could have been in a hotel in New York or London. A few Filipino items—mango frappé, *pili* nuts, *lapu-lapu* in browned butter, and bamboo shoot salad—hinted at the hotel's location in America's most important imperial colony in Asia. But the meal made clear that Western food was a marker of class and refinement.[1]

This chapter explores how American reformers attempted to transform culinary knowledge and practices in the Philippines during the forty-eight years when the country was an American colony. I show how food, a basic object of everyday life, was used as a signal of cultural change by American reformers. I first describe how the public schools transformed thinking about food. Girls studied domestic science and home economics, and boys studied agriculture. Both further developed their culinary knowledge in secondary schools, vocational schools, and universities. Next, I look at food advertisements from popular Philippine magazines and newspapers. American food companies claimed superiority over their Filipino competitors and used slick artwork, ad copy, and allusions to Filipino and American culture to cultivate consumers' desires. Last, I examine popular cookbooks from the Philippines. These publications connected the products in the advertisements to the lessons on cooking from schools using European and American recipes. Together, these three areas—education, advertising, and cookbooks—attempted to Americanize the Filipino palate.

Before examining these reform efforts, I review how Americans regarded Filipino food at the start of the twentieth century.

"Not of a Kind or Quality to Support White People"

Most Americans arriving in the Philippines after the Spanish-American War did not want to eat Filipino food. Businessmen like Charles Morris asserted that Manila's restaurants were "primitive in character" and offered "little more than rice and fruits for sale."[2] Similarly, American teacher Herbert I. Priestley deemed the food in Bicol to be "not of a kind or quality to support white people."[3] The food was not enticing to American soldier John Clifford Brown, despite his monotonous army diet of hardtack and canned beef. "I have yet to see a soldier who would tackle any of the cooked dishes," he said, "and a soldier will try almost anything."[4] The American surveyor José de Olivares labeled Filipino customers at roadside restaurants as "vindictive and treacherous—just the kind of people that all good Americans desire to keep away from."[5] American reformers thus had many motives to transform Filipino food and impose American culinary standards. They first targeted the schools by introducing lessons on cooking, eating, and farming.

A New Way of Understanding Food

American public schools transformed Philippine daily life. They introduced lessons in civics, self-government, and vocational training and, most notably, made English the national language. American teachers, confident that their new curriculum was a vast improvement over the Catholic educational system of the Spanish period, brought lessons in nutrition, hygiene, and agriculture.

The 1929 publication *A Tentative Guide for Health Education in Elementary Schools* demonstrates the new importance of food instruction in its lists of the yearly objectives of food instruction for teachers from grades 1 through 6. Grade 1 students were to learn the greater nutritional benefits of imported canned condensed milk than those of *carabao* (buffalo) milk and the superiority of Western whole grains to rice. Grade 2's lessons stressed etiquette: eating slowly, sitting down while chewing, and chewing one's food thoroughly. Grade 3 taught students how to identify foods that strengthened bones and teeth, and grade 4 focused on memorizing the nutritional value of whole grains, fruits, vegetables, and milk. Grade 4 also advocated the elimination of *merienda*, or midday snacks between meals. Grades 5 and 6 targeted hygiene, with lessons on protecting food from dirt and flies, the use of clean individual drinking cups, and consuming water for proper digestion.[6]

After grade 6, food instruction was divided by gender. Girls trained in kitchens and boys trained on farms. Alice Fuller's *Housekeeping: A Textbook for Girls in Public Intermediate Schools of the Philippines* lists the recipes that girls in middle school were required to learn, such as hot cakes, corn bread, muffins, biscuits, drop sponge cakes, jelly rolls, doughnuts, and cookies. University home economics and domestic science classes standardized food instruction even further. The Philippine Normal School, the country's teachers college, required all female students, regardless of major, to take three semesters of domestic science, one year of botany with an emphasis on food values, one year of physiology with an emphasis on female hygiene, and one year of domestic science.[7] All female students at the University of the Philippines took two courses on the principles of cooking, nutrition, home arts, and citizenship training. The university's general catalog even listed a course devoted to "the intelligent selection of imported goods as well as those locally produced."[8] Food thus was an integral part of a female student's education.

Filipino boys studied how to farm and export cash crops like sugar, tobacco, and coconuts. Schools like the Silliman Institute in Dumaguete tailored their instruction to specific regions and climates so seventh-grade boys could specialize in the culture and care of papayas, bananas, pomelos, oranges, lemons, Chico cacao, and tobacco.[9] Their textbooks praise farmers and underscore their importance to the nation's future. Edwin Bingham Copeland, the director of agriculture for the public schools, wrote in his textbook *Elements of Philippine Agriculture* that Filipino boys studying agriculture were "not only preparing themselves for the most general industry of these islands, but are helping by their work, in school after school, in the uplifting of their people." Copeland urged Filipino students to study hard and surpass Hawai'i in sugar and Ceylon (Sri Lanka) in coconut production.[10] Another school that focused on farming was the Central Luzon Agricultural School in Muñoz, the 658-hectare home to 1,038 students who ran their own movie house, sawmill, general store, bank, and printing press. Profits from these student-run businesses paid for a local granary, gardens, and poultry and hog projects. The Philippine government tried to replicate Central Luzon's success with new campuses in Mountain Province, Camarines Sur, Samar, Abra, and Palawan. In addition, it created 272 rural high schools, fourteen farm schools, and 274 settlement farm schools.

The public schools changed more than just how food was prepared and produced. American educators credited them for creating a Philippine middle class with new tastes and preferences for consumer goods. As M. E. Polley wrote in 1929,

Education has created in the large middle class desires for comforts, luxuries, and pleasures of modern life far in excess of the desires for these blessings among the upper class two decades ago, and they are satisfying those desires by wearing better clothing, eating better food, living in better and more sanitary homes, having more diversions, traveling more and with better means of transportation, and giving their children better education.[11]

Thus, a range of imported products entered the country, and advertisers cultivated the Filipino consumer desire for new goods.

New Items for Old Recipes, Old Items for New Recipes

Food advertisements capitalized on public school lessons by invoking hygiene, nutrition, and sanitation. Ads asserted that American goods were symbols of sophistication and worldliness available to Filipino consumers halfway around the world and that they were better than Filipino items simply because they were American. In addition, they were easily adaptable to Filipino daily life and conveniently bridged differences between Filipino and American culture.

Many ads contended that American goods were superior because they met government inspection standards. For example, an advertisement for Hershey's Chocolate in 1938 announced, "Every tin of Hershey's 'Breakfast' Cocoa must conform to U.S. Government and Bureau of Health standards for fat content and fineness of powder."[12] Another advertisement in 1931 for Libby's boasted that its cold storerooms met high sanitation and hygiene standards.[13]

Ads expanded on the theme of American superiority by invoking nutrition. Condensed milk ads repeatedly stressed their products were more nutritious than native *carabao* (buffalo) or coconut milk and connected them to the country's future by stating that milk was essential to the individual success of Filipino children. A 1927 Horlick's ad stated that malted milk gave "the glow of health to pale cheeks," "a sparkle in the eye," and a chance for a Filipino boy "to head his class."[14] Carnation connected its evaporated milk to the nation's future, stating, "Happy, healthy babies bring joy to your home. They represent the country's future wealth."[15] These appeals made milk into a product larger than food; they became essential to the country's future.

Other ads combined American and Filipino images to suggest the mingling of Western power and taste in Philippine settings. The National Biscuit Company, the predecessor of today's Nabisco, printed images of George Washington, the U.S. Capitol dome, and the Stars and Stripes on its biscuit tins.[16]

Jacob's Milk Crackers announced that its crackers could be consumed "at meal time, between meals, for hungry boys and girls, afternoon tea or *merienda*."[17] It underscored this adaptability with an image of a Filipina mother dressed in the traditional clothing alongside her son dressed in Western attire. Del Monte provided the most literal depiction of Philippine-American imagery in a 1926 ad for Queen Anne cherries. The ad illustrated the journey from central California to a *bahay kubo*, or *nipa* hut, in the Philippine province. It further appealed to Filipino readers by presenting a mother and son in everyday clothing walking home from the market with canned goods. These ads told Filipino consumers that Filipinos could easily welcome these products into their homes, regardless of class or location.[18]

Ads for Heinz Tomato Ketchup and Lea & Perrins Worcestershire Sauce blended traditional Filipino dishes and recipes with American products. A 1926 Heinz ad offered ketchup with *lechon*, or spit-roasted pig, traditionally served as a fiesta dish. The typical *lechon* sauce combined brown sugar, lemongrass, and minced pork offal, so pairing it with ketchup was very different. Heinz romanticized this departure by depicting tomato ketchup next to Filipino items such as a *parol* (decorative star), a *bahay kubo* (*nipa* hut), and a clay *palayok* (pot).[19] A 1929 ad for Lea & Perrins offered a recipe for *adobo*, the Philippine national dish, that included Worcestershire sauce. Lea & Perrins made its case for adding this Western condiment to a familiar recipe by saying, "Great cooks in the most outstanding hotels and clubs in the world are using the famous sauce." The recipe called for three pounds of pork, one and a half cups of vinegar, one tablespoon of salt, eight cloves of garlic, and a half cup of water. After marinating, browning, and braising the pork, the cook added one tablespoon of Lea & Perrins to finish the sauce.[20] In this way, any Filipino could easily incorporate American condiments into favorite dishes.

Recipes also inspired this essay's third subject: cookbooks, which gave Filipinos instructions for making new dishes, especially the ones from Europe and the United States. They were an extension of lessons from the classroom and enabled home kitchens in the Philippines to become familiar with other traditions and cuisines.

Reading and Cooking New Dishes in Filipino Kitchens

Cookbooks provided practical instructions and directions for cooking Western dishes. They served as primers for the proper preparation and selection of ingredients as well as references for basic nutrition and hygiene. Most cookbooks that were published in the Philippines contained recipes from France,

Spain, and the United States reflected the publishers' desire to bring foreign cooking into Filipino homes.

Two cookbooks exemplify this desire to popularize European cookery: Rosendo Ignacio's *Aklat ng pagluluto* and Crispulo Trinidad's *Pasteleria at reposteria* offered classical French and traditional Spanish recipes to Tagalog readers.[21] Although *Aklat ng pagluluto's* first two chapters focused on hygiene and sanitation, the rest of the book was a collection of classical French and Spanish recipes. For example, the chapter on sauces had recipes for mayonnaise, hollandaise, white espagñole, and white velouté. The soup chapter included Parisien pot-au-feu, consommé with cream, codfish stew, and asparagus. The chapter on beef described preparations for oxtails, meatballs, roast beef, filled beef rolls, tongue, and pigs' trotters, along with Spanish stewed *bacalao, bacalao* in mayonnaise, and Mallorca calamares. Finally, the baking chapter had French basics like flour doughs, flans and custards, flans with fruit, puddings with fruit, pastry creams, sugared fruits, meringues, cakes, tarts, breads, wafers, biscuits, doughnuts, and rolls. To combat the heat, the book suggested iced-cheese, milk, butter, pineapple, coconut, Chantilly, milk flower, Burgundy, and hollandaise sorbets. *Aklat ng pagluluto* was the guidebook for Tagalog readers eager to bring French culinary techniques into their homes.

The second cookbook, *Pasteleria at reposteria*, contained translations into Tagalog of French, German, British, and Spanish baking recipes, especially those for basic doughs and fillings, tarts filled with Gruyere cheese, almonds, toasted rice, chocolate, licorice, and raisins. There were pastels, timbals, and empanadas filled with truffles, almonds, crab, oysters, lamb, poultry, hot onions, fish, and vegetables. Basic pastry sauces and creams such as Spanish, German, crème pâtissière, and two kinds of béchamel accompanied fillings of vanilla, chocolate, toasted rice, caramel, almonds, fruits, pistachios, cider, peppermint, cherry, apple, and potatoes. In dramatic fashion, the cookbook ended with a chapter on soufflés.

The majority of popular cookbooks in the Philippines, however, were written in English or Spanish and usually were published by the government. *Everyday Cookery for the Home*, in both English and Spanish, by Sofia Reyes de Veyra, was printed in 1934 by the Philippine Education Company. De Veyra adapted recipes from the *Ladies' Home Journal* to suit the needs, conditions, tastes, and temperament of a Filipino audience. The book did include Filipino recipes such as those for baked *lapu-lapu* (grouper), *bangus* (milkfish) loaf, *camote* (sweet potato) waffles, glacéed *camote*, mango whip, mango fluff, *ubi* (purple yam) pudding, *pinipig* (toasted rice) cookies and macaroons, *buko* (coconut) ice cream, *pili* (box tree) nut brownies, and *calamansi* (calamondin) syrup punch. But there were six times as many American recipes in the cookbook as Filipino recipes.[22]

One cookbook originally published in 1922 and republished in 1978 showed how Filipinos gradually embraced their food over time. *Good Cooking and Health in the Tropics*, by Mrs. Samuel Francis Gaches, is full of American, Spanish, and Asian recipes. Gaches believed that Filipinos deserved better food, and her book complains about the state of country's food supply. She explains how inefficient transportation and distribution translate into high prices for seafood. She criticizes unregulated market vendors for what she dubbed "the Oriental custom of having no fixed price but making everything a matter of haggling."[23] Although the cookbook does offer a few Filipino recipes written by two Filipina nurses educated in the United States, most of them are for American food.[24] In 1978, the book was reprinted with a new introduction by Carlos Quirino. He writes that even though the original 1922 edition had just a few Filipino recipes, Filipino cuisine had become popular in sophisticated circles two generations since the book's original printing. Filipino dishes were now served "in grand parties and buffets" and in a "proliferation of Filipino restaurants." Pride in Filipino cuisine had finally arrived. Quirino celebrates the past by praising the Filipinos, for even though they had "adapted the cakes and desserts and preserves and salads from the American era, [they] preferred the Mechados, Cocidos and Rellenos of the Spaniards, the Humba, Taucho, *pansit* of the Chinese."[25]

Conclusion

The exchange of food went in both directions. Filipino recipes appeared in the United States after Philippine independence in 1946, especially as immigration from the Philippines to the United States increased with the passage of the Immigration Reform Act of 1965. Nora V. Daza's *Galing-Galing: The First Philippine Cookbook for Use in the United States* targeted Filipinos abroad who missed the flavors of home. Private school and church cookbooks printed adobo recipes, and the *Los Angeles Times Cookbook* gave adobo mainstream treatment in 1981.[26] The long story of food exchanges between the United States and the Philippines now flipped as Americans tried adobo for themselves.

Today, the Manila Hotel retains many of the features from 1936. Much of the building is the same, with the grand ballroom, the promenade by Manila Bay, and the facade remaining largely intact. What has changed is the hotel's own kitchens' pride in Filipino food. Menus in the Manila Hotel now feature

Filipino specialties alongside Western fare. A hotel guest can now choose between a breakfast of *tapsilog*—a combination of cured meat, garlic fried rice, and a fried egg—or a continental breakfast. The country's food tastes are now shaped by a transnational population proud of its regional culinary traditions and open to new ideas brought to the country by overseas foreign workers. American education, advertising, and cookbooks tried to change the Filipino palate. But favoring Western cuisine at the expense of Filipino cuisine no longer works. Today, Filipino food combines pride in the past and a careful selection from the present.

Notes

1. Dinner Menu, Manila Hotel, March 18, 1936, New York Historical Society.
2. Charles Morris, *Our Island Empire* (Philadelphia, 1899), 408–9.
3. Herbert I. Priestley to Ethel Priestley, September 4, 1901, Herbert I. Priestley Papers, Bancroft Library, UC Berkeley.
4. John Clifford Brown, *Diary of a Soldier in the Philippines* (Portland, ME: Lakeside Press, 1901), 54–55.
5. José de Olivares, *Our Islands and Their People: As Seen with Camera and Pencil* (New York: N. D. Thompson Publishing, 1899), 553, 761.
6. Department of Public Instruction, *A Tentative Guide for Health Education in Elementary Schools* (Manila: Bureau of Education, 1929), 13–29.
7. Bureau of Education, *Philippine Normal School Bulletin no. 30: Catalogue for 1909–1910* (Manila: Bureau of Education, 1909), 16, 22–23.
8. University of the Philippines, *General Catalogue, 1958–1959* (Quezon City: University of the Philippines Press, 1958), 315.
9. *Silliman Truth*, April 1, 1917, 2–3.
10. Edwin Bingham Copeland, *Elements of Philippine Agriculture* (New York: World Book, 1908), 2.
11. M. E. Polley, "Public School System of the Philippines," *School and Society* 30 (October 19, 1929): 544–48.
12. Advertisement for Hershey's Cocoa, *Philippine Magazine*, January 1938, 65.
13. Advertisement for Libby's, *Liwayway*, August 14, 1931, 48.
14. Advertisement for Horlick's, *Graphic Magazine*, December 31, 1927, back cover.
15. Advertisement for Carnation Milk, *Philippine Magazine*, November 1, 1936, back cover.
16. Advertisement for National Biscuit Company, *Liwayway*, December 23, 1932, 47; and Advertisement for National Biscuit Company, *Excelsior*, January 10, 1933, 14.
17. Advertisement for Jacob's Milk Crackers, *Graphic Magazine*, April 20, 1929, back cover.
18. Advertisement for Del Monte, *Liwayway*, June 11, 1926, back cover.
19. Advertisement for Heinz, *Liwayway*, April 2, 1926, back cover.
20. Advertisement for Lea & Perrins, *Liwayway*, February 1, 1929, 18.
21. Rosendo Ignacio, *Aklat ng Pagluluto: Hinango sa lalòng bantóg dakilàng aklát ng pagluluto sa gawîng Europa at sa Filipinas, na kapuwà nasusulat sa wikàng kastilà, at isinataglog ng boong katiyagâan ni Rosendo Ignacio* (Manila: Ikalawang pagkalimbag, 1919); Crispulo Trinidad, *Pasteleria at reposteria: Francesa at Española: Aklat na ganap*

na naglalaman ng maraming palacada sa pag-gaua ng lahat ng mga bagay-bagay na matamis at mga pasteles (Manila: Limbagan ni J. Martinez, 1919).

22. Sofia Reyes de Veyra, *Everyday Cookery for the Home* (Manila: Philippine Education Company, 1934).

23. Mrs. Samuel Francis Gaches, *Good Cooking and Health in the Tropics* (Manila: Bureau of Printing, 1922), 118.

24. The items listed as Filipino that appear in the cookbook are *atchara, bataw, buko, bulanglang sitaw, cardillo*, chicken with *malungay* leaves, escabeche, fish tortilla, fresh corn, *gabi*, guava, *kilawin, lagat* lobster or shrimp, *lutong talunan, makapuno* preserves, *mongo guisado, mongo* pods, *pakam, paksiw, paksiw* pig's *pata, patani, patola, pesa* chicken, *pesang isda*, picadillo with potatoes, *pinakbet, puso, sarciado* cabbage, *sinigang* beef, *sinigang* fish, *sinigang, sitaw*, stuffed broiled fish, *talong diningdeng, tachio, tinola* chicken, *upo diningdeng*, and *upo guisado*. The ice-cream flavors are *atis*, coconut, *makapuno*, mango, pineapple, *pinipig*, and *ube*.

25. Carlos Quirino, *Culinary Arts in the Tropics Circa 1922* (Manila: Regal Publishing, 1978), 32.

26. Nora V. Daza, *Galing-galing: First Philippine Cookbook for Use in the United States* (Manila: Carnation Philippines, 1974); Christ the King Parish Guild, *Favorite Recipes* (Kansas City, MO: Circulation Services, 1968); Buckley School, *Buckley's Best* (Sherman Oaks, CA: Buckley Mothers Club Cookbook Committee, 1973); *Los Angeles Times California Cookbook*, ed. Betsy Balsley (New York: Abrams, 1981).

9

"Oriental Cookery"

Devouring Asian and Pacific Cuisine during the Cold War

MARK PADOONGPATT

"Cooking is considered an art in the Orient," Ruby Erskine explained to students in her cooking class at the Women's Auxiliary to the Salt Lake Chapter of Life Underwriters in Utah. "And the food in the Orient," Erskine added as she used chopsticks to stir-fry vegetables in an electric skillet, "is a happy combination of good eating and good health." It was 1970, and Erskine had been teaching courses like these with "tremendous enthusiasm" for several years throughout Salt Lake City. She regularly spoke on the topic of "Oriental cookery" in front of church and civic groups, organized Oriental-themed benefit dinners, and once demonstrated the preparation of Oriental food at the Winder Stake House, where she served it for lunch.[1] At one point, Erskine even flirted with the idea of publishing an Oriental cookbook. She treated the cuisine as an art form, making sure to emphasize in teaching demonstrations how to delicately mince and julienne vegetables for stir-fry dishes. But Erskine also assured her students, almost all of whom were white housewives, that Oriental cooking was not simply the "most delicious in the world" but could also transform them into ideal, economically efficient, suburban homemakers. Or as she once told a local newspaper, "Oriental cooking is pleasing to the palate, the profile, and the pocketbook."[2]

Erskine's experiences as an expert on Asian culinary practices reveal quite a bit about race, gender, and class in Cold War U.S. society. First, the popularity of her cooking classes and banquets among white housewives, as well as the fact that Christian groups and church community centers such as the Winder Stake House sponsored such events, suggests that a number of white Americans had a deep interest in the cultural practices of Asia. While white Americans' fascination with the "Orient" is certainly not new, as it dates back to the Revolutionary period, what is significant is that the interest in Asian food practices occurred simultaneously with the formation of suburban whiteness, a cultural crackdown, in U.S. society.³ In addition, this fascination *preceded* the arrival of a large number of Asian immigrants, in places that were overwhelmingly white and, in many cases, historically hostile to Asians. Salt Lake City was roughly 90 percent white when Erskine spread the gospel about Oriental cooking.⁴ Indeed, locals described her as someone who held the "secrets of the Far East" based solely on her knowledge of Asian cooking practices. But for Erskine to operate as *the* authority on Asian cuisine meant that she either learned to cook Asian dishes from a member of the local Asian population—and thus committed an act of severe cultural and racial appropriation—or she learned the cooking practices on her own. But where did she learn? And how? Erskine's experiences raise important questions about why U.S. citizens became fascinated with food culture from Asia and the Pacific more broadly, what enabled their access to Asian cuisine, how they introduced it to U.S. consumers, and the way in which food configured categories of race, gender, and class in the Cold War period.

The story of how and why a white suburban housewife from Utah like Ruby Erskine evolved into an Asian culinary expert and a vessel of Far East secrets—and why such "secrets" meant anything at all—is, at heart, a story of U.S. global expansion in Asia and the Pacific after World War II. Erskine traveled to Japan sometime in the 1950s to be with her husband, Jasper, who was stationed there after the war as a U.S. Army officer.⁵ The United States was strengthening its occupation of and influence over Japan while it was recovering from the effects of two U.S. atomic bomb attacks on both the natural and built environment and the psyche of Japanese people. The United States saw this devastation as an invitation. Accordingly, U.S. officials decided to restructure Japan's postwar economy to become more like the United States, using it as a primary model for future American aspirations outside Europe.⁶ It was in this context that Erskine "fell in love" with Asian cuisine, learning how to prepare Japanese food from the couple's domestic servant, whom she described as a "fantastic Japanese cook."

In this chapter, I use Erskine's story to show how white American women participated in the romance and tragedy of U.S. global expansion, by examining the historical relationship of Asian/Pacific cuisine, politics, and identity formation during the Cold War, both "at home" and abroad. I argue that a history of Asian/Pacific food culture uncovers the way in which after the war, the U.S. Empire turned foodways into a central site of identity formation for white American women, specifically suburban housewives. Most important, white American women's fascination with Asian/Pacific cuisine sustained the empire by adapting local food cultures and systems to the taste and appetites of U.S.

consumers. Their so-called discovery of new Asian/Pacific cooking practices, their role in transforming foods from sustenance to commodities, and the standardization of recipes in cookbooks certainly shaped attitudes and feelings that made U.S. citizens support U.S. intervention in the region. But the story I tell contends that these acts were also mechanisms of domination (not simply a justification), as food became linked to processes of U.S. global expansion that strengthened neocolonial relationships between the United States and the countries and peoples of Asia and the Pacific.

In recent years, a number of scholars have explored the significance, for both Asians and Asian Americans, of America's postwar economic and military expansion into Asia and the Pacific. One topic that has received a great deal of attention is the Orientalist representations that emerged during America's efforts to win the hearts and minds of Asian people. Scholars like Christina Klein and Naoko Shibusawa argue that liberal U.S. policymakers and cultural producers—novelists, playwrights, filmmakers, journalists—constructed and disseminated racialized and gendered images of Asia and the Pacific as Cold War allies as well as nations in need of American guidance on "modernization" and democracy.[7] According to Jodi Kim, the Cold War in Asia must be considered "at once a geopolitical, cultural, and epistemological project of imperialism and gendered racial formation undergirding U.S. global hegemony."[8] This project reconfigures Asian Americans from the yellow peril into ethnically assimilable model minorities.[9]

But these representations also have had a profound impact on the ground. For Asian immigrants and Asian Americans, images that depict them as assimilable "foreign friends" contradict their treatment in U.S. society. Despite the symbolic passage of the 1952 Immigration Act, which acknowledges the racism built into the 1924 Immigration Act, Chinese, Japanese, and Filipino Americans continue to fight racial and gender discrimination as they struggle to find a "feeling of belonging."[10] What these authors agree on is that Cold War cultural productions—and, to a lesser extent, immigration policy—racialized Asian Americans as perpetual foreigners who remain outside the social, political, economic, and cultural boundaries of the United States.

Building on this scholarship on the history of Asian Americans and the Cold War, I use foodways—the production, representation, and consumption of a food—to understand how U.S. Cold War interventions in Asia and the Pacific played out in everyday life. Rather than add to the large body of work on cultural representations, I illustrate the everyday life of empire and how the political economy of food shapes race, gender, and class. I do so by extending philosopher Lisa Heldke's concept of "cultural food colonialism." In *Exotic*

Appetites, she defines cultural food colonialism as an "attitude problem" characterized by whites' passion for cooking, eating, and appreciating food that is rooted in a European colonial thirst for authenticity, adventure, and novelty. They find and appropriate "exotic culture" in the cuisine of economically dominated or Third World people, which was used to justify, and was justified by, political and economic forms of U.S. colonialism and imperialism.[11]

I broaden and deepen Heldke's concept in two ways: First, I place it in the historical context of the Cold War in order to claim that cultural food colonialism is more than just an "attitude" that works alongside and helps make more powerful political and economic forms of imperialism and colonialism. Instead, white women's access to and consumption of Asian/Pacific cuisine is an actual colonial practice in and of itself. The goal is to shift attention away from debates over whether or not people like Ruby Erskine were "liberal multiculturalists" or racists or imperialists or all of these. Focusing on the individual feelings of these women detracts from a much larger, more central issue: that culinary tourism fueled the rise of service-based economies in Asia and the Pacific. Second, Heldke does not adequately explain how and why an analysis of foodways can enrich our understanding of colonialism and imperialism in ways that an analysis of architecture, literature, art, or music have not or, perhaps, cannot. As each of the contributors to this book makes clear, one reason why foodways provides a unique framework is that it demonstrates how social hierarchies of power have been inscribed on bodies by categories created and maintained by other human senses besides sight, namely, taste and smell.

Epicurean Delights and Enchanting Encounters

In the 1950s and 1960s, several white Americans enjoyed Asian/Pacific cuisines in restaurants across the United States. Although they frequented Chinese restaurants in the late nineteenth and early twentieth century (when it was considered slumming), during the postwar period, Asian food became even more popular, along with the growing number of Chinese restaurants around the country. And even though dining out at an Asian restaurant was still relatively unusual, a night on the town that included indulging in lobster fried rice and beef in black bean sauce was still a meaningful social and cultural experience. During this time, most Chinese restaurants served Cantonese and Mandarin dishes in addition to the more familiar "chop suey": a stir-fried dish of meat, eggs, bean sprouts, cabbage, and celery in a thickened sauce. Restaurant owners also catered to non-Asian guests, creating Western-style menus with combination dinners offering a choice of dishes from either column A or column B. Owners also decorated their restaurants in ways that played up to white fantasies of Asia and the Pacific. In the 1950s, for example, Trader Vic's tiki-themed restaurant at the Savoy Hotel in New York City became a huge hit, with customers coming in droves for the tropical drinks, especially the mai tais.[12] Although Trader Vic's purported to serve Polynesian fare, it served mainly Cantonese dishes, which included *rumaki* (Polynesian hors d'oeuvre usually made with water chestnuts and duck or chicken liver wrapped in bacon), crab Rangoon (deep-fried wontons filled with crab and cream cheese), and Calcutta lamb curry, as well as egg rolls, fried rice, wonton soup, barbecued pork, almond chicken, and beef with tomato. Restaurants like Trader Vic's were so popular that they inspired copycats like the Kon-Tiki Club in Chicago, which advertised "Escape to the South Seas!" and offered a complete Cantonese dinner for $1.85 to $3.25.[13] The craze for Polynesian-style restaurants serving Cantonese food continued well into the 1970s. They popped up in different parts of the United States, such as the Oriental Luau, an eatery on a commercial strip in New Jersey that featured a popular all-you-can-eat "Hawaiian smorgasbord."[14] Furthermore, several restaurants were designed to provide an upscale dining experience for food connoisseurs and, of course, celebrities. In 1960s New York City, Bruce Ho's Four Seas restaurant catered primarily to a white, "very good high clientele" who came to enjoy assorted seafood Cantonese, lobster rolls, spare ribs, and sizzling pork *wor ba* (over rice).[15]

While some people traveled from their suburban homes into the city for a taste of Asia and Pacific, others traveled across the Pacific Ocean. In the 1950s, west Los Angeles homemaker Marie Wilson moved to Thailand and had her first encounter with Thai cuisine. Apprehensive and slightly disgusted at first, Wilson eventually became smitten with Thai food for its unique, rich, and highly seasoned dishes that "happily" combined its Indian and Chinese origins. She discovered the greatest pleasure, however, in the cuisine's hot and spicy flavors: "Thais don't care whether their food is hot . . . we soon learned that hot food was only a Western idea but we never gave up trying to convince our cooks [that hot] was better."[16] At the same time, Meda Croizat traveled across the Asian continent and became "Gung Ho for Oriental Cookery." By the late 1960s, Croizat, a gourmet chef, home economics teacher, and "international hostess" from Santa Monica, California, had had more than twenty years of experience with Chinese (as well as French) cooking and had developed a taste for Thai food, a cuisine described by Croizat also as unique because of the "spiciness of the curries and by the unusual and abundant fruits." She especially liked the *mee krob*, a sweet crispy noodle dish that was a "favorite with all of us."[17]

The experiences of U.S. Peace Corps volunteers (PCVs) offer further evidence of how white U.S. citizens, specifically women abroad, approached Asian/Pacific food with curiosity and excitement. PCVs in Thailand fondly remembered their first tastes and smells of Thai food when recalling their Peace Corps assignments during the mid- to late 1960s.[18] Marianne May Apple, a volunteer from San Diego, assigned to Trat Province in southeastern Thailand, typed a letter to her parents on May 24, 1966, explaining, "The food really takes getting used to. It all has a distinctive taste and most of it is so hot that you think you're on fire."[19] In another letter to her sister later that year, Apple wrote:

> My teacher . . . usually invites me to lunch on Sat[urday] after I finish teaching. Last time we had crab eggs and blood—good[,] believe it or not! . . . I think I will write a Thai cookbook . . . because I have so many recipes that are of more a variety that those in the book at home.

At her parents' request, Apple photographed the Thai ingredients and dishes and suggested that the family plant a small Thai pepper plant and find lemongrass and Kaffir limes in order to make "authentic" Thai food.[20]

Taste, smell, and sight defined U.S. citizens' encounters with Asian/Pacific "epicurean delights," thereby providing a powerful way to anchor ideas about race, ethnicity, and nation in the postwar world. In Marie Wilson's *Siamese Cookery*, the first Thai cookbook published in the United States, she promises readers that "new herbs and spices will fill your house with appetizing odors and make meal time and exciting adventure."[21] The spiciness or heat of some of the foods indeed awoke new parts of the palate for the culinary adventurers. But they also allowed white American women to map the Cold War world and its people according to other senses besides sight. Taste and smell also helped them apply meaning to cultural and national differences. As another woman observed, "Satay vendors and their charcoal braziers are a regular feature of the streets. There is a smell of grilled meat mixed with the pungent aroma of fresh red chilies and peanuts typical to this part of the Far East."[22]

As anthropologists have demonstrated, sensory perception like taste and smell are cultural as well as physical acts, in that they are infused with meanings and ways of knowing that are socially constructed and historically specific.[23] Janeth Johnson Nix suggests in her cookbook that taste is culturally specific but implies that it is timeless:

> [The] contrast of sweet and sharp, bitter and bland, soft and crisp, subtle and strong. Even hot and cool—not temperatures but flavor. The Chinese, like the

Indians, feel that "hot" foods (like bitter melon and curry) cool you off, and that "cool" foods (like rice and yogurt) warm you up.[24]

The love affair with Asian and Pacific food surpassed simply wanting to consume new and exciting tastes and flavors. White American women wanted to learn how to prepare the dishes. This required more intimate contact with members of the local population, particularly domestic servants, which had both negative and positive consequences. According to Marie Wilson, Thai cooks and servants were "indispensable" to helping foreigners adjust in Thailand, especially to shop at the local market and prepare meals. But Wilson also recalled being "either 'squeezed' on the food money, or forced to care for dozens of the cooks' ne'er-do-well relatives, or fed poorly cooked food, or just not fed enough. We felt put upon, deprived, and bullied."[25] Even though her servants introduced the family to Thai cuisine, they apparently often left a bad taste in their mouths.

Other interactions were much more pleasant and involved a semblance of equal exchange, mutual understanding, and emotional bonds. Johnson Nix, a home economist and food writer from California with a self-described "insatiable appetite" for Oriental cooking, learned to cook by trial and error while living in Japan in the 1960s—going to shops, buying what looked interesting, and trying to concoct something edible. When Nix improved her culinary skills, she began giving lessons in American cooking to Japanese women, with whom she also exchanged recipes and cooking methods.[26] This sharing of recipes and cooking methods was not uncommon. For example, in December 1962 on the Japanese island of Okinawa, a Japanese woman, referred to by *Stars and Stripes* newspaper only as "Mrs. Thomas H. Luke," demonstrated how to deep-fry spring rolls to a small group of white American women in her Oriental cooking class at the Naha AB Community Center.[27]

Although white American women had wonderful memories of preparing and consuming Asian/Pacific cuisine, these memories were more feelings and longings for colonialism, or "imperialist nostalgia." They found becoming acquainted with an exotic culture to be exciting. But they received enormous pleasure in food culture because it was during a meal that they felt truly revered, respected, and catered to by "others" whose main goal was to satisfy their needs. Several accounts of this colonial thirst for adventure to be quenched by Asian/Pacific food culture appeared in newspapers and oral histories, but the cookbooks from this period best capture the attitude of cultural food colonialism.

In *The Original Thai Cookbook*, Jennifer Brennan, who lived in East Asia and Southeast Asia for more than twenty years during the Cold War, invites readers to experience the romance awaiting them: "It is dusk in Bangkok and you are going out to dinner. The chauffeured Mercedes 280 sweeps you from your luxury hotel through streets lined with large, spreading trees and picturesque tile-roofed wooden shops and houses." Upon arriving at your elegant Thai home, she continues, you are "greeted by an exquisite, delicately boned Thai woman, youthful but of indeterminate age" and served a "parade of unfamiliar and exotic dishes."[28] In her 1958 cookbook, *The Far Eastern Epicure*, author Maria Kozslik Donovan also takes readers on a journey through Indonesian food culture. Donovan, a housewife from Cook County, Illinois, who once lived in a bungalow on the hills of Java overlooking paddy fields, revealed that European colonialism attracted her to Indonesia and influenced her views before she arrived there.[29]

> My culinary visit to the East began with Djakarta. . . . all I knew about the place was that the Dutch called it Batavia, that there was a canal there, a luxury hotel (old travel brochures mentioned it as the Ritz of the Far East!), a club with a classical façade ("ou la Colonie s'amusait!"), and that before the war one could get the best Rijsttafel in the world there.[30]

One could argue that the burst of new tastes and flavors experienced in Asian/Pacific cuisine alone offered enough novelty for white American women. In fact, Brennan once stated that she fell in love with Thai food because of its "indescribable mixture of flavors."[31] For Donovan, Indonesian food, too, was an "intoxicating mixture" of "Chinese, Indian, and Polynesian" influences that reflected the history of cultural blending in the country.[32] And when she visited Singapore, she introduced readers to yet another place with a different variety of cuisines, "where all tastes are catered to."[33]

These women craved more than just the food, however; they also wanted to be treated like royalty. In other words, white American women became enchanted with Asian and Pacific food culture in large part because they enjoyed the services provided by local natives. During her visit to Indonesia, Donovan's experience of a *rijsttafel*, a formal Indonesian banquet consisting of a variety of dishes served with rice, serves as a powerful example of the centrality of service to constructing the fantasy of culinary adventure in the Asian Pacific. Donovan raves in her cookbook about the *rijsttafel* and provides a dish-by-dish account of the Javanese feast in which a series of "boys" brought out dishes and served the guests. "The first boy appears, . . . barefoot, but in a scrupulously clean linen uniform. The little black Moslem cap is placed firmly on his head. He brings the rice, the basis of the Rijsttafel, and serves you."[34] Donovan then describes in detail the range of dishes that the Indonesian "boys" deliver while the "smell of spices tickles our noses in the meantime": "Opor Daging (slices of beef braised in coconut milk), Daging Ketjap (pork flavored with garlic and soybean sauce), Goreng Ati (fried calf's liver), salted and dried fish fried in oil, red hot chilies, and krupuk—frothy wafers made with shrimp and egg white."[35] After the last boy brings out *atjar* (pickled vegetables), "he steps back and takes his place in the row of silent figures who now watch you from the corners of their eyes."

Donovan states in no uncertain terms that the *rijsttafel's* aura of colonial splendor is what gives it its charm. In fact, it was the Dutch who instituted the *rijsttafel* as a "tradition" during its colonial occupation of Indonesia in the late nineteenth and early twentieth century. The Dutch colonists wanted to impress their visitors with an array of exotic dishes that demonstrated not only the mul-tiethnic character of Indonesia but also showcased the abundance of their col-ony.[36] Even after Indonesia gained independence from Dutch rule in the late 1940s, Donovan explains joyfully that in the 1950s, Dutch businessmen still gath-ered at the Hotel Robertson, a guesthouse facing the famous canal in the capital city of Jakarta, to enjoy the "traditional" *rijsttafel*. She writes, "In solemn silence, they ate through many courses, nostalgically evoking the past grandeur of Bat-avia, when the Rijsttafel was never less than forty dishes!"[37] But more import-ant, despite her attention to the exotic flavors, tastes, and textures, Donovan pays equal, if not more, attention to the actions and behaviors of the Indonesian servants, young boys with bare feet and clean uniforms who, in representing a cross between rural backwardness and civility, are subordinate in status. They are childlike, subservient, and do not talk back. Thus, cuisine and service made Asia and the Pacific into a colonial paradise. Such was the romance of Asian/Pacific food: it offered more than sustenance; it offered a lifestyle.

Some of the Asian and Pacific food cultures reflect the convergence and influ-ence of many different empires and colonial forces. Macao, a small city on the southern coast of China near Hong Kong, is one of those places, where Portu-guese, Chinese, and American powers collided in the postwar period. In *Far East-ern Epicure*, Donovan describes her visit in the 1950s and again paints an idyllic colonial backdrop for the reader. "The Pousada Inn in Macao awakens at sun-set," described Donovan. "In the soft glow of the twilight the blemished, decaying stucco façade is transformed into a stage setting for a Mediterranean romance."[38] But it was the cuisine that made "pocket-sized Macao" a place where one could get a taste of not just China but the world. Tourists wandered around on the city's sidewalks and indulged in food that was hardly "Chinese"—such as olives and garlic, Portuguese wine, "eels a la Pousada," and "Chicken Mozambique."

Donovan also profiles a chef, Angelo, who operated an open-air kitchen on a Macao street. She describes his latest possession, a "three-legged barbeque stove streamlined with the same efficient touch that marks all American products," which he "received from a Chicago store after choosing it from a mail-order catalogue." According to Donovan, Angelo had never traveled outside Hong Kong but had become increasingly "restless" because of an interaction he had had with an American businessman who wanted to open a Portuguese drive-in restaurant in Los Angeles. During one visit, the businessman found Angelo's food to be delicious and, upon returning to California, wrote to recruit him to come to California and work as a "blue-ribbon chef" at his restaurant.[39]

Donovan's account vividly captures the way Portuguese, Chinese, and American influences played out in the textures of everyday life. The food of Macao certainly reflects this collision, particularly Angelo's recipe for Chicken Mozambique, a dish that combines Portuguese and East African ingredients and flavors. Angelo got the recipe from African soldiers stationed on the island to "protect" Macao from invasion.

During the 1600s, the Portuguese Empire transported thousands of African slaves from one colony, in Mozambique, to Macao, where they sought to establish another colonial outpost.[40] As the African soldiers patrolled Macao, they often came into direct conflict with the local Chinese population. But more important, Portuguese influence and control over Macao waned after World War II as the result of both its struggle for independence from Portuguese rule and global independence movements. It was during this decline of formal European colonialism (formal British rule in Hong Kong ended as well) in Asia that the United States began insinuating itself into everyday Macanese life. Angelo's interaction with the American businessman and his purchase of a new, "modern" American grill from what was most likely a department store catalog underscore U.S. economic and cultural infiltration. Macao's food culture provides a glimpse of cultural mixing embedded in old-style European colonialism and imperialism, as was the case in Indonesia. Yet this cultural mixing also was clearly about the influence of a new burgeoning global power: the United States. White American women's growing fascination with Asian/Pacific cuisine food was not simply a feeling or attitude; it was part of the United States' global expansion into Asia and the Pacific that secured and facilitated access to new markets, new people, and, thus, new cuisines.

U.S. Global Expansion, Tourism, and Food Culture in Asia and the Pacific

The United States emerged from World War II as the new global power and embarked on a campaign to secure the world for capitalism by defeating communism. The Cold War between the United States and its allies and the Soviet Union and its allies was an intense global competition that sparked political tension, a military defense buildup, and anxiety over the possibility of nuclear annihilation. Just as important, the ascendance of the United States as the preeminent world leader coincided with the explosion of Third-World anticolonial movements in Africa, Asia, and Latin America, which led to numerous interventions, by both the United States and the Soviet Union, into the "darker nations."

Some scholars have explored the role of U.S. cultural production in the formation of postwar U.S. global supremacy. In *Cold War Orientalism*, Christina Klein argues that while the Truman administration forged a U.S. domestic culture of containment, "liberal" U.S. political elites turned their attention to building stronger relations with their allies, especially in Asia and the Pacific. These liberal officials formulated what she calls a "global imaginary of integration," a comprehensive way of viewing the world as a place with open pathways between those nations whose differences could be resolved and overcome by forging intellectual and emotional bonds.[41] After the defeat of Nazi Germany and amid the growing anticolonial movements for self-determination, the United States had to assure itself and the rest of the world that its new position as the leader of the Free World did not simply mean business as usual, that is, the continuation of white supremacy by way of colonial rule. U.S. officials understood that overt force and violence were no longer acceptable as means to gain political and economic dominance, especially with the natives fighting back. Fueled by the ideology of "modernization," the post–World War II U.S. Empire opened access to new markets and tried to secure the supremacy of global capitalism by promoting development, democracy, and cultural understanding.[42] Thus, U.S. empire building in the Cold War demanded more than the defensive posture of communist containment. Equally important was the *integration* of Latin America, Africa, Asia, and the Pacific.

White American women who traveled in and tasted the foods of Asia and the Pacific did so as a direct result of U.S. global expansion. During this period, the U.S. State Department expanded the definition of "tourist" from "sightseeing traveler" to "the bona fide non-immigrant who desires to make a temporary visit to a foreign country for any legitimate purpose." In other words, it defined the American traveler as an agent, representative, and diplomat of the United States around the world. As Ruby Erskine did, many accompanied their husbands, who went as military officials, diplomats, businessmen, ambassadors, volunteers, teachers, scholars, and tourists. Marie Wilson traveled to Thailand to marry her fiancé, a Fulbright scholar teaching English in

Bangkok. Meda Croizat journeyed wherever her husband, Marine Colonel Victor Croizat, was assigned. Janeth Johnson Nix made her extensive trip to the "Orient" after her husband's company transferred him to Kobe, Japan, in 1967. Wilson, Croizat, and Johnson Nix joined hundreds of thousands of U.S. citizens who traveled around the world. In 1947, approximately 200,000 Americans had valid passports. During the mid-1950s, more than one million U.S. citizens went overseas, and by 1959, around seven million took trips abroad. While only 500,000 tourists visited Asia and the Pacific that year, there was a great deal of interest in the region, in large part because of the boom in travel writing. James Michener's *The Voice of Asia*, for instance, made Asia real to U.S. citizens, as did other travel writers who introduced the peoples and cultures of Asia and the Pacific through newspapers, magazines, and films.[43]

White women's participation in culinary adventure illustrates the central role of women in the development of the informal U.S. Empire after World War II, with U.S. tourism in Asia and the Pacific during the Cold War operating as a "soft" version of U.S. Empire. These women's appropriation of Asian and Pacific food practices was fueled by the development of tourist infrastructure at a moment when "Third World" countries, having recently won independence from colonial rule, were trying to establish their economic autonomy. In fact, as Christina Klein shows, the boom in U.S. tourism in Asia and the Pacific was intertwined with U.S. global expansion, even sharing the same material infrastructure. Not only did the U.S. federal government play a role in funding the construction of airstrips around the world, but the tourist industry itself also functioned as a colonial economy in which self-determination shifted from local populations to outside interests and entities: the U.S. corporation and the U.S. consumer.

Members of the travel industry identified the construction of a tourist infrastructure—airports, airstrips, hotels, golf courses, shopping centers, and restaurants—as both a necessity for U.S. travelers to access foreign places and a prime strategy for the economic development of the "Third World." The U.S. government and private companies like Pan American Airlines helped develop this infrastructure, and U.S. travel agents contributed as well. Travel agents encouraged the professionalization and consolidation of worldwide travel organizations, strengthened relationships between travel agents and government officials, joined the public and private sectors, lobbied governments to ease travel regulations in immigration policy, and, most important, secured capital investment to finance the modernization of the Third World's tourist infrastructure.

The Pacific Area Travel Association (PATA) is an example of how U.S. travel agents helped develop the tourist infrastructure in Asia and the Pacific that facilitated culinary tourism. In 1952, PATA was established in order to increase tourism and encourage U.S. travelers to "discover the Pacific." PATA, originally named the Pacific Interim Travel Association when it held its first meeting at a conference in Honolulu, advertised the region of Asia and the Pacific to investors as the next big consumer product. PATA's main mission was to help the people and cultures of Asia and the Pacific "move from post-WWII conditions of poverty to a position of global leadership."[44] In addition to assisting with postwar recovery efforts, PATA's vision paralleled U.S. attempts to use cultural exchange and understanding as a weapon in the Cold War. "Tourists bring wealth into a country," wrote U.S. Secretary of Commerce Luther H. Hodges, "wealth in the form of good will and understanding; wealth in the form of foreign exchange, vitally needed for international trade."[45] So PATA officials did more than just sell tourist packages; they sold the *idea* of U.S. tourism as an expression of postwar American global leadership and benevolence.

Thailand is a prime example of how PATA promoted tourism in Cold War Asia and the Pacific, as PATA officials worked with Thai leaders and the Thai government to make tourism the country's top priority for its postwar national development. In the late 1950s, Thai leaders had very little interest in tourism, as the country did not have an organized tourist industry, only 871 standard tourist rooms, and roughly 50,000 visitors per year, most of whom stayed in Bangkok for an average of only two to three days.[46] But PATA officials saw Thailand as a site with untapped tourist potential. In a 1958 report written for the U.S. Department of Commerce, PATA listed Thailand's location as the "air center" of Southeast Asia, its "raw materials" of spectacular temples, "exceptionally interesting classical Thai dancing," friendly people, and "colorful" way of life as key ingredients for profitable tourist destination.[47] Someone, it urged, just needed to package it. PATA suggested that the Tourism Organization of Thailand (TOT) work closely with the Thai government and especially with outside "specialists" and business leaders with private capital. It also laid out guidelines and ten-year projections, based on empirical research, for Thai leaders to follow if they wished to cash in on the booming industry: (1) network with other Asian and Pacific nations to develop regional tourism; (2) ensure the construction of 1,200 new, first-class hotel rooms at a price of $18 million; (3) create a long-term promotional and marketing program; and (4) eliminate government red tape and restrictions on travelers, such as expediting customs procedures, reducing immigration paperwork, and liberalizing visa "formalities." In 1959, the Thai government appeared to have seriously considered PATA's recommendations, making the Tourism Authority of Thailand (TAT) a part of its development planning. By the mid-1960s, the Thai government decided to invest heavily in an infrastructure for tourists. With luxury hotels erected for tourists as well as Thailand's wealthy socialites, the tourist-centered approach to economic development replaced anything resembling urban planning or policy in large cities like Bangkok.

PATA's effort to turn spaces like Bangkok into tourist playgrounds challenges what scholars have come to call "cultural imperialism." While the use of the term itself implies the destruction, eradication, and replacement of a culture with the cultural practices of a "superior" culture as an act of domination, this was not how the political economy of tourism functioned. As U.S. travel agents remade Asia and the Pacific to meet their particular vision of postwar development, they also were acutely aware that they had to preserve, protect, and respect other cultures. In essence, PATA officials fought to maintain cultural traditions in Asia and the Pacific at the same time that they destroyed them. In Thailand, for instance, PATA recommended that the country "encourage the preservation of Thai art and customs" and concluded that further "study will have to be given to ways and means of retaining their charm and preventing its deterioration and commercialization."[48]

U.S. tourism altered Asian and Pacific food culture as dramatically as it did the urban landscape and beaches. The transformation of the food culture during this period best captures the way U.S. tourism breathed life into the U.S. Empire. As a vital aspect of U.S. global capitalist expansion, the growth of tourist industries forced countries like Thailand to become service-based economies catering to the desires of both U.S. consumers and national wealthy elites, but at the expense of the local population's needs. For example, the growing number of hotels in Thailand allowed Thai chefs to interact more closely with U.S. officials and distinguished travelers. Thai sous-chefs learned fruit, vegetable, ice, and butter carving specifically to entertain tourists.[49] In Bangkok in the 1960s, Thai restaurants catering to private dining experiences with a Western sequence of courses began to appear along with a range of foreign restaurants—Korean, Lebanese, Japanese, Italian, French, Mexican—in part to attract U.S. diplomats, businessmen, and military officials.[50] Classical Thai dinner-and-dance shows also lured more wealthy tourists and visitors, who could experience "authentic" Thai food in a palace-like setting of "Old Siam."[51] Hawai'i, too, a U.S. colony deeply entangled in U.S. militarization and tourism since the late 1800s, underwent considerable changes as its tourist industry set travel records during this period. The island of Hawai'i became a playground for U.S. military servicemen and other travelers captivated by the hula. By the late 1950s, Hawai'i's tourist industry ranked third behind sugarcane and pineapple in economic importance and brought in 35 million tourist dollars annually, as much as Las Vegas did.[52]

U.S. culinary tourism in Asia and the Pacific further reveals that the Cold War was as much about global capitalist *integration* as it was about global communist *containment*. The U.S. travel industry facilitated U.S. Empire, acting literally as an arm of modernization and development that made Asian and Pacific countries and islands accessible for U.S. tourist gustatory consumption. The U.S. tourist industry created, maintained, and justified unequal encounters based on race, gender, and class.

Oriental Cookery in Cold War Suburban America

White women who encountered food cultures of Asia and the Pacific attempted to replicate the enchantment after returning home to fulfill their role as suburban housewives in the United States. One way that they did this was to introduce family and friends to their culinary discoveries by hosting Asian-inspired dinner parties. With the advent of the electric skillet, suburban homemakers were able to prepare Asian and Pacific dishes more efficiently while also using the skillet as the main attraction of a dinner party. An article from *Pacific Stars & Stripes* in May 1958 suggested that women "orient their diet" by using their electric skillets to make sukiyaki for party guests wanting to cook their own Japanese sukiyaki.[53]

Cooking "Oriental" was important because exposing friends and family to new, exotic flavors held the promise of elevating white American women's social and cultural status *outside* the confines of the home. In *Simple Oriental Cookery* (1960), author Edna Beilenson encourages readers to prepare the unfamiliar but simple recipes in her cookbook to entertain party guests. Beilenson opens with a poem in which she tries to erase for her readers any reservations they might have about Asian and Pacific dishes:

> From China, Hawaii
> From the Far-and Near-East
> We bring you these dishes
> On which you can feast
> They're really quite simple;
> They're really quite good;
> And really quite different
> From our Western food!
> You'll like Sukiyaki
> And Chinese Chow Mein;
> You'll come back to the curries

Again and again!
So don your kimono
Your sari or lei;
And fix your next party
The old Eastern way!

The poem clearly reveals that Beilenson imagined her reading audience to be fellow white American women, specifically suburban housewives, who were searching for ways to make themselves more interesting through food practices. She emphasizes how different the cuisine is from "our Western food" and invites white women to playfully dress up in a "kimono . . . sari or lei" and act as walking, breathing exotic decorations during themed dinner parties. The poem illuminates how white women could use "Far-and Near-East" dishes to elevate their *public* status in a private sphere.

One challenge they faced when hosting an Asian/Pacific–inspired dinner party was to make the exotic familiar to the American palate while trying to maintain the food's novelty and foreignness. One of the more effective, and undoubtedly inventive, strategies was giving Asian/Pacific dishes a "different twist" that fused "Oriental" and "American" foods. In 1962, Marian Manners offered some advice in a *Los Angeles Times* article that encourages suburban homemakers to plan an exciting Hawaiian-themed backyard Labor Day dinner party that will provide "glamour at little price in time and effort for the hostess."[54] Hawai'i, Manners insists, is the perfect theme for a party because of the island's Chinese, Japanese, Korean, Filipino, and Portuguese influences, which meant the "foods of these people can be combined in an exotic, but not too bizarre, cook-out supper." The "not too bizarre" dishes she suggests included a "Macadamian Pilaf," which required simply sprinkling Hawaiian macadamia nuts over an American rice pilaf, and "Kim Chee Dip," a blended mixture of Korean *kimchi* (spicy pickled cabbage) and cream cheese. Combining or sometimes blending together (for better or worse) what was considered Asian/Pacific and American foods was a method used to appeal to a novice's palate. But it was also an act that tapped into a broader discourse of global cultural exchange and understanding. In concocting the "Kim Chee Dip," white women not only tried to represent the seamless, harmonious mixing of "East" and "West" (and perhaps in this case failed)—they reinforced their status as worldly middle-class individuals.

In addition to dinner parties, white American women sought to display their identity and expertise in Asian/Pacific food by teaching courses on Oriental cookery. Cooking classes carried important meaning during the Cold

War era, particularly for women who tried to exercise autonomy outside their role as domestic housewives. In *Homeward Bound*, Elaine Tyler May points out that home economics courses and programs proliferated during these years as educators and counselors refashioned women's education to fit domestic tasks and attend college to "become interesting wives for educated husbands" or accept a career as a "professional homemaker."[55] In Santa Monica, California, Jennifer Brennan taught cooking classes to introduce Los Angelenos to Thai cuisine. Brennan's previous teaching experience with Chinese and Indian cooking prompted her to teach evening Thai cooking classes for white housewives in the recreation room of her apartment building.[56] Her thirty-dollar courses, based on participation instead of demonstration, were wildly popular and often overcrowded.

Moreover, in several cases throughout the 1960s, Oriental cooking was used to bolster civic engagement. In Los Angeles's San Gabriel Valley, the Alhambra–San Gabriel Chapter of the Daughters of the American Revolution, an organization for women who were direct descendants of men who participated in the American Revolution, selected "Oriental Hour" as the theme for a benefit brunch held at the Edison Company's offices in February 1963. Margo Wells, a home economist, showcased a luncheon at which she provided a "cooking demonstration of Oriental foods," its quick preparations, and the versatility of the electric skillet.[57] Teaching cooking courses thus became an opportunity for white American women to enter the public sphere and build community.

Several white American women also wrote some of the first Asian/Pacific cookbooks in the United States, which were filled with recipes appropriated from China, Japan, Thailand, Indonesia, India, and Hawai'i. Writing cookbooks meant more than introducing new cuisines, cooking methods, and ideas for dinner parties, as it allowed white American women to act as authorities on Asian/Pacific cuisines in U.S. society. Describing in written form the cooking methods that had been passed down orally enabled these women to establish expertise and ownership of a food culture different from their own. Translating "inaccessible" cooking methods into "recipes" during the Cold War standardized and thus "modernized" Asian/Pacific food practices into an exact science in which ingredients could be measured, cooked, and replicated inside the home with new appliances. Also, being the first to present recipes in the English language turned white American women into authorities because they, by default, appeared to be the only ones with knowledge of this subject.[58]

In addition, writing an ethnic cookbook served as a platform for white housewives to further present themselves as worldly, cultured individuals and explorers of foreign cultures with exciting stories to tell. As cultural outsiders, they had to convince their audience of adventurous readers that the collection of Asian and Pacific recipes was indeed authentic and vastly different. To achieve this, they described in detail their extensive travel through Asian and Pacific countries and their submersion in other ways of life. They demonstrated their knowledge of Asian ingredients and their mastery of cooking techniques. Above all, they played up their personal relationships with "native informants" in order to authenticate recipes and also to show their willingness to accept exotic others. Janeth Johnson Nix claims in *Adventures in Oriental Cooking* that

> almost all of my life I've been surrounded by Orientals as friends, and for at least twenty years I've made very special demands upon them: "Tell me what it is. Show me how to do it." Most of them are Japanese, Chinese, or Korean; some are nationals, some are second or third generation, all have been heroically obliging. You will meet many of them in this book.[59]

What is fascinating about these Oriental-inspired dinner parties, cooking classes, and cookbooks is not merely that it helped configure Asians and Pacific Islanders as exotic others within the frame of Orientalism. It is fascinating because it happened in a space and time—in the historical imagination—characterized by mass consumption, suburbanization, nuclear bomb scares, and, most important, cultural and political conformity exemplified by U.S. citizens turning inward to the domestic sphere. All of this contributed to the consolidation of whiteness. Yet the evidence suggests that U.S. Cold War intervention in Asia and the Pacific also shaped the contours of race, gender, and class in profound ways. Alongside meatloaf and frozen TV dinners, U.S. citizens prepared and consumed Peking duck and chicken curry. White suburban homemakers used Asian/Pacific food culture to carve some room and maneuverability under Cold War gender conventions as they moved outside their domestic role and into the public sphere.

Taste and smell mattered. In a moment of conformity to whiteness when nearly everything *looked* the same—houses, appliances, cars, and even the housewives themselves—one way in which they distinguished themselves was to deliver new flavors, tastes, smells, and stories. White American women used the exotic tastes and flavors of Asian/Pacific cuisine to make themselves appear more interesting, cultured, and unusual in order to stand out from other suburban homemakers. The more exotic and thrilling the food, the better. Their relationship to Asian/Pacific food culture simultaneously allowed them to challenge gender conventions and enter into postwar middle-class whiteness, thus shaping their racial and class position. Above all, they benefited from U.S. intervention in Asia and the Pacific, which granted them access to the "raw material" of Asian/Pacific food and a chance to become players in U.S. global expansion.

Conclusion

In this chapter, I examined the historical roots of the relationship of Asian/Pacific food culture, politics, and identity formation in the context of U.S. global expansion during the Cold War. Placing the history of white American women's encounters with "Oriental cookery" in the context of the U.S. Cold War intervention in Asia and the Pacific, I argued that Asian/Pacific food culture is one of the best ways to uncover the way that the post–World War II U.S. Empire turned foodways into a site of identity formation for white American women, particularly suburban housewives. I also showed how food became linked to imperialism and neocolonialism that extended beyond personal attitudes and cultural representations. Food practices are significant because they show us that food, as a practice of everyday life, help people make sense of the world around them. Thus food practices operated as a form of exploitation and exercise of power along racial, gender, and class lines in late twentieth-century U.S. society.

This story broadens and deepens the narrative of U.S. Cold War history by challenging the boundaries separating "foreign policy" from "domestic affairs" that prevent a more complex and accurate portrait of U.S. society. We see that ordinary U.S. citizens participated in the Cold War on the ground. They imagined themselves as members of a global community who tried to build meaningful relationships through supposedly equal cultural exchanges and understanding. Therefore, we must take into account how U.S. global expansion shapes U.S. social, political, economic, and cultural milieus, and must examine how U.S. policies affect everyday life in other countries and in what capacity. The history of Asian/Pacific foodways in the United States is an excellent place to start.

Notes

1. I use the term "Oriental" at many points throughout this chapter because I want to place in front of readers the exact terminology used to describe Asian and Pacific Islander food and peoples during this period. I have tried to replace "Oriental" with "Asian/Pacific" when possible, but I have kept it where I believe it is useful for understanding white Americans' attitudes toward and assumptions about Asia and the Pacific.
2. Winnifred Jardini, "The Secrets of the Far East," *Deseret News*, February 13, 1970.

3. For an excellent discussion of early American Orientalism, see John Kuo Wei Tchen, *New York before Chinatown: Orientalism and the Shaping of American Culture, 1776–1882* (Baltimore: Johns Hopkins University Press, 1999).

4. U.S. Census 1970, *Social Explorer & U.S. Census Bureau* (Washington, DC: U.S. Government Printing Office, 1972, P1–P9.

5. National Archives and Records Administration, *U.S. World War II Army Enlistment Records, 1938–1946* [database on-line] (Provo, UT: Ancestry.com Operations Inc., 2005), original data: Electronic Army Serial Number Merged File, 1938–1946 [archival database]; World War II Army Enlistment Records, Records of the National Archives and Records Administration, Record Group 64, National Archives, College Park, MD.

6. Odd Arne Westad, *The Global Cold War* (Cambridge: Cambridge University Press, 2007), 24.

7. Christina Klein, *Cold War Orientalism: Asia in the Middlebrow Imagination, 1945–1961* (Berkeley: University of California Press, 2003); Naoko Shibusawa, *America's Geisha Ally: Reimagining the Japanese Enemy* (Cambridge, MA: Harvard University Press, 2006).

8. Jodi Kim, *Ends of Empire: Asian American Critique and the Cold War* (Minneapolis: University of Minnesota Press, 2010), 237.

9. Robert G. Lee, *Orientals: Asian Americans in Popular Culture* (Philadelphia: Temple University Press, 1999), 146.

10. Charlotte Brooks, *Alien Neighbors, Foreign Friends: Asian Americans, Housing, and the Transformation of California* (Chicago: University of Chicago Press, 2009); Shirley Jennifer Lim, *A Feeling of Belonging: Asian American Women's Public Culture, 1930–1960* (New York: New York University Press, 2006); Mae Ngai, *Impossible Subjects: Illegal Aliens and the Making of Modern America* (Princeton, NJ: Princeton University Press, 2004).

11. Lisa Heldke, *Exotic Appetites: Ruminations of a Food Adventurer* (New York: Routledge, 2003), xv–xviii.

12. Andrew Coe, *Chop Suey: A Cultural History of Chinese Food in the United States* (Oxford: Oxford University Press, 2009), 147.

13. Ibid.

14. Ibid., 216.

15. Harley Spiller, "Chow Fun City: Three Centuries of Chinese Cuisine in New York City," in *Gastropolis: Food and New York City*, ed. Anne Hauck-Lawson and Jonathan Deutsch (New York: Columbia University Press, 2009), 143.

16. Marie M. Wilson, *Siamese Cookery* (Rutland, VT: Tuttle, 1965); and Cecil Fleming, "A Happy Task—Getting to Know Thai Cuisine," *Los Angeles Times*, January 6, 1966.

17. Jean Murphy, "She's Gung Ho for Oriental Cookery," *Los Angeles Times*, August 31, 1967.

18. Peter Lee, interview conducted by Robert Klein, August 4, 2004, Returned Peace Corp Volunteer Oral History Collection, John F. Kennedy Presidential Library, Boston; Jerolyn "Jerri" Minor, interview conducted by Susan Luccini, March 27, 2008, Returned Peace Corps Volunteer Oral History Collection, John F. Kennedy Presidential Library, Boston.

19. Marianne May Apple, Returned Peace Corps Volunteer Personal Papers, John F. Kennedy Presidential Library, Box 13, 8–9, Boston.

20. May Apple, Returned Peace Corps Volunteer Personal Papers, July 26, 1966, 14; November 10, 1966, 33.
21. Wilson, *Siamese Cookery*, 16.
22. Maria Kozslik Donovan, *The Far Eastern Epicure* (Garden City, NY: Doubleday, 1958), 59.
23. See Mark Smith, *Sensing The Past: Seeing, Hearing, Smelling, Tasting, and Touching in History* (Berkeley: University of California Press, 2007), 3.
24. Janeth Johnson Nix, *Adventures in Oriental Cooking* (San Francisco: Ortho Books, 1976), 9.
25. Wilson, *Siamese Cookery*, 12.
26. Nix, *Adventures in Oriental Cooking*, 3.
27. "Spring Rolls Coming Up," *Pacific Stars & Stripes*, December 20, 1962, 7.
28. Jennifer Brennan, *The Original Thai Cookbook*, 3, 4; quoted from Heldke, *Exotic Appetites*, 101.
29. Ancestry.com, *Cook County, Illinois Marriage Index, 1930* Janeth Johnson Nix, *Adventures in Oriental Cooking 1960* [database on-line]. Provo, UT, Ancestry.com Operations Inc., 2008, original data: Cook County Clerk, comp., *Cook County Clerk Genealogy Records* (Chicago: Cook County Clerk's Office, 2008).
30. Donovan, *Far Eastern Epicure*, 17.
31. Barbara Hansen, "Students Learn by Doing: Thai Cookery with a British Accent," *Los Angeles Times,* May 12, 1977.
32. Donovan, *The Far Eastern Epicure*, 19.
33. Ibid., 65–68.
34. Ibid., 23.
35. Ibid., 24.
36. Sri Owen, *Indonesian Regional Food & Cookery* (London: Frances Lincoln, 1999), 22; Michael Krondl, *The Taste of Conquest: The Rise and Fall of the Three Great Cities of Spice* (New York: Random House, 2007) 261.
37. Donovan, *The Far Eastern Epicure*, 40.
38. Ibid., 131.
39. Ibid., 132–33.
40. Zhidong Hao, *Macau: History and Society* (Hong Kong: Hong Kong University Press, 2011), 63.
41. Klein, *Cold War Orientalism*, 23, 41–49.
42. For a discussion of how modernization theory informed U.S. foreign policy and its similarities to U.S. imperialism at the turn of the nineteenth century, see Michael E. Latham, *Modernization as Ideology: American Social Science and "Nation Building" in the Kennedy Era* (Chapel Hill: University of North Carolina Press, 2000), chap. 2.
43. See Klein, *Cold War Orientalism*, chap. 3.
44. Chuck Y. Gee and Matt Lurie, eds., *The Story of the Pacific Asia Travel Association* (San Francisco: Pacific Asia Travel Association, 1993), xiii.
45. Harry G. Clement, "The Future of Tourism in the Pacific and Far East" (Washington, DC: U.S. Department of Commerce, Bureau of Foreign Commerce, 1961), iii.
46. Christopher J. Baker and Pasuk Phongpaichit, *A History of Thailand* (New York: Cambridge University Press, 2005), 149; and Clement, "The Future of Tourism," 127.
47. Clement, "The Future of Tourism," 127.

48. Ibid., 135.
49. Brennan, *The Original Thai Cookbook*, 29.
50. Philip Cornwel-Smith, *Very Thai: Everyday Popular Culture* (Bangkok: River Books, 2006), 18; Penny Van Esterik, *Food Culture in Southeast Asia* (Westport, CT: Greenwood Press, 2008), 90.
51. Van Esterik, *Food Culture in Southeast Asia*, 90.
52. "Tourist Boom Establishes Hawaii Records," *Los Angeles Times,* October 31, 1954, A15.
53. "Orienting Your Diet: Japan's Food Is Fun to Eat," *Pacific Stars & Stripes*, May 23, 1958, 11.
54. Marian Manners, "Brimful of Goodies for Hungry Mainlanders: Hawaii Calls Gourmet." *Los Angeles Times*, August 30, 1962.
55. Elaine Tyler May, *Homeward Bound: American Families in the Cold War Era* (New York: Basic Books, 1999), 72–73.
56. Hansen, "Students Learn by Doing."
57. "Oriental Theme Selected," *Los Angeles Times*, February 14, 1963.
58. Heldke, *Exotic Appetites*, 105–10.
59. Nix, *Adventures in Oriental Cooking*, 3.

10

Gannenshoyu or First-Year Soy Sauce?

Kikkoman Soy Sauce and the Corporate Forgetting
of the Early Japanese American Consumer

ROBERT JI-SONG KU

On September 19, 2007, the Kikkoman Corporation placed a full-page color advertisement in the *New York Times* commemorating the company's fiftieth anniversary in America. The ad is essentially a letter of thanks to America from Yuzaburo Mogi, the company's chairman and CEO. "Arigato, America," the ad reads in large letters. A large photographic cutout of a smiling, grandfatherly Mr. Mogi appears beneath the 160-word letter, accompanied on the left by a bottle of Kikkoman soy sauce hovering over a special gold emblem expressly designed for this occasion. The emblem, announcing "50th Anniversary in America," is flanked by two dates, 1957 and 2007. To the right of Mogi is a caption identifying the chairman as a "member of the family that founded the company more than three centuries ago" and who "helped make Kikkoman one of the world's leading food brands."

"Thank you, America, for 50 great years," begins Chairman Mogi's letter:

Thank you for making Kikkoman one of America's best-loved food brands. We are honored and humbled by the generous welcome you have extended to us since we started marketing our soy sauce in America 50 years ago.

A lot has changed since then, but one thing remains the same. Our core product, naturally brewed soy sauce, is still made just as it was more than 300 years ago—slowly fermented and aged for full flavor like a fine wine.

Over the last half century, you have embraced our soy sauce, teriyaki, and other authentic seasonings and products. You have made us a part of the American pantry. And as we celebrate our golden anniversary with you, we thank you for welcoming us into your homes and your hearts, and we look forward to sharing a place a the table with you for many years to come.

At the bottom of the ad, under the interlocked fingers of the genial-looking chairman, are the details of Kikkoman's fiftieth-anniversary sweepstake, promising great prizes, including a trip to Japan, no purchase necessary.

Far from being a singular event, this ad was a small snippet of a wider, all-out marketing blitz choreographed by the Kikkoman Corporation for the better part of 2007. In observance of the anniversary, the company replaced the standard labels on many of its products with newly designed commemorative ones and replaced the signature red caps on some bottles of soy sauce with festive gold ones. Earlier in the year, before more than forty journalists gathered at San Francisco's city hall, the president of the San Francisco Board of Supervisors proclaimed June 5, 2007, as the city's "Kikkoman Day." It was here in 1957 that Kikkoman established Kikkoman International, Inc., and Kikkoman Day marked the fiftieth anniversary of that occasion.[1]

The festivities in San Francisco were followed a few months later by a gala in Washington, DC, held across the street from the White House at the U.S. Chamber of Commerce. With a guest list of more than two hundred business and political luminaries, the event featured congratulatory speeches by, among others, Carlos M. Gutierrez (secretary of commerce), Jim Doyle (governor of Wisconsin), and Tommy Thompson (former secretary of health and human services). During the proceedings, congressional members announced that a resolution recognizing Kikkoman's fifty years in the United States had been submitted to both houses of Congress.[2]

Governor Jim Doyle's conspicuous role in the Chamber of Commerce gala was not incidental. In May 2003, the Kikkoman Foundation pledged a million dollars to the University of Wisconsin–Madison to establish the Kikkoman Laboratory of Microbial Fermentation. This gift was connected to another Kikkoman anniversary, the thirtieth anniversary of the company's first U.S.-based soy sauce production facility, established in Wisconsin's Walworth County in 1973. The opening of this plant was momentous, as Kikkoman was arguably the first Japanese company to establish a production facility on U.S. soil.[3]

In *Kikkoman Chronicles*, a book commissioned by the company on the history of the Kikkoman Corporation, the author, Ronald E. Yates, writes:

> The Kikkoman Soy Sauce plant (in Walworth) is generally conceded to be the first full-blown Japanese manufacturing facility ever constructed in the United States. . . . While it's true that Japan's Sony Corp. opened a television picture tube assembly plant that it had previously purchased near San Diego in 1972, it wasn't producing a product from scratch the way Kikkoman's Walworth plan was. Nor was it producing a 100 percent Japanese product like brewed soy sauce.[4]

Figure 10.1. Kikkoman's Golden Anniversary advertisement published in the *New York Times* on September 19, 2007. Photograph by the author.

But perhaps of greater interest, especially in respect to Kikkoman's presence in America, is a historical tidbit revealed elsewhere in Yates's book about an event that took place a century earlier.

According to Yates, in 1868, "the same year that the Emperor Meiji wrested power from the Tokugawa Shogunate," Saheiji Mogi (a forebear of the current chairman Mogi) shipped kegs of Kikkoman soy sauce (called *shoyu* in Japanese) to Hawai'i and California in an effort to expand the Kikkoman brand internationally.[5] "By 1868, the Mogi clan was shipping soy sauce to Hawaii and California—traveling with some of the first Japanese immigrants to both places, writes Yates."[6] This detail is reiterated in the book's conclusion:

> Someone once said that you cannot discover new oceans unless you have the courage to lose sight of the shore. It's a great definition of risktaking. Losing sight of Japan's shore is something the Kikkoman Corporation has been doing for almost half of its 300-plus-years of existence. It began when members of the Mogi clan began shipping kegs of Kikkoman brand soy sauce to Hawaii and California in 1868—the same year Japan opened its doors to the world after almost 300 years of self-imposed isolation. And it didn't stop there. Kikkoman went on to set up a subsidiary in San Francisco in 1957 that has become a benchmark model of how to introduce a relatively unknown product (Japanese shoyu) to the mainstream U.S. market.

Yates's evocation of the year 1868, when juxtaposed with 1957 and 2007, raises an obvious question: If Kikkoman soy sauce was indeed shipped to Hawai'i and California at the onset of the Meiji era, why would that not qualify as the first instance of its marketing in America? Yates's account obfuscates as much as it reveals. In one instance, Yates states that Kikkoman soy sauce was shipped *to* Japanese immigrants in Hawai'i and the United States as early as 1868. But he also states that the soy sauce *traveled with* them, implying that the immigrants purchased it before leaving Japan. If Yates's account of Kikkoman's start in America is true, why, then, not commemorate 1868, instead of 1957, as Kikkoman's first year in America? Moreover, if Kikkoman soy sauce was indeed shipped to Hawai'i and the United States as early as 1868, were there any Japanese immigrants in either location to receive it? That is, was the Japanese population large enough to make it financially viable for Kikkoman to ship its soy sauce over such a long distance?

In both the *New York Times* ad and Kikkoman's corporate website, as well as in the fulsome press coverage of the soy sauce maker's anniversary celebration, 1957 is emphatically referred to as either the "start" of Kikkoman soy sauce "marketing" in America or the year in which the soy sauce first "entered" U.S. markets. Senate Resolution 323—introduced during the first session of the 110th Congress on September 20, 2007, by Senators Herbert Kohl (D-WI) and Russell Feingold (D-WI)—recognizes "Kikkoman Foods, Inc., for its 50 years of operations in the United States." (Apparently, the resolution confused Kikkoman Foods, Inc., the subsidiary overseeing the Walworth plant, for Kikkoman International, Inc., the company's San Francisco–based marketing arm.) The resolution also recognizes Kikkoman as "celebrating its 50th anniversary of business in the United States during the year 2007"; as having "established sales operations in San Francisco, California, in 1957"; as annually shipping "over 30,000,000 gallons of soy sauce throughout North America"; as "one of the first Japanese companies to have a major manufacturing plant in the Unites States"; as continuing "to make steadfast commitment to the economic and culinary vitality of the United States"; and as having remained for fifty years "steadfast in its devotion to promoting international cultural exchange." The document concludes by resolving that the Senate

1. recognizes the importance of the contribution made by Kikkoman Foods, Inc., to the cultural and economic vitality of the United States; and
2. commends Kikkoman Foods on its 50 years of marketing and operations in the United States.[7]

As the resolution directly states and various media widely announced, the golden anniversary celebration very clearly commemorated the 1957 installation of Kikkoman International, Inc., in San Francisco.

But how significant is Yates's revelation that Kikkoman shipped its soy sauce to Japanese in Hawai'i and California as early as 1868? Surely, if this were the case, these earliest Japanese immigrants could not have received the product as a gift; that is, they must have bought it. Therefore, can we consider 2007 as Kikkoman's 139th anniversary in America? In fact, there is irrefutable evidence that on numerous occasions not long *after* 1868 and long *before* 1957, Kikkoman soy sauce was marketed to, exported to, and consumed by a sizable group of Americans. Thus, if not the first instance of Kikkoman soy sauce being marketed in the United States, what does 1957 really commemorate? And what is Yates implying when he describes the San Francisco subsidiary as first introducing Japanese soy sauce to the "mainstream U.S. market"? Of course, what Yates is really saying here is that the soy sauce was indeed marketed to some Americans before 1957. Who exactly, then, is part of this so-called mainstream, and who is outside it? What do these three dates—1868, 1957, and 2007—really signify?

The answer, it turns out, is obliquely hinted at in the Kikkoman newspaper ad, when Mogi describes Kikkoman soy sauce as a "naturally brewed soy sauce . . . still made just as it was more than 300 years ago—slowly fermented and aged for full flavor like a fine wine." With this self-characterization, Kikkoman reveals a marketing strategy that attempts to establish the legitimacy of its own soy sauce while alluding to what it sees as the dubiousness of some of its competitors' soy sauces that do not undergo a similar process of slow fermentation. Referred to by some as "non-brewed," "hydrolyzed," or "chemical" soy sauce, and often American made, alternative types of soy sauce are widely consumed the world over, and, owing to its lower cost compared with that of the traditionally long-brewed type, will most likely increase in popularity. By repeatedly stressing that its soy sauce is "naturally brewed," "slowly fermented," and "aged," Kikkoman is strongly insinuating that non-brewed soy sauces are "unnatural" and therefore inauthentic. They are, in a word, fake.

To drive home this point, Kikkoman even went as far as to ask an international food arbitrator—the United Nation's Codex Alimentarius Commission—to bar U.S. soy sauce makers from using the term "soy sauce" when marketing their non-brewed products. Undeterred, the U.S. makers parried by essentially accusing Kikkoman of unfair essentialism: "All we want is for the standard for soy sauces to be all-inclusive," argued a U.S. delegate to the commission. "We have people who make naturally brewed and the hydrolyzed. We just have to make sure the product is safe and compatible, that's all."[8]

But in hitching the "authentic soy sauce" advertising strategy to the San Francisco office's fiftieth anniversary, Kikkoman not only is deliberately questioning the legitimacy of its competitors' soy sauces but also is consciously characterizing another thing as an ersatz version of what that thing purports to be. By essentially erasing the history of Kikkoman's marketing presence in Hawai'i and the United States between 1868 and 1957, the company is asking whether those who consumed its soy sauce during this period are, in fact, authentically American. In other words, Japanese Americans, who constituted a major overseas market for Kikkoman soy sauce for many decades before 1957, are simultaneously likened to fake soy sauce and defined as ersatz Americans.

Read against the interwoven backdrops of early Japanese history in Hawai'i and California, and the current debate taking place among soy sauce manufacturers over the very definition of soy sauce, it is apparent that Kikkoman's *New York Times* ad and the associated golden anniversary celebration reveal a series of assertions, conjectures, and implications that radiate far beyond Mogi's simple desire to say, "Arigato, America."

First-Year Soy Sauce?

On May 17, 1868, a little less than a century before Kikkoman established its San Francisco office, the first large group of Japanese to sail for Hawai'i boarded the *Scioto*, a ship ferrying 149 contract laborers—141 men, six women, and two children—from Yokohama to Honolulu.[9] The only Japanese to disembark on the islands earlier—long before James Cook "discovered" them in 1778—were most likely shipwrecked Japanese sailors who drifted ashore.[10] None of them left any trace. According to Yamato Ichihashi in his landmark 1932 study, *Japanese in the United States*, the earliest Japanese document noting the arrival of Japanese in Hawai'i is 1803, whereas the earliest Hawaiian document dates this to 1832, "when a small number of Japanese castaways were brought to Honolulu on board an American sailing vessel."[11] "Thus it seems evident that a number of Japanese by accident reached both Hawai'i and California in those early years but neither were induced nor cared to remain," writes Ichihashi. "They returned to their native land as soon as they found opportunity to do so."[12]

In contrast, the passengers aboard the *Scioto* were not compelled to go ashore because of some unfortunate nautical mishap. Indeed, Hawai'i was their intended destination, even if most "had no accurate idea of where they were going"; they simply "expected to become wealthy."[13] Specifically, they came to work in Hawai'i's burgeoning sugar plantations under a three-year contract brokered by an enterprising—albeit unscrupulous, by most accounts—American businessman named Eugene M. Van Reed. Known as the *gannenmono*, or "first-year people," to indicate that they migrated during the first year of the Meiji Restoration, this pioneering group consisted of "a few samurai, a hairdresser, cooks, potters, printers, saké brewers, tailors, and woodworkers."[14] Also among them was a stowaway, who kept a diary of the passage. In his entries was an inventory of the ship's provisions, which included items indispensable to the Japanese diet: more than five hundred bags of rice (mostly brown, which some of the passengers passed the time by polishing during the long journey), miso (a paste made of fermented soybeans, barley, and rice in varying combinations), and soy sauce.[15]

W. Mark Fruin, author of *Kikkoman: Company, Clan, and Community*, one of the volumes in the Harvard Studies in Business History series, writes that in 1838, Saheiji Mogi "petitioned for and received central government registration of the brand name Kikkoman and unknowingly began what would become a century-long crusade for brand recognition of his family's flagship shoyu, Kikkoman." This sort of assertive business maneuver was "a rather unusual move for the time," observes Fruin. While the Mogi family sold soy sauces under a variety of brand names, "Kikkoman was the pride of the family, its private label."[16] Even the name, Kikkoman, is special. The word is composed of three characters, the first two (*kikkō*) meaning "tortoise shell" and the third (*man*) meaning "ten thousand." Because *kikkō* also can mean hexagon, the brand's logo is a hexagon with the character *man* in the middle.[17] In what turned out to be one of many shrewd moves in expanding his prized brand overseas, in 1879, Mogi registered Kikkoman in California "as a legally recognized brand name, a move that predated the same legal protection in Japan by six years."[18] By 1906, the brand had been registered in every U.S. state.[19]

As Ronald Yates asserts in his Kikkoman-commissioned book, if Saheiji Mogi shipped kegs of soy sauce to Hawai'i 1868 *with* Japanese immigrants, it must have been aboard the *Scioto*, and the soy sauce inventoried in the stowaway's diary must have borne the Kikkoman label. But if the kegs were shipped *to* Japanese immigrants aboard a different vessel that same year, the *gannenmono*, who constituted the entirety of the Japanese population on the islands during those early years, had to have been the intended buyers. (Almost twenty years passed before another of shipload of Japanese went to Hawai'i.) As contract laborers subject to precise, if not coercive, contractual conditions, this first group of Japanese, once on the islands, had to buy everything they would need, including grocery items such as rice and soy sauce. Considering Saheiji Mogi's bold tactics to internationalize the Kikkoman brand as early as the first half of the nineteenth century—a business gambit not attempted by his more hidebound Japanese competitors—the *gannenmono*'s soy sauce in all probability was Kikkoman.

Casting a bit of doubt on this conjecture, however, is the fact that nowhere in Fruin's meticulous account of the company's history is there any mention of any soy sauce, let alone the Kikkoman brand, being shipped to Hawai'i — or anywhere else outside Japan, for that matter—in 1868. Indeed, the earliest mention of Kikkoman's international exposure is 1872, when Saheiji Mogi entered the soy sauce in the Amsterdam World's Fair, followed a year later at the Austria World's Fair, where it received a letter of commendation for excellence. A gold medal awarded at the 1883 Amsterdam World's Fair further exposed Kikkoman to an international audience and stimulated consumer demand both in and beyond Japan. Mogi promptly capitalized on the growing exposure by raising the price of Kikkoman soy sauce at home higher than that of his domestic competitors. According to Fruin, Mogi also raised imports, most notably to Hawai'i and California, "where the kegs of Kikkoman were particularly prized by the increasing number of Japanese immigrants."[20]

But this did not happen until the late 1880s, or perhaps even later, when the Japanese population in Hawai'i had begun to rise significantly. For nearly two decades after the *Scioto* landed there, the Japanese government stopped send-ing laborers to Hawai'i. Rumors of maltreatment of the *gannenmono* by the plantation hierarchy, as well as news of abuse of fellow Asians, the Chinese in particular, had reached Japanese authorities and been reported in the press.[21] Moreover, as Hilary Conroy notes, "The Japanese were determined that West-ern nations should not have reason to regard Japan as an Oriental storehouse of coolie labor like China. And to them the case of the *Gannen Mono* savored not only of coolie trade but even of kidnapping."[22] The harsh conditions of plantation life eventually compelled forty *gannenmono* to return to Japan before fulfilling their three-year contracts, with thirty-nine formally accusing Hawai'i's plantations of cruelty and breach of contract.[23] For several years, the plantations, eager for laborers, implored Japan to reconsider its policy, and Japan finally assented in 1884. Representing the restart of Japanese labor to Hawai'i were the passengers aboard the *City of Tokyo*, which arrived in Hono-lulu on February 8, 1885, with nearly 950 men, women, and children aboard.[24]

It is a safe guess that the *City of Tokyo*, like the *Scioto* before it, stocked large quantities of soy sauce as part of the provisions for the long voyage. How could it have not, given the indispensability of soy sauce to the Japanese diet? It is equally safe to guess that the Japanese immigrants brought along a large reserve, knowing that soy sauce and other Japanese food items would be difficult to find in Hawai'i, where then the Japanese made up only a negligible fraction of the overall popu-lation. The demographic outlook, however, changed considerably as more Japa-nese laborers followed in subsequent years. By 1890, more than 12,000 Japanese were living in Hawai'i, making up roughly 14 percent of the overall population, and by 1896, the number had doubled, as had the percentage. By 1920, more than 109,000 Japanese resided there, representing nearly 43 percent of its population.[25] By 1924, more than 200,000 Japanese (including those who decided to return to Japan) had made the passage to Hawai'i.[26] This translated into not only a substan-tive labor force carrying out the backbreaking work of plantation life under the relentless heat of the tropics, but also innumerable kegs of soy sauce consumed by a newly emerging community of Japanese, who, although thousands of miles from home, still hankered for a familiar taste of Japan.

What label did the soy sauce ferried by the *City of Tokyo* display? The odds are overwhelmingly in Kikkoman's favor. According to Fruin, by 1939, Kik-koman exported one-tenth of its entire production to locations outside Japan, with half going to "countries in the yen currency block (largely Manchuria and North China, excluding Korea and Taiwan), and most of the remainder went to Hawai'i and America's West Coast with their considerable Japanese and Jap-anese-American population."[27] No other Japanese brand came anywhere close to having such a large overseas market. All indications point to Kikkoman soy sauce's being in Hawai'i with the Japanese laborers when it mattered most during those early and, no doubt, arduous days. Whether it was 1868, when the *Scioto* transported the first group of Japanese workers to Hawai'i, or 1885, when the *City of Tokyo* resumed the practice, or the early decades of the twentieth century, when Kikkoman soy sauce became a multinational export item and most likely the first soy sauce to cross the Pacific, Kikkoman truly deserves the title of *gannenshoyu*, or "first-year soy sauce."

California Dreamin'

Of course, even if a ship transporting Kikkoman soy sauce berthed at a Hawaiian dock in 1868, it would be a mistake to qualify the year as the start of Kikkoman's presence in America, since Hawai'i was not yet a part of the United States. Neither was it in 1885, even if, as Arthur Power Dudden argues,

> The unbroken continuity between modern Hawaii's epochs constitutes a remarkably singular chapter of American history in the Pacific. Nineteenth-century Hawaii before the United States annexation of 1898 was replete with Americans and American influences. Twentieth-century Hawaii after annexation is the history of the Territory and the State of Hawaii.[28]

Before 1893, when annexationists, composed mainly of acquisitive American businessmen, dethroned Queen Lili'uokalani, the last monarch, behind the cover of armed U.S. sailors, Hawai'i had been a sovereign kingdom, first established in 1810 when Kamehameha the Great unified the islands, by brute force, under his exclusive reign. For a brief period after the queen's deposition (1894–1898), as the U.S. Congress and presidency debated the merits of annexation, Hawai'i operated as a republic, with Sanford B. Dole as its first and only president. The surprisingly effortless American victory over a once formidable European power in the Spanish-American War of 1898 convinced many in Washington, DC, of Hawai'i's strategic importance, and President William McKinley signed the Newland Resolution on July 7, approving the annexation of Hawai'i to the United States. Statehood followed nearly half a century later, with President Dwight Eisenhower signing on August 21, 1959, the presidential proclamation admitting Hawai'i into the Union "with equal footing with other states."[29] Thereafter, Hawai'i would be known interchangeably as the Fiftieth State, the Aloha State, and, as the poet Eric Chock sardonically characterized the island's overdevelopment, "real estate."[30]

Consequently, while it is entirely possible that a shipment of Kikkoman soy sauce was sent to Hawai'i in 1868, that obviously does not equate it with being sent to the United States. But as Yates also claims, if kegs of Kikkoman soy sauce were sent to Japanese immigrants in the Golden State the same year, that is altogether another matter. California, following the Treaty of Guadalupe Hidalgo that ended the Mexican-American War, became the thirty-first state to join the Union in 1850. Thus, anything that Japan shipped to California in 1868 meant that it was sent to the United States. It also means that 2007 marks the 139th year of Kikkoman soy sauce in America and not merely the fiftieth year, as the *New York Times* ad states. But before attempting to make sense of Kikkoman's strategy of possibly moving up the starting point in order to posit a particular meaning—whatever that might be—to the finish line, there is another, more urgent, question to address regarding the year 1868. Although as Ernest Hemingway might put it, "it's pretty to think" that Kikkoman soy sauce was sent to California in the same year the *Scioto* transported the *gannenmono* to Hawai'i, if indeed it was sent, was there anyone—least of all, the Japanese immigrants—there to receive it?

As was the case with Hawai'i, castaway sailors and fisherman were likely the first Japanese to come ashore on North America. It has been estimated that some sixty Japanese vessels vanished in the Pacific Ocean between 1617 and 1875, so one can only guess at how many survivors—if any—providentially found dry ground on North America.[31] According to Yamato Ichihashi,

> As early as 1803 eleven such castaways returned (to Japan) from America; in 1830 a Spanish vessel rescued twelve shipwrecked Japanese and brought them to California; in 1841 Manjiro (Nakahama), a fisherman, was blown to sea with two of his companions, and was picked up and brought to America, where he remained for about ten years, returning to Japan shortly after the arrival of Perry in that Country. The romantic story of Joseph Heco, a castaway Japanese boy, picked up and brought to San Francisco in 1850, has been already told at some length; also mention has been made of numerous cases of castaways, whose problems Heco assisting in solving.[32]

Accidental arrivals notwithstanding, the consensus among historians of early Japanese immigration to the United States is that the first *contingent* of Japanese to traverse the Pacific with the manifest intention of settling in the United States traveled on the Pacific Mail Company's PMSS *China*, which docked at San Francisco Bay on May 27, 1869. Leading the exploratory expedition was a German arms dealer, John Henry Schnell, who had made a small fortune in the feudal domain of Aizu in Japan's Fukushima Prefecture. According to John E. Van Sant, with the support of Matsudaira Katamori, an influential daimyo (a feudal lord and vassal of the shogun) of Aizu, Schnell "devised a plan to establish a colony of Aizu settlers in California that would produce tea and silk," believing that the "venture would be profitable for Aizu, which had lost most of its land to the central government as a result of the civil war."[33]

Aboard the *China* were Schnell and a mere seven Japanese men and women, including his samurai-class wife, Jou. Later that year, sixteen additional Aizu denizens arrived, followed by several others months later. Together, the enterprising group, which numbered thirty-five at the most, established the Wakamatsu Tea and Silk Farm Colony on six hundred acres of land purchased by Schnell in the Gold Hill district of Coloma, the reputed site where a sawmill operator, James Marshall, first discovered specks of gold dust in 1848, precipitating the start of the California Gold Rush. Thus it came to pass that the Wakamatsu colonists—whose dreams of riches were dashed in less than two years owing to a lack of resources, mainly water—became "the largest group of Japanese in the United States to that time."[34] No less than the state of California and the Japanese American Citizens League, the oldest and largest Japanese American civil rights organization in the country, recognize the Wakamatsu colony as the first Japanese immigrants to the United States.[35]

As with the case of Hawai'i, some thorny questions complicate Yates's claim that Kikkoman soy sauce either traveled with or was shipped to Japanese immigrants in California in or around 1868. For Yates's chronology to hold true, the Japanese in California for whom the soy sauce was intended had to have been the Wakamatsu colonists. There were no other large groups of Japanese immigrants in California—or anywhere else in the United States, for that matter—during that time. This is not to say that there were no Japanese *people* there. As early as 1858, the Japanese government dispatched embassies to a number of leading Western nations, including the United States. The first mission to the United States, consisting of seventy-one people, left Japan aboard an American vessel, the *Powhatan*, on February 13, 1860, arriving in San Francisco on March 29.[36] In addition, students were sent overseas to Europe and the United States at the behest of the Meiji government to obtain knowledge of the West, or they went on their own. Estimates are that between 1868 and 1900, some nine hundred students came to the United States to study.[37] According to Gary Okihiro, in San Francisco alone, "student laborers were the largest group within a growing Japanese American community that numbered about 3,000 in 1890."[38]

There is also the obvious incongruity of dates in the hypothesis linking Kikkoman to the Wakamatsu colony. While Yates cites 1868 as the year of the soy sauce shipment, the first group of Wakamatsu colonists did not arrive in San Francisco until May 27, 1869. In order for Yates's hypothesis to be tenable, the PMSS *China* not only needed to have held Kikkoman soy sauce as cargo but also must have left Japan in the previous calendar year. While the date of *China*'s arrival is well documented (it was widely covered by the California press), the date of departure is hard to pin down. If the ship sailed during the latter days of 1868, the voyage would have lasted more than 150 days. Recall that the *Scioto*, which traveled only half the distance to Hawai'i, took thirty-four days to reach its terminus. The *Powhatan*, which ferried the embassy mission in 1860, took a mere forty-five days to cross the entire Pacific Ocean to California. Of course, the *China* may have taken a more circuitous route. As a mail carrier, the ship could very well have had to make several stops along the way. Or perhaps the ship was subject to extended layovers en route. Whatever the case, in all likelihood, Kikkoman was the first soy sauce to reach the United States, if not in 1868 or 1869, then certainly by 1879, when Kikkoman was legally registered as a recognized brand name in California. But perhaps the question of whether the steamer that transported the Wakamatsu colony also transported Kikkoman soy sauce is ultimately a trivial matter. Of far greater significance on a symbolic—if not a mythological—level is the mere suggestion that the year 1868, the first year of the Meiji era, was the inaugural year of Kikkoman soy sauce in America.

Willful Forgetting

In his acknowledgments, Yates lists only individuals in the Kikkoman "family"—corporate communications consultants, staff members of the president's office, directors of divisional operations, managers of production facilities, corporate board members, and Chairman Yuzaburo Mogi himself. As a commissioned author, did Yates play the neutral role of amanuensis and simply repeat the version of company lore as it was told to him? If so, what does Kikkoman gain by putting its soy sauce in the pantry of the first Japanese immigrants to Hawai'i and the United States? If the *gannenmono* and the Wakamatsu colony were in fact the first groups of Japanese to reach Hawai'i and the United States, then, as the soy sauce that accompanied these immigrants, the Kikkoman brand can justifiably boast an equally compelling narrative. In other words, Kikkoman soy sauce, too, is an immigrant. What can be more "American" than to advertise oneself as an original immigrant in a country billed as a land of immigrants, where the Statue of Liberty, Ellis Island, and Angel Island—the immigration station in San Francisco Bay that operated between 1910 and 1940—are revered as sacred national landmarks? Then again, what if it turns out *not* to be the case, that the 1868 proposition is merely company propaganda?

Hence the necessity of the 2007 golden anniversary: Given the difficulty of verifying the 1868 claim, Kikkoman does not need either to vouch for or disavow it but merely to allow the legend to linger. Meanwhile, with the ex post facto designation of its San Francisco subsidiary as the "official" moment of its American origin, the company is able to generate a tremendous amount of free and decidedly fawning publicity—as evidenced by the lavish media coverage and Senate resolution—at a critical juncture in its three-hundred-years-plus history. This second tale of origin, however, is not without its own complications. On closer inspection, the circumstances behind the apotheosis of the San Francisco venture appear to belie the significance placed on it by the company. In fact, the establishment of Kikkoman International, Inc., in 1957 represents not the start but, rather, the *restart* of Kikkoman soy sauce sales in the United States, which had been interrupted by America's entry into World War II.

In 1957, Kikkoman filed an application with the Japanese Ministry of Finance requesting permission to export a significant amount of capital overseas. Filed with the San Francisco subsidiary in mind, the request included a prospectus, which, among other details, indicated the scope of Kikkoman's U.S. operations before the war:

> For the past 50 years, our company has been exporting its product, Kikkoman Soy Sauce, to the United States (and Hawaii). These exports were intended mainly to meet the demands of persons of Japanese ancestry in the United States. The volume of [our] exports in the years preceding the outbreak of World War II (1940) was 21,000 *koku* [833,769 gallons at 1 *koku* = 39.7 gallons], which amounted to 95 per cent of the total consumption of soy sauce in the United States.[39]

When trade relations between Japan and the United States resumed after the war, Kikkoman's desire to pick up where it last left off proved unfeasible. The toll of the war on its niche base was detrimental, as the near monopoly once enjoyed by Kikkoman in the Japanese American and Japanese Hawaiian communities had all but evaporated. During its absence, opportunistic entrepreneurs established several soy sauce production facilities in Los Angeles, Chicago, and other mainland locations, as well as four in Hawai'i alone. In fine American fashion, venturesome immigrant capitalists had filled the lacunae left behind by Kikkoman. At least one of these still survives as the Aloha

Shoyu Company, established by five local Japanese families in Kalihi, a suburb of Honolulu, in 1946. More than surviving, the company appears to be thriving, with a growing market extending outside the islands, and celebrity endorsements from Olympic gold medal figure skater Kristi Yamaguchi and renowned restaurateur Sam Choy.[40]

Suddenly faced with competition from local soy sauce producers upon its return to U.S. markets, and with little chance of restoring its exports to prewar levels, Kikkoman adopted a radical strategy: Instead of lamenting the loss of its traditional customer base—namely, the Japanese and other Asian communities in California and Hawai'i—the company set its sights higher: on the Caucasian market. The prospectus filed with the Ministry of Finance spells this out by noting "an unusual postwar phenomenon":

> The feeling Caucasians in general hold toward Japan have improved remarkably in the United States, and their interest in and the reputation among them of Japanese food products has gradually improved.
>
> Observing this clearly, our company commissioned some experts in the United States to conduct a thorough study on the possibility of getting Caucasians to use soy sauce in their diets. This led to our great confidence that soy sauce is a promising product [in the United States].[41]

The original objective of Kikkoman's San Francisco venture was therefore twofold: first, to regain as much as it could of the not-so-insignificant soy sauce market that it had had in the United States and Hawai'i before the war and, second (and much more important), to begin attracting Caucasian or European Americans to its soy sauce—an exotic brew in the minds of all but a handful of Americans then—in hopes of tapping into an endless source of potential growth and future profit for the company.

Thus, what the 2007 anniversary celebrated was not the start of Kikkoman soy sauce marketing in America at some point during the second half of the nineteenth century, but the start of its dedicated marketing to *white* Americans five years after the end of the U.S. military occupation of Japan. The ramification of this is not without significance. What it means is that for the golden anniversary celebration to be tenable, Kikkoman must first *disavow* or *excise* its relationship with Japanese Americans before 1957. In effect, Japanese Americans must be deliberately culled from the heterogeneous American population, and their equal standing *as* Americans must be placed in doubt. In other words, they must be racially quarantined in order for Kikkoman's corporate marketing strategy to make sense.

The most egregious instance of Japanese Americans suffering the igno-miny of racial quarantining was, of course, during World War II, when nearly 120,000 Japanese Americans were forcibly removed from their homes and livelihoods along the entire length of the West Coast, and interned in con-centration camps in some of the most desolate locations in the country. Kik-koman's golden anniversary, therefore, was accompanied by a huge amount of irony: Just as the start of the war led to the racial quarantining of Japanese Americans, so too did the establishment of Kikkoman International, which resulted in the racialized disqualification of the same population as legitimate Americans. If the internment camps can be justified by the violent military competition between two powerful nations, the rationale for the fiftieth anni-versary of Kikkoman rests on the market competition among powerful soy sauce producers. Complicit in this act of racial erasure, then, are no less than the city of San Francisco, with its Kikkoman Day proclamation, and the U.S. Senate, which passed a resolution bestowing a congressional stamp of approval on Kikkoman's truncated version of its history in the United States.

The Sway of Authenticity

What started out centuries ago as an indispensable pantry item in East and Southeast Asian cuisines has become global. The culinary importance of soy sauce is no longer limited to the traditional foods of countries such as Japan, China, Korea, Philippines, Thailand, and Vietnam but now serves as a generic, umami-rich flavoring agent and a more complex-tasting substitute for salt in foods associated with a whole host of non-Asian countries. The chaotic bricolage of recipes archived on the Food Network's website is one possible indicator of the increasing global use of soy sauce. A simple key word search of an unlikely pairing of soy sauce with Gorgonzola cheese, for example, yields a rib-eye steak sandwich courtesy of the network's resident Italian cuisine personality, Giada De Laurentiis.[42] A search of soy sauce with the word "Creole" yields a recipe for Brandied Duck Liver Mousse with Cre-ole Mustard Sauce from the immensely popular Emeril Lagasse, regarded as a master of New Orleans cuisine.[43] Meanwhile, the Kikkoman Corpora-tion has on its website a cookbook titled *World Soy Sauce Cooking*, which offers evocative recipes that contain soy sauce, from nearly a hundred differ-ent countries. These recipes, most of which were provided by their national embassies in Japan, include *dajaj mashwi*, a chicken dish from the Hash-emite Kingdom of Jordan; *karhai*, a chicken dish from the Islamic Republic of Pakistan; *lachania*, a pork and cabbage dish from the Hellenic Republic;

oksegryte, a beef stew from the Kingdom of Norway; *filetes con aceitunas y vino blanco*, a beef and olive dish from Spain; *churrasquinho*, a grilled beef dish from the Federative Republic of Brazil; shrimp *ceviche* from the Republic of Ecuador; curry and rice with sauce *arachide* from the Republic of Côte d'Ivoire; *akoho sy voanio*, a chicken and coconut stew from the Republic of Madagascar; and, incredibly, *chop suey* from Canada.[44]

Not surprisingly, this internationalization of soy sauce use translates into an expanded global trade of the product. Behind the smiling visage of the chairman in the *New York Times* ad is a decades-long tug-of-war between Kikkoman and its chief American rivals over a growing global soy sauce market. Kikkoman has already won the battle for America by vanquishing the two largest chemical soy sauce brands, La Choy and Chun King (both owned by the industry giant ConAgra Foods), to become the best-selling soy sauce in the United States. A generation ago, La Choy and Chun King were the most recognized and top-selling brands in America, the Coke and Pepsi of American soy sauces. But by 1971, Kikkoman had overtaken Chun King as the second best-selling brand after La Choy, which relinquished the top spot to Kikkoman five years later.[45]

The next battle, however, is on a much larger stage. In direct competition against Kikkoman beyond the United States is, once again, La Choy, the largest American producer of "bottled" soy sauce, whose top export markets include Jamaica, Haiti, Greece, St. Martin, and Belize.[46] The largest producer of "packet" soy sauce—the tiny, individually portioned packets commonly given away by Chinese take-out restaurants—is Kari-Out, yet another widely profitable chemical soy sauce brand.[47] Thus, Kikkoman appears to have set its sights on competing with these and other chemically produced brands both in and beyond the United States.

The *New York Times* ad highlights a crucial strategy employed by Kikkoman's marketing wing to sway public opinion in its favor: the promise of authenticity. While not unique to Kikkoman, the strategy is particularly well suited to the Japanese company's efforts to distinguish itself from its American competitors. The gist of Kikkoman's message is as simple as it is blunt: We, the Japanese, produce *real* soy sauce; they, the Americans, produce *something else*. This message is made clear in the ad in Chairman Mogi's description of Kikkoman soy sauce as an example of "naturally brewed soy sauce . . . still made just it was more than 300 years ago—slowly fermented and aged for full flavor like a fine wine." This self-characterization is the centerpiece of Kikkoman's current global advertising campaign. A visitor to Kikkoman's website, for example, is offered the following counsel on shopping: "As a general rule of thumb, it is best to avoid chemically manufactured sauces. . . . Kikkoman soy sauces are naturally brewed, made from three ingredients—soybeans, wheat and salt."[48] An inquisitive shopper may ask, What are the ingredients found in other brands? The label on a bottle of La Choy soy sauce provides one answer: water, salt, hydrolyzed soy protein, corn syrup, caramel color, and potassium sorbate.

Although not referenced by name, Kikkoman's American competitors are discredited for producing ersatz soy sauce, a poorly simulated product made merely to suggest the presence of the real thing. If Kikkoman can be compared with fine wine, then by inference, American brands like La Choy and Kari-Out are the equivalent of artificially flavored grape soda blended with cheap alcohol. By repeatedly underscoring its three-centuries-long tradition of brewing soy sauce, Kikkoman is sounding a warning to every potential buyer: *Don't be duped. Beware of other brands. Beware of fakes.*

Here is where the two discursive threads stemming from Kikkoman's golden anniversary celebration come together as one—and the result is not necessarily beneficial for either Kikkoman or Japanese Americans. Through its marketing strategy, Kikkoman characterizes chemically produced soy sauce as *too American* and Japanese Americans as *not American enough.* What makes this assertion especially compelling is the fact both can trace their beginnings to Japan. That the ancestry of Japanese Americans goes back to Japan is self-evident. Not so obvious is that the technology for chemical soy sauce production also originated in Japan—and it was Kikkoman that led the way.

Immediately after World War II, during the Occupation, Kikkoman was responsible for a radical industrywide change in the manufacture of soy sauce. The shortage of raw materials, such as soybeans, wheat, and salt, necessitated experimentation with alternative ingredients and means of production. In 1948, Kikkoman, which operated under the name Noda Shoyu from 1917 to 1964, introduced a "semichemical" soy sauce, which was based on a method that had existed in Japan since the 1920s. According to Mark Fruin, "The company had felt compelled to develop and to popularize these newer methods because Occupation officials, as an answer to crop shortages, had recommended that soy sauce producers give up fermentation altogether in favor of the faster and less expensive process of mixing hydrochloric acid and hydrolyzed vegetable protein."[49]

Although most Japanese soy sauce makers returned to producing fermented soy sauce by the 1950s, the chemical method, which critics charge is inferior in terms of taste and aroma, took hold in United States by the time Kikkoman established its office in San Francisco in 1957, the year that also marks the corporate forgetting of Japanese Americans fifty years into the future.

Notes

1. "Kikkoman Celebrates 50th Anniversary in America," *Kikkoman News*, available at http://www.kikkoman.com/news/2007news/03.shtml (accessed June 12, 2008).

2. "Kikkoman's 50th Anniversary Party Held in D.C.," *Kikkoman News*, available at http://www.kikkoman.com/news/2007news/06.shtml (accessed June 12, 2008).

3. "Kikkoman Gifts Creates UW–Madison, State and International Partnership," *University of Wisconsin–Madison News*, available at http://www.news.wisc.edu/releases/8707.html (accessed June 12, 2008).

4. Ronald E. Yates, *The Kikkoman Chronicles: A Global Company with a Japanese Soul* (New York: McGraw-Hill, 1998), 84.

5. Ibid., 24, italics added.

6. Ibid., 126.

7. S.R. 323 (110th), available at GovTrack, http://www.govtrack.us/congress/billtext.xpd?bill=sr110-323 (accessed July 21, 2008).

8. Kim Severson, "Global Food Fight? Why, Soytainly!" *San Francisco Chronicle*, August 25, 2002, available at http://www.sfgate.com/cgi-bin/article.cgi?f=/c/a/2002/08/25/MN70302.DTL (accessed January 15, 2006).

9. Gary Y. Okihiro, *Cane Fires: The Anti-Japanese Movement in Hawaii, 1865–1945* (Philadelphia: Temple University Press, 1992), 20.

10. John E. Van Sant, *Pacific Pioneers: Japanese Journeys to American and Hawaii, 1850–90* (Urbana: University of Illinois Press, 2000), 99.

11. Yamato Ichihashi, *Japanese in the United States: A Critical Study of the Problems of the Japanese Immigrants and Their Children* (Stanford, CA: Stanford University Press, 1932), 19.

12. Ibid., 21.

13. Hilary Conroy, *The Japanese Frontier in Hawaii, 1868–1898* (Berkeley: University of California Press, 1953), 27.

14. Okihiro, *Cane Fires*, 20.

15. Okihiro, *Cane Fires*, 21; Van Sant, *Pacific Pioneers*, 106.

16. W. Mark Fruin, *Kikkoman: Company, Clan, and Community* (Cambridge, MA: Harvard University Press, 1983), 59.

17. See www.kikkoman.com/corporateprofile/overview/index.shtml (accessed March 11, 2013).

18. Fruin, *Kikkoman*, 60.

19. Yates, *The Kikkoman Chronicles*, 24.

20. Fruin, *Kikkoman*, 59–60.

21. Ichihashi, *Japanese in the United States*, 24.

22. Conroy, *The Japanese Frontier*, 15.

23. Gary Y. Okihiro, "The Japanese in America," in *Japanese American History: An A-to-Z Reference from 1868 to the Present*, ed. Brian Niiya (New York: Facts on File, Inc., 1993), 2.

24. Okihiro, *Cane Fires*, 23–25.

25. Ichihashi, *Japanese in the United States*, 31–32.

26. Ronald Takaki, *Pau Hana: Plantation Life and Labor in Hawaii, 1835–1920* (Honolulu: University of Hawai'i Press, 1983), 45.

27. Fruin, *Kikkoman*, 274, 286.

28. Arthur Power Dudden, *The American Pacific: From the Old China Trade to the Present* (New York: Oxford University Press, 1992), 49.

29. Gavan Daws, *Shoal of Time: A History of the Hawaiian Islands* (Honolulu: University of Hawai'i Press, 1968).

30. Eric Chock, "Poem for George Helm: Aloha Week 1980," in *Last Days Here* (Honolulu: Bamboo Ridge Press, 1990).

31. Van Sant, *Pacific Pioneers*, 22.

32. Ichihashi, *Japanese in the United States*, 48–49.

33. Van Sant, *Pacific Pioneers*, 123.

34. Ibid., 125.

35. Ibid., 118.

36. Ichihashi, *Japanese in the United States*, 48–47.

37. Paul R. Spickard, *Japanese Americans: The Formation and Transformation of an Ethnic Group* (New York: Twayne, 1996), 10.

38. Okihiro, "The Japanese in America," 3.

39. Michael Gerlach, "Trust Is Not Enough: Cooperation and Conflict in Kikkoman's American Development," *Journal of Japanese Studies* 16, no. 2 (summer 1990): 423.

40. Aloha Shoyu, available at http://www.alohashoyu.com (accessed on August 1, 2008).

41. Gerlach, "Trust Is Not Enough," 423.

42. The Food Network, available at http://www.foodnetwork.com/food/recipes/recipe/0,,FOOD_9936_29792,00.html (accessed July 12, 2008).

43. The Food Network, available at http://www.foodnetwork.com/food/recipes/recipe/0,,FOOD_9936_19821,00.html (accessed July 12, 2008).

44. Kikkoman Corporation, available at http://www.kikkoman.com/cookbook.html (accessed July 12, 2008).

45. Fruin, *Kikkoman*, 286.

46. Jennifer 8. Lee, *The Fortune Cookie Chronicles: Adventures in the World of Chinese Food* (New York: Twelve, 2008), 170.

47. Ibid., 174.

48. Kikkoman Corporation, available at http://www.kikkoman.com/soysauce/index.shtml (accessed July 2, 2008).

49. Fruin, *Kikkoman*, 263.

PART III

Fusion, Diffusion, Confusion?

11

Twenty-First-Century Food Trucks

Mobility, Social Media, and Urban Hipness

LOK SIU

Just as I turned into the parking lot, I suddenly realized I had no idea what Jae Kim, the founder of Chi'Lantro Food Trucks, looked like, and I had forgotten to ask for some mark of identification when we confirmed our meeting. But without giving it a second thought, I rushed toward the front door of Asia Café, a major Austin, Texas, landmark for delicious northern Chinese food. There stood a young man in his late twenties or maybe early thirties, wearing dark blue jeans, a stylish pullover sweater, and black sneakers. He had his face down, looking intently at his iPhone and furiously tapping his thumbs on the screen. He did not resemble the typical image of a restaurant owner, if there is such a thing. He was young, much younger than one would expect a successful food truck entrepreneur to be. Still, I suspected he was Jae Kim. I asked tentatively, "Jae?" He looked up immediately, giving me that familiar slightly surprised and confused look. I suppose I do not look like a typical university professor, either. In any case, the feeling of surprise was mutual; neither of us fit the stereotypical image of our profession. To avoid any awkward silence, I quickly introduced myself, and he noted that Asia Café was full (the rain had not kept people away) and suggested that we go somewhere quieter instead. We walked down a short way to a cupcake bakery, and with coffee and cupcakes in hand, we sat down at one of the tables.

My meeting with Jae Kim was a result of my ongoing interest in Asian Latino food. In the late 1990s in New York City, I was introduced to the Chinese Latino restaurants[1] on the Upper West Side of Manhattan. Having done research on diasporic Chinese in Latin America, I was fascinated with restaurants that had names like "La Caridad 78," "Flor De Mayo," or "Dinastia China," which had self-consciously named their cuisine Chinese-Latin, or Spanish and Chinese, or Comida China y Criolla.[2] When I moved to Austin, Texas, a few years ago, I missed the juicy and flavorful *pollo Asado* and the tangy sweet and

231

succulent *plátanos maduros* of those Chinese Latino restaurants. Fortunately, one day during the "Cultural Politics of Food" course I was teaching at University of Texas at Austin, a student mentioned her favorite local food truck, Chi'Lantro, which serves "Korean tacos." My eyes lit up in my excitement at the emergence of yet another "Asian Latino" food concept, this one drawing on Korean and Mexican traditions. Soon thereafter, I visited Chi'Lantro and had my first taste of bulgogi beef tacos. Think of thinly sliced beef—marinated in a sauce made of garlic, soy sauce with a hint of sugar, and sesame seeds—grilled and then wrapped in a warm corn tortilla and topped with minced onions, thinly chopped cabbage, cilantro, and hot sauce. Absolutely delicious! With those first tacos I was hooked, and since then have been eating Korean tacos and exploring the food truck phenomenon.

Food trucks seem to have exploded on the national stage in the late 2000s. While the previous generation of food trucks was quite diverse, in general they were perceived as offering cheap, "authentic" (often read as "ethnic" or "low culture") food consumed primarily by the working class or sometimes thought to be the only option available in the area. Now, although food trucks still have a reputation for being affordable, they have been transformed into something modern, hip, cutting-edge, and mainstream. In this chapter I try to make sense of how food trucks, once situated at the margins of food culture, have become so popular and widely embraced in the past few years. I explore the reemergence and growing presence of food trucks in American society and ask, What cultural and social forces made food trucks such a popular phenomenon? What kinds of desires and impulses drive and are reflected in the proliferation of food trucks? Who are the new owners, workers, and consumers of these new food trucks? My findings are drawn from the preliminary ethnographic fieldwork I conducted in 2011 on the "Asian fusion" food trucks Chi'Lantro and Peached Tortilla, both based in Austin, Texas. By "Asian fusion," I am referring to food created from at least two culinary traditions, one from Asia (Korea, Japan, China, Vietnam, and the like). Whereas Chi'Lantro was inspired by Korean and Mexican food traditions, Peached Tortilla traces its roots to various parts of Asia and Southern (American) food. What follows is a collage of ethnographic vignettes that bring together some of the disparate forces that enabled the emergence of this new food truck culture at the beginning of the twenty-first century. I suggest that the particular constellation of changes in media technologies, food entertainment, and the national economy has played a critical role in laying the groundwork for the proliferation, as well as the explosive reception, of food trucks in the past few years.

Entrepreneurship, Youth, and Cultural Mixing

One of the most conspicuous aspects of these Austin-based Asian fusion food truck entrepreneurs is their youth. The owner of Chi'Lantro Food Trucks, Jae Kim, is twenty-eight years old, was born in South Korea, and migrated to United States at the age of eleven. He attended a boarding school in Ojai, California, and later switched to a public school in Orange Country, California. In college, he studied business, and after graduating, he followed his girlfriend to Texas. Even though his relationship did not blossom, his business ambitions did. After working for a few years in the marketing department for a large grocery store chain in Texas, he decided to start his own business. To my surprise, though, this was not his first entrepreneurial enterprise, as he had owned and operated a coffee shop in Irvine, California, when he was only twenty-one. Building on that experience and knowledge, Jae Kim, twenty-six at the time, did three months of research before he single-handedly launched his first "mobile catering" business in February 2010. Using his own savings, he worked alongside his first employee, his cook Julia, to perfect the daily operations of the food truck business. When asked where he got his culinary inspiration for Korean tacos, he referred to his childhood growing up in ethnically diverse Los Angeles.

> I grew up in a mixed community where there was a large presence of Mexicans and Asians. I used to eat Mexican food all the time, and of course, I ate lots of Korean food at home. . . . Being in Texas, Mexican food, especially tacos, is everywhere. So, I guess it made sense for me to mix Korean and Mexican staples together.

For Jae, his personal experience of living close to both Asian and Mexican communities and having access to their foods was the inspiration for his culinary experimentation. He first tried different recipes at home, and once they passed his taste test, he served them to patrons and got feedback from them. Gradually, he perfected each dish and then the menu.

The early days were a struggle, not only because he was understaffed and quite literally was working around the clock, but also because he did not have enough customers. He recalls, "I was working twenty hours a day, six days a week for a very long time. . . . I remember the first day I opened my truck, I earned $9; the second day I got $4. For weeks I had to throw away buckets of food." Korean tacos, which had made their debut in Los Angeles in 2008, were still unknown in Austin. But after the annual "South by Southwest" festival in mid-March, when his Korean BBQ Taco food truck became widely publicized through Twitter, Facebook, and other social media, he finally made a breakthrough. Still, for the next six to eight months, Jae had to work tirelessly with his cook to ensure the survival and success of his business. When his work schedule finally became unsustainable, he wisely hired another person, who became his right-hand man, and slowly but steadily he expanded his business. Today, Jae Kim runs three Chi'Lantro trucks in Austin and plans launch another in Houston in summer of 2012.

Jae's story is one of great success. While some may find his youth surprising, being young is typical of most of the food truck entrepreneurs and workers I met in Austin. For instance, like Jae Kim, Peached Tortilla food truck owner Eric Silverstein also started his business when he was in his late twenties, after he decided to change his career from law to business. Eric, whose father is Jewish American and whose mother is Chinese American, was born and raised in Japan until the age of ten, after which his family moved to Atlanta, Georgia. Drawing on his knowledge of Asian and American Southern food, he launched Peached Tortilla, which offers an eclectic menu of items like *banh mih* tacos and burritos, Chinese BBQ burritos, and crab cake sliders.

When I asked about the general youthfulness of people in the food truck business, both Kim and Silverstein cited the demanding nature of the work, explaining that it is a business requiring long hours, hard work, and complete dedication. In fact, both described their employees as being under the age of thirty and male. Eric:

> It's impossible to do this with a family. For sure, my business has taken a toll on my relationship [with my girlfriend]. Working on the food truck is hard on my body. I used to go to sleep late at night (around 2 or 3 a.m.) because that's what time it is after our night shift is over and after the truck is thoroughly cleaned, and I wake up around 9 a.m. so I can get the lunch shift ready. And it is like that day after day. It is hard work. The hours are long. You have no life when you start this business. You've got to do it when you are young.

In addition, I suppose financial risk also is easier to weather when one is young and without family responsibilities.

Their youth aside, something about their transnational and multicultural experience informs their culinary creations. Their choice of food experimentation indexes their familiarity and sustained contact with different ethnic cuisines, which, I assume, comes from their experience of migration and/or being part of a multicultural community.

Refashioning Food Trucks

My earliest memory of food trucks is associated with the ice-cream trucks that drove around on summer afternoons, churning out a familiar tune that remains with me today. Then, there were the trucks serving burgers or tacos that were parked outside constructions sites, hospitals, and industrial areas. Those are the old-style food trucks I remember from my childhood days in Los Angeles. Today's food trucks could not be more different. Taking advantage of the latest food trends and culinary experiments, they exude an urban hipness that draws the young, cosmopolitan, self-proclaimed "foodies." How did this makeover happen?

There are many factors. Since the 1990s, the number of food shows on television has exploded, like those in which Rachael Ray, Guy Fieri, and Bobby Flay teach us how to make delicious meals. Shows like Anthony Bourdain's *No Reservations* take us around the world and allow us to vicariously experience exotic cuisines of distant countries. Cooking competitions, like *Iron Chef,* feature top chefs around the country and judges who offer thoughtful and articulate critiques of their food. All the while and without our realizing it, we are being introduced to a new world of food consumption. These shows give us a sense of adventure and experimentation, a taste for "refined" cuisine and food presentation, and a vocabulary to describe the myriad flavors and textures. In this way, the mass media not only activated a desire for food experimentation and a curiosity for exotic ethnic cuisines, but they also instilled a more self-conscious approach to preparing, tasting, and talking about food. In a way, the media helped create a generation of food consumers who are more willing to try new dishes, have a broader knowledge of food in general, and have more confidence in assessing taste.

When modernized food trucks are reintroduced in this new context, their "newness" is attributed to more than their innovative menus. What sets them apart from their restaurant counterparts is their mobility. It is this style of food service and consumption, in addition to their food, that attracts people to food trucks. The adoption of seemingly more trendy and experimental dishes separates them from the earlier generation of food trucks, which we tend to associate with traditionally conceived menus: burgers and fries or Mexican tacos and burritos. The new trucks also are extremely eager to brand themselves with clever names and bold designs. But the mobility of food trucks offers a different commensality from conventional restaurants. Food trucks go to where their consumers are likely to be found. They park near bars, malls, and special events. They also park together and form clusters to attract more people; tables and chairs are set beside these trucks in an informal eating area. Mainstream audiences suddenly rediscovered a "new" food phenomenon, which actually is no more than a modernized version of the old with a few twists. Food magazines that once favored elite restaurants now feature articles on specific food trucks, thus affirming their acceptance into the foodie world. Websites and social media continue to showcase, follow, and facilitate conversation about food trucks. The Food Network even televised a national competition to find the most successful food truck operators. By 2010, food trucks had achieved mainstream status and managed to obtain an approving nod from the foodie world for their culinary and entrepreneurial innovation.

The intensified use of social media also helps spread the word about restaurants and foods. Food blogs and web reviews play a critical role in sharing information and allowing ordinary people to give "honest" and unfiltered opinions about their food experience. This democratization of information sharing has shifted the power of food critique and the ability to influence "taste" from the mouths of "experts" to those of ordinary consumers (or at least users of social media). Websites like Yelp offer a platform for people to post their comments and to influence consumption practices. Today, the Internet is a key site for people to learn about and shape particular food trends, to evaluate and to choose which restaurants to visit and foods to eat, and to help bring business to certain institutions or to kill it. In short, social media have become a crucial site of advertisement for all restaurants, not just food trucks. I suggest, however, that food trucks are much more dependent on social media than their brick-and-mortar counterparts are, precisely because they are mobile and need to steer customers to their site, which continually changes. Sustained and consistent communication with customers via websites and social media, then, is crucial to the survival of these food trucks.

Mobile yet Connected

The Internet and social media have facilitated the reemergence of food trucks in many ways. Because food trucks lack a permanent physical address, they rely heavily on the Internet to communicate with their consumers and to inform them of their precise location at a particular time. For instance, if people discover a food truck they like by chance, social media enable them to find out exactly when and where to find that food truck again. Indeed, their permanent address is not necessarily a site that is represented by a number on a particular street; it is their web page.

Food trucks usually move around within a circuit of designated sites in a city. Some trucks have one rented location or a set of locations where they regularly park. Others drive around, depending on what parking areas are available. Of course, for any food-related business, having a website today is like being listed in the Yellow Pages in the pre-Internet world. It is a common, even expected, method of establishing a presence. For the food trucks in Austin, having a web presence is further necessitated by the fact that they lack a permanent location. Food truck owners, therefore, rely heavily on the Internet to post information about where they are, where they will be and upcoming special events, and also respond to their clients' positive and negative comments. Because food trucks rely so heavily on their web presence to attract customers, they are highly sensitive and responsive to web postings about their business. During one of our interviews, food truck owner Eric Silverstein scanned his smart phone and read to me a Twitter posting: "My three favorite food trucks/trailers are now Chi'Lantro, East Side King, and Peached Tortilla." He explained, "This tells me how my food truck is doing. I am being grouped with Chi'Lantro and East Side King, two of the top performers. This is how I know how my business is doing." At the Yelp website, I also noticed his active presence in responding to negative reviews. In one instance, he offered the Yelp commenter to come by for a free lunch in order to make up for an earlier bad experience.

Because of the food trucks' heavy reliance on the Internet, it is not surprising that the majority of food truck consumers are part of the Internet generation, those people who are technology, Internet, and social media savvy, people for whom being wired or online is second nature and whose experiences are usually mediated by the web. The main determinant here is not necessarily age but familiarity with and reliance on the Internet. In many ways, the instant popularity, spread, and success of food trucks in the twenty-first century reflect the lifestyle shift for one large segment of U.S. society, exemplifying the mobility that relies on intensive connectivity.

Producing Urban Hipness

According to Jae Kim, the social media are what helped catapult Chi'Lantro into Austin's food scene (and beyond), which in turn generated both visits to the truck and hard capital. For him, the sales and media attention he received during the South by Southwest (SXSW) festivities in Austin gave him the necessary exposure he needed. SXSW is primarily a music festival that takes place every year in Austin. It was initiated to increase tourism and business activities for Austin's entertainment sector during spring break, when the university population is away. Although SXSW first started as a music festival, over the years it has expanded to other fields, including education and technology. It is one of Austin's biggest events, with thousands of young musicians, technology entrepreneurs, educators, and tourists from all over the country visiting Austin for one week in March. Young professionals and artists revel in a youth culture embedded in music and technology. With their latest phone gadgets in hand, the participants text, Twitter, and blog about the latest trends emerging from SXSW.

For Chi'Lantro, the social media coverage it received during the SXSW week helped get it out of the red. Most of its business comes from catering parties hosted by the music, technology, and entertainment companies participating in SXSW. Because they are mobile kitchens, food trucks make ideal catering units and offer a different approach to conventional catering services. Known for their food innovation and urban hipness, with a nod to counterculture, food trucks coincide with the general ethos of SXSW's alternative culture. At a "food truck" panel sponsored by the University of Texas's Center for Asian American Studies, Jae frankly stated, "We prepare for SXSW six months in advance, and we make more during the festival than we do the rest of the year. Well . . . let's say at least as much as the rest of the year."

With the buzz generated during "South by South West," Kim's business picked up. Since the first year of its participation in SXSW, Chi'Lantro has gained a national profile, having been featured in popular media such as the Food Network, the Cooking Channel, the *New York Times*, Fox News, *GQ* magazine, *San Francisco Chronicle*, and CNN. Only a little more than years after its debut, Chi'Lantro has become a tourist attraction for many visitors to Austin. Indeed, on one Saturday morning in April 2012, when my family and I went downtown to pick up some Korean tacos from Chi'Lantro, we met a family visiting from Galveston, Texas. While waiting for the truck to open its doors, the Galveston family and I struck up a conversation. The mother of the group graciously offered to allow our family of four to order first. Pointing to her group of about a dozen people, she insisted, "There are a lot of us here, so go ahead and order first. Your kids are probably hungry." Pausing for a moment, she continued,

> We are [originally] from Guam, now living in Galveston, and we are on our way to a Dallas concert where Guam musicians are playing. We specifically planned our trip so we can pass through Austin for some Korean BBQ tacos, which we've heard so much about. We don't want Mexican tacos, we can get that anywhere [in Texas]. We want something different . . . Korean BBQ tacos.

Indeed, I was reminded that it was precisely this seemingly exotic mix that attracts people from all over to Chi'Lantro and other food trucks like it. In a state where Mexican tacos are standard fare, people are intrigued by something different, something extraordinary but still familiar. The fact that it is delicious, of course, makes it that much more worthwhile to seek out.

The Right Place at the Right Time

The first time that many college students and young professionals visit Chi'Lantro and try their specialty kimchi fries (among other popular dishes), they often do so after a night of barhopping. When young Austinites end a night of fun, they are grateful to find a variety of mobile food trucks parked right in the heart of downtown, where many bars and entertainment venues are located. Chi'Lantro and other food trucks thus have become part of the urban hip geography by specifically targeting young professionals and college students seeking late-night snacks. Thriving on the media buzz that highlights their creative, experimental, and ethnic fusion dishes, the food trucks have been branded with a certain cosmopolitanism that attracts urban youth seeking the latest food trends. According to Jae Kim,

> People are more willing to try new foods when they are a little drunk and with a group. After partying for a little while, when they get hungry, they want some food. And we make it convenient for them by being within walking distance. They look at the menu and get curious about kimchi fries. With some peer pressure, they try it for the first time. And most of the time, they come back when they are sober to try it again, to see if they really did like it. After that, they get hooked.

Kimchi fries are made of "caramelized Kimchi, a mound of sizzling Korean BBQ, chopped grilled onions, cheddar and Monterey Jack cheese, cilantro, magic sauce, sriracha and sesame seeds. All set on top of a pile of crispy French fries" (http://www.chilantrobbq.com/menu). As someone who is not a big fan of french fries, I hesitated ordering the kimchi fries, but after my first bite, I have been converted, not to fries in general, just kimchi fries. The combination of slight spicy, savory, sweet, and tartness make this dish unimaginably good.

While being part of the night scene in Austin has converted many people to kimchi fries and Korean BBQ tacos, the downtown presence of the truck during lunch hour[3] has expanded and sustains another group of followers. During the day, the truck serves primarily white-collar office workers in the downtown area where restaurants are abundant. Unlike the earlier generation of food trucks that often parked in locations where there was less competition and most of whose consumers were working-class folks, today's food trucks are situated in more accessible and prominent locations that attract white-collar workers and the middle class. The fact the today's food trucks can compete well with the more established downtown businesses illustrates their success in filling a particular niche that is based on both taste and price, which in turn are shaped by the media and the economy.

For some of the more established food trucks, renting a spot in a downtown parking lot offers a permanent venue, which makes it easier to grow their business. The predictability of being at a regular spot at a regular time gives clients a sense of certainty that if they go there, they will find the food truck of their choice. For despite the predominance of the Internet in contemporary life, not everyone is attached, or wants to be attached, to their mobile devices. Having a semipermanent location, then, helps reach a broader population, a population that may not be tech savvy but still is interested in the latest food trends. Most, if not all, food truck owners start without a regular spot. As they become more established, they may be able to rent a place in a parking lot. Location, of course, is everything, and even though the food truck business is still in a somewhat nascent stage in Austin, the cost of renting a spots in a parking lot is climbing. Interestingly, for most food truck owners in Austin, the end goal is to earn enough money to underwrite a brick-and-mortar business. The food trucks, then, are expected to generate both the capital and the consumer base to ensure the future success of a "real" restaurant.

Keeping the Costs Down

In many ways, the rise of food trucks cannot be disassociated from a particular economic moment. For young business entrepreneurs with limited capital and proven experience, starting a small business can be extremely challenging. The food trucks offer a great entry point precisely because they require a relatively small initial capital investment but intensive labor. Whereas Jae Kim used his personal savings to start his business, Eric Silverstein consolidated funds from his savings, investors' money, and bank loans. With approximately $70,000 to $80,000 of funds set aside to ensure both their business and personal economic survival for six months to a year, they embarked on their venture. In the beginning, each of them in his own business served simultaneously as the manager, cook, server, public relations officer, cleanup leader, and every other position.

Mindful of the current economy, food truck owners are extremely careful when pricing their food. Most dishes cost from four to seven dollars.

According to Eric Silverstein, his clients are extremely sensitive to price, and he is well aware that pricing dishes above seven dollars will lead to fewer sales. "There is a certain threshold or price limit that people are comfortable with when it comes to buying food [from food trucks]. It is simply not sustainable if I raise the prices above that threshold," he remarks. While the depressed state of the economy certainly has influenced the pricing of dishes, people's expectations also play a role. People assume that food from food trucks will be less expensive than that served in brick-and-mortar restaurants, so they are surprised, sometimes even outraged, when they find slightly higher prices at food trucks. For Eric and other food truck entrepreneurs, then, the challenge is to provide innovative, high-quality food at an affordable price.

Eric Silverstein also noted that people in Austin are still quite hesitant to try new foods, whether they are new combinations of well-known cuisines or different ethnic cuisines that have not yet entered into mainstream food trends.

> People want familiar food with an extra something. It's hard to get them to try really different food—especially Asian food—that is completely new to their food repertoire. It just doesn't work here. Texas is different from Washington [State] and California in that sense. They are less familiar with Asian fusion, in general. So, it's been a challenge.

Unlike Korean BBQ tacos, which borrow from the two most common and popular foods—Tex-Mex and BBQ—in Austin (and Texas more generally), Eric's food is a mix of Vietnamese, Thai, and Southern dishes that do not automatically resonate with Austin's local food culture, despite the large Vietnamese presence in Austin and Texas's proximity to the American South. It is important to remember that even though non-Texans may see Texas as part of the American South, Texans do not see it that way. Instead, they have a strong sense of Texan identity that is distinct from the American South and, more generally, the rest of the United States. In fact, the idea of the "Republic of Texas" is still very much alive in Texan cultural consciousness. The two dominant foods in Texas are BBQ and Tex-Mex, so Korean BBQ tacos, burritos, and quesadillas do not stray too far.

Conclusion: The Food Trucks of the Twenty-First Century

New food trends reflect the social concerns and aspirations of the time. For instance, in the United States, comfort food was characteristic of the economically depressed decade of the 1930s, and California cuisine and Japanese sushi, both status foods, emerged during the booming 1980s, along with the yuppie generation and Japan's rising economy.[4] The past two decades introduced fusion cooking, the slow food movement, and the organic food movement. Today, food trucks are the latest addition to the food scene. Even though they have been around for decades, food trucks have undergone a dramatic transformation and achieved mainstream status. Ice-cream trucks, old-style food trucks that offer coffee and pastries in the morning, and those that serve the more conventional burgers and tacos are still in operation. But when we speak of food trucks today, what comes to mind are not those old-style food trucks but the ones with catchy names (like Chi'Lantro and Peached Tortilla) and stylish designs, food trucks that serve the latest food trends and updated comfort foods. The question that arises, then, is why are food trucks so popular today? Indeed, what factors contribute to the reinvention, popularization, and mainstreaming of food trucks? What does the rapid proliferation of food trucks tell us about the current state of our cultural, social, and culinary world? My findings thus far are from research I did in Austin, so many of the details cannot be generalized to the food trucks in other cities like New York, Seattle, Los Angeles, and San Francisco.[5] Place and locality help determine how the food truck phenomenon transpires in these different cities. Nonetheless, I want to highlight several forces that have contributed to the general spread of food trucks across the nation.

The popularization of media and mobile technologies has been crucial to the recent success of food trucks. The mobile devices that allow us to access the Internet at any time have given food trucks a more effective way of communicating with and building a consumer base. Because food trucks do not have a permanent location, they rely on the Internet—through their own web page, Facebook web page, or Twitter—to keep their customers abreast of where they are. This constant online communication is necessary to ensure that consumers know where to find the food trucks and for food truck entrepreneurs to maintain a base of followers. For some people (especially young people and the professional class), being online is now an ordinary aspect of everyday life. While the popularization of Internet usage has been instrumental in revitalizing food trucks in this way, it has also rejuvenated, quite literally, the image of food trucks. Today's food truck entrepreneurs and consumers identify themselves as young, urban, cosmopolitan, and/or professional. Internet media have brought this particular segment of consumers to the mobile food service, thereby revamping the image of food trucks and creating a new food phenomenon. Food trucks are no longer relegated to the margins of society and the edges of cities. Competing effectively with well-established restaurants in the heart of the city, they now are hip, urban, and thoroughly mainstream.

Food truck customers also belong to a cohort of people who have been socialized, through television, into a more diversified world of food consumption. They have been introduced to exotic dishes served in faraway places. At home, in the United States, they have experienced fine dining, modernized comfort foods, ethnic foods of all kinds, and fusion cooking. Their craving for food diversity and innovation, however, has been tempered by the current economic recession. In the 1980s and 1990s, when the economy was booming, the cultural ideal of food consumption was to go to an elegant, expensive restaurant. Now, though, it has become socially accepted, even culturally fashionable, to find tasty "cheap eats." In a depressed economy, being budget conscious is now a concern for most people, not just for the working class. Food trucks, on the one hand, have a lingering stereotype of offering affordable food, which appeals to the budget conscious. Their presumably lower overhead costs suggest lower-priced food as well. On the other hand, these new food trucks are serving the latest food trends, which are usually associated with cutting-edge restaurants with famous chefs. In some ways, food trucks fill the vacuum created by the increased demand for innovative, tasty food and the unwillingness or inability of consumers to eat at expensive restaurants.

I conclude with a word about the "Asian Latino" fusion food that is becoming popular in Austin and other urban areas. By Asian Latino fusion, I am referring to the mix of at least two cooking traditions associated with Asia and with Latin America. While "fusion" in the 1990s often meant the combination of Asian (usually Japanese and Chinese) and European (usually French) influences, the fusion of today has a broader reference, one that includes both Asian and Latino influences. Korean BBQ tacos are prime examples of Asian Latino fusion. How do we make sense of their invention and subsequent wide acceptance? I suggest that this new kind of fusion—the invention of dishes that draw from various Asian and Latino cooking traditions—actually reflects the changing demographics of various cities in the United States as well as the cross-ethnic intersections and interactions between Asian and Latino populations. As Jae Kim pointed out, it was his experience of living in a largely Latino and Asian community and eating Mexican food and Korean food that led to his creation of Korean BBQ tacos and burritos.

Asians and Latinos are the fastest-growing immigrant populations in the United States. Neighborhoods and cities are being transformed, producing new kinds of conversations and connections. Asian Latino fusion, I believe, represents and indexes an emergent cultural form that resulted from these groups living close to each other and engaging in a process of interaction, exchange, and cultural invention.

Notes

I sincerely thank Robert Ji-Song Ku for his thoughtful comments and suggestions. This chapter has been enriched by his input, though I take full responsibility for all its shortcomings. Without Robert's Zen-like patience and support, this chapter could not have been finished in time for this publication.

1. By Chinese Latino restaurants, I am referring to a wide range of restaurants that serve a combination of Chinese food and food from a Latin American or Caribbean country.

2. Lok Siu, "Chino Latino Restaurants: Converging Communities, Identities, and Cultures," *Afro-Hispanic Review* 27, no. 1 (spring 2008): 161–71. These restaurants are established by diasporic Chinese who have migrated to the United States from Latin America and the Caribbean. Note that these restaurants do not serve "fusion" cuisine, understood as food created from a mix of culinary traditions, spices, and/or ingredients. Instead, their menus reflect the coexistence (separate but together) of two cuisines conventionally known as "Chinese" and "Latino." Moreover, the food they serve is not fusion per se, in the sense of newly created dishes that draw on two different food traditions. In any case, the restaurants offer the possibility of consuming, at the same time, both "Chinese" and "Latino" dishes, thereby bringing together people of various backgrounds drawn to those two different culinary traditions. For a more detailed discussion of these restaurants, refer to Siu, "Chino Latino Restaurants."

3. Unlike many cities in the United States, the lunch hour for Austin businesses is always and everywhere set from noon to 1 p.m. This makes it possible for the food trucks to park for just a few hours, usually 11 a.m. to 2 p.m., when they can maximize their lunch sales in just a few working hours. This aspect of Austin culture gives food trucks a predictable schedule.

4. See Sylvia Lovegren, *Fashionable Food: Seven Decades of Food Fads* (New York: Macmillan, 1995); and Theodore C. Bestor, "How Sushi Went Global," in *The Cultural Politics of Food and Eating: A Reader*, ed. James L. Watson and Melissa I. Caldwell (Malden, MA: Blackwell, 2005), 13–20.

5. Since moving to Northern California a few months ago, I have become abundantly aware of just how much place—local culture, population, expectations, and regulations—has shaped the development of the food truck phenomenon. The differences between the food truck culture of Austin and that of the Bay Area are too many to cover in this chapter.

12

Samsa on Sheepshead Bay

Tracing Uzbek Foodprints in Southern Brooklyn

ZOHRA SAED

In southern Brooklyn, at the very tip of the borough where the beaches are the main attraction, runs Ocean Avenue. Along this long street, which begins on Emmons Avenue and ends near Prospect Park, is a long stretch of apartments, which, in the 1980s, were managed by Turks, Tatars, and Uzbeks. The buildings were hardly six stories high and nearly identical, distinguishable only by a few shades of brick, yellow or red. My childhood was spent zipping from one building to the next, playing in basements with the reckless freedom of childhood. My friends were the children of the superintendents who lived and worked in these apartments, so we were able to sneak in through all the nooks and crannies, playing hide and seek, and even crawling into the large dryers in the basements. The thread that held us together around the neighborhoods and in school was the Turkic languages: Tatar, Uzbek, Kazakh, and Turkish. But something else equally important bound us together: Turkic food.

The memory of my childhood is filled with an abundance of smells and tastes amid moored boats and seagulls that flew in a flurry above our heads. The most memorable is the taste of minced lamb tucked into dough and baked as *samsa* or fried as *bulani*. How can I ever forget Emmons Avenue in autumn, the view of the bay on a sunny day, a thermos of steaming black tea with cardamom, sweetened for the small family trips? Cupped in our warm hands, these treats simply melted in our mouths. The mini savory pies were celebratory foods; making them required all hands to be on deck. These labor-intensive meals were prepared by groups of women who gathered before special events such as picnics or holidays. Together, they painstakingly "knotted" the pastry, the Uzbek term for wrapping dumplings or other filled pastries.

Nomadic Culinary Roots

In the Uzbek household, the fundamental meal is a rice dish known as *osh* or *palau* (also called *pilov* or *pilaf*, as it is more familiarly known in the West). Variations of the *palau* traveled to India with the Moguls and became *biryani*, which means "fried" in Farsi, just as korma is *qourma*, which means "fried" in Turkic. *Quorma* was then taken as *gourmeh* in Iranian Farsi and turned finally by the French into "gourmet." Given this etymological lineage, how can korma *not* taste delicious?

Lamb is the main protein on the Central Asian table. The meat is steamed, broiled, grilled, stewed, or tucked into pastry dough and either baked to form *samsas* or fried to make *chiborek* or *bulani*. Beef makes an appearance in noodle soups, like *laghman*, but rarely. Chicken, although present in roasts or kebabs, is not nearly as popular as lamb. Central Asian cuisine is a gastronomic testimony of a nomadic past, which is why there is such an abundance of lamb, goat, dairy (mostly yogurt), briny cheese, sausages, and dried meats. Lamb is famously made into shish kebabs and grilled on an open wood fire. The origins of shish kebab is *shush kebab*, a Farsi term that means "lungs roasted." Lungs salted, skewered, and roasted in an open fire was a quick meal on the go along the mountains and steppes. The popular term used by Russians and Turks is *shashlik,* which some claim has Turkic origins meaning "hurried" or fast food, while others argue that it is a variation of the *seekhlik*, which means "with a stick."

Vegetables are a rarity in the Central Asian diet. The national fruit is the melon, known as *kherbuza,* which means "donkey-goat" in Farsi. The story behind the *kherbuza* is that only after a donkey and a goat ate the melons did the king see it fit for the people to eat the fruit. The other national fruit is the watermelon, or *tarbuz,* a variation of the *kherbuza,* which translates into the more humorously literal "wet goat." The joke is that even our fruits are named after animals.

Ka'zi, or horsemeat made into sausage, is a specialty among Turkic people. Even though the meat is considered taboo according to Islamic food laws, the Uzbeks allowed themselves some flexibility by slaughtering lame horses according to halal rules, rendering the meat permissible. Other religious Uzbeks made *ka'zi* passable in the Muslim Uzbek diet by telling a folk story that grants permission through *macru,* a religious concept that allows for a gray area in Islamic law. *Macru* permits some flexibility for eating animals for which the rules are unclear, such as rabbits.

This flexibility is not tolerated in Muslim countries outside Central Asia, however. In Saudi Arabia, Uzbek migrant workers caught preparing horsemeat are deported from the country. In Afghanistan, Uzbeks are referred to as "donkey eaters" because of the rumor of Uzbeks making sausages, an unfamiliar food item to Afghans, who prefer their meat dried.

Ka'zi is considered the ideal meat for winter, since it is purported to have heating properties, and in this regard, Central Asian traditional medicine is similar to the Ayuverdic and Chinese health traditions. Horses, like chickens and turkeys, are believed to have warming effects on the body, and so they are considered a cure for those who are sensitive to the cold, have poor circulation, or even suffer from incontinence. Medicinal eating is a rationale that allows for the eating of *ka'zi*, a culinary tradition that traces back to the Mongols.

The horse holds an important position in Central Asian mythology. The word for "name" in the Turkic language is *ot,* which also means horse. The tradition of preparing and selling *ka'zi* was not brought to the United States by the Uzbeks who had come via Afghanistan. Perhaps the derogatory reputation of horsemeat and living in a more religious society affected their taste and longing for these sausages. Instead, *ka'zi* made its debut on the streets of Brooklyn after the year 2000 with the third wave of Uzbek immigrants to southern Brooklyn. This group came directly from Uzbekistan.

The addition of potatoes to the Uzbek diet has an indirect connection to the Civil War in America, during which cotton was not exported to Europe. The shortage of cotton led to the Russian conquest of Tashkent in 1865, Samarkand and Bukhara in 1868, and Khiva in 1873. To satisfy the need for cotton, cotton fields replaced wheat fields. To make up for the lack of wheat, the Russian government sent train cars filled with a New World tuber, which served as a substitute starch in Uzbekistan in the late nineteenth century. Potatoes came in by the freight car load. My grandfather once recalled how the people at first thought the *khatichka* were rocks that the Russians had brought to throw at the people. This is perhaps why the word for potato in Uzbek is an alteration of *kartoshka*, the Russian term. But that was then. Today, the people of post-Soviet Uzbekistan refer to potatoes by the proper Russian term *kartoshka*. For the Uzbeks of the diaspora who migrated after the 1917 Bolshevik invasion, however, the word is still *khatichka*, which I always heard as Khadija, said quickly like a sneeze. I grew up thinking the potato was named after a woman.

The suspicion regarding vegetables is not limited to the "Russian rocks" of old, for even local vegetables, like zucchini and squash, are referred to as "pot scrubbers." According to tradition, vegetables are either fed to livestock or dried and used to scrub pots. During the Soviet era, Moscow's greed for cotton destroyed Uzbekistan's food crops, and starvation spread across most of Central Asia in the early years of Sovietization, which brought about changes in traditional foods. Soviet propaganda photographs—like a famous one by Max Penson—depicted images of joyous, cotton-picking Uzbeks, with baskets full of vegetables from their farms and new technology from Russia. In reality, Uzbekistan faced dire conditions in which families were forced to sell the wood beams supporting the roof of their homes for a few loaves of bread. Others consumed compressed bricks of cottonseed after the oil was harvested; many died from this lethally indigestible meal.

In more fortunate homes, meat dishes were stretched with the addition of vegetables; lamb was reinforced by potatoes or replaced with pumpkin. Potatoes were mashed and added along with the meat to make steamed lamb dumplings known as *mantu*. Soon, potatoes were given starring roles, such as in special pastry dishes known as *khanum*. These knish-like pastries, filled with mashed potatoes, were otherwise known as "ladies." What all this meant was that the potato was finally integrated into the Uzbek table as an inexpensive, but filling, meal.

Through Sovietization, new ethnic groups were relocated to Uzbekistan. Tatars, who were deported from Crimea, were relocated to Tashkent and the outer towns of Uzbekistan. They brought their love of *chiborek*—or *bulani*, depending on what side of the Amu Darya (Oxus River) you were standing on—along with them. Closely related to the Uzbek steamed dumpling *mantu* is the Korean *mandu*, which appears to have been introduced to Korea in the sixteenth century under the Mongols, when Uighurs played a leading role in governing Korea. In the first half of the twentieth century, thousands of Koreans were forcibly relocated to Uzbekistan and returned the *mantu* to its origin in the form of *mandu*. The Koreans also introduced fresh salads and pickled vegetables. The most popular of these among Uzbeks is a salad called *yongoqli chim chi*, which, coincidentally or not, sounds awfully like *kimchi*, the ubiquitous Korean pickled vegetables. Made of julienned carrots, *yongoqli chim chi* is now an integral part of a typical Uzbek home meal and is regularly served in Uzbek restaurants. The migration of Russians to Uzbekistan meant that there was also plenty of vodka, despite Islam's taboo against alcohol. Now the Soviet era may be over, but vodka is still a part of the post-Soviet Uzbek table.

The Uzbek version of *mantu* features spices strongly associated with the Middle East, such as a generous amount of cumin and black pepper. *Mantus* are typically served with a minty yogurt sauce. Popular throughout Central Asia, *mantus* has numerous regional variations. In Afghanistan, they are sometimes filled with cooked meat and served with *kormas* made of lentils and diced carrot. Uzbek *mantus* are filled with meat and red onions; tradition requires that their size be no bigger than the center of a palm of a hand.

A favorite dish among the Turks is *manti,* which are very tiny dumplings, something Uzbeks call *chichwara,* but tied up like tortellini. Whenever I see tortellini, I think of Marco Polo chatting with Kubla Khan somewhere on the steppes.

From the very beginning, food traditions in Central Asia were already criss-crossed with the multiple tastes and aromas of the Middle East and East Asia. Long before their migration to the United States, Central Asians set their table with the culinary offerings of the Americas, the Middle East, and East Asia. And let us not forget South Asia: chili sauce is a reminder that the winds blew from that direction as well.

A Turkic Palimpsest in Southern Brooklyn

By name alone, Sheepshead Bay sounds like the ideal culinary location for Central Asians nostalgic for the lamb's head soups of their homelands. In truth, the neighborhood was named for the once abundant sheepshead fish. It is, for the most part, an Italian, Irish, and Jewish neighborhood that is separated by a bridge from Manhattan Beach, a wealthier neighborhood. The majority of Central Asians who now reside there sought out southern Brooklyn through word of mouth from earlier Turkic immigrants.

Sheepshead Bay was my childhood neighborhood. I grew up there in a small pocket of vibrant and varied Central Asians. This community expanded as an older, more established community of Turks and Tatars befriended newly arriving Afghan Uzbeks, helping them find work as superintendents in apartment buildings along Ocean Avenue, from south of Prospect Park all the way down to the beach. Over time, these new arrivals found work as fram-ers in frame shops, as rug dealers in Persian rug stores, and as neighborhood shopkeepers. The commonalities of the Turkic languages kept their connec-tions strong. During the 1980s and 1990s, in an expression of unity, the various Turkic-language groups gathered to march together in pan-Turkic spirit at the Turkey Day Parade under a common red and white star crescent flag. This was quite a controversial move, as many Turkic people felt loyal to their particular Kazakh, Uzbek, or Afghan flags. But the collective need for communal cel-ebration and social networks proved more urgent.

Reportedly, the first New York City–based Central Asian organization com-posed of a unified community was founded in 1927. The numbers were small, consisting mainly of Turkic-speaking people who wished to preserve their lan-guage. Although the organization was open to all Muslims, regardless of ethnic affiliation, including African Muslims, there was a respectable representation of Turks, who had migrated from Turkey. Because of immigration restrictions, however, the community of Turkic people was not able to grow. From 1944 to 1947, following the Stalin-era deportation from their lands, Crimean Tatars came to New York, many of them survivors of the Crimean genocide of 1944.

Founded in 1964, the American Tatar Association opened an office in Flushing, Queens, where large communities of Asians now reside. This was an important year in the migration of Turkic people from Turkey and from Central Asia, including my father, then a teenager, and my grandfather. At the time, the two of them were in Karachi, Pakistan, awaiting word that would grant them entry into the United States. The good news finally arrived, but tragically, as they prepared for the long journey, my grandfather suddenly died, and the loss left my father bereft and his desire to move to the United States dissipated. He thus stayed in Pakistan, worked as a waiter at a café, finished his dental degree, and returned to Afghanistan. In Karachi, he witnessed waves of Turkic people—Uzbeks, Kazaks, and Uighurs—living in the Turkistan Anjuman, a community housing center in Karachi. They all were biding their time while waiting to leave for the United States. My father finally ended up coming to New York in 1980, and he came very much like the majority of Afghan and Uzbek immigrants of that time, with a family in tow. The one-dollar bill and the quarter that he once received as a tip while working as a waiter at Tawana House Café in Karachi are now framed, serving as homage to the dream of a teenager who once wished he could come to America with his father.

During the late 1970s and 1980s, Sheepshead Bay and Brighton Beach became the principal places where Afghan Uzbeks came to settle. They found a home in the community established by earlier immigrants, complete with a halal butcher shop, an ethnic grocery store, and a small mosque. Owing to the rise in popularity of Afghan food during the 1980s, many opened restaurants. All the while, as many Afghan Uzbeks prospered, they began to move away from the neighborhood, and by 1991, a great number had resettled in the middle-class suburbs of New Jersey and Long Island. Throughout it all, the Uzbek families maintained a traditional family structure in which women stayed home as homemakers. When they did work outside the home, it was mostly part time.

Wedding halls were popular places to gather and eat, and meetings there kept the community socially connected. More than any other event, weddings were the main attraction. In order to become a member of the Turkistan American Association, all members were required to attend one another's weddings and funerals. Indeed, to miss a life event of this magnitude meant losing one's social position in the community. In a community in which eating at home or at communal dinners was of paramount importance, there was little need for fast-food Uzbek restaurants. Nonetheless, after the Soviet-Afghan War, Afghan food was unpopular among Russian immigrants in Brooklyn. Even though the cuisine was becoming increasingly popular among the general New York public, especially in Manhattan and Queens, Russian New Yorkers kept their distance from both Afghan restaurants and Afghan New Yorkers, despite often sharing the same zip code.

The economic disaster in independent post-Soviet Uzbekistan is what caused a new wave of migration—economic refugees—to enter the United States. Not surprisingly, many moved to the same neighborhoods that earlier waves of Central Asian immigrants had established. This time, though, the new immigrants did not come as families. Instead, most were employed by affluent Russian immigrants in need of affordable domestic servants. Due in part to Uzbekistan's crumbling health sector after 2004, Uzbek migrant workers were predominantly educated women, most of them pharmacists, medical doctors, and surgeons. In New York City, however, they served as nannies and elder care assistants for Russian families. While riding the subway, I often chatted with older Uzbek women who once worked in the health sector in Uzbekistan but chose to work as a nanny in Brooklyn. Being a nanny in New York City meant earning three times what a physician made in Tashkent. The money was hard to resist, even if the long hours were nearly impossible.

From Halal Meat Shops to Fast-Food Joints

The Central Asian community in Brooklyn was built on several layers of migration involving different groups of Central Asians—Tatars, Turks, Uzbeks (including Afghan Uzbeks), and Kazaks—before, during, and after the Soviet era. Each of these groups left an indelible mark on the restaurant culture of New York City. What is remarkable about the recent growth of Uzbek and Uighur restaurants in Sheepshead Bay and Brighton Beach is their ability to weave back and forth between two of the more established communities in these neighborhoods, the Russian and the Turkish.

In the mid-1990s, Turkish restaurants began opening along the strip of newly renovated Emmons Avenue. With the new condos and the tearing down of the summer bungalows that were built in the 1930s came a strip mall and even a casino boat that promised to bolster the economy of this neighborhood. Most of the new Turkish restaurants specialized in kebabs, and these Turkish kebab restaurants thrive to this day. Even the smaller, more residential streets feature eateries that specialize in shish kebabs or *shashlik*. Accordingly, it would not be unthinkable to refer Sheepshead Bay by the culinarily appropriate moniker "Shish Kebab Bay."

Café Kashgar on Brighton Beach Avenue is a narrow restaurant with meals rarely costing more than ten dollars. The affordable price is not the only magnet that draws hungry Central Asians to the restaurant; the perfectly knotted *mantus* and *samsas*, as well as the succulent sticks of roasted lamb, also brings them in droves. The tiny TV screen in the corner of the establishment perpetually flickers with Uzbek television shows and films, and at times, there also are Russian movies. The clientele are gold-toothed natives of Tashkent, Baku, or Moscow, and the mood is always jovial. The wait staff is fluent in Russian, Uzbek, and Tajik. Invariably, a tableful of patrons arrive bearing their own bottles of vodka and drink to their own reflections, as the restaurant has cleverly positioned large mirrors on both sides of the walls to make the space look bigger than it actually is. Café Kashgar was the first of its kind to open in Brooklyn. After years of working in the kitchens of other restaurants in the United States, the owner, a Uighur with green eyes, decided to open his own restaurant where the meat was halal. "You can't find food safe to eat here, so I opened my own restaurant," he once told me as I waited for my take-out order to arrive.

The first wave of Turkic immigrants to Brooklyn opened halal butcher shops and ethnic groceries that catered to the specific needs of the community, which was composed primarily of families with traditional patriarchal structures intact. In contrast, the third wave chose to open small restaurants that featured all the foods missed at home. There was a ready-made clientele for this: the growing number of single workers, childless couples who came for work, and those who had left grown children back in Uzbekistan. Like the Pakistani restaurants along Brooklyn's Coney Island Avenue that cater to twenty-four-hour cab drivers, these Central Asian restaurants offered shish kebabs that were different from those sold in Turkish shish kebab restaurants. The Turkish version is "dry"; the Central Asian version is skewered with extra fat. Even the *mantu* is made in a similar fashion—salty and fatty to suit the desires of Uzbek migrant workers leaving for work late at night to Manhattan Beach or to one of the luxury condos on Brighton Beach a few steps from the tiny restaurants lit up with fluorescent lamps and a few framed photographs of Samarkand and Bukhara.

The neighborhood housewives of my childhood, women who dressed up and took turns visiting one another at their small apartments and cooking meals together, are now a distant memory. Gone is the time when *mantu, chiborek, samsa,* and *chichwara* all were readily available under the supervision of these women. To the new generation of working women and third-wave bachelor workers, these women of the older generation are now stuff of legends. The new generation of Central Asians does not rely on mosques or community centers to provide a sense of community; often lacking the bond of family or children to pull them home each evening, they instead rely on restaurants to serve as venues of community building. It is in restaurants where they gather to share the foods of their homelands and recall and reimagine a shared past and envision a collective future.

The Sovietization of Uzbekistan brought Uzbeks and Russians closer together, even if that sense of closeness had residues of colonial hierarchies lingering among those who moved to the United States. The Russian language connected these communities, as did the Russians' Orientalist nostalgia for Samarkand, Bukhara, and Tashkent, which contributed to the success of local restaurants catering to the fad of hookah lounges and Arabian Nights-inspired decor. Elaborate Uzbek restaurants with Orientalist names like Ali Baba or 1001 Nights are the more recent examples. These new restaurants, replete with cushions, scarves, and a rotund statue of the Molla Nasruddin, evoke an old Uzbek palace that satisfies the Russians' nostalgia for their own private East. There is irony in the realization that the neighborhood is more welcoming of restaurants that feature faux mosque-like architectural design than actual mosques that serve the area's Muslim community. In fact, any talk of building a mosque is met with vehement protests, a reminder that the ethnic and racial divide of Brooklyn is not merely a thing of the past but a feature of the present.

From halal butcher shops to garish orientalist restaurants, the food imprint of Central Asian Americans does not begin and end with kebabs. The growing community has moved beyond the narrow place where Borough Park and Ditmus Park rub shoulders to encompass a neighborhood composed of ethnic shops, halal butchers, and restaurants. The neighborhood comes to life during weddings—and most colorfully during *nowruz*, commonly referred to as the Persian New Year. Commemorating the first day of spring and the March equinox, *nowruz* is celebrated not only by Iranians but also by people across the Central Asian diaspora.

Uzbek television has a strong following both online and via satellite. Typically, the production crew is made up of former actors and actresses from the Tashkent Theater; they perform in dance programs, plays, and films that can be viewed on the TV sets of restaurants that have their doors open to the street. This is yet another way that Central Asians have created networks that crisscross geographic borders. Often, language and food connect Turks to Tatars to Uzbeks to northern Afghans to Uighurs. In this regard, pan-Turkism is not merely a romantic notion. Rather, it is a lived reality for immigrants, a vital form of support for new immigrants to locate work, to find marriage partners, and to build business alliances.

The importance of the Central Asian restaurants to the lives of Central Asian Americans in southern Brooklyn goes beyond the culturally digestible themes of "Ali Baba." Ironically, it is inside the walls and on the tables of Orientalist-inspired trappings that many of the traditional foods that have been lost through the confusion and chaos of migration have been rediscovered. *Ka'zi*, whether made of beef or horse, was once a culinary art form forgotten by the Uzbek American household. It now can be enjoyed in the neighborhood restaurant. The Uighurs of northwestern China have reintroduced the traditional way of preparing *mantus* and handmade noodles to the immigrant Central Asian population that had, like most other immigrant groups, adapted speedier versions of these foods as they adjusted to the American way of life. It is now possible once again to taste *mantus* and *samsas* wrapped in handmade dough instead of mass-produced wonton wrappers or store-bought puff pastry sheets.

I am tired of the term "authentic" when applied to culture and, especially, to the crossroads of cultures that make up Central Asian cuisine. But I cannot deny that the new wave of Central Asians has brought with them tastes, aromas, and cooking techniques that were long forgotten by the earlier generation that had become used to dousing their *bulani* and *chiborek* with ketchup. The end of the Soviet era brought about a reunion of sorts in southern Brooklyn. Sitting side by side, elbow to elbow, in restaurants on Emmons Avenue and Coney Island Avenue are the multitudinous people who share the Turkic language and food. Among them are Afghan Uzbek Americans, like myself, speaking Uzbek that predates the linguistic influence of Russian, although the Uzbek spoken here now is littered with English words. As I sit in one of these restaurants laughing along with an Uzbek TV show, I order another plate of steamed lamb dumplings and think to myself how delicious life in Brooklyn is.

13

Apple Pie and *Makizushi*

Japanese American Women Sustaining Family and Community

VALERIE J. MATSUMOTO

In 1930s Los Angeles, Natsuye Fujimoto, a second-generation Japanese American teenager, compiled a booklet she entitled "Recipes (Japanese)." Carefully documenting the food her family enjoyed and considered Japanese, she included dishes ranging from "Nasu-Ni (Sautéed Eggplant)" and traditional New Year's "Ozoni" soup, to "Shrimp Salad" and "Baked Flat Fish" with "Pesha Meru" (béchamel) sauce.[1] The notation "Serves 5"—the number in the Fujimoto family—on many of the recipes suggests that these dishes constituted part of the family's regular diet. Fujimoto's "Shrimp Salad" with pineapple and cucumber shows how Japanese immigrant families adapted the idea of the Western salad, dressing theirs with Japanese sweet wine, vinegar, ginger, and mustard. Her "Baked Flat Fish" recipe called not for baking the fish in an oven, with which many Japanese immigrants were unfamiliar, but frying it on a stove; and the "Pesha Meru" sauce served over the fish contained the butter, flour, and egg yolks of a classic French sauce. The recipe for "Chinese Steamed Castella" hinted at even earlier histories, referencing both a Chinese cooking technique and the "Castella" cake linked with the influence of Portuguese traders in Japan. The Fujimoto family's culinary practices offer glimpses of the process by which women have transmitted, adopted, and combined elements of Japanese American culture.

The food prepared by nisei (U.S.-born second-generation) women in the pre-World War II period reflects their efforts not only to sustain family and ethnic community but also to cross social and cultural boundaries. In chapter 19 of this book, Delores Phillips draws attention to such crossings in the 1999 cookbook *Madhur Jaffrey's World Vegetarian*, which she examines as an endeavor to "transform space in ways that resist the customary boundaries of nation and culture." Second-generation Japanese Americans grew up in an era of exclusion, when boundaries between racial groups in the U.S. West were defined by restrictive housing covenants, alien land laws, laws against interracial marriage, and discrimination in the workplace and recreation. If Jaffrey's cookbook "imagines the eater as a global citizen," the nisei's culinary activities in the 1920s and 1930s reaffirm their sense of themselves as American citizens with deep attachments to ethnic cultural practices.

In the context of race relations before World War II, the second generation's preparation and consumption of Western dishes can be read as a sign of interest in new flavors and a way of claiming and demonstrating their Americanness. Their tastes also showed the influence of regional demographics and interactions with other minority groups in Southern California. At the same time, nisei women continued to prepare the traditional holiday food and experiment with familiar Japanese dishes. Drawing on both the ethnic press and oral history, I examine in this chapter young Japanese American women's engagement with foodways, at home and in their clubs, with a focus on prewar Los Angeles.[2] Given women's primary culinary responsibilities, they played a creative role in shaping both the mundane and festive elements associated with ethnic culture.

Japanese Americans before World War II

Natsuye Fujimoto and her family were part of the growing Japanese American population on the West Coast in the early twentieth century. By the 1890s, the growing stream of Japanese laborers immigrating to Hawai'i and the continental United States reflected elite dreams of Japanese colonial expansionism as well as the pragmatism of displaced farmers seeking economic opportunities and avoiding military service by going abroad.[3] Although white nativists who had clamored for the passage of the Chinese Exclusion Act of 1882 now began to press for restrictions on Japanese immigration, Japan's political clout as a rising world power at the turn of the century delayed these measures. The 1908 Gentlemen's Agreement between Japan and the United States halted the influx of Japanese laborers, but a loophole permitted the entrance of the wives and family members of earlier residents. Their arrival before the 1924 Immigration Act steadily narrowed the gap in the sex ratio in the immigrant community. Indeed, due in part to the legal loophole facilitating family reunification and growth, the nisei became the biggest prewar group of second-generation Asian Americans. By 1910, Los Angeles County boasted the largest concentration of issei (first-generation immigrants) and nisei, numbering 8,641 in the continental United States, and by 1930, this number had increased to 35,000, half of whom were U.S.-born nisei. The emergence of the second generation hastened the development of family-centered communities. Ethnic newspapers like the *Rafu Shimpo* and *Kashu Mainichi* in Los Angeles vied for nisei readers by offering English-language sections edited by fellow nisei. In Southern California, most issei and nisei engaged in agriculture, fishing, and gardening and operated small businesses, such as the restaurants owned by Natsuye Fujimoto's father.[4]

Like many other Asian Americans and other people of color in the U.S. West, Japanese Americans faced formidable obstacles in all areas during the 1920s and 1930s. A battery of laws hampered their economic pursuits, marital choice, and political involvement, and residential segregation limited where they could live. Sometimes they were denied service in, or faced limited access to, restaurants, theaters, swimming pools, and other public facilities.

Over the past decade, research by historians like Eiichiro Azuma has shown how issei and nisei leaders tried to maneuver, despite the sometimes crushing intersection of U.S. and Japanese imperial movements.[5] Azuma asserts that "the Issei's concepts of the 'Pacific era' and their children as a 'bridge of understanding' between the United States and Japan glamorized a future role for the nisei beyond the borders of the American nation."[6] The racial barriers they faced in the United States made this concept particularly appealing, although as David Yoo points out, "Very few of the second generation could have served as true bridges, since they lacked adequate knowledge of Japanese language, history, and culture."[7] Still, mindfulness of their parents' and their own vulnerability spurred the nisei's efforts to promote "Pacific understanding" and harmonious interracial relations. The occasional newspaper reports of Japanese food prepared by nisei youth clubs for white women's organizations and local "international festivals" exemplify small steps toward the acceptance the Japanese Americans hoped to gain from the dominant society. They also echo the part that issei and nisei envisioned the second generation's playing in facilitating amity between Japan and the United States. In their using ethnic food as a diplomatic gesture of goodwill, women were expected to serve as ambassadors.

During this era of exclusion, both issei and nisei formed their own organizations for peer support, fostering camaraderie and gaining access to material resources through gendered and generational networks. Nisei youth clubs were widespread in cities like Los Angeles and San Francisco. By the eve of World War II, the *Rafu Shimpo*'s estimates of the number of nisei youth organizations in Southern California ranged from four hundred to six hundred, with young women raising the number.[8] Young Women's Christian Association (YWCA) and church-sponsored clubs were particularly numerous, as club membership offered girls a place of acceptance and understanding, as well as a vehicle through which to gain parental approval for social and recreational activities.

The Importance of Food to the Nisei's Social World

Japanese American women's culinary work and creativity were important to their families and communities, shaping one of the most cherished markers of ethnicity. According to Susan Kalčik, "Foodways can be charged with emotion and significance for both old and new Americans because food is potentially a symbol of ethnic identity."[9] Providing food was also one of the ways in which women helped build and sustain their social networks. In accordance with Western and Asian gender roles, girls and women prepared most of the food, which constituted a major arena of unpaid female labor and a vital element of Japanese American gatherings. As prewar ethnic newspapers documented, food was important to the nisei world, whether prepared for a family holiday or a group fund-raising event. No report in the 1920s of an outing, meeting, wedding, or club social would be complete without a reference to the "good eats" that were enjoyed.

The role of food in the urban nisei's social world offers a lens through which to explore what Vicki Ruiz terms "cultural coalescence," the process by which immigrants and their children select, maintain, adapt, and create cultural forms, drawing from as many influences as societal circumstances permit.[10] Their choices—and the broader evolution of American foodways—show both an attachment to the familiar and the appeal of novelty. Donna Gabaccia views this "tension between people's love of the familiar and the pleasure they find in desiring, creating, and experiencing something new" as a key to identity and culture.[11] Nisei women's efforts both to maintain ethnic cultural practices and to experiment with other cultural influences are particularly evident in their foodways.

As they engaged in cultural coalescence in everyday life, urban nisei women pondered the impact of the "modern girl," the younger, style-conscious, consumerist avatar of the "new woman" who had emerged in the late nineteenth and early twentieth century. In China, Japan, Europe, Australia, South Africa, and the United States, social critics in the 1920s voiced alarm at what they viewed as the modern girl's preoccupation with fashion, cosmetics, romance, dancing, and dating. In Los Angeles's Little Tokyo, immigrants and older nisei likewise expressed concern about the second generation's idealization of modernity as epitomized by American popular culture. Even though young women's flapper fashions and makeup drew censure, other aspects of Western culture were smoothly integrated into the Japanese American community. As a *Rafu Shimpo* headline announced in 1936, "Western Dish Predominant Nisei Palate."[12] Clearly, culinary activities may have offered nisei girls a parentally approved avenue by which to claim modern femininity and Americanness.

Indeed, culinary experimentation also interested issei women like the mother of Mary Nishi Ishizuka, who excelled at both Japanese and Western cooking—she made mouth-watering *tsukemono* (pickles) and sukiyaki, as well as corn chowder. Ishizuka remembered fondly the "bottles and bottles of root beer that she made for us."[13] As did the Filipina women about whom Dawn Mabalon writes in chapter 7, many Japanese women shared their culinary knowledge with their friends. Urban issei women also became acquainted with new dishes through their jobs as domestic workers in white households and from neighbors. For example, Setsuko Matsunaga Nishi recalled that her mother learned from an African American neighbor how to bake deep-dish apple pie. Issei Taka Honda attended adult classes in English and cooking at the Nora Sterry School in west Los Angeles, where she learned how to prepare a Thanksgiving dinner. "And she learned how to make pumpkin pie," her daughter Rose recounted, as well as banana nut bread and cookies—"we had peanut butter cookies coming out of our ears."[14] Many issei women kept up with the latest Japanese recipes through women's magazines like *Shufu no tomo*, and those with English-language skills consulted American guides such as *The Joy of Cooking*.

Both nisei daughters and their issei mothers were eager to improve their culinary skills, as reflected by the popularity of cooking classes in the Japanese American community. The classes offered by the Japanese YWCA in Los Angeles included not only sewing and Japanese literature but also "Japanese and western style culinary art."[15] Other groups also sponsored classes. For example, the Midori Kai, an "uptown ladies club," advertised lessons in baking and making puddings as well as Japanese dishes.[16] Girls' organizations also sometimes offered cooking lessons. In 1928 the young nisei women members of the Blue Triangle Club, affiliated with the YWCA, favored culinary training over handicrafts and etiquette.[17]

The "New" Japanese American Cuisine

These cooking classes were often explicitly aimed at preparing women for their anticipated roles as wives and mothers, thereby reinforcing traditional gender roles. In 1927 the *Rafu Shimpo* joked about culinary skills as a means of attracting male romantic interest: "Well, anyway the way to the men's hearts are through their stomachs."[18] With domestic harmony in mind, the Midori Kai proclaimed the household art of cooking to be a necessity for every wife and mother; wives were invited to attend their classes so that "their husbands will always want to eat at home."[19] The *Rafu Shimpo* similarly encouraged women to take the Japanese YWCA's Japanese cooking classes, saying, "Girls, here's one way you can make your husbands happy. They may be tired of ham and eggs every morning."[20] A decade later, a forum of college nisei men and women in Northern California reported that men believed that cooking skills were essential for women and that most college women students were either majoring in home economics or taking cooking classes. All present agreed that "we shall want both American and Japanese cooking in our homes."[21]

These examples make it clear that from the 1920s, Japanese Americans were interested in not only Japanese but also Western dishes. As the "ham and eggs" remark suggests, some aspects of European American cuisine may have quickly found a place in urban Japanese American homes. Other ethnic cuisines were appealing as well, especially Chinese and Chinese American food. For instance, in 1927 the Japanese YWCA hired a chef to teach women how to prepare chop suey.[22] The Blue Triangles, whose ambitions matched their adventurous palates, decided in 1928 to learn how to cook the "favorite dishes of all the countries."[23]

Nisei women also tried the recipes offered by the *Rafu Shimpo* newspaper. In a time when few ethnic cookbooks were written in English, the Japanese American newspapers in Los Angeles and San Francisco constituted an important resource for second-generation women who wished to prepare Japanese dishes, and clearly many of them did. In 1936 the *Rafu Shimpo* reported in a special supplement, "In many of the American homes of Japanese descent, we find that a large part of the food habits handed down by the elders are being perpetuated," adding optimistically that "Japanese meals will continue to be served . . . long after the first generation will have passed on."[24] To further this aim, and perhaps in response to its readers' interest, in 1940 the *Rafu Shimpo* offered a pamphlet of "15 popular" reprinted Japanese recipes for the price of ten cents.[25]

Indeed, the Japanese American test of a "good housewife" was the preparation of boiled rice, the staple of the Japanese diet. Nisei daughters—and second-generation Chinese American women like Jade Snow Wong—faced a rigorous judgment of their domestic skills, to which the cooking of rice was critical.[26] Acknowledging this, the *Rafu Shimpo* helpfully imparted the "secret" of making good boiled rice. Drawing on this mainstay of the Japanese household, readers also found tips on how "left-over rice may add variety" to the menu, making return appearances in dishes such as stuffed bell peppers.[27] These recipes also reflected Depression-era strategies for making more expensive ingredients go further by stretching them with less costly starches.

By the mid-1930s, nisei women appear to have been most interested in three areas of cuisine: "Japanese," "American," and "Chinese." In this, they both reflected and bucked the larger trend of the homogenization of the national diet stemming from the growth of giant food companies, technologies of preservation and distribution, and a flood of culinary advice dispensed via radio, cookbooks, and newspapers.[28] Harvey Levenstein notes that "the center of gravity of American cookery"[29] shifted from New England to the Midwest at this time—a shift that may have been hastened in California by the influx of midwestern migrants in the early twentieth century. To the nisei, "American" food seemed to mean the kind of meat-and-potatoes fare popular among transplanted midwesterners. In 1936 the *Rafu Shimpo* focused a special supplement on these three categories, taking pains to distinguish between "Real Tempura" and "Occidental Fritters" and to explain how "Original Sukiyaki" differed from the "U.S. Variety."[30] This may indicate the nisei's interest in preserving cultural practices and flavors and also the introduction of certain Japanese dishes—like sukiyaki—to the perhaps more adventurous West Coast. As the newspaper blithely predicted, "It won't be long before the American people will come to adopt Japanese dishes in their homes."[31] This optimistic pronouncement accompanied the photo of apparently European American "college girls learning the technique of handling chopsticks at a restaurant in Tokyo."[32] The image and caption suggest that at least some Japanese Americans perceived cultural adaptation as more than a one-way process. Hopes for the future appreciation of Japanese cuisine by mainstream America may have been linked with hopes for the increased social acceptance of Japanese Americans.

Food and Ethnicity

Japanese American experiences with racial barriers as well as cultural trends in the larger society both reinforced the appeal of Chinese food to the nisei. In the early twentieth century, Chinese food, particularly chop suey, gained enormous popularity in urban America, embraced as a sign of cosmopolitanism by customers who were unaware that their favorite dishes were unknown in China and had been developed by creative immigrant entrepreneurs adapting to local tastes.[33] The issei and nisei joined a diverse clientele who enjoyed chow mein and egg foo yung. For Japanese Americans, Chinese restaurants were important as sites where they could be sure of a welcome, as denial of service at white-owned restaurants deterred many issei and nisei from entering them. As nisei Katsumi Kunitsugu pointed out, "You go into just any old restaurant, and sometimes the waitresses wouldn't serve you. They don't tell you to get out, they just never came around to take your order."[34] In Los Angeles, Chinese eateries such as San Kwo Low, Far East, and Manshu Low offered tasty, affordable food and often served as the setting for Japanese American wedding receptions and organizational banquets.

A New, Multicultural Cuisine

Hopeful that food might serve as a cultural bridge, the *Rafu Shimpo* presented a vision of the nisei kitchen that highlighted technological advancements in tandem with the continuation of "traditional Japanese dishes."[35] For nisei women and housewives across the country, commercially prepared canned foods were a convenience and bore a prized stamp of modernity. To the pre-war nisei, modernity was often linked with Western culture. In the ethnic press, recipes for foods such as "Magic Mayonnaise" and "Parisian Dressing" frequently called for commercially processed ingredients. In this spirit, the *Rafu Shimpo* writer's description of the well-stocked kitchen included "a colorful assortment of packaged and canned foods, quite a number of which were unmistakably Japanese." Chilling in the refrigerator were "containers of fruit juices and tomato juice" while "packages of quick-frozen meats and vegetables" from the market waited in the freezer section. In the lean years of the Great Depression, this rosy image reflected more aspiration than reality, projecting women's culinary creativity as an instrument for social transformation. Nonetheless, the writer had high hopes that "nisei housewives" might improve Japanese cuisine by adapting "scientific American features" and thus "blaze the path to a new Pacific understanding through the food that will be served in the homes of America and Japan."[36]

Women's culinary experimentation and improvisation stimulated the development of hybrid forms that became part of Japanese American cuisine. A recipe for *pakkai* (sweet-and-sour spareribs),[37] reflected this hybridization. Among the ingredients were *katakuriko* (Japanese starch made from dogtooth violets), *shoyu* (soy sauce), green chilis (an element of regional Mexican American cuisine), and a can of pineapple, hinting at the labor migration routes of Chinese and Japanese from Hawai'i to the continental United States. In the process of cultural coalescence, Japanese immigrants and their children drew on a rich array of culinary traditions in the multicultural landscape of the U.S. West.

Cities, especially, offered the nisei opportunities to try new dishes. Fumiko Fukuyama Ide recalled how for the first time, as a junior high school student, she bought a dish of macaroni and cheese at the cafeteria: "I loved it! I never knew such things existed." On the way home after studying at the downtown central library while she was attending Belmont High School, she and her friends would stop at Thrifty Drugstore for cherry cokes and ice-cream sodas. A special treat was a jaunt to the Pig 'N Whistle —"THE dessert place to go to"—which introduced her to delights such as mocha chocolate cake and carrot cake.[38]

The city nisei's taste for a variety of foods can be found in journalist Larry Tajiri's paean to his favorite snacks, which included *nabeyaki udon* with home-made noodles at a café in Little Tokyo; tacos and a cup of *champorrado* (Mexican hot chocolate) on Olvera Street in the Mexican section nearby; hamburgers and onions from a drive-in; and a bowl of clam chowder at a waterfront restaurant.[39] A variety of cultural influences and the integration of Japanese and U.S. holidays can be seen in the array of recipes in the *Kashu Mainichi* as well. In the spring of 1938, for example, home cooks could find instructions for a Lenten pineapple-strawberry salad, *sake no miso shiru* (miso soup with salmon), a Ukrainian Easter dessert, *kashiwa mochi* (a sweetened rice confection) for Japanese Boys' Day, Mother's Day angel food cake, and a German potato salad to serve fifty.[40]

City families living in or near an ethnic enclave were more likely to have access to—and to be able to afford—a range of Asian and Western ingredients. Natsuye Gwen Fujimoto's family recipes called for a wide array of Japanese vegetables, seaweed, herbs, and nuts, such as *warabi* (bracken), *wakame* (seaweed), *renkon* (lotus root), and *ginnan* (gingko nuts), reflecting the size and vibrancy of the southern California ethnic communities. The *Rafu Shimpo's* recipes were geared to Japanese American kitchens stocked with both Western and Asian supplies and to cooks who wished to broaden their culinary repertoire. In its "Hints for Housewives," women were taught how to prevent mildew in soy sauce containers and how to keep *nori* (dried seaweed) and *senbei* (Japanese crackers) crisp, as well as how to preserve the aroma of coffee or tea and how to determine the safety of eating oysters.[41]

In the early 1940s, the *Rafu Shimpo's* recipe section—by then a regular feature—affirmed nisei women's continuing interest in both Japanese cultural practices and culinary diversity. The array of dishes covered mirrored the various influences and synthesis in the nisei's lives. For instance, a discussion of *tsukemono* (Japanese pickles), without which a "Japanese meal is never complete," might share the page with recipes for cream sponge cake and baked lemon pudding.[42] The nisei were also encouraged to try "'Good neighbor' dishes from south of the border," such as "Enchilada Luncheon Pie" and "Mexican Chicken," although they were so heavily adapted to the mainstream U.S. (and possibly Japanese American) palate that it is questionable whether a Mexican cook would recognize their origin.[43] Reflecting the urban nisei girls' involvement in clubs, the newspaper offered "sure fire" and "can't miss" cookie recipes for "your next club tea"[44] or for the club cookie sales that had become "quite the fad these days."[45]

The preparation and consumption of food became a bonding experience for nisei girls, particularly as part of their club activities, which thrived in West Coast cities like Los Angeles. Together, they experimented with making foods unfamiliar to their parents, like seafoam candy and fudge, and they cemented ties of gender and generation at club teas and "progressive dinners" during which each course would be served at a different club member's home. They often utilized their culinary skills on behalf of their organizations, holding box-lunch socials and cookie sales to raise money for club activities and social service projects.

Food and Gender

Joint activities among nisei girls' and boys' clubs sometimes reinforced traditional gender roles, as young women were usually expected to provide "the eats." When the Blue Triangle girls' club and the UCLA Bruin Club (mostly male at that time) went on a hike on Mount Baldy in 1928, the two clubs promised that "the girls will furnish all the provisions from sandwiches to 'nigiri-meshi' [Japanese rice balls] and the boys will have enough to eat. . . . There will be no danger of starvation."[46] While this arrangement may have been based on the young women's having initiated the hike, it was common for girls to supply the food for such gatherings. When a combined Christian Endeavor group from Union Church drove to Eagle Rock for an outdoor meeting, the girls brought the provisions. With tongue in cheek, a reporter described a sumptuous feast: "The 'light' refreshments which the girls fixed up consisted of ten spring chickens, chipped beef on toast, asparagus with mayonnaise, roasted venison, barbecue, etc. Everybody was so hungry that the food disappeared quickly."[47] Girls' clubs were even sometimes asked to prepare and serve the food for boys' club events, as in the case of the YMCA (Young Men's Christian Association) Hi-Y Club's "Father-Son Banquet." The *Rafu Shimpo* declared, "The success of the party was due to the splendid way in which the Girl Reserves from M.E. and Union Church cooked and served the dinner."[48] Paying fifty cents per plate, the guests consumed "gambelorious quantities of nutritious filaments."[49] Two years later, the girls' clubs proved to be a great help to the Oxy Hi-Y boys in "all their banquets, entertainments, and many other ways." The young men found "that it was hard to do many things without the help of the fairer sex."[50]

The boys' clubs, however, also occasionally reciprocated, treating the girls' organizations to festivities in appreciation of their help. When a *Rafu Shimpo* reporter asked rhetorically, "Did the Girl Reserves and the Hi-Y Boys enjoy the social party that was given by the boys in honor of the Girl Reserves and [their adviser] Mrs. Leech?" the answer was, "Hope to kiss the flea they did!" This social, attended by forty nisei, began "with the game of Domestic Science," and adhering to the prevailing gender conventions, the reporter commented, "It is remarkable how many of the kitchen utensils the boys knew."[51] Still, not surprisingly, a girl proved to have greater culinary familiarity: "Celia had the most names and she received a prize which she shared with a boy." After playing various games, "the merrymakers went to another room, and there partook of heavy refreshments." While this reference indicates that the food was more substantial than punch and cookies, it also suggests the gendering of the food and the association of "heavy refreshments" with males.[52]

Box-lunch socials, popular in the late 1920s, also reveal the nisei clubs' reinforcement of conventional gender roles, as well as their cultural adaptation, and combined opportunities for flirtation and fund-raising. This practice, probably brought to California by white migrants from the Midwest, showcased and commodified young women's domestic skills. Young men purchased both the food and the company of the maker. In 1926, in order to raise money to install showers (for the boys) at the Japanese M.E. Church gym, the Epworth League youth held a box-lunch social. "All girls who plan to attend," the *Rafu Shimpo* reminded, "are earnestly asked to bring box lunches. These will be auctioned, so make something enough for two."[53] The reporter underscored the assumed differences in male and female appetites: "Remember, even if you are a light-eater, boys always have a big appetite."[54] In 1931, the All Around Girl Reserves held a highly successful Valentine box lunch social, raising more than sixty dollars to send delegates to the annual Girl Reserves summer conference. The Valentine social ended with "each boy dancing with the fair maker of his lunch."[55] Such events allowed nisei girls to push the boundaries of coed socializing in the immigrant community, display their culinary ability, and raise funds for group endeavors. In addition to strengthening bonds among their nisei peers, young women used their cooking skills to foster friendly interracial relations.

Not only did they provide many of the "good eats" for Japanese American organizations, these young women sometimes introduced Japanese food to groups outside the community.[56] In the 1930s, for example, when sukiyaki became a trendy dish in Southern California, nisei girls prepared it for their own birthday parties and gatherings and were also called on to cook and serve it for interethnic college organizations and European American society events. In 1931, when a white Girl Reserves group requested "a real Japanese dinner," their nisei Girl Reserve hosts decided to serve sukiyaki, with soup and salad.[57] While the nature of the "salad"—*sunomono* (salad dressed with vinegar) or Waldorf?—remains ambiguous, the inclusion of this wording suggests the influence of Western notions about how meals should be organized and offers a glimpse into the process of cultural coalescence. This occasion also exemplifies how nisei girls served as representatives of the ethnic community, using food as a cultural bridge.

Holiday Foods

From the mid-1920s to World War II, ethnic holiday food was very important to Japanese Americans, urban and rural. As Micaela di Leonardo found in her study of Italian Americans in California, the planning and presentation of festive dishes and other rituals are female responsibilities, part of the women's work of maintaining kinship ties.[58] In chapter 7 of this book, Dawn Mabalon describes how even in the difficult years of the Great Depression, Filipino American women provided an array of delicacies for the birthdays and other celebrations that drew families together. Chinese American women also cooked special holiday foods that signified wishes for health, wealth, and longevity. Issei and nisei women, too, played a crucial role in preparing the symbolic dishes central to the celebration of family, community, and shared ethnicity.

Rice cakes, a central New Year's food, required elaborate, often communal, preparation, which is called *mochi tsuki*. Rose Honda remembered that relatives and friends would gather a few days before New Year's for the festive occasion. Her mother would soak and steam sweet glutinous rice, which would then be dumped into a large concrete mortar. The men would take turns pounding it rhythmically with wooden mallets, two at a time, while the women would wet the *mochi*. When it had reached a smooth consistency, the women would remove the rice and quickly shape the hot, sticky mass into small round rice cakes. Everyone who came to help with the *mochi tsuki* would take some home. After putting part of it aside for their New Year's soup, Rose's family would toast the fresh *mochi* and eat it with soy sauce and sugar or a mixture of *kinako* (toasted soybean flour) and sugar. "It was so good," Rose remembered. "And to this day, I just love it."[59]

New Year's Day—Oshōgatsu—was the major holiday for Japanese Americans, whose ways of celebrating varied somewhat depending on the region of Japan they had come from. For most of them, it was imperative to have a fresh start for the New Year, with a clean house and a bath the previous night. Since supposedly no work should be done on New Year's Day, the women spent hours preparing a variety of symbolic dishes invoking health and good fortune for the year to come. Most Japanese families thus began New Year's Day with *ozōni*, a clear soup in which the rice cakes floated, symbolizing prosperity. When people visited their friends to share good wishes for the new year, they enjoyed the *ogochisō* (feast) prepared by the issei and nisei women of the household, which might include *mame* (sweetened black beans, a homonym for "health"), *kazunoko* (fish roe for fertility), *kinpira* (spicy strips of burdock root), *kamaboko* (steamed fish cakes), *nishime* (a cooked vegetable dish), *makizushi* (rolled sushi), *inarizushi* (rice in fried sweetened tofu pouches), and *yōkan* (a sweet bean confection), accompanied by green tea, and, for the adults, saké (rice wine).[60]

Before World War II, the coverage of ethnic festival food in the newspapers shifted to reflect the changing demographics and the coming of age of the second generation. In the earlier years at holiday time, the *Rafu Shimpo* ran detailed educational articles, sometimes reprinted from the Japanese press, on the proper presentation and symbolic significance of foods like *mochi* (rice cakes) and *mame* (black beans). For example, in 1936, *Rafu* staff writer Mitsuko Yoshii compared New Year celebrations in Japan and the United States, explaining that the Japanese served foods associated with prosperity, longevity, and good health. "American New Year dinners apparently place emphasis on the appearance of the table" and accoutrements such as shining silverware and expensive candlesticks; by contrast, she said that the Japanese had "deep sentimental definitions embedded in the food itself."[61]

As youngsters, the urban second generation enjoyed a mixture of New Year's observances. As Nellie Nimura wrote in 1931 in a New Year's greeting to the editor of the *Rafu Shimpo*, "I'm getting a quite a dose of this Japanese American harmony idea. Danced just about all night of New Year's Eve a la American style and getting up early the same morning to eat historic 'o-zoni' and other antiquated foods."[62] Nimura happily slept through the rest of the day, getting up in time to hear the football game score. Her letter suggests that she lived in her parents' household as a daughter—perhaps a younger daughter—who was not required to do any of the Oshōgatsu (New Year) work. One might even speculate that Nimura's breezy attitude toward holiday harmony may have suffered a serious challenge when her turn came to face the tasks of preparing the *ozōni* and all the "antiquated dishes" she so readily ate.

By the end of the 1930s, the swelling ranks of the nisei had matured and increasing numbers of second-generation women had begun to shoulder the primary responsibilities in their parents' and their own households. As nisei handled more of the food preparation, the newspapers explained not only the significance of the dishes but also the instructions for making them. At this time, recipes for special New Year's dishes appeared seasonally in both the *Kashu Mainichi* and the *Rafu Shimpo*.[63]

By this time, obvious tensions were arising between the time-consuming work of producing Oshōgatsu food and the urban nisei's inclination to celebrate the holiday in more Western fashion. In 1941, a journalist reported,

> With each new year, the traditional Japanese-style New Year's Day with its dishes after dishes of Japanese food becomes more outmoded. The young folks don't see much sense in wasting the precious New Year's Eve hours in working over a hot stove for foods they'd just as soon do without, while the issei parents are beginning to agree with them.[64]

Nevertheless, traditional recipes were reprinted for the benefit of nisei whose parents "feel that New Year's wouldn't be New Year's without kazunoko, omochi and the rest."[65] Of course, many of the second generation did enjoy eating *ozōni, nishime*, sushi, and *yōkan*. But given the amount of work involved in preparing these foods, the desire to please the issei and a sense of filial duty clearly became major factors in nisei women's decisions about how to celebrate the New Year. Japanese American cultural practices, cherished and challenged, then faced severe testing during World War II.

Food after World War II

Japanese American family and community life on the West Coast was shattered by the forced uprooting and incarceration during the war. Both issei and nisei struggled to adjust to the crude communal facilities in desolate regions of the country. Nisei artist Miné Okubo's drawings of the barracks, latrines, and mess halls and her description of the camp food convey the disruption of prewar family routines and diet. Confined in the Topaz camp in Utah, Okubo observed, "Often a meal consisted of rice, bread, and macaroni, or beans, bread, and spaghetti. At one time we were served liver for several weeks, until we went on strike."[66] Increasingly, many people—especially the youth—began to spend mealtimes with their peers rather than family members. As Heidi Kim explains in chapter 6, mess hall dining became a potent and problematic symbol of the fragmentation of the nuclear family in the camps. Although mess hall dining was only part of the wartime hardships faced by Japanese

Americans, it exemplifies their loss of autonomy and the impact of mass exclusion and incarceration on the family structure. After the war, resettlement presented challenges as well.

After the war ended in 1945, Japanese Americans were permitted to return to the West Coast, where they faced lingering racial hostility, residential segregation, and a swelling labor force. Jobs and housing were hard to find, and the issei and nisei scrambled to find wage-paid work. Many men went into gardening, while women entered the garment industry and, if lucky, clerical work. As the *Rafu Shimpo* showed, the focus of the early postwar years was survival, during which time growing numbers of the second generation—whose median age was seventeen at the outset of war—began to marry and form families.

Postwar nisei households reflected the sexual division of labor that prevailed in mainstream society and the immigrant community. Whether as daughters or wives, Japanese American women were responsible for the bulk of domestic work. One of their key responsibilities was food preparation. In January 1946, soon after the *Rafu Shimpo* resumed publication, a woman reader suggested including a "cooking recipe column," saying, "I know lot of nisei girls will be looking forward to something like that." Mirroring prewar gastronomical preferences, she added, "Try and add variety by printing Chinese, American, and Japanese recipes, whenever possible."[67] Perhaps at her prompting, for about a year the *Rafu* ran a weekly "Today's Recipe" column, starting on February 5 with directions for the Chinese dish "Celery Chow Yuk," followed on February 9 by simple recipes for a Japanese shrimp concoction and "Nasu no Goma-Shoyu," a minimalist eggplant dish. All the featured dishes were Chinese or Japanese. The short lists of ingredient (two pounds of eggplant were the only ingredient in the "Nasu no Goma-Shoyu" recipe) may reflect the fledgling skills of novice cooks as well as postwar budgets and the need to economize. Although by 1947 recipes no longer appeared in the *Rafu*, notices of cooking classes did.

Community cooking classes similarly reflected Japanese American tastes and economic pressure. In July 1947, Mrs. Matsuo, a "well-known dietician," began teaching classes at the International Institute in East Los Angeles for young adults and teenagers interested in Italian, American, and Japanese cuisine.[68] Mindful of budgetary concerns and growing families, she demonstrated "new culinary methods of preparing one pound of meat to serve six or eight persons."[69] The American Red Cross (ARC) also offered cooking classes to issei and nisei, with an emphasis on thrift, assuring prospective students, "Careful selections and good cooking can help you win a bout with continued

269

high food prices."[70] Notably, the ARC gently challenged gender divisions in the kitchen by issuing an invitation to "brides, husbands, and experienced home-makers" to attend the classes.[71]

As Japanese American families returned and communities took root, girls' club activities resurged in Southern California by the late 1940s. The Atom-ettes, who began as a group of sixth graders attending the West Los Angeles United Methodist Church, are an example. As for the prewar nisei girls' clubs, service was an important component of the Atomettes' activities, and they had great impact on church traditions after the war. Rose Honda, one of their two advisers, explained:

> They were the ones who started the bazaar. They called it May Bazaar, and . . . they went out to the strawberry fields, and picked the strawberries, and made strawberry jam, and sold it. They were the ones who started the Easter break-fast. . . . They did all the cooking, and they must have served 50 or 75, or more people—seven girls.[72]

As did the nisei girls' clubs before the war, the Atomettes used culinary skills to raise morale and strengthen community ties.

Conclusion

From the 1920s to the 1950s, second-generation girls and women nourished their communities, preparing the food for a wide variety of private and public events ranging from club socials and church fund-raisers to weddings. They maintained Japanese cultural practices through cooking staples like rice and special symbolic holiday dishes. At the same time, they introduced other cui-sines into the ethnic community, adjusting the flavors to suit Japanese Ameri-can tastes. The girls' club offerings, the food sections of the ethnic press, and family recipes like those of Natsuye Fujimoto reveal the eclectic influences and delight in experimentation that have expanded Japanese American foodways. Through their multifaceted culinary work, nisei women affirmed ties of ethnic culture and community, claimed modern femininity and Americanness, and demonstrated creativity in cultural adaptation.

Notes

1. Natsuye (Gwen) Fujimoto, "Recipes (Japanese)," Hirasaki National Research Center, Japanese American National Museum (JANM). Many thanks to Jane Nakasako and the other JANM staff and docents who assisted with this research.
2. By foodways, I mean the ideas and practices associated with food.

3. Eiichiro Azuma, *Between Two Empires: Race, History, and Transnationalism in Japanese America* (New York: Oxford University Press, 2005), 23–31.

4. Fujimoto's father's restaurants—the Park Restaurant and the New Star Restaurant—in Los Angeles served items like hamburgers and turkey sandwiches.

5. Azuma, *Between Two Empires*.

6. Ibid., 138.

7. David K. Yoo, *Growing Up Nisei: Race, Generation, and Culture among Japanese Americans of California, 1924–49* (Urbana: University of Illinois Press, 2000), 32.

8. The *Rafu Shimpo* holiday issue for December 22, 1939, 16, estimated that there were nearly six hundred nisei clubs in Southern California; in the December 23, 1940 holiday issue, 16, Sadae Nomura refers to "400 active nisei organizations." Four hundred appears to be a reasonable estimate.

9. Susan Kalčik, "Ethnic Foodways in America: Symbol and the Performance of Identity," in *Ethnic and Regional Foodways in the United States: The Performance of Group Identity*, ed. Linda Keller Brown and Kay Mussell (Knoxville: University of Tennessee Press, 1984), 44. Kalčik points out, "We are now not so much concerned with defining ethnicity as a category whose characteristics and traits we want to list but as a social process in which the relationship of individuals and groups and the communication of identity are significant" (44).

10. Vicki L. Ruiz, *From Out of the Shadows: Mexican Women in Twentieth-Century America* (New York: Oxford University Press, 1998), xvi.

11. Donna R. Gabaccia, *We Are What We Eat: Ethnic Food and the Making of Americans* (Cambridge, MA: Harvard University Press, 1998), 229.

12. *Rafu Shimpo*, October 11, 1936.

13. Mary Nishi Ishizuka, interview by Valerie J. Matsumoto, August 4, 2009.

14. Rose Honda, interview by Valerie J. Matsumoto, July 30, 2009.

15. *Rafu Shimpo*, March 28, 1927.

16. *Rafu Shimpo*, March 7, 1927.

17. *Rafu Shimpo*, October 15, 1928.

18. *Rafu Shimpo*, February 28, 1927.

19. *Rafu Shimpo*, March 7, 1927. This pronouncement may have come from the reporter rather than the Midori kai.

20. *Rafu Shimpo*, October 18, 1926.

21. See Kimi Kanazawa, "The Nisei Come of Age," *Kashu Mainichi*, May 24, 1936.

22. *Rafu Shimpo*, July 25, 1927.

23. *Rafu Shimpo*, October 15, 1928.

24. *Rafu Shimpo*, October 11, 1936.

25. *Rafu Shimpo*, January 7, 1940.

26. See Jade Snow Wong, *Fifth Chinese Daughter* (1945; repr., Seattle: University of Washington Press, 1989), 57–59.

27. Ibid.

28. Harvey Levenstein, *Paradox of Plenty: A Social History of Eating in Modern America*, rev. ed. (Berkeley: University of California Press, 2003), 24–39.

29. Ibid., 37.

30. *Rafu Shimpo*, October 11, 1936.

31. Ibid.

32. Ibid.
33. Jennifer 8. Lee, *The Fortune Cookie Chronicles: Adventures in the World of Chinese Food* (New York: Twelve, 2008), 56–65.
34. Katsumi (Hirooka) Kunitsugu, interview, *REgenerations Oral History Project: Rebuilding Japanese American Families, Communities, and Civil rights in the Resettlement Era* (Los Angeles: Japanese American National Museum, in collaboration with Chicago Japanese American Historical Society, Japanese American Historical Society of San Diego, and Japanese American Resource Center/Museum, 2000), 262.
35. *Rafu Shimpo*, October 11, 1936.
36. Ibid.
37. Ibid.
38. Fumiko Fukuyama Ide, interview by Valerie J. Matsumoto, March 27, 2001.
39. *Kashu Mainichi*, November 26, 1933.
40. *Kashu Mainichi*, March 25, 1938; April 4–5, 13–14, 25, 1938; May 7, 12, 1938. The recipe for potato salad was printed by request.
41. Ibid.
42. *Rafu Shimpo*, February 4, 1940.
43. *Rafu Shimpo*, January 4, 1942, 10. The defining ingredient in both recipes appears to have been one tablespoon of chili powder.
44. *Rafu Shimpo*, March 3, 1940. I beg to differ with the food editor regarding the "sure fire" nature of the brown sugar cookies.
45. *Rafu Shimpo*, December 7, 1941.
46. *Rafu Shimpo*, January 1, 1928. The Bruin Club was responsible for planning half the program.
47. *Rafu Shimpo*, July 25, 1926.
48. Ibid.
49. Ibid.
50. *Rafu Shimpo*, March 12, 1928. The Oxy Hi-Y boys reciprocated with a leap-year dinner in honor of the S.O.F. and All Around Girl Reserves.
51. *Rafu Shimpo*, June 20, 1926.
52. *Rafu Shimpo*, June 20, 1926. The boys appear to have varied cooking skills:
    The sandwiches, which were made by Danar Abe and his gang, must have been good because it went around three or four times. If the sandwiches were good, the Hungarian Goulashes [sic] which was made by the honorable secretary of the Hi Y Club was even better. . . . At the end of the social, the secretary was mobbed by the girls who wanted the recipe.
53. "Box-Lunch social at M.E. Church by Epworth Youths," *Rafu Shimpo*, November 29, 1926.
54. Ibid.
55. "Financial Success Marks All Around Lunch Social," *Rafu Shimpo*, February 23, 1931. By this time, dancing had become a feature of the nisei box-lunch social, expanding the opportunity for male-female socializing and flirtation. For more examples of box-lunch socials held by girls' clubs, see "Two Events on Program of Emba Girl Reserves," *Rafu Shimpo*, May 25, 1931; "Sea Breeze Plan Idea for Emba's Box Lunch Social," *Rafu Shimpo*, June 8, 1931; and "Cherry Blossom Club Plan Benefit Box Lunch Social," *Rafu Shimpo*, November 15, 1931.

56. Jade Snow Wong recounts how she cooked Chinese food for her friends at Mills College in *Fifth Chinese Daughter*, 155–61.

57. *Rafu Shimpo*, December 6, 1931. See also *Rafu Shimpo*, April 22, 1937, for a nisei club sukiyaki party.

58. Micaela di Leonardo, *The Varieties of Ethnic Experience: Kinship, Class, and Gender among California Italian-Americans* (Ithaca, NY: Cornell University Press, 1984), 215.

59. Honda, interview.

60. For a description of an urban family's mixture of Japanese and U.S. New Year's customs in Seattle, see Monica Sone, *Nisei Daughter* (Seattle: University of Washington Press, 1953), 80–86.

61. *Rafu Shimpo*, holiday issue, December 24, 1936, 9.

62. *Rafu Shimpo*, January 5, 1931. Nimura's brief letters appeared for a while as a regular feature entitled "With Apologies to Will Rogers." It seems that she was a local nisei living in Boyle Heights in east Los Angeles.

63. The New Year's recipes were credited to Dr. P. M. Suski (i.e., Suzuki), an influential issei leader and the father of Louise Suski, the first nisei editor of the *Rafu Shimpo*'s English-language section. He also wrote a book to help the nisei learn the Japanese language.

64. *Rafu Shimpo*, December 28, 1941.

65. Ibid.

66. Miné Okubo, *Citizen 13660* (1946; repr., Seattle: University of Washington Press, 1983), 143.

67. *Rafu Shimpo*, January 31, 1946, 1. Her letter to the editor was signed "Miss T. K."

68. "Cooking lessons," *Rafu Shimpo*, July 25, 1947, 1; "Cooking class," *Rafu Shimpo*, October 18, 1947, 1. Mrs. Matsuo also offered a class on making varieties of chop suey; see *Rafu Shimpo*, September 6, 1947.

69. "Cooking class," *Rafu Shimpo*, October 18, 1947, 1.

70. "Reports Cooking Classes by ARC," *Rafu Shimpo*, September 20, 1947, 1. Unfortunately there were no follow-up reports of who signed up for the classes.

71. "Reports Cooking Classes by ARC," *Rafu Shimpo*, September 26, 1947, 1.

72. Rose Honda, *REgenerations Oral History Project*, 80. Mary Ishizuka was the other Atomettes' adviser.

14

Giving Credit Where It Is Due

Asian American Farmers and Retailers as Food System Pioneers

NINA F. ICHIKAWA

A tour through any supermarket yields rich anthropological information: who lives nearby, what they like to eat, how they clean their bathtubs. Much has changed in American supermarkets since 1965, when the Hart-Cellar Act lifted harsh regulations on Asian immigration. Most have added an "Asian" or "Oriental" section, with products like sesame oil and soy sauce for shoppers who wish to begin experimenting "outside their lane" (literally). But what about the neighboring aisles? How have Asian American farmers and retailers transformed so-called American food, as well as our understanding of it? Beyond supermarkets are Asian restaurants identifiable with virtually every region that are now ubiquitous in any American mall or downtown area. But again, how have Asian American food pioneers influenced what is served at *non*-Asian restaurants? For answers, we must dig below the place of consumption and look at the role of Asian Americans at other points in the food system.[1]

This chapter is a broad overview of the ways in which Asian American contributions to agriculture and food retail have altered the trajectory of American food. It examines how Asian Americans stimulated market innovation and increased the availability of fresh fruits and vegetables. While Asian immigrants to the United States and their descendants have participated in the entire range of American economic activity, their consistent participation in these earlier stages of the food system is notable and deserves a closer look as we write the ever evolving story of American food culture.

The term "food system" is commonly defined as the entirety of steps required to feed a population, including farming and livestock husbandry, harvesting, processing, packaging, transporting, marketing, consuming, and disposing.[2] What Marion Nestle calls the "vast 'food-and-fiber' system" is estimated to generate a trillion dollars or more in sales every year in the United States and employs about 17 percent of the country's labor force.[3] Many agricultural economists and environmentalists favor the beginning-to-end perspective of food system analysis, which seeks to reintegrate elements of food production into the understanding and, ultimately, the price of a table-ready home or restaurant meal.[4]

Taking into account the entire food system enables the recognition of negative externalities, such as the cost of pesticides or water pollution, as well as the effects of government intervention and changes in the labor market. On the West Coast, where Asian immigration has historically concentrated, Asian American contributions to all aspects of this food system were pivotal. For example, before their incarceration during World War II, Japanese Americans in California not only dominated the strawberry industry but also had a significant stake in the production of lettuce, tomatoes, celery, spinach, peas, onions, garlic, and snap beans. In other words, they grew or sold many of the "mainstream" crops sold to the "mainstream" market. These Japanese Americans cleared land, enriched soil, and did backbreaking work alongside Sikhs, Punjabis, Filipinos, Koreans, Chinese, Chicanos, and European Americans. Production was so high that after Executive Order 9066 was issued, authorizing the removal of Japanese Americans, local media and the U.S. Department of Agriculture (USDA) officials fretted whether the wartime food supply could survive the sudden absence of Japanese American farmers.[5] To prepare for the economic fallout from this disturbance, the government conducted a detailed survey and appraisal of Japanese American–owned properties and farms.[6]

Asian Americans were pioneering farmers, literally building soil that to this day forms the fertile foundation of farms that still exist. California's agricultural industry is now the most profitable in the country, with $43.5 billion in revenue in 2011.[7] Nearly half of all fruits, nuts, and vegetables grown in the United States are produced in California. During the twentieth century, Americans slowly increased their consumption of fresh fruits and vegetables, and while Asian Americans sought to capitalize on this by investing in farming and food retail at rates disproportionate to their numbers, they also drove the change.[8] But the Asian American contribution was not limited to the fields; the birth of "California cuisine" is another example of how Asian American farmers and retailers transformed America's food system.

California Cuisine—Who Built it?

Alice Waters came of age during the postwar explosion of mass-manufactured foods that Harvey Levenstein, author of *Paradox of Plenty: A Social History of Eating in Modern America*, calls the "Golden Age of Food Processing."[9] Brand names were replacing family recipes, and despite consumers' excitement over the mass availability of cheap processed foods, for Waters and her middle-class white contemporaries, something was amiss.[10] The food they had grown up with felt denatured, anonymous, and remote. Improved logistics chains favored efficiency over locality, and grower-packer-shipper operations were becoming larger and more powerful. Because *terroir* did not have a cultural value, the identity of individual farmers and the distinctive story of their unique growing practices, water, and seeds were becoming irrelevant and unimportant to the everyday consumer.

During a study abroad trip, Waters fell in love with the aesthetic pleasures of French cuisine. Back home, as she made plans to open a restaurant, she and her team began considering how to recreate the French food culture, notably its freshness, seasonality, and tangible relationship between producers and consumers. While East Coast high-end restaurants continued to shape themselves in the European mold, Waters wanted to know what a *California* apple really tasted like and how to best serve it to her customers. She wanted to highlight local ingredients.

This proved difficult. The food available from wholesale suppliers at the time was increasingly frozen, processed, or simply old after being shipped across logistics lines that were evolving into the world's most advanced food delivery system. Neighborhood food specialty shops were giving way to larger and larger supermarkets. The subsequent concentration of power in the American food industry among fewer and fewer large manufacturers and retailers meant less variety and fewer options for customers and shorter profit margins for farmers.[11]

Waters found a solution to her problem in Asian American farms, fishmongers, and retailers, who maintained the "Old World" emphasis on freshness and flavor over shelf life and convenience. "The Chinese markets were crowded and chaotic, but they had chickens that tasted like chicken," notes biographer Thomas McNamee, author of *Alice Waters and Chez Panisse: The Romantic, Impractical, Often Eccentric, Ultimately Brilliant Making of a Food Revolution*, referring to either the San Francisco or the Oakland Chinatown.[12] Waters learned to navigate Chinese American markets from the Chinese food maven Cecilia Chiang, herself a renowned chef and restaurateur. The first meal at Chez Panisse, the restaurant founded by Waters in 1971, featured duck from San Francisco's Chinatown and fruits and vegetables likely sourced from a Japanese American produce market in Berkeley called U-Save. "When it's seasonal, it's cheaper. When it's seasonal, it's the best," says Bill Fujimoto, a local produce buyer and an early sourcer for Chez Panisse.

Figure 14.1. Nectarines at Kozuki Farms, Parlier, California, 2011. Photograph by the author.

Asian American Markets: Linking Farmer, Eater, and Restaurateur

When ingredients are king, a buyer with good contacts is a kingmaker. Waters knew she needed a more reliable way of getting raw ingredients beyond trips to Chinatown, so she solicited Fujimoto, a third-generation Japanese American. His family store was less than a mile from Chez Panisse, in an area that came to be called the "Gourmet Ghetto" for its concentration of innovative food shops and restaurants. Fujimoto and his staff played a pivotal role in shaping the culinary future of the fledgling restaurant. As Waters recalls,

> All during the first years of Chez Panisse, [Fujimoto] was like the Shell Answer Man: "Where can I get the best oranges?" "Oh, well I think I can get them up at this farm, I'll get you a box and you see what you think." . . . Many of the people we buy from now are people we were introduced to by Bill, many, many years ago. We fell in love with what he was selling, and then we just followed that through and ended up getting connected with this beautiful group of local organic farmers.[13]

Many of Fujimoto's picks enjoyed star treatment on the plates of Chez Panisse when the restaurant menu began identifying the source of the ingredients. Although now common practice in gastronomically ambitious American restaurants, the practice of crediting farms by name on the menu was considered an oddity at the time. Among the first farms to gain prominence in this manner was the Japanese American Chino Farms, near San Diego, which, according to McNamee, produced "some of the most delicious fruits and vegetables Alice had ever tasted, in stupendous variety."[14] In a rare departure from Waters's local-only rule, products from Chino Farms were flown directly from the field to the restaurant. A new job title was born at Chez Panisse: "professional forager." For many of these modern-day foragers, entering an Asian American market in California—be it Chinese, Japanese, or Southeast Asian—was to be awed. It also was a learning experience, which gave rise to more expansive and inventive menus for the restaurant.

Fujimoto approached his role as a purveyor of produce with equal parts of salesmanship and mentorship. He nurtured farmers with an eye to their shared success, taking risks that others would not and beseeching restaurateurs like Waters to join the risk taking. The idiosyncrasies of second-generation Chicano farmworkers and now farm owners, of Japanese Americans resurrecting prewar orchards, and of idealistic white hippies and back-to-the-landers Fujimoto treated as assets and gave them an open door when large chain grocery stores would not. He, Waters, and the sourcers who later worked for the restaurant agreed on what is now considered essential to this new California cuisine: the interdependence of flavor, freshness, and source verification. In other words, they were unified in the fundamental belief that integrity in growing practices leads directly to higher-quality products that would ultimately be discerned by the patrons of Chez Panisse.

Meanwhile, Asian American retailers on the East Coast were also beginning to take advantage of new ingredients, sourcing, and techniques. As Pyong Gap Min, author of *Ethnic Solidarity for Economic Survival: Korean Greengrocers in New York City*, explains, the Korean corner grocery stores that have proliferated in New York City since the 1980s played a significant role in providing fresh, visually pleasing produce to urban centers.[15] Because they were often excluded from the tight-knit Italian and Jewish wholesale markets, Korean grocers were forced to source independently. This meant forging relationships with farms that were not only smaller but also closer. The Korean grocers paid close attention to the detailed trimming, packaging, and presentation of fruits and vegetables, which led to a greater demand for them. Innovations like the addition of salad bars to neighborhood delis, the introduction of Asian fruits

Figure 14.2. Golden Bowl Supermarket, Fresno, California, 2012.
Photograph by the author.

and vegetables, and greater attention to the appearance of produce helped
solidify New York City's transition from Italian and Jewish greengroceries to
those operated by Korean Americans.[16] Directly benefiting from this rise of
New York City's Korean-run greengrocers were the East Coast Asian American farmers and retailers, who previously had had a much smaller customer
base of multiethnic immigrant consumers. Moreover, their proximity to New
York City and emerging relationship with Korean greengrocers meant that
they now had access to a more affluent consumer base in a concentrated media
market.[17]

Another East Coast city that directly benefited from Asian American farmers
and sourcers was Boston, where two immigrants from Japan, Michio and Aveline
Kushi, founded the pioneering natural foods distributor Erewhon in 1966.[18] Just
a little more than two decades earlier, "Japs Not Welcome" signs were ubiquitous
on the West Coast, where Japanese Americans struggled with the fallout of World

War II. Here, on the other side of the country, thanks to the Kushis, northeasterners were having their first tentative tastes of brown rice, seaweed, and soy sauce. The Kushis were instrumental in training a generation of natural foods distributors. Eventually, many of those they trained began to sell their own house brands by replicating the Kushis' model of contracting directly with organic producers. One of these emulators was Paul Hawken, a "green business" guru and the cofounder of the garden supply chain Smith & Hawken. Hawken cut his teeth in the business working as the second manager of the Kushis' store.

From the Kushis and the genre of store they spawned, Americans learned about fermented soybean paste and the ancient curdled soybean squares invented by the Chinese.[19] These newly available health food stores—often located in college towns like Boulder and Ann Arbor—supplemented stores found in traditional Asian American ethnic enclaves. Together, they brought a wider variety and greater understanding of Asian foods to the general American public. They also helped validate traditional Asian health principles with regard to food, by translating and making them more accessible to English-speaking audiences. Companies like Eden Foods and Hain Celestial are direct beneficiaries of this legacy. Today, the natural food industry is a multibillion-dollar business, with many of the smaller companies started by Erewhon affiliates being bought out by multinational food companies like General Mills and Kraft Foods.[20]

Asian American Farmers: Fruit and Vegetable Innovators

Fred Lee is a third-generation Chinese American vegetable grower. His family farm, Sang Lee Farms in Long Island, New York, began by selling exclusively Chinese vegetables to the wholesale Chinese restaurant market.[21] Eyeing market consolidation and other factors driving down the prices of wholesale sales, Sang Lee Farms successfully morphed into an all-retail business selling both American and Chinese vegetables to a mixed clientele. Fred and his wife, Karen, invented various techniques to bring their products to a changing market, including "stir-fry packs," premixed bags of Asian vegetables packaged with appropriate sauces. The Lees' efforts demystified Cantonese mainstays like *gai lan* and *bok choy* for the mostly non-Chinese clientele that came to their farm stand and farmers' markets. Later, through partnerships with inner-city community groups, they taught the art of stir-fry to food stamp recipients in New York City.[22]

At one time, Fred Lee's father maintained a second farm in southern Florida to serve the northeast winter market. He belongs to a long tradition of Chinese

American growers and retailers in Florida. Lue Gim Gong, the "Citrus Wizard of Florida," pioneered the hybridization of frost-resistant oranges in 1911 and was later recognized for his successful—and profitable—hybridizations of citrus, apples, tomatoes, and peaches. Today, Florida has the third-largest number of Asian American–owned farms. Numbering more than six hundred, Florida trails only California and Hawai'i.[23]

Although Sang Lee Farms is relatively well known, it is just one of the thousands of Chinese American food businesses whose culinary and agricultural roots can be traced to southern China. Known as the "vegetable basket" of China, with its abundant seafood and temperate weather, this area has been instrumental to the diversification of U.S. farming, by sending migrants like Fred Lee's grandparents, and through its food traditions. Southern China has contributed to the food diversity of the United States by helping increase not only the amount but also the types of vegetables consumed by the general population. According to wok expert and Chinese cooking teacher Grace Young, before the spread of stir-fry cooking in the United States, "Most Americans were not accustomed to eating such minimally cooked vegetables. Especially vegetables tasting like vegetables.[24] Through farming and marketing innovations, this hallmark of Cantonese cooking is now commonplace in the American diet.

A wide swath of the American population has struggled over the years to adhere to the government's recommendation to eat more plant products. Asian Americans have consistently consumed a comparatively higher proportion of fruits and vegetables, and they have also helped provide them to the general public. Before his death in 1926, Japanese American George Shima (born Kinji Ushijima) built a multimillion-dollar fortune in potato farming and distribution. Although he pleaded with California Governor Hiram Johnson to reject the anti-Asian hysteria of the time, his entreaties were ignored. The 1913 Alien Land Law sought to derail farmers, like Shima, who had bought and reclaimed inexpensive marsh, swamp, and other low-quality fields and turned them into highly profitable farmland.[25] It is these Asian American farmers who literally prepared the ground for later migrants, where the story usually begins. For example, according to Mark Bittman, the author of *Food Matters: A Guide to Conscious Eating*, "The [Central] valley became widely known in the 1920s and 1930s, when farmers arrived from Virginia or Armenia or Italy or (like Tom Joad) Oklahoma and wrote home about the clean air, plentiful water and cheap land."[26] Yet the first Japanese farmworkers arrived to the valley in the 1890s, and according to *California Japantowns*, "By 1910, the Japanese population in Fresno County was 2,233, with 122 businesses and 9 organizations; and doubled in size by 1920 to 5,732 residents with 187 businesses."[27] There was significant Asian American farming presence in the valley before and through the period Bittman describes. Harvey Levenstein calls the internment of Japanese Americans a major blow to the availability of fresh vegetables in wartime, a period during which fresh vegetables were not rationed but sugar, meat, butter, and canned foods were. He credits the revival of the Victory Gardens program as filling in the gaps.[28] Today, 63 percent of all farms operated by Asian Americans produce "specialty crops"—a category that includes fruits, nuts, vegetables, nursery, and greenhouse operations—compared with 9 percent of non–Asian American farms.[29]

The Census of Agriculture, a data-gathering device for farming administered by the federal government, first began to record national numbers for Asian Americans in 2002, without disaggregating by ethnic group or country of origin.[30] A separate framework counts, calculates, explains, and supports "alternative farming," an umbrella term that includes organic, biodiverse, agro-ecological, and other agricultural techniques in the ideological minority of American farming. Despite their long experience in many different types of farming in both Asia and the Americas, Asian American farmers rarely appear in either framework. Just one Asian American farmer was profiled in a USDA national roundup of organic farmers, and few Asian Americans are leaders of influential groups like the National Organic Standards Board or the National Sustainable Agriculture Coalition.[31]

Many of the early generations of Asian American farmers have either moved out of agriculture or expanded their operations into larger, more profitable, and more established businesses. Success stories include Tanimura & Antle, a network of fresh vegetable farms in California and Arizona, which was formed by a partnership between a Japanese American family farm and a packing company owned by Dust Bowl émigrés. It is now one of the largest lettuce companies in the United States, selling internationally about half a billion dollars a year in romaine, iceberg, and specialty lettuces. In 2003, former California Governor Arnold Schwarzenegger named A. G. Kawamura, a third-generation Japanese American fruit and vegetable grower, as California's secretary of agriculture. Kawamura's family's trajectory is similar to the Tanimuras': Once sharecroppers, they moved into fertilizer sales, then a growing and shipping company, then their current company, Orange County Produce. His family was one of the lucky ones, able to hold on to land and property through incarceration, and prosper as California's property values skyrocketed. Histories of early Asian American farming are full of families that were not as lucky, however. One farmer named Katsuko Hirata despaired at her double challenge of wringing life from the land and respect from her neighbors:

Figure 14.3. Boxes and storage shed at Kozuki Farms, Parlier,
California, 2011. Photograph by the author.

A wasted grassland
Turned to fertile fields by sweat
Of cultivation:
But I, made dry and fallow by
tolerating insults[32]

Asian American farmworkers today are more likely to be Hmong, Mien,
Lao, Chinese, Filipino, or Vietnamese, and live in the Upper Midwest,
Deep South, or anywhere along the rich growing area of the West Coast.
Between 2002 and 2007, Minnesota saw a fourfold increase in Asian American farmers, and their products now dominate at many farmers' markets
in Minnesota and Wisconsin.[33] While some have received aid from the U.S.
government for their role in the Vietnam War, their continuing struggles
echo earlier generations of Asian American farmers, prompting the USDA

in 2012 to fund outreach and training programs to Asian American and Pacific Islander farmers in Arkansas, Ohio, California, and Hawai'i.[34] But these new Asian American farmers lack access to land and capital and are often excluded from profitable marketing channels. They are sometimes stymied by American business practices and are the most vulnerable to wild price fluctuations due to industry consolidation and market speculation. Whether or not they will choose to remain in farming is an open question.

Conclusion

The story of American food is one of macrotrends like economics, trade flows, and women entering the workforce and deciding they liked it. Farmers already are planning for the large-scale environmental impacts of climate change and water scarcity. But our ways of eating also are affected by the mundane details of everyday life: where we live, whom we talk to, what we learn in school. At key points in the development of our collective concept of "American food," a process still deeply in flux, Asian Americans have made significant contributions that have altered both our eating habits and the common story of that eating.

Why, then, are significant landmarks like California cuisine, Florida citrus, or the common green bean *not* seen as Asian American milestones? It may be due to accidental oversight, intentional exclusion, or self-exemption. Even after decades in business and a devoted consumer base, the tendency toward modesty does not escape many Asian American food entrepreneurs. When contacted by the *New York Times* in 2005 for an article on the store he built and championed, Glenn Yasuda, cofounder of the Berkeley Bowl Market and another partner in the California cuisine movement, could barely muster words for the reporter. "All the markets are pretty good. We do the same thing," he said before insisting that he had work to attend to and abruptly ending the interview.[35]

This modesty may also pertain to a universal challenge of telling the history of food: history's farmers, grocers, butchers, and waiters were often poor and lacked the political power to tell the story of their contributions. Many moved out of food work entirely as soon as their children gained citizenship and access to American education and the white-collar economy. But a new generation of immigrants and their children still use food production as survival: The latest Census of Agriculture counted 20,417 Asian American farm operators, with Asian Americans entering the profession at higher rates than any

Figure 14.4. California Department of Labor safety poster written in Hmong. Fresno, California, 2012. Photograph by the author.

other racial group besides Native Americans.[36] As in the past, Asian American farmers continue to focus on diversified fruit and vegetable cultivation, the higher-margin "specialty crops" that allow their farms to be smaller and more labor intensive, yet reap higher profits.[37] Asian American retailers continue to source unique products and devise creative ways of selling them, influencing both the production stream before them and the tastes of consumers. They are writing the American food story of the future and probably will not ask for credit. But they deserve it. Thanks to them, American food and farming is stronger, healthier, and better able to provide something of enduring value to the American diet.

Notes

1. Mitchell Davis, "Eating Out, Eating American: New York Restaurant Dining and Identity," in *Gastropolis: Food & New York City,* ed. Annie Hauck-Lawson and Jonathan Deutsch (New York: Columbia University Press, 2009), 304.

2. One version is Cornell University's "Discovering the Food System Glossary," available at http://www.discoverfoodsys.cornell.edu/glossary.html.

3. Marion Nestle, *Food Politics: How the Food Industry Influences Nutrition and Health* (Berkeley: University of California Press, 2002), 11.

4. This includes, among others, the Prince of Wales, who began the Accounting for Sustainability Project and lectures on the role of proper pricing of agricultural and other goods to reflect environmental and other externalities.

5. Editorial, "Jap Eviction Brings Threat of Crop Losses," *San Francisco News,* March 28, 1942.

6. "List of Evacuee-Owned Properties, March 12, 1943." National Archives and Records Administration, Western Region.

7. California Department of Food and Agriculture statistic.

8. From 1987 to 1997, there was a per-capita increase of consumption of fresh fruits (10 percent) and vegetables (14 percent); this, however, is under government recommended levels. See Phil R. Kaufman et al., "Understanding the Dynamics of Produce Markets: Consumption and Consolidation Grow," U.S. Department of Agriculture, Economic Research Service, Information Bulletin no. 758, August 2000.

9. Harvey Levenstein, *Paradox of Plenty: A Social History of Eating in Modern America* (Berkeley: University of California Press, 2003).

10. See Sallie Tisdale, *Best Thing I Ever Tasted: The Secret of Food* (New York: Riverhead Books, 2001).

11. Raj Patel, *Stuffed & Starved: From Farm to Fork, the Hidden Battle for the World Food System* (London: Portobello Books, 2007), 13. The hourglass diagrams illustrate the pinching of food distribution systems caused by retail and manufacturing consolidation.

12. Thomas McNamee, *Alice Waters and Chez Panisse: The Romantic, Impractical, Often Eccentric, Ultimately Brilliant Making of a Food Revolution* (New York: Penguin, 2007), 32.

13. "Eat at Bill's: Life in the Monterey Market," DVD recording, Churchill Orchard / Tangerine Man Films, 2008.

14. McNamee, *Alice Waters,* 192.

15. Pyong Gap Min, *Ethnic Solidarity for Economic Survival: Korean Greengrocers in New York City* (New York: Russell Sage, 2008), 54–55.

16. Sam Dolnick, "A New York Staple, Korean Grocers Are Dwindling," *New York Times,* June 1, 2011.

17. Davis, "Eating Out, Eating American," 302. Davis, vice president of the James Beard Foundation, compares New York with "Paris vis-à-vis France before anything that could be called French cuisine had coalesced," for its power in defining the national taste.

18. William Shurtleff and Akiko Aoyagi, *History of Erewhon-Natural Foods Pioneer in the United States, 1966-2011* (Lafayette, CA: Soyinfo Center: 2011), 12.

19. I believe that it was because of the Kushis that the Japanese term was adopted in the United States for many items that also have Chinese and Korean provenance, such as miso, tofu, and nori. That said, Pancho Villa Taqueria in San Francisco's Mission District aims for neutrality with a menu reference to its Soy Bean Cake Burrito.

20. See Samuel Fromartz, *Organic, Inc.: Natural Foods and How They Grew* (Boston: Houghton Mifflin Harcourt, 2006).

21. Nanette Maxim, "Grown in the USA," *Gourmet,* September 2000.

22. Fred and Karen Lee, interview with Nina F. Ichikawa, October 10, 2010.

23. 2007 Census of Agriculture—State Data. U.S. Department of Agriculture, National Agricultural Statistics Service.

24. Grace Young, interview with Nina F. Ichikawa, December 21, 2011.

25. Don and Nadine Hata, "George Shima: The Potato King of California," *Journal of the West* 25, no. 1 (1986): 55–63.

26. Mark Bittman, "Everyone Eats There: California's Central Valley Is Our Greatest Food Resource. So Why Are We Treating It So Badly?" *New York Times Magazine,* October 14, 2012.

27. From *California Japantowns,* an online history project of the California Japanese American Community Leadership Council, available at http://www.californiajapantowns.org/fresno.html.

28. Levenstein, *Paradox of Plenty*, 85.

29. 2007 Census of Agriculture—Asian Farmers Factsheet, Washington, DC: U.S. Department of Agriculture, 3.

30. The Census of Agriculture has come under repeated scrutiny by farming equity groups for its failure to accurately count farmers of color. See Rural Coalition/Coalicion Rural and Federation of Southern Cooperatives Land Assistance Fund, "A Time to Change: A Report by the Assessment Conversations Team," ACT Report (Washington, DC: Rural Coalition and the Federation of Southern Cooperatives, 2010), 14.

31. Deborah Wechsler, "Lon Inaba and Family, Inaba Produce Farms," in *The New American Farmer: Profiles of Agricultural Innovation*, ed. Valerie Berton, 2nd ed. (Beltsville, MD: Sustainable Agriculture Network, 2005), 175. The Inaba family profiled in this government-funded publication chose to emphasize to the interviewer that owing to the history of discrimination their family faced as former farmworkers, they placed a priority on fair wages and decent housing for their mostly Latino workforce.

32. From the Japanese American National Museum's permanent exhibit. Other first-person examples are *The Issei of the Salinas Valley: Japanese Pioneer Families*, published in 2010 by the Salinas Valley Japanese American Citizens League and available from the National Steinbeck Center, Salinas, CA.

33. Mark Steil, "Ag Census Shows Number of Minnesota Farms Holds Stable," *Minnesota Public Radio*, February 4, 2009.

34. "USDA Announces Assistance for Socially Disadvantaged Farmers and Ranchers," New Release no. 0266.12, August 8, 2012.

35. Sharon Waxman, "You Think You've Got Tomatoes," *New York Times,* August 3, 2005.

36. U.S. Department of Agriculture, National Agriculture Statistics Service, *2007 Census of Agriculture: Demographics Factsheet*. Note: The 88 percent increase in Native American operators is largely due to a change in counting methods by the USDA. Asian American operators have increased by 40 percent, while the national average is a 7 percent increase.

37. U.S. Department of Agriculture, National Agricultural Statistics Service, "2007 Census of Agriculture: Asian Farmers Factsheet."

15

Beyond Authenticity

Rerouting the Filipino Culinary Diaspora

MARTIN F. MANALANSAN IV

A few years ago, I took one of my regular jaunts to Woodside, a neighborhood in the borough of Queens, New York City, where I first lived after arriving in the United States in 1984. Since the 1990s, the neighborhood has become increasingly populated by a variety of Asian Americans, including Korean, Chinese, Indian, Thai, and Filipino Americans. Along Roosevelt Avenue, from roughly Sixtieth to Seventieth Avenue, is Little Manila, where Filipino stores, bars, and restaurants can be found in abundance.

On this day, I took a couple of my American-born and -raised foodie friends to a Filipino restaurant called Ihawan (Tagalog for "grilling over fire"). All three of us ordered the house specialty, which was the barbecued meats—pork and chicken that came with rice and *achara* (pickled green papaya). Amid various food aromas; brightly colored posters of the Philippines, including forthcoming concerts by Philippine-based film and music celebrities; and the gleaming Formica and melamine dishes, my friends and I began to eat. Our silence was occasionally disrupted by the clinking of forks and spoons against the plate, the smacking of lips chewing, and the buzz of Tagalog spoken by the clientele around us. After a couple of minutes of silent contemplative eating, my friend Roger blurted out in his inimical and somewhat sarcastic manner, "Interesting!"

My other friend, Elaine, and I looked at each other and then at Roger. Like an impromptu duet, we simultaneously and incredulously queried, "Interesting? That's all you have to say?"

Roger explained that he could not "locate" or "place" the food. He had not had Filipino food before, he said, and thought it was a little bit Thai because the meats were kind of sweet and also "Chinesey" because of the rice, but he was curious about where the "Filipino-ness" or Filipino angle was in the food. He then asked whether this was considered "authentic" Filipino food, or given the restaurant's New York location, was this a "watered-down" or an "Americanized" version?

Before I could answer, Elaine chimed in, saying that since we were in a Filipino restaurant and the food was prepared by Filipino cooks and served by Filipino waitresses, it had to be Filipino. Just the "atmosphere" alone, according to her, made it "authentically Filipino." I tried to say something profound despite being amused and annoyed at the same time, but failed.

During uncomfortable moments like this one, when conversations about food and authenticity emerge from cosmopolitan encounters in global cities, I feel compelled to offer a more critical reconsideration of authenticity, particularly culinary authenticity in relation to migration and diaspora. While I see myself as less an expert and more a "participant-observer/ native," I have specific investments in this particular kind of project. In this chapter I describe the notion of Filipino culinary authenticity and the diasporic homecoming or return. What kinds of emotional and material ideas and meanings circulate in these sorts of encounters by the various actors or subjects involved? What are the roles of emotions, feelings, affects, and senses in the expressions and articulations of Filipino culinary inauthenticity and diasporic return? How are notions such as "Filipino-ness" attached to and/or detached from notions of authenticity, identity, body, nation, and migration?

I follow the wonderful examples of chapters 7 and 8 on Filipino cuisine and foodways by Dawn Bohulano Mabalon and Alex Orquiza Jr., respectively, in this book. Both chapters map out the historical trajectories and legacies of the cuisine from the late nineteenth century until immediately after World War II, and my understanding of the complexity of Filipino cuisine is influenced and informed by their ideas. In my chapter, I use ethnography[1] and discourse analysis to describe post-1965 experiences, particularly of identity, authenticity, and diasporic return. I present two cases for analysis of the issues and questions I outlined earlier. The first case is a Christmas meal in a Filipino American home in Queens, New York. The second case is the Philippines episode of the television series *Anthony Bourdain: No Reservations*. With these two cases, I revisit the notions of authenticity and diasporic return in relation to feelings, affects, sensuality, and embodiment. I then analyze these notions as a part of a larger project on the politics of consumption and food among Filipinos and Filipino Americans in both the Philippines and the United States. First, I explore two ideas or concepts that have a direct bearing on my chapter: authenticity and diasporic homecomings or return.

Authentic for Whom?

Authenticity hovers over the heads of immigrants like the persistent aroma of fried fish or cured meats. As the incident at the Ihawan restaurant demonstrates, this can be amusing, annoying, or, at times, both. Immigrants encounter notions and questions of authenticity because they are almost always seen as strangers being slowly integrated into the preexisting "native" culture. Questions about authenticity and the immigrant condition revolve around primordial places, times, and bodily experiences. They also concern origins, hence the question predictably asked of immigrants or people who "look" or "sound" like immigrants: "Where do you come from?"

Authenticity, whether it applies to people, food, or other experiences, pivots on the notion of origin or roots, which explains my friend Roger's attempts to "locate" the food at the Ihawan restaurant. Being able to "place" things and persons is a way to legitimize one's own knowledge and to assess the relative strangeness and/or acceptability of the thing or person in question. It is also a way of differentiating oneself from others.[2] Authenticity follows that famous and rather simplistic dictum "You are what you eat." That is, authenticity thrives on the idea of the essence and purity of origins and selfhood that are conventionally understood as unchanging or static.[3]

Many of the recent discourses on culinary authenticity have come from adventurous eaters and food experts who identify themselves as "foodies." Foodies are often associated with an "insider" knowledge of food or some kind of vernacular expertise about food as a mark of cosmopolitanism and class distinction.[4] As food scholars who have deconstructed "culinary authenticity" assert, the crux of all claims of culinary authenticity is its *constructedness*.[5] In other words, there is nothing inherent in the food that makes it "authentic"; rather, authenticity emerges from the shifting standards, conventions, cultural, and class backgrounds of the person authenticating the phenomenon at hand. Therefore, an individual's various positions—including class standing, cultural background, and other historical markers—shape, alter, and control the understanding of authenticity. In short, authenticity is not based on a timeless set of standards or criteria.

The everyday lived experience of immigrants and notions of culinary authenticity are often entwined. "Immigrant foods" and questions about culinary authenticity, particularly in the West, are joined with the "ethnic connection."[6] The term "ethnic," at least in the United States, has come to signify otherness, of being separate from the so-called mainstream or what is construed as all-American. Whatever is seen as *not* part of the mainstream is routinely labeled ethnic, a label signifying that the ethnic subject's origin lies "elsewhere," that is, anywhere but "here." Immigrant food is thus categorized as ethnic food precisely because of its alterity and difference, and "ethnic food" is almost always subject to questions about authenticity. It is interesting to note here that "all-American" pertains to foods like pizza, taco, chips, and hamburgers that belonged to early immigrant culinary cultures that have been since integrated into popular practice. In other words, questions about authenticity and ethnic food are not intrinsic to the cuisine or particular criteria but to the dominant/mainstream and marginal/non-mainstream food choices and tastes that are constantly shifting.[7]

Return to Where?

Popular ideas about authenticity and diasporic homecoming or return are interconnected. Diaspora refers to people leaving their homelands or places of birth and subsequently becoming "dispersed" into other countries. Once there, they become part of the larger population and, at the same time, apart from it. But the premise of diaspora is never just about *leaving* a place of origin; instead, a cyclical notion of diaspora is contingent on a *return* to the homeland. The diasporic subject leaves only to return. Diasporic return is often portrayed as a romanticized end point, a moment characterized as either a rediscovery or a recovery of authenticity, a heroic and redemptive closure, or an idealized final destination of all diasporic odysseys and linear migratory movements. As I argue in this chapter, return is a complicated process with ambivalent and contradictory routes, meanings, and practices that are embodied and enacted. When enacted through food, diasporic return is a performative arena in which the tensions and contradictions about space, nationhood, gender, sex, class, and citizenship unfold and play out through tastes, smells, digestion, and commensality.

Diasporic return is made up of various motivations, temporalities, and modalities. Some scholars use a typology of various modes of diasporic return, which include provisional returns, forced returns, or the kind of returns that exists primarily in the imagination. Diasporic return is also a mediated concept shaped and inflected by biographies, histories, and power structures.[8]

As anthropologist Louisa Schein suggests, however, despite all its inflections, diasporic return is primarily made up of corporeal and sensory experiences and practices that are embedded in a specific form of erotics.[9] She further observes that the homeland is a site for "both capital accumulation and for erotic entanglements."[10] Therefore, engagements with the homeland are pivotal to the enunciations of the sexual, sensual, national, and erotic, and to this I add the gustatory.

A person need not be *physically* relocated in the homeland to enable a return. The sensual experiences of food often become events of both imagined and real diasporic homecomings. Accordingly, the taste and smell of food can be a way to travel back "home." Food often transports eaters to places and times associated with happiness or unhappiness. While fond food memories often stir feelings of solace via nostalgia (hence the term "comfort food"), less happy gastronomic recollections can provoke uneasiness, distress, or discomfort. Food, therefore, is a sensory, emotional, and pneumonic trigger for remembering the homeland and the past, as well as evaluating one's present situation or future predicament. Past experiences and specific rituals, such as those concerning food, enable a sort of "homecoming" through senses, emotions, and other embodied experiences. Thus, diasporic return occurs not only in the moment of physically setting foot on homeland *soil*; it also can be through emotion-filled and memory-ridden food events in the "elsewhere," as illustrated in the following story of a Philippines holiday meal that took place thousands of miles from the Philippines archipelago.

A Filipino Christmas Meal in New York City

In December 2005, I and several Filipinos and non-Filipinos went to a Christmas celebration at the home of an old family friend. In addition to a variety of salads and desserts, the guests were served three main dishes. The first was a beef stew that Melissa, our hostess, said was her "Christmas stew," an old family recipe. The second was a stuffed, semiboneless chicken dish called "chicken *gallantina*." The third dish was a big bowl of what was called "Filipino-style spaghetti."

The house was decorated in festive red and green ornaments that were echoed in the colors of each of the three main dishes. The stew had chunks of beef, green peas, red bell peppers, and slivers of hot dog (in red casings) in a tomato-based sauce. The stuffed roast chicken was sliced to reveal a filling consisting of red bell peppers, ground pork, raisins, and, again, long strips of red hot dogs. The Filipino-style spaghetti had a sweet-sour tomato sauce that included, yet again, the ubiquitous red hot dog.

Several guests, including myself, were highly amused at the intentional color synchronization of food and decor. The non-Filipino guests were more interested in whether the main dishes were "representative" of food in festivities "back there" in the Philippines. While there was no actual mention of authenticity, this question was at the core of the dinner conversation.

Some of the Filipino guests responded—once safely out of earshot of the hostess—by being defensive; they said that while some of these dishes are served in many Filipino homes, other, "more Filipino" dishes would better "represent" the culture, nation, and people. Some discussed their own family culinary traditions involving specific dishes that, they claimed, were more "representative" and "truly Filipino."

Others were appalled and perplexed by the hostess's overindulgent use of hot dogs, which, according to a couple of Filipino guests, were not at all Filipino. Elsa, a middle-aged Filipina, disagreed, maintaining that hot dogs had been part of Filipino culture since the Americans, especially American GIs, introduced them and that they had become a Filipino staple. She added that it was a typical breakfast and snack food in many households. It reminded her of her own childhood, in which the hot dog, resplendent in it red casing, was a gleaming, greasy (from the frying pan) delicacy in the middle of a plateful of rice.

While many in the group agreed, some whispered—so as not to offend the hostess—that it still was "tacky" to have hot dogs in all the main dishes. A couple of Filipino guests even went as far as to remark that the meal embodied a very *masa*, meaning plebeian taste, and that it was a disgrace to suggest to non-Filipinos that Philippine cuisine was not "classy."

Several people were clearly uncomfortable with the "hot dog" theme and insisted that there was a better and more "authentic substitute" for the hot dogs, such as Spanish chorizo or chorizo de Bilbao. As a Filipino woman huffed, "We would not have served these dishes with hot dogs—it does not show the true 'native' dishes that we have back home." But an older man named Bert, who had been in the United States since the late seventies, admonished the woman. He said that if we really wanted "native" food, then we would not even be talking about chorizo as an authentic Filipino ingredient. He asked, "Didn't chorizo come from Spain?" People nodded, and some added that the spaghetti and the *gallantina* also were not "originally" from the Philippines. "In fact," Bert said, "the Christmas stew, which is our hostess's family heirloom recipe, is actually *afritada*, which, if we are going to be strict about it, is from Mexico or Spain."

The Christmas dinner was a disappointment for some of the guests, especially the Filipino Americans, because for them, the meal did not meet their subjective definition of authenticity. But wise old Bert had another view. As he confided to me, along with a couple of other guests, "The real issue here is not authenticity because if it is, then many of these Filipino guests would have to admit that they would have used hot dogs in these dishes. Back home, isn't that what we do? It is actually very authentic, although not pleasing [in regard to authenticity]." Bert's rather circuitous statement about authenticity made sense to some of the guests. Others, like myself, still sought other explanations.

While food—and particularly the food of holidays—may be the trigger for memories of home, some of these memories may not be pleasant, satisfactory, or even palatable. This Christmas meal in a Filipino immigrant home in New York City was not about comfort, warmth, or other positive feelings; nor was it about the warm emotions typically attributed to home cooking and "native" foods. The meal made some of the people uncomfortable because they had to confront and "return" to the unwanted tastes and flavors they thought they had left behind.

For reasons of class distinctions and immigrant pride, the imagined return to a Filipino home/land distorts the teleology of ideas like "you are what you eat" because that may or may not approximate who you think you are or were. In other words, eating can confound, distort, and/or unsettle your sense of identity and belonging. Some of the guests' dis-identification with their home-land may be a way of refusing the linearity and simplistic essentialism that surrounds questions of authenticity. This immigrant food event of a Christmas meal does not offer an easy or direct emotional link with national identity and belonging, warm nostalgic returns, or clear mappings of authenticity. Rather, such an event provides critical moments for reflecting about diaspora, especially if compared with the narrative of an *actual* return to the Philippine homeland as seen in a popular television food show.

Elusive Homecomings: Or the *Lechon* and a Filipino American's Return

Anthony Bourdain: No Reservations, a food series that aired on the Travel Channel from 2005 through 2012, is a prime example of culinary travel's narratives and discourses about the complications of authenticity and diasporic returns. In this series, the celebrity chef and author Anthony Bourdain took an eclectic approach to the spaces and practices of eating around the world. Totally catholic—or, should I say, imperial—in his tastes, he explored and ingested everything from mass-driven cuisines to haute cuisines in presentation, ingredients, and ambience.

The Philippines episode, which aired in 2009, was highly unusual in one important way. Usually a committee of experts chose the show's location, but this time, the trip to the Philippines was selected through a competition in which the show's fans made a case for a specific country and cuisine of their choice. Most of their submissions were video proposals of fans trying to persuade Bourdain and his staff of the merits and advantages of going to a specific country or region. One video, from Augusto, a Filipino American from Long Island, New York, caught their attention. He used a smart, energetic, and witty strategy to convince the show's producers of the culinary desirability of the Philippines.

Bourdain was captivated by Augusto's tenacity and yet amusing arguments, and his proposal made the initial cut, meaning that he was called into the show's production offices for a face-to-face conversation—all of which, of course, was videotaped. Bourdain expressed disappointment when he met Augusto, for instead of the enthusiastic young man captured on tape, Augusto was reserved and rather pensive. (Also, to Bourdain's great disappointment, he had not seen *Apocalypse Now*, which was filmed in the Philippines.) Gone were the amusing anecdotes and snippets of information, the bright smile, and photogenic, sunny personality. In his place was a young man with a rather morose and almost melancholic composure. Bourdain thus told the audience that he had been ready to give up on the Philippines but then reluctantly decided to take a chance on Augusto and plunge into the unknown, mainly because he knew he had a large Filipino audience that was upset that he had not yet visited their country, even though he had been to numerous other locations in Southeast Asia. "This is getting to be embarrassing," Bourdain admitted.

As part of his narrative, Augusto, a Filipino American, told the audience that his parents never taught him much about Philippine culture and traditions because they wanted him to succeed by becoming assimilated to mainstream American culture. It was not until he reached college that he realized that most of his Asian friends had very strong connections to their heritage. He consequently felt a sense of shame for not having the sort of belonging or attachment to his parent's homeland that all his Asian American college friends apparently possessed. In fact, before the trip to the Philippines with the *No Reservations* crew, Augusto had been to the Philippines just once.

The show's narrative in the Philippines begins without Augusto; he does not appear until the second half of the episode. Rather, Bourdain tells us that he "stumbles into this Philippines journey on [his] own." In reality, of course, he navigates the labyrinth of Manila and its environs not on his own but with the assistance of several native guides, such as Ivan, "who gives food tours of Manila." These guides lead Bourdain through Manila's old Chinatown and into various wet markets and street stalls. The guides are represented as authoritative cultural brokers who open the country's culinary doors and provide the necessary historical and cultural contexts for Bourdain's signature rhapsodic and often irreverent rants and reflections.

Midway through the program, Bourdain flies to the Visayas, the Philippines' central islands, and specifically to the city of Cebu. Here, he finally meets Augusto, who is still, according to Bourdain, in a kind of gloomy haze. Bourdain becomes "concerned."

What makes this episode compelling is that Bourdain, a television personality, provides an unusual rendering of a young Filipino American as "uneasy" about being back in his parents' homeland, his place of "origin." While Bourdain shares a meal with him, the camera captures Augusto with a forlorn face, looking sadly at his plate of food. He constantly seems to be drowning in some sort of internal turmoil, whether over an opulent meal at a notable restaurant or with his extended family at a dinner at his relatives' home. Overtaken by concern over Augusto's emotional, if not spiritual, well-being, Bourdain tries to remedy the situation by organizing a grand feast on his behalf. Indeed, Augusto's mood shifts significantly over what is described as the best *lechon* (roast pig) in the world at the center of the feast.

During this epic meal, strange things begin to occur. The *lechon*—considered by many to be the national dish of the Philippines—begins to transform Augusto, who appears to be awakened from his melancholy by the crunch of the roasted pigskin. The ambivalence and emotional detachment that appeared to permeate Augusto's very being just moments ago have now vanished. At one point during the meal, Augusto declares that he is very much an American, even though he appears to be not completely comfortable with this realization. He is, however, as evidenced by his bright smile and decisive demeanor as he devours the roast pig, to be at ease with his newfound "Filipino-ness."

Instead of demonstrating his characteristic smugness over what could be considered a magical feat of awakening a young Filipino American from his existential stupor, Bourdain refuses to take credit for the transformation. Despite what could have been a triumphant ending to both his and Augusto's Philippine odyssey, Bourdain is satisfied with leaving things alone. Still, Bourdain feels something is still amiss, that there may be something to the common belief that "Filipinos are too nice."

What I take this to mean is that Bourdain feels that Filipinos have failed to create a visible and marketable presence in the food world, much less to possess a strong sense of culinary and national identity. He regards this failure as a possible explanation for Augusto's malaise. But instead of exploring this supposition further, Bourdain drops the subject, preferring to "leave it to the experts" to figure it out. Despite the lack of narrative closure, in the end a content Augusto is seen smiling with his Cebu family. Ultimately, it is as if food were an adequate denouement to his vexed diasporic return to his homeland.

Another reading, I think, would be more accurate. Instead of allowing Augusto to settle comfortably into the homeland culture that Bourdain and his crew have constructed in the episode, I believe that Augusto's uneasy and difficult affective moments cannot be so easily blanketed by smiles, delicious foods, and commensal gatherings. Indeed, this uncomfortable moment can be juxtaposed with that of the Christmas meal in New York City. Viewed together and against each other, these two uneasy culinary moments regarding the Filipino diaspora returns my discussion to my examination of culinary authenticity and diasporic return.

Conclusion: Messy Emotions and Alternative Culinary Itineraries

Augusto's return and the tensions of the Christmas meal in New York City, I believe, are not an arrival at a condition of easy authenticity but an uncomfortable encounter with *inauthenticity*. By this, I do not mean to resurrect authenticity and take questions about culinary authenticity *literally*. Instead, following Lisa Heldke's *Exotic Appetites: Ruminations of a Food Adventurer* and Josee Johnston and Shyon Baumann's *Foodies: Democracy and Distinction in the Gourmet Foodscape*, I propose dismantling or deconstructing the very notion of authenticity and dislodging it from its underexamined position in food scholarship, particularly as the discourse that concerns immigrant food.

On the one hand, I regard authenticity as a kind of constructed "settledness" or static adherence to origins, identity, and belonging. On the other hand, I see inauthenticity *not* as a lack of authentic elements (whatever they may be) but as a historically and cultural negotiated state and process of emotional discomfort and affective refusal to adhere to an easy mapping of identity. In other words, in the case studies in this chapter, inauthenticity is a way to break apart the static notions of" Filipino-ness" by refusing to obey the strictures and clichés of food and identity.

In the *No Reservations* episode, inasmuch as I disagree with Bourdain's statement about Filipinos' failing to become more visible and have a clear presence in the culinary world, I do agree with him that Augusto's return is not ultimately a shift from shame to pride. That is, what he experienced was not an embrace of his putative Filipino-ness. Instead of taking Bourdain's statement as a condemnation of Filipino cultural failure, I see it as an entry to a discussion of Filipino culinary and diasporic experiences. Following J. Jack Halberstam's queering of failure,[11] I take the scenes of breakdowns and botched attempts, such as the hot dog fiasco in the Christmas meal and Augusto's lingering sense of sadness, as opportunities to better understand the complexity of food. Issues and meanings of food are not always pleasant. In fact, to insist on the positive aspects of food consumption ignores the blind spots in our critical understanding of the complicated ways in which people, particularly immigrants, relate to their homelands and their cuisines.

From these two cases, it is clear that we need to confront rather than evade Filipino and Filipino American identifications and disidentifications, the coexistence of pride and shame, and the often disorderly travels and travails of migrants or diasporic subjects. Filipino cuisine is not just pristine localized practices and institutions; it is also formed by multiple culinary convergences, attempted adaptations, and "outside" influences. It is a product of individual and/or collective meanings and practices, like the Filipino hot dogs in the red casings. This is the messy reality of any cuisine, whether it is called fusion, diffusion, or confusion.

Returns to the homeland by diasporic subjects need not be about some sort of psychic or affective completion brought about by a telos that often replaces shame with pride, failure with success, a regaining of something lost through migration or expatriation. As we all know, food is often the most accessible medium of return. Diasporic homecomings, whether imagined, as in the Christmas meal, or actual, as in Augusto's case, also are uneasy confrontations with filial and other affective and sensual/sensory ties. Often, these confrontations do not result in happiness or "authentic" encounters with one's cultural/ethnic provenance. I suggest that Augusto's awkwardness and the tensions among the Christmas meal guests are not due to the failure of food to do its work of authenticating homecoming natives. Rather, these situations speak to the indeterminacy and instability of diasporic links among body, desire, place, and time. Not all culinary travels and diasporic homecomings end in a single destination of "you are what you eat," and not every diasporic return ends with settling into one's place of "origin."

The Christmas meal and Augusto's visit to the Philippines are not entirely upbeat; neither resulted in unambiguous moments of happy smiles and satisfied bellies. But it is not always necessary to equate diasporic return with stable or secure authentic personhoods. Instead, these two examples show that diasporic returns are often insubordinate or recalcitrant forms of practices, institutions, and meanings that constitute diasporic phenomena. Moreover, these forms can be sensory, emotional, and other embodied experiences that refuse to be attached to linear romantic/nationalist directionality and simplistic filial links to homelands. Interestingly, Augusto's story did not culminate with his embrace of his Filipino-ness, and the story of the Christmas meal did not end with satisfied guests. But are these outcomes undesirable? Why should we expect only positive endings, only contented emotional destinations? I suggest that such expectations lead to political, cultural, and emotional dead ends and impasses, just as discussions of authenticity usually result in feelings of emptiness.

The Christmas meal guests' uneasiness with the hot dogs and Augusto's emotional state leave many ideas unexplored and just as many questions unanswered. What I offer here are not definitive answers or conclusive opinions but suggestions for creatively rerouting or reorienting the ways that we confront immigrant/diasporic culinary cultures and the notion of authenticity. I am confident such a process will help us better understand the complex role of food and consumption in our lives.

Consumption is never a complete process. While it can lead to satiation, it can also lead to more hunger, more queries, and lingering discomforts. And while we might wish that Augusto's trip and the Christmas meal had gratifying endings, such facile conclusions can leave us with a shallow satisfaction that, in turn, starts a spiral of eating, drinking, and consuming, which then leads to endless questions about authenticity and identity. I argue that this accomplishes very little other than to sustain an endless reprisal of arguments over which food is authentic and which is not. Instead, let us think of new and challenging ways of thinking and talking about food, migration, and return. Let us find new political recipes and cultural itineraries that might lead to a more sustaining and capacious way of dealing with culinary cultures and immigrant lives.

Notes

I would like to the thank my coeditors and comrades Anita Mannur and Robert Ku for being such pleasant and intellectually nourishing collaborators. The research funds for this chapter were provided by the Campus Research Board and the Departments of Anthropology and Asian American Studies at the University of Illinois.

1. I did my ethnographic fieldwork on Asian American immigrant culinary cultures in Queens, New York, for fifteen months between 2005 and 2010.
2. Lisa Heldke, *Exotic Appetites: Ruminations of a Food Adventurer* (New York: Routledge, 2003), 23–44.
3. Ibid.
4. Josee Johnston and Shyon Baumann, *Foodies: Democracy and Distinction in the Gourmet Foodscape* (New York: Routledge, 2010), 69–96.
5. Ibid.
6. Ibid.

7. For an excellent historical examination of American "ethnic" cuisines, see Donna Gabbacia, *We Are What We Eat: Ethnic Food and the Making of Americans* (Cambridge, MA: Harvard University Press, 1998).

8. Lynellen Long and Ellen Oxfeld, eds., *Coming Home: Refugees, Migrants and Those Who Stayed Behind* (Philadephia: University of Pennsylvania Press, 2004). For an ethnographic account of the diasporic return of Chinese American youth, see Andrea Louie, *Chineseness across Borders* (Durham, NC: Duke University Press, 2004).

9. Louisa Schein, "Diaspora Politics, Homeland Erotics, and the Materializing of Memory," *positions: east asia cultures critique* 7, no. 3 (1999): 697–729.

10. Ibid., 699.

11. J. Jack Halberstam, *Queer Art of Failure* (Durham, NC: Duke University Press, 2011).

PART IV

Readable Feasts

16

Acting Asian American, Eating Asian American

The Politics of Race and Food in Don Lee's Wrack and Ruin

JENNIFER HO

What kind of Vedic rabbit hole of temporally acausal connections have we tumbled through? I mean, holy mother of Carl Gustav Jung, throw down the I Ching, man, this is heavy, the serendipity of this, the Deschampsian plum-pudding wheel of karma that's spun me off in this direction.

Don Lee, *Wrack and Ruin*, 289

Greedy land developers. Estranged Korean–Chinese American brothers. Chocolate ice cream. Buddhist precepts written on paper airplanes. Organic brussels sprouts. These are but a few of the plot elements that propel Don Lee's second novel *Wrack and Ruin* (2008). Lyndon Song, former world-renowned sculptor, is besieged by visitors to his organic brussels sprout farm, including his Los Angeles wannabe movie producer brother, who is also a former Wall Street embezzler; an aging and washed-up Hong Kong martial arts film star; a former art curator turned *shiatsu* masseuse; and two environmental activists trying to save the snowy plover from a golf course developer. Although clearly a satire, at the heart of Lee's novel is an organic message that emphasizes the interconnected nature of all beings and experiences as well as a respect for the land and for the linkages among people, animals, and the food we produce and consume. In this novel, to act Asian American and to eat Asian American become forms of political engagement rooted in a desire to be understood outside a dominant white hegemonic culture and outside stereotypical and Orientalized portraits of Asian Americans and foodways.

Wrack and Ruin continually upends expectations of model minority stereotypes and self-consciously questions what it means to be an Asian American artist and, by extension, what it means to act Asian American: what it means to live as an Asian American in our day and age. Food serves as an organizing device, as well as a plot element, yet not in the ways that one would typically associate with the term "Asian." Food in many ways centers this novel, but not as a simple or simplistic ethnic symbol, signifier of racial difference, material of assimilation, or sign of hybridization. In this chapter, I expand on Anita Mannur's observation that "the deliberate recasting and reframing of which foods are deemed 'exotic,' un-American, and desirable can be read as a strategic attempt to understand and undermine the continuing link between Asian Americans and their foodways."[1] Mannur recognizes that decoupling food from ethnicity and race releases Asian American identities from being exoticized and racialized through stereotypical associations with food and eating, thereby making them objects of consumption rather than subjects who are "consumers and producers of American taste mechanisms."[2] Indeed, *Wrack and Ruin* does not fetishize authentic Asian-ethnic foodways; instead, Lee's invocations of food and eating become political acts through their apolitical affiliations, calling on readers to understand action and eating as forms of racialized politics through their de-ethnicized materiality.

Race versus Ethnicity: The Meaning of "Asian American"

"'You know the problem with us?" Woody said to Lyndon. "We're fucking typical Asian men. We don't talk. We're emotionally inaccessible.'"

Don Lee, Wrack and Ruin, 145

As the title of my chapter suggests, there is a way in which one can act Asian American as well as eat Asian American, but what does that really mean? What does it mean to act or to eat "Asian American"? Is this about one's identity, one's behavior, one's performance, or the materiality of the food items that one is consuming? Moreover, just what *is* this adjective, "Asian American"?

"Asian American" acts as a racial rather than an ethnic descriptor, meaning that it is not tied to a particular Asian ancestral homeland or ethnic national identity. Rather, "Asian American" exists as a constructed, political marker, one created during the 1960s civil rights movement.[3] Scholars and journalists like Daryl Maeda, William Wei, Frank Wu, and Helen Zia traced the development of a racialized Asian American community and the rise of the Asian American movement, specifically its development as a political affiliation encompassing various Asian-ethnic groups.[4] To be Asian American in the late 1960s and early 1970s was to affirm one's difference from the white mainstream majority as an oppressed nonwhite "other" in solidarity with people of color.

After the civil rights era, the term "Asian American" has been used most in academic and activist arenas to demarcate a group of people who have ancestral roots in Asia and whose experiences in the United States remain marked by a history of disenfranchisement: exclusionary immigration and naturalization laws, antimiscegenation statutes, housing discrimination, illegal incarceration as enemy aliens, and, today, racial targets as terrorists. In other words, those who either consider themselves Asian American from a census perspective or who choose this term out of an activist sense of shared history are distinguished through their difference. To be Asian American means that one's nationality may always be called into question owing to one's racial difference; accordingly, citizenship for Asian Americans is always suspect.

This definition has plagued the field of Asian American studies and Asian American literature (from the points of view of both the literature and the literary criticism). A look at novels labeled "Asian American literature" reveals that they are written by people who may identify as Asian American but whose works usually cohere around a single Asian ethnicity. Chinese American writer Gish Jen centers her stories on Chinese American families.[5] Indian American author Jhumpa Lahiri describes the lives of Indians in the diaspora.[6] Korean American Chang-rae Lee populates his novels with Korean and Korean American characters,[7] and Vietnamese American Monique Truong's novels focus on Vietnamese characters living both inside and outside the United States.[8] Most Asian American novelists feature Asian-ethnic characters who share the ethnic ancestry of their authors. While there are notable exceptions[9] (Don Lee being among them), Asian American authors usually write about the ethnic group to which they belong, and works of Asian American literature are usually defined by the Asian ethnicity of the writer as well as the protagonists and/or characters of the novels.

Similarly, Asian American scholarship, whether literary criticism or ethnography in general, tends to focus on questions of Asian ethnic specificity, for example, how Filipino Americans, Cambodian Americans, and Japanese Americans navigate their worlds or how they have been perceived as Asian ethnic "others" within a larger U.S. historical framework.[10] Seldom do scholars of Asian American studies define the term "Asian American" in their works, relying on assumptions about what this racial umbrella term means and whom it covers. I am not criticizing scholars who use the term in this manner; indeed, almost all researchers of Asian American people and literature (myself included) make assumptions about the definition of "Asian American." However, it still begs the question about the efficacy of this term and what it means, exactly, to act and eat as one who identifies as Asian American, since this is a racialized, political term that has currency only in a U.S. context. As the literary critic Sau-ling Cynthia Wong explains, "Asian America" is a concept that does not travel well, so to talk of an "Asian American" diaspora "is simply quite meaningless," since "the loosely held and fluctuating collectivity called 'Asian Americans' will dissolve back into its descent defined constituents as soon as one leaves American national borders behind.["]11 What unites Asian Americans in the United States is their shared difference with other people of Asian descent.

Asian American literature and scholarship thus concentrate on Asian ethnic peoples, experiences, and histories. Likewise, food is usually thought of as being ethnic rather than racially specific. Restaurants in the United States generally serve cuisine tied to an Asian nation (pan-Asian fusion restaurants notwithstanding), and the way that we talk about the Asian ethnic food that we cook and consume is through ethnic-national markers. We eat Chinese soup dumplings, Japanese miso soup, Korean *bibimbap*, Thai curry, Indian samosas, Vietnamese *banh mih* sandwiches, and Filipino chicken adobo. There are notable Asian and American hybrids—the fortune cookie[12] and California roll[13] come readily to mind—but outside pan-Asian fusion dishes[14] and the local Hawaiian dish *loco moco*,[15] there are no truly Asian American foods, and we generally do not talk about, think about, or cook Asian American food.

Despite the lack of a coherent Asian American cuisine, eating Asian American—or eating as an Asian American—can be understood as a form of political engagement, a recognition of the political and racialized moniker that the term "Asian American" connotes. This means that eating Asian American and acting Asian American are forms of social engagement, awareness, and activism, a means of distinguishing Asian American practices from mainstream, hegemonic, or assimilative norms. In other words, Asian American eating and acting become active forms of resisting Asian stereotypes that demean, belittle, and objectify Asian Americans, stereotypes that usually are trafficked through foodways.[16] To eat and to act Asian American is to acknowledge the ways in which Asians in America have been subjected to institutional forms of white supremacy and a complicated history of racialization that has pitted them against other minority groups.[17]

Acting and Eating Asian American in *Wrack and Ruin*

Their food finally came, two waitresses bringing out all of their backed-up orders at once, the grilled asparagus and eggplant, yakitori, the duck breast marinated in sake, tempura, braised short ribs with daikon, fried softshell crabs, soba salad, gyoza, marinated mackerel, steamed egg custard, ohitashi, and potato croquettes. There wasn't enough room on the table for everything, the rims of plates stacked on top of one another. Looking at the spread in totality, they realized they'd ordered way too much food. Still, they dug in.

Don Lee, *Wrack and Ruin*, 213

Don Lee is among a handful of Asian American writers who have explored different Asian ethnic American characters and perspectives in his works of fiction. The Korean American Lee does indeed write about Korean American characters. But his first short story collection, *Yellow: Stories* also contains Chinese American, Japanese American, Filipina, black, mixed-race Filipino-white, black–Korean Amerasian, Latino, and white American characters.[18] Set in the fictional world of Rosarita Bay in Northern California, *Yellow* is a short-story cycle in which a minor character from one story appears as a major character in a later story.[19] Even though the characters are clearly described using ethnic and racial signifiers, the stories themselves (with the exception of the last one) do not make race a central conceit or force. Instead, Lee creates stories about artistic ambition, loneliness, romantic disappointments, the ambivalence of impending parenthood, and coming to terms with various kinds of losses: romantic, familial, career, and youth.

With *Wrack and Ruin*, Lee returns to the fictional world of Rosarita Bay.[20] This time, instead of providing numerous snapshots of the various residents in this sleepy California coastal village, Lee concentrates on a pair of siblings, Lyndon and Woody Song. These half Korean and half Chinese American middle-aged brothers have been estranged from each other for more than sixteen years because of Woody's embezzlement of his clients' (which include the Song parents) funds when he worked as a financial planner with Credit Suisse First Boston. The novel alternates between Lyndon's and Woody's third-person narrations in consecutive chapters, with each brother's chapters taking place entirely from his perspective rather than from that of an omniscient narrator.[21] During the 2005 Labor Day weekend, the novel pivots from Lyndon's organic brussels sprout farm to different locales around Rosarita Bay, featuring the characters who attach themselves to one of the brothers: Sheila Lemke, Lyndon's ex-girlfriend and Rosarita Bay's mayor; Yi Ling Ling, a B-list martial arts movie star whom Woody brings to his brother's farm for the weekend; JuJu LeMay, Lyndon's best friend and Ling Ling's new paramour; Laura Diaz-McClatchy, a former art curator turned *shiatsu* masseuse; Dalton Lee, an acclaimed independent film director and collaborator on Woody's latest film deal; and Trudy Nguyen, a Vietnamese American adult transnational and transracial adoptee and little sister of Woody's former best friend, Kyle Thorneberry. The various debacles hinted at in the novel's title—the physical, emotional, mental, and financial devastations and debilitations that afflict both Lyndon and Woody—and the brothers' estrangement itself provide the tension in the novel. Central is the question of whether Lyndon will sell his twenty-acre farm to the Centurion Group, a development company that is constructing a luxury housing complex around a premiere golf course, serves as the novel's major plot device, with Woody's business interests hinging on whether he will be able to convince his brother to sell his farm.

Although it may seem obvious to say that this Korean American author's third published book is a work of Asian American fiction, its Asian American elements are self-conscious ruminations that raise questions about the issue of identity politics, the relationship between race and aesthetics, the responsibility (if any) of artists of color to their racial communities and the larger society, and the challenges of upending stereotypes by giving characters rich inner and outer lives, characters who just happen to be people of Asian ancestry. Lee's first collection of short stories, *Yellow*, features different inhabitants of Rosarita Bay, both Asian American and non–Asian American, and *Wrack and Ruin* adds a variety of characters to Rosarita Bay, some of whom hail from the Asian diaspora. In addition to the Chinese Korean Song brothers, whose story anchors the narrative, there is the multiracial Laura Diaz-McClatchy, a woman who is initially described through Lyndon's unspoken appraisal of her as a "petite, late thirties, Latina,"[22] but who later discloses to Lyndon that her middle name is Kobayashi and that her Japanese mother trained her in the family's generations-old tradition of *shiatsu* message.[23] Some of the residents of Rosarita Bay from *Yellow* briefly reappear in a single paragraph as a nod to his first work of fiction: Hank Low Kwon; Dean Kaneshiro; Caroline Yip; Eugene Kim; Evelyn Yung; Janet McElroy, whom Lee notes is "a half-black, half-Korean psychotherapist"; and Brian, the "adopted Amerasian son"[24] of Evelyn Yung.[25]

The characters in Lee's work have both typical and atypical traits and histories associated with Asians in America. Trudy Nguyen, the Vietnamese adopted daughter of a wealthy WASP family, rejects her parents' money and name upon returning to the United States after a trip to Vietnam. Trudy confesses to Woody that her unsuccessful attempt to find her birth parents "'made me realize I didn't belong there, in Vietnam,'" yet her closing question, "'But where did I belong?'" reinforces the kinds of cultural confusion that many Asian transracial adoptees feel, and it also reflects the psychological and emotional state of many Asian Americans (adoptees and non-adoptees alike) who question their ability to really feel a sense of belonging in the United States as a racial minority.[26]

In addition, Lee subverts the stereotypes associated with Asian Americans, most notably that of being hyperaccomplished and overachieving. When Lyndon muses about how different he is from his compulsively driven, competitive brother, he notes that "their parents hadn't been particularly demanding in that regard, never meting out any bourgeois, upwardly mobile, model-minority pressure for their sons to go Ivy League."[27] Upending the stereotype of Asian Tiger parents who push their children to excel at all costs, Lee casts Woody's quest for success as an internal manifestation, one that derives from the brotherly favoritism he perceives his parents bestowing on Lyndon rather than from external Asian parental forces.[28] The slacker, pot-smoking Lyndon is portrayed as someone who succeeds despite his lack of aspirations, as he describes himself as one who has "'always taken a principled stand against ambition and discipline,'" a clear departure from the model minority Asian American.[29]

Yet beyond subverting stereotypes, *Wrack and Ruin* is most self-consciously an Asian American novel due to its central preoccupation with the dilemma that Asian American artists, whether of fine arts, films, or novels, face in struggling to produce art that is "art" rather than "Asian" or "Asian American." As the art historian Alice Yang observes,

> There is, first of all, little agreement as to what constitutes Asian American art, as such. Is it simply a descriptive label referring purely to the racial background of the artist? Or does the term serve a critical purpose designating a kind of art with shared concerns, vocabularies, and histories that imply the combination of Asian and Western modes? If so, what does Asian American art look like? Can there actually be a common denominator, given the many different ethnic groups that are covered under the rubric, not to mention the wide array of interests and stylistic approaches adopted by individual artists?[30]

While Yang's rhetorical questions cohere around the dilemma that the conceptual category of "Asian American art" produces, they are equally instructive in thinking about how to define creative works labeled as "Asian American."[31] Should artists of Asian descent living in the United States always be known through a racialized or ethnicized lens (the Asian American sculptor, the Taiwanese director, the Korean American writer) rather than simply as a sculptor, a director, or a writer? Just what makes a work of art, or a novel like *Wrack and Ruin*, Asian American?

Remembering back to when he was an international sensation in the art world, Lyndon notes that "apparently he was not an artist. He was an Asian-American artist."[32] While the "he" in this quotation refers to Lyndon, it could just as easily refer to the author, Don Lee, who ponders the boxes placed on Asian American artists when, through the perspective of Asian American filmmaker Dalton Lee (who could easily be Don Lee's fictional alter ego), he observes,

> "Why are we stuck with comfort women, picture brides, geishas, and greengrocers, with exploring our roots and searching for our birth parents and examining

what it means to be Asian American? I mean, come on, why does it always have to be about race and identity? I'm sick to death of race and identity."[33]

Filmmaker Lee goes on to acknowledge that "nothing happens in this country without the involutions of race. But if we let it dictate what we can and cannot do and start limiting ourselves as artists, then we're no longer free."[34]

The frustration inherent in Lee's alter ego/author statement about racial labels that confine and constrain artists of color from producing their work, irrespective of these labels, speaks to the complex racial politics in Lee's novel. Again, using one of his characters as a mouthpiece for his own beliefs, Lee comments on the opinions of some in contemporary writing circles who believe that writers of color receive literary attention not because of the quality of their work but because of the color of their skin: "'His latest peeve is with minority writers. He claims most of their books would never have seen the light of day if they'd been white, that they're getting the benefit of literary affirmative action. He's coming off as vaguely racist.'"[35] Spoken to Lyndon in a flashback scene by his soon-to-be girlfriend, Sheila Lemke, about her soon-to-be-ex-husband, Stephen, Lee uses this scene to further complicate the pressures facing Asian American artists. They are perceived by white society as being nothing but affirmative-action no-talents who don't deserve fame and recognition because they are capitalizing on their ethnic ancestry and, at the same time, they are being interpreted by the general public as producing art that "is about assimilation and diaspora, about racism and post-colonialism," which is what Lyndon discovers when he is interviewed by critics who choose to see shades of the DMZ and Marco Polo and Korean aphrodisiacs in his sculptures, even though this was not how he wanted his work to be read.[36] Indeed, as art critic Margo Machida affirms, "amid such diversity, where differences frequently outweigh similarities and all that might be held in common is a presence in this nation, the fact that there is a wide and divergent range of perspectives among Asians in the United States should come as no surprise."[37] While the diversity and differences among Asians in America should come as "no surprise," Don Lee's description of the flattening of artists of Asian heritage into representative "Asian American artists" whose work must always demonstrate an essentialized Oriental ethos reinforces the political nature of Asian American art.

Lee also singles out the pressures placed on Asian American artists by critics, both Asian American and non–Asian American. Filmmaker Dalton Lee complains about "the white hegemony" who "like it when we segregate ourselves."[38] Lyndon appears caught in a double bind by Asian American critics who initially slam the sculptures he creates out of made-up ideograms for "exploiting his ethnicity, of being a phony, of falsely exoticizing his work in order to cash in." Lyndon is declared "the Uncle Tong of the art world."[39] Yet in a subsequent sculpture series on birds and fish, Lyndon "got shellacked by the Asian-American pundits as well, this time for not including any discernible Asian references. . . . They rebuked him for trying to deny his cultural heritage and whitewashing himself. For being, in short, a Twinkie."[40] Through Lyndon's and Dalton's perspectives, Lee raises questions of identity politics that plague Asian American artists: the unrealistic and unfair expectations placed on Asian American writers to simultaneously produce art that speaks responsibly to Asian American communities, that does not self-Orientalize, and that still rings true to the vision of the artist of Asian descent.

What are the politics invoked in producing Asian American art or acting Asian American? Perhaps it is simply that being Asian American cannot be confined to a singular definition or art form. Again, quoting Machida:

Not only is there no such thing as a singular or definitive contemporary Asian experience in America, but with the convoluted mingling of influences in a world where mobility reigns and boundaries between cultures are increasingly porous the broad range of Asian reactions to life in this nation are not reducible to limited paradigms such as assimilation versus separatism, tradition versus modernity, or East versus West.[41]

Just as there is no single or definitive Asian American experience, there is no singular or definitive identity surrounding the term "Asian American." To be Asian American, one must simply identify as Asian American. To use this label self-consciously and self-referentially is to acknowledge the political force of history that this term encompasses. Don Lee's recognition of forces like white hegemony and the damned-if-you-do-and-damned-if-you-don't attitude of Asian American critics demonstrates that he is not advocating for a deracinated existence for Asian Americans. Although Lyndon and Dalton each identify as Asian American, Lee has each of them question what it means to be Asian American. These are the questions that author Don Lee himself appears to be wrestling with, as *Wrack and Ruin* tries to work out a balance between what it means to exist as part of the Asian diaspora in the United States, one who may eat Asian ethnic food and watch martial arts films from time to time but who is also a wind surfer and a brussels sprout farmer and an activist trying to save an endangered bird species.[42]

If acting Asian American in *Wrack and Ruin* becomes a political statement, so, too, does eating represent a type of Asian American politics for the Asian diasporic characters of Rosarita Bay. One of the notable aspects of Lee's novel, and part of what makes it a truly Asian American novel, is that all the characters of Asian descent appear to be of the second generation, and their eating habits reflect the kinds of tastes found among Asian Americans who are not of the immigrant generation and who are highly Americanized.[43] While this novel may not seem at first to be about eating, the primacy of foodways—all that we associate with the cultivation, production, and consumption of food— permeates the narrative. Indeed, food—or, more specifically, meals—becomes an organizing force in *Wrack and Ruin*, and the plot circulates around when the main characters, Lyndon and Woody, sit down to eat, wake up to eat, prepare meals, indulge a food craving, or eat out in various diners, restaurants, and bars. During a massage session with Laura Diaz-McClatchy, Lyndon gets a whiff of chocolate ice cream, which leads him to eat strawberry yogurt as a substitute for the ice cream he craves (and that isn't in his freezer), which is the prelude to his simple dinner of zucchini and chicken stir-fry with rice. The following day he runs into Laura, and they both indulge their desire for chocolate ice cream at a local shop, Udderly Licious, and while walking around town and eating their cones, Lyndon asks Laura to go to dinner with him, which in turn leads to various plot progressions in character development and narrative revelations. The initial whiff of chocolate ice cream and Lyndon's desire for consuming ice cream propel his character into action, and scenes of consumption—the ice-cream shop, the bar where Laura gives him her phone number, the Japanese restaurant where they go on their date—figure prominently in the narrative, serving as integral settings for the unfolding of the novel.

In this opening chapter, Lee demonstrates that his Asian American protagonist indulges in meals one would assume would be part of his Asian ethnic heritage, such as cooking rice in a rice cooker and preparing a stir-fry meal for dinner, yet his consumption of strawberry yogurt and chocolate ice cream suggest more typically American tastes. I draw this distinction not to assert that Lee is deliberately trying to ethnicize or racialize Lyndon as "Asian" through an association with cooking rice and stir-fry. On the contrary, while Lyndon does eat foods that conform to his Asian palate, his eating habits run the gamut of ethnic cuisines. The meals that Lyndon and other Asian American characters enjoy throughout the novel are, in many ways, truly American, representing a multiracial, multiethnic American food landscape that twenty-first-century diners assume are commonplace. The characters in *Wrack and Ruin* eat Mexican enchiladas, Japanese tapas, gourmet dark chocolate, chili, chowder, grilled cheese sandwiches, burgers, eggs, lattes, bagels, pasta carbonara, and, of course, brussels sprouts. Commenting on the fluidity of consumptive practices and tastes of residents in New York City's extraordinarily diverse neighbor-hood of Flushing, Queens, Martin Manalansan describes the influence of "Asian pan-ethnic sentiments" that "have been influential in eroding the cul-tural borders between Asian consumers of various cuisines."[44] Like Manalan-san's Asian ethnic informants, the characters in Lee's narrative have developed Asian pan-ethnic gustatory and gastronomic practices in keeping with the panoply of foodways found in America.

Indeed, what is most important about Asian American consumption in this novel is its plurality and diversity. To eat Asian American is not to limit one-self or to be limited by Asian ethnic food practices. But it also does not mean repudiating the food of one's ethnic heritage. Asian American characters eat a variety of foods that may or may not be from their ethnic tradition. But just as he portrays their identities as second-generation Asian Americans, Lee por-trays these characters and the food they eat as more than simply the sum of their Asian ethnic identities. They are more than just Asian American type-cast personalities acting in ways typically or, more accurately, stereotypically associated with Asian American characters. The Asian Americans in this novel possess a depth and complexity belied by their initial introduction, which is in keeping with the way that actual flesh-and-blood Asian Americans exist in real life: as more complex individuals than are rendered through two-dimensional portraits in typical mass media outlets.[45] Perhaps most refreshingly, Lee does not portray Asian Americans as struggling with their ethnic or racial identity. Food is not the barometer for how authentic or inauthentic they feel about their Asian heritage. Instead, food is just one more cultural product for inges-tion, signaling an acceptance of the characters' Asian American-ness through the range of what they consume, which includes both Asian and non-Asian foodstuffs.

A case in point is brussels sprouts. While eating a midday meal of grilled cheese and tomato sandwiches in the farmhouse kitchen, Ling Ling asks Lyn-don whether he actually likes brussels sprouts, which leads Lyndon into a Forest Gump–like catalog of all the ways that he knows how to prepare them: "He knew how to sauté them, bake, them, steam, fry, boil, braise, roast, stew, and blanch them. He knew how to serve them lyonnaised, au gratin, and a la barigoule."[46] Through the symbol of brussels sprouts, we can understand the political implications of acting and eating in *Wrack and Ruin*. The primary tension in the novel is whether Lyndon will sell his organic brussels sprout farm to the Centurion group so it can build a golf course on his property. For Lyndon, the farm and his relationship to his crops and the land are a synergis-tic part of who he is, linking him to nature. He realizes that "whether he was here or not, it would go on, this cycle, for thousands of years, like it had before him. Knowing this was humbling. It made him feel insignificant, and paradoxically that feeling was useful, freeing. He would do whatever it took to keep this farm."[47] The farm and the brussels sprouts that he grows connect Lyndon to a larger cycle of nature, which he is both a part of and apart from, demonstrating his organic connection to his farm.

In this narrative, it is this message—the organic part of it—that speaks to the political nature of acting and eating. In an early scene, Lee describes Lyndon's ruminations on why he farms organically:

> Lyndon hated it, the idea of it, the residue of all those pesticides and herbicides on the sprouts, the trace elements of toxins seeping into the earth and contaminating it for decades. But, contrary to assumptions, Lyndon wasn't a reformer. He wasn't some sort of idealistic, hippie-dippy enviro-activist, not even a vegetarian. He just wanted to farm in a way that was simple and pure, and keep his life uncomplicated.[48]

Lyndon's organic sensibilities aren't simply for environmental or dietary reasons, since he is neither a green activist nor a vegetarian. Instead, his refusal to sell to the Centurion Group and to turn his farm into a piece of overly processed, toxic commercialized real estate signals his desire to be interconnected with nature. At the end of the Labor Day weekend, Lyndon finds himself attached to people in his community and making choices that demonstrate his awareness of how his life is tied to the lives of others, as well as how much he is tied to the land. The novel emphasizes an organic connection among the characters that illuminates how intertwined everyone's lives truly are.

Food becomes the arena for this organic interrelatedness. Udderly Licious—or, more specifically, the two teenagers working behind the ice-cream counter—also reappears throughout the novel, demonstrating the connectedness of various characters with food and with one another. In fact, the two teenaged ice-cream scoopers, Jan de Leuw and Andre Meeker, initially figure as background characters to the main narrative. Yet what develops during the weekend and throughout the novel is the prominence of these two seemingly minor characters: from Lyndon's brief encounter with Jan as they pass each other in Laura's *shiatsu* waiting room; to Woody and Trudy's witnessing of Jan and Andre's lovemaking while riding bareback on a horse; to the revelation that Jan and Andre are part of an environmental terrorist organization, the Planet Liberation Front (or PLF) and, as such, are responsible for two events that severely affect Lyndon's and hence Woody's lives: they release an elephant at the chili and chowder festival, and they accidently release turpentine into Lyndon's irrigation pond. This last act of unintended harm, by Jan and Andre, make them responsible for the novel's denouement and subsequent resolution of what will happen to Lyndon's organic brussels sprout farm, illuminating the intertwined nature of Lee's narrative, which begins and ends with the influences of the seemingly minor ice-cream scooper (and bearer of the chocolate ice-cream fragrance that lingers on the *shiatsu* mat): Jan de Leuw.

This may be food's central feature in this novel; Lee's "organic" message that everything is truly interconnected. The series of coincidences, reunions, and serendipitous meetings are integral to the novel's overall theme of organic unity. In the first chapter, while Laura is treating Lyndon's neck spasm by massaging other parts of his body, she tells him that "'it's all connected. . . . Everyone assumes that things are isolated, but they're not. Every part speaks to another.'"[49] Lyndon begins the novel as a hermetic and isolated individual and spends the weekend, and the bulk of the narrative, coming to terms with the many different encumbrances and relationships that he has with his family, lovers, enemies, friends, and friends of friends. Lee emphasizes the sense of connection and community, of interconnection and interrelatedness, that the characters all share with one another.

While the characters exist as individuals with their own separate stories, Lee highlights the organic wholeness of the narrative through the confluence of the characters' various story lines in the climax of the novel. In the penultimate chapter, all the characters we have been following converge on Lyndon's farm, through either their direct presence or their indirectly influential actions, all of which culminate in the dramatic unlocking of the barn door and the secret that Lyndon harbors there. While Ed Kitchell (head of the Centurion Group) and local sheriff Stephen Lemke (ex-husband of Lyndon's ex-lover) believe that the barn is full of marijuana, the open barn doors reveal an elaborate art sculpture of "bent rods and wires, hammered sheets and plates, all welded together and twisting intricately into thousands of branches . . . a sandblasted, oxidized, patinaed grove, which shimmered in luminous shades of red, orange, black, blue and green."[50] The metal jungle that Lyndon had been working on for seventeen years "was not art," as the narrator pointedly tells us, but an organic creation that mirrors the messy, conjoined nature of humans existing together, a metaphor for the interrelationships of the characters themselves:

> It was a single, massive linked sculpture that would be impossible to separate from the barn, that could never be dismantled or moved or installed in any gallery or museum. And while the individual parts were lovely and exquisite, with

their workmanship and detail, the whole made no sense—no sense at all. It had no shape, no definition, no pattern or apparent meaning.[51]

The sculpture in the barn is like life itself, integrally linked together without apparent purpose or meaning and impossible to separate one part from another. This is also the message in Lee's narrative: that Lyndon and Woody, try as they might, cannot escape the bonds connecting them to others, in ways large and small, in the narrative, bonds that become solidified through the shared meals and their relationship to various foods and foodways in *Wrack and Ruin*.

Conclusion: Right Actions and the Call to Social Justice

The Fourth Noble Truth was that the end of suffering could be attained through the pursuit of morality, meditation, and wisdom, as described by the Eightfold Path: right view, right intention, right speech, right action, right livelihood, right effort, right mindfulness, right concentration.

Don Lee, *Wrack and Ruin*, 320

In the brief concluding chapter of *Wrack and Ruin*, Woody and Lyndon are joined together: no longer does one brother's perspective exclude the other. Instead, the narrator allows us into each sibling's actions and thoughts, and the novel ends with a scene of commensality: the two brothers join in eating dinner. By combining Lyndon's and Woody's perspectives in this final chapter, Lee emphasizes the organic message of his novel: that the two brothers, who are vastly different from each other and who may never be the best of friends, are nonetheless connected to each other. Both have suffered emotional, psychological, and physical injuries throughout the weekend. Quite literally, both brothers are wounded: Woody is on crutches with a broken toe and sprained ribs, and Lyndon has a sprained knee and his left arm in a sling. Each brother sustained his injuries because he put himself in harm's way while rescuing others, and each brother does so not once but twice, hurting himself in order to protect someone else.[52] Lyndon and Woody, in other words, try to do what is right. According to the epigraph to this conclusion, the end to suffering can be achieved by following a path of right living; one of the central tenets of Buddhism is understanding the sense of interconnectedness that all beings, human and nonhuman, share with one another.

Right living and right action are prominent ideas in this novel, emphasizing the themes of organicism and justice. The fact that Lyndon does not sell his farm to the Centurion Group but to a nonprofit land conservancy group can be interpreted as the right action, the right thing for Lyndon to do in terms of his organic connection to the environment. It can also be seen as an act of environmental justice: his decision is the opposite of moral or ethical compromise and affirms the values of preservation and conservation.

Indeed, the idea of doing the right thing, despite failure and injury, is continually emphasized throughout the narrative. Trudy acknowledges that while she and her partner, Margot, had been unable to save the snowy plover, a bird species displaced when the Centurion Group began constructing the golf course and luxury homes, the birds' demise at the hands (or beaks) of predatory ravens causes Trudy to become introspective: "But you know, I'm okay with it. I can accept it. It's part of the natural cycle of things, not something caused by people, so we did our job. Now we're going to another project, in Hawaii."[53] Trudy understands that while it was regrettable that the plover chicks could not be saved, the attempt was worthwhile, and she and Margot will continue their environmental activism in another location. Trudy's circumspection reinforces the idea of organicism promoted in the novel, as earlier she tells Woody: "'We have the atoms of our ancestors in each of us. You have Mahatma Gandhi, the Buddha, inside you right now! The whole planet, everyone dead and alive, is breathing together! Isn't that remarkable to think?'"[54] Trudy's exhortation reinforces the message that we can obtain from Lee's narrative: we all are interconnected, and we all are part of an organic whole. Whether we are hurt in the process of right action or we are able to save others is not the point; the point is that it is always worthwhile to act because our actions tie us to a larger community.

Don Lee creates an Asian American community in this novel not by creating stereotypes of Asian behaviors; instead, his community in *Wrack and Ruin* is populated by many people who just happen to be Asian American, along with their identities as farmers, actresses, environmentalists, and artists. Yet the deliberateness of creating a work that has so many characters of Asian ethnic descent—and of having two Asian American characters, Lyndon and Dalton, question the notion of how Asian American art is perceived—speaks to the politics always inherent in the term "Asian American." My last claim is that Lee's invocation of the term "Asian American" in his novel signals an understanding of racial rather than ethnic or national politics. His characters do not think about being Korean or about their U.S. citizenship. Their concerns deliberately pertain to how they, as Asian American artists of color, are interpreted by others, as racially Asian in America, as always interpellated through their racial identity. To invoke terms like "Asian American" is always to invoke issues of racial politics and what it means to be a racial minority with the weight of anti-Asian racism and oppression that circulates within the term "Asian American."

Actions and eating in an Asian American politicized framework remind readers that our most prosaic, everyday consumptive choices, whether what we consume in our kitchens or the local cinema multiplex or the art museum can become a call to social justice. The meals shared and food farmed in Lee's narrative underscore the organic connections among land, people, and items of consumption that transcend traditional boundaries of ethnicity and race and complicate our notion of affiliation and affinity. As literary critic Wenying Xu observes, "Sharing food plays a central role in the formation of social groupings. . . . We eat together, and sometimes cook together, to affirm our feelings of family, community, friendship, love, and comfort."[55]

The last pages of the novel depict the antagonistic brothers eating, their enmity not resolved but briefly suspended during their shared meal, one that Lyndon prepares: steamed rice, grilled steaks, and braised brussels sprouts, which are described in fine detail: "He had browned slices of thick diced bacon, sautéed them with shallots, added chicken stock, thyme, parsley, as well as some sherry, salt, and pepper, and a bay leaf, then the sprouts, brought everything to a boil, and simmered it, covered, for fifteen minutes."[56] Although Lee leaves us with a recipe for brussels sprouts, what he actually leaves readers with is a sense of interconnectedness, of briefly being in-the-moment and harmonious, with someone who is close enough to be your brother but whom you may regard as your greatest enemy. In this novel, food serves to temporarily, if not permanently, bind people together. The last line of Lee's novel may very well describe not only the meal that Woody and Lyndon eat together but the narrative that readers of *Wrack and Ruin* have just consumed: "Now he served the sprouts with the steak and the rice to his brother—a simple meal, not much to it, just the basic elements, but filling."[57]

Notes

1. Anita Mannur, *Culinary Fictions: Food in South Asian Diasporic Culture* (Philadelphia: Temple University Press, 2010), 173.

2. Ibid., 177.

3. I want to be very clear that when I use the term "Asian American," I do so in the racialized and politicized sense, which recognizes the social construction of "Asian American" as a racial signifier but also acknowledges that just because race is constructed, it does not mean that it is not real or that its effects (institutional racism/white privilege and supremacy) are not deeply felt and experienced.

4. For more on the history of the Asian American movement, see Daryl Maeda, *Chain's of Babylon: The Rise of Asian America* (Minneapolis: University of Minnesota Press, 2009);

William Wei, *The Asian American Movement* (Philadelphia: Temple University Press, 1993); Frank Wu, *Yellow: Race in American beyond Black and White* (New York: Basic Books, 2003); and Helen Zia, *Asian American Dreams: The Emergence of an American People* (New York: Farrar, Straus & Giroux, 2001).

5. See the following books by Gish Jen: *Typical American* (Boston: Houghton Mifflin, 1991); *Mona in the Promised Land* (New York: Vintage Books, 1997); *The Love Wife* (New York: Vintage Books, 2005); and *World and Town* (New York: Knopf, 2010).

6. See the following books by Jhumpa Lahiri: *Interpreter of Maladies* (New York: Mariner Books, 1999); *The Namesake* (New York: Mariner Books, 2004); and *Unaccustomed Earth* (New York: Knopf, 2008).

7. See the following books by Chang-rae Lee: *Native Speaker* (New York: Riverhead Books, 1996); *A Gesture Life* (New York: Riverhead Books, 1999); *Aloft* (New York: Riverhead Books, 2004); and *The Surrendered* (New York: Riverhead Books, 2010).

8. See the following books by Monique Truong: *The Book of Salt* (Boston: Houghton Mifflin Harcourt, 2003); and *Bitter in the Mouth* (New York: Random House, 2010).

9. See the following books by Don Lee: *Yellow: Stories* (New York: Norton, 2001); and *Wrack and Ruin*). Other Asian American writers who have either written outside their Asian ethnic ancestry or have included Asian ethnic American characters beyond those of their heritage are Shawn Wong, *American Knees* (New York: Simon & Schuster, 1995); Susan Choi, *American Woman* (New York: Harper, 2003); and Han Ong, *Fixer Chao* (New York: Farrar, Straus & Giroux, 2001). This, of course, does not include American writers of Asian ancestry writing about non-Asian American characters; for example, the works of Sigrid Nunez, with the exception of her first novel *Feather on the Breath of God* (New York: HarperCollins, 1995), which feature non-Asian Americans or de-racinated characters who appear to identify as white. For more on Asian American writers writing about non–Asian American characters and the definition of Asian American literature, see my "The Place of Transgressive Texts in Asian American Epistemology," *Modern Fiction Studies* 56, no. 1 (2010): 205–25.

10. Works by such eminent scholars such as Yen Le Espiritu, *Asian American Women and Men: Labor, Laws, and Love* (Lanham, MD: Rowman & Littlefield, 2008); Josephine Lee, *Performing Asian America: Race and Ethnicity on the Contemporary Stage* (Philadelphia: Temple University Press, 1997); Huping Ling, *Asian America: Forming New Communities, Expanding Boundaries* (New Brunswick, NJ: Rutgers University Press, 2009); and Ronald Takaki, *Strangers from a Different Shore: A History of Asian Americans* (New York: Little Brown, 1990) all use the phrase "Asian American" in the titles of their works, yet the works themselves look at specific Asian ethnic examples, even while acknowledging the racialized aspects of Asian ethnic Americans in their studies.

11. Sau-ling Cynthia Wong, "Denationalization Reconsidered," *Amerasia Journal* 21, nos. 1and 2 (1995): 17–18.

12. For a detailed genealogy of the fortune cookie as an American invention, see Jennifer 8. Lee, *The Fortune Cookie Chronicles: Adventures in the World of Chinese Food* (New York: Twelve, 2009).

13. See Trevor Corson, *The Zen of Fish: The Story of Sushi from Samurai to Supermarket* (New York: HarperCollins, 2007).

14. How much one can consider pan-Asian food to be "Asian American" food may be debatable; however, given the plethora of pan-Asian eateries in the United States and the

popularity of fusion cuisine in general in the United States, pan-Asian dishes and Asian-fusion food seem to be uniquely Asian and American creations. For a good analysis of pan-Asian fusion food, nationalism, and narratives see Anita Mannur, "Easy Exoticism: Culinary Performances of Indianness," in her *Culinary Fictions: Food in South Asian Diasporic Culture* (Philadelphia: Temple University Press, 2010).

15. *Loco moco* is a favorite dish among people living in Hawai'i. It was developed at a Japanese American–owned diner in the late 1940s and is composed of a hamburger patty on a bed of rice, topped with a fried egg and gravy. Here, rice, a staple of many Asian cuisines, and a hamburger, the quintessential American food, are combined into an Asian American food staple as *loco moco*, which does not seem to be widely known outside the Hawaiian Islands.

16. The subject of my first book, *Consumption and Identity in Asian American Coming-of-Age Novels* (New York: Routledge, 2004), argues in part that the Asian American bildungsroman featuring foodways tied to ethnic identity serves as a counterdiscourse to the racist depictions of Asians in America that have been conflated through their association with various foodways. For example, Chinese immigrants were vilified as rat eaters.

17. Specifically, I am thinking about the model minority myth, which is mainly associated with Asian Americans and valorizes their accomplishments as minorities in America, with the unspoken comparison with African Americans, Latinos, and Native Americans, implying that these supposedly "darker" minority communities should also pick themselves up by their bootstraps and achieve success as Asian Americans did. For more on a critique of the model minority myth, see Rosalind Chou and Joe Feagin, *The Myth of the Model Minority: Asian Americans Facing Racism* (Boulder, CO: Paradigm Publishers, 2008); and Stacy Lee, *Unraveling the "Model Minority" Stereotype: Listening to Asian American Youth* (New York: Teacher's College Press, 1996).

18. The term "Amerasian" refers specifically to the children of a male U.S. serviceman and an Asian woman that were conceived during one of the many wars in Asia that the United States participated in during the twentieth century.

19. Readers familiar with the geography of the California Bay Area will quickly recognize the town of Half Moon Bay, disguised as the fictionalized village of Rosarita Bay. Similarly, San Vincente stands in for San Mateo, although other prominent cities, such as Los Angeles and San Francisco, exist as themselves, as do the major freeways running through these coastal towns and hamlets.

20. Told in the genre of a neo-noir detective-style novel, Lee's first novel, *Country of Origin* (New York: Norton, 2004), takes place in Japan, and hinges on the search for what happened to a black-Japanese Amerasian woman, Lisa Countryman.

21. The one rupture of the focalization taking place through the perspective of one of the Song brothers can be seen in chapter 9, which opens with the declaration that "the first annual Rosarita Bay chili and chowder festival was a miniature version of the town's larger, more established pumpkin festival. . . . An inspector from the San Vincente County Health Department was on-site to ensure that the guidelines for food treatment, per its environmental health standards, were being strictly enforced" (284). While Lyndon could ostensibly have this information, he is not introduced until a page and a paragraph later.

22. Lee, *Wrack and Ruin*, 15.

23. Ibid., 25.

24. Lee, *Yellow*, 286. Readers of *Yellow* will remember Brian and his brother Patrick as the half-Filipino, half-white sons of Davis and Lita Fenny.

25. While the Asian ethnicities mentioned in *Wrack and Ruin* include Korean, Chinese, Filipino, Samoan, Japanese, and Vietnamese, notably absent are characters from the South Asian diaspora. Indeed, the novel's Asian American characters in this work and in Lee's other works are predominantly East Asian American. Although Lee is not responsible for including all Asian ethnicities (to do so would be impossible, given the breadth and scope of what the term "Asian American" covers), I believe it is worth noting that even as his novel attends to certain members of the Asian diaspora, it is not a comprehensive look at what it means to be Asian American.

26. Lee, *Wrack and Ruin*, 193.

27. Ibid., 72.

28. The reference to "Tiger parents" is a play on the "Tiger mother" stereotype promulgated by Amy Chua's *Battle Hymn of the Tiger Mother* (New York: Bloomsbury Publishing, 2011), which seems less about how to properly parent in the Asian style and more an exercise in narcissistic memoir writing.

29. Lee, *Wrack and Ruin*, 76.

30. Alice Yang, *Why Asia?* (New York: New York University Press, 1998) 104.

31. Yang's book is listed among the works that Don Lee referenced while writing *Wrack and Ruin*, and her influence can be most strongly seen in Lyndon's internal flashback during his date with Laura Diaz-McClatchy when he recalls his former life as a celebrated Asian American artist.

32. Lee, *Wrack and Ruin*, 219.

33. Lee, *Wrack and Ruin*, 267. The character Dalton Lee seems to be modeled partly on Asian American director Justin Lin (*Better Luck Tomorrow*) through the similarity of the two independent filmmakers who made a splash at the Sundance film festival with their Asian American movies. However, the ideas about the constraints placed on Asian American artists, as well as the fact that Dalton Lee's character is an avid windsurfer, suggests that Don Lee (also a self-proclaimed avid windsurfer, according to his website, www.don-lee.com) is using Dalton Lee as a mouthpiece for his own frustrations with being pigeonholed as an Asian American writer.

34. Lee, *Wrack and Ruin*, 268.

35. Lee, *Wrack and Ruin*, 81. Nam Le, a writer who was born in Vietnam, raised in Australia, educated in the United States, and currently divides his time between the United States and Australia, also ruminates, through his fictional characters, about the belief among writers that "ethnic literature's hot" (9) and that writers of color "exploit" (10) their ethnic backgrounds and life experiences in order to win book contracts. For more, see Nam Le, "Love and Honor and Pity and Pride and Compassion and Sacrifice," the first story in Le's debut collection *The Boat* (New York: Knopf, 2008).

36. Lee, *Wrack and Ruin*, 219.

37. Margo Machida, *Asia/America* (New York: Asia Society Galleries and the New Press, 1994) 67.

38. Lee, *Wrack and Ruin*, 267.

39. Ibid., 220–21.

40. Ibid., 222.

41. Machida, *Asia/America*, 108.

42. Indeed, Lee continues to wrestle with the question of what defines Asian American art in his latest novel, *The Collective* (New York: Norton, 2012).

43. The only character of Asian descent who is not American is Yi Ling Ling. But as someone who was born in Hong Kong (a very cosmopolitan city), educated in England, and travels around the globe as a goodwill ambassador (she is headed for Vietnam at the novel's close), Ling Ling is, in many ways, the kind of world citizen unbound by simple allegiances of nation and race that Eleanor Ty writes about: "one of those mobile, cosmopolitan citizens" (141). For more, see Eleanor Ty, *Unfastened: Globality and Asian North American Narratives* (Minneapolis: University of Minnesota Press, 2010).

44. Martin Manalansan IV, "The Empire of Food," in *Gastropolis: Food and New York City*, ed. Anne Hauck-Lawson and Jonathan Deutsch (New York: Columbia University Press, 2009), 102.

45. For more on the connection between mass-media and popular culture depictions of Asian Americans and food that have typecast them as stereotypes, see my *Consumption and Identity*.

46. Lee, *Wrack and Ruin*, 86. By saying "Forest Gump–like catalog" I am referring to the scene in the film *Forest Gump* in which Bubba lists all the ways he knows how to prepare shrimp, an extensive cataloging that appears to last for several days.

47. Lee, *Wrack and Ruin*, 164–65.

48. Ibid., 50.

49. Ibid., 18.

50. Ibid., 313–14.

51. Ibid., 315.

52. Lyndon first pushes Yi Ling Ling out of danger when the roof of the Boat House bar collapses; the following day he pushes his ex-girlfriend, Sheila Lemke, out of the way of a rampaging elephant set loose during the chili and chowder festival. Woody rescues Margot and Trudy from the same rampaging elephant; the following morning, while rushing Lyndon's dog Bob to the vet, he breaks his foot and strains his neck in a car accident, all in an attempt to save Bob's life.

53. Lee, *Wrack and Ruin*, 277.

54. Ibid., 189.

55. Wenying Xu, *Eating Identities* (Honolulu: University of Hawai'i Press, 2008) 3.

56. Lee, *Wrack and Ruin*, 332–33.

57. Ibid., 333.

17

Devouring Hawai'i

Food, Consumption, and Contemporary Art

MARGO MACHIDA

For contemporary visual artists of Asian and Pacific backgrounds, tropes of food—embedded in lived experience and intermeshed with themes of place, material culture, commerce, and migration—provide a plethora of multi-sited metaphors and iconographies for global circulation, intersections, and cross connections among peoples and cultures. This growing body of work, here mainly by artists from Hawai'i of Asian or part-Asian backgrounds, offers insights into the expressive formation of globally mediated localism that underscores how the local is shaped and transformed by the global, and how diverse external influences have long been appropriated and reworked for local needs and circumstances.

Over the past few decades, the study of food has accelerated across a range of disciplines. Multifaceted issues of food, foodways, and food politics—sometimes addressing volatile matters like access to natural resources, land, and sources of nourishment to sustain diverse populations—have similarly become subjects for art. Fundamental to existence, food is an indispensable component of human culture that confers a common connection and source of contention between peoples. As a locus for social identification and a signifier of collective presence, food is a medium for sharing and exchange, its practices and rituals a bearer and catalyst of historical and personal memory and a vehicle for symbolic resistance and social critique. Food equally exists in complex relation to material culture and, like other commodities, acquires histories, values, and "social lives" through human usage that are invested with multiple layers of meaning.[1] Issues of food and nutrition—including dietary preferences, and its production, procurement, preparation, presentation, and consumption—thus open in many directions to examine individuals' and groups' understandings of their connections to place, other human beings, their historic and cultural origins, and relations of power.

Besides connecting human beings, food is tied to basic biological requirements for survival; has material, symbolic, and sentimental value; and bridges the sacred and profane. Resonant and evocative, food's links to bodily appetites and sensory experiences invite considerations of the immediate needs and desires driving human behavior. Associating bodily imagery with food offers a medium for artists' contention with wider social, cultural, and historical issues. Closely tying individual and collective experiences, the body serves as a sign of presence and physical engagement in the world, a focal point for social and historical texts, and a manifestation of the artist as a performing subject. For instance, in the 2005 work *Lovely Hula Hands* by Puni Kukahiko, multiple incarnations of a sinuously undulating, seminude hula girl cast in edible chocolate and molded by this Native Hawaiian artist from mass-produced tourists' souvenirs, challenge how the figure of the Polynesian woman and, by implication, Polynesia itself, are being served up for Western delectation.[2]

Based on my current research with artists of Asian and indigenous Hawaiian backgrounds, the following artworks suggest the breadth of expressive and critical possibilities presented by food as an entry point to trace and question the continuum of historical trajectories, geopolitical conditions, and systems of production, distribution, and consumption that have brought together peoples and cultures from around the world in many Pacific lands. Besides emphasizing the United States' long-standing and intimate ties to Hawai'i and the Pacific region, these projects—many by artists of mixed descent who reside in both Hawai'i and its continental U.S. diaspora—cast into relief the distinctive character of Hawai'i as a dynamic transpacific zone of contact and mixing between indigenous and migrant peoples. Here the native presence often has a profound influence on diasporic Asian lives, sensibilities, and perceptions of place. Indeed, the first immigrants from Asia—Chinese sailors who soon married Native Hawaiian women—had arrived in Hawai'i by the late eighteenth century.[3] Drawing on recorded interviews with individual artists who use food-related imagery and themes to assert larger social claims of citizenship, positionality, and belonging, these works offer insights into the complex social and physical environments of Hawai'i and island nations in the Pacific region. Their art, being open to the complexity of lived experience in the islands, delineates topographies, human relations, societal positions, and emotional responses shaped by indigenism, the historic impact of colonialism, annexation, settler cultures, and an outside military presence; by sociocultural hybridization via migration and transnational flows of labor, capital, goods, and ideas; and by international tourism and its marketing through tropes of an idyllic tropical paradise.

Figure 17.1. Puni Kukahiko, *Lovely Hula Hands*, 2005, chocolate, 9" × 3" × 3", University of Hawai'i Commons Gallery, Honolulu. Collection of the artist.

Circulations

Lynne Yamamoto

New England–based, Honolulu-born sculptor Lynne Yamamoto is intrigued by the ways in which people's lived experiences, material circumstances, and the environment of Hawai'i have been transformed and imprinted by larger systemic conditions. Stirred by personal associations, her scrutiny of specific items, including foods, consumer goods, and the built environment, is based on an affective experience of her physical surroundings, influenced by her heritage as the descendant of Japanese migrant plantation workers, some of whom worked as servants in the households of American missionary families. Her background has made Yamamoto sensitive to the class and racialized hierarchies of the island society in which she was raised. Through poetically evocative assemblages of objects, a hands-on artisanal use of materials, and a research-based investigative approach, she works outward from the personal to produce layered engagements with historic patterns of global circulation across national and cultural boundaries.

The 2010 installation entitled *Genteel* has three major components: *Grandfather's Shed (Lana'i City, Island of Lana'i)*, a small-scale rendering in marble of a humble work shed built of salvaged and scrap materials by the artist's grandfather; *Insect Immigrants, after Zimmerman (1948) (Hawai'i)* composed of white linen

Figure 17.2. Lynne Yamamoto, *Provisions, Post-War (Pacific Asia and U.S.)*, detail of installation view, *Genteel*, 2010, vitreous china, Oresman Gallery, Smith College, Northampton, MA. Photograph by Lynne Yamamoto. Courtesy of the artist.

doilies roughly embroidered with images of local insects; and *Provisions, Post-War (Pacific Asia and U.S.)*, containing sculptural objects based on popular commercial foods ubiquitous in Hawai'i and the Asia-Pacific region. In *Provisions, Post-War (Pacific Asia and U.S.)*, white vitreous china castings of mass-produced food containers that Yamamoto associates with Hawai'i's working-class cuisine—SPAM vienna sausage, evaporated milk, and sardines—are arrayed in a row like a typical shop display. Among these prosaic provisions recalled from the artist's postwar childhood, SPAM has a particular resonance because its introduction is linked to the World War II American military presence in the islands. War is "probably the single most powerful instrument of dietary change in human experience," since basic resources on a mass scale are diverted toward the war effort.[4] Spurred in part by the civilian population's wartime food shortages and the military's need for nonperishable foods to feed the troops in the field, SPAM became an internationally recognized commodity. SPAM, with its distinctive label and package, a round-edged rectangular metal can, is a processed pork product developed by the Hormel Foods Corporation in 1937. Integrated into numerous ethnic dishes in Hawai'i, including the popular Japanese-derived finger food SPAM *musubi*, SPAM has since been absorbed into many nations' diets and modified to suit local tastes.[5] Transported along with military supplies, SPAM followed the

U.S. armed forces' progress, ultimately reaching populations across the Pacific and Europe. Today residents of Hawai'i, Guam, and the Northern Mariana Islands are reputed to be the largest consumers of SPAM per capita in the United States and its territories. Partly as a legacy of the expanded U.S. troop presence in Pacific Asia after World War II, there currently are sizable markets for SPAM also in Japan and Okinawa, the Philippines, South Korea, and China.

Michael Arcega and Michel Tuffery

Yamamoto's engagement with the transpacific circulation and consumption of processed Western foods and their relationship to war finds symmetry in a series of mixed-media works directly incorporating SPAM by Manila-born, San Francisco–based conceptual artist Michael Arcega. His 2001 *SPAM/MAPS: World* consists of a world map based on the European-devised Mercator projection, whose landmasses are formed entirely of carved slabs of hardened SPAM, a mock-cartographic device emblematic of "America's ongoing influence on many nations."[6] The related 2007 work, *SPAM/MAPS: Oceania*, concentrates on the numerous Pacific island nations in which SPAM became "a standard source of meat" in the wake of that global conflict.[7] Along the same lines, during the 1990s New Zealand–based sculptor Michel Tuffery produced a series of life-size renditions of steers fashioned from flattened corned beef tins to reference the historic impact of colonialism, Western influences, war, and global trade on island life in oceanic cultures, through their increasing dependence on, and taste for, such imported goods, which have often become local status items associated with Western-style modernity.[8] Tuffery, who is of Samoan, Tahitian, Cook Island, and European descent, has also spoken publicly of the destructive impact of the absorption of this food into contemporary oceanic diets, leading to the spread of dietary diseases like diabetes and generating substantial waste that finds its way into the surrounding ocean.[9]

Whereas Arcega's *SPAM/MAPS* series incorporates a perishable food and Tuffery's slyly humorous reconstructions gesture to the living animals from which these highly processed meat products are derived, Yamamoto is more interested in referencing the commercial goods themselves. Rather than simply reproducing such easily recognizable popular consumer goods, the artist defamiliarizes each item by casting its simple manufactured form in unadorned vitreous china, a glazed ceramic material today typically used in sinks and toilets. Seeking to shift the viewers' perception, the artist strips out readily identifiable traits, thereby disengaging the objects from their familiar incarnation as visibly branded goods. The artist, long fascinated by the "circles of meaning

Figure 17.3. Michael Arcega, *SPAM/MAPS: World*, 2001, SPAM luncheon meat and pins, 3′ × 4′ × 2″. Courtesy of the artist.

that emanate from different objects," here invites audiences to see them afresh and to more closely contemplate, as she puts it, "the idea of the SPAM can, and what that means in a larger sense."[10] Indeed, the use of vitreous china as a sculptural medium amplifies commercial products' association with larger historic patterns of global trade and emphasizes the long-standing connections between the Asian Pacific and the Atlantic worlds by evoking the circulation of highly valued Chinese porcelain wares, which were exported to Europe and then to Britain's North American colonies beginning in the mid-1700s.

Keith Tallett

Keith Tallett, a mixed-media artist who lives on the Big Island of Hawai'i, has an abiding interest in Hawaiian popular culture, especially those aspects that retain a close connection to the land. Tallett creates a distinctly local sensibility by scavenging imagery and materials from his immediate surroundings, using techniques from vernacular idioms like tattooing and surfboard shaping to inform and to augment his formal training in studio art. His conception of what it means to be local comes from his mixed lineage as the descendant of indigenous Hawaiians and Portuguese who migrated from the Madeira Islands in the 1880s to work in Hawai'i's sugar plantations. Throughout his formative years, Tallett gained great respect for the resourcefulness of both sides of his family to sustain themselves. Among the relatives that Tallett cites as having affected his life is his maternal grandmother's second husband, who was of Chinese descent. Besides producing much of their food by raising livestock and planting small gardens,[11] Tallett watched his father crafting surfboards, his uncle carving wood and weaving fishnets, and his grandmother sewing much of the family's clothing and traditional Hawaiian quilts—all influences and skills he credits with shaping his approach to art making, the materials he seeks out, and the subjects and life ways that most attract his attention.[12]

In striving to "explore the blurred lines that define authenticity" and informed by his own mixed heritage, Tallett is captivated by the ways in which living things, goods, and ideas from around the world have long been accepted, assimilated, and transformed by the native society.[13] Locally cultivated foods, therefore, figure prominently as subjects in the artist's recent pieces. These include nonindigenous fruits like the Cavendish banana, and "invasive species" like the strawberry guava (which often crowds out native plants), both of which have become part of Hawai'i's cuisine. *Tattoo Williams,* for example, is a 2010 series of color inkjet prints produced from digital photographs featuring a type of Cavendish banana known as the Williams. The Cavendish, whose origins are traced to Southeast Asia, is one of more than seventy banana species. One of the world's most widely grown types today, it can be found on farms and agricultural estates extending from the Philippines and Southeast Asia to India, as well as in Africa, the Caribbean, and Central and South America. Named after William Spencer Cavendish, the sixth duke of Devonshire (1790–1858), whose greenhouse in England nurtured an early specimen, the Cavendish was brought to Samoa in the 1830s by the English missionary John Williams before being transported to Fiji, Tonga, and other regions in the Pacific.[14] Introduced into Hawai'i around 1855, the Cavendish was, for a time, a significant export crop.[15] Although the Hawaiian Islands remain the largest grower of bananas in the United States,[16] they no longer are a major commercial producer for sales abroad.[17] Nevertheless, in the context of Hawai'i, such imagery evokes the local impact of U.S. corporations with multinational operations like the United Fruit Company (and its successor, Chiquita Brands International) and the Standard Fruit Company (now Dole Food Company). This imagery also has historic, material, and biotic linkages—via cultivation, crossbreeding, and transplantation—which arose in the post-Columbian age as globalized networks of circulation designed to enrich Western interests joined ecosystems and plantations to distant markets.

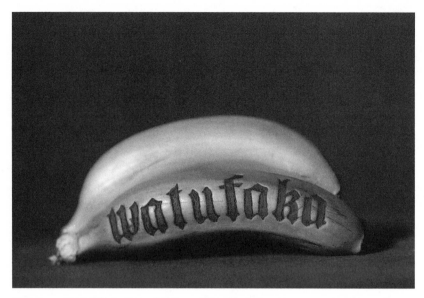

Figure 17.4. Keith Tallett, *Tattoo Williams (Watufaka)*, 2010. Banana, tattooed by artist. Archival inkjet print on cotton rag, dimensions variable. Courtesy of the artist.

Using a tattoo gun, a modern mechanical inking device designed to rapidly imprint indelible markings on human flesh, Tallett hand-inscribes Cavendish bananas harvested near his home with various texts, numbers, and maps that he associates with Hawai'i. Each photograph in the *Tattoo Williams* series documents, for the artist, the permanent "residue" that results from the act of tattooing directly on the fresh skin of highly perishable fruit.[18] Among these inscriptions are an outline drawing of the Hawaiian Island chain, as well as "Watufaka," a local pidgin English slang expression (translated as "what you fucker?"), and "808," the islands' area code. Both "Watufaka" and "808" are emblazoned on the bananas in ornate Old English script to resemble the gang and prison tattoos that are a familiar feature of contemporary continental U.S. urban street culture, music, surf, and hip-hop fashion, which themselves have been adapted and marketed in Hawai'i to identify with island-style localism. In incorporating such overt commercial influences into his work, Tallett takes an ecumenical view of the role that popular devices like logos have in the social environment, as an expression of "local pride" and a means of allowing diverse people (including those born outside the islands) to identify with and support local culture and interests.

Since subsistence farming and fishing, and gathering staples like fruit remain important to many people in Hawai'i, the use of bananas as a central motif in *Tattoo Williams* stresses that this locally available food is not regarded simply as a lucrative commercial crop but has become another means by which Hawai'i provides for its peoples' needs. Much as gang tattoos reinforce group solidarity, by tattooing fruit Tallett is asserting a symbolic claim on local resources for his fellow Hawaiians, thereby signaling their common purpose as primary stakeholders in the islands' fate. The impetus for Tallett's work and his focus on intersections between the vernacular and the commercial remain immediate, personal, and grounded in what appears around him. He thus regards the use of an expression popularized throughout the region like "Watufaka" and the similar slogans "Aloha Army," "Soljah," and "Warrior" as organic to the contemporary island sensibility. Such colloquial sayings are a familiar way of giving voice to common attitudes in Hawai'i toward outsiders, since they appear regularly on locally produced T-shirts and car bumper stickers, and even tattooed on people's backs—and also convey the defiant, deeply ambivalent attitude of many born and raised in Hawai'i toward their economic overdependence on outside markets and tourism. Or as Tallett puts it, "Welcome to sunny Hawai'i and [now] get the fuck out."[19]

Despite the artist's confrontational posture, *Tattoo Williams*—which is part of a larger body of photographs, paintings, and mixed-media sculptures entitled *Militia*—does not seek to advance any specific politics or program of local resistance. Rather, by loosely using the metaphor of a volunteer citizen force mobilized for the islands' defense, Tallett regards such eye-catching images and phrases as "tools" to help spur awareness of the need to protect Hawai'i's land, environment, and resources. This stance both embodies the artist's pragmatic concern with how local land and resources are used and allocated and points to how control over these matters is very differently perceived by powerful outside interests like agribusinesses, the tourist industry, and real estate developers.

Kalo as a Cultural Signifier and Locus of Resistance

For many people in Hawai'i, the cultivation of indigenous food plants and the teaching of traditional agricultural practices that respect the land and its resources are seen as vital to perpetuating the values and spiritual beliefs of its native culture. Central among these plants is the *kalo*, also known as taro. A tuber, it was introduced to the islands by the Hawaiians' seafaring ancestors millennia ago and is a staple food in the indigenous Hawaiians' diet as the source of poi. *Kalo*, considered a traditional ancestor of the Hawaiian people, is a hallowed figure in the Kumulipo, the Hawaiian creation chant. In this sacral tradition, Hāloa, the *kalo* plant, originally emerged from the grave of the stillborn first son of the union between the Sky Father Wākea and his daughter Hoʻohōkūkalani, following the deceased sibling's burial in island soil.[20] Accordingly, Native Hawaiians trace their genealogy through the land and thus see their social relationships as based on this shared ancestral lineage.

In pieces produced over the past decade, not only do representations of the *kalo* regularly appear as a key motif, but also the living plants themselves have been directly incorporated into art installations. In an island context in which taro farming is actively pursued in efforts to reinvigorate Hawaiian culture and to foster ecologically sustainable agricultural practices based on traditional uses of the land, art projects involving *kalo* serve a valuable dual purpose. They preserve the integrity of indigenous tradition even as they advance public engagement by extending the contemporary life worlds of Native Hawaiians to galleries and museums.[21]

Kaili Chun

The wide-ranging works of Honolulu-born sculptor and installation artist Kaili Chun, who describes herself as a Native Hawaiian of indigenous, Chinese, and European ancestry, engage the ongoing "challenge[s] of continuing to exist as a Hawaiian," given their displacement from the land and loss of agency extending from the initial penetration by U.S. settlers and business and military interests through the wholesale importation of foreign labor and commercial and industrial development.[22] In expressing an indigenous standpoint, Chun was inspired by the 1970s renaissance of Hawaiian culture that began when activists revived and reasserted the Native Hawaiian language and culture in all its forms—arts, crafts, music, and dance, as well as traditional agricultural, healing, and deep-water navigational skills. To this end, Chun apprenticed herself to Wright Bowman Sr., a master Hawaiian wood carver and canoe builder, and she also pursued academic training in architecture and studio art. Drawing on those precedents, her approach is quite contemporary even as it concurrently embodies a distinctively "Hawaiian epistemology" that derives from a primal spiritual connection to place.[23] For Chun, this outlook is not motivated by an atavistic or romantic idealization of the precontact past but conveys a prevailing Native Hawaiian ethos grounded in a cultural view of local topography formed around the sacralization of the *ʻāina*, the land itself.

For an untitled installation from the mid-1990s, Chun fashioned a group of fired, glazed ceramics to resemble *pōhaku*, a common local volcanic stone, as a compound sign to embody the land of Hawaiʻi and the people who arose from it. To convey a sense of how Hawaiians remain "bound, manipulated, and whitewashed" by ways of thinking that arose in the wake of their culture's "colonization and commodification," each rocklike form is tightly encircled with rebar—twisted steel rods used to reinforce poured concrete—and inlaid with screws and bullet casings.[24] All these materials were discarded construction and military supplies scavenged by the artist from the Pearl Harbor Naval Shipyard. Through the incorporation of these man-made elements, Chun is simultaneously alluding to the employment of many Native Hawaiians by the shipyard (part of the sizable U.S. military presence on the islands) and to how the physical environment is being radically transformed by non-Hawaiian interests.

In another equally evocative project that features a living *kalo* plant, Chun also affirms that the spiritual values that are the basis of Hawaiian culture endure. In this untitled installation from the late 1990s (ca. 1996–1998) a *kalo* plant that was immersed in running water and set in a cairn-like basin fashioned from volcanic rock flourished for the duration of the exhibition. Symbolically protecting the installation's living focal point is an encircling ring of polished wooden spears crafted by the artist and suspended by chains from the ceiling, their menacing sharpened tips aimed outward. For Chun, this arrangement emphasizes that the *kalo* provides the "very foundation of life, in body, mind, and mythology" in the Hawaiian tradition and underscores the common responsibility to protect and care for the land—*mālama 'āina* in Hawaiian—which everywhere provides for the physical and spiritual nourishment of humankind.[25]

Puni Kukahiko and Maika'i Tubbs

A sprouting *kalo* plant likewise serves as the centerpiece for *Makua Bound*, a jointly conceived 2007 installation by O'ahu-based Native Hawaiian artists Puni Kukahiko and Maika'i Tubbs, both of whom are of mixed heritage that include East Asian ancestries. The piece is a tribute to Mākua Valley, a sacred O'ahu site appropriated and fenced off by the U.S. military in the 1940s for use as a live-fire target range. *Makua Bound*'s main component is an anthropomorphic personification of the valley in the shape of a woman—its curved female form an allusion to the Earth Mother, Papa (or Papahanaumoku, wife of the Sky Father Wākea), who is said to have given birth to the islands. The figure, pinioned on the gallery wall by the same kind of chain-link fence that currently denies access to the valley, was cast from Kukahiko's own body, utilizing a cocoonlike mold fabricated from tightly wrapped layers of transparent packing tape. Cut away from its encapsulating mold and reassembled, the resulting planterlike concave form was packed with mulch, fertile insect-laden soil, and spent bullet casings gathered from the valley floor. Once this moist mixture began to decompose, the artists planted *kalo* shoots that flourished in the figure during the exhibition. Since Mākua, according to Kukahiko, "is not just a valley, she is our mother," the installation demonstrates that the indigenous connection to the land of Hawai'i is akin to a close familial relationship— and hence, new life, with appropriate cultivation and care, will reemerge on these neglected sites despite long years of depredation.[26]

The 2010 piece *Mobile Taro Lo'i (Camo design)*, part of Keith Tallett's *Militia* series, consists of clear plastic buckets filled with bright green taro plants (the artist's preferred term) immersed in water and conveyed on a working four-wheeled flatbed garden cart decorated in a stylized camouflage pattern. Because the Hawaiian word "lo'i" refers to irrigated terraces or taro patches, the artist regards this whimsical design as a fitting response to the current situation of the Hawaiian homelands. Tallett contends that indigenous families, once they are deemed eligible, can wait for years on a long list before finally being granted a "postage stamp spot [of land]"[27] in the relatively small areas that the state government has designated for exclusive Hawaiian settlement under the Hawaiian Homes Commission Act of 1920.[28] Because many are denied access to even this limited land base, Tallett has embodied the Native Hawaiians' need to fashion an enduring form of "portable culture" for themselves—no matter how partial or jerry-rigged—in the figure of a wagon-mounted mobile taro patch that is readily transferable and available for immediate replanting wherever local conditions allow.

Plantation Legacies and Food Politics

It should be no surprise to find art in Hawai'i—the only state in the nation with a majority Asian population—that evokes the plantation system, its historic heritage, and its impact on present-day demographics. Beginning with the Chinese in the 1850s, the forebears of many artists of Asian ancestry arrived in Hawai'i as field laborers under contract to the American sugar and pineapple planters whose companies came to dominate the islands' economy by the late nineteenth century. The first commercial sugar plantation was established on the island of Kaua'i by New Englanders in 1835, on land leased for that purpose from King Kamehameha III. Hawaiians in general and foreigners were not permitted to possess land until 1850. But following the enactment of three reform laws, the Great Māhele (1848), the Alien Land Ownership Act, and the

Figure 17.5. Keith Tallett, *Mobile Taro Lo'i* (Camo design), 2010. Mixed media, dimensions variable. Site-specific installation at AGGROculture, The Arts at Marks Garage, Honolulu. Photograph by Sally Lundburg. Courtesy of the artist.

Kuleana Act (both 1850), the right of alien residents to buy and sell land was deemed important to securing the "foreign capital, skill, and labor to develop the agricultural resources" of Hawai'i.[29] Nonetheless, sugar growers subsequently acquired most of this newly privatized land, so that by 1890, "three out of four privately held acres were owned by haoles or their corporations."[30] (*Haole* is the Hawaiian term for a Caucasian.)[31] The land and the wealth it generated for the sugarcane industry thus was concentrated in the hands of a small group of families, many being the descendants of American missionaries who played a crucial role in the overthrow of the indigenous monarchy in 1893 and successfully lobbied for the U.S. annexation of Hawai'i in 1898. The commercial interests of the corporations that these families founded, collectively known as the "Big Five," consequently also dominated the islands' emerging import, shipping, and banking industries.[32]

The subject of the plantation, often situated in personal standpoints and centered on coextensive topics like family, food, and foodways, has led visual artists to explore the profound impact of this chapter in local ethnic history. Since the present is the partial creation of the past, these projects have expanded awareness of the dominance of the plantation system in molding the islands' economy, political infrastructure, and historic relations of different groups. Such efforts have also fostered an interest in the multifaceted formation and makeup of the overlapping labor diasporas that constituted the plantation communities, and the transnational connections that linked worldwide plantation economies by conveying agricultural workers, plants, and animals across oceans and continents. Owing to the escalating clamor for imported labor, many of the plantations had multiethnic populations that not only included large numbers of Asians—Chinese, Japanese, Okinawans, Filipinos, and Koreans—but also Portuguese, Puerto Ricans, Spaniards, Norwegians, and Germans. Initially, Native Hawaiians were part of this shifting polyglot workforce, but their participation soon declined because of their deaths from foreign diseases and a disinclination to work in these demanding, often harsh, conditions.

Trisha Lagaso Goldberg

The mixed-media work of Honolulu-born sculptor and conceptual artist Trisha Lagaso Goldberg, a descendant of Filipinos who worked in Hawai'i's sugarcane and pineapple fields, conjures a vision of hybrid localism that intertwines the histories, symbols, values, and expectations associated with various ethnic groups. The artist, conceiving of Hawai'i as a complicated and frequently contradictory corelational space for social interchange, works from a triangulated vantage point that is equally informed by her forebears' experiences of plantation life, the common legacies of U.S. colonialism in Hawai'i and the Philippines, and the omnipresent influence of Native Hawaiian culture. Influenced by an appreciation for graphic, interior, and fashion design, Lagaso Goldberg's current work freely appropriates items closely associated with local hybrid materials and popular culture—food, clothing, adornments, and mass-produced memorabilia enjoyed by tourists and locals alike—that the artist considers typical of the creolized "pidgin-local" sensibility that has emerged in Hawai'i.

The subject of agricultural labor has appeared in a number of Lagaso Goldberg's works over the past decade. Among them is the *Sakada* Series (2006), a trio of wall pieces fabricated from sheets of hard, reflective Plexiglas that are dedicated to her maternal and paternal grandfathers, first-generation Filipino immigrants (known as *sakadas*) who worked on the sugarcane plantations. The square format and symmetrical design of these large plaquelike objects echo the syncretic form of traditional Hawaiian quilts. The hand-sewn quilt, introduced to Hawai'i by American missionaries in the nineteenth century, was adapted by Native Hawaiian women using their own designs and motifs of cultural and spiritual significance, including local food plants like the *ulu* (breadfruit) and the *kalo*.[33] Goldberg renders her interpretation of these quilt designs in an unconventional material to provoke viewers to reconsider how these intercultural objects have been subsumed by Hawai'i's commercialized landscape while also foregrounding symbols—the *bolo* (machete), the pickax, and the hoe—specific to another "historically invisible" local presence, Filipino fieldworkers whose labor has gone largely unheralded.[34]

Over the past few years, in mixed-media and performative works, Lagaso Goldberg has experimented with producing linear "ground drawings" made from granulated sugar, a concept suggested by Hawai'i's cane fields as depicted on local maps.[35] The use of sugar as a medium to represent the product of her family's labor provides the artist with a tangible connection to the past. Sugar also summons warm memories of the artist's Filipina grandmothers, their cooking for their relatives and other migrant workers on the plantations, and the sticky rice, sugar, and coconut milk confection known in the Ilocano dialect as *kankanen* that was prepared for their families and sold for consumption in nearby towns like Hilo.[36] The artist, who is too young to have shared in her family's experience of the sugar industry, reimagines the period by joining elements of plantation landscapes and social milieus. To develop this visual-mnemonic approach that she terms "memory-maps," the artist interviewed her parents to elicit their recollections of the physical environments that they and their parents had known in "intimate, difficult, sometimes painful ways.[37] In addition, she conducted research in the Hawai'i state archives on the Big Island of Hawai'i's Olaa Sugar Company, covering the 1930s to 1940s when her family members worked there, as well as historic photographs and aerial maps of plantations throughout the islands.

In *Eshu Veve for Olaa Sugar Company*, (ca. 2010/2011), a work currently in progress, Goldberg is extending her interest in the intertwined relations of plantation life, family, labor, and food, to her African American husband's family history. The selection of Eshu, which her husband suggested, recognizes an important African *orisha*, or deity, in the Yoruba religious pantheon, who is the protector of crossroads and travelers. The artist, conceiving of Hawai'i as the junction in which both their lives have converged, pondered how the world-spanning plantation system itself became the common link that brought their forebears to this nation—as Filipino contract labor brought to Hawai'i beginning in the early 1900s, and as enslaved Africans transported to the Caribbean and the American South from the sixteenth to the nineteenth century.[38]

Figure 17.6. Trisha Lagaso Goldberg, *Eshu Veve for Olaa Sugar Company*, 2011, mixed media, dimensions variable. Photograph by the author. Courtesy of the author.

By engaging her husband and young son in this effort, Goldberg is jointly devising a familial ritual to honor their combined cultural legacies by gathering together, mixing, and personalizing the signs of their various ancestors. Yet she is also aware that such an intimate, quasi-ceremonial project, intended to provide a "real function" in her family's life, would not necessarily fit comfortably in a public activity like performance art.[39] In June 2011, the artist and her husband collaborated in presenting and documenting, via digital photography, an exploratory "staging" of this concept in a borrowed artist's studio in Honolulu's Chinatown.[40] In a "ground drawing" made from long white lines of sugar carefully strewn on the studio floor, Lagaso Goldberg combined a schematic map of the Olaa plantation with a *veve*, a religious symbol originating in Africa that is associated with Haitian voodoo ceremonies in which substances like cornmeal and wood ash are sprinkled on the ground to summon ancestral spirits. The piece's resulting impermanent pattern, although not meant to replicate existing devotional rituals, is also reminiscent of detailed sand paintings in Tibetan Buddhist and traditional Navajo spiritual practices, as well as the elaborate cosmograms found in many cultures.

Using the computer-aided design and fabrication techniques devised for the *Sakada* series, Lagaso Goldberg had the final pattern cut into a sheet of

Plexiglas. With a flour sifter and this stencil-like Plexiglas device as a guide, she transferred the full-sized outline to the studio floor. The sugar was dispensed slowly and mindfully in a meditative process that Lagaso Goldberg equates with activating the circuit of historic connections joining her and her husband to each other and to their respective forebears. Over the subsequent half hour, the couple silently circled the design, placing food offerings and objects of personal significance—raw rice, black-eyed peas, wine, cheese, water, spools of thread, a tiny airplane—at selected points to note and to honor their combined ancestors. While the impulse that animates *Eshu Veve for Olaa Sugar Company* is primarily personal, the project nevertheless speaks to larger ongoing processes in which the traditions and belief systems of successive diasporic groups in the Americas are being reshaped, repurposed, and merged according to the particular needs of their times, places, and circumstances.

Alan Konishi

Currently based in Los Angeles, Honolulu-born mixed-media artist Alan Konishi grew up in rural Wai'anae, one of the poorest areas on O'ahu and the former site of a major plantation and sugarcane refinery active through the mid-1940s. As the descendant of two generations of agricultural laborers, Konishi has an abiding interest in local history that is rooted in immigrant labor. His awareness of this period is shaped by his nisei (second-generation) Japanese American father's accounts of plantation life and his Laotian immigrant mother's experiences as a seamstress in the local Hilo Hattie garment factory. Influenced by the legacies of plantation life and U.S. warfare and expansionism in the Pacific, Konishi's art has delved into charged subjects like cultural assimilation, ethnic ambivalence and self-erasure, institutionalized discrimination, and uneasy intergroup relationships defined by class and ethnic stratification.

A pair of sculptures from 2006 entitled *Yellow Peril (Remember Pearl Harbor?)* and *Yellow Peril (Am I White Yet?)* are cast bronze representations of foods Konishi associates with local plantation life: *musubi*, a traditional Japanese cold rice ball usually wrapped in dried seaweed known as *nori*, and pineapple, a plant indigenous to South America whose large-scale cultivation in Hawai'i began in the early twentieth century. In *Yellow Peril (Remember Pearl Harbor?)*, twin *musubi* resembling hand grenades nestle ominously in Konishi's rendering of the kind of mass-produced disposable Styrofoam (or plastic) bento box used for take-out meals in Hawai'i. Its companion piece, *Yellow Peril (Am I White Yet?)* consists of a mismatched pair of rough-hewn scrub brushes, each with rows of jagged bristles, in the guise of tiny pineapples.

Figure 17.7. Alan Konishi, *Yellow Peril (Remember Pearl Harbor?)*, 2006, cast bronze, 6" × 14". Courtesy of the artist.

The *musubi* was brought to Hawaiʻi by Japanese arriving in the 1880s, the majority of them farmers and peasants from southern Japan, where this readily transportable fare was consumed while working in the fields.[41] Reflecting Konishi's concern that the social pressures on ethnic groups to assimilate is an inherent form of colonization, the metaphorical militarization of a food associated with the Japanese presence becomes his assertion of how a cultural heritage should be considered a powerful "weapon," its recovery providing Hawaiʻi's Japanese communities with the ultimate means of "decoloniz[ing] ourselves."[42] In Hawaiʻi, "we've been brought up . . . to separate ourselves from our roots," and accordingly he perceives that these overly accommodating tendencies, which reached their apex during World War II, were forced on the local Japanese population over decades of anti-Japanese sentiment and discrimination.[43] The period immediately following the outbreak of the war in 1941 was especially difficult. While the majority of Japanese in Hawaiʻi, unlike those on the U.S. mainland, were not removed to internment camps, most nonetheless felt compelled to promptly destroy everything—family shrines, Japanese-language books, ethnic clothing, and personal mementos—linking them with Japan. At the time, it was commonly accepted that the "supreme proof of loyalty for Hawaiʻi's Japanese was to be anti-Japanese," but many of them continued to seek acceptance by blending into the dominant culture long after hostilities ceased.[44]

To demonstrate how the past informs the present—and in particular how the "irrational fear of another culture is still very much part of the American psyche"—Konishi deliberately modeled *Yellow Peril (Remember Pearl Harbor?)*

after a modern disposable bento box, instead of from the round tin pails (also referred to as bento boxes) that once were carried into Hawaiʻi's cane fields by Japanese plantation workers.[45] Whereas Japanese in Hawaiʻi are no longer actively discriminated against, he sees a close equivalent between their historic treatment and current attitudes toward other immigrant groups, like Latinos and, especially, Muslims after 9/11.

The refashioned pineapples in *Am I White Yet?* convey a far more ambivalent message by speaking to Konishi's profound personal discomfort following his acceptance into an elite local private school where he was made acutely aware of the class and regional disparities separating him from his peers. Here Konishi, having spent much of his childhood outdoors, evokes the heightened self-consciousness of a teenager in new surroundings whose skin tone was typically darker than that of the other students. He relates, "I remember scrubbing [my skin] hard to get the brownness off. So I wanted to make a brush that symbolized that angst."[46] Konishi's transmutation of a scrub brush's bristles into tiny pineapples, with their characteristically sharp spiny leaves and thick skin, shows how painful such acts of psychic self-erasure can be.

While this sculpture originated as the private symbol of a difficult period in the artist's life, it also gives Konishi a larger metaphor for the response of earlier generations of Japanese immigrants in confronting difference as a non-white minority in the United States. The artist's referencing of self-inflicted emotional wounds internalized by Asians as racialized subjects in the United States resonates with psychoanalytical concepts like "racial melancholia" and "abjection," which are currently invoked to address the social trauma of people of color who are unable to assimilate entirely into the state of whiteness on which full "psychic citizenship" in the West is premised.[47] Indeed, as Konishi describes his own sense of youthful unease, "This was something felt from the beginning: the need to assimilate, to become part of a status quo."[48]

Mat Kubo

Oʻahu-born mixed-media and performance artist Mat Kubo was raised in Honolulu and spent time in various cities across the mainland United States prior to moving to San Antonio, Texas, in 2009. For Kubo, the fourth-generation descendant of Japanese immigrant plantation workers, food is the locus for sculptural works crafted in Hawaiʻi that function as touchstones to the evolution of the local socioeconomic environment, and also for a series of socially oriented performance projects staged in Hawaiʻi and on the mainland aimed at engaging participants in an active interchange during the artist's preparation of shared meals.

Figure 17.8. Mat Kubo, *Big Five* (full view and detail with pineapple open), 2004, bronze, steel, 4" × 4" × 11". Courtesy of the artist.

The design of *Big Five*, a sculptural object from 2004, makes ironic use of the pineapple—here emblematic of Hawai'i—as an mini-memorial to the corporate oligarchy that shaped the islands' economy and the contested events that led to the ascendancy of the five companies that dominated 96 percent of the local sugar industry by 1933.[49] This distinctive stand-alone piece—whose design recalls commercial pineapple-shaped ceramic cookie jars—is made from cast and patinated bronze, a material that Kubo chose for its close association with antiquity, permanence, and monumentality in Western culture. To produce *Big Five*, Kubo bisected an actual pineapple, complete with spiky leafed crown—its upper and lower halves each hollowed out and separately cast. The final "product" is presented either whole or split into constituent components, exposed to reveal five bullets hiding at its base. Cast from live shells, the ammunition is aimed skyward like lethal missiles in a Cold War silo. The object alludes to the "Bayonet Constitution," an 1887 document signed by Hawaiian King Kalākaua under threat of U.S. military force that severely reduced the monarchy's power while enfranchising local men of American and European descent. This incident presaged the 1893 coup d'état led by Caucasian businessmen and supported by U.S. Marines that overthrew the sovereign Hawaiian kingdom, deposing its last reigning monarch, Queen Liliʻuokalani. Among the coup's leaders was Sanford Dole, the son of a missionary family and relative of James Dole, who founded the Hawaiian Pineapple Company (later the Dole Food Company) on Oʻahu in 1901. Sanford Dole served as the Republic of Hawaiʻi's only president until securing the islands' 1898 annexation. For Kubo, the concealment of bullets in *Big Five's* bronze core is a counterpart to the intimidation underlying the U.S. takeover and the Big Five's emergent economic and political power. This disturbing legacy, in the artist's perception, is all too often ignored or unrecognized, or even sometimes deemed praiseworthy outside the islands and even by local residents.

As a city-raised artist concerned with political activism, the trajectory of Kubo's performative work is shaped by his ongoing involvement with urban community and youth groups. Viewing food as a tangible connection between people that is basic to survival and also immediately gratifying, he uses foods as a platform to encourage conversation. The interest in sharing food—which, in Kubo's experience, breaks down social barriers by encouraging greater intimacy and trust between people—emerged out of the artist's apprehension over shifting social conditions in the islands caused by Honolulu's fast-paced urban lifestyle and the demographic shifts that occur as new groups take up residence in the city. These changes, which lead people to become increasingly distanced from one another, contrast sharply with Kubo's recollection of social relations in Hawaiʻi's ethnic communities during his youth. This was a time, he recalls, when individuals usually knew their neighbors, watched out for one another, and willingly shared the fruit and vegetables from their backyard gardens.

In June 2008 Kubo launched *OffTheGrid: ActionFunUrbanSurvivalism,* a performance-based project centered on issues of sustainability in Hawaiʻi for an exhibition entitled Eco/Logic. For this activity, Kubo chose to live for three weeks on only what he could "hunt, gather, glean, and trade" during daily excursions to different Honolulu neighborhoods.[50] Seeking immediate public feedback, the artist kept an active web blog that solicited visitors to track and comment on his activities in real time. During this challenge, Kubo asked strangers for permission to take spare fruit from their yards while offering food from his own property in exchange. Finding that many of those he met were open to accepting this proposal, Kubo was encouraged in his belief that nascent local relationships based on neighborly reciprocity and cooperation could be reactivated, despite the changing social climate. Calling attention to "the kinds of . . . relationships we need to forge and nurture if we intend to sustain ourselves here in Hawaiʻi" underscored his central conviction that we "need each other to survive."[51]

Kubo's subsequent ventures in Hawai'i and on the mainland often revolved around cooking for others—especially the cuisine Kubo associates with the Japanese presence in the islands—and stressed the importance of face-to-face contact and interchange. Kubo's use of cooking and sharing food as an art medium, mounted in a variety of settings to which he is invited, including art museums, galleries, schools, and private homes, is devoted to modeling alternatives to existing social relations through mutuality and sharing. The deliberate contextualizing of these projects as performance art serves a pivotal strategic function for the artist, as it directs the participants' attention to an occurrence that might otherwise be assumed to be a simple social gathering. Kubo views such activities as small-scale actions by which artists can "hack into existing systems and use them for our advantage," in support of social change.[52]

In 2008 and 2009, a half-year-long sequence of performances entailed Kubo's preparation of a variety of meals at private and public sites in Hawai'i. Entitled *Cook for You, Cook for Me*, the series culminated in two stagings at Honolulu's Contemporary Museum. In this highly visible setting, the artist made *nabe*, a hearty stew or souplike winter concoction originating in rural Japan, from a recipe regularly cooked by his maternal grandmother. Throughout each of these events, Kubo, against a backdrop of projected images and recorded conversations from earlier performances in the series, prepared this traditional one-pot dish for groups of twenty museum visitors at a time. For him, *nabe* was the "perfect metaphor for connecting over food," as in this style of eating, family members add ingredients and dine together from a communal pot of bubbling broth.[53] Indeed, whereas Japanese food is customarily served as individual portions with separate utensils and dishes, eating *nabe* allows for the "breakdown of everyday reserve and a sense of fusion or solidarity among the diners."[54]

Kubo's projects find recent precedents in those of Argentine-born Thai artist Rirkrit Tiravanija, who gained international attention in the early 1990s by cooking Thai food for museum visitors in makeshift on-site kitchens. These open-ended approaches, with their emphasis on sociability and the creation of temporary spaces for exchange around shared activities, resonate with the notions of "relational aesthetics" propounded by French critic and curator Nicolas Bourriaud, whose writings Kubo cites as an influence. In the 1990s Bourriaud famously argued that contemporary art should be about "ways of living and models of action" that are anchored in immediate contexts of human interaction.[55] Food-related activities that seek out audience participation and that aim to breach perceived boundaries between art and life, also have had well-documented precedents in American conceptual and performance art since the 1960s. Among them is American artist Allan Kaprow's 1964 *Eat*, a "happening" in which the event used foods to engage audiences in more interactive ways. In pursuing an avant-garde art practice "inseparable from real life," Kaprow propounded the use of everyday materials and processes that included the ways in which food "is grown, prepared, eaten, digested, and composted."[56] Kubo has extended such life-based, performative models by making conversational interchange a major element in his artistic practice and by also moving beyond art contexts to solicit participants from popular venues like social media sites and Craigslist.

Gaye Chan

Two of Honolulu-based Gaye Chan's best-known public collaborative projects since the late 1990s are *Downwind Productions* and *Eating in Public*. Each includes spirited critiques, mounted from different angles, of the damage being done to Hawaiʻi's land and resources by corporate and state interests. These undertakings, conceived in the tradition of agitprop by this Hong Kong–born conceptual artist and cultural activist, use metaphor and ambiguity to address conflicted issues of food production and resource distribution in the islands. Chan, whose work likewise is influenced by Bourriaud, conceives of her collaborative undertakings as a "relational practice" mediated by a complex sense of "poetics," which is centered on establishing points of encounter for people to make conscious choices about their actions in relationship to Hawaiʻi's physical and social environment.[57]

DownWind Productions, a multimedia venture cofounded in 1999 by Chan and cultural historian Andrea Feeser and joined by sociologist Nandita Sharma, is an effort to provide a highly visible critique of the extensive environmental, human, and cultural costs of the development of the beachfront area surrounding Waikiki, the islands' economic dependence on the international tourist industry, and the U.S. military infrastructure. Appropriating two well-established commercial formats to serve their dissident agenda—informational websites and coffee table books—the collaborators developed a pair of related projects: a slickly rendered, web-based mock "travel site" (which went online in 2002) that also sells satiric ersatz souvenirs of their own creation, and a colorfully illustrated volume entitled *Waikīkī: A History of Forgetting & Remembering* (2006).

For the website, the perspectives of a diverse range of people who live and work in the Waikiki area were elicited. To indicate how all their views, along with other social and commercial pressures, exist simultaneously in Waikiki, and influenced by the concept of "contrapuntal analysis," the collaborators use multiple recollections and sources to counter the sort of clichéd, overly circumscribed representations of the area that primarily serve the tourist industry.[58] Situating this broadly inclusive approach in the context of social justice, this representational strategy emphasizes that issues of tourism and development are located in larger global networks of social and economic relations.

Waikiki, a vacation-oriented beachfront neighborhood of Honolulu that had already been a retreat for Hawai'i's royalty in the nineteenth century, is today routinely decried by critics as an overdeveloped thicket of commercial high-rises, hotels, restaurants, malls, souvenir stands, and prepackaged entertainments that exploit indigenous traditions. The *DownWind* home page provides active links corresponding to the three commonly used terms by which people in Hawai'i are primarily identified: *kanaka maoli* (indigenous Hawaiian), *kama'aina* (island-born or long-term nonindigenous resident), and *haole* (Caucasian).[59] No matter which category the visitor chooses as a point of access into the website's content, she or he is presented with the same map of Waikiki on which more than 136 locales are marked with active links. One of these web portals—all of which display images, texts, and anecdotes closely connected to each of the different areas—reveals maps and historic images of local streams associated with traditional indigenous land divisions known as *ahupua'a*. These once well-irrigated farming areas, extending from nearby mountain slopes to the Waikiki seashore, contained land that was used to grow *kalo*, along with other resources required for the Native Hawaiians' sustenance before their watercourses were diverted by unrestrained real estate development and commercialization.

In the ongoing *Eating in Public* series, which began in 2003, Chan and Sharma aspire to effect change by making a local impact via social microinterventions. The collaborators' turn to this more direct, real-world approach emerged from their recognition of the limits of *DownWind* as a conceptually oriented art project dealing with issues of representation.[60] *Eating in Public*, an umbrella title for a group of interrelated works in progress, is documented on its website (http://www.nomoola.com) and periodically exhibited in art venues in Hawai'i, North America, and Europe. In this evolving, long-term undertaking, Chan and Sharma (along with an informal array of supporters) subversively seek to "insert themselves" into the local system of food production and distribution by periodically operating alongside and outside existing networks.[61]

These activities, listed on the website under categories like "gardens," "weeds," "bins," and "stores," include the establishment of a "free store" and the home manufacture and distribution of wire recycling bins to augment the limited number and availability of those provided by the state of Hawai'i, many of which are commandeered by private groups, including charities. The collaborators' interest in advancing local self-sufficiency and in providing unmonitored venues as "autonomous spaces of exchange," is inspired by diverse models.[62] Their influences include San Francisco's Diggers, a 1960s radical community-action group who foresaw a society without private property; their seventeenth-century namesake (an agrarian Protestant movement that formed small egalitarian communities in England); and the time-honored English tradition of the commons, which had once allowed widespread access to rural land and its resources.[63]

The first of the food-oriented projects involved the planting, without permission, of papaya seedlings on a strip of public land adjacent to the chain-link fence erected by a prominent private institution devoted to the education of Native Hawaiian children. Seeking alternative ways of relating to control over local land, Chan and Sharma solicited passersby—through an official-looking sign put up for the purpose—to help tend the growing crop and harvest mature papayas for their own use. Another project, entitled *Free Grindz* (meaning "free food" in local pidgin), was exhibited in San Francisco in 2011.[64] This work consists of a rough-hewn, tablelike object whose multiple compartments hold reams of blank stationery, mailing supplies, and rubber stamps imprinted with recipes for preparing dandelion, purslane, and amaranth, edible plants that typically are considered weeds. This practical arrangement, reminiscent of an old-fashioned postal hutch, gives audience members a means of exchanging information about the location and preparation of a wild food source that is abundant almost everywhere, including Hawai'i, yet is commonly ignored or stigmatized. Attitudes like these—despite the growing sympathy for sustainable management of natural resources—are prevalent not only because of the dominance of commercially cultivated fruit and vegetables in mass venues like supermarkets but also because of the uneasy associations this type of nourishment may have with poverty, scarcity, outdoor foraging, and filth. This negative connection, all too often ascribed to people of lower class, ethnic, and nondominant backgrounds, also applies to immigrant groups who grow and consume foods that others may regard as "weird."[65]

Since the collaborators view the sharing of seed as an ancient worldwide practice that today is under threat from modern agribusiness, their project draws on elements of this prototypical design to install a number of unmonitored "seed-sharing stations" around demographically varied areas of metropolitan Honolulu and sites outside the islands.[66] Each of these entities—here

Figure 17.9. Gaye Chan and Nandita Sharma, *Eating in Public*, Free Garden at Kailua, Hawai'i, 2003–2012, site-specific installation, acrylic and ink on plywood, dimensions variable. Photograph by Gaye Chan. Courtesy of the artist.

presented in the form of smaller open-shelved display racks made from scrap or recycled wood—are stocked with a variety of seed packets and stationery supplies, allowing onlookers to readily take, share, and transmit food seeds. The racks, installed for at least one year, sport an eye-catching self-explanatory sign entitled simply "Share Seeds," along with a web address, and are crafted individually to fit the demands of a variety of well-trafficked indoor locations, such as arts institutions, coffee shops, libraries, farmers' markets, churches, and community centers. Seen against the marked decrease in biodiversity accelerated by corporate moves to bioengineer and patent plants, the collaborators argue that such a visible effort raises awareness of the need to retain and circulate multiple nutritious seed varieties (including ancient grains nearing extinction) as vital to the future of the islands, the planet, and their expanding populations. Taken together, the *Eating in Public* series emphasizes an ethics that places primary responsibility on the individual to decide how she or he will act and to determine how each will relate to other people in a changing global environment.

Interestingly, "Share Seeds" has echoes in Trisha Lagaso Goldberg's 2006 piece *Biag ti agtrabajo (The Lives of Laborers)*. This mixed-media installation has framed inkjet print photographs of *malunggay* (also known as *kalumungay* or Moringa tree) and *paria* (bitter melon vine) cuttings, both widely grown in Africa and Asia, eaten in the Philippines, and used by Filipinos in Hawai'i, including the artist's grandmother who often served *malunggay* with fried fish. Grown in backyards in Hawai'i, the dark green leaves of the *malunggay* tree are used like spinach and even heralded as a "super food" in the Philippines, where it also has medicinal purposes. Yet in Hawai'i, the *malunggay* generally remains an ethnic specific food and is sometimes associated with poverty. Although as an adult, Lagaso Goldberg recognizes and highlights these plants' inherent value as a working-class Filipino staple that sustained plantation families, she still recalls her childhood embarrassment over bringing non-Filipino friends to the house because of this food's pungent aroma when stewed.[67]

Coda

Equally motivated by purpose and passion, the preceding artists' works, using food-centered metaphors, symbols, emblems, and actions, demonstrate how social meanings are being manifested, negotiated, and imbued with communicative force—and even marshaled to facilitate change in the present-day world. Despite differences in these Asian American and Native Hawaiian artists' backgrounds and concerns, a distinguishing trait of all the art discussed is its worldly orientation. Rather than providing autonomous objects and performative activities for the sole contemplation of sympathetic cognoscenti, the artists want their endeavors to be immersed in the immediate world around them and thereby to provide for a positive real-world function. Even where these artists engage the material and social impact of large-scale forces, such as historic Western expansion or modern globalization, their apprehension of them stays rooted in local and personal experience through multisensory encounters with surrounding objects, spaces, and people.

All of them born between the late 1950s and 1980s, these artists, in part because of the period in which they studied art, are influenced by conceptualism (in which underlying concepts are deemed to be more significant to art making than materials or aesthetics), as well as by intellectual currents inflected by critical theory, feminism, and postcolonial theory that have strongly affected ethnic, indigenous, visual culture, and performance studies. For artists with moral imaginations informed by a relational aesthetic, food also acts as a modality for sociality, even as a means to directly engage with other people. As such, these artists' interest in having an impact on public behavior and in promoting critical awareness of social problems is not unique to contemporary Asian Americans or Native Hawaiians.

Alongside a range of work on kindred sociohistoric themes by other groups of color in the United States, a parallel to Native Hawaiian art is evident in Native American art, in light of the importance of land and the sustenance it offers to indigenous peoples. For example, in *Corn Blue Room*, a 1998 multimedia installation by Tuscarora artist Jolene Rickard, six braids of dried corn are suspended from a gallery ceiling to signify the six nations in the Iroquois Confederacy. Here, as the central feature of an installation confronting a hydroelectric project's partial displacement of Rickard's tribe from its ancestral land in Upstate New York, corn embodies the artist's conviction that working together to grow this ancient crop and sharing the traditional knowledge of its cultivation from one generation to the next is necessary to the continued physical, cultural, and spiritual cohesion of her people.[68] Like *kalo*, corn has a spiritual and material significance as a revered staple food that sustains a native people, and art offers means by which this living presence can be manifested.

Ultimately, artistic projects like these, linked as they are to the distinct worldviews and empathetic interventions of creative individuals, offer access to the daily lives, internal conceptions, and group identifications of diverse peoples of color. By being both spatially and historically located, such socially engaged undertakings also speak to the entangled contacts, cultural overlays, and mutual transformations, reaching across boundaries and centuries, which increasingly constitute contemporary human societies.

Notes

1. See Arjun Appadurai, ed., *The Social Life of Things: Commodities in Cultural Perspective* (Cambridge: Cambridge University Press, 1986).

2. Puni Kukahiko, in Joleen Oshiro, "World Views: UH Graduate Art Students Use a Variety of Materials to Comment on Daily Life," *Honolulu Star-Bulletin*, December 12, 2004. Also see Puni Kukahiko, artist's statement, in *Changing Hands: Art without Reservation*, vol. 2, *Contemporary Native North American Art from the West, Northwest & Pacific*, by David Revere McFadden and Ellen Napiura Taubman (New York: Museum of Arts and Design, 2005), 34.

3. According to J. Kēhaulani Kauanui, among Native Hawaiians, the most common cross-racial pairings in postcontact Hawai'i were between Native Hawaiian women and white men. By the 1870s, however, with the growing influx of Chinese male workers, Hawaiian women who intermarried increasingly "partnered and reproduced with Chinese men." See J. Kēhaulani Kauanui, *Hawaiian Blood: Colonialism and the Politics of Sovereignty and Indigeneity* (Durham, NC: Duke University Press, 2008), 133.

4. Sidney W. Mintz, *Tasting Food, Tasting Freedom: Excursions into Eating, Culture, and the Past* (Boston: Beacon Press, 1996), 25.

5. For a discussion of how SPAM was incorporated in a range of local ethnic cuisines in Hawai'i, see George H. Lewis, "From Minnesota Fat to Seoul Food: Spam in America and the Pacific Rim," *Journal of Popular Culture* 34 no. 2 (fall 2000): 90–92.

6. Michael Arcega, *SPAM/MAPS*, available at http://arcega.us/section/240417_SPAM_
MAPS.html (accessed December 29, 2011).

7. Ibid.

8. Judith A. Bennett, *Natives and Exotics: World War II and Environment in the Southern
Pacific* (Honolulu: University of Hawai'i Press, 2009), 226–27.

9. Michel Tuffery, in Isabelle Genoux, "Povi Tau Vaga—The Clash of the Bulls—Performed
at the Third Asia Pacific Triennial of Contemporary Art," Pacific Arts Online, October 23, 2000, available at http://www.abc.net.au/arts/artok/performance/s202947.htm
(accessed May 11, 2011).

10. Lynne Yamamoto, telephone interview with Margo Machida, November 28, 2010.

11. According to the 2000 U.S. Census, about 20 percent of Native Hawaiians live in
poverty; overall they have the lowest mean family income and the highest family
poverty rates of any major ethnic group in the Hawaiian Islands. See Shawn Malia
Kana'iaupuni, Nolan J. Malone, and Koren Ishibashi, *Income and Poverty among Native
Hawaiians: Summary of Ka Huaka'i Findings* (Honolulu: Kamehameha Schools, PASE,
05-06:5, 2005), available at http://www.ksbe.edu/spi/PDFS/Reports/Demography_Well-
being/05_06_5.pdf (accessed October 18, 2012).

12. Keith Tallett and Sally Lundburg, e-mail correspondence with Margo Machida, November 4, 2011.

13. Keith Tallett, Artist's Statement, available at http://keithtallett.com/?page_id=431
(accessed December 28, 2011).

14. Dan Koeppel, *Banana: The Fate of the Fruit That Changed the World* (New York: Plume,
2008), 135–41.

15. David Livingston Crawford, *Hawaii's Crop Parade: A Review of Useful Products Derived
from the Soil in the Hawaiian Islands, Past and Present* (Honolulu: Advertiser Publishing
Company, 1937), 52. Also see Koeppel, *Banana*, 140.

16. "Crop Profile for Bananas in Hawaii," June 2003, available at http://www.ipmcenters.org/
cropprofiles/docs/hibananas.html (accessed October 14, 2011).

17. Virginia Scott Jenkins, *Bananas: An American History* (Washington, DC: Smithsonian
Institution Press, 2000), 9.

18. Keith Tallett and Sally Lundburg, e-mail correspondence with Margo Machida, November 18, 2011.

19. Keith Tallett, interview with Margo Machida, Pa'auilo, Hawai'i, June 15, 2011.

20. On the origins and significance of the kalo plant, see "Pōhaku ku'i 'ai Collection,"
Bishop Museum, Honolulu, available at http://www.hawaiialive.org/realms.php?sub=
Wao+Kanaka&treasure=342&offset=0 (accessed December 29, 2011). See also "Canoe
Plants of Ancient Hawai'i: KALO," available at http://www.canoeplants.com/kalo.html
(accessed December 29, 2011).

21. Some Hawaiian artists view their art making as coextensive with an array of life-based
practices aimed at sustaining native culture and traditions. For instance, O'ahu-based
artist and activist community leader Eric Enos is the cofounder and executive director of the Cultural Learning Center at Ka'ala Farm (founded in 1976). The center is
dedicated to teaching traditional Hawaiian values and skills, including the care of the
land and cultivation of *kalo* and other native plants. One of his sons, the prolific painter,
muralist, and illustrator Solomon Enos, likewise pursues projects that provide concrete
means by which "art, the land and the people can all take care of and inspire each other."

See Solomon Enos, "About Solomon," available at http://www.solomonenos.com/about. html (accessed December 24, 2011).

22. Kaili Chun, telephone interview with Margo Machida, September 20, 2007.

23. See Manulani Aluli Meyer, *Ho'oulu: Our Time of Becoming: Collected Early Writings of Manulani Meyer* (Honolulu: 'Ai Pōhaku Press, 2003), 76–202.

24. Kaili Chun, interview with Margo Machida, Honolulu, Hawai'i, May 22, 2006.

25. "The Significance of Kalo (Taro)," available at http://www.mauiranchland.com/kalo. html (accessed September 22, 2007). This article cites Edward S. C. Handy, Elizabeth G. Handy, and Mary Kawena Pukui, "Native Planters in Old Hawaii, Their Life, Lore, and Environment," *Bishop Museum Bulletin* 233 (1972).

26. Puni Kukahiko, interview with Margo Machida, Honolulu, Hawai'i, June 28, 2007.

27. Keith Tallett and Sally Lundburg, e-mail correspondence with Margo Machida, November 4, 2011.

28. See "Hawaiian Homes Commission Act," Hawaiian Home Lands Trust, Department of Hawaiian Homelands, available at http://www.hawaiianhomelands.org/hhc/laws-and-rules/ (accessed December 29, 2011).

29. Sally Engle Merry, *Colonizing Hawai'i: The Cultural Power of Law* (Princeton, NJ: Princeton University Press, 2000), 94.

30. Ronald Takaki, *Pau Hana: Plantation Life and Labor in Hawaii* (Honolulu: University of Hawai'i Press, 1983), 18.

31. Mary Kawena Pukui and Samuel H. Elbert, *Hawaiian Dictionary* (Honolulu: University of Hawai'i Press, 1986), 58.

32. Gary Y. Okihiro, *Pineapple Culture: A History of the Tropical and Temperate Zones* (Berkeley: University of California Press, 2009), 99–100, 116–17.

33. See Reiko Mochinaga Brandon and Loretta G. H. Woodward, *Hawaiian Quilts: Tradition and Transition* (Honolulu: Honolulu Academy of Arts, 2004), 14–18.

34. Trisha Lagaso Goldberg, interview with Margo Machida, Honolulu, June 9, 2007.

35. Trisha Lagaso Goldberg, e-mail correspondence with Margo Machida, May 29, 2011.

36. Trisha Lagaso Goldberg, telephone interview with Margo Machida, July 8, 2011. Also Trisha Lagaso Goldberg, e-mail correspondence with Margo Machida, November 30, 2011.

37. Trisha Lagaso Goldberg, e-mail correspondence with Margo Machida, May 29, 2011.

38. Between 1500 and 1880, most enslaved Africans shipped to the Americas via the transatlantic slave trade were bound for the Caribbean sugar plantations. See Kenneth Pomeranz and Steven Topik, *The World That Trade Created: Society, Culture, and the World Economy 1400 to the Present* (Armonk, NY: Sharpe, 2006), 89.

39. Trisha Lagaso Goldberg, interview with Margo Machida, Honolulu, June 25, 2011.

40. I was invited by Trisha Lagaso Goldberg to view this private staging of *Eshu Veve for Olaa Sugar Company*, which took place in Honolulu on June 25, 2011.

41. Rachel Laudan, *The Food of Paradise: Exploring Hawai'i's Culinary Heritage* (Honolulu: University of Hawai'i Press, 1996), 53.

42. Alan Konishi, interview with Margo Machida, Honolulu, June 16, 2007.

43. Ibid.

44. Gary Y. Okihiro, *Cane Fires: The Anti-Japanese Movement in Hawaii, 1865–1945* (Philadelphia: Temple University Press, 1991), 229.

45. Alan Konishi, e-mail correspondence with Margo Machida, December 27, 2011. Note that the term "bento" by itself refers to a type of meal rather than the container in which

the meal is served. Bento containers take many forms, ranging from variously shaped, boxlike conveyances to elaborate lacquerware. The etymology of the Japanese word can be traced to a Chinese slang term for "convenient" or "convenience," originating in the Southern Song dynasty (1127–1279).

46. Konishi, interview.

47. David L. Eng and David Kazanjian, "Introduction: Mourning Remains," in *Loss: The Politics of Mourning* (Berkeley: University of California Press, 2003), 16.

48. Konishi, interview.

49. Okihiro, *Pineapple Culture*, 117.

50. Mat Kubo, "The Statement, ActionFunUrbanSurvivalism, 2008," available at http://mat-kubo.blogspot.com/2008/08/statement.html (accessed December 31, 2011). Documentation and objects used in this project were included in the art exhibition Eco/Logic (July 29–September 6, 2008) at The Arts at Marks Garage, Honolulu.

51. Kubo, "The Statement."

52. Mat Kubo, e-mail correspondence with Margo Machida, November 25, 2011.

53. Ibid.

54. Naomichi Ishige, *The History and Culture of Japanese Food* (London: Kegan Paul, 2001), 235.

55. Nicolas Bourriaud, *Relational Aesthetics* (Dijon: Les presses du réel, 2002), 13.

56. Allan Kaprow, *Essays on the Blurring of Art and Life* (Berkeley: University of California Press, 1993), 204–5.

57. Gaye Chan, interview with Margo Machida, Honolulu, June 20, 2011.

58. See Edward W. Said, *Culture and Imperialism* (New York: Knopf, 1993).

59. See Downwind Productions website, http://www.downwindproductions.com/.

60. Chan, interview.

61. Barbara Kirshenblatt-Gimblett, "Playing to the Senses: Food as a Performative Medium," *Performance Research* 4, no. 1 (1999): 12. See her discussion of other artists who similarly work directly with, or critique aspects of, the food system, including its production, distribution, exchange, and consumption.

62. Kirshenblatt-Gimblett, "Playing to the Senses."

63. Gaye Chan and Nandita Sharma, "Gardens," *Eating in Public*, available at http://www.nomoola.com/gardens/diggers_p6.html (accessed December 31, 2011).

64. Gaye Chan and Nandita Sharma, "Free Grindz," *Eating in Public*, available at http://www.nomoola.com/weeds/index.html (accessed January 1, 2012).

65. Chan, interview.

66. Gaye Chan and Nandita Sharma, "Seeds," *Eating in Public*, available at http://www.nomoola.com/seeds/index.html (accessed October 16, 2012).

67. Trisha Lagaso Goldberg, interview with Margo Machida, Honolulu, June 9, 2007.

68. Jolene Rickard, "Jolene Rickard Speaks . . . ," in *Reservation X: The Power of Place in Aboriginal Contemporary Art*, ed. Gerald McMaster (Seattle: University of Washington Press, 1999), 127.

18

"Love Is Not a Bowl of Quinces"

Food, Desire, and the Queer Asian Body in
Monique Truong's The Book of Salt

DENISE CRUZ

Monique Truong's *The Book of Salt* (2003) is a foodie reader's fantasy. The novel abounds with tantalizing, mouth-watering concoctions: duck braised with port-drenched figs, tarts crisped with sugared butter, ripe quinces gently simmered in honeyed water. But for the characters in the novel, these delicacies are rendered all the more fascinating because they are created by Bính, the queer Vietnamese chef who works in Gertrude Stein and Alice B. Toklas's Parisian household. It was, in fact, this surprising morsel of real-life intimacy—the relationship between Vietnamese laborers and two of U.S. modernism's most famous figures—that inspired Truong's novel. In interviews about *The Book of Salt*, Truong recalls finding a revelation in the pages of the *Alice B. Toklas Cook Book*, which is both a cookbook and a memoir of Toklas's life with Stein. "In a chapter called 'Servants in France,'" remembers Truong,

> Toklas wrote about two Indochinese men who cooked for [them] at 27 rue de Fleurus and at their summer house in Bilignin. . . . When I got to the pages about these cooks, I was, to say the least, surprised and touched to see a Vietnamese presence—and such an intimate one at that—in the lives of these two women.[1]

A small, forgotten tidbit thus became the premise for *The Book of Salt's* narrator, Bính, Truong's fictionalized version of the couple's live-in chef.[2] Following Bính as he travels from French Vietnam to Stein and Toklas's French households, the novel interweaves a present set in 1934 with a narrative that traces Bính's evolving diasporic, queer Vietnamese identity.

I begin with the origin of Truong's novel because it serves as an appropriate anecdotal *amuse bouche* for my own interests in *The Book of Salt*. Bính's talents are influenced by Vietnam's imperial history, his diasporic exile in France, and the queer desires circulating in and out of his employers' homes. Those who delight in his food are amazed by the incongruity of French haute cuisine prepared by Vietnamese hands and the construction of these dishes in queer domestic space. Acutely aware of these dynamics, Bính both draws pleasure from and resists them. Indeed, Truong's novel is notable because its palate defies mimetic links among ethnic bodies, cultures, and food. Her play with the culinary questions unidirectional narratives that cast the West as a controlling network of desire and consumption. Food reveals the hitherto unacknowledged presence of Vietnamese laborers in the overlapping global and domestic spaces. Imagining, describing, and eating food become a means of potentially subverting the hierarchies in these realms and of constructing nonnormative familial intimacies.[3] Yet while food allows access to these new formations, it also reveals their necessary limits. My analysis of *The Book of Salt* thus explores the politics and implications of a representational strategy that simmers together the literary and the culinary to produce immiscibilities rather than fusions. Ultimately, *The Book of Salt* highlights how food does and does not stand in for authenticity, how language can and cannot represent objects or people, and how queer desire both fuels and is fueled by Asian bodies.

My chapter builds on recent work that has reclaimed the importance of foodways to Asian American literature and culture. Asian American critics have long been suspicious of presumed connections linking food, the body, and authenticity. Often, this criticism centers on the questions of whether or not an Asian American author is capitulating to a mainstream U.S. market; in readings that decry representations of food as "food pornography," food markets the ethnic subject as not just palatable but also enticing. In part, this recipe for mainstream market success does work. As Anita Mannur has tracked, novels that focus on food or capitalize on an interest in food (e.g., Amy Tan's *The Joy Luck Club*) have been quite successful commercially.[4]

Working against this suspicion about representational foodways, recent studies by Mannur, Jennifer Ann Ho, and Wenying Xu draw on early foundational work by scholars like Sau-Ling Wong to reclaim the critical potential of the culinary in Asian American literature.[5] For these scholars, Asian American and South Asian authors use the culinary to unsettle the normative and limiting dynamics of citizenship, diaspora, identity, community, and globalization. Their efforts question the connections between Asian bodies and food and the dynamics of knowing and consuming the Asian other.[6] They reaffirm the importance of food in Asian American novels not as trope or metaphor but as a means of exploring processes critical to identity, subject, and community formations.[7] Historically, they contend, this argument makes sense because of the centrality of food to how Asian Americans have been racialized by mainstream U.S. cultural representations, which often pitch Asians and Asian food as either "disgusting" or exotic. Examinations of food in Asian American literature thus offer a complicated response to how food has been employed by both Asian authors and U.S. constructions of Asia and Asians.[8] The importance of domestic spaces to the creation and consumption of food in Asian American literature provides opportunities to uncover the complicated matrices of gender, sexuality, and class that structure Asian American identities and communities, as well as possibilities of imagining new alternatives. Yet these critics also are aware of the complexities of these alternatives. As Mannur observed of South Asian diasporic texts, "the 'culinary' most typically occupies a seemingly paradoxical space—at once a site of affirmation and resistance."[9]

What do we do, then, with a text like Truong's and its careful play with the very seductiveness of not only food but also the seductive allure of its preparation by Asian hands? Truong certainly is interested in exposing and critiquing cycles of objectification and consumption, yet she also explores methods of resistance that are much more complicated than Bính's outward rejection of these dynamics. For although the novel subverts the Western appetite for an Asian other, *The Book of Salt* also extends this critique by reversing the usual directionality of this desire, so that Bính takes pleasure in and relishes the knowledge that others desire him. *The Book of Salt* thus complicates the networks of pleasure and desire that circulate between Asian laborers and their employers. Bính clearly refuses yet wants to be desired, and this combination of motive and response articulates the complexities of queer diasporic Vietnamese subjectivity, an experience characterized by a need for recognition. This admixture of catering to, relishing, and withdrawing from circuits of desire emerges in the kitchens of Bính's Messieurs and Mesdames and in the secrets woven into his recipes.

In this chapter, I explore this complex intersection of the culinary and the literary in *The Book of Salt*. First, I examine Truong's representation of food—its production and consumption and the circulation of recipes—as critical to Bính's manipulation of those who desire to know and control him. Building on Xu's and David Eng's exploration of queer intimacies in the novel, I next analyze the connections between the culinary and networks of queer desire, arguing that through the representation of preparing and sharing meals, *The Book of Salt* imagines formations of queer communities. I then turn to what makes Truong's work truly unusual: the novel's emphasis on language, negation, and the literary. *The Book of Salt* calls attention to both the culinary and the literary, and to the possibilities and shortcomings of both genres of production in imagining queer diasporic identities and communities. I end with a brief coda that turns to a very different iteration of the dynamics that I explore in *The Book of Salt*: the representation of Hung Huynh in the reality television show *Top Chef*— to acknowledge the widespread and continued consumption of Asian domestic and affective labor.

Consumption and Circulation

In the opening descriptions of his life as a chef, Bính reveals that he is quite aware of how his body and labor circulate. Indeed, even though Bính's agency in Paris may be limited, Truong illuminates his awareness of imperial epistemologies and his ability to maneuver within hierarchical structures of knowledge. His Parisian employers, he confides, fall into three different categories. In the first, after a "catlike glimpse" of his face (16), his employers dismiss him immediately.[10] The second group is inquisitive and suspicious and "behave as if they have been authorized by the French government to ferret out and to document" his presence on "their hallowed shores" (16). The third category, in his terms, is "the collectors" (18), who quickly hire him. These men and women, though, are ultimately "never satiated by my cooking. They are ravenous. The honey that they covet lies inside my scars." Although the collectors may be more "subtle," they are nevertheless "indistinguishable from the type twos except for the defining core of their obsession. They have no true interest in where I have been or what I have seen. They crave the fruits of exile, the bitter juices, and the heavy hearts" (19).

In this environment—in which the desire to know is linked to consumption of the colonized Asian body, a body that is exiled and estranged in the metropole—Bính's incredible skills as a chef present opportunities to reverse the epistemological structures and hierarchies of labor and empire in Paris. The preparation of food becomes a means of breaking the bounds separating Bính from his employers. For him, his work as a chef gives him opportunities to experience what Xu calls "some self-determination and dignity," and the production and serving of culinary creations are processes of delightful— and, most important, pleasurable—manipulation.[11] His Mesdames may direct him in the kitchen, but he knows that he retains control over what enters their mouths: "Three times a day, I orchestrate, and they sit with slackened jaws, silenced" (19). Even more delicious: his Mesdames don't even realize his power. He gleefully confides in us:

> It is your ignorance, Madame, that lines my pocket, gives me entry into the lesser rooms of your house, allows my touch to enter you in the most intimate of ways. Madame, please do not forget that every morsel that slides down your dewy white throat has first rested in my two hands, coddled in the warmth of my ten fingers. What clings to them clings to you. (153–54)

The passage of Bính's creations from his hands to his Mesdames' mouths reverse assumptions about the hierarchy of American employers over Asian workers or, in broader terms, the French and U.S. empires and their exploitation of Asian bodies. This description moves from rooms in the house, to literal and metaphorical pockets, to the interior cavities of the body. But in the eroticism of this moment, something else is also at work. Bính's pleasure stems from this intimate transgression, but the sticky cling of residues that transfers from his working fingers to his Mesdames' throats is tinged with violence and forced entry. Here, even the disrupted hierarchies—of West over East, transnational American over exiled Asian, Madame over servant—ultimately cannot escape the logic of heterosexual violence that has been foundational to imperial structures of power.

In addition to acts of production and consumption, the culinary also gives Bính opportunities to remind himself (and, though they may not realize it, his employers) that their control and knowledge is not all-encompassing. Tantalizing and then refusing to give his employers what they crave, he constantly provokes questions and withholds answers.[12] This back-and-forth serves as both survival strategy and amusing game. His Mesdames assume that the exquisite taste of Bính's dishes originate not in his talents, skill, or work as a chef but from some withheld secret ingredient:

> Like children, gullible and full of wonder, they always ask, "What is your secret?"
>
> Do I look like a fool? I ask myself each time. Please, Madame, do not equate my lack of speech with a lack of thought. . . . They all believe in a "secret" ingredient, a balm for their Gallic pride, a magic elixir that anyone can employ to duplicate my success. Its existence downplays my skills, cheapens my worth. . . . If there is a "secret," Madame, it is this: Repetition and routine. Servitude and subservience. Beck and call. (153–54)

In this response, Bính mocks Madame's ignorance, her failure to recognize that his skill in the kitchen comes not merely from the ingredients alone but from years of difficult service.

Yet again, I want to stress the complexities of Truong's novel, for despite Bính's angry dismissal of these questions and his contention that the true secret of his culinary expertise stems from the invisible labor that provides these dishes, he often does include secret ingredients in his recipes. These components give Bính moments of pleasure in an environment in which his desires are dismissed and rendered invisible. In one example, Bính lies to an inquisitive Madame, telling her that the secret to his perfect omelet is a touch of freshly grated nutmeg, a spice that, when added to eggs, results in a final product "laced with the taste of handsoaps and the smell of certain bugs whose crushed bodies emit a warning order to the others" (154). Yet only a page earlier, Bính reveals that his recipe does, in fact, include a secret: a second tablespoon of melted butter carefully tucked inside the omelet just as it begins to puff. Throughout the novel, Bính reveals other surprising ingredients, from peppercorns steeped in milk for gingered ice cream (186) to black truffle shavings on *salade cancalaise*. These secrets leave the taster with a question, a feeling that there is "something deeper," "a lingering lace of a feeling on the tongue" (186). His revision of recipes is yet another way to exercise power over his employers, and these elements and techniques can be withheld, misrepresented, or openly shared. He enjoys eluding his Mesdames' and Messieurs' will to know, as these unrecognizable tastes are a method of escape from questions, explicit and implicit, about where he is from or why he is in France.

The novel also highlights the exploitation of the Asian laborer through Bính's recognition that the act of preparing a culinary masterpiece often also requires acts of violence. *The Book of Salt* stresses that the most delicious recipes require some sort of sacrifice, from the death of a young animal to the realization that while the taste of a meal might linger on the tongue, the labor and sacrifice required to learn and master a dish often disappears once the results are consumed. The most memorable of these shared revelations are recipes taught to Bính by Toklas. Lamb á la Toklas (Bính's private name for his Madame's recipe for roast lamb) requires a pré-salé lamb. These lambs are raised in salt marshes on the northern coast of France. According to Toklas, they need no seasoning, for they "are salted and seasoned from the raw beginning." When roasted to a succulent, perfect brown, their tender and mouthwatering flesh is a "reminder of why we kill and eat the young" (178). In another example, Bính remembers learning how to suffocate pigeons, a technique that Miss Toklas uses to preserve the blood in the bird, so that the result is a plumper and juicier bite. The process requires Bính to use the sense of touch in ways that are excruciating, as he uses his fingers to press on the bird's throat and eventually to feel the quickening of the bird's heart as its life is extinguished. Although "the difference in the end result . . . is spectacular . . . the required act is unforgivable" (68).[13] The horror of strangling a pigeon or carefully cultivating and then butchering a lamb stems from the fact that these animals are killed in this way to increase the diner's pleasure. Although Bính masters these techniques, he is nevertheless haunted by them, for he becomes complicit in a cycle of consumption and erasure that also affects him. Bính's reaction to these acts of culinary sacrifice thus critiques dynamics of continued exploitation and the invisibility of their extensive and lingering effects.

Food and Networks of Queer Intimacy

In *The Book of Salt,* the culinary also offers, at least for ephemeral moments, access to nonnormative communities and intimacies that work against imperial and heteropatriarchal structures. After characterizing his employers (the collectors) into three distinct categories, the novel takes an unexpected turn as soon as Alice B. Toklas opens the door to the Toklas-Stein residence on the rue du Fleurus. Indeed, like Bính, we expect Stein and Toklas to fall into one of these categories. Yet what is most striking about Bính's relationship with them is that they are in many ways unlike his other employers. Instead, the bounds of this queer domestic household allow for alternative formations that include temporary, queer affiliations between expatriate modernist and Vietnamese laborer. Bính, GertrudeStein (one word in *The Book of Salt*), and Toklas create, even for small and tiny moments, a familial intimacy. The unique queer and diasporic household on the rue de Fleurus thus temporarily allows for cross-class affiliations that are not otherwise available amid the overarching structures of empire and globalized labor.

These fleeting moments of community and connection often stem from opportunities to share a meal or to learn and revise a recipe. The novel highlights the affinities shared by Bính and Toklas, both of whom are subject to the whims of GertrudeStein and her desires. Toklas, like Bính, seems most comfortable and at home in the kitchen. The two share a cautious admiration for each other and their shared cooking talents. Like Bính, Madame Toklas also relies on secrets (like a prized gazpacho recipe made without salt): "Intrigue," Bính confides in us, "is what my Madame aspires to in all of her creations" (179). Bính and Toklas are joined in this queer affinity that is also about their labor—the behind-the-scenes orchestrations that make Stein's life enjoyable.

Yet even with these close connections to his Mesdames, Bính is constantly reminded that lasting intimacies are impossible. One example centers on a simple preparation of eggs. In the novel, Bính falls in love with Marcus Lattimore, and after their first night together, he struggles to find an excuse for his absence. He lies about his whereabouts and tells his Mesdames that he failed to return home because he was drunk and asleep after consuming an entire bottle of rum given to him by Lattimore. Dismayed at the thought that someone has taken advantage of Bính, Toklas (who introduced him to Lattimore), invites the chef to prepare a simple "meal *en famille*, as the French would say." Such a simple repast,

> a platter of fried eggs and a loaf of bread placed in the center of a family's table are never an insult. It is a ritual in intimacy. It is food that has no business with the outside world, food that no hired cook would ever dare serve. A family member, maybe a friend, but never a servant. I understand my Madame's gesture perfectly. With Miss Toklas on one arm and GertrudeStein on the other, I step into the circle that Miss Toklas has in that moment drawn. There is no visible trace of its outline, but I always know that it is there. I have sensed its presence in all of the households that I have been in. (102)

Truong uses the present tense to convey the immediacy of Bính's emotional response to Toklas's offer, its temporal binding "in that moment." Bính can imagine his inclusion into this intimate circle as family member and not servant, an opportunity represented by the promise of food created without fuss or bother, the intimate simplicity of eggs and bread served for loved ones. Bính finds, however, that when faced with this completely unexpected gesture, he cannot continue to lie. He guiltily discloses the truth and in doing so, is "excommunicated yet again from that perfect circle that is at the center of every home" (103).

In contrast to such disappointments, a few pages earlier Truong presents an alternative formation of queer Vietnamese community over a meal laced with the flavors of diasporic longing. Bính meets a "man on the bridge," the fictionalized version of Nguyen Ai Quoc / Ho Chi Minh, who invites him to an intimate dinner for two. This meal is unique in *The Book of Salt*, as it is the only scene in which food is prepared for Bính and not by him. Again, Truong disrupts the links between ethnic and national identity and food. The flavors of this meal are haunting and memorable for the diners because they are drawn from the chef's experiences in many locations. With Nguyen Ai Quoc, Bính becomes the diner and experiences the sensual pleasures of food, so often orchestrated by his own hand. The pleasure, for Bính, though, is not of exotic consumption but of familiarity, the recall of long forgotten memories and taste associations, the surprise of Asian cuisine and partnership in an unexpected location, and the experience of dining with a countryman who is familiar with its flavors. The menu can only be described as flavored by the diaspora. In reflecting on the meal, Bính appreciatively notes that it is "not Chinese food" or "American, either" but food made by a Vietnamese chef, who, Nguyen Ai Quoc tells him, "will always cook from all the places where he has been. It is his way of remembering the world" (99). Bính delights in the undeniable bitterness of watercress, perhaps unrecognizable to a Parisian palate but instantly identified by Bính, especially when it is quickly wilted in a searing hot pan. Salt-and-pepper shrimp are flavored with fleur de sel, morels, and brown butter. The meal is also a seduction; throughout the meal, the two men flirt over a game of questions and answers as Bính guesses the ingredients of each course. The tongue, Bính reminds us, cannot lie, for a diner cannot deny the sensation of taste. In this meal, food allows him to immediately forge an intimate connection with another Vietnamese man. The two men, connected by exile and their presence in a place where their bodies are constantly marked as curiosity, enjoy a momentary reprieve from this scrutiny, over a quiet dinner that takes place in an empty restaurant.

The novel's placement of these moments of intimacy alongside one another, the promise of a shared meal (ultimately withheld, in the case of Stein and Toklas, and realized, in the case of the man on the bridge), also attest to the immiscibilities that are critical to Truong's exploration of potential queer affiliations across class, race, and nation. *The Book of Salt* imagines, through food, a sensibility that is more than the politics of the plate. Each of these scenes is similar in that the representation of queer community, family, or connection is tied to the fleeting pleasure of food, the taste on the tongue that, while perhaps memorable, is also ephemeral. Thus Bính's desire for and connection to foundational figures—whether those belonging to Vietnamese nationalism or literary high modernism—in the end do not last, and food, rather than representing unquestioned forms of ethnic authenticity or easy possibilities for community, instead underscores painful and bitter realizations.

Translation, Description, Negation: Or When a Pear Is Not a Pear

In *The Book of Salt*, the culinary is both literal and literary, and the language and literary construction of food is critical to Truong's examination of the complexities of labor, the diaspora, and queer community formations. In this section, I turn to the novel's engagement with the culinary through the literary. Truong's choice of Gertrude Stein and Alice B. Toklas is crucial because they are, in David Eng's terms, "poster children of queer liberal pluralism," and because of Stein's unique relationship to language and the literary and her deeply fraught representations of race and class.[14] Truong's play with language and translation clearly responds to Stein's own fascination with raced and classed others, manifested most famously—and infamously—in *Three Lives*. Through works like *Three Lives* (and especially *Melanctha*), scholars have wrestled with the difficult combination of aesthetic and formal innovation—trademarks of Stein's high modernism—and her construction of tragic immigrant, working-class, or racialized bodies.[15] The novel's setting, however, already undermines the presumed hierarchies that would set this U.S. modernist figure apart from and above the Vietnamese laborer working in her home. In Paris and Bilignin, both Stein and Bính are expatriates and exiles. Both are viewed as curiosities, Stein for her relationship with Toklas, and Bính for his racialized body. Most important, both have difficulty communicating in French. Although the novel itself is written in English, the narrative we read is presumably an English translation of French or Vietnamese. Bính and Stein thus meet on the common, linguistic ground of their mutually awkward and limited French. These layers of multiple transformations and reconfigurations, together with Bính's own slippery unreliability as a narrator, highlight Truong's exploration of the possibilities of language and narrative, on one hand, and the novel's undermining of the assumed power dynamics of Stein as an elite modernist and Bính as merely the represented object, on the other.

The novel's interest in the possibilities and failures of language and representation is closely tied to the culinary. In a method that recalls Stein's own literary strategies, Bính quickly learns to develop a practice of communication by means of negation, a character trait that was inspired by Toklas's descriptions of her cook, Trac.[16] Truong explicitly ties this form of communication to the global marketplace. He develops this strategy in the Parisian markets as the act of pointing to and then rejecting objects, cuts of meat, and ingredients becomes critical to his navigation of Paris. For although "communication in the negative is not the quickest and certainly not the most esteemed form of expression," he recognizes that "for those of us with few words to spare it is the magic spell, the incantation, that opens up an otherwise inaccessible treasure trove" (18). The strategy of communication by means of negation is critical to "those" like Bính, those who lack fluency in French and find themselves participating in the global markets of Paris as simultaneously a purchaser, a laborer, and an object of desire.

In maneuvering the ins and outs of Parisian markets through negation, Bính subverts a global marketplace that depends on and denies his labor and objectifies his body as an exotic trophy and curiosity object.

But the act of translation or, to be more accurate, the failed capacities of translation also counter those who, like Stein, read, catalog, represent, and ultimately exploit Asian laborers. "GertrudeStein, love is not a bowl of quinces" illustrates this response. In context, this quotation refers to a game that Stein plays with Bính. The game begins early on in his employment at rue du Fleurus, when he discovers that he cannot remember the French word for pineapple. Frustrated, he stammers that he wants "buy a pear . . . not a pear" (35) and then twists his body into the shape of a pineapple to convey his meaning. Stein finds the combination of Bính's coinage and charade intensely amusing, and every evening, they gather at the dining table with an assemblage of objects that is reminiscent of her catalog in *Tender Buttons*. Stein, Bính tells us, has a seemingly infinite hoard of buttons, glass globes, and other knick-knacks, "a whole world stashed away" (35) in drawers and cubbies. Stein points, and Bính defines, always through negation. Her beloved poodle Basket is a "dog not a friend" and Pepe, a Chihuahua, is a "dog not a dog" (36). After four years of playing the game, Stein, tired of objects and family dogs, raises the level of discourse, asking Bính, "How would you define love?" (33).

This question marks the end of the game. Bính's answer, however, also emphasizes the shifting connections between the Vietnamese laborer and his employer, between the "other" represented, and the modernist writer who attempts to represent him. Bính refuses to submit to Stein's attempt to learn more about his carefully guarded past, her desire to taste what he has previously called the bitter fruits of exile. "Ah," he thinks,

> a classic move from the material to the spiritual. GertrudeStein, like the collectors who have preceded her, wants to see the stretch marks on my tongue. . . . I point to a table on which several quinces sit yellowing in a blue and white china bowl. I shake my head in their direction, and I leave the room speechless. (36)

As with many moments in *The Book of Salt,* Bính's explanation of this game is entangled in a subnarrative: his painful memories of his love for an American man who eventually exploits Bính's affection to get ahold of one of Stein's unpublished manuscripts. At the end of this chapter, Bính tells us that even when ripe, quinces "remain a fruit hard and obstinate, —useless, GertrudeStein, until they are simmered, coddled for hours above a low steady flame. . . . GertrudeStein, love is not a bowl of quinces yellowing in a blue and white china bowl, seen but untouched" (40). Bính's strategy has already fueled the literary technique that has become associated with Gertrude Stein's style, for "she is affirmed by [his] use of negatives and repetition" (34). This scene is full of ironies. As Catherine Fung notes, the conversation turns on a "metaphysical pun" (a pear not appear), which depends on Truong's English version of Binh's recasting of an exchange that supposedly occurs in French (pear in French, notes Fung, is "*poire*" and appear is "*apparaître*").[17] The novel disrupts presumptions about origins and reverses dynamics of colonial mimicry.[18] Just as we find out later that Stein has written a manuscript based on Bính, here her trademark technique is imitation. Yet the metaphor's beautiful bitterness articulates Bính's compromised position and also serves as a reminder that even though he might believe that he can subvert the representational logics of empire and labor, these moments are, in the end, only fleeting and fragile.

The plea that initiates this game—Bính describing what he wants to buy and how he must contort his body in order to express this desire—illustrates the novel's constant, delicate threading together of multiple forms of economies and consumption. The wish that cannot be fulfilled—and the object, taste, or emotion that escapes expression—are linked to the novel's interest in where and how language fails and to the lack of awareness of Asian laborers in global and colonial networks. Tropes of negation and repetition are thus ultimately also tied to these bodies and their histories. A pear is thus not a pear, and love is not a bowl of quinces. The taste of salt can be linked to four different sources—blood, sweat, tears, or the sea. Highlighting both multiplicities and failures, Truong's intersection of the literary and the culinary thus compels us to consider more carefully how we think about, know, and collect the Asian body.

Coda

Four years after Monique Truong published *The Book of Salt*, the Vietnamese-born and classically trained chef Hung Huynh was revealed as the winner of the Bravo reality competition *Top Chef*. Although in terms of genre, Truong's contemporary novel is far different from that of reality television, I end this chapter with a comparison of Huynh and Bính to highlight the persistence of these representational and narrative patterns. Both Truong's novel and Hung Huynh's portrayal on *Top Chef* illuminate the continuing and vexed complexities that are still attached to Vietnamese and Asian laboring bodies and to the networks that continue to consume and desire them. Hung Huynh illustrates a similar incongruity to Bính's—a Vietnamese body that could execute French culinary technique with precision—yet who initially seemed to refuse the role of grateful Vietnamese migrant. What I'm interested in here is the crafting of Hung Huynh's persona on *Top Chef* and his transition in the show from the cold-hearted villain to his final metamorphosis into the grateful immigrant who recognizes his Vietnamese "soul." My brief analysis considers how *Top Chef* (aided certainly by Huynh's own behavior) made this transformation.

Huynh quickly stood out in the third season of *Top Chef* for his amazing technical skills. Nonetheless, despite the consistent praise for his culinary technique and precision, the show characterized him as manipulative, cold, and calculating. Editors and producers used the contestant's self-professed strategy of crafting a "win-at-all-costs *Top Chef* persona."[19] He was often shown racing around the kitchen, oblivious to those in his path (he later explained that he used this tactic to unnerve and even annoy his fellow contestants). In the mis-en-place relay race, a challenge in which the contestants are assigned different tasks, he furiously butchered four different chickens in record time. His speed, precision, and technical mastery became part of his evolving character on the show as someone who was cold and calculating. "Even Hung's biggest detractors," note the editors of *The Top Chef Cookbook*, "had to be astonished by his technical skills, honed while working at Guy Savoy in Las Vegas. He could bone a chicken in seconds, whip up a killer sous vide, re-create a classic dish at Le Cirque, and even build a trippy Smurf-like village out of cereal."[20] Huynh's portrayal on *Top Chef* was drawn from his behavior on the show, his strategy for winning, and the careful editing that is central to any reality competition. Ultimately, this construction also depended on Huynh's refusal of intimacy with other contestants, with the judges who tried to advise him, and with Bravo's viewers. Eventually, this combination led to the persistent observation that Huynh, although he consistently exhibited culinary technical mastery, also produced dishes that lacked heart and soul. "Hung," reflected *Top Chef* host Padma Lakshmi, "works on technique . . . I do think there's something to be said from really cooking, um, with your palate and cooking with love and all that. I don't think that Hung doesn't bring love to his cooking, I just think he approaches it from a much different, [*sic*] from a technician's standpoint."

In the final episodes of *Top Chef*, Huynh's persona quickly, and rather amazingly, began to shift. In these closing moments, he began to reclaim both an immigrant narrative and nostalgic longing for his Vietnamese culture as the true inspiration for this work. As if in direct response to the judges' critiques regarding his lack of passion and soul, Huynh began emphasizing the importance of his Vietnamese family. This new version of him centered on the proper reclaiming of this Asian heart and soul, a process that supposedly inspired his victory. Frank Bruni, writing for the *New York Times* blog *Diner's Journal*, recaps this sudden and dramatic character turn:

> I also thought [Hung] might be a goner for another reason: the transparent groveling and obsequiousness of his remarks to the judges' panel in last week's episode and in this one's. On the heels of a comment that he didn't seem to cook with enough heart or soul, Hung suddenly morphed—at least semantically—into one big, red beating heart that had been marinated for 24 hours in essence of soul.
>
> Anytime a judge asked him a question, a Hung response went something like this: "I was just cooking with my heart! I have so much love in my cooking! My cooking is about love and soul and, oh, did I mention heart? Did I mention the soulful cooking of my mother and my grandmother and my aunt and my uncle and our next-door neighbor and how it took up a permanent place in my own heart, which is so full of the love of cooking?"[21]

Part of Bruni's satirical humor is its accuracy; Huynh spoke often about his family as the inspiration of his cuisine and as the source for his passion for cooking, and both the fervor and the frequency with which he used these strategies were surprising. Moreover, he suddenly dropped the cool demeanor that had become his trademark during the show, and the closing episode featured shots of a tearful Huynh overcome with gratitude and joy.

The conclusion of *Top Chef* rescripted Hung Huynh, and the finale linked his triumphant victory to his display of an immigrant's gratitude, hard work, motivation, and determination.[22] His participation in the competition was pitched as leading to an important lesson. Experience in the United States (albeit a highly fictionalized and manipulated form of "real" experience) supposedly led not to assimilation but to a sentimental reclaiming of difference and its value. The editors of the *Top Chef* cookbook, released a few years after Huynh appeared, confirm this story; in the introduction to Huynh's section of the book, they describe him as "driven by an inspiring immigrant narrative."[23] In his finale blog, Judge Ted Allen adamantly defends Huynh and alludes to this plot of immigrant striving:

I have never agreed with the notion that Hung's food lacked "heart" or "soul." Ever. You see it in every knife stroke, and you taste it in (almost) every dish. Yes, he has seemed less than cuddly with his competitors at times—I think that's really what Hung's detractors are reacting to. We should consider, though, that most of that was really the product of editing, prodding by interviewers, a few ill-chosen remarks, and a not-very-convincing job of trying to be the Santino/Jeffrey/Marcel/Stephen [*Top Chef* "villains" from previous seasons] that Hung thought the show wanted him to be—a natural hazard of this wildly successful reality format. Set that stuff aside for a moment, and chew on this: What drives a young man to become that excellent with a knife, that relentless with his curiosity about cooking techniques? Who else in this cast has worked harder to master the classics and to explore new frontiers in food, to scratch and claw all the way into the kitchen at Guy Savoy in Vegas, a restaurant so exacting that it's hard to draw parallels?[24]

What Allen asks his readers to mull over is the indescribable and, for the presumed Bravo viewer, seemingly unfathomable immigrant desire and motivation. Ultimately, even for Allen, even though Huynh may have been masterful with his knife skills or palate, it is his motivation as a Vietnamese migrant that truly secured his *Top Chef* victory. This production of Hung Huynh as learning how to correctly perform as a grateful immigrant subject—a model minority chef—also presumably made him more palatable as racialized object ("Chew on this," offers Allen). The consistent invocation of terms like heart, soul, and passion are important, for these emotional registers are the means through which Huynh can form intimate relationships with the *Top Chef* viewers. Allen's post also highlights Huynh's production as an Asian sexualized subject for both queer and straight viewers of the Bravo network; his cheeky title, "Well, Hung," recalls popular U.S. representations of Asian masculinity as effeminate.

Clearly, the reality television star Huynh and Truong's fictionalized Bính are far different in their representations of Vietnamese queer masculinity. What Huynh's case does show, however, is that the fictional dynamics in *The Book of Salt* have very real counterparts. Both Truong's novel and the treatment of Huynh in *Top Chef* illustrate the ongoing exploitation and consumption of Asian domestic and affective labor that, even when visible, still remains too easily dismissed and forgotten. Indeed, the happy ending of *Top Chef* opposes Bính's careful refusal of such easy versions. Rather, Truong's intervention is to dwell in complexities. For although another narrative of empowerment might, perhaps, momentarily taste sweeter, it would also be unpalatable precisely because such a story would deny the lingering bitterness of historic and continued exploitations.

Notes

1. Houghton Mifflin Harcourt, press release for *The Book of Salt* by Monique Truong, available at http://www.hmhbooks.com/booksellers/press_release/truong/#questions.
2. Truong combines portrayals of two Vietnamese cooks, Nguyen and Trac, in her own construction of Bính. See Anita Mannur, review of *The Book of Salt*, by Monique Truong, *Gastronomica: The Journal of Food and Culture* 4, no. 3 (summer 2004): 120–21.
3. For other analyses of Truong's novel, see chapter 2 of David Eng, *The Feeling of Kinship: Queer Liberalism and the Racialization of Intimacy* (Durham, NC: Duke University Press, 2010), which focuses on queer affiliations and temporality; Catherine Fung, "A History of Absences: the Problem of Reference in Monique Truong's *The Book of Salt*," *Novel: A Forum on Fiction* 45, no. 1 (2012): 94–110; Y-Dang Troeung, "'A Gift or a Theft Depends on Who Is Holding the Pen': Postcolonial Collaborative Autobiography and Monique Truong's *The Book of Salt*," *Modern Fiction Studies* 56, no. 1 (2010): 113–35; and Wenying Xu, *Eating Identities: Reading Food in Asian American Literature* (Honolulu: University of Hawai'i Press, 2008).
4. Anita Mannur, *Culinary Fictions: Food in South Asian Diasporic Culture* (Philadelphia: Temple University Press, 2010), 10–19.
5. For earlier work that focuses on Asian American food and literature, see Sau-Ling Cynthia Wong, *Reading Asian American Literature: From Necessity to Extravagance* (Princeton, NJ: Princeton University Press, 1993); Monica Chiu, *Filthy Fiction: Asian American Literature by Women* (New York: Altamira Press, 2004); Eileen Chia-Ching Fung, "'To Eat the Flesh of His Dead Mother': Hunger, Masculinity, and Nationalism in Frank Chin's *Donald Duk*," *LIT: Literature, Interpretation, Theory* 10 (1999): 255–74; and Wilfried Raussert and Nicole Waller, "Past and Repast: Food as Historiography in Fae Myenne Ng's *Bone* and Frank Chin's *Donald Duk*," *Amerikastudien/American Studies* 40, no. 3 (1996): 485–502. See also Jeffrey Partridge, "The Politics of Ethnic Authorship: Li-Young Lee, Emerson, and Whitman at the Banquet Table," *Studies in the Literary Imagination* 37, no. 1 (spring 2004): 101–25; and Wilfried Raussert, "Minority Discourse, Foodways, and Aspects of Gender: Contemporary Writings by Asian-American Women," *Journal x: A Journal in Culture and Criticism* 7, no. 2 (2003): 184–204.
6. Mannur, *Culinary Fictions*; Xu, *Eating Identities*; Jennifer Ho, *Consumption and Identity in Asian American Coming-of-Age Novels* (New York: Routledge, 2005).
7. Xu, *Eating Identities*, 2; Mannur, *Culinary Fictions*, 1–17.
8. Xu, *Eating Identities*, 8.
9. Mannur, *Culinary Fictions*, 8.
10. Monique Truong, *The Book of Salt* (Boston: Houghton Mifflin Harcourt, 2003). Page numbers of quotations from this book are in parentheses.
11. Xu, *Eating Identities*, 140.
12. My reading of Bính's subversive strategies is conversant with Eng's and Xu's examination of subversion and agency. See Eng, *The Feeling of Kinship*, chapter 2; and Xu, *Eating Identities*, 127–47.
13. Xu helpfully also traces the trope of pigeons in *The Book of Salt* to Bính's relationship with his mother.

14. Eng, *The Feeling of Kinship*, 74.

15. See, for example, Corinne E. Blackmer, "African Masks and the Art of Passing in Gertrude Stein's *Melanctha* and Nella Larsen's *Passing*," *Journal of the History of Sexuality* 4, no. 2 (1992): 230–63; Laura Doyle, "The Flat, the Round, and Gertrude Stein: Race and the Shape of Modern(ist) History," *Modernism/Modernity* 7, no. 2 (2000): 249–71; Michaela Giesenkirchen, "Ethnic Types and Problems of Characterization in Gertrude Stein's Radcliffe Themes," *American Literary Realism* 38, no. 1 (2005): 58–72; and John Carlos Rowe, "Naming What Is Inside: Gertrude Stein's Use of Names in *Three Lives*," *Novel* 36, no. 2 (2003): 219–43.

16. Xu, *Eating Identities*, 128.

17. Fung, "A History of Absences," 101.

18. I am thinking here of Homi Bhaba, "Of Mimicry and Man: The Ambivalence of Colonial Discourse" in *The Location of Culture* (London, New York: Routledge, 1994), 85–92.

19. Kate Krader, "Top Chef Winner's Tips," *Food & Wine*, February 2008, available at http://www.foodandwine.com/articles/top-chef-winners-tips.

20. Lianna Krissoff and Leda Scheintaub, eds., *Top Chef: The Cookbook* (San Francisco: Chronicle Books: 2008).

21. Bruni, Frank, "The Top Chef Finale: Of Bad Lobster and Tame Cake," *Diner's Journal*, October 4, 2007, available at http://dinersjournal.blogs.nytimes.com/2007/10/04/the-top-chef-finale-of-bad-lobster-and-tame-cake/.

22. The portrayal of Huynh reminds me of Christina Klein's work on narrative of sentiment and integration in Cold War Asian American relations. See Christina Klein, *Cold War Orientalism: Asia in the Middlebrow Imagination, 1945–1961* (Berkeley: University of California Press, 2003).

23. Krissoff and Scheintaub, *Top Chef*, 207.

24. Ted Allen, "Well, Hung," October 3, 2007, available at http://www.bravotv.com/top-chef/blogs/ted-allen/well-hung.

19

The Globe at the Table

How Madhur Jaffrey's World Vegetarian Reconfigures the World

DELORES B. PHILLIPS

The figuration of the world traveler that Jaffrey describes and the autobiographical fashioning of self in her cookbooks already have been analyzed. But an addition to this analysis is the configuration of Jaffrey's world. In other words, her books' "gastropoetics" have been analyzed, but the gastocartographies that she maps—or elides—have not. The conventional thinking about global cuisine follows two archetypal configurations: that of each culture bringing to the table its special flavor, its unique inflection of signature tastes or that of the multinational corporation—McDonalds, Taco Bell, KFC— that represents a branded flavor recognized everywhere, with a chain opening in each country and region and adapting its flavors to suit local tastes. Both rely on familiar, readily recognizable flavors, but they oppose each other in ways that underscore the special problems of globalization, power, privilege, and consumption.

Madhur Jaffrey's cookbook, entitled *Madhur Jaffrey's World Vegetarian*, does something in between. In this chapter, I first identify the cartographies that structure Jaffrey's text, analyzing how *World Vegetarian* reconfigures globalism by placing South Asian ingredients, cooking methods, tastes, and textures at the epicenter of global vegetarian cuisine, thereby redistributing the forces of culinary globalization by positioning South Asian cooking at the center of global power. Consequently, Jaffrey readjusts the geographic orientation of the currents moving global influence as India becomes everywhere. In this way, her book distances notions of globalization from twentieth- and twenty-first-century economics and its association with an East-meets-West or North-meets-South dialectic. Even as she brings the globe to the table, though, I argue that she reifies differences that threaten her cookbook's task of bridging cultural gaps. Next I contrast Jaffrey's model of the world to that of other world travelers. I contend that Jaffrey uses her cookbook to oppose the shape of the world as imagined by such globetrotters as the McDonalds burger-eater abroad, the U.S. vegetarians with only iceberg lettuce for company but whose privilege grants them access to exotic foods, and the multinational agricultural corporation, whose hegemonic structures construct globalization in terms of market share and distributions of labor. I focus on the last as the most important and least visible of these contrasts, as the multinational agribusinesses provide the ideal complement to Jaffrey's world vegetarian. I examine the problematic relationships between the First and Third Worlds as they emerge in both Jaffrey's figure of the Third World woman and the manner in which U.S. multinationals feed—and feed on—the Third World spaces that are one of the engines driving their profits.

Consequently, I read the "world" in *World Vegetarian* as a noun instead of an adjective, a noun that can easily become a verb configuring and disseminating knowledge and power.[1] Rather than consider the world vegetarian as a well-traveled cosmopolite whose expansive palate is fed morsel by morsel, I read the world as a supranational entity mapped in a vegetarian mode. Its legend comprises ingredients and measurements: spices and flavors mark boundaries, national and territorial; techniques and directives reveal topography. All cosmopolites travel in a world that facilitates their momentum. Kwame Appiah's airport conversations and Aihwa Ong's flexible citizens operate in modes of circulation that also describe the circumference of the world, a material one that they all inhabit.[2] The body that refuses national limits is a body whose movements, real or imagined, configure a model of a world with unclear borders.

Regional cookbooks that attempt to transform space in ways that resist the customary boundaries of nation and culture offer such means of accomplishing this configuration. *Madhur Jaffrey's World Vegetarian* is one of them. In keeping with the aesthetic of mapping the globe, Jaffrey's objective is comprehensiveness. At 758 pages and with more than 650 recipes for preparing beans, peas, lentils, nuts, vegetables, grains, and dairy products, *World Vegetarian* gathers flavors and food styles from around the globe, organizes them in categories that make them easy to find, and presents them to the reader in a format that is easy to read, with instructions that are easy to follow. The dust jacket states that the book contains "dishes from five continents [that] touch on virtually all the world's best loved flavors for an unsurpassed selection of vegetarian fare." A comprehensive reference for worldwide vegetarian cuisine, the text is global in its expanse: *World Vegetarian* contains more than two hundred recipes for vegetables, with "at least a dozen recipes for eggplant alone."[3] The book offers access to all corners of the globe: in a single meal, a diner can span several continents, sampling the local flavors from each. The book promises both authenticity and access; food becomes the substrate of the multicultural transaction. The range of recipes for eggplant—cited as a twenty-page exemplar of varied, delicious treatments—offers global variations of a single ingredient, as opposed to the global spread of a single brand with its narrow range of signature flavors.

The ostensible purpose of Jaffrey's cookbook is to transform the reader into a world vegetarian similar to the author, although she is not a vegetarian and has written many other, nonvegetarian cookbooks. To achieve this, the book strives for inclusiveness in both its content and its audience. The first line of the introduction proclaims, "This book is written for everyone." Although her next clause narrows "everyone" by classifying its members according to their vegetarian status, the idea that the book's audience is the entire globe is emphasized. Her book's "everyone" is the raceless, amorphous mix of all of us, bound together in our need to eat and our desire to sample new flavors. In reading and imagining, cooking and eating, we all become the world vegetarians of the book's title. If the book strives for comprehensiveness, then it also does not restrict its audience according to race or socioeconomic background. Jaffrey does not address only those who can afford fresh lychee or Kobe beef; instead, her readers are both the "sophisticated food enthusiasts [and the] impoverished students" whom she sees waiting in the same line at the stand to buy Asian noodles in London.[4] Rather than concentrating on diversity defined by racial differences overcome by universal commonalities, Jaffrey focuses on a diversity defined by socioeconomic difference overcome by the blurring of borders that make a wide variety of foods affordable to a culturally heterogeneous body of diners.

As Shameem Black observes, *World Vegetarian* conforms in most ways to the conventional definitions of cosmopolitanism.[5] In addition to her goals of limitless inclusion and comprehensive cataloging, Jaffrey imagines the eater as a global citizen by using herself as a model. This eater is already at home everywhere, and the cookbook provides the means by which she can dine everywhere at once: she eats at home in the world. The cookbook does not, however, create the cosmopolitan subject because it observes an already existing condition. Instead, her reason for writing this book derives from Jaffrey's observations of globalism's pervasive effect on culinary culture. She notes, "We seem to be heading toward a softening of boundaries between all cuisines."[6] She does not imply the erasure of difference or the abdication of personal preference or cultural allegiance in favor of a complete lack of differentiation in which all influences converge in a single culinary tradition (the ultimate in fusion cuisine). While culinary traditions may share certain features, Jaffrey does not suggest that all foods everywhere are the same. Her book highlights culinary commonalities and uses them to create meals based on shared flavors. She also describes the cultural specificities of each dish, describing the differences in a system of cultural exchange and interchange that equalizes their values.[7]

The analyses of the cosmopolitanism of Madhur Jaffrey's cookbooks look at her internationality, her narrative voice, and her reader's internationality. Her cookbooks also construct space, using familiar tactics to represent nations. If her previous works mapped India for her reader, then her task in *World Vegetarian* is to map the world and populate it with readers, eaters, and cooks from around the globe, uniting them over meals both real and imagined. In this way, she practices a special form of gastrocartography: mapping space through taste. By following conventional maps, which are less about accurate reproductions of space than they are about depictions of space that support ideological and rhetorical objectives, Jaffrey's book is disinterested in the territorialization exemplified by the many maps that represent foreign spaces.[8] Instead it is interested in mapping spaces in ways that populate them but leave the reading and eating suspended above and between cultures yet engaged with them in constant material production and reproduction. Ultimately, regional cookbooks—including Jaffrey's de-regionalized cookbook—share the same basic features of cartography: they initiate a relationship between territory and knowledge. Indeed, engaging with *World Vegetarian* is to come to know space intimately, in the most embodied fashion possible.

Madhur Jaffrey's *World Vegetarian* and Global Gastrocartographies

In her *World Vegetarian*, Madhur Jaffrey depicts cultural spaces by describing culinary habits. She connects eating bodies and literal spaces in somatic, sentimental ways, incorporating her readers in her construction of the world. This world is not of the past; it is of the present and the future. It is "dynamic and imaginative," encouraging readers to place themselves in its crucial formative moments.[9] She both brings lands together and distinguishes them through shared flavors. The imagined communities of Benedict Anderson, invoked by Shameem Black in her analysis of Jaffrey's cookbooks, are not just the recipes' cultural designations but also the global communities of its readers that the book creates. These communities thus achieve more than simply an abstract understanding of cultural production. Instead, Jaffrey tries to connect them to real spaces occupied by eating people. Her representations of space defy the dimensions of conventional cartography, although the mapping of space in *World Vegetarian* follows many of its functions. The bonds between eating people that constitute the substrate of her mapping blur the distinctions of maps from other forms of literary and artistic production by instantiating the logic governing them all. The result of the cartographies that she draws is a sense of place that implies the wideness of the world but still is small enough to fit into a single bite.[10]

Beans and split peas are a good example of Jaffrey's gastrocartography. In counting the number of ways in which beans and split peas can be cooked, Jaffrey recounts recipes as the footprints marking her travels across nations, starting with

> a 6000-year-old dish, the famous khichri of India, that combines split peas and rice in a stew and seasons it with cumin seeds and ginger, and going on to an unusual and elegant black bean soup from Costa Rica flavored with green coriander and green peppers, . . . a whole world that remains unexplored.[11]

Jaffrey's work plunges into this unexplored terrain, orienting her reader in this world. To do this, she begins with a temporal engagement and then moves geographically along the axis of the global South. Jaffrey and her reader move through space bean by bean.

These gastrocartographies do not configure space nation by nation in ways that make their boundaries as distinct as one might find on a map or a globe, and Jaffrey further rearranges the map by juxtaposing countries in seemingly random alignments. The ordering of the recipes mixes them geographically, inviting readers to stride quickly across borders.[12] Rather than the familiar ordering of the world, with nations in their conventional places, the ordering principle is gastronomic resonances that guide the taster through unfamiliar terrain by means of shared flavors. For example, the section on the various preparations of cabbage reveals the logic of ordering that transcends geography by offering landscapes of taste. *Tang Chu Bow Pai Tsai* from China (Sweet-and-Sour Cabbage) on page 148 shares the sweetness of sugar and marmalade with the dried red currants in Turkey's *Tembel Dolma* (Cabbage with Rice and Currants) on the following page and complements the spicy bite of the former's ginger with the latter's piquancy of cinnamon and black pepper. The recipe for *Tembel Dolma* is followed by the Indonesian *Sambal Kol* (Stir-Fried Green Cabbage with Spicy Red Paste), which graduates from black to cayenne pepper. Borders draw nations closer as they delineate their spatial separation. The book maps national character not simply by the flavors unique to each country but by the similarities and differences of recipes that serve as national ambassadors. Meanwhile, the distinct political units of Jaffrey's gastrocartographies create embodied citizens whose biopower—enacted in consumption and digestion—contributes to Jaffrey's larger project of democracy and freedom.

Jaffrey nonetheless includes some stateless foods, dishes that are assigned to no locale and are instead suspended beyond even the fluctuating geographies of taste mapping the cookbook. The Curried Red Cabbage with Cranberry Juice recipe following *Sambal Kol* is a stateless invention of Jaffrey's own making, a dish that combines the Indian flavors she learned as a girl with new, American flavors she learned as an adult: "I grew up with neither red cabbage nor cranberry juice. America has taught me to use both."[13] Like Jaffrey's recipe for Corn with Ginger, Cauliflower Stir-Fried with Ginger and Cilantro, Peas with Ginger and Sesame Oil, and Whole Wheat Couscous with Cumin and Cauliflower,[14] Curried Red Cabbage with Cranberry Juice lacks the national designations of other dishes.

> I came up with [Curried Red Cabbage with Cranberry Juice] one Christmas when I wanted to braise red cabbage with Indian seasonings. I also did not want to use any red wine, whose tartness and color helps to keep the red cabbage red. And so I came up with the idea of substituting cranberry juice and was very happy with the results. . . . The fennel seeds add a very special, sweet flavor, which I have loved since childhood.[15]

This recipe inclines toward diasporic yearning: it instructs in the preparation of a Christmas dish that retains the deep reds of the holiday season in the United States[16] yet is refracted by nostalgia for foreign shores, signified by Jaffrey's use of curry powder. While coriander, peppercorns, and cloves are perhaps the stereotypical inclusions in the Christmas flavor palate (an always already "foreign" assemblage of spices with a lengthy imperialist history), turmeric, chilies, cumin, and brown mustard seeds are perhaps new faces at the feast. This dish maps taste as it marks attenuation and as it also maps the world by bringing together disparate cultural influences in a single mouthful.

In her presentation of the universality of rice, subject to the modifications of color, length, and density demonstrated in the color photos, Jaffrey artfully arranges this staple grain of the world in a single tableau. She complements the visual array in the color photos with a description of the geographic specificities of its worldwide consumption:

> In all of Asia and many parts of the Mediterranean I find it remarkable that everybody prefers their own rice. If you are used to eating rice, you are used to

eating a particular rice and nothing else quite satisfies. . . . In Bali, you will hear that the only perfect rice is the plump Balinese one, grown under the watchful eye of the goddess Sri. The Japanese, who could export cheap rice from California, will pay six times as much for their own because they insist that it is sweeter and has more texture. The Italians prefer their own risotto rice, while the Greeks and Turks, who have similar rices, will prefer to eat what they grow. In India, much of the west coast thinks that that the best daily rice is their partially milled red rice and in the south, it is "boiled rice," a parboiled, medium-grain rice that sits on every single plate and banana leaf.[17]

In the globalized array of foods, rice is subject to its own provinciality. However, among the plain rice dishes on pages 375 and 376, only the basmati rice recipe of India has a national identity. Meanwhile, the nationalized rice dishes on pages 377 and 378 exhibit the morphological differences that mark them as exotic: Plain "Forbidden" Black Rice is so visually striking that Jaffrey declares that "you almost need to create a meal around it," and its color, paired with grilled red peppers with romesco sauce or surrounded with "sliced summer tomatoes and mozzarella—with fresh basil and extra-virgin olive oil, of course"—creates a dish whose visual appeal complements its gustatory richness. The black, red, white, and green color contrasts are the basis for a culinary consumption of the exotic other, and the gastrocartographies of these plates surround China by Italy and Spain.

In mapping the globe through its rice and her insistence on national preferences, Jaffrey establishes two things about American rice consumption: first, that American rice is an inferior product that can be most suitably treated according to the American-style food rules that privilege speed and ease over flavor and texture; and, second, that American appetites for rice follow a more fickle model of cosmopolitanism, one marked by scant attention and superficial engagement. In writing about the international tastes for provincial varieties of rice, she describes American appetites for the exotic: "It is only in America, where rice is still not in the blood, that every new rice is embraced as the wonder of the day."[18] Meanwhile, in her instructions for preparing Plain Long-Grain Rice, Jaffrey acknowledges that cooks in a rush may not have time to wash and soak their rice, so offers a recipe to accommodate these conditions. In advising her readers which variety to cook, she writes: "It is best to use American-style long-grain rice here. It would be a pity to waste the basmati."[19] This is more than simply an acknowledgment that different ingredients should be prepared according to best practices in accordance with their provenance. If an ingredient requires a specific touch, of course it is wasteful to gloss over necessary steps, ruining the ingredient or cheating the eater of its flavorful promise. Indeed, the recipe for *Tengai Saadam* (South Indian Coconut Rice) on page 382 uses long-grain white rice, preparing it according to the recipe Jaffrey provides a few pages earlier. The language of waste, however, puts American-style long-grain rice into a wholly different register. It does not require care and is part of the dismissive regimen that both alienates American vegetarians from their counterparts around the globe and makes them into culinary cultural dilettantes.

Cross-referencing the index with the book's geographic regions reveals uneven geographical distributions of the recipes' origins. It is here that the cartography of the volume becomes clear: most of the recipes are Indian, placing India at the epicenter from the globe, which radiates outward from South Asia and across the global South. This means that Jaffrey's cosmopolitanism is that of an Indian traveler at home in the world, which is supported by a map drawn to reflect this specific cosmopolitical engagement. This in turn complements Jaffrey's intervention in the debates of gastropoetics, shifting it away from authenticity and toward an expansive sense of self by creating a world that accommodates her movements.[20] Both Jaffrey's gastrocartographic and gastropoetical practices accord with Black's observations of how *World Vegetarian* "construct[s] an expanded sense of [Jaffrey's] own Indianness" as India constitutes the geographic home orienting the book.

World Vegetarian's recipes for eggplant provides a clear sense of how a single ingredient can map the globe in ways that establish Indianness as its base. About eggplant, Jaffrey writes: "Almost every nation in the world cooks it," unlike chickpea flour, which is, according to Jaffrey, "known in limited parts of the East and West and totally unknown in others. It deserves better." Jaffrey continues,

> How they cook it is what makes the dish regional or national. If there are mustard and fennel seeds in it, it must be Bengali. If it is creamed with olive oil and lemon, it has to have a Middle Eastern or a Greek/Turkish bias. If it is cooked with honey, it could be Moroccan.[21]

This passage is open to a number of interpretations that point toward how an ingredient can be used as a tool for mapping a global gastrocartography. However, in the twenty pages of eggplant recipes, a significant number are from South Asia, and the majority of South Asian recipes are from India. The number of eggplant recipes is distributed according to national origin: four for India; two each for Turkey, Hong Kong, and Sri Lanka; one for Korea,

Trinidad, Japan, China, Palestine, Afghanistan, Pakistan, and Indonesia; and one also for a stateless, Tuscan-inspired recipe.

By itself, the prominence of South Asian eggplant recipes may not be noteworthy (although Monsanto's work with *Bt brinjal*, examined briefly later, provides a counterpoint for Jaffrey's use of eggplant as a gastrocartographic key). The index also devotes five columns to Indian recipes—significantly more than those of any other nation and more than those of whole other regions combined. The representation of South Asian recipes thus redraws the map to enlarge South Asia and shrink other nations. The five columns of Indian recipes are complemented by a much shorter, but no less rich, selection of Sri Lankan recipes. Other South Asian recipes are scattered throughout the book and configure space in interesting ways: Bombay-Style Green Mango Pickle, Bengali-Style Green Beans, and Madras-Style Spicy Yogurt Drink stand apart from the rest of India as geographies of style rather than as national representatives. Other recipes work their own geographic alchemy: Kashmir is granted a degree of sovereignty by Kashmiri-Style Tea and a chutney of its own; so, too, is Palestine, with a complete meal of Eggplant with Garlic, Rice with Lentils and Browned Onions, and Tomato-Cucumber Salad.[22] In this way, the world of *World Vegetarian* is one with deep roots in South Asia.

The book's globalism is not necessarily along the axis of India's increasing cultural and financial power abroad. Indeed, how the book maps the globe may reflect how its author has experienced the world, as Shameem Black argues and as Anita Mannur examines at length in her book *Culinary Fictions*. As a cosmopolitan Indian who has traveled widely, Jaffrey tries global cuisines in each locale in which she sets foot and translates them, not just for other world travelers who set out from other points of origin, but also for the much narrower culinary lexicon of a woman who learned her culinary skills as a child in India. This means that the book recasts the globe to show the flows of global capital and reimagines the globe as resisting these flows. To observe that *World Vegetarian* is an image of a culinary world as seen through the eyes of a woman on the move does not account for Jaffrey's observations about her audience in the earlier sections of the book, even as it acknowledges that she speaks from a position of authority as an Indian woman who cooks. In other words, it is perhaps true that Jaffrey's book is a translation of her own culinary experiences around the world. She offers only her own, subjective view of a world shaped by her own hands, relying on her relatively limited expertise to reproduce these dishes, inflecting them with her own accents as she prioritizes taste over an accuracy that she may fail to reproduce. Rather than attempt to produce Indonesian Corn Soup using imprecise techniques not honed by decades of culturally specific practice, Jaffrey must use her own expertise to produce reliable results.[23] Reading her book in this way, however, does not fully account for the cultural transactions between Jaffrey and her readers and between Jaffrey and the cooks on whose authority her culinary representations rely.

Trouble at the Global Table: The Mysterious Case of the Disappearing Third World Woman

One of the features of cartography that Ian J. Barrow describes is that maps obscure territory even as they establish territorialization.[24] The maps that Jaffrey draws pose the same risk to less-than-careful readers, obscuring the lives of those living on the ground even as they show how to reproduce them. The book's invocation of the Third World woman is one such area of elision. In other words, Jaffrey's maps highlight and then remove certain global citizens. Jaffrey's introduction to the section of the text listing recipes for beans uses a universalized image:

> The oldest women of the house—generally my grandmother—would place a few handfuls of lentils, split peas, or beans into the big metal plates we each held. Quite automatically, we drew the legumes to the edge nearest our bodies. Then, in an ancient ritual, enacted as if in a half-remembered dance, we began pushing the lentils toward the far side one by one, plucking up and discarding all sticks and stones as we did so. Sometimes we sang, sometimes we gossiped, sometimes we were lost in our own silences.
>
> As we were doing this in India, Chinese, Syrians, Mexicans, and Peruvians were doing the same in their own courtyards, gardens and kitchens.[25]

The culturally specific activity of a group of Indian women cleaning lentils echoes the identical activity in households around the world, households in India, China, Syria, Mexico, and Peru that are distinguished by cooking processes and economic privilege from the West and the global North. Removed from their cultural contexts and placed next to one another in a global system, cooking methods thus adhere to the same model of globalization that Gayatri Spivak describes in *Imperatives to Reimagine the Planet*, in which "globalization is achieved by the imposition of the same system of exchange everywhere."[26] Cooking methods bring the globe into a coherent culinary whole by establishing a uniformity that can be achieved only by placing individual elements in a system of knowledge that levels their values even as it acknowledges culturally specific points of origin. In other words, the globe assumes familiar contours by pointing out that these women's labor is the same everywhere and is of value to Western readers because it will put them in touch with something important about themselves by pointing out their difference from them.

In her description, Jaffrey offers a poem that "unites us all," by the Armenian poet Zahrad, entitled "A Woman Cleaning Lentils":

> A lentil, a lentil, a lentil, a stone.
> A lentil, a lentil, a lentil, a stone.
> A green one, a black one, a green one, a black. A stone.
> Suddenly a word. A lentil.
> A lentil, a word, a word next to another word. A sentence.
> A word, a word, a word, a nonsense speech.
> Then an old song.
> Then an old dream.
> A life, another life, a hard life. A lentil. A life.
> An easy life. A hard life. Why easy? Why hard?
> Lives next to each other. A life. A word. A lentil.
> A green one, a black one, a green one, a black one, pain.
> A green song, a green lentil, a black one, a stone.
> A lentil, a stone, a stone, a lentil.[27]

As this poem suggests, cooking binds our bodies in a way that the very global economy that grants us access to esoteric ingredients divides and isolates us. Cleaning, cooking, and eating beans reminds us of "what our ancestors did to plow the earth and wrest from it foods to nourish us . . . something we of the supermarket culture have quite forgotten."[28] This very act of remembrance makes Jaffrey very thoroughly, very bodily Indian as it also conjoins her Indian woman's body to other women's bodies halfway around the world. The contours of the globe conform to the shape of each body participating in the "half-remembered dance" that reinforces family and cultural bonds as it feeds other hungry bodies. However, Jaffrey has outlined a curious axis of remembrance: she cites India, China, Syria, Mexico, and Peru as countries in which women still perform the ritual of cleaning beans. Women in the United States and western Europe apparently do not participate, as they constitute the "supermarket culture" whose amnesia has unhitched its members from the rest of the world.[29] South and East exemplify an earthbound globality that can teach North and West how to reconnect with the very substance of life. For Jaffrey, becoming global in this way entails an act of remembrance, in which food recovers its links to the processes used to prepare it and to the other eating bodies around the world. What this means is that the body of the Third Woman becomes the shuttle in the transaction between the inauthentic, amnesiac body and the site of healthful authenticity that proliferates in Third World spaces.

There are two specific, yet interlinked problems with this figure concerning images of Third World women in many regional cookbooks. The first, most immediate, problem is that she vanishes. Jaffrey's woman cleaning lentils appears early in the text and then nowhere else, jettisoned in favor of the trappings of First World modernity to include the image of limitless mobility. Two pages after the "ancient ritual" of cleaning lentils by sliding them one by one across a large metal plate while gossiping and singing with other women and by also implying that this is a global practice, Jaffrey begins her list of steps for preparing legumes with a disavowal of canned beans—beans that the woman preparing lentils will never eat but that their First World counterparts will reflexively use. Jaffrey's list follows the logic from acquisition to consumption as she moves from buying, storing, picking over and washing, soaking, cooking, and seasoning beans. Over these steps, especially in seasoning the beans by pouring spiced, heated ghee or oil over them, the specter of the Third World woman hovers. But by the time we get to the recipe from Costa Rica for Black Beans with Rice, or "Spotted Rooster," on page 14, she has fled. Describing the ubiquity of this dish, Jaffrey writes, "So pervasive is Costa Rica's national breakfast dish, even the local McDonald'ses and Burger Kings feel the need to have it on their menus." Because fast-food restaurants have this local dish on their menus, the Third World woman whose labor is so romanticized in the tedium of plucking stones and twigs from the beans disappears in favor of the other international flavors of the fast-food chains and their connections to globalization and international commerce.

The second problem with using the Third World woman is that Jaffrey depends on a structure of separation and alienation, a mode of forgetting, or "half remembrance," to intensify her power in the text. This means that her alienation from the readers becomes essential to the sentimentality that connects her to the readers. The pages of the cookbook putatively invite them into her previously unknowable, desirable life. But in actuality, they do not: the imprecise handful of lentils poured onto her *thali* becomes the precisely measured one cup that is used in *Tarka Masoor Dal* (Red Lentils with Cumin and Scallion) or in *Masoor Dal Hyderibadi* (Red Lentils Hyderibadi) once we step out of the kitchen of Jaffrey's youth and into the kitchen where we will prepare her grandmother's bean dishes.[30] This is a woman whom we can imagine but whom we cannot know. We almost get to know her as Jaffrey points out her labor, but then the text sidesteps her life. The distinction is much more sharply represented in the poem about picking lentils, in which the proximity of lentils to stones highlights their similarity in shape, size, and shared space even as it underscores their difference by distinguishing an undesirable hard life from a desirable easy one. We all are lentils and stones in the same pile, segregated only by the hardness and ease of our everyday lives. The act of separating the two questions that very act of separating the hard and undesirable from the soft and is a song of solidarity. You, whose life is hard: I recognize the proximity of my easy life so very close to your own, and it is this small act of picking over lentils that calls attention to this closeness. Yet once the page is turned, the bag of lentils from the supermarket obviates the activity in the poem. We no longer have to pick over my lentils, and we no longer have recognize my closeness to the song's metaphor of little stones and twigs that can crack our teeth, even as we prepare the dish that welcomes us into your home. We can pick through the lentils—but only if we want to. Meanwhile, the "hard lives" of Third World women everywhere season our food. Although we eat their food, we suffer none of their privations. By the time the page has turned, we have stepped out of the Third World.

The reason why Jaffrey's invocation of the Third World woman is problematic is because, despite the call to solidarity in Jaffrey's description of women cleaning lentils, there remains an incommensurability between the First and Third Worlds. In this gap lies the difference in privilege that segregates the First World woman from her Third World sisters, precisely because neither can cross the span between them. Other, even more complex figures populate this space. One of them is the busy Indian woman who, in 2005, made headlines in the *New York Times* by buying frozen and ready-made food. Twenty-four-year-old Rujuta Jog of Bangalore, a recently married office worker, was guilty of buying her yogurt and using Pillsbury flour to make rotis. She works forty hours a week outside her home and spends part of what she makes on "ready-to-drink packaged Nestlé buttermilk, prepared ginger-garlic paste and even frozen chickens [she doesn't] have to clean." For her, they save time and are inexpensive. Even the markets where a Mumbai woman might buy her produce have changed, selling pasta alongside basmati rice and offering the same range of international vegetables and fruits that I can buy at the Whole Foods around the corner from my home. As culinary influences and products become available in the markets where the Third World woman shops, the recipes that she prepares will not be subject to translation because they will not have to be translated; they already are framed in the familiar lexicon of canned beans, prepared meats, and vegetables such as broccoli and iceberg lettuce.[31] Increasingly, developing countries are experiencing the same culinary drift, for example, in colonial India, according to Parama Roy's *Alimentary Tracts*. The problem is that in order to maintain their credibility, these shifts must go unremarked in regional cookbooks.

Culinary representations, which allegedly offer a true cultural communion, still take advantage of the Third World woman, romanticizing her labor and making her impoverishment the base for authenticity. If she had a choice, would she grind her spices using a stone? Would she trust her food to an unevenly heated grate? Does she envy the easier life of the First World woman? What substitutions does she make in her recipes before they are translated, to hide what she may lack, correct mistakes, or improve on her recipes? Why are these recipes unstable even in their rawest incarnations? And how do we flatten her world so that only one figure may emerge globally as the trusted cook: a woman with a covered head and worn hands, kneeling in native garb in front of raw ingredients? Meanwhile, not only does the text conveniently dispose of her when she is no longer needed, but the world in which she lives looks vastly different on the ground from the one described as "authentic."

This means that the Third World Woman participates in what Timothy Brennan calls "the image-function of the periphery."[32] He describes the Third World woman's value best in regard to the lack of modernity of the villages of rural India or Latin-America, which allows the Third World woman to stand at the cultural periphery as "a countersystem of value, a hope." She is emblematic of the periphery's charms, which Brennan sees as having to do with "the art of conversation, the decrease of speed, the altruistic act of hospitality, and the decommercialization of artistic performance, all of them important psychological and emotional outlets for the negative energy overwhelming a metropolis characterized by anxiety, fear, and restlessness"—and, I would add, ennui, alienation, and other hungers of the spirit that a meal from a rustic kitchen can readily satisfy.[33] To put it uncharitably, like the artist whose work is imitated at the Luxor and the trees cultivated in Mandalay Bay in Las Vegas, and the folk doctor whose identifications of plants contribute to the medicines of large pharmaceutical interests, the regional cookbook writer often borrows liberally with little meaningful attribution. Jaffrey's mapping of the globe prompts a response to Brennan's challenge to those who borrow what he calls the "cultural inventions" of others: "Ideas routinely stolen from other civilizations are sold to a docile public without even a thought to paying for the goods taken." I repeat that challenge here in regard to how it affects the relationship of culinary representations with the bodies of women who model its practices, and the royalties paid to regional cookbook authors, because the pillaging of the Third World woman's knowledge and the oversimplification of her home and habits resonate with his argument, though they may differ in kind but not degree. Brennan writes:

> In an entertainment economy like our own, where fatuous scriptwriters in Hollywood are paid large sums for options on some micro-twist to a clichéd story line . . . there is not even a hint that there might be legal claim under the principle of intellectual property rights to folk healing or the copied designs of a theme hotel. If the demand for royalties might in the latter case be absurd, let us by all means make it anyway to underline the absurdity of a system that sells patents on vitamins, on story lines, and in the future (why not?) on the air. To ask for payment is to expose the process of appropriation occurring asymmetrically on behalf of a country that seeks to extend its national property rights laws universally.[34]

Can the Third World woman whose recipes for *tarka* appear in Jaffrey's instructions for living in communion with the world; can this woman insist on a generous slice of the royalty payments that are the invisible underside of the regional cookbook's engagement with authenticity? What is her due?

The World Farmer: Multinational Agribusiness and International Food Politics

The flip side of the world vegetarian that Jaffrey maps may not be the provincial vegetarians eating iceberg salads garnished with pallid, grainy tomato slices in the continental United States, nor is it the world's meat eaters consuming slabs of cooked flesh. Nor is it the world travelers who trust no food unless a familiar logo adorns the package. It is perhaps another pair of world travelers: Cargill and Monsanto, two of the world's largest agribusinesses. A perhaps not so minor aspect of these travelers is that U.S. corporations have legally protected personhood that grants them a range of rights along with suprahuman privileges.[35] Among these is the ability to have a real presence in multiple locales at the same time: If Madhur Jaffrey's world vegetarian is a woman with a foot on every continent, then Cargill and Monsanto are even more dexterous world travelers. Unlike people, multinational corporations maintain a real presence in many spaces in simultaneity and perpetuity, a feat that Jaffrey attempts to teach her readers in the assembly of a multinational meal. Unlike the feast that I prepare that focuses the world on my plate, the plural presences of multinational corporations work as components of a monolithic organism designed to produce food. For example, Cargill's production strategy creates phosphate fertilizer in the United States that is then used in Argentina and the United States to grow soybeans to be pressed for oil; the soybean meal is then sent to Thailand to grow chickens to be processed, cooked, and packaged for sale in Japan and Europe.[36] But whereas Jaffrey's world traveler celebrates difference and diversity, the multinational corporation's touch is a homogenizing one.[37] As it intervenes in local economies and communities, Cargill is Cargill, whether it is in Egypt, the United States, or Brazil. Rather than be altered by its experiences in other spaces as Jaffrey has been and her readers will be, the multinational corporation alters these spaces, sometimes to devastating effect.[38]

For example, when describing the role of multinational corporations in the mustard oil crisis of 1998, Vandana Shiva implies that the casualties prompting the ban might be laid at the feet of Monsanto as it sought to export soybeans to India. To prod the Indian government into taking action against local producers of mustard oil, it was widely believed that agents of the corporation tainted the oil, killing and sickening people to drum up the hysteria that resulted in a ban against an ingredient that Shiva identifies as central to Indian cultural identity. The poisonings and the consequent ban neatly coincided with the U.S. government's exemption of agricultural commodities from the May 1998 trade sanctions imposed as a punitive measure against India's nuclear weapons tests. Shiva suggests that heavy corporate lobbying, coupled with underhanded tactics, succeeded in granting U.S.-based multinationals a larger market share of the global South. In answer to why the multinational corporations would go to such lengths to move their seeds, Shiva responds that global pressures from First World markets resulted in a surplus of soybeans that they could not sell. "How to get rid of all this increasingly unsaleable produce?" she asks. "The answer could be to dump it on the Third World, in countries such as India, where the public had not yet been alerted to the possible dangers of GM [genetically modified] crops." A temporary market share is not in Monsanto's long-term interest, though the elimination of mustard plants is. Shiva explains:

> By encouraging the Indian government to ban the sale of mustard oil throughout the country, the food multinationals were provided with a perfect market opening for their products—which would enable them to dominate, and on a permanent basis, the market in that country for vegetable oil. And, if traders cannot sell mustard oil, they will not buy mustard from farmers and farmers will stop growing it. This will lead to the extinction of a crop that is central to India's

farming system and food culture. Once mustard oil has gone out of cultivation, even were the ban on mustard oil to be lifted, we would still remain dependent on soyabean for our edible oil. If the government were to allow us one day to reintroduce mustard oil it could only be a patented genetically engineered variety—as Monsanto has already patented all the brassica grown in India.

Shiva indirectly connects Monsanto's desire to monopolize edible oil to food riots in Indonesia as dependence on global market forces increased the price of oil, putting it out of reach for the average Indonesian consumer. Her indictment of their deeds places at the feet of Monsanto and Cargill the responsibility for global civil unrest rising from a lack of affordable food.[39]

At the time of this writing, the Indian government is suing Monsanto for biopiracy, claiming that its attempt to patent *Bt brinjal*, an indigenous species of eggplant used in a wide range of dishes and exported abroad, constitutes theft of a native crop. This is the first legal action of its kind anywhere.[40] The public outcry against Monsanto's "frankencrop" variety of *Bt brinjal* prompted the government to ban it in 2010 for an indefinite period of time, stating that the corporation's work on GM varieties of native plants violates India's Biological Diversity Act of 2002. If Jaffrey's use of eggplants in *World Vegetarian* as the model for a widely available ingredient allows her to map global spaces using the different preparations of this vegetable, then Monsanto's attempt to genetically modify and then market *brinjal* works along a different axis. It is an example of an attempt to gain biological control over various local foods and economic control over the people who eat them.

It perhaps would be overreaching to speak of the iniquities of Jaffrey's book in the same breath as those of U.S.-based multinational corporations. She does not differentiate between the authentic and the inauthentic or the global and the local that leads to the conflict between farmers and the multinational corporations that exploit their labor, intrude on regional markets, and draw local populations into penurious relationships with global capital. But her cookbook does display—and attempts to overcome—a parallel with the relationship that these corporations maintain with the local populations on which they depend for their profits. In other words, Jaffrey's invocation of the Third World woman and her mapping of the world replicate the structure of this conflict.

Despite the tension between the hypervisibility and the invisibility of the laboring women in her cookbooks, Jaffrey's work serves as a crosscurrent against the practices of large-scale agribusiness that map a similar, complementary geography: Jaffrey, born in India, travels to Britain and then the United States, where she writes a book that maps a consumable world;

Monsanto, ConAgra, and Cargill, born in the United States, move abroad to establish global networks of production and consumption. Jaffrey describes the book as "[her] handpicked collection of the world's best vegetarian recipes for you to cook at home. . . . Of course the recipes are chosen from my point of view and reflect my taste."[41] As Shameem Black argues, the "world vegetarian" of the title is actually Jaffrey herself, a world traveler whose book constitutes her travel narrative. In it, she advocates a model of cosmopolitan engagement with the world. However problematic this engagement, it binds people bodily to one another by connecting the fundamental aspects of human life. It is perhaps something of an overstatement to suggest that the book participates in a form of global ecological activism, but the question must be asked: Is the woman cleaning lentils the same as the woman counting the suicide seeds that might have claimed her husband's life?[42] This implies that the book opens an ecocritical commentary on the relationship among people, plants, eating, and living in a cosmopolitan mode. It is in the comparison between the objectives of *Madhur Jaffrey's World Vegetarian* and the activity of the multinational corporation that quite a different picture of the world emerges, in which global eats and eating the globe yield to the more complicated cartographies mapping how and what we consume.

Notes

1. My chapter examines the concept of worlding (particularly as pertains to the Third World woman) in ways that are in keeping with Gayatri Spivak's notion of how the Third World is worlded. She articulates this idea in *A Critique of Postcolonial Reason: Toward a History of the Vanishing Present* (Cambridge, MA: Harvard University Press, 1999).
2. In thinking through models of cosmopolitanism, Bruce Robbins invokes Neil Smith's rethinking of space:

    As Neil Smith has suggested, rethinking the imperfections of democracy requires rethinking space: the pertinent subnational and supranational units of agency and communication, differentials of a scale that rule out many of our most frequent moralizing, universalizing gestures and demand a politics that is also differential. The most generous and useful way to begin rethinking cosmopolitanism, it seems to me, is neither as ideal unplaceableness nor as sordid elitism, but as a way of relativizing and problematizing the scale and the units of democracy.

    Pheng Cheah and Bruce Robbins, eds., "Comparative Cosmopolitanisms," *Cosmopolitics: Thinking and Feeling beyond the Nation* (Minneapolis: University of Minnesota Press, 1998), 261.
3. Madhur Jaffrey, *Madhur Jaffrey's World Vegetarian* (New York: Clarkson Potter, 1999), ix.
4. Ibid., viii.
5. Shameem Black, "Recipes for Cosmopolitanism," *Frontiers: A Journal of Women Studies* 31, no. 1 (2010): 1–30.

6. Jaffrey, *World Vegetarian*, viii.

7. Gayatri Chakravorty Spivak, *Imperative zur Neuerfindung des Planeten* [*Imperative to Reimagine the Planet*] (Vienna: Passagen-Verlag, 1999), 44.

8. Ian J. Barrow's *Making History, Making Territory: British Mapping in India, c. 1756–1905* (New Delhi: Oxford University Press, 2003) is an excellent, comprehensive study of the connection between cartography and British imperialism in India.

   Matthew Henry Edney's *Mapping an Empire: The Geographical Construction of British India, 1765–1843* (Chicago: University of Chicago Press, 1997) states that "imperialism and mapmaking intersect in the most basic manner. Both are fundamentally concerned with territory and knowledge . . . . To govern territories, one must know them" (1).

   Madhur Jaffrey's books exhibit not necessarily a colonial, imperialist relationship between cooking and tourism (warnings about which abound in Lisa M. Heldke's *Exotic Appetites*) but perhaps a postcolonial desire for supranational citizenship. The basic mechanisms, however, that power the imperialist dynamic among map reader, cartographer, and space precede the mechanisms that undergird representations of space in culinary writing.

9. According to Ian J. Barrow,

   > The land [the cartographers of India] depicted had histories of ownership and occupation and that, if carefully crafted, their maps could portray those histories in an effective and seemingly direct manner. But they were also aware that they could make their maps more appealing, authoritative, and beguiling if they used maps as a way of incorporating the past into the present. In other words, map makers would not only show how the present political situation was derived from what had occurred previously, they would also invite their readers, through a perusal of symbols, juxtapositions, and wording of the map, to relive and once more participate in those moments in the past which made the present possible. The history that they wrote and drew into a map was dynamic and imaginative; it encouraged the map viewers to place themselves in the crucial formative moments of the past. (1–2)

   Barrow's book is not about "how modern mapping contributed to the imagining of an Indian nation."

   > Nor do I examine the processes whereby an essentialized nation may have been projected into the past as a way of buttressing Indian nationalist agendas. Instead, I focus on how colonial cartography depicted histories of British territorial possession in India, and how these histories helped the British to make themselves legitimate as rulers while also reinforcing the construction of a British sense of national identity. Hence, this book is not about the construction of an Indian geo-body, but about the making of a British colonial territorial state. (12–13)

   His work instead highlights how mapping obeys ideological impulses. In other words, the maps he analyzes are not about what they represent but are about something else: the management of space. Similarly, regional cookbooks do the same: designating spaces through flavor palates and national dishes. Thus, Jaffrey's book is largely disinterested in faithful reproductions of space in dry, ethnographic tones. It is however, interested in engaging the cartographer's basic tools to create a decolonized, transnational space of porous borders, albeit a mappable, manageable space nonetheless.

10. Jaffrey's construction of place in her mapping of the world closely resembles the literary cartographies analyzed by Rick Van Noy in his *Surveying the Interior: Literary Cartographers and the Sense of Place* (Reno: University of Nevada Press, 2003). Quoting Wallace Stegner, he writes: "A place could require poetry because it is more than the sum feelings, and concepts—gives us what we call the sense of place. To bring it into being, we need a complex intersection of cartography and literature, a charting of interior and exterior landscapes" (xvi).

11. Jaffrey, *World Vegetarian,* ix.

12. According to Shameem Black in "Recipes for Cosmopolitanism," "As her cookbooks register and direct an audience's inchoate desire to engage affectively with a wider world, they promote imaginative border crossing through the readerly and performative labor of cooking" (2).

13. Jaffrey, *World Vegetarian,* 151. Anita Mannur offers a detailed analysis of Jaffrey's diasporic desire in *Culinary Fictions: Food in South Asian Diasporic Culture* (Philadelphia: Temple University Press, 2010), describing how Jaffrey serves her audiences in the United States: "As a diasporic subject who has adapted her cuisine for American kitchens, Jaffrey enables cooks in American kitchens to take pleasure in the complexity of Indian flavors that might be easily created with American spices and ingredients" (195). Mannur also describes a community of Indians living abroad: "Placing patriotism squarely in the middle of her agenda, Jaffrey's words are also directed to an audience of responsible and 'patriotic' Indians in the United States who care enough about their nation's culinary image to portray an 'authentic' version of Indianness in the space of their homes" (34).

14. Jaffrey, *World Vegetarian,* 171, 162, 257, 498.

15. Ibid., 707.

16. The red and white colors of the U.S. Christmas season were made permanent by Haddon Sundbloom's famous paintings of Santa Claus as part of a Christmastime advertising campaign by Coca-Cola. See Bruce D Forbes, *Christmas: A Candid History* (Berkeley: University of California Press, 2007), 92–93. This means that Jaffrey's stateless dish is the odd stepchild of a global commercial culture, which complicates in interesting ways the book's critique of multinational corporations.

17. Jaffrey, *World Vegetarian,* 371.

18. Ibid.

19. Ibid., 376.

20. Shameem Black writes in "Recipes for Cosmopolitanism":
    Gastropoetics are often discussed in the language of authenticity and fraudulence, read as ways of inventing ties to an ancestral imagined community or as performances of fakery that exploit the enhanced social capital associated with the foreign and the novel. Jaffrey's intervention in this debate, I suggest, is to construct an expanded sense of her own Indianness (and, implicitly, of other ethnic and national affiliations of her readers). (20)

21. Jaffrey, *World Vegetarian,* viii, ix.

22. Ibid. 699–700, 207, 657, 650, 659–60, 191–92, 404, 638.

23. Ibid., 584.

24. Barrow, *Making History, Making Territory,* 48.

25. Jaffrey, *World Vegetarian*, 3.

26. Spivak, *Imperative*, 44.

27. Jaffrey, *World Vegetarian*, 3.

28. Ibid.

29. Ibid.

30. Ibid., 68, 69.

31. Monica Bhide, "As Cash Flows In, India Goes Out to Eat," *New York Times*, April 20, 2005, available at http://www.nytimes.com/2005/04/20/dining/20indi. html?sq=mumbai%20working%20women%20frozen%20food (accessed February 24, 2009).

32. Timothy Brennan, "The Economic Image-Function of the Periphery," in *Postcolonial Studies and Beyond*, ed. Ania Loomba, Suvir Kaul, Matti Bunzl, Antoinette Burton, and Jed Esty (Durham, NC: Duke University Press, 2005), 101–24.

33. Ibid., 118.

34. Ibid., 118–19.

35. This statement is a simplification of the debate surrounding corporate personhood, which Susanna K. Ripken examines at length in her article "Corporations Are People Too: A Multi-Dimensional Approach to the Corporate Personhood Puzzle," *Fordham Journal of Corporate & Financial Law* 15, no. 1 (2009): 97–177). In this chapter, I rely on the theory that corporations are real entities.

36. Byeong-Seon Yoon, "Who Is Threatening Our Dinner Table?," *Monthly Review: An Independent Socialist Magazine* 58, no. 6 (November 2006): 57.

37. Yoon writes: "By promoting specialization in agriculture, TNACs [transnational agriculture corporations] are increasing environmental degradation, reducing the diversity of genetic resources, expanding the supply of standardized production, and imposing uniformity on agricultural production" ("Who Is Threatening Our Dinner Table?," 61).

38. Yoon writes:

    > Developed countries have been providing a variety of subsidies to agriculture, resulting in an abundant production of cheap food. However, in developing countries where hunger is prevalent and food is scarce the result of this global system of production is to promote not the independence of the national food supply and self-sufficiency but increasing dependence. This is why flour imports to developing countries increased from a mere 10 percent in the 1950s to 57 percent in 1980, and why agricultural products emanating from developing countries are directed not at their own needs but at the wants of the rich economies managed by the TNACs. Hence the local economy in the underdeveloped economies is not expanded and people's often dire food needs are not met. ("Who Is Threatening Our Dinner Table?," 61–62)

39. Vandana Shiva, "The Mustard Oil Conspiracy," *Ecologist* (2001): 27–29.

40. Jonathan Benson, "India Files Biopiracy Lawsuit against Monsanto Says Biotech Giant Is Stealing Nature for Corporate Gain," *Gerson Healing Newsletter* 26, no. 6 (2011): 7–8.

41. Jaffrey, *World Vegetarian*, viii.

42. Andrew Malone of the *UK Daily Mail* covered this trend, citing the case of Shankara Mandaukar as an example of Indian farmers driven by debt to kill themselves. See Andrew Malone, "The GM Genocide: Thousands of Indian Farmers Are Committing Suicide after Using Genetically Modified Crops," *UK Daily Mail*, November 2, 2008,

available at http://www.dailymail.co.uk/news/article-1082559/The-GM-genocide-Thousands-Indian-farmers-committing-suicide-using-genetically-modified-crops.html (accessed October 28, 2012). The debate over the connection between Monsanto seeds—bred to yield only one harvest but to produce no viable seed, thereby guaranteeing that the farmer will buy them annually from Monsanto—and an increase in the deaths of farmers moved by despair to kill themselves because they were drowning in debt is a contentious one. A study published by the International Food Policy Research Group disputes this connection. See Guillaume P, Gruère, Debdatta Sengupta, and Purvi Mehta-Bhatt, *Bt Cotton and Farmer Suicides in India: Reviewing the Evidence* (Washington, DC: International Food Policy Research Institute, October 2008).

20

Perfection on a Plate

Readings in the South Asian Transnational Queer Kitchen

ANITA MANNUR

During the last decade, a wide corpus of writing about food in diasporic contexts has emerged in ethnic studies and its interlocutory fields of gender, race, and sexuality studies. One such work is Krishnendu Ray's *Migrant's Table,* a sociological inquiry that maps the foodways of Bengali American households in the United States.[1] Through a series of interviews and thick ethnographic research, Ray establishes the central desires and ideas at stake in the Bengali American culinary imaginary. But implicit in his analysis, as with several inquiries into foodways in the domestic space, is the notion that food preparation in the home is yoked to an unyielding form of heteronormativity. Whether they seek to reinforce or bring their own spin to Bengali home cooking, cooks in the home are almost always described as "wives" and "mothers," so that South Asian diasporic foodways are mapped by an implicit heteronormativity. Nonetheless, the home space is one of the least likely spaces to guarantee what I refer to as unyielding heteronormativity. The kitchen is always already a homosocial space that allows for articulations of same-sex intimacy to emerge through and against the strictures of a regimented heteronormativity. Culinary narratives are particularly rich sites for examining the queer potentialities and promises of desire, precisely because food preparation in the domestic space is heavily invested in the ideologies of heteronormativity. When cooking is about the queer and when it refuses the narrative of unequivocal happiness, it establishes alternative logics. If cooking is resignified to complicate heteronormativity, it can be about pleasure, not teleologically oriented to a "happily ever after" that often implicitly circumscribes a narrative of heteronormativity, but about an alternative, affective fulfillment that understands pleasure without insisting on happiness or happily ever afters. Two recent queer South Asian diasporic texts that intervene into this discursive rendering of sexuality are the 2006 novel *Bodies in Motion* and the 2006 film *Nina's Heavenly Delights.* In examining the queerness of these texts, one visual and one written, I hope to push scholarship about food studies toward the linkages between food and sexuality.[2] Through a British Asian film and a Sri Lankan American novel, I also hope to further expand the transnational purview of Asian American studies, so that the questions asked are more definitive than the objects interrogated.[3]

Perfectly Queer

In her pathbreaking work on queer diasporas and South Asian public cultures, cultural critic Gayatri Gopinath theorizes the position of impossibility vis-à-vis the articulation of a queer female subjectivity. For Gopinath, the "foregrounding of queer female diasporic subjectivity is not simply an attempt to bring into visibility or recognition a heretofore invisible subject."[4] Rather, the queer subject is always an impossible subject in the context of a heteropatriarchal structure that delegitimizes queer female subjectivity. Certainly, the impossibility of imagining queer female subjectivity helps explain the latent queer narrative of the relationship of the two female leads in Gurinder Chadha's 2000 crossover hit, *Bend It Like Beckham*. In the film, a pair of soccer-playing friends, Jess and Jules, find their friendship tested because of a mutual love for their coach. In between, the film's comedy emerges from misunderstandings that would view Jules and Jess as queer. After all, what could be queerer than two soccer-playing girls? But according to one reviewer, if the film forecloses the possibility of queer desire, it is because of the implicit homophobia of the diasporic Indian audience. Chadha, as one reviewer notes, "originally planned to include a lesbian romance between the characters of Jess [Parminder K. Nagra] and Jules [Keira Knightley], but "chickened out" at the last minute for fear of offending and upsetting Indian audiences." On the website AfterEllen.com, Sarah Warn notes:

> In a perfect world, a small-budget British film starring an unknown Indian actress as a girl who overcomes sexist and cultural barriers in order to play soccer while falling in love with another girl would become a word-of-mouth phenomenon and ultimately generate millions in U.S. and international box office revenue. But this isn't a perfect world, and the *Bend It Like Beckham* director knew that wasn't going to happen; something had to give, and that something was the lesbian romance.[5]

Notable in Warn's description is the notion that in a perfect world, a lesbian romance can exist without offending the patriarchal structures of the

Indian diaspora. Although this is framed as impossibility, the implied "perfect ending" and perfection itself maintain an ambiguous relationship to the elusive concept of happiness, in which queer subjectivity comes into play. When the perfect ending eludes queer female subjects, particularly Asian diasporic female subjects, it behooves us as cultural critics to develop a more nuanced reading strategy to interrogate the terms under which cultural work seems to deliberately and strategically make available the perfect ending that also brings happiness.[6]

Known best for her hard-hitting documentary films, Indo-British filmmaker Pratibha Parmar frequently uses a strong critical lens through which to address the inequities plaguing the lives of minorities who negotiate inequities based on race, class, gender, sexuality, and disability. Her films have the pedagogic function of focusing on issues that are both politically complex and visually rich while rendering visible the hidden stories of women's strength as they negotiate the complexities of racial, sexual, and cultural oppression. In *Sari Red*, a short elegiac film to Kalbinder Kaur Hayre, a young Sikh woman killed in 1985 in a racist attack in England, Parmar investigates the presence of private and public violence in the lives of Indo-British woman. Parmar's collaboration with Alice Walker produced the documentary *Warrior Marks*, which positioned her as a voice in global conversations about women's bodies and responsibilities to other women. As Parmar explained,

> It was amazing. . . . It was a small film that we were doing and we thought it would be seen by a few people, but actually it really sparked off a whole international debate. It's been really gratifying because I've literally seen how a film can trigger social change and change attitudes in people.[7]

In addition, her landmark film *Khush* was praised for its engagement with the narratives and voices of queer people of color in India and Britain. Through its use of first-person testimonial, it brings to light the pleasures and pains of living as a queer South Asian subject.

With such radically oriented works, it is curious that Parmar's most recent film and her first feature film depart from this tradition to produce a film that Ellen Dengel-Janic and Lars Eckstein suggest "seeks the company of other major 'exotic' foodies . . . and counters the provocative thrust of its gender politics in fantasy world of sensuous universalism."[8] The focus on food in Parmar's *Nina's Heavenly Delights* has led some cultural critics, perhaps unsurprisingly, to lament the demise of Parmar's commitment to radical politics.[9]

But I argue that a closer engagement with the politics of food in this film provides an alternative conceptual map for understanding the radical freight of Parmar's vision.[10]

Nina's Heavenly Delights, Parmar's first feature-length film, tells the story of Nina Shah, an Indian from Glasgow, Scotland. After an extended, self-imposed exile in London, Nina returns to Glasgow to attend her father's funeral. As she begins the emotionally taxing work of settling his affairs, she learns that her father, a well-respected chef at the New Taj Restaurant and the winner of the "Best of the West" Curry Competition, gambled away his prized restaurant. The family restaurant is now owned by Lisa, a young woman who is having trouble keeping it afloat. The film's intrigue develops as her father's former rival from Glasgow's Indian community seeks to buy the failing restaurant from a well-intentioned but clueless Lisa. But rather than giving into pressure from her family to abandon her late father's foolish dream, Nina joins forces with Lisa to hold on to the restaurant. And what better way to do this than to enter the Best of the West cooking battle one last time in order to restore her father's good name and keep the restaurant in the family? Not surprisingly, her major rival in the competition is restaurateur Sanjay, one-half of the father-and-son team who is preying on the New Taj Restaurant. Sanjay, coincidentally, happens to be Nina's former fiancé. Indeed it was in order to escape an arranged marriage with him that prompted her to leave Glasgow for London. In any case, Nina and Lisa join forces to perfect their culinary skills, eventually winning the contest. Somewhat predictably, Lisa and Nina fall in love through the process of cooking with and for each other.

But as the film moves toward its conclusion, a few queer moments disrupt its seemingly sugary-sweet narrative. Among these moments that I call queer and that Ellen Dengel-Janic and Lars Eckstein call transgressive are the fact that Nina's sister is secretly a champion Scottish highland dancer; Nina's best friend Bobbie is a drag queen; and Nina's brother is secretly married to a white Scotswoman. Nina's networks of intimacy, then, are decidedly queer in that all of her closest loved ones chip away at the Indo-Glaswegian edifice of heteropatriarchy. Eckstein and Dengel-Janic find these moments troubling because they appear to flatten the multiple social constraints in Nina's life. They interpret Nina's father's words, "In cooking as in life, no matter what the recipe says, always follow your heart," as a sign of the "effortless transcendence of all social obstacles through the power of love."[11] But in the face of a failing capitalist enterprise, the immigrant restaurant, Nina's attempts to hold on to what is also a part of her can also be read as a refusal of social norms. If the restaurant is a kind of metonym for Nina herself and if she can prevent her father's restaurant from falling into her former suitor's hands, it also is possible to read this moment as queerly disruptive, not merely transcendent, because it is an effort to retain sexual autonomy and resist heteropatriarchy while holding on to the means of production.

Through all this, it is Nina, the queer subject, who is responsible for maintaining the legacy of her father and who keeps the restaurant in the traditionally defined family. Elizabeth Buettner argues that restaurant culture in Britain is largely defined through male patriarchy and notes that *Nina's Heavenly Delights* "destabilizes the image of the restaurant as an exclusively male arena."[12] Nina departs from tradition in the route she takes to creating a winning dish. Rarely does she cook alone. When she goes shopping for ingredients, Lisa and Bobbie accompany her in the garishly colored, Bombay film–themed van. When they arrive at the shop, the three dance and prance around, disrupting the quiet of the space. When they sample food from their competitors' restaurants, all three eat together. Cooking is thus resignified as a collective activity to be shared among loved ones.

Even though the film makes remarkable strides in subverting the genre of the typical foodie film, at moments it seems to play into the conventions of the genre, such as during a particularly engaging scene during which a spicy vegetarian dish is prepared.

As onions sizzle in a full-screen shot, the word "ginger" is superimposed on the screen. Chili powder is added to the pot, and the word "turmeric" floats across the screen. The ingredients are stirred together, and beans are added as the words "garam masala" appear. Curry leaves are added into the sauté along with cauliflower, and the word "garlic" is thrown into the mix. Tomato pieces are accompanied by "cumin." "Coriander" follows with pieces of torn spinach. As the dish is plated and finished to complete a visually perfect ensemble, Lisa prepares to take a bite. At the precise moment the spoon crosses into the realm of the palatal, Nina's sensory response to the dish disrupts the viewer's visual pleasure as she declares, "Oh this is shite!" This moment of cognitive dissonance between the food on screen and the sensations they evoke for the person tasting the food ruptures the moment of filmic culinary pornography. The perfectly composed scene is disrupted by the viewer's awareness that the character's on-screen disgust at what she has just consumed is anything but a scene of perfect chemistry. Here, then, I depart slightly from Elizabeth Buettner's reading of this film. She suggests that in the film, the correct flavors meld together to produce harmony, placing "female chemistry at [the] heart" of the film. Although chemistry is at play, the chemistry evidenced in the "failed" dish cannot be described as "perfect." [13]

Figure 20.1. A "perfect" dish comes together. Frame enlargement from *Nina's Heavenly Delights* (2006).

As the film draws to a close, it is clear that Nina and Lisa will live happily ever after, that they will win the contest, and that they will retain control of her father's restaurant. All this is perhaps predictable and reminiscent of several other films in the romantic comedy foodie genre. But up to the very end, the film allows for the presence of a queer subtext. In deciding what dish to prepare for the contest, Nina follows her mother's suggestion and prepares a meal of tender baby lamb simmered in ginger and garam masala, followed by pomegranate chicken with rose petals and a light ginger sherbet for dessert, the very same meal served at her parents' wedding banquet. But lest we think that this is a reproduction of heterosexual norms, Bobbie, the drag queen friend, first intervenes to request his personal favorite dish, chicken *xacuti*, be added to the menu. Later, Nina also finds out that the mother she has feared was far from the perfect wife. That is, even though her mother was married to Mohan Shah, she was secretly in love with someone else. In short, the wedding banquet, which outwardly might have signified a kind of normative reinstallation of heterosexuality, is undercut by a latent queerness. After all, even the gaudy host of the show refers to Nina and Lisa's menu as a "wedding banquet fit for queens."

In locating spaces of queer female desire, or what Gopinath terms "vibrant livable spaces of possibility," Parmar's film produces a film that does more than present queer subjects in everyday spaces to the point that they appear as viable and nontransgressive.[14] Perhaps, then, what is so queer about the film is

Figure 20.2. The "perfect dish," which tastes like "shite," is thrown into the trash. Frame enlargement from *Nina's Heavenly Delights* (2006).

that it ends happily ever after. A fairytale ending may seem excessive, but it is precisely in that space of excess, in that space of fantasy, that these subjects who seem real also seem impossible. Certainly the tongue-in-cheek humor of the film seems all too cognizant that it is indulging in a kind of fairytale excessive bliss in suggesting that everyone ends up happily ever after. During the final moments of the Best of the West Curry Competition, the host of Korma TV announces the winner:

> Nina Shah's Mogul menu was beautifully prepared with each and every one of the delicate flavors complementing each other perfectly. But Sanjay Khanna confounded our senses with a meal of sheer technical perfection. A difficult choice between perfection and heavenly delight. But in true fairy tale style, the heart wins out and tonight's award goes to the pursuit of heavenly delight!

Heavenly delights are pitted against perfection so as to call attention to the fact that these competing discourses cannot *not* be in contention with each other. Yet by the end of the contest, it is not perfection that wins but the fairytale queer romance. And if this were not enough, the final scene of the film is an ensemble Bollywood performance in which all the cast members dance together, lip-synching to a hit song by 1970s pop queen Nazia Hassan. As actors take their place in this dance sequence, set against an impossibly idyllic blue sky, Bobbie takes center stage, dressed in his drag queen ensemble. As the song ends, the camera slowly pans out, revealing that the scene is staged in front of a green screen. The film crew and the director come into focus, and it becomes clear that this final dance sequence, "Love in a Wet Climate," is a cinematic fantasy made possible by the clever manipulation of the visual.

Earlier I referred to Sarah Warn's suggestion that in a perfect world, one might encounter viable lesbian relationships, ones that are not deemed impossible in the way that *Bend It Like Beckham* seems so insistent on reinforcing. But in consistently repudiating the idea that Nina's food is perfect and in refusing the term "perfect," Parmar's film, I believe, makes clear that desire—or, her term, "delight"—can exist even in imperfect scenarios. The multiple culinary moments signal that this perfection is never attainable in any form. The wedding banquet does not represent a perfect marriage but a flawed one. The delectable dish on screen was visually perfected but tasted like "shite." Sanjay's desire to be perfect does not help him win the competition. Perfection is not as tenable as fantasy. Indeed, fantasy and pleasure reinforce the moments of heavenly queer delight in this film.

Female Intimacies in the Sri Lankan American Kitchen

Analogous to the ways that *Nina's Heavenly Delights* uses cooking to reinforce rather than undermine queer love, in the erotically charged novel *Bodies in Motion*, by Sri Lankan American author Mary Anne Mohanraj, perfection is elusively presented as something that, though possible, is not always the ultimate goal. One character that appears in two chapters of the novel refuses a narrative of compulsory heterosexuality in the kitchen. In the first instance, I use the term "refuse" to signal a rejection in favor of alternative epistemologies. In the second instance, it signifies a re-fusing of ideology, one that creates a different kind of assemblage to negotiate the heterotopic space of the kitchen.

Mohanraj's *Bodies in Motion* is a multigenerational novel about two extended families, the Vallipurams and the Kandiahs, and their lives in Sri Lanka, Britain, and the United States from 1939 to 2002. In the novel, the possibility of inhabiting queerness is enabled by the culinary. In their search for a place to feel at home in the world, the characters continually negotiate the vicissitudes of immigration, war, and displacement affecting their everyday lives. From the onset, the heterosexual seams stitching together the tapestry of this sprawling extended family are carefully unraveled. Marriage rarely acts as a guarantor of unyielding heteronormativity; instead, moments of queerness gently chip away at the edifice of heterosexuality around which the architecture of family life is built.

Figure 20.3. "Love in a Wet Climate." As the song ends, the scene cuts to the green screen revealing the staging of the scene. Frame enlargement from *Nina's Heavenly Delights* (2006).

One such narrative in the novel emerges through the character Mangai Vallipuram, a woman who remains unmarried into her old age. Like most of the characters in this novel, Mangai's story occupies little space in the larger narrative; only two vignettes among the twenty that make up the novel specifically focus on her. Introduced in the chapter entitled "Seven Cups of Water," her story is completed in the epilogue "Monsoon Day." We first encounter her character in 1948, when Mangai is seventeen, and do not meet her again for another forty-eight years, when she is sixty-five years old. Spatially, the novel makes an analogous move; whereas Mangai is first introduced in the northern city of Jaffna, the final section takes place in Colombo. From the first chapter in which her character is introduced, Mangai is marked as a queer subject. In the early days of Mangai's brother Sundar's marriage, his new wife, Sushila, finds herself unfulfilled affectively and sexually by her husband. Sushila thirsts for intimacy, and each night after the household goes to sleep, she enters the kitchen in search of water to quench that desire. Over a week, the exchange of water becomes decidedly more erotically charged, moving from a literal embodiment of thirst to a more figurative one. Mangai describes the intimacy of sharing water as follows:

I picked up the cup, raise it to my lips. I filled my mouth with water, soaking the dry roof of my parched tongue. I turned to face her, still enclosed in the circle of her arms. I leaned forward, placed my lips on hers, and gave her water. She sucked the water deep down her throat, swallowed, and I felt the motion in my lips, making each mouthful smaller and smaller, each transfer taking longer and longer, until the cup was not just empty, but dry.[15]

Sushila might be able to satisfy her thirst, and Mangai also feeds her sexual appetite, so that it quickly becomes apparent that these clandestine nightly encounters are working through and against the implicit heteronormative logic of the domestic culinary space. When satisfying thirst alone is not enough, Mangai resorts to more creative ways to engender thirst. Creating a paste of red chili peppers, she applies the fiery substance to Sushila's body. The burning sensations on Sushila's body are calmed by careful caresses, as water alone is not an effective salve to the incendiary pain. For Mangai, intolerant of spicy food, the swirling of chili paste on her tongue combines intense pain and pleasure. "I wanted to suffer for her," she explains, articulating the sting of the pain with the pleasure of intimacy. Although these encounters are short lived—Sushila is unwilling to leave her husband for Mangai, fearing social censure—they haunt Mangai throughout her life. More important, they begin to form a space to think about the queer potentialities of the kitchen even as Sushila vehemently forecloses the possibility of entering a visible relationship. Just as the water spills out of the container, so too does queerness spill into and over the edges of the heteronormative home. Even though Mangai and Sushila never cross paths again, the strategic placement of this vignette early in the narrative, one of the few taking place in the kitchen, is important in its hinting at the queer intimacies enabled through shared palatal preferences.

Although Mangai does not reappear, her story is reintroduced at the novel's close. At this moment the narrative centers on Mangai's weekly ritual of preparing an elaborate meal of rice, fish, leeks, potatoes, and eggs, large enough, she notes, "to feed a man four times her size" that only she will consume.[16] Mangai's meal, the final meal—and scene—of the novel, is an elaborate act of producing a kind of culinary perfection that is not about creating a network of care in a conventional sense. She is decidedly not the kind of maternal caretaker who cooks for a heteronormative family. Each week as she prepares the meals, she is aware that the neighborhood girls gather around the perimeter of her home, "peer[ing] in through cracks, over windowsills" as she cooks.[17] Despite their voyeurism, Mangai "waits until they are settled before she begins to cook. It is another part of the unspoken bargain with her neighbors."[18]

Meal preparation is only part of what makes this moment of gastro-pornography interesting. As she cooks, Mangai disrobes; as she stirs the potatoes, she undoes the hooks on her sari blouse; while the leeks braise in a pan with turmeric and salt, she unwraps the layers of her sari. She gradually prepares the meal, removing articles of clothing along the way. When her meal is prepared, she is completely naked in the kitchen and completely mindful that the whole time she has been under the children's watchful gaze. At no point are the children ever invited to join her meal, but Mangai performs for them nonetheless. But in the solitary gesture of refusing to cook for children, she refuses to become wedded to an ideological system that requiring women's labor to be a kind of pedagogy, teaching the next generation of "wives" and cooks how to prepare meals for their families. Rather, her pedagogical moves invite a network of girls to contemplate that cooking can be about bodily pleasure and sensual self-affirmation; that cooking is not about becoming a good wife to a future husband; that cooking can be about pleasure and communing with the self. The text notes, "Mangai could tell the girls that this kind of cooking is not learned by watching, or even by teaching—that it is only the passage of time that grinds the lessons into the muscles and bones. But she cannot be bothered."[19] In addition to framing cooking as a learned bodily knowledge is the absence of caring about how others feel, the disinterest in feeding others that she feels might be understood as part of what makes her a resiliently queer figure. Consider the closing words of the novel:

> When the fish is ready, Mangai turns off the last burner. She takes a plate down from the shelf, battered tin. She fills a tin cup with cold water. She serves herself rice, fish, leeks, potatoes, eggs. There is enough on her plate to feel a man four times her size. She undoes the tie on her underskirt and lets it fall to the floor. Mangai carries the plate and cup over to the wall; she sits down, cross-legged on the dirt floor, with her naked back against the wall, with the water sliding down, running along her wrinkled skin, over her ribs, pooling in the hollows of her hips. She takes a drink from the cup, and a sharpened edge cuts the corner of her lip. She balances the plate on her bony right knee, and, shuddering with pleasure, she eats.[20]

Although Mangai derives pleasure from this solitary act of eating, one might consider this a form of disaffection in the terms that Martin Manalansan proposes. For Manalansan, disaffection is an alternative mode of domesticity. As he explains, "[Disaffection] is not resplendent in its heteronormative structurations, but is fraught with the intrusions and intersections of contradictory non-maternal feeling, interests and desires that emerge out of the banal repetitive routines of domestic labor."[21] Mangai enjoys cooking, but she is not interested in cooking for others. Her disaffection inhabits an alternative mode of domesticity insofar that cooking is about making herself happy, but not about making others happy in the conventional ways in which women are imagined to be happy homemakers who will willingly slave over a hot stove to prepare intricate meals for loved ones. Yet this space becomes one of female intimacy, albeit not because Mangai necessarily wishes it to be so.

> There are no boys outside, only girls. That is one of the rules, strictly enforced, by the parents, not by Mangai. Only girls outside, to see what they will become in time . . . she brings her neighbors more pleasure as present scandal than she ever could as past expulsion. It is at times like this that they have an excuse to tell her story again. . . . It will give them something to talk about for days. . . . In a way, it's almost a gift she gives them. Perhaps they know it, but she does not do it for them.[22]

Read in this way, Mangai ceases to be a pitiable figure or even a cause célèbre for triumphing over adversity: she is neither unhappy nor happy. Rather than viewing her as a failed subject who falls out of narratives of normative couplehood, I suggest that she is a queer single figure whose everyday demeanor embodies a kind of resilience precisely because her narrative is not about being happy or unhappy.[23] Her cooking, which, as she puts it, is about "sustain[ing] her in a normal day," positions her as a subject who has managed to overcome various kinds of violence, both as a result of her position as an ethnic Tamil and as a queer woman.[24] While neither vignette discloses in detail what happens to Mangai, we learn that in the intervening years spanning the civil war, she was shot and that the neighbors, scandalized by the "woman who had lived with her servant Daya for decades, in a house with only one bed[,] a woman they had insulted, behind her back, and to her face," left her for dead bleeding out on the floor of her home while they looked the other way.[25] She is thus guilty of both being the wrong ethnicity and not being in a conventionally normative relationship. There is a re-fusing of what violence looks like: the censure against the ethnicized body is linked to homophobic violence. In either case, she is that queer figure, an assemblage, whose very presence disturbs the community in which she lives. She refuses to allow the failure of entering into couplehood to exile her from the kitchen. Even though she may not be a conventional figure, preparing food in the home space to reproduce a kind of culinary nationalism, she does not stop cooking. Indeed, she almost takes an intense pleasure in cooking only for herself, thus embodying a kind of culinary resilience because cooking is about making herself happy. According to literary scholar Madelyn Detloff, the concept of resilience stands in opposition to resistance as a mode of engaging trauma.

> Resilient writing differs from redemptive writing in its refusal to make loss into a metaphor for something else. It diverges from the "unspeakable" hypothesis by recognizing the attempts of survivors to invent, if necessary, new methods of recognizing and communication, without suggesting that those methods are always and only symptom's of trauma's inescapable hold. Another way to describe resilient writing would be to suggest that it respects the dynamic relationships between the particularity of suffering and the temporality of living, of continuing on after, even in the midst of, suffering. Resilience then might be seen as a complex adaptation to traumatic circumstances—but an adaptation that does not "get over" or transcend the past as redemptive narratives imply. Rather, the past, like the "patch," becomes part of the continuously emerging present.[26]

Mangai's affective landscape thus negotiates between a sense of disaffection and resilience: disaffection because her work is about a kind of queer pleasure that does not simply seek to reproduce culinary subjects in the next generation, and resilience because she is not interested in being redeemed through her cooking and because she continues to live even after she negotiates the difficulties of everyday living in a homophobic and xenophobic context. Mohanraj's novel thus resituates the figure of the cook in the home so that her pedagogical imperative is not always about being a "wife" or "mother" or, for that matter, a partner in a coupled situation. In remapping the contours of South Asian foodways, Mohanraj allows for other topographies not circumscribed by an implicit heteronormativity. Food indexes queer resilience because it is through and against the act of preparing meals that Mangai, amid this narrative of a sprawling family, has the last word in the novel.

There is a startling symmetry in the simultaneous refusal of both the film and the novel to invest in perfection as an uncomplicated objective. Happiness in both works is not about creating the perfect meal, but about creating possibilities in spaces that are typically inhospitable to the forms of desire that the characters in these cultural works desire. In the texts' broader cultural context, the discourse of multiculturalism, a terrain on which works like *Bodies in Motion* and *Nina's Heavenly Delights* are consumed, there is an expectation of pleasure and joy in the act of cooking and eating. One expects the act of consumption to be about pleasure. Eating food is about producing happiness. One feels better about difference if one can eat the food of the other. Eating often is predicated on the notion that the commensal tradition is about celebration and perfect endings. After all, if sharing meals is not about happiness, what, arguably, is the point of commensality and conviviality? Works like Parmar's and Mohanraj's unsettle the notion that food must always be narrated in heteronormative frameworks. In the moments of "failure" are moments of possibility and desire.[27] Beyond the happily ever afters are moments of nonperfect delight and failure.

In an interview on the website afterellen.com, Pratibha Parmar, fully aware of how her film might indeed be read as a "failure" for being "too happy," commented:

> British Asian films are only allowed to be a certain kind of film. . . . [Critics approve] as long as the Asians are portrayed in stereotypical ways or they bring their cultural baggage with them. If it had been a real kind of misery-fest with Nina slashing her wrists because she's in love with a woman, the critics would have loved it.[28]

According to such a worldview, when the queer subject continues to cook and continues to live, it becomes possible to embrace the queerness of failure and the happily never afters; to relish meals that are not perfect but delightful; and to smile just a little with Mangai's happiness in the face of failure when she declares, "None of those meals came out perfectly—somehow she always managed to ruin them. Secretly, she was glad."[29]

Notes

1. Krishnendu Ray articulates these ideas in his *The Migrant's Table: Meals and Memories in Bengali American Households* (Philadelphia: Temple University Press, 2004).
2. In chapter 18 of this volume Denise Cruz signals the possibility of understanding food in a queer matrix. Also see Anita Mannur, *Culinary Fictions: Food in South Asian Diasporic Cultures* (Philadelphia: Temple University Press, 2010).
3. I borrow the idea of subjectless discourse in Asian American critique from Kandice Chuh, *Imagine Otherwise: On Asian Americanist Critique* (Durham, NC: Duke University Press, 2003).
4. Gayatri Gopinath, *Impossible Desires: Queer Diasporas and South Asian Public Cultures* (Durham, NC: Duke University Press, 2004), 15–16.
5. Sarah Warn, "Dropping Lesbian Romance from *Beckham* the Right Decision," afterellen.com, last modified November 2003, available at http://www.afterellen.com/archive/ellen/Movies/beckham.html.
6. Sara Ahmed, *The Promise of Happiness* (Durham, NC: Duke University Press, 2010).

7. Karman Kregloe, "Pratibha Parmar Makes Change," afterellen.com, last modified June 6, 2007, available at http://www.afterellen.com/people/2007/6/pratibhaparmar?page=1,1.

8. Ellen Dengel Janic and Lars Eckstein, "Bridehood Revisited: Disarming Concepts of Gender and Culture in Recent British Asian Film," in *Multi Ethnic Britain 2000+*, ed. Lars Eckstein, Barbara Korte, et al. (Amsterdam: Rodopi, 2008), 59.

9. Amandine Ducray's comparative analysis of Gurinder Chadha and Pratibha Parmar's films explores the tensions between their mainstream and independent films. Exploring how the question of audience and issues of access fundamentally alter the nature of filmmaking, Ducray provides a thoughtful analysis that examines the myriad meanings of both filmmakers' films. See Amandine Ducray, "Conflit, feminité et identité diasporiques: Le pouvoir de la representation chez Parmar et Chadha," *Anglophonie: French Journal of English Studies* 27 (2010): 305–17.

10. In recent years, some of the major voices in independent feminist South Asian film have turned to the romantic foodie comedy as profit-making ventures to help offset the funding for independent films. Dengel-Janic and Eckstein, no doubt, are referring to some of the recent South Asian diasporic collaborations on films about food—Gurinder Chadha's collaboration with Paul Berges on *Mistress of Spices* (2005), as well as her film *It's a Wonderful Afterlife* (2010), and Deepa Mehta's role as screenplay writer for *Cooking with Stella* (2009)—that, though beyond the scope of this chapter, like *Nina's Heavenly Delights*, are aimed at a mainstream global audience and are seen as works that depart from these directors' previous work. All these films, I would argue, use food in subtle ways to provide a counternarrative to easy exoticism.

11. Dengel Janic and Eckstein, "Bridehood Revisited," 58.

12. Elizabeth Buettner, "Chicken Tikka Masala, Flock Wallpaper and 'Real' Home Cooking: Assessing Britain's 'Indian' Restaurant Traditions," *Food and History* 7, no. 2 (2009): 203–30.

13. Ibid., 223.

14. Gopinath, *Impossible Subjects*, 194.

15. Mary Anne Mohanraj, *Bodies in Motion* (New York: Harper Perennial, 2006), 30.

16. Ibid., 275.

17. Ibid., 268.

18. Ibid.

19. Ibid., 271.

20. Ibid., 275.

21. Martin Manalansan, "Servicing the World: Flexible Filipinos and the Unsecured Life," in *Political Emotions*, ed. Janet Staiger, Ann Cvetkovich, and Ann Reynolds (New York: Routledge, 2009), 215–28.

22. Mohanraj, *Bodies in Motion*, 272.

23. Michael Cobb's analysis of singledom as "failure" is an important critical corollary to my argument. Cobb's brilliant analysis of the reviled status of the single articulates well with my point about Mangai's queer and reviled status. Cobb notes, "Part of the reason being single is terrible is that it's been made into a mystifying condition, marked by failure, characterized by an almost unassimilable oddity, despite its always threatening ubiquity." See Michael Cobb, *Single: Arguments for the Uncoupled* (New York: New York University Press, 2012), ebook.

24. Mohanraj, *Bodies in Motion*, 269.

25. Ibid., 273.

26. Madelyn Detloff, *The Persistence of Modernism: Loss and Mourning in the Twentieth Century* (Cambridge: Cambridge University Press, 2009), 14–15.

27. I understand failure here to be more of a generative position in the context that Judith Halberstam describes in *The Queer Art of Failure*: "Under certain circumstances failing, losing, forgetting, unmaking, undoing, unbecoming, not knowing, may in fact offer more creative, more cooperative, more surprising ways of being in the world." See Judith Halberstam, *The Queer Art of Failure* (Durham, NC: Duke University Press, 2011), ebook.

28. Karman Kregloe, "Pratibha Parmar Makes Change," afterellen.com, last modified June 6, 2007, available at http://www.afterellen.com/people/2007/6/pratibhaparmar?page=1,1.

29. Mohanraj, *Bodies in Motion*, 271.

BIBLIOGRAPHY

Abelmann, Nancy, and John Lie. *Blue Dreams: Korean Americans and the Los Angeles Riots.* Cambridge, MA: Harvard University Press, 1997.

Adams, Wanda A. *The Island Plate: 150 Years of Recipes and Food Lore from the* Honolulu Advertiser. Waipahu, HI: Island Heritage Publishing, 2006.

Ahmed, Sara. *The Promise of Happiness.* Durham, NC: Duke University Press, 2010.

Appadurai, Arjun. "How to Make a National Cuisine: Cookbooks in Contemporary India." *Comparative Studies in Society and History* 30, no. 1 (January 1988): 3–24.

Appadurai, Arjun, ed. *The Social Life of Things: Commodities in Cultural Perspective.* Cambridge: Cambridge University Press, 1986.

Ashcroft, Bill, Gareth Griffiths, and Helen Tiffin. *The Empire Writes Back: Theory and Practice in Post-colonial Literatures.* 2nd ed. London: Routledge, 2001.

Avakian, Arlene Voski, ed. *Through the Kitchen Window: Women Explore the Intimate Meanings of Food and Cooking.* New York: Berg, 1997.

Azuma, Andrea. *Food Access in Central and South Los Angeles: Mapping Injustice, Agenda for Action.* Los Angeles: Urban and Environmental Policy Institute, 2007.

Azuma, Eiichiro. *Between Two Empires: Race, History, and Transnationalism in Japanese America.* New York: Oxford University Press, 2005.

Balsley, Betsy, ed. *Los Angeles Times California Cookbook.* New York: Abrams, 1981.

Bangarth, Stephanie. *Voices Raised in Protest: Defending North American Citizens of Japanese Ancestry, 1942–49.* Vancouver: University of British Columbia Press, 2008.

Barbas, Samantha. "'I'll Take Chop Suey': Restaurants as Agents of Culinary and Cultural Change." *Journal of Popular Culture* 36, no. 4 (spring 2003): 669–86.

Barrow, Ian J. *Making History, Making Territory: British Mapping in India, c. 1756–1905.* New Delhi: Oxford University Press, 2003.

Beck, Louis. *New York's Chinatown: An Historical Presentation of Its People and Place.* New York: Bohemia Publishing, 1898.

Belasco, Warren, and Philip Scranton. *Food Nations: Selling Taste in Consumer Societies.* New York: Routledge, 2002.

Bestor, Theodore C. *Tsukiji: The Fish Market at the Center of the World.* Berkeley: University of California Press, 2004.

———. "How Sushi Went Global." In *The Cultural Politics of Food and Eating: A Reader*, ed. James L. Watson and Melissa L. Caldwell, 13–20. Malden, MA: Blackwell, 2005.

Bennett, Judith A. *Natives and Exotics: World War II and Environment in the Southern Pacific.* Honolulu: University of Hawai'i Press, 2009.

Besa, Amy, and Romy Dorotan. *Memories of Philippine Kitchens: Stories and Recipes from Far and Near.* New York: Stewart, Tabori & Chang, 2006.

Bhabha, Homi. *The Location of Culture.* London, New York: Routledge, 1994.

Black, Jane. "The Kimchi Fix." In *Best Food Writing 2010*, ed. Holly Hughes, 175–78. New York: Marlowe, 2010.

Black, Shameem. "Recipes for Cosmopolitanism." *Frontiers: A Journal of Women Studies* 31, no. 1 (2010): 1–30.

Blackmer, Corinne E. "African Masks and the Art of Passing in Gertrude Stein's *Melanctha* and Nella Larsen's *Passing.*" *Journal of the History of Sexuality* 4, no. 2 (1992): 230–63.

Bloom, Leonard. "Familial Adjustments of Japanese-Americans to Relocation: First Phase." *American Sociological Review* 8, no. 5 (1943): 551–60.

Bonner, Arthur. *Alas What Brought Thee Hither? The Chinese in New York, 1800–1950.* Madison, NJ: Fairleigh Dickinson University Press, 1997.

Bonus, Rick. *Locating Filipino Americans: Ethnicity and the Cultural Politics of Space.* Philadelphia: Temple University Press, 2000.

Bourriaud, Nicolas. *Relational Aesthetics.* Dijon: Les presses du réel, 2002.

Brandon, Reiko Mochinaga, and Loretta G. H. Woodward. *Hawaiian Quilts: Tradition and Transition.* Honolulu: Honolulu Academy of Arts, 2004.

Brooks, Charlotte. *Alien Neighbors, Foreign Friends: Asian Americans, Housing, and the Transformation of California.* Chicago: University of Chicago Press, 2009.

Brown, John Clifford. *Diary of a Soldier in the Philippines.* Portland, ME: Lakeside Press, 1901.

Brown, Linda Keller, and Kay Mussell, eds. *Ethnic and Regional Foodways in the United States: The Performance of Group Identity.* Knoxville: University of Tennessee Press, 1984.

Buaken, Manuel. *I Have Lived with the American People.* Caldwell, OH: Caxton Printers, 1948.

Buchholdt, Thelma. *Filipinos in Alaska.* Anchorage: Aboriginal Press, 1996.

Buckley School. *Buckley's Best.* Sherman Oaks, CA: Buckley Mothers Club Cookbook Committee, 1973.

Buell, Evangeline Canonizado. *Twenty Five Chickens and a Pig for a Bride.* San Francisco: T'Boli Publishing, 2006.

Buenaventura, Steffi San. "Filipino Folk Spirituality and Immigration: From Mutual Aid to Religion." *Amerasia Journal* 22, no.1 (1996): 217–32.

Buettner, Elizabeth. "Chicken Tikka Masala, Flock Wallpaper and 'Real' Home Cooking: Assessing Britain's 'Indian' Restaurant Traditions." *Food and History* 7, no. 2 (2009): 203–30.

Bulosan, Carlos. *America Is in the Heart: A Personal History.* Seattle: University of Washington Press, 1973.

Center for Oral History. *The Oroku, Okinawan Connection: Local-Style Restaurants in Hawai'i.* Honolulu: Social Science Research Institute, 2004.

Chan, Sucheng. *Asian Americans: An Interpretive History.* Boston: Twayne, 2001.

———. *Survivors: Cambodian Refugees in the United States.* Urbana: University of Illinois Press, 2004.

———. *This Bittersweet Soil: The Chinese in California Agriculture, 1860–1910.* Berkeley: University of California Press. 1989.

Chapek, Ralph, Inc. *1979 Donut Industry Survey.* Santa Barbara, CA: Ralph Chapek, Inc., 1979.

Chappell, George S. *The Restaurants of New York.* New York: Greenberg, 1925.

Cheah, Pheng, and Bruce Robbins, eds. *Cosmopolitics: Thinking and Feeling beyond the Nation.* Minneapolis: University of Minnesota Press, 1998.

Chen, Da. *Emigrant Communities in South China.* New York: Institute of Pacific Relations, 1940.

Chiu, Monica. *Filthy Fiction: Asian American Literature by Women*. New York: Altamira Press, 2004.

Chock, Eric. *Last Days Here*. Honolulu: Bamboo Ridge Press, 1990.

Choi, Susan. *American Woman*. New York: Harper, 2003.

Chou, Rosalind, and Joe Feagin. *The Myth of the Model Minority: Asian Americans Facing Racism*. Boulder, CO: Paradigm Publishers, 2008.

Choy, Sam. *Sam Choy's Island Flavors*. New York: Hyperion, 1999.

Christ the King Parish Guild. *Favorite Recipes*. Kansas City, MO: Circulation Services, 1968.

Chua, Amy. *Battle Hymn of the Tiger Mother*. New York: Bloomsbury Publishing, 2011.

Chuh, Kandice. *Imagine Otherwise: On Asian Americanist Critique*. Durham, NC: Duke University Press, 2003.

Cobb, Michael. *Single: Arguments for the Uncoupled*. New York: New York University Press, 2012.

Cobble, Dorothy Sue. *Dishing It Out: Waitresses and Their Unions in the Twentieth Century*. Urbana: University of Illinois Press, 1991.

Coe, Andrew. *Chop Suey: A Cultural History of Chinese Food in the United States*. Oxford: Oxford University Press, 2009.

Coe, Sophie D. *America's First Cuisines*. Austin: University of Texas Press, 1994.

Collingham, Lizzie. *Curry: A Tale of Cooks and Conquerors*. Oxford: Oxford University Press, 2006.

———. *The Taste of War: World War Two and the Battle for Food*. London: Allen Lane, 2011.

Collins, Kathleen. *Watching What We Eat: The Evolution of Television Cooking Shows*. New York: Continuum, 2009.

Conroy, Hilary. *The Japanese Frontier in Hawaii, 1868–1898*. Berkeley: University of California Press, 1953.

Coontz, Stephanie. *The Way We Never Were: American Families and the Nostalgia Trap*. New York: BasicBooks, 1992.

Cordero-Fernando, Gilda, ed. *The Culinary Culture of the Philippines*. Manila: Bancom Audio-vision Corporation, 1976.

Cornwel-Smith, Philip. *Very Thai: Everyday Popular Culture*. Bangkok: River Books, 2006.

Corson, Trevor. *The Zen of Fish: The Story of Sushi from Samurai to Supermarket*. New York: HarperCollins, 2007.

Costa, LeeRay, and Kathryn Besio. "Eating Hawai'i: Local Foods and Place-Making in Hawai'i Regional Cuisine." *Social & Cultural Geography* 12, no. 8 (2011): 839–54.

Counihan, Carole, and Penny Van Esterik, eds. *Food and Culture: A Reader*. New York: Routledge, 1997.

Crawford, David Livingston. *Hawaii's Crop Parade: A Review of Useful Products Derived from the Soil in the Hawaiian Islands, Past and Present*. Honolulu: Advertiser Publishing, 1937.

Crosby, Alfred W., Jr. *The Columbian Exchange: Biological and Cultural Consequences of 1492*. 30th anniversary ed. Westport, CT: Praeger, 2003.

Cwiertka, Katarzyna J. *Modern Japanese Cuisine: Food, Power and National Identity*. London: Reaktion, 2006.

Cwiertka, Katarzyna, and Boudewijn Walraven, eds. *Asian Food: The Global and the Local*. Honolulu: University of Hawai'i Press, 2001.

Dalby, Andrew. *Dangerous Tastes: The Story of Spices*. Berkeley: University of California Press, 2000.

David-Perez, Enriqueta. *Recipes of the Philippines*. Manila: Capitol Publishing House, 1956.

Davis, Mike. *City of Quartz: Excavating the Future in Los Angeles*. New York: Vintage Books, 1992.

Daws, Gavan. *Shoal of Time: A History of the Hawaiian Islands*. Honolulu: University of Hawai'i Press, 1968.

Day, Kristen. "Being Feared: Masculinity and Race in Public Space." *Environment and Planning* 38, no. 3 (2006): 569–86.

Daza, Nora V. *Galing-Galing: First Philippine Cookbook for Use in the United States*. Manila: Carnation Philippines, Inc., 1974.

de Guzman, Jean-Paul. "Beyond 'Living La Vida Boba': Social Space and Transnational Hybrid Asian American Youth Culture. *Amerasia Journal* 32, no. 2 (2006): 89–102.

de Olivares, José. *Our Islands and Their People: As Seen with Camera and Pencil*. New York: N. D. Thompson Publishing, 1899.

de Veyra, Sofia Reyes. *Everyday Cookery for the Home*. Manila: Philippine Education Company, 1934.

Detloff, Madelyn. *The Persistence of Modernism: Loss and Mourning in the Twentieth Century*. Cambridge: Cambridge University Press, 2009.

di Leonardo, Micaela. "The Female World of Cards and Holidays: Women, Families, and the Work of Kinship." *Signs* 12, no. 3 (1987): 440–53.

———. *The Varieties of Ethnic Experience: Kinship, Class, and Gender among California Italian-Americans*. Ithaca, NY: Cornell University Press, 1984.

Diehl, Michael, et al. "Acculturation and the Composition of the Diet of Tucson's Overseas Chinese Gardens at the Turn of the Century." *Historical Archeology* 32, no. 4 (1998): 19–33.

Diner, Hasia. *Hungering for America: Italian, Irish and Jewish Foodways in the Age of Migration*. Cambridge, MA: Harvard University Press, 2001.

Donovan, Maria Kozslik. *The Far Eastern Epicure*. Garden City, NY: Doubleday, 1958.

Doyle, Laura. "The Flat, the Round, and Gertrude Stein: Race and the Shape of Modern(ist) History." *Modernism/Modernity* 7, no. 2 (2000): 249–71.

Ducray, Amandine. "Conflit, feminité et identité diasporiques: Le pouvoir de la representation chez Parmar et Chadha. *Anglophonie: French Journal of English Studies* 27 (2010): 305–17.

Dudden, Arthur Power. *The American Pacific: From the Old China Trade to the Present*. New York: Oxford University Press, 1992.

Dunlop, Fuchsia. "Strange Tale of General Tso." In *Authenticity in the Kitchen*, ed. Richard Hosking, 165–77. Blackawton: Prospect Books, 2006.

Dusselier, Jane. "Does Food Make Place? Food Protests in Japanese American Concentration Camps." *Food & Foodways* 10 (2002): 137–65.

Eckstein, Lars, et al., eds. *Multi Ethnic Britain 2000+*. Amsterdam: Rodopi, 2008.

Edney, Matthew Henry. *Mapping an Empire: The Geographical Construction of British India, 1765–1843*. Chicago: University of Chicago Press, 1997.

Eng, Christina. "In My Mother's Kitchen." In *Best Food Writing 2002*, ed. Holly Hughes, 314–21. New York: Marlowe, 2002.

Eng, David L. *The Feeling of Kinship: Queer Liberalism and the Racialization of Intimacy*. Durham, NC: Duke University Press, 2010.

Eng, David L., and David Kazanjian. *Loss: The Politics of Mourning*. Berkeley: University of California Press, 2003.

Espina, Marina. *Filipinos in Louisiana*. New Orleans: A. F. Laborde, 1988.

Espiritu, Yen Le. *Asian American Women and Men: Labor, Laws, and Love.* Lanham, MD: Rowman & Littlefield, 2008.

Farquhar, Judith. *Appetites: Food and Sex in Post-Socialist China.* Durham, NC: Duke University Press, 2002.

Fernandez, Doreen. *Kinilaw: A Philippine Cuisine of Freshness.* Manila: Bookmark, 1991.

———. *Palayok: Philippine Food through Time, on Site, in the Pot.* Manila: Bookmark, 2000.

———. *Tikim: Essays on Philippine Food and Culture.* Manila: Anvil Publishing, 1994.

Fine, Gary Allen. *Kitchens: The Culture of Restaurant Work.* Berkeley: University of California Press, 1996.

Foucault, Michel. *Archaeology of Knowledge.* New York: Vintage Books, 1982.

———. *Discipline and Punish: The Birth of the Prison.* New York: Vintage Books, 1995.

———. *Madness and Civilization: A History of Insanity in the Age of Reason.* New York: Vintage Books, 1988.

———. *The Order of Things: An Archaeology of the Human Sciences.* New York: Vintage Books, 1994.

Fromartz. Samuel. *Organic, Inc.: Natural Foods and How They Grew.* Boston: Houghton Mifflin Harcourt, 2006.

Fruin, W. Mark. *Kikkoman: Company, Clan, and Community.* Cambridge, MA: Harvard University Press, 1983.

Fuchs, Lawrence H. *Hawaii Pono: A Social History.* New York: Harcourt, Brace & World, 1961.

Fujikane, Candace, and Jonathan Y. Okamura, eds. *Asian Settler Colonialism: From Local Governance to the Habits of Everyday Life in Hawai'i.* Honolulu: University of Hawai'i Press, 2008.

Fung, Catherine. "A History of Absences: The Problem of Reference in Monique Truong's *The Book of Salt.*" *Novel: A Forum on Fiction* 45, no. 1 (2012): 94–110.

Fung, Eileen Chia-Ching. "'To Eat the Flesh of His Dead Mother': Hunger, Masculinity, and Nationalism in Frank Chin's *Donald Duk.*" *LIT: Literature, Interpretation, Theory* 10 (1999): 255–74.

Furiya, Linda. *Bento Box in the Heartland: A Food Memoir.* Emeryville, CA: Seal Press, 2006.

Gabaccia, Donna R. *We Are What We Eat: Ethnic Food and the Making of Americans.* Cambridge, MA: Harvard University Press, 1998.

Gabaccia, Donna R., and Dirk Hoerder, eds. *Connecting Seas and Connected Ocean Rims.* Leiden: Brill, 2011.

Gaches, Samuel Francis. *Good Cooking and Health in the Tropics.* Manila: Bureau of Printing, 1922.

Gee, Chuck Y., and Matt Lurie, eds. *The Story of the Pacific Asia Travel Association.* San Francisco: Pacific Asia Travel Association, 1993.

Gerlach, Michael. "Trust Is Not Enough: Cooperation and Conflict in Kikkoman's American Development." *Journal of Japanese Studies* 16, no. 2 (summer 1990): 389–25.

Ghent Urban Studies Team, ed. *The Urban Condition: Space, Community, and Self in the Contemporary Metropolis.* Rotterdam: 010 Publishers, 1999.

Giesenkirchen, Michaela. "Ethnic Types and Problems of Characterization in Gertrude Stein's Radcliffe Themes." *American Literary Realism* 38, no. 1 (2005): 58–72.

Glick, Clarence E. *Sojourners and Settlers: Chinese Migrants in Hawai'i.* Honolulu: Hawai`i Chinese History Center, 1977.

Gopinath, Gayatri. *Impossible Desires: Queer Diasporas and South Asian Public Cultures.* Durham, NC: Duke University Press, 2004.

413

Gordon, Andrew. "Indiana Jones and the Temple of Doom: Bad Medicine." In *Food of the Gods: Eating and the Eaten in Fantasy and Science Fiction*, ed. Gary Westfahl, et al., 76–85. Athens: University of George Press, 1996.

Greeley, Alexandra. "Pad Thai." *Gastronomica: The Journal of Food and Culture* 9, no. 1 (winter 2009): 78–82.

Greenbaum, Fred. "The Social Ideas of Samuel Gompers." *Labor History* 7, no. 1 (1966): 35–61.

Guimary, Donald L. *Marumina Trabaho*. Lincoln, NE: iUniverse, 2006.

Halberstam, Judith. *The Queer Art of Failure*. Durham, NC: Duke University Press, 2011.

Haley, Andrew. *Turning the Tables: Restaurants and the Rise of the American Middle Class*. Chapel Hill: University of North Carolina Press, 2011.

Han, Kyung-Koo. "Noodle Odyssey: East Asia and Beyond." *Korea Journal* 50, no. 1 (spring 2010): 60–83.

———. "Some Foods Are Good to Think: Kimchi and the Epitomization of National Character." *Korean Social Science Journal* 27, no. 1 (2000): 221–35.

Hao, Zhidong. *Macau: History and Society*. Hong Kong: Hong Kong University Press, 2011.

Hata, Don, and Nadine Hata. "George Shima: The Potato King of California." *Journal of the West* 25, no. 1 (1986): 55–63.

Hauck-Lawson, Annie, and Jonathan Deutsch, eds. *Gastropolis: Food and New York City*. New York: Columbia University Press, 2009.

Heldke, Lisa. *Exotic Appetites: Ruminations of a Food Adventurer*. New York: Routledge, 2003.

Henderson, Janet Wald. *The New Cuisine of Hawaii: Recipes from the Twelve Celebrated Chefs of Hawaii Regional Cuisine*. New York: Villard Books, 1994.

Hendler, Glenn. "The Limits of Sympathy: Louisa May Alcott and the Sentimental Novel." *American Literary History* 3, no. 4 (winter 1991): 685–706.

Hirsch, Dafna. "'Hummus Is Best When It Is Fresh and Made by Arabs': The Gourmetization of Hummus in Israel and the Return of the Repressed Arab." *American Ethnologist* 38, no. 4 (2011): 617–30.

Hiura, Arnold. *Kau Kau: Cuisine and Culture in the Hawaiian Islands*. Honolulu: Watermark Publishing, 2009.

Ho, Jennifer. *Consumption and Identity in Asian American Coming-of-Age Novels*. New York: Routledge, 2005.

———. "The Place of Transgressive Texts in Asian American Epistemology." *Modern Fiction Studies* 56, no. 1 (2010): 205–25.

Houston, Jeanne Wakatsuki, and James D. Houston. *Farewell to Manzanar: A True Story of Japanese American Experience during and after the World War II Internment*. New York: Houghton Mifflin Harcourt, 2002.

Hsu, Madeline. *Dreaming of Gold, Dreaming of Home: Transnationalism and Migration between the United States and Southern China, 1882–1943*. Stanford, CA: Stanford University Press, 2000.

Ichihashi, Yamato. *Japanese in the United States: A Critical Study of the Problems of the Japanese Immigrants and Their Children*. Stanford, CA: Stanford University Press, 1932.

Ignacio, Rosendo. *Aklat ng Pagluluto: Hinango sa lalòng bantóg dakilàng aklát ng pagluluto sa gawîng Europa at sa Filipinas, na kapuwà nasusulat sa wikàng kastilà, at isinataglog ng boong katiyagâan ni Rosendo Ignacio*. Manila: Ikalawang Pagkalimbag, 1919.

Ishige, Naomichi. *The History and Culture of Japanese Food*. London: Kegan Paul, 2001.

Jacobs, Jane. *The Death and Life of Great American Cities*. New York: Vintage Books, 1992.

Jaffrey, Madhur. *Madhur Jaffrey's World Vegetarian*. New York: Clarkson Potter, 1999.

Jen, Gish. *The Love Wife*. New York: Vintage Books, 2005.

———. *Mona in the Promised Land*. New York: Vintage Books, 1997.

———. *Typical American*. Boston: Houghton Mifflin, 1991.

———. *World and Town*. New York: Knopf, 2010.

Jenkins, Virginia Scott. *Bananas: An American History*. Washington, DC: Smithsonian Institution Press, 2000.

Johnston, Josee, and Shyon Baumann. *Foodies: Democracy and Distinction in the Gourmet Foodscape*. New York: Routledge, 2010.

Joo, Rachael Miyung. "Chamoe." *Massachusetts Review* 45, no. 3 (2004): 285–94.

Jung, John. *Sweet and Sour: Life in Chinese Family Restaurants*. Los Angeles: Yin and Yang Press, 2010.

Kamp, David. *The United States of Arugula: How We Became a Gourmet Nation*. New York: Broadway Books, 2006.

Kana'iaupuni, Shawn Malia, Nolan J. Malone, and Koren Ishibashi. *Income and Poverty among Native Hawaiians: Summary of Ka Huaka'i Findings*. Honolulu: Kamehameha Schools—PASE, 05-06:5, 2005.

Kaprow, Allan. *Essays on the Blurring of Art and Life*. Berkeley: University of California Press, 1993.

Kauanui, J. Kēhaulani. *Hawaiian Blood: Colonialism and the Politics of Sovereignty and Indigeneity*. Durham, NC: Duke University Press, 2008.

Kelly, James. "Loco Moco: A Folk Dish in the Making." *Social Process* 30 (1983): 59–64.

Kim, Claire. "Imagining Race and Nation in Multiculturalist America." *Ethnic and Racial Studies* 27, no. 6 (2004): 987–1005.

Kim, Jodi. *Ends of Empire: Asian American Critique and the Cold War*. Minneapolis: University of Minnesota Press, 2010.

Kirshenblatt-Gimblett, Barbara. "Playing to the Senses: Food as a Performance Medium." *Performance Research* 4, no. 1 (1999): 1–30.

Kitayama, Shinobu, and Hazel Rose Markus. "Culture and the Self." *Psychological Review* 98, no. 2 (1991): 224–53.

Klein, Christina. *Cold War Orientalism: Asia in the Middlebrow Imagination, 1945–1961*. Berkeley: University of California Press, 2003.

Kodama-Nishimoto, Michiko, Warren Nishimoto, and Cynthia Oshiro. *Talking Hawai'i's Story: Oral Histories of an Island People*. Honolulu: University of Hawai'i Press, 2009.

Koeppel, Dan. *Banana: The Fate of the Fruit That Changed the World*. New York: Plume, 2008.

Koerner, Mae Respicio. *Filipinos in Los Angeles*. Charleston, SC: Arcadia Publishing, 2007.

Kotani, Roland. *The Japanese in Hawaii: A Century of Struggle*. Honolulu: Hawai'i Hochi, 1985.

Krissoff, Lianna, and Leda Scheintaub, eds. *Top Chef: The Cookbook*. San Francisco: Chronicle Books, 2008.

Krondl, Michael. *The Taste of Conquest: The Rise and Fall of the Three Great Cities of Spice*. New York: Random House, 2007.

Ku, Robert Ji-Song. "'Beware of Tourists If You Look Chinese' and Other Survival Tactics in the American Theatre: The Asian(cy) of Display in Frank Chin's *The Year of the Dragon*." *Journal of American Drama and Theatre* 11 (spring 1999): 78–92.

———. Review of *Chop Suey: A Cultural History of Chinese Food in the United States*, by Andrew Coe. *Gastronomica: The Journal of Food and Culture* 10, no. 4 (fall 2010): 93–94.

————. Review of *Curry: A Tale of Cooks and Conquerors*, by Lizzie Collingham. *Food and Foodways* 16, no. 1 (January 2008): 98–102.

Ku, Robert Ji-Song, and Alexandra Suh. "Asian American Literature, Post-1965." In *Crossing into America: The New Literature of Immigration*, ed. Louis Mendoza and S. Shankar, 314–26. New York: New Press, 2003.

Kwong, Peter. *Chinatown, N.Y.: Labor and Politics, 1930–1950*. New York: New Press, 1979.

Lahiri, Jhumpa. "Indian Takeout." In *Best Food Writing 2000*, ed. Holly Hughes, 301–4. New York: Marlowe, 2000.

————. *Interpreter of Maladies*. New York: Mariner Books, 1999.

————. *The Namesake*. New York: Mariner Books, 2004.

————. *Unaccustomed Earth*. New York: Knopf, 2008.

Lai, Him Mark. *Chinese American Transnational Politics*. Urbana: University of Illinois Press, 2010.

Latham, Michael E. *Modernization as Ideology: American Social Science and "Nation Building" in the Kennedy Era*. Chapel Hill, NC: University of North Carolina Press, 2000.

Laudan, Rachel. *The Food of Paradise: Exploring Hawaii's Culinary Heritage*. Honolulu: University of Hawai'i Press, 1996.

Le, Nam. *The Boat*. New York: Knopf, 2008.

Lee, Chang-rae. *Aloft*. New York: Riverhead Books, 2004.

————. *A Gesture Life*. New York: Riverhead Books, 1999.

————. *Native Speaker*. New York: Riverhead Books, 1996.

————. *The Surrendered*. New York: Riverhead Books, 2010.

Lee, Don. *The Collective*. New York: Norton, 2012.

————. *Country of Origin*. New York: Norton, 2004.

————. *Wrack and Ruin*. New York: Norton, 2009.

————. *Yellow: Stories*. New York: Norton, 2001.

Lee, Erika. *At America's Gates: Chinese Immigration during the Exclusion Era, 1882–1943*. Chapel Hill: University of North Carolina Press, 2003.

Lee, Erika, and Judy Yung. *Angel Island: Immigrant Gateway to America*. New York: Oxford University Press, 2011.

Lee, Jennifer 8. *The Fortune Cookie Chronicles: Adventures in the World of Chinese Food*. New York: Twelve, 2009.

Lee, Josephine. *Performing Asian America: Race and Ethnicity on the Contemporary Stage*. Philadelphia: Temple University Press, 1997.

Lee, Robert G. *Orientals: Asian Americans in Popular Culture*. Philadelphia: Temple University Press.

Lee, Sharon Heijin. "The Story of Gimchi Chigae." *Massachusetts Review* 45, no. 3 (autumn 2004): 381–85.

Lee, Stacy. *Unraveling the "Model Minority" Stereotype: Listening to Asian American Youth*. New York: Teachers College Press, 1996.

Levenstein, Harvey. *Paradox of Plenty: A Social History of Eating in Modern America*. Rev. ed. Berkeley: University of California Press, 2003.

Levine, Susan. *School Lunch Politics: The Surprising History of America's Favorite Welfare Program*. Princeton, NJ: Princeton University Press, 2008.

Lewis, George H. "From Minnesota Fat to Seoul Food: Spam in America and the Pacific Rim." *Journal of Popular Culture* 34 no. 2 (fall 2000): 83–105.

Lewis, Henry T. *Ilocano Rice Farmers: A Comparative Study of Two Philippine Barrios*. Honolulu: University of Hawai'i Press, 1971.

Lim, Shirley Jennifer. *A Feeling of Belonging: Asian American Women's Public Culture, 1930–1960*. New York: New York University Press, 2006.

Ling, Huping Ling. *Asian America: Forming New Communities, Expanding Boundaries*. New Brunswick, NJ: Rutgers University Press, 2009.

Linn, Brian McAllister. *Guardians of Empire: The U.S. Army and the Pacific, 1902–1940*. Chapel Hill: University of North Carolina Press, 1997.

Longstreth, Richard. *The American Department Store Transformed, 1920–1960*. New Haven, CT: Yale University Press, 2010.

———. *City Center to Regional Mall: Architecture, the Automobile, and Retailing in Los Angeles, 1920–1950*. Cambridge, MA: MIT Press, 1997.

———. *The Drive-In, the Supermarket, and the Transformation of Commercial Space in Los Angeles, 1914–1941*. Cambridge, MA: MIT Press, 2000.

Loomba, Ania, Suvir Kaul, Matti Bunzl, Antoinette Burton, and Jed Esty, eds. *Postcolonial Studies and Beyond*. Durham, NC: Duke University Press, 2005.

Lovegren, Sylvia. *Fashionable Food: Seven Decades of Food Fads*. New York: Macmillan, 1995.

Lowe, Lisa. *Immigrant Acts: On Asian American Cultural Politics*. Durham, NC: Duke University Press, 1996.

Machida, Margo. *Asia/America*. New York: Asia Society Galleries and New Press, 1994.

Maeda, Daryl. *Chains of Babylon: The Rise of Asian America*. Minneapolis: University of Minnesota Press, 2009.

Maki, Mitchell T., Harry H. L. Kitano, and S. Megan Berthold. *Achieving the Impossible Dream: How Japanese Americans Obtained Redress*. Urbana: University of Illinois Press, 1999.

Manalansan, Martin F. "Cooking Up the Senses: A Critical Embodied Approach to the Study of Food and Asian American Television Audiences." In *Alien Encounters: Asian Americans in Popular Culture*, ed. Thuy Linh Tu and Mimi Nguyen, 179–93. Durham, NC: Duke University Press, 2007.

———. "The Empire of Food: Place, Memory, and Asian 'Ethnic Cuisines.'" In *Gastropolis: Food and New York City*, ed. Annie Hauck-Lawson and Jonathan Deutsch, 93–107. New York: Columbia University Press, 2009.

———. "Prairiescapes: Mapping Food, Loss, and Longing." *Massachusetts Review* 45, no. 3 (2004): 361–65.

———. "Servicing the World: Flexible Filipinos and the Unsecured Life." In *Political Emotions*, ed. Janet Staiger, Ann Cvetkovich, and Ann Reynolds, 215–28. New York: Routledge, 2009.

Mannur, Anita. *Culinary Fictions: Food in South Asian Diasporic Culture*. Philadelphia: Temple University Press, 2010.

———. "Model Minorities Can Cook." In *East Main Street: Asian American Popular Culture*, ed. Shilpa Davé, Leilani Nishime, and Tasha G. Oren, 72–94. New York: New York University Press, 2005.

———. Review of *The Book of Salt*, by Monique Truong. *Gastronomica: The Journal of Food and Culture* 4, no. 3 (summer 2004): 120–21.

Masumoto, David Mas. *Four Seasons in Five Senses: Things Worth Savoring*. New York: Norton, 2003.

Matejowsky, Ty. "SPAM and Fast-Food 'Glocalization' in the Philippines." *Food, Culture, Society* 10, no. 1 (2007): 24–41.

May, Elaine Tyler. *Homeward Bound: American Families in the Cold War Era*. New York: Basic Books, 1999.

Mazumdar, Sucheta. "The Impact of New World Food Crop on the Diet and Economy of China and India, 1600–1900." In *Food in Global History*, ed. Raymond Grew, 58–78. Boulder, CO: Westview Press, 1999.

McFadden, David Revere, and Ellen Napiura Taubman. *Changing Hands: Art without Reservation 2: Contemporary Native North American Art from the West, Northwest & Pacific*. New York: Museum of Arts and Design, 2005.

McKeown, Adam. "Transnational Chinese Families and Chinese Exclusion, 1875–1943." *Journal of Ethnic Studies* 18, no. 1 (1999): 73–110.

McMaster, Gerald, ed. *Reservation X: The Power of Place in Aboriginal Contemporary Art*. Seattle: University of Washington Press, 1999.

McNamee, Thomas. *Alice Waters and Chez Panisse: The Romantic, Impractical, Often Eccentric, Ultimately Brilliant Making of a Food Revolution*. New York: Penguin, 2007.

Merry, Sally Engle. *Colonizing Hawai'i: The Cultural Power of Law*. Princeton, NJ: Princeton University Press, 2000.

Meyer, Manulani Aluli. Hoʻoulu: *Our Time of Becoming: Collected Early Writings of Manulani Meyer*. Honolulu, HI: ʻAi Pōhaku Press. 2003.

Min, Pyong Gap. *Ethnic Solidarity for Economic Survival: Korean Greengrocers in New York City*. New York: Russell Sage, 2008.

Minnick, Sylvia Sun. *Samfow: The San Joaquin Chinese Legacy*. Fresno, CA: Panorama Books, West Publishing, 1988.

Mintz, Sidney W. *Sweetness and Power: The Place of Sugar in Modern History*. New York: Penguin, 1986.

———. *Tasting Food, Tasting Freedom: Excursions into Eating, Culture, and the Past*. Boston: Beacon Press, 1996.

Mohanraj, Mary Anne. *Bodies in Motion*. New York: Harper Perennial, 2006.

Monrayo, Angeles. *Tomorrow's Memories: A Diary, 1924–1938*. Honolulu: University of Hawai'i Press, 2003.

Montoya, Carina Monica. *Los Angeles's Historic Filipinotown*. Charleston, SC: Arcadia Publishing, 2009.

Morris, Charles. *Our Island Empire*. Philadelphia, 1899.

Mullins. Paul. *Glazed America: A History of the Doughnut*. Gainesville: University Press of Florida, 2008.

Mullins, Paul, and Sally Levitt Steinberg. *The Donut Book: The Whole Story in Words, Pictures & Outrageous Tales*. North Adams, MA: Storey Publishing, 2004.

Mullins, Paul, and Steve Penfold. *The Donut: A Canadian History*. Toronto: University of Toronto Press, 2008.

Murray, Alice Yang. *Historical Memories of the Japanese American Internment and the Struggle for Redress*. Stanford, CA: Stanford University Press, 2008.

Nestle, Marion. *Food Politics: How the Food Industry Influences Nutrition and Health*. Berkeley: University of California Press, 2002.

Ng, Franklin. "Food and Culture: Chinese Restaurants in Hawai'i." In *Chinese America: History and Perspectives—The Journal of the Chinese Historical Society of America*, 13–22.

San Francisco: Chinese Historical Society of America and UCLA Asian American Studies Center, 2010.

Ngai, Mae. *Impossible Subjects: Illegal Aliens and the Making of Modern America*. Princeton, NJ: Princeton University Press, 2004.

Niiya, Brian, ed. *Japanese American History: An A-to-Z Reference from 1868 to the Present*. New York: Facts on File, 1993.

Nix, Janeth Johnson. *Adventures in Oriental Cooking*. San Francisco: Ortho Books, 1976.

Nunez, Sigrid. *Feather on the Breath of God*. New York, HarperCollins, 1995.

Ochs, Elinor, and Merav Shohet. "The Cultural Structuring of Mealtime Socialization." *New Directions for Child and Adolescent Development* 111 (spring 2006): 35–49.

Ohnuki-Tierney, Emiko. "The Ambivalent Self of the Contemporary Japanese." *Cultural Anthropology* 5, no. 2 (May 1990): 197–216.

———. *Rice as Self: Japanese Identities through Time*. Princeton, NJ: Princeton University Press, 1993.

Okada, John. *No-No Boy*. Seattle: University of Washington Press, 1979.

Okihiro, Gary Y. *Cane Fires: The Anti-Japanese Movement in Hawaii, 1865–1945*. Philadelphia: Temple University Press, 1991.

———. *Pineapple Culture: A History of the Tropical and Temperate Zones*. Berkeley: University of California Press, 2009.

Okihiro, Michael. *AJA Baseball in Hawaii: Ethnic Pride and Tradition*. Honolulu: Hawaiʻi Hochi, 1999.

Okubo, Miné. *Citizen 13660*. Seattle: University of Washington Press, 1946.

Oliver, Melvin, and Thomas Shapiro. *Black Wealth, White Wealth: A New Perspective on Racial Inequality*. New York: Routledge, 2006.

Omi, Michael, and Howard A. Winant. *Racial Formation in the United States: From the 1960s to the 1990s*. New York: Routledge, 1994.

Ong, Aihwa. *Buddha Is Hiding: Refugees, Citizenship, the New America*. Berkeley: University of California Press, 2003.

Ong, Han. *Fixer Chao*. New York: Farrar, Straus & Giroux, 2001.

Osorio, Jonathan Kay Kamakawiwoʻole. *Dismembering Lahui: A History of the Hawaiian Nation to 1887*. Honolulu: University of Hawaiʻi Press, 2002.

Owen, Sri. *Indonesian Regional Food & Cookery*. London: Frances Lincoln, 1999.

Padoongpatt, Tanachai Mark. "Too Hot to Handle: Food, Empire, and Race in Thai Los Angeles." *Radical History Review* 110 (spring 2011): 83–108.

Pai, Sona. "Mangoes, Memories and Automobiles." In *Best Food Writing 2010*, ed. Holly Hughes, 291–96. New York: Marlowe, 2008.

Partridge, Jeffrey. "The Politics of Ethnic Authorship: Li-Young Lee, Emerson, and Whitman at the Banquet Table." *Studies in the Literary Imagination* 37, no. 1 (spring 2004): 101–25.

Patel, Raj. *Stuffed & Starved: From Farm to Fork, the Hidden Battle for the World Food System*. London: Portobello Books, 2007.

Pettid, Michael J. *Korean Cuisine: An Illustrated History*. London: Reaktion, 2008.

Pollan, Michael. *In Defense of Food: An Eater's Manifesto*. New York: Penguin, 2008.

———. *Omnivore's Dilemma: A Natural History of Four Meals*. New York: Penguin, 2006.

Pomeranz, Kenneth, and Steven Topik. *The World That Trade Created: Society, Culture, and the World Economy 1400 to the Present*. Armonk, NY: Sharpe, 2006.

Pukui, Mary Kawena, and Samuel H. Elbert. *Hawaiian Dictionary*. Honolulu: University of Hawaiʻi Press, 1986.

Quirino, Carlos. *Culinary Arts in the Tropics circa 1922*. Manila: Regal Publishing, 1978.

Rath, Eric C., and Stephanie Assmann, eds. *Japanese Foodways Past and Present*. Urbana: University of Illinois Press, 2010.

Raussert, Wilfried. "Minority Discourse, Foodways, and Aspects of Gender: Contemporary Writings by Asian-American Women." *Journal x: A Journal in Culture and Criticism* 7, no. 2 (2003): 184–204.

Raussert, Wilfried, and Nicole Waller. "Past and Repast: Food as Historiography in Fae Myenne Ng's *Bone* and Frank Chin's *Donald Duk*." *Amerikastudien / American Studies* 40, no. 3 (1996): 485–502.

Ray, Krishnendu. "Domesticating Cuisine: Food and Aesthetics on American Television." *Gastronomica: The Journal of Food and Culture* 7, no. 1 (winter 2007): 50–63.

———. "Ethnic Succession and the New American Restaurant Cuisine." In *The Restaurants Book: Ethnographies of Where We Eat*, ed. D. Beriss and D. Sutton, 97–114. New York: Berg, 2007.

———. *The Migrant's Table: Meals and Memories in Bengali American Households*. Philadelphia: Temple University Press, 2004.

Ray, Krishnendu, and Tulasi Srinivas, eds. *Curried Cultures: Globalization, Food, and South Asia*. Berkeley: University of California Press, 2012.

Roberts, J. A. G. *China to Chinatown: Chinese Food in the West*. London: Reaktion, 2002.

Rowe, John Carlos. "Naming What Is Inside: Gertrude Stein's Use of Names in *Three Lives*." *Novel* 36, no. 2 (2003): 219–43.

Ruiz, Vicki L. *From Out of the Shadows: Mexican Women in Twentieth-Century America*. New York: Oxford University Press, 1998.

Rustomji, Roshni. "American Dhansak and the Holy Man of Oaxaca." *Massachusetts Review* 45, no. 3 (2004): 309–18.

Said, Edward. *Culture and Imperialism*. New York: Knopf, 1993.

Salyer, Lucy E. *Laws Harsh as Tigers: Chinese Immigration and the Shaping of Modern Immigration Law*. Chapel Hill: University of North Carolina Press, 1995.

Sanchez, George. *Becoming Mexican American*. New York: Oxford University Press, 1995.

Saxton, Alexander. *Indispensable Enemy: Labor and the Anti-Chinese Movement in California*. Berkeley: University of California Press, 1971.

Schlosser, Eric. *Fast Food Nation: The Dark Side of the All-American Meal*. New York: Perennial Books, 2002.

Schmitt, Robert C. *Historical Statistics of Hawai'i*. Honolulu: University Press of Hawai'i, 1962.

Schwartz, Shepard. "Mate-Selection among New York's Chinese Males." *American Journal of Sociology* 56, no. 6 (May 1952): 562–68.

Shapiro, Laura. *Perfection Salad*. Berkeley: University of California Press, 2008.

Shaw, Angel Velasco, and Luis H. Francia, eds. *Vestiges of War: The Philippine-American War and the Aftermath of an Imperial Dream*. New York: New York University Press, 2002.

Shibusawa, Naoko. *America's Geisha Ally: Reimagining the Japanese Enemy*. Cambridge, MA: Harvard University Press, 2006.

Shiva, Vandana. "The Mustard Oil Conspiracy." *Ecologist* (2001): 27–29.

———. *Stolen Harvest: The Hijacking of the Global Food Supply*. Cambridge, MA: South End Press, 2000.

Shortridge, Barbara G., and James R. Shortridge, eds. *The Taste of American Place: A Reader on Regional and Ethnic Foods*. Lanham, MD: Rowman & Littlefield, 1998.

Shouse, Heather. *Food Trucks: Dispatches and Recipes from the Best Kitchens on Wheels.* Berkeley, CA: Ten Speed Press, 2011.

Shurtleff, William, and Akiko Aoyagi. *History of Erewhon-Natural Foods Pioneer in the United States, 1966–2011.* Lafayette, CA: Soyinfo Center, 2011.

Silva, Noenoe. *Aloha Betrayed: Native Hawaiian Resistance to American Colonialism.* Durham, NC: Duke University Press, 2004.

Simpson, Caroline Chung. *An Absent Presence: Japanese Americans in Postwar American Culture, 1945–1960.* Durham, NC: Duke University Press, 2001.

Singson, Precious Grace. "Sally's Lechon: An Outpost of Eating America." *Amerasia Journal* 32, no. 2 (2006): 79–87.

Siu, Kin Wai Michael. "Red Packet: A Traditional Object in the Modern World." *Journal of Popular Culture* 35, no. 3 (2002): 103–25.

Siu, Lok. "Chino Latino Restaurants: Converging Communities, Identities, and Cultures." *Afro-Hispanic Review* 27, no. 1 (spring 2008): 161–71.

Smith, Mark. *Sensing The Past: Seeing, Hearing, Smelling, Tasting, and Touching in History.* Berkeley: University of California Press, 2007.

Soja, Edward W. *Postmodern Geographies: The Reassertion of Space in Critical Social Theory.* London: Verso, 1989.

Sone, Monica. *Nisei Daughter.* Seattle: University of Washington Press, 1979.

Song, Miri. *Helping Out: Children's Labor in Ethnic Businesses.* Philadelphia: Temple University Press, 1999.

Spickard, Paul R. *Japanese Americans: The Formation and Transformation of an Ethnic Group.* New York: Twayne, 1996.

Spivak, Gayatri. *A Critique of Postcolonial Reason: Toward a History of the Vanishing Present.* Cambridge, MA: Harvard University Press, 1999.

———. *Imperative zur Neuerfindung des Planeten (Imperative to Reimagine the Planet).* Vienna: Passagen-Verlag, 1999.

Sta. Maria, Felice Prudente. *The Governor-General's Kitchen: Philippine Culinary Vignettes and Period Recipes, 1521–1935.* Manila: Anvil Publishing, 2006.

Stannard, David H. *Before the Horror: The Population of Hawai'i on the Eve of Western Contact.* Honolulu: Social Science Research Institute, University of Hawai'i, 1989.

Suehiro, Arthur. *Honolulu Stadium: Where Hawaii Played.* Honolulu: Watermark Publishing, 1995.

Sumida, Stephen. *And the View from the Shore: Literary Traditions of Hawai'i.* Seattle: University of Washington Press, 1991.

Swislocki, Mark. *Culinary Nostalgia: Regional Food Culture and the Urban Experience in Shanghai.* Stanford, CA: Stanford University Press, 2009.

Takaki, Ronald. *Pau Hana: Plantation Life and Labor in Hawaii, 1835–1920.* Honolulu: University of Hawai'i Press, 1983.

———. *Strangers from a Different Shore: A History of Asian Americans.* New York: Little Brown, 1990.

Takei, George. *To the Stars: The Autobiography of George Takei, Star Trek's Mr. Sulu.* New York: Pocket Books, 1994.

Tamura, Eileen. *Americanization, Acculturation, and Ethnic Identity: The Nisei Generation in Hawaii.* Urbana: University of Illinois Press, 1994.

Tashiro, Kenneth A. *'Wase Time!': A Teen's Memoir of Gila River Internment Camp Days.* Bloomington, IL: AuthorHouse, 2005.

Tchen, John Kuo Wei. *New York before Chinatown: Orientalism and the Shaping of American Culture, 1776–1882.* Baltimore: Johns Hopkins University Press, 1999.

Tisdale, Sallie. *Best Thing I Ever Tasted: The Secret of Food.* New York: Riverhead Books, 2001.

Tompkins, Kyla Wazana. *Racial Indigestion: Eating Bodies in the 19th Century.* New York: New York University Press, 2012.

Toribio, Helen, ed. *Seven Card Stud with Seven Manangs Wild: An Anthology of Filipino American Writing.* San Francisco: T'Boli Publishing, 2002.

Trask, Haunani Kay. "Settlers of Color and 'Immigrant' Hegemony: 'Locals' in Hawai'i." *Amerasia Journal* 26, no. 2 (summer 2000): 1–24.

Trinidad, Crispulo. *Pasteleria at Reposteria: Francesa at Española: Aklat na ganap na naglalaman ng maraming palacada sa pag-gaua ng lahat ng mga bagay-bagay na matamis at mga pasteles.* Manila: Limbagan ni J. Martinez, 1919.

Troeung, Y-Dang. "'A Gift or a Theft Depends on Who Is Holding the Pen': Postcolonial Collaborative Autobiography and Monique Truong's *The Book of Salt.*" *Modern Fiction Studies* 56, no. 1 (2010): 113–35.

Truong, Monique. *Bitter in the Mouth.* New York: Random House, 2010.

———. *The Book of Salt.* Boston: Houghton Mifflin Harcourt, 2003.

Tsai, Ming, and Arthur Boehm. *Blue Ginger: East Meets West Cooking with Ming Tsai.* New York: Clarkson Potter, 1999.

Tuchman, Gaye, and Harry Gene Levine. "New York Jews and Chinese Food: The Social Construction of an Ethnic Pattern." *Journal of Contemporary Ethnography* 22, no. 3 (October 1993): 382–407.

Tuon, Bunkong. "Cambodia: Memory and Desire." *Massachusetts Review* 45, no. 3 (2004): 319–20.

Ty, Eleanor. *Unfastened: Globality and Asian North American Narratives.* Minneapolis: University of Minnesota Press, 2010.

Vallangca, Robert. *Pinoy: The First Wave.* San Francisco: Strawberry Hill Press, 1977.

Van Esterik, Penny, *Food Culture in Southeast Asia.* Westport, CT: Greenwood, 2008.

Van Noy, Rick. *Surveying the Interior: Literary Cartographers and the Sense of Place.* Reno: University of Nevada Press, 2003.

Van Sant, John E. *Pacific Pioneers: Japanese Journeys to American and Hawaii, 1850–90.* Urbana: University of Illinois Press, 2000.

VOICES: A Filipino American Oral History. Stockton: Filipino Oral History, 1984.

Wang, Oliver. "to live and dine in kogi l.a." *Contexts* 8, no. 4 (fall 2009): 69–73.

Watson, James L., ed. *Golden Arches East: McDonald's in East Asia.* Stanford, CA: Stanford University Press, 1997.

Watson, James L., and Melissa L. Caldwell. *The Cultural Politics of Food and Eating: A Reader.* Malden, MA: Blackwell, 2005.

Wei, William. *The Asian American Movement.* Philadelphia: Temple University Press, 1993.

Westad, Odd Arne. *The Global Cold War.* Cambridge: Cambridge University Press, 2007.

Williams-Forson, Psyche. *Building Houses out of Chicken Legs: Black Women, Food, and Power.* Chapel Hill: University of North Carolina Press, 2006.

Williams-Forson, Psyche, and Carole Counihan, eds. *Taking Food Public: Redefining Foodways in a Changing World.* New York: Routledge, 2011.

Wilson, Marie M. *Siamese Cookery*. Rutland, VT: Tuttle, 1965.

Wong, Alan. *Alan Wong's New Wave Luau: Recipes from Honolulu's Award-Winning Chef*. Berkeley: Ten Speed Press, 1999.

———. *The Blue Tomato: The Inspiration behind the Cuisine of Alan Wong*. Honolulu: Watermark Publishing, 2010.

Wong, Bernard. *Patronage, Brokerage, Entrepreneurship and the Chinese Community of New York*. New York: AMS Press, 1988.

Wong, Jade Snow. *Fifth Chinese Daughter*. 1945. Reprint, Seattle: University of Washington Press, 1989.

Wong, Sau-Ling Cynthia. "Denationalization Reconsidered." *Amerasia Journal* 21, nos. 1 and 2 (1995): 1–27.

———. *Reading Asian American Literature: From Necessity to Extravagance*. Princeton, NJ: Princeton University Press, 1993.

Wong, Shawn. *American Knees*. New York: Simon & Schuster, 1995.

Wong, Wayne. *American Paper Son: A Chinese Immigrant in the Midwest*. Ed. Benson Tong. Urbana: University of Illinois Press, 2006.

Woon, Yuen-Fong. *Social Organization in South China, 1911–1949: The Case of the Kuan Lineage of K'ai-p'ing County*. Ann Arbor: Center for Chinese Studies, University of Michigan, 1984.

Worcester, Dean. *The Philippines: Past and Present*. New York: Macmillan, 1914.

Wu, David Y. H., and Sidney Cheung, eds. *The Globalization of Chinese Food*. London: Routledge Curzon, 2002.

Wu, Frank. "The Best 'Chink' Food: Dog Eating and the Dilemma of Diversity." In *Gastronomica Reader*, ed. Darra Goldstein, 218–31. Berkeley: University of California Press, 2010.

———. *Yellow: Race in America beyond Black and White*. New York: Basic Books, 2002.

Xu, Wenying. *Eating Identities: Reading Food in Asian American Literature*. Honolulu: University of Hawai'i Press, 2008.

Yamaguchi, Roy. *Hawaii Cooks: Flavors from Roy's Pacific Rim Kitchen*. Berkeley, CA: Ten Speed Press, 2003.

———. *Roy's Feasts from Hawaii*. Berkeley, CA: Ten Speed Press, 2007.

———. *Roy's Fish and Seafood*. Berkeley, CA: Ten Speed Press, 2005.

Yang, Alice. *Why Asia?* New York: New York University Press, 1998.

Yang, Young-Kyun. "Jajangmyeon and Junggukjip: The Changing Position and Meaning of Chinese Food and Chinese Restaurants in Korean Society." *Korea Journal* 45, no. 2 (summer 2005): 60–88.

Yano, Christine. "Side-Dish Kitchen: Japanese American Delicatessens and the Culture of Nostalgia." In *The Restaurants Book: Ethnographies of Where We Eat*, ed. D. Beriss and D. Sutton, 47–63. New York: Berg, 2007.

Yates, Ronald E. *The Kikkoman Chronicles: A Global Company with a Japanese Soul*. New York: McGraw-Hill, 1998.

Yee, Alfred. *Shopping at Giant Foods: Chinese American Supermarkets in Northern California*. Seattle: University of Washington Press, 2003.

Yoo, David K. *Growing Up Nisei: Race, Generation, and Culture among Japanese Americans of California, 1924–49*. Urbana: University of Illinois Press, 2000.

Yoo, David K., ed. *New Spiritual Homes: Religion and Asian Americans*. Honolulu: University of Hawai'i Press and UCLA Asian American Studies Center, 1999.

Yu, Renqiu. "Chop Suey: From Chinese Food to Chinese American Food." *Chinese America: History and Perspectives* 1 (1989): 87–99.

———. *To Save China, to Save Ourselves: The Chines Hand Laundry Alliance of New York.* Philadelphia: Temple University Press, 1992.

Zia, Helen. *Asian American Dreams: The Emergence of an American People.* New York: Farrar, Straus & Giroux, 2001.

Zubaida, Sami, and Richard Tapper. *Culinary Cultures of the Middle East.* London: I. B. Tauris, 1994.

CONTRIBUTORS

WANDA ADAMS was born and raised on the island of Maui, growing up in verdant ʻIao Valley where her parents owned a small hotel and restaurant. She learned to cook at the hands of her Portuguese grandmother, helped her grandfather in his sprawling garden, and simply could not be kept out of the hotel kitchen. Besides serving as the food editor for Hawaiʻi's major daily newspaper, the *Honolulu Advertiser*, Adams has penned numerous cookbooks and books about local food in Hawaiʻi.

DENISE CRUZ is an assistant professor of English at the University of Toronto. She is the author of *Transpacific Femininities: The Making of the Modern Filipina* and the editor of Yay Panlilio's *The Crucible: An Autobiography of "Colonel Yay," Filipina American Guerrilla*. Her research, which centers on the use of spatial and geographic frameworks to analyze gender and sexuality in national and transnational culture, has appeared in *American Quarterly*, *American Literature*, *Modern Fiction Studies*, and *PMLA*.

ERIN M. CURTIS is a PhD candidate in the Department of American Studies at Brown University, where she also holds an MA in public humanities. Her dissertation, "World Donut: Cambodians, Donut Shops, and Los Angeles, 1979–Present," examines Los Angeles's Cambodian doughnut shops in relation to the history of mass food production, U.S. refugee policy, and the city's physical and cultural landscapes. She lives in Los Angeles, where she works as an assistant curator at the Skirball Cultural Center.

JENNIFER HO is an associate professor in the Department of English and Comparative Literature at the University of North Carolina at Chapel Hill, where she teaches courses in contemporary American, multiethnic American, and Asian American literature. Her first book, *Consumption and Identity in Asian American Coming-of-Age-Novels*, examines the intersection of coming-of-age, ethnic identity formation, and foodways in late-twentieth-century coming-of-age narratives and American popular culture. Her current book manuscript, "Telling Stories, Making Knowledge: Racial Ambiguity in Asian American Culture," investigates the theme of racial ambiguity and Asian American culture through diverse subjects like transracial/transnational adoptees, Tiger Woods, and mixed-race literature.

NINA F. ICHIKAWA is the food and agricultural editor for *Hyphen*, a print and online magazine profiling the culture, arts, and politics of Asian America. In 2011, she was named Food and Community Fellow by the Institute for Agriculture and Trade Policy, a fellowship for writers and activists "working to create a just, equitable and healthy food system in the United States." She is a co-convener of AAPI Food Action and worked as an assistant to the Obama administration's

"Know Your Farmer, Know Your Food" program at the U.S. Department of Agriculture. She has written for *Rafu Shimpo*, *Nikkei Heritage*, *Civil Eats*, and *Gist* and is the fourth-generation descendant of Northern California Japanese American flower growers.

HEIDI KATHLEEN KIM is an assistant professor in the Department of English and Comparative Literature at the University of North Carolina at Chapel Hill. She has published articles on various topics in nineteenth- and twentieth-century American literature, such as the Mississippi Chinese and the novels of William Faulkner (*Philosophical Quarterly*) and the Louisiana Francophone anti-slavery novel *Le vieux salomon*. Her article on the public discussion of plastic surgery and racialized appearance as it affected the *Korematsu* landmark Supreme Court case on the Japanese American incarceration appeared in a special issue of the *Journal of Transatlantic American Studies*. She is currently finishing her first book manuscript, "Invisible Subjects: Asian Americans in Postwar U.S. Literature," and is editing an incarceration memoir, correspondence, and artwork of the Hoshidas, a Japanese American family in Hawai'i.

ROBERT JI-SONG KU is an associate professor of Asian and Asian American studies at Bing-hamton University of the State University of New York. He has previously taught at Cal Poly, San Luis Obispo, where he chaired the Department of Ethnic Studies, as well as Hunter College of the City University of New York, where he directed the Asian American studies program. His writings appear in a wide array of publications, including *Amerasia Journal*, *Journal of Asian American Studies*, *Food and Foodways*, and *Gastronomica*. He is the author of *Dubious Gastron-omy: The Cultural Politics of Eating Asian in the USA* and is currently coediting a book on *hallyu* (the Korean Wave) in the United States.

HEATHER R. LEE is a doctoral candidate in American studies at Brown University. Her disserta-tion, "Chinese Restaurants in the United States: A History of Migration, Labor, and Entrepreneur-ship, 1850–1943," explains how the Chinese used a loophole in America's anti-Chinese immigra-tion laws to develop the Chinese restaurant industry into what it is today. To tell this complex story without archival material, she is creating an online platform for the public, organizations, and researchers to share materials on Chinese restaurants. Extending this effort to bridge public and academic interests, she has interned at Museum of Chinese in America in New York City and the Wing Luke Museum in Seattle, and curated exhibits on Chinese restaurants in the United States. She has published essays on migration, food, and Asian American histories. She has an MA in public humanities from Brown University and a BA and MA in history from Emory University.

DAWN BOHULANO MABALON, a third-generation Pinay born in Stockton, California, is an associate professor of history at San Francisco State University. She received her PhD in Ameri-can history at Stanford University. She is a coauthor of *Filipinos in Stockton*, a coeditor of *Filipi-nos in San Francisco*, and the author of *Little Manila Is in the Heart: The Making of the Filipina/o American Community in Stockton, California*. She is the cofounder of the Little Manila Foun-dation, which works for the preservation and revitalization of the Little Manila Historic Site in Stockton, and is a national trustee of the Filipino American National Historical Society.

MARGO MACHIDA is an associate professor of art history and Asian American studies at the University of Connecticut. Born and raised in Hawai'i, she is a scholar, independent cura-tor, and cultural critic specializing in Asian American art and visual culture studies. Her most recent book is *Unsettled Visions: Contemporary Asian American Artists and the Social Imaginary*, which received the 2011 Cultural Studies Book Award from the Association for Asian American Studies. She is a coeditor of the volume *Fresh Talk / Daring Gazes: Conversations on Asian American Art*. She received the 2009 Lifetime Achievement Award from the National Women's Caucus for Art. She is currently working on her next book, "Resighting Hawai'i: Global Flows and Island Imaginaries in Asian American and Native Hawaiian Art."

MARTIN F. MANALANSAN IV is an associate professor of anthropology and Asian American studies and the Conrad Professorial Humanities Scholar at the University of Illinois at Urbana-Champaign. He is an affiliate faculty member in the gender and women's studies program, the global studies program, and the unit for criticism and interpretive theory. He is the author of *Global Divas: Filipino Gay Men in the Diaspora*, which was awarded the Ruth Benedict Prize in 2003. He is editor and/or coeditor of several anthologies of essays. Currently, he is the social science review editor for *GLQ: A Journal of Gay and Lesbian Studies*, and was on the editorial board of the *American Anthropologist*, the flagship journal of the American Anthropological Association. His current book projects include the ethical and embodied dimensions of the lives and struggles of undocumented queer immigrants, Asian American immigrant culinary cultures, sensory and affective dimensions of race and difference, and Filipino return migration.

ANITA MANNUR is an associate professor of English and Asian / Asian American studies at Miami University, Oxford, OH, and an associate editor of the *Journal of Asian American Studies*. She is the author of *Culinary Fictions: Food in South Asian Diasporic Culture* and has written widely on the topic of food in Asian American contexts. Her work has appeared in *Cultural Studies, Amerasia Journal, Massachusetts Review, MELUS*, and *Journal of Commonwealth and Postcolonial Studies* as well as the collections *Taking Food Public, East Main Street: Asian American Popular Culture*, and Asian *American Studies after Critical Mass*. She is the 2012 recipient of the Early Career Award from the Association for Asian American Studies.

VALERIE J. MATSUMOTO is a professor in the Department of History and the Department of Asian American Studies at the University of California, Los Angeles. Her book *Farming the Home Place: A Japanese American Community in California, 1919–1982* examined three generations of men and women. She also coedited the essay collection *Over the Edge: Remapping the American West*. Her essays on Asian American women artists appeared in *Asian American Art: A History, 1850–1970*. Her book on nisei girls' clubs is forthcoming. In 2006, she was the first recipient of the Hoshide Distinguished Teaching Award from the UCLA Asian American Studies Center and, in 2007, received the UCLA Distinguished Teaching Award.

RENÉ ALEXANDER ORQUIZA JR. is an Andrew W. Mellon postdoctoral fellow in American Studies at Wellesley College. He teaches Asian American studies and the Philippine-American relationship. He was a Fulbright scholar in the Philippines and a lecturer in history at the University of the Philippines, Diliman Center for International Studies. He is currently working on a project that connects the attempt to Americanize Filipino food to economic, political, and social forces of the American Empire. He received his PhD in History from the Johns Hopkins University in 2012.

MARK PADOONGPATT is an assistant professor in the interdisciplinary degree programs at the University of Nevada, Las Vegas. His research and teaching interests are wide ranging, covering twentieth-century U.S. history, Asian / Pacific American studies, comparative race and ethnicity, immigration, U.S. Empire, urban/suburban communities, food, and leisure. His work has appeared in the *Radical History Review* and *A People's Guide to Los Angeles*. He is currently at work on a manuscript exploring the history of Thai Americans in Los Angeles in the context of U.S. global expansion in Asia and the Pacific during the second half of the twentieth century.

DELORES B. PHILLIPS is an assistant professor of postcolonial literature and theory and codirector of the Postcolonial Research Group at Old Dominion University. She received her PhD in postcolonial literature from the University of Maryland in 2009. Her current book project is "In Questionable Taste," about the relationship between cultural and culinary representations in cookbooks, memoirs, and fiction.

ZOHRA SAED is a coeditor of *One Story, Thirty Stories: An Anthology of Contemporary Afghan American Literature*. Her poetry has appeared in *Voices of Resistance: Muslim Women on War, Faith and Sexuality*, edited by Sarah Hussein; *Speaking for Herself: Asian Women's Writings*, edited by Sukrita Paul Kumar and Savita Singh; *Seven Leaves One Autumn*, edited by Sukrita Paul Kumar and Savita Singh; and, most recently, *Sahar Muradi & Zohra Saed: Misspelled Cities*. She is currently a PhD candidate at the Graduate Center of the City University of New York.

LOK SIU is an associate professor of ethnic studies at University of California, Berkeley. Trained as a cultural anthropologist, she works on the areas of diaspora, transnationalism, cultural citizenship, racial and gender formation, cultural politics of food, and Asians in the Americas. Her books include *Memories of a Future Home: Diasporic Citizenship of Chinese in Panama* and two coedited volumes, *Asian Diasporas: New Formations, New Conceptions*, and *Gendered Citizenships: Transnational Perspectives on Knowledge Production, Political Activism, and Culture*. She is currently working on two book projects: a volume of essays tentatively entitled "Transnational Asian America: New Theories and Methodologies in Asian American Studies," and an ethnography that explores Asian Latino intersections through food, art, and memory. Her exploration of Asian Latino food has included research on Chinese Cuban restaurants.

OLIVER WANG is an associate professor of sociology at California State University, Long Beach, specializing in popular culture and race/ethnicity. He is the author of the forthcoming *Legions of Boom: Filipino American Mobile Disc Jockey Crews of the San Francisco Bay Area*. He writes on music/culture for National Public Radio, the *Los Angeles Times*, and KCET's ArtBound.

SAMUEL HIDEO YAMASHITA is the Henry E. Sheffield Professor of History at Pomona College in Claremont, California, where he has taught since 1983. He is currently working on two long-term food projects. The first is a history of Japanese food, and he has given several public lectures on the subject, including "The Beginnings of 'Japanese' Food" and "The Cost of Victory: The Hunger of Evacuated Children in Wartime Japan." The latter will be published as "The Food Problem of Evacuated Children in Wartime Japan, 1942–1945" in *Food in Zones of Conflict*. "Licking Salt for the Nation: Food and Diet in Wartime Japan, 1937–1945" will appear in the forthcoming *Cuisine, Consumption and Culture: Food in Contemporary Japan* edited by Theodore Bestor. His second food project is a study of Pacific Rim fusion cuisine, and he is completing a short history of Hawai'i Regional Cuisine.

CHRISTINE R. YANO is a professor and chair of the anthropology department at the University of Hawai‘i. She is the author of *Tears of Longing: Nostalgia and the Nation in Japanese Popular Song, Crowning the Nice Girl: Gender, Ethnicity, and Culture in Hawai‘i's Cherry Blossom Festival, Airborne Dreams: "Nisei" Stewardesses and Pan American World Airways,* and the forthcoming *Pink Globalization: Hello Kitty's Trek across the Pacific.*

Abelmann, Nancy, 28n63

abjection, 341

Acapulco trade, 149-50

Achieving the Impossible Dream (Maki, Kitano, and Berthold), 145n28

Adams, Wanda, 34, 37, 39, 43, 45, 49n1

adobo, 150, 157-67, 170, 181, 183, 306

adoption, of Chinese children, 2-3

Adventures in Oriental Cooking (Nix), 203

affective labor, 357, 368

Afghan: communities in the U.S., 249-50; cuisine, 251; immigrants, 250

Afghan Uzbek Americans, 254

African American(s): in Los Angeles, 84, 88; representations, 2; studies, 6

agrarian Protestant movement, 347

Aklat ng pagluluto (Ignacio), 182

Albers, Clem, 128

Alice B. Toklas Cook Book (Toklas), 354

Alice Waters and Chez Panisse (McNamee), 275

Alien Land Laws, 255, 281, 334

Alimentary Tracks (Parama), 384

Allen, Ted, 368

Allison, Anne, 34

Aloha Shoyu Company, 221-22

Amerasian, 307, 320n18

America Is in the Heart (Bulosan), 150, 166

American cuisine, 14, 36

American Federation of Labor (AFL), 63-65

American food system: Asian American contributions to, 275-85; size, 274-75. *See also* Asian American(s), farmers; Asian American(s), retailers

American Red Cross (ARC), 269-70

American School Food Service Association, 38

American Tatar Association, 250

Americanization, 164; of Japanese Americans, 126, 133; of Southeast Asian refugees, 3; through food, 32-36, 39-40, 51n13, 164, 177-81

Amsterdam World's Fair, 215

Anderson, Benedict, 374. *See also* imagined communities

Angel Island, 58-59, 220

Angelenos, 14

anticolonial movements, 196

Appadurai, Arjun, 31, 44

Appiah, Kwame, 372

Arcega, Michael, 327-28. See also *SPAM/MAPS: Oceana*; *SPAM/MAPS: World*

area studies, 6

Asian American(s): art, 309, 317, 322n42; artists, 309-11; contribution to American food system, 275-85; contribution to California cuisine, 275-78; cultural hybridity, 90; ethnic identity, 305; farmers, 280-85; identity politics, 311; images, 3, 6; literature, 306, 355-56; meanings, 1, 7, 304-6, 311, 317-18, 318n3; model minorities, 188, 320n17; movement, 304; as a racial category, 1, 7-8; racialization, 2-4, 6, 90, 188, 305-6, 356; retailers, 278-80, 285; subjectivity, 8; yellow peril, 126, 131-33, 133

Asian American studies, 3, 306; intersection with food studies, 3; transnational scope, 394

Asian fusion cuisine, 232, 241, 243

Asian Latino fusion cuisine, 8, 243

Asian/Pacific cuisine: American women as experts, 186-87, 200-201; early American fascination, 189-90; rise to popularity, 200-204; white women's interest, 190-95
Asociación de loncheras, 78
assimilation: agents, 39; culinary, 31-35, 44; discourse on, 3, 35, 44; of Japanese Americans, 126, 132
Atomettes, 270
Austria World's Fair, 215
authenticity, 4, 7-8, 213, 223-24, 289-91, 297-99, 313, 355, 378, 382; culinary, 289-90, 292-94, 297. *See also* inauthenticity
Azuma, Eiichiro, 257

bagoong, 101, 149, 150, 155, 160, 161, 162
banh mih, 234, 306
Banham, Rayner, 15
Barbas, Samantha, 90
Barrow, Ian J., 380, 389n9
Bayonet Constitution, 342
Beilenson, Edna, 200-201. See also *Simple Oriental Cookery*
Bend It Like Beckham (film), 394, 400. *See also* Chadha, Gurinder
Bengali American, 393
Berges, Paul, 407n10. See also *Mistress of Spices*
Berkeley Bowl Market, 284
Biag ti agtrabajo (The Lives of Laborers), 348-49. *See also* Lagaso Goldberg, Trisha
bibimbap, 306
Big *Five*, 342-43. *See also* Kubo, Mat
Biological Diversity Act of India, 387
biopower, 376
Bittman, Mark, 281. See also *Food Matters: A Guide to Conscious Eating*
Black, Shameem, 373-74, 378-79, 388, 390n12. *See also* "gastropoetics"
Bodies in Motion (Mohanraj), 8-9, 393, 400-405; gastro-pornography, 402-3; heteronormativity, 400, 406; queer moments, 400, 403-5
Bollywood, 399
Bolshevik invasion, 247
Book of Salt, The (Truong), 8, 354-56; authenticity, 355; colonial mimicry, 365; diaspora, 362-63; labor, 359, 363-64; queer community formation, 357, 360-62; queer desire, 355; queer diasporic Vietnamese subjectivity, 356-57
Bourdain, Anthony, 235, 294-97. See also *No Reservations*
Bourriaud, Nicolas, 344-45. *See also* "relational aesthetics"
box-lunch socials, 265
Brennan, Jennifer, 192-93, 202. See also *The Original Thai Cookbook*
Brennan, Timothy, 384-85
Brillat-Savarin, Jean Anthelme, 2
Bruni, Frank, 367
Bt brinjal, 379, 387. *See also* Monsanto
Buaken, Manuel, 162. See also *I Have Lived with the American People*
Buettner, Elizabeth, 397
Building Chickens out of Chicken Legs (Williams-Forson), 2
bulani, 245, 246, 248, 254
Bulosan, Carlos, 150. See also *America Is in the Heart*
Byrne, Ray, 89

cafeteria ladies, 6, 31-33, 38-42, 50n3; agents of assimilation, 39; entrepreneurs, 41
Caldwell, Allison, 79, 93n9
California cuisine, 8, 111, 114-15, 241, 275; Asian American influence, 275-78; emergence, 275-78; movement, 284
California Gold Rush, 4, 219
Cambodian American, 24
Cambodian Doughnut Dreams (film), 23
Cambodians in the U.S.: arrival in the United States, 13; employment, 13, 16; entrepreneurs, 13-19, 24-25; entry into donut business, 13-14, 16; ethnic enclaves, 22; first-generation, 23, 24; history as refugees, 14; identity, 22-24
Camp Pendleton, Oceanside, California, 13
cannery, 4, 148, 156, 160, 161
Capra, Frank, 133. See also *Prelude to War*
Cargill, 385-88
Cavendish, William Spencer, 329
Census of Agriculture, 282, 284, 287n30

Central Asian: cuisine, 246, 254; community organizations, 249-50; food, 246-49; groups, 251; immigrants, 249-51, 253-54; neighborhoods, 249-54; restaurants, 252, 254. *See also* Turkic; Uzbek

Central Asian Americans, 253

Chadha, Gurinder, 394, 407n9, 407n10. See also *Bend It Like Beckham*; *It's a Wonderful Afterlife*; *Mistress of Spices*

Chan, Gaye, 345-48. See also *DownWind Productions*; *Eating in Public*

Chan, Sucheng, 23. See also *Survivors: Cambodian Refugees in the United States*

Chen, Ta, 67

Chiang, Cecilia, 276

child labor: in donut shops, 19; in ethnic businesses, 18-19; in school cafeterias, 42-43

Child Nutrition Archives, 32

Child, Julia, 110

children: as consumers, 35; as decision makers, 35

China, racialized discourse on, 2-3

Chinatown, 54, 59-60, 105, 162-65, 276-77, 295; as place of residence for other ethnic groups, 165; tourism, 60. *See also* "slummers"; "slumming"; "rubberneckers"

Chinese American: food, 90, 260; markets, 276, 280-81

Chinese Consolidated Benevolent Association, 65-66

Chinese Exclusion Laws, 54, 57, 63, 256; strategies to circumvent, 57-58

Chinese food, 2-4, 261; depictions of, 54; mainstream popularity, 54; as a symbol of Americanization, 164; as the ultimate "ethnic" American fast food, 5

Chinese Hand Laundry Alliance, 64-65

Chinese Latino restaurants, 232, 244n2

Chinese Restaurant Association, 65. *See also* Chinese Restaurant Workers and Merchants' Association

Chinese Restaurant Workers and Merchants' Association, 65

Chinese restaurants, 4, 189-90; Americanized restaurants, 62; business structure, 61, 64; in California, 164-66; early history, 4,

59-60; in Hawai'i, 101-2; labor conditions, 54-55, 61-63, 65-77; labor conflicts, 61-62, 65-67; labor organizing, 63-65; labor structure, 54-55, 61-62; in New York, 54, 59-61; opinions on, 54, 60; regulation of, 65-66; as a space for ethnic groups, 165-66, 261

China Salvation Times (newspaper), 64

Chinese, racialized discourse on, 2-3

Chock, Eric, 217

Choi, Roy, 79, 80, 84, 89, 91

chop suey, 4, 54, 60-61, 72n1, 90, 164-66, 167, 189, 260-61; an American staple, 61; symbol of cosmopolitanism, 261

Choy, Sam, 106, 109, 111, 113, 115-17, 120n39, 222

Christian Century (magazine), 138

Chun, Kaili, 332-33

citizen(s): flexible, 372; global, 256, 373

citizenship, 3, 24, 34-35, 38, 43-44; culinary 6, 31-32, 34, 43-45; and property ownership, 171; psychic, 341; supranational, 389n8

City of Tokyo (ship), 216-17

civil rights: movement, 304; organization, 219; violation of, 125, 132

Civil War, American, 247

Cold War, 7, 186-98; American military expansion, 188, 195; cultural exchange programs, 198; culture of containment, 196; policy of integration, 196, 200; promotion of tourism, 197-200; role of food, 187-89, 191, 195; role of white women, 187-89, 191, 196; U.S. cultural production, 188, 196. *See also* imperialism, U.S.

Cold War Orientalism (Klein), 196

colonial mimicry, 365

colonialism: European, 193-95; Japanese, 256; in Oceana, 327; Russian, 247; Spanish, 149, 178. *See also* colonialism American in the Philippines

colonialism, American, in the Philippines: advertising American goods, 180-81; American public school system, 152-53, 177-70; civilizing mission, 152-53; cooking lessons in schools, 178-79; creation of middle-class consumption practices, 179-80; dislocation of small landholders, 151;

colonialism, American (*continued*):
domestic science, 152-53; gendered education system, 152-53, 177, 179; promotion of Western cookbooks, 181-84; provincial poverty, 151-52; racialization of Filipinas/os, 153; racialization of Filipina/o food, 153, 178; shaping Filipina/o diet, 7, 147, 152-53, 171, 177-84, 189, 192, 336
comfort food, 38, 44, 241-43, 292
compulsory heterosexuality, 400
ConAgra, 224, 388
Congressional Committee on the Wartime Relocation and Interment of Civilians (CWRIC), 126
Conroy, Hilary, 216
"contrapuntal analysis," 346
Cook, James, 214
Cook for You, Cook for Me, 344. *See also* Kubo, Mat
Cooking with Stella (film), 407n10. *See also* Mehta, Deepa
Coontz, Stephanie, 141
Copeland, Edwin Bingham, 179. *See also Elements of Philippine Agriculture*
Corn Blue Room, 350. *See also* Rickard, Jolene
corporations: lobbying, 386; personhood, 385
cosmopolitanism, 88, 373-74, 377-78, 388n2. *See also* multicultural, cosmopolitanism
Country of Origin (Lee) 32n20
Crimean genocide, 250
Crimean Tatars, 250
Critique of Postcolonial Reason (Spivak), 388n1
cuisines: Afghan, 251; American, 14, 36; Asian fusion, 232, 241, 243; Asian Latino fusion, 8, 243; Asian/Pacific 187, 189-91, 193, 195, 201; California, 8, 111, 114-15, 241, 275; Central Asian, 246, 254; fiesta, 149; Filipina/o, 149-51, 162-63, 177, 182-84, 298; Filipina/o American, 8, 148, 163, 166-71; fusion, 243; haute-meets-street, 79; Indonesian, 193; national, 36; regional, 112-13, 115; school lunch, 32; street cuisine, 79; Uzbek, 248-49. *See also* Thai cuisine
culinary: citizenship, 6, 32, 43-45; pornography, 397; tourism, 189, 198, 200

Culinary Arts in the Tropics (Quirino),153
Culinary Fictions (Mannur), 379, 390n13
"cultural coalescence," 258, 262, 266. *See also* Ruiz, Vicki
"cultural food colonialism," 188-89, 192. *See also* Heldke, Lisa
cultural imperialism, 199
curry, 4, 41, 112, 190, 192, 203, 224, 306, 376

Dalby, Andrew, 4
dance halls, 155, 163
Daughters of the American Revolution, 202
Day, Kristin, 81
Daza, Nora V, 183. *See also Galing-Galing: The First Philippine Cookbook for Use in the United States*
De Laurentiis, Giada, 223
De Veyra, Sofia Reyes, 182. *See also Everyday Cookery for the Home*
De Witt, John, Jr., 133
Dengel-Janic, Ellen, and Lars Eckstein, 395, 407n10
Detloff, Madelyn, 405
Di Leonardo, Micaela, 266
diaspora, 5, 289, 291, 324, 362-63; Asian American, 305; Asian, 4, 311, 321n25; Central Asian, 253; Filipina/o, 288-89, 292-94; Indian, 305, 395; queer, 394; South Asian, 321n25, 393; Uzbek, 247. *See also* diasporic homecoming; queer, diasporic Vietnamese subjectivity
diasporic homecoming, 289, 291-94, 297-99; through food, 292
Dikon, Roger, 103-4, 106, 110, 120n39
Diner, Hasia, 148-49
disaffection, 403, 405. *See also* Manalansan, Martin
discourse analysis, 289
dog, as meat, 2, 9
Dole, Sanford B., 217, 343
domesticity, 403-4
domestic science, 152-54, 156, 177, 179, 265. *See also* home economics
domestic work, 259, 269
Donovan, Maria Kozslik, 193-95. *See also Far Eastern Epicure, The*

donut, history in Los Angeles, 15

donut shops, Cambodian-owned: apprentice-ship arrangement, 16; business model, 16-22, 28n58; business strategies, 19-22; as community spaces, 22; competition, 21, 28n56; diversity of customers, 21-24, 28n58, 28n61; emergence, 16; labor source 18-19; popularity, 14, 26n6, 26n9; preservation and promotion of Cambodian culture, 22-23; relationship with neighborhoods, 21-22; as sites of cultural negotiation, 15; as spaces of Americanization, 23-34; viability as a business enterprise, 16-19

DownWind Productions, 345-46. *See also* Chan, Gaye; Feeser, Andrea; Sharma, Nandita

Dr. Seuss, 133. *See also* Geisel, Theodore

Ducray, Amandine, 407n9

Dudden, Arthur Power, 217

Dusselier, Jane, 126

Eat, 344. *See also* Kaprow, Allan

eating dogs, controversy on, 2

Eating in Public, 345-48. *See also* Chan, Gaye

Edible Schoolyard Project, 34-35

Eisenhower, Dwight, 217

Elements of Philippine Agriculture (Copeland), 179

Ellman, Mark, 104, 109, 111, 120n39

encloso system, 157

enemy aliens, 35, 305

Eng, David, 356, 363

English Standard Schools, 118n7; as de facto segregation, 118n7

Eshu Veve for Olaa Sugar Company, 337-39. *See also* Lagaso Goldberg, Trisha

ethnic businesses, labor source, 18

ethnic enclaves, 22. *See also* Chinatown; Little Manila; Little Phnom Penh; Little Tokyo; Manilatown; Valerio Gardens

Ethnic Solidarity for Economic Survival (Min), 278

ethnography, 8, 97n58, 232, 289, 305, 393

Everyday Cookery for the Home (De Veyra), 182

Executive Order 9066, 275. *See also* incarcera-tion, of Japanese Americans

Exotic Appetites: Ruminations of a Food Adventurer (Heldke), 188-89, 297, 389n8

Facebook, 234, 242

family, as a rhetorical device, 141. *See also* nuclear family

Far Eastern Epicure, The (Donovan), 193-94

Farewell to Manzanar (Houston and Houston), 138-41

fast food, "ethnic" American, 4

Feeser, Andrea, 345. See also *DownWind Productions*; *Free Grindz*

Ferguson, Amy, 105, 108, 110-11, 120n39. *See also* Southwestern Cuisine

Fernandez, Doreen, 149-50, 153

Filipina/o: culinary authenticity, 289; cuisine, 149-51, 162-63, 177, 182-84, 298; diaspora, 288-89, 292-97

Filipina/o American(s), 3, 147, 188; cuisine, 148; foodways, 14; gender roles, 166-67; history, 148; identity, 148, 149, 171; restau-rants, 162-63; during WWII, 170-71. *See also* Little Manila

Filipina/o American cuisine, 8, 148, 163, 166-71; emergence, 163, 166, 171; women's contribution in shaping, 166

Filipino Federation of America (FFA), 155-56

Fine, Gary, 34

Flay, Bobby, 114, 235

flexible citizens, 372

Food and Foodways (journal), 3

food blogs, 90, 236

"food documenting," 90

Food Matters: A Guide to Conscious Eating (Bittman), 281

Food Network, 223, 236

food politics, 8, 323, 334, 385

food pornography, 355

food studies: inter- and multidisciplinarity, 3, 5-6; intersection with Asian Ameri-can studies, 3; intersection with sex and sexuality studies, 394; transnational and diasporic framework, 5 food system: literature on, 5; definition, 274. *See also* American food system

food trucks, 8, 231-44; affordability, 240-41, 243; Asian fusion cuisine, 232, 234, 241-42; customers, 239-40, 243; entrepreneurs, 233-34, 240-41; financial risks, 234; mobility, 235-37, 240; as a reflection of culture, 80-81; rise to mainstream popularity, 232, 235-36, 242-44; as a signifier of "urban-ness," 81, 242; urban hipness of, 235, 237-39; use of social media and the Internet, 79-80, 82, 234, 236-38, 242; working conditions, 233-34. See also *loncheras*; *nueva* trucks

foodies, 79, 235, 290; Asian Americans, 89-90

Foodies: Democracy and Distinction in the Gourmet Foodscape (Johnston and Baumann), 297

foodways: definitions, 148, 188, 312; site of identity formation, 187, 204

forager, professional, 278

Foucault, Michel, 1

442nd Regimental Combat Team, 131, 142

Free Grindz, 347

Fruin, W. Mark, 214-16. See also *Kikkoman: Company, Clan, and Community*

Fujimoto, Bill, 276-78

Fujimoto, Natsuye, 255, 256, 263, 270

Fuller, Alice 179. See also *Housekeeping*

Fung, Catherine, 365

fusion cuisine, 8, 80, 91, 232, 239, 241, 243, 298, 306, 320n14, 355, 373

Gabaccia, Donna, 258

Gaches, Mrs. Samuel Francis, 183. See also *Good Cooking and Health in the Tropics*

Galing-Galing: The First Philippine Cookbook for Use in the United States (Daza), 183

Gannenmono, 214-16, 218, 220

Gannon, Beverly, 108, 111, 114, 115, 120n39

gastrocartographic key, 379

gastrocartography, 371, 374-80

Gastronomica (journal), 3

"gastropoetics," 371, 378, 390n20. *See also* Black, Shameem

gastro-pornography, 402-3

Geisel, Theodore, 133. *See also* Dr. Seuss

Gelt, Jessica, 81

Genteel, 325. *See also* Yamamoto, Lynne

Gentlemen's Agreement, 256

global citizens, 256, 373

globalization, 380; culinary, 371, 380-81

Gold, Jonathan, 82

Gold Rush, 3, 219

"Golden Age of Food Processing," 275. *See also* Levenstein, Harvey

Gompers, Samuel, 63. See also *Meat vs. Rice*

Good Cooking and Health in the Tropics (Gaches), 183

Google Maps, 82

Gopinath, Gayatri, 394, 398

"Gourmet Ghetto," 277

Grandfather's Shed, 325. *See also* Yamamoto, Lynne

Great Depression, 61, 148, 155, 157-59, 171, 260, 262, 266

Great Māhele, 334

green groceries, 8, 279

Halberstam, J. Jack, 297. *See also* Halberstam, Judith

Halberstam, Judith, 408n27. *See also* Halberstam, J. Jack

haole, 39, 335, 346

Hart-Cellar Act, 274. *See also* immigration, Reform Act of 1965

Hawai'i: dependence on imported food, 102; history, 98-100, 217, 335, 343-44; influence of race and class on food practices, 100-101; interracial marriages, 350n3; local diet, 100-102; military presence in, 116, 119n15, 326-27, 331, 333; race relations, 98-101, 103; racialized education system, 99-100, 118n7; racialized politics, 100; racialized sports league, 100; as a transpacific zone of contact, 324

Hawai'i regional cuisine (HRC), 6, 98, 106-17; contributions, 115-17; critique of racist and colonial food practices, 117; founding chefs, 106, 120n39; immigrant and indigenous Hawaiian influence on, 112-14; local food campaign, 103-8, 111-13, 115-17; rise to popularity, 109-11; target market, 114-15

Hawai'i Regional Cuisine, Inc., 111

Hawai'i Restaurant Association, 111

"Hawaiian epistemology," 332

health food movement, 8

Heldke, Lisa, 188-89, 297, 389n8. *See also* "cultural food colonialism"; *Exotic Appetites*

Hell to Eternity (film), 141

Helping Out: Children's Labor in Ethnic Businesses (Song), 18

Hemingway, Ernest, 218

Henderson, Janice Wald, 119-20

Hendler, Glenn, 140, 145n41

heteronormative structuration, 403

heteronormativity, 9, 393, 400, 402-03, 406

heteropatriarchy, 394, 396-97

Hirabayashi, Gordon, 132. See also *Hirabayashi v. United States*

Hirabayashi v. United States, 132

Hirsch, Dafna, 43-44

Hiura, Arnold, 43

home economics, 39-40, 141, 152, 177, 202, 260; as a career path for women, 39-40; emergence, 39; movement, 39-40. *See also* domestic science

Homeward Bound (May), 202

homosociality, 393

Hong Kong, 58, 194-95

Hotel Employee and Restaurant Employee Union (HERE), 63-65

Housekeeping: A Textbook for Girls in Public Intermediate Schools of the Philippines (Fuller), 179

Houston, James D., 138. See also *Farewell to Manzanar*

Houston, Jeanne Wakatsuki, 138-41, 143. See also *Farewell to Manzanar*

hummus, 42, 43, 44, 52

Huynh, Hung, 357, 365-66

I Have Lived with the American People (Buaken), 162

Ichihashi, Yamato, 214, 218. See also *Japanese in the United States*

identity politics, 308, 311

Ignacio, Rosendo, 182. See also *Aklat ng pagluluto*

imagined communities, 374. *See also* Anderson, Benedict

immigration: Act of 1924, 188, 256; Act of 1952, 188; discrimination in, 1; Reform Act of 1965, 183. *See also* Hart-Cellar Act

immigration, of Chinese, 54-59, 66, 324; to Hawai'i, 334; immigrants in the military, 55, 68-70; internal migration in the U.S., 59; to New York, 55; practice of "interdependence," 67, 69, 71; push factors, 56, 66; remittance 57, 70-71; transpacific family network 55, 67-71. *See also* Chinese Exclusion Laws

immigration, of Filipinas/os to the U.S. before 1965: to Alaska, 148, 154, 156; as aliens, 155; as American nationals, 154-55; to California, 154, 162-63; emigrants, 151-52, 154; entrepreneurship, 162-64; experiences during the Depression, 155, 159-60, 171; family separation, 154; family structure, 154, 166; to Hawai'i, 152, 154, 336-8; immigrant diet, 147-48, 154-55, 157-60; immigrants in cities, 162; immigrants in the U.S. military, 170-71; interracial marriage, 161; labor, 148, 154-56; labor organizing, 155-56, 161; life in canneries, 160-62; life in farm labor camps, 156-60, 167-68; to New York 154, 162; old-timers, 147; provincial ethnic identities, 148-49; push factors, 151-54; racialization, 153, 155; to Washington state, 154, 163

immigration, of Japanese, 256; to California 218-20, 256, 281-82; to Hawai'i, 211, 213-17, 220, 325, 340

Imperatives to Reimagine the Planet (Spivak), 380

imperialism, U.S.: 7, 187-89, 191, 195, 196-97, 200-204, 358; in Asia and the Pacific, 187-188; cultural producers as agents, 188; informal empire,197; tourism as an imperial practice, 198-200; white women's role in, 177-78, 187-89. *See also* colonialism, American, in the Philippines

imperialist nostalgia, 192

inauthenticity, 289, 297, 313, 329, 382, 387. *See also* authenticity incarceration camps, 7, 125, 143n2; assembly camps, 143n2; assembly centers, 130, 143n2; Gila River, 131; Heart Mountain, 129; management of, 128-30; Manzanar, 126, 139; as a site of Americanization, 129

incarceration of Japanese Americans, 35, 223, 268-69, 282; camp workers, 131-32; challenge to legality of military orders, 132, 144n20; communal living and dining, 127-36; depictions of incarcerees and their families; 131-34, 136-38; family separation, 125-36, 143, 144n20; food rationing, 128-29; incitement of patriotism, 131-32; juvenile delinquency and discontent, search 133-37; incarceree or internee rights, 130; nisei in military service, 131-33, 142; nuclear family as a unit of management, 130; propaganda of compassionate government, 133; redress and reparation campaign, 138-39, 145n28; resettlement, 130-32, 134, 136, 138, 268-27; sentimental depictions of family separation, 138-41. *See also* incarceration camps; mess halls, in incarceration camps

Indonesian cuisine, 193

industries, in Los Angeles: aerospace, 15, 26n16; high-technology, 16, 27n20; tire, 15

Insect Immigrants, after Zimmerman, 325. *See also* Yamamoto, Lynne

internment, 143n2. *See* incarceration, of Japanese Americans

Islamic food laws, 246-47

Italian Americans, 266

It's a Wonderful Afterlife (film), 407n10

Jaffrey, Madhur, 8, 225, 371-83, 385, 387; as a cosmopolitan Indian, 379; version of cosmopolitanism, 378. *See also Madhur Jaffrey's World Vegetarian*

Japan: American military in, 187, 197; economic restructuring after World War II, 187

Japanese American Citizens League (JACL), 129, 134, 138, 219

Japanese American cuisine, 262-63, 266-67; hybridization of, 262-63

Japanese Americans: Americanization, 126, 133, 259-60; Americanness, 256, 258, 260, 270; domestic workers, 259; gender roles and dynamics, 258-60, 264-65, 267, 269; holidays and food, 266-68; issei, 256-57, 259; nisei women, 255, 258-62; nisei youth clubs, 257, 264, 270, 272n55; racial discrimination, 255-57

Japanese in the United States (Ichihashi), 214

Jen, Gish, 305

Johnson Nix, Janeth, 191-92, 196, 203. See also *Adventures in Oriental Cooking*

Johnston, Josee, and Shyon Baumann, 297. See also *Foodies: Democracy and Distinction in the Gourmet Foodscape*

Josselin, Jean-Marie, 103, 104, 105, 106, 109, 111, 114, 115, 120n39

Joy Luck Club, The (Tan), 355

Kalākaua (King), 342

Kalčik, Susan, 258, 271n9

kamaʻaina, 346

Kamehameha (the Great), 217

Kamehameha III, 334

Kamehameha Schools, 99, 119n12

kanaka maoli, 346

Kane, Mac, 78, 95n37, 97n42. See also *loncheras*

Kaprow, Allan, 355. See also *Eat*

Kawamura, A. G., 282

Keller, Thomas, 110

Khmer Rouge, 13, 23

Khush (film), 395

Kikkoman: American competitors of, 224-25; awards, 215; disavowal of ties with Japanese Americans, 222; history in the U.S., 7, 209-12, 214-15, 218-26; as an immigrant, 220; international expansion, 223-24; marketing strategy, 208-9, 213, 222-25; promotion as "natural" and "authentic," 224-25; *white* consumer market, 222. *See also* soy sauce

Kikkoman Chronicles (Yates), 209, 211

Kikkoman: Company, Clan, and Community (Fruin), 214-15

Kikkoman Day, 209

Kikkoman Laboratory of Microbial Fermentation, 209

Kim, Jae, 231, 233-34, 237-40, 243

Kim, Jodi, 188

kimchi, 4, 41, 88, 201, 239, 248

King Kamehameha III, 334

kinship, 18, 266

Klein, Christina, 188, 196-97

Konishi, Alan, 339-41. See also *Yellow Peril (Remember Pearl Harbor?)*; *Yellow Peril (Am I White Yet?)*

Korean Americans, 279

Korean greengrocers, 8, 278-79

Kubo, Mat, 341-44. See also *Big Five*; *Off-TheGrid: ActionFunUrbanSurvivalism*; *Cook for You, Cook for Me*

Kukahiko, Puni, 324, 333. See also *Lovely Hula Hands*; *Makau Bound*

Kuleana Act, 335

labor: laws on children, 42; movement, 64

labor unions, 63-65; racial exclusion, 63. See also American Federation of Labor (AFL); Hotel Employee and Restaurant Employee Union (HERE)

Ladies' Home Journal, 182

Lagaso Goldberg, Trisha, 336-38, 348. See also *Eshu Veve for Olaa Sugar Company*; *Biag ti agtrabajo (The Lives of Laborers)*

Lagasse, Emeril, 109, 223

Lahiri, Jhumpa, 305

Lakshmi, Padma, 366

Laudan, Rachel, 37, 43

Latin Americans, of Japanese descent, 130

Latinos, 84, 88, 97n58, 341

laulau, 113

lechon, 159, 161, 170, 171, 181, 294, 296

Lee, Chang-rae, 305

Lee, Don, 8, 303-4, 307-18, 320n20. See also *Wrack and Ruin*

Lee, Fred, 280-81

Levenstein, Harvey, 261, 275, 282. See also *Paradox of Plenty*

Levine, Susan, 33. See also *School Lunch Politics*

liberal multiculturalists, 189

Lie, John, 28n63

Lili'uokalani (Queen), 217, 343

Little Manila, 147, 162-63, 166, 168, 288. See also Manilatown

Little Phnom Penh, 22

Little Tokyo, 258

Lived Practice, 36

Local 37, 151

Local 211, 64-65

locavore, 108

loco moco, 113, 306, 320n15

loncheras, 78-79, 82, 86-88, 91, 92n6; 92-93n7, 95n37; as "authentic" street cuisine, 79; consumers of, 87; destinations, 87; hybrid type, 79; invisibility of, 91; luxe, 79, 93n11; scholarship on, 97n58; semi-permanent, 78; transient, 78, 87, 95n42; use of social media, 91. See also food trucks

Los Angeles Riots, 28n63. See also Abelmann, Nancy; Lie, John

Los Angeles Times Cookbook, 183

Lovely Hula Hands, 324. See also Kukahiko, Puni

Lowe, Lisa, 81

Lozada, Eriberto P., Jr, 35

lumpia, 113, 149, 168, 169, 170

Macao, 194-95

Machida, Margo, 8, 310-11

macru, in Islamic law, 246

Madhur Jaffrey's World Vegetarian, 8, 255, 371-88; cosmopolitanism, 373-78; gastro-cartography, 374-78; gastropoetics, 378; purported inclusivity of, 373; representation of Third World women's labor, 381-83; South Asian origin, 379. See also Jaffrey, Madhur

Maeda, Daryl, 304

Mak, Stephen, 130

Makau Bound, 333. See also Kukahiko, Puni; Tubbs, Maika'i

Manalansan, Martin, 403. See also disaffection

Manguera, Mark, 79

Manilatown, 162. See also Little Manila

Mannur, Anita, 304, 355-56, 379, 390n13. See also *Culinary Fictions mantu*, 248, 252, 254

Manzanar Fishing Club, from Barbed Wire to Barbed Hooks, The (film), 146n46

Manzanar riots, 126

Marshall, James, 219

Martinez, Raul, 78

masculinity: Asian, 368; queer, 368; white working-class, 63

Mavrothalassitis, George, 105, 109, 111, 112, 113, 115, 120n39

May, Elaine Tyler, 202. See also *Homeward Bound*

McDonald's, 4, 163, 371, 372, 382

McKinley, William, 217

McNamee, Thomas, 276, 278. See also *Alice Waters and Chez Panisse*

Meat vs. Rice: American Manhood against Asiatic Coolieism (Gompers), 63

Mehta, Deepa, 407n10. See also *Cooking with Stella*

Meiji Restoration, 214, 220

Melanctha (Stein), 363

"memory-maps," 337. *See also* Lagaso Goldberg, Trisha

Merriman, Peter, 103, 105-8, 111, 114, 120n39

mess halls, in incarceration camps, 145n20, 268; as battlegrounds for Americanization, 7, 126; homogenized organization of, 127-29; regulations in, 130; as a site of family breakdown, 126-36, 140

Mexican-American War, 218

Mexican Americans, 149

Mexico, 149-50, 380

Michener, James, 197. See also *Voice of Asia, The*

Migrant's Table (Ray), 393

migration, chain, 55

Militia, 331, 334. *See also* Tallett, Keith

Min, Pyong Gap, 278. See also *Ethnic Solidarity for Economic Survival*

Mintz, Sidney, 4

Mistress of Spices (film), 407n10

mobile catering, 233

Mobile Taro Lo´i, 334-35. *See also* Tallett, Keith

mochi, 155, 263, 266, 267,

model minority, 188; myth, 320n17; stereotype, 303

modernization, 188, 196-97, 200; ideology, 196; theory, 206n42

Mogi, Saheiji, 211, 214-15

Mogi, Yuzaburo, 208, 213, 220, 224

Mohanraj, Mary Anne, 400, 405-6. See also *Bodies in Motion*

Monsanto Company, 379, 385-88, 391-392n42; attempt to patent *Bt brinjal*, 387; frankencrop, 387

Montoya, Carina Monica, 162

motherhood, ideology on, 34

movements: agrarian Protestant, 347; anticolonial, 196; Asian American, 304; California cuisine, 284; civil rights, 304; health food, 8; home economics, 39-40; labor, 64; organic food, 242; regional cuisine, 108; slow food, 242; Southwestern cuisine, 108

multicultural: cosmopolitanism, 3; triumphalism, 81

multiculturalism, 3; discourse on, 405

multinational corporations, 386-87; homogenizing impulse, 386

Mydans, Carl, 132-33

National Food Service Management Institute, 32

National Organic Standards Board, 282

National Organic Sustainable Agriculture Coalition, 282

National Restaurant Association, 64

National School Lunch Program, 33

natural food industry, 280

neocolonialism, 188, 204

Nestle, Marion, 274

New Deal, 155

New York City Food Truck Association, 80

New York Restaurant Keepers Association, 64

Newland Resolution, 217

Nina's Heavenly Delights (film), 8-9, 393, 395-401, 405, 407n10; culinary pornography, 397; heteronormativity, 396-97, 406; queer moments, 396-98. *See also* Parmar, Pratibha

Nisei Daughter (Sone), 127

No Reservations, 235, 289, 294-95, 297. *See also* Bourdain, Anthony

No-No Boy (Okada), 144n20

Nowruz, 253. *See also* Persian New Year

nuclear family: as a battleground for assimilation, 126; images of, 141; as a myth, 143; as a symbol of assimilation, 132

nueva trucks, 79, 81-82, 84-91, 94n30, 95n37, 97n57; consumers of, 86-89, 94n30; deliberate policy of abandonment of, 84, 86; as destinations, 87-88; "geographical parameters" of, 82-85, 87, 96n46; "geographically conservative" types, 84; mobility of, 82-84, 87; as symbols of diversity, 81; use of social media, 82, 86, 91. *See also* food trucks

Obama, Michelle, 34

obesity, childhood, 33

OffTheGrid: ActionFunUrbanSurvivalism, 343. *See also* Kubo, Mat

Okada, John, 144n20. See also *No-No Boy*

Okihiro, Gary 4, 219

Okubo, Miné, 136, 268

Omi, Michael, and Howard Winant, 1. *See also* race, critical studies

Ong, Aihwa, 22, 24, 372. *See also* flexible citizens

oral history, 32, 126, 134, 135, 192, 256

organic food movement, 242

"Oriental," 204n1

"Oriental cookery," 7, 204; American women as experts of, 186-87, 200-201; rise to popularity, 200-204; white women's early interest, 190-95

Orientalism, 188, 203; Russian, 253

Original Thai Cookbook, The (Brennan), 192-93

Pacific Area Travel Association (PATA), 197-99

Pacific Citizen (newspaper), 129, 137

Pacific Interim Travel, 198. *See also* Pacific Area Travel Association

Padovani, Philippe, 105, 106, 120n39

pan-Turkism, 253-54

Paradox of Plenty (Levenstein), 275

Parmar, Pratibha, 395-98, 406, 407n9; radical politics of, 395-96. See also *Sari Red*; *Khush*; *Warrior Marks*

Pasteleria at reposteria (Trinidad), 182

Peace Corps volunteers (PCVs), 191

Persian New Year, 253. See also *Nowruz*

Philippine Education Company, 182

Philippine Normal School, 179

Philippines: Acapulco trade, 150; Chinese traders, 149; dialects, 149; diet at the turn of the twentieth century, 149-50; elite food, 149-50; middle class consumption, 180; plebeian food, 150; precolonial diet, 149; as a U.S. colony, 149

PMSS *China* (ship), 218-20

"Polarities of Food Culture," 36. *See also* Lived Practice; Wilks, Richard

political economy, 188, 199

Portuguese: immigrants, in Hawai'i, 328, 336; traders in Japan, 255

Powhatan (ship), 219-20

Prelude to War (film), 133. *See also* Capra, Frank

Provisions, Post-War, 326. *See also* Yamamoto, Lynne

psychic citizenship, 341

Public Performance, 36

queer: of color in India and Britain, 395; community formation, 357, 363; desire, 356, 394, 398; diaspora, 394; diasporic Vietnamese subjectivity, 393, 395; female subjectivity, 394-95; masculinity, 368

queerness, 8, 398, 400, 402, 406

Quirino, Carlso, 183. See also *Good Cooking and Health in the Tropics*

quorma, 246

race: critical studies, 1; effects on social discourse, 1; popular understanding, 1-2; privilege, 89; topography of, in Los Angeles, 89

Racial Indigestion: Eating Bodies in the 19th Century (Tompkins), 2 racialization, 1; of Asians in the U.S., 3-4; of Asian Americans, 2-4, 6, 90, 188, 305, 356; through food, 1-2; through the body and sentiments, 3. *See also* Omi, Michael, and Howard Winant

racial melancholia, 341

Ray, Krishnendu, 393. See also *Migrant's Table*

reality television. See also *Top Chef*

reformers, American, 7, 102, 177-78

refugee (s): policies on, 28n45; Southeast Asian, 3. *See also* Cambodians in the U.S.; Vietnamese

regional cuisine, 112-13, 115; movement, 108. *See also* California cuisine; Hawai'i Regional Cuisine (HRC); Southwestern cuisine

Reinitz, Bertram, 54-55, 61

"relational aesthetics," 344. *See also* Bourriaud, Nicolas

Relocation Center, 143n2. *See also* incarceration camps

resilience, concept of, 405

restrictive housing covenants, 255

rice, 30, 32, 36, 43, 60, 72n1, 147, 149, 150-52, 156-62, 164-71, 190, 201, 214, 246, 260, 266, 268, 288, 312, 318, 383; *palau*, 246; as part of *rijsttafel*, 193; production in the U.S., 154; representation of universality, 376-78

Rickard, Jolene, 350. See also *Corn Blue Room*

rijsttafel, 193-94

Robbins, Bruce, on models of cosmopolitanism, 388n2

Rohrback, Judge D. W., 155

Roy, Parama, 384. See also *Alimentary Tracks*

"rubberneckers," 60. *See also* Chinatown, tourism

Ruiz, Vicki, 258. *See also* "cultural coalescence"

Russian: colonialism, 247; migration, 248, 251. *See also* Sovietization

Sakada Series, 336, 338. *See also* Lagaso Goldberg, Trisha

samsa, 245, 246, 252, 254

San Buenaventura, Steffi, 148

Sanchez, George, 149

Santa Anita Assembly Center, 128

Sari Red (film), 395

Schein, Louisa, 291

Schnell, John Henry, 218-19

School Food Services, 37-38, 50n4

school lunch, 6, 31-36; campaigns on, 34; cuisine, 32; as an icon in Hawai'i, 42-43; as a locus of assimilation, 32-36, 44; nostalgia of, 32, 34, 37, 44-45; as a site of culinary citizenship, 32, 45; subsidized programs, 34

School Lunch Politics (Levine), 33

Schwarzenegger, Arnold, 282

Scioto (ship), 214-18, 220

Senate Resolution 323, 212

Service industry, 6, 55, 62, 67

Sex and the City (television show), 2

sexual division of labor, 166, 269-70

Sharma, Nandita, 345-47. See also *DownWind Productions*; *Free Grindz*

Shibusawa, Naoko, 188

Shin-Manguera, Caroline, 79

Shiozaki, Cory, 146n46. See also *Manzanar Fishing Club*

shish kebab, 246, 251, 252

Shiva, Vandana, 386-87

Siamese Cookery (Wilson), 191

Silverstein, Eric, 234, 237, 240, 241

Simple Oriental Cookery (Beilenson), 200-201

Simpson, Caroline Chung, 132-33

sinigang, 159, 160, 162, 163, 171, 185n24

slow food movement, 242

"slummers," 60. *See also* Chinatown, tourism

slumming, 189. *See also* Chinatown, tourism; "slummers"; "rubberneckers"

Smith, Neil, on space, 388n2. *See also* space

social media. *See also* food trucks; *loncheros*; *nuevo* trucks

Soja, Edward W., 16, 27n20

Sone, Monica, 127. See also *Nisei Daughter*

Song, Miri, 18. See also *Helping Out*

South Asian: cooking, 8, 371-80; diaspora, 321n25, 393; diasporic texts, 356

South by Southwest festival, 233, 237-38

Southwestern cuisine, 105, 108; movement, 108. *See also* Ferguson, Amy

Soviet Union, 196

Soviet-Afghan War, 251

Sovietization, 247-48, 253

soy sauce, 101, 102, 112, 149, 154, 157, 158; Chun King, 224; hydrolyzed or chemical, 213, 225; La Choy, 224, 225. *See also* Kikkoman

space, 374; Neil Smith's formulation of, 388n2; representation of, 374

SPAM: in ethnic dishes, 326; international popularity, 326; link to American military, 326-27; *musubi*, 4

SPAM/MAPS: Oceana, 327. *See also* Arcega, Michael

SPAM/MAPS: World, 327-28. *See also* Arcega, Michael

Spanish-American War, 178, 217

Spivak, Gayatri, 380, 388n1. See also *Imperatives to Reimagine the Planet*

SS *President Coolidge* (ship), 58

Sta. Maria, Felice Prudente, 150

Stannard, David, 100-101

statist ideology, 34

Stegner, Wallace, 390n10

Stein, Gertrude, 363. See also *Three Lives*; *Melanctha*

Strehl, Gary, 105, 106, 110, 120n39

suburbanization, 187-88

"supermarket culture," 381

supranational citizenship, 389n8

Surveying the Interior: Literary Cartographers and the Sense of Place (Van Noy), 390n10

Survivors: Cambodian Refugees in the United States (Chan), 22-23

sushi, 4, 112, 241, 267, 268

sustainability, in food practices, 8, 343

taco truck(s): Korean, 7; wars, 92-93n7

tacos, 78, 80, 235, 239, 242, 263; *banh mih*, 234; Korean, 4, 81, 88, 90, 96n51, 232, 233, 238, 241

Taishan County, China, 56

Takei, George, 125. See also *To the Stars*

Tallett, Keith, 328-31, 334-35. See also *Tattoo Williams*; *Militia*; *Mobile Taro Lo´i*

Tan, Amy, 355. See also *Joy Luck Club, The*

Tattoo Williams, 329-31. *See also* Tallett, Keith

Tentative Guide for Health Education in Elementary Schools, A, 178

teriyaki, 30, 41, 88, 112, 142, 208

Thai cuisine, 190-193, 199, 202; early interest in, 190-193; popularization in the U.S., 200-204

Thailand, rise of tourism industry, 198-99

Three Lives (Stein), 363

Tiravanija, Rirkrit, 344

To the Stars (Takei), 125

Tompkins, Kyla Wazana, 2. See also *Racial Indigestion: Eating Bodies in the 19th Century*

Top Chef (television show), 8, 357, 365-66

Top Chef Cookbook, The, 366

tourism: in Asia Pacific, 197; Chinatown, 60; culinary, 189, 198, 200; Hawai'i, 199; infrastructure development, 197; in Thailand, 198-99

Tourism Authority of Thailand (TAT), 198

Tran, Diep, 89

transnational, 5

Trask, Haunani Kay, 118n4, 122n97

Treaty of Guadalupe Hidalgo, 218

Trinidad, Crispulo, 182. See also *Pasteleria at reposteria*

Truman, Harry S, 196

Truong, Monique, 8, 305, 354-65. See also *Book of Salt, The*

Tsai, Ming, 110

Tubbs, Maika'i, 333. See also *Makau Bound*

Tuffery, Michel, 327

Tule Lake, 134-36; rebels, 134-35; riots, 133-34, 136

Turkic: food, 245; immigrants, 249-51; languages, 245-49; migration to the U.S., 250-52; organizations, 249-50

Turkish restaurants, 251-52

Turkistan American Association, 250

Twitter, 79, 82, 87, 91, 234, 237-38, 242

Ty, Eleanor, 322n43

Tydings-McDuffie Act, 172n4

Uighur, 248; migration to Uzbekistan, 248; of northwestern China, 254; restaurants, 251-52

United Nation's Codex Alimentarius Commission, 213

urban utopianism, 81
U.S. Department of Agriculture (USDA), 33, 36, 275, 282-83
U.S. Department of Commerce, 198
U.S. Department of State, 196
Uzbek: cuisine, 8, 248-49; diaspora, 247; diet, 246-48; immigrants, 249-51; migrant workers, 246, 251; neighborhoods in the U.S., 249-50; new wave of U.S. migration, 251; restaurants, 251, 253
Uzbekistan, during Sovietization, 247-48, 253

Valerio Gardens, 22
Van Noy, Rick, 390n10. See also *Surveying the Interior*
Van Sant, John E., 219
Vietnam War, 283
Vietnamese: community in Austin, Texas, 241; diasporic queer subjectivity, 354, 356; queer community, 361; refugees, 13
Voice of Asia, The (Michener), 197

Waikīkī: A History of Forgetting & Remembering, 345
Wakamatsu Tea and Silk Farm Colony, 219-20
Walker, Alice, 395. See also *Warrior Marks*
War Relocation Authority (WRA), 126-31, 133-34, 138, 143, 143n2
War Relocation Authority Centers, 128
Warhol, Andy, 276
Warrior Marks (Walker), 95
Wartime Civilian Control Agency, 143n2
Waters, Alice, 34-35, 105, 111, 113, 275-78. *See also* California cuisine; Edible Schoolyard Project
Wei, William, 304
White House Garden, 34
White supremacy, 196, 306
Wilks, Richard, 36. *See also* "Polarities of Food Culture"
Williams-Forson, Psyche, 2. See also *Building Chickens out of Chicken Legs*

Wilson, Marie, 191-92, 196. See also *Siamese Cookery*
Wong, Alan, 103, 106, 109, 110-17, 120n39
Wong, Sau-Ling Cynthia, 305, 355
World War II, 7-8, 15, 35, 68, 126, 132, 170, 326
Worldling, 388n1. See also *Critique of Postcolonial Reason;* Spivak, Gayatri
Wrack and Ruin (Lee), 8, 303-4, 307-18, 321n25; Asian American identity, 311-13, 317; as an Asian American novel, 309; identity politics, 311; questions of authenticity, 313; subversion of stereotypes, 308-09. *See also* Lee, Don
Wu, Ellen, 134
Wu, Frank, 304

Xu, Wenying, 318, 356

Yamaguchi, Kristi, 222
Yamaguchi, Roy, 103, 104, 106, 107, 109-11, 113-16, 120n39
Yamamoto, Lynne, 325
Yang, Alice, 309
Yasuda, Glenn, 284
Yates, Ronald E., 209, 211-12, 215, 218-20. See also *Kikkoman Chronicles*
yellow peril, 126, 131-33, 188. *See also* Asian American(s)
Yellow Peril (Am I White Yet?), 339, 341. *See also* Konishi, Alan
Yellow Peril (Remember Pearl Harbor?), 339-41. *See also* Konishi, Alan
Yellow: Stories (Lee), 307-08
Yelp, 90, 236-37
Yoo, David, 257
Yoon, Byeong-Seon, 391n37, 391n38
Yoon, Sang, 89
Young Men's Christian Association (YMCA), 264
Young Women's Christian Association (YWCA), 257, 259-60

Zia, Helen, 304
Zoot-suiters, 134